Domain-Specific Bodies of Knowledge in
Project Management – **Volume 3**

Building a Body of Knowledge in Project Management in Developing Countries

Domain-Specific Bodies of Knowledge in Project Management

Print ISSN: 2811-0889
Online ISSN: 2811-0897

Series Editor: Mohan M Kumaraswamy
(The University of Hong Kong, Hong Kong)

Published:

Vol. 3 *Building a Body of Knowledge in Project Management in Developing Countries*
edited by George Ofori (London South Bank University, UK)

Vol. 2 *Managing Information Technology Projects: Building a Body of Knowledge in IT Project Management*
edited by Srinath Perera (Western Sydney University, Australia) and Robert Eadie (Ulster University, UK)

Vol. 1 *Building a Body of Knowledge in Construction Project Delivery, Procurement and Contracting*
edited by Giovanni C Migliaccio (University of Washington, USA) and Pramen P Shrestha (University of Nevada Las Vegas, USA)

Domain-Specific Bodies of Knowledge in
Project Management – **Volume 3**

Building a Body of Knowledge in Project Management in Developing Countries

Editor-in-Chief: Mohan M Kumaraswamy
The University of Hong Kong, Hong Kong

Editor
George Ofori
London South Bank University, UK

World Scientific

NEW JERSEY • LONDON • SINGAPORE • BEIJING • SHANGHAI • HONG KONG • TAIPEI • CHENNAI • TOKYO

Published by

World Scientific Publishing Co. Pte. Ltd.
5 Toh Tuck Link, Singapore 596224
USA office: 27 Warren Street, Suite 401-402, Hackensack, NJ 07601
UK office: 57 Shelton Street, Covent Garden, London WC2H 9HE

Library of Congress Cataloging-in-Publication Data
Names: Ofori, George, editor.
Title: Building a body of knowledge in project management in developing countries / editor, George Ofori, London South Bank University, UK.
Description: Hackensack, NJ : World Scientific, [2023] | Series: Domain-specific bodies of knowledge in project management, 2811-0889 ; vol. 3 | Includes bibliographical references.
Identifiers: LCCN 2022061355 | ISBN 9789811224713 (hardcover) | ISBN 9789811224720 (ebook) | ISBN 9789811224737 (ebook other)
Subjects: LCSH: Project management--Developing countries. | Industrial management--Developing countries. | Knowledge management--Developing countries.
Classification: LCC HD69.P75 B845 2023 | DDC 658.4/04--dc23/eng/20221222
LC record available at https://lccn.loc.gov/2022061355

British Library Cataloguing-in-Publication Data
A catalogue record for this book is available from the British Library.

For any available supplementary material, please visit
https://www.worldscientific.com/worldscibooks/10.1142/11950#t=suppl

Desk Editors: Nambirajan Karuppiah/Nicole Ong

Typeset by Stallion Press
Email: enquiries@stallionpress.com

To my brothers and sisters: Kwame Siaw, Amma Ankyaa,
Kwabena Opuni, Yaa Oduraa, Afua Antwiwaa, Kwame Boateng,
and Adwoa Acheamponmaa.
This is for you.
I thank you for your prayers and support all these years.

https://doi.org/10.1142/9789811224720_fmatter

Foreword

When I was a student in Glasgow, I took summer vacation work in 1962, 1963, and 1964 with a local contractor. It proved to be my most valuable and inspirational experience. The Site Manager to whom I reported was one Charlie Robinson, who at that time was Britain's Basketball Team Captain. He had attributes to which I could never aspire. He was BIG. Not only was he big in stature, his personality also matched it. Charlie always created a presence wherever he was and whoever's company he was in. He could demonstrate leadership to the workforce and inspired them every day to achieve more than they had the day before. Charlie also appeared as a leader amongst the senior managers and especially to little people like me. I remember with clarity to this day on being forcibly harangued when he said, "Estimating, Planning, Workforce Management, Quality Management, Cost Control — that's what this job's all about AND they don't teach you THAT at University." He was right — in those days civil engineering and construction degrees were entirely technical subjects with no mention of management.

After some years of experience in industry, I spent my academic work trying to remedy Charlie's criticism. I was not alone, but in a small minority to start with. Up to the late 1980s, the institutionalized view of Civil Engineering education and training was that Civil Engineering was design-based and required only scientific, technical, and analytical education and training. Most professorial heads of university departments of

Civil Engineering were structural engineers. Any futuristic proposal for course development invariably involved "more analysis." Any thought of including management or construction technology in education and training was not dismissed but was just met with a blank stare, showing no understanding. Although the push for change had already started in the 1960s, progress was limited to a few universities. We, at Loughborough, formed strong bonds with the companies that employed our graduates and therefore took the lead on course content and year out training from these companies that were not from the institutions who would send other academics to review our courses. These academics did not represent industry. We would quote the companies' views to the Institution of Civil Engineers (ICE) Joint Board of Moderators and have some uncomfortable discussions. My view was that the discomfort was theirs.

The ICE attempted to shape and influence the content of undergraduate degrees through their "Guidelines for Undergraduate Courses." However, a wider take-up of the need to change the above narrow focus began to emerge. Notably, in 1985, the ICE held a conference entitled *Civil Engineers for the 1990s* at Kingston Polytechnic (as it was named then), where one substantive conclusion was: "Engineering studies should be taught in the context of both design AND CONSTRUCTION" (The emphasis on "AND CONSTRUCTION" was the authors', not mine). The importance of this conclusion was that the previous published ICE guidelines for undergraduate courses in Civil Engineering contained no reference to "CONSTRUCTION", the management of construction or even the management of design.

The conference report went on to say that, after the technical subjects, the remaining time for other subjects which might not be easily quantified:

- SHOULD include management subjects, relevant legislation, and health and safety.
- MIGHT include law in an engineering context as well as planning and civil engineering history.
- PERHAPS a foreign language.

The above represented a "small" breakthrough against the institutionalized view of undergraduate teaching. At that time the employment pattern of civil engineering graduates was: Contractors 35%; Consultants 20%; Local authorities 10%; Water authorities 15%; and Out of civil engineering 15%.

So, it was clear that graduates joining contractors were not being well prepared by their undergraduate degree. Also, the entrenched view at the time was that those going into design did not need management training. The concept of managing the design process was quite alien and would take longer to be accepted. But the battle was won, and more and more universities included management and technology in their courses.

The ICE's Joint Board of Moderators' Guidelines for undergraduate degrees has grown into a much more structured and detailed document.

The annexes covering the content are as follows:

Annex B: Design in Degree Programs
Annex C: Sustainability in Degree Programs
Annex D: Health and Safety Risk Management in Degree Programs
Annex E: Industrial Placements in Degree Programs
Annex F: Professionalism, Ethics, Diversity, and Inclusion in Degree Programs
Annex G: Site Visits in Degree Programs
Annex H: Industrial Influence and Input in Degree Programs
Annex I: Surveying in Degree Programs.

This is more broadly based than in the earlier days with more recognition of the breadth of careers. Design is upfront and in the first place of the content descriptions. Construction is not given equal status but surfaces in other annexes. Annex H: Industrial Influence and Input into Degree Programs is specifically required, a significant advance from when we had our industrial sponsors attend an accreditation and the professor who was chair advising me that the panel were not happy with their presence. The link between universities and industry in the development of graduates and professional engineers should have no barriers.

Annexes C to H contain the broadening subjects beyond scientific, technical, and analytical subjects. This gives modern civil engineering degrees a broader base. I would have been happier if two of the annexes had been "Construction and Design Management" and "Construction

Technology." I think it important to know how what is designed can be constructed and also how design and construction are managed. Industrial placements, Site Visits and Industrial Influence, and Input in Degree Programs go somewhere toward this, but the formal inclusion seems weaker. Moreover, Construction Technology and Construction Management could be formally taught, supported by Industrial Placements, Site Visits, and Industry Influence.

The guidelines seem to stop just short of addressing what careers the graduates might aspire to and how best to prepare them — for example, to develop well-balanced careers in Design and in Construction, ideally with holistic approaches to address issues such as Sustainability; Health and Safety; Risk Management; Professionalism, Ethics, Diversity and Inclusion. Indeed, I believe that there are only two meaningful performance metrics for engineering and construction departments: (1) the graduates get good well-paid jobs; and (2) that research output is applied. Both these require the engineering and construction departments to have sound, productive, and meaningful working relationships with companies in industry.

Now we have project management, including the management of design as well as of construction, taught in both undergraduate and masters courses, and project management features strongly in both PhD and funded research projects.

Loughborough's MSc in Construction Management was started in 1966, being the second such MSc in the world, beaten to the start by Stanford whose MSc is nine months older. The MSc aimed to cover all the Construction Management content that was not presented in a structured way by earlier education and training. Roy Pilcher's book, *Principles of Construction Management*, was then probably the only construction management book with a substantive numerical content, others being descriptive and anecdotal. The subject had not, at that time, matured into a reasonably distinct discipline, with a recognizable group of subjects. Later books built on the content of the MSc program and began to provide the structured form of the subject. My colleague Frank Harris and I produced a text in 1977, which is currently in its eighth edition, so we know that there is a market of engineers seeking the knowledge of construction management.

The content of books and publications, research work, and teaching material by staff at Loughborough grew out of the students' projects, which represented about one-third of the course in the MSc. I remember discussing with the staff of Balfour Beatty a research project to develop computer-aided estimating at a time when there was no computer-aided estimating. Computers and estimating had not come together. In the discussion, the Balfour Beatty staff asked, "Have you thought about...naming a specific issue..." I took an MSc student's report from the shelf and tabled it. "Ah but you won't have considered...naming another topic..." I tabled another student report. By the time the conversation ended, we had five student reports on the table and Balfour Beatty were ready to enter a development project with us.

Similarly, the teaching material relating to construction in developing countries has, by and large, been produced by the course's international students, of whom there are and were many. They have provided a rich source of material that has relevance. The standing of the MSc Course in Construction Management was strong amongst the international community, and we were engaged by the UK Overseas Development Administration and later the International Labour Organization to produce four PhD graduates from Sri Lanka and to establish an MSc Course at the University of Moratuwa. A good number of Loughborough staff visited Moratuwa during its formative years.

In addition, Loughborough later launched an MSc program in "construction" targeted on international students from developing countries. Separately, and not specifically including Management, but linking to grassroots needs, our department created an institute entitled Water Engineering in Developing Countries (WEDC) providing education, training, development, and research opportunities in this domain, while focusing on developing countries. It is now called the Water Engineering Development Centre.

Since Charlie's criticism (as in the first paragraph of this Foreword), project management has progressed in developed economies. Project management has also progressed in developing countries but not as much due to the greater challenges. You could almost say Charlie's comments would still mostly apply to developing countries today as they had then. We must put that right and *Building a Body of Knowledge in Project Management in Developing Countries* should make a major contribution.

This book is part of a World Scientific Book Series with the headline title of *Domain Specific Bodies of Knowledge in Project Management.* This series recognizes that Project Management operates in many domains, and therefore aims to address current and emerging issues in specific domains capturing and building on best practice and proven principles also outlining insightful ways forward. Amongst the texts are *Developing a Body of Knowledge for Green Construction Project Management*; *Building a Body of Knowledge in IT Project Management*; and *Building a Body of Knowledge in Construction Project Delivery, Procurement and Contracting*.

Each book in the series is edited by a distinguished editor who also contributes to the chapters together with a long list of expert authors. The distinguished editor for *Building a Body of Knowledge in Project Management in Developing Countries* is George Ofori. George has also authored 5 chapters, contributed to two other chapters, and assembled 53 authors to create the total of 26 chapters.

A body of knowledge in project management in developing countries is a timely contribution. Most texts deal with project management in developed economies; you could argue that the academic and professional communities have, to a degree, neglected developing countries by not providing enough attention. From my own experience, some time ago, when I was reviewing international-aid–related projects, it was clear that international companies rarely left behind a legacy of competence in project management after completion of aid-funded projects. This seemed a set of missed opportunities. On the other hand, even international organizations often get things wrong in developing countries. They tend to fall short in understanding the situation and in factoring in the special conditions, constraints, and the context that exists. Project Management in Developing Countries is a discipline that needs clearer definition, description, and areas for development. This book should inspire academics, researchers, and funding agencies to develop the discipline and create opportunities for the development of a construction industry that can deliver effectively and economically in developing countries.

This book is welcomed and you could say it is overdue.

The first part sets out the rationale of the book beginning with a review of the present state of project management in developing countries. The first chapter concludes that project management in developing countries is an important set of skills; it argues for the development of a body of knowledge to guide both practice and research. In the next chapter, the problems are highlighted of importing project management without sufficient adaptation to local conditions. Project management in developing countries faces far greater challenges. As a result, the performance of project management in developing countries is much poorer than in industrialized economies.

The following part of the book attempts to define the knowledge areas with developing countries' perspectives. This includes chapters on Project Schedule Management, Project Cost Management, Quality Management, Communication Challenges, Risk Management, Procurement Management, and Stakeholder Management. This represents a comprehensive review of key areas giving a framework of areas that need developing.

The next part is on "Additional Important Areas of Knowledge" in this context. This begins with a review of project performance indicators. To achieve the important goal of value for money, issues about embedding facilities management knowledge are reviewed. Also addressed in this part are Post-Disaster Reconstruction Projects. These projects, resulting from disasters, usually face chaos and need to respond to the circumstances that have been created. By definition, these projects cannot be well structured and are usually fragmented in organization and management. The issues of estimating, which are difficult enough in industrialized countries, are considered from a developing country perspective, by examining the Indian context. This is followed by reviewing the knowledge in developing and implementing construction industry improvement programs. The final chapter in this part deals with Project Leadership in construction in developing countries and ends with suggestions for project leadership development.

The following part of the book gives examples of Project Management in Brazil, India, China, and South Africa. Nearing the end of the book the penultimate section is on the future. It is noted that the discipline of Project Management in Developing Countries is growing and receiving contributions from many sources. An action plan is then provided to bring together and further develop the body of knowledge of project management for developing countries with useful suggestions on what it might look like.

The book ends with rousing conclusions. Project Management needs an increasingly important set of skills and has many areas to address and much progress to make in filling gaps and dealing with misconceptions in its own body of knowledge. The case for the development of a body of knowledge is powerfully made, particularly to guide practice and research on project management in developing countries.

Researchers, practitioners, and students of project management in developing countries will find this book inspirational and it should drive them to greater achievement.

I think even Charlie Robinson would be impressed.

Ronald McCaffer
Emeritus Professor
Loughborough University, UK

https://doi.org/10.1142/9789811224720_fmatter

Preface

I was glad when I was approached by the series editor of the book series *Domain-Specific Bodies of Knowledge in Project Management*, Professor Mohan M. Kumaraswamy, to put together a book on a body of knowledge of project management for developing countries. He encouraged me by saying this would be the first book of the new series launched by World Scientific Publishing Company, a publisher which I knew well during my Singapore days. Although I was busy at that time with the work on another book which I had been commissioned to write, I did not hesitate in taking up this task because I had considered the absence of such a guide on project management which addresses the needs of the developing countries to be urgently necessary to fill the vacuum which was constraining project performance and effectiveness in those countries.

I am very happy that the book has been released. For many reasons, it took much longer to complete this book than I had expected. First, it was initially difficult to assemble the authors of the chapters on the topics I had suggested. Then, a very small number of those who had accepted the initial invitation did not show any enthusiasm to go forward with the project, and I had to find replacements for them. Second, the deadlines I had set proved to be too ambitious. Moreover, they had to be moved, on several occasions, for particular authors. Finally, I had to work on this book at the same time as the other book I have mentioned above.

The 26 chapters in this book, together, enable me to say that the authors and I have met the original goal of the book which was: "to present a state-of-the art account of the field of project management, and present a body of knowledge of the field for the developing countries." We have also realized the book's objectives which were to present the current state of knowledge on project management by considering the trends, and how they widen the content and scope of the field; to explore the need for a special body of knowledge of project management for the developing countries; to determine the nature of the field of project management in the developing countries and discuss the relationships between the proposed new field and the established bodies of knowledge; and to consider the future prospects of the field of project management in developing countries and how it might influence mainstream project management. The chapters in this book present the current situation of project management. They assess its merits and weaknesses and its applications in various sectors and in all countries. Then they go on to focus on the developing countries and explore the development of the body of knowledge of project management for guiding the undertaking of projects in this group of countries.

I am really grateful to all the 52 other authors for the high-quality chapters in this book. I am thankful that they accepted my initial request to write chapters for the book. I am also grateful that they responded to my requests and those of the publishers' production team in a timely manner, most of the time. To the fellow authors, I say, let us hope that our book makes an impact. The strategic importance of our subject makes it critical that action is taken to realize some of the proposals we have made in this book. I will do my part in that regard by promoting the book at every opportunity. I hope you will make your contribution to this effort too.

I am grateful to Mr John Stuart, Senior Commissioning Editor of World Scientific, for encouraging me at different stages of this endeavor. He has been very patient with me but his gentle reminders and sharing of his experience with books such as this one were very helpful. I also thank the Series Editor, my old friend Mohan Kumaraswamy, for the intellectual support and, similarly, the occasional gentle enquiries on progress, as well as reminders.

This book initiates a discussion on the need for a project management body of knowledge that is tailored to the needs and contexts of the developing countries, and enables projects in those countries to be undertaken effectively and efficiently. It is a major contribution to the field of project studies in general.

In the end, this will not be the first book of the new series of World Scientific but I believe it will be a significant one, and I am also of the opinion that it has been worth the wait. It will be a worthwhile initiative if World Scientific were to commission a follow-up book on the subject of a project management body of knowledge for developing countries in 2032, if not earlier.

I strongly urge readers of the book to help in making the development of the DCPMBOK a reality. It is needed in the developing countries to help the long-term advancement of these countries, and improve the quality of life of a large proportion of the world's population.

George Ofori
London
February 2023

https://doi.org/10.1142/9789811224720_fmatter

About the Contributors

George Ofori is a former Dean of the School of the Built Environment and Architecture at the London South Bank University, UK. He has also worked at the National University of Singapore, Kwame Nkrumah University of Science and Technology (KNUST), Ghana, and in industry. He is a graduate of KNUST and University College London, where he obtained his PhD degree and was also awarded a DSc degree. He is a Fellow of the Ghana Academy of Arts and Sciences and Fellow of the Chartered Institute of Building, Royal Institution of Chartered Surveyors, and Society of Project Managers (Singapore). His main subject of research is the improvement of the capacity and capability of the construction industry, especially in developing countries. He also undertakes research on Productivity in Construction, Sustainable Construction, Leadership, and Professionalism and Ethics. He has undertaken assignments in advising many governments (especially those of developing countries) and international agencies on the construction industry. He is a member of the International Board of CoST, the Infrastructure Transparency Initiative, and the Board of Trustees of Engineers Against Poverty, UK. He can be reached at oforig3@lsbu.ac.uk

Gonzalo Lizarralde is a professor at the School of Architecture at the Université de Montréal, Canada. He has taught at the University of Cape Town (South Africa), McGill University (Canada), the International University of Catalunya (Spain), and Universidad del Valle and Universidad

Javeriana (Colombia). Gonzalo is the holder of the Research Chair Fayolle-Magil Construction in architecture, construction and sustainability. He is also the director of the IF Research Group and the leader of the Disaster Resilience and Sustainable Reconstruction Research Alliance. He is a founding member of i-Rec, an international network of specialists in disaster-risk reduction and reconstruction. He is the author of the books, *Unnatural Disasters*, and *The Invisible Houses*, and the co-author of the book, *Rebuilding after Disasters*. He is a Member of the College of New Scholars, Artists and Scientists of the Royal Society of Canada, the country's first system of multi-disciplinary recognition for intellectual leadership. He can be reached at gonzalo.lizarralde@umontreal.ca

Holmes Páez is an Associate Professor at the Department of Civil Engineering at the Pontificia Universidad Javeriana in Colombia. He is an expert in construction management and economics, organizations, institutions, and governance in the construction industry. He explores the role of technology and human behavior in organizational change in the built environment. He has experience in research and consultancy in climate change adaptation in Latin America. He is also the director of a graduate program at the Department of Civil Engineering at Pontificia Universidad Javeriana. He can be reached at paez.holmes@javeriana.edu.co

Benjamin Herazo is the Research Project Coordinator of the IF Research Group at the Université de Montréal, Canada. He is an architect with a Master's degree in economics and a PhD from the Faculty of Environmental Design at Université de Montréal. He has previously spent 15 years as an associate professor, director, and Dean at the Environmental Studies School at Javeriana University in Colombia. He also had experience in architectural firms and has been a consultant and researcher in environmental management. Benjamin is a member of the Research Chair Fayolle-Magil Construction in architecture, construction, and sustainability. He is a consultant and member of boards of directors of different organizations in Montreal. His PhD dissertation focused on how sustainable development contributes to the alignment between strategic and tactical management in the building sector. He can be reached at bj.herazo.cueto@umontreal.ca

Martin Morgan Tuuli is a Professor of Construction Business and Project Management and Deputy Rector of the Ghana Institute of Management and Public Administration (GIMPA), Ghana, in charge of Academics, Research, Training and Advisory Services, and a former Dean of the GIMPA Business School. Professor Tuuli holds a BSc in Building Technology from the Kwame Nkrumah University of Science and Technology, Ghana, and a PhD in Construction Project Management from the University of Hong Kong. Professor Tuuli has an international outlook and over 20 years of consultancy, professional and research/academic experience. His consultancy and professional experience have been in the context of developing, implementing, evaluating, and commercially managing infrastructure and development projects and programs. He has managed significant research projects and his works are published and cited in top journals in his field on the human factor and technology issues required to sustain the efficiency and effectiveness of projects and programs and project-based organizations. He can be reached at mtuuli@gimpa.edu.gh

Ebenezer Adaku is an Associate Professor of Operations and Project Management and Head of Department of Management Science at the GIMPA Business School, Ghana Institute of Management and Public Administration (GIMPA), Ghana. He holds a PhD in Civil and Environmental Engineering with specialization in Infrastructure Economics and Systems from the University of Stuttgart, Germany. His research interests include causes of construction project cost and time overruns; social capital and its effects on project performance in developing economy environments; and occupational safety and health (OSH) management on construction projects. His research has been published in *International Journal of Managing Projects in Business*, *International Journal of Production Economics*, *Production Planning & Control*, among others. He can be reached at eadaku@gimpa.edu.gh

Eric Zunouh Banye is an international development management professional with more than 17 years of experience in portfolio, program, and project management. He is currently the Country Programme Coordinator for the United Nations Industrial Development Organisation and previously worked with SNV-Netherlands Development Organisation as the

Country Sector Leader for Agriculture for several years. He has implemented projects funded by agencies including the European Union, African Development Bank, World Bank, United States Agency for International Development, B&M Gates Foundation, and private sector projects. He holds Master's and Bachelor's degrees from the University of Ghana. He is a Certified Project Management Professional (PMP), a Fellow of the Institute of Project Management Professionals (FPMP), and a Member of the Institute of Directors (MIoD). He is also a PhD Candidate in Project Management at GIMPA Business School, Accra, Ghana. His research interests are in project sustainability, green economy, organizational capability, performance measurement, strategic management, procurement management, agile project design and implementation, financial management, resource mobilization, public–private partnership projects, and multi-stakeholder processes and gender issues in projects. He can be reached at eric.banye@st.gimpa.edu.gh.

Annette S. Tettey is a Quantity Surveyor at SKOL Consult Ltd. She has been principally involved in the planning and management of a significant number of projects in commercial and mixed-use development in Ghana. She has a bachelor's degree in Quantity Surveying from the Kwame Nkrumah University of Science and Technology (Ghana); and a Master's degree in Construction Project Management from Loughborough University (UK). Her career and research interests are in contract administration; construction planning, scheduling and control; cost planning and management; construction innovation; and the use of digital technologies in the built environment. She can be reached at senamtettey@gmail.com

Hemanta Doloi is an Associate Professor in Construction Management in the Faculty of Architecture, Building and Planning at the University of Melbourne, Australia. He is the director of the Smart Villages Lab (SVL) that focuses on data-driven research in the area of 'rural construction and development' under the auspices of the Smart Villages program. He leads the trans-disciplinary research in smart villages for developing solutions for affordable housing and infrastructure systems, generating new theories for education and governance, and empowering rural communities. Hemanta won the Australian Institute of Quantity Surveyors' Infinite Value award in Teaching and Research — recognizing the excellence of scholarship impacting the wider community in the profession. He has authored works which have been published widely in the areas of project management, infrastructure planning and policy, construction economics and management and Smart Villages. He serves as a member of the editorial boards of a number of prestigious journals including the *International Journal of Project Management, Built Environment Project and Asset Management*, and *Construction Innovation: Information, Process, Management*. He is a founding Chair of the *International Conference on Smart Villages and Rural Development (COSVARD)*. He can be reached at hdoloi@unimelb.edu.au

Nii A. Ankrah is a Senior Lecturer in Quantity Surveying and Deputy Head of the Department of Civil Engineering in Aston University, UK. He has extensive research experience in organizational behavior and project management in construction. He has delivered outcomes from funded research projects in construction health and safety, supply chain management, dispute resolution, cradle to cradle and circular economy in the built environment and has produced many papers in these areas. These projects have focused on improving construction performance through better health and safety management, more effective management of resources, and supply chain management. He also undertakes cost consultancy for construction companies. He delivers training in these areas in the UK and internationally. He can be reached at n.ankrah@aston.ac.uk

Emmanuel Manu is an Associate Professor in Quantity Surveying and Project Management at the School of Architecture, Design and the Built Environment at Nottingham Trent University, UK; a Fellow of the Higher Education Academy; and a Member of the Association for Project Management. His teaching responsibilities span the initiation of projects, project procurement and contract practice. He has over eight years of experience researching construction supply chains, the circular economy, sustainable procurement, and social value, and has collaborated with industry partners to deliver research and consultancy projects in these areas. He has also supervised and examined several doctoral research projects in construction and project management. His research activities have led to the publication of technical reports, chapters in books, and refereed articles in highly ranked journals and conference proceedings.

Prior to joining the academic field, he worked in private practice as a Quantity Surveyor, where he developed expertise in contract administration, procurement, and cost management. He can be reached at emmanuel.manu@ntu.ac.uk

Pantaleo D. Rwelamila (PD) is Professor Emeritus of Project Management and Procurement Systems at the University of South Africa, and a 'B' Rated researcher by the South African National Research Foundation (NRF) as an internationally acclaimed researcher. He is a Joint Coordinator of CIB W107: Construction in Developing Countries; Past President of the South African Council for Project and Construction Management Professions; and former Editor (until 2021) of African Academy of Business and Development (AABD) proceedings. He was a member of a core team of investigators on the Future of the City Centre project. He has authored more than two hundred peer-reviewed journal papers, chapters in books and papers in conference proceedings. He is a visiting professor at the Institute of Social and Economic Research, Rhodes University in South Africa. He can be reached at mutajwaarwelamila@gmail.com

Fidelis Emuze, PhD, is Professor and Head of the Department of Built Environment at the Central University of Technology, Free State (CUT), South Africa. Lean construction, health, safety, and well-being and sustainability constitute the primary research interest of Dr Emuze, who is a National Research Foundation (NRF) C rated researcher who has published over 300 research outputs. He is the editor of books published by Routledge which include *Value and Waste in Lean Construction*, and *Valuing People in Construction*, and co-editor of *Construction Health and Safety in Developing Countries* (also published by Routledge). He authored the *Construction Safety Pocketbook for South Africa* (published in English, Sotho and Afrikaans). Dr Emuze is the International Coordinator of CIB W123 — People in Construction Working Commission. He can be reached at femuze@cut.ac.za

L.G. Mollo is a Senior Lecturer in the Department of Built Environment at the Central University of Technology, Free State, South Africa. He holds a PhD in Construction Management from the Nelson Mandela University (NMU); his thesis is entitled: "Framing the Reduction of

Human Failures in Construction: A Mixed-Methods Training-Within-Industry (TWI) Study." He holds a master's degree in Quantity Surveying from NMU from where he graduated in 2017. He has industrial experience from working with different construction organizations on a part-time basis. His research focuses on construction management, construction health and safety, lean construction and building energy management. He can be reached at lmollo@cut.ac.za

Bankole Awuzie is an Associate Professor in the Department of Built Environment, Faculty of Engineering, Built Environment, and Information Technology at the Central University of Technology, Free State, South Africa. He holds a PhD in Built Environment (Construction Project Management) from the University of Salford, UK and an MSc in Construction Project Management from the Robert Gordon University, Scotland. He is a rated researcher of the South African National Research Foundation (NRF). His research interests are in the smart, sustainable, and circular built environment knowledge domains. He can be reached at bawuzie@cut.ac.za

Imriyas Kamardeen is Professor and Head of Construction Management at Deakin University, Australia. He is also the Editor-in-Chief of the international journal *Construction Economics and Building*. His research predominantly lies in improving health, safety and wellbeing in the construction industry; he has, to date, authored six book on this theme. Imriyas holds a PhD in Building from the National University of Singapore, is a Fellow of the Higher Education Academy, UK and a Fellow of the Australian Institute of Building. He can be reached at imriyas.kamardeen@deakin.edu.au

Abid Hasan is a Lecturer in the School of Architecture and Built Environment at Deakin University, Australia. He holds a PhD in Construction Management from the University of South Australia. He also holds a Master of Technology degree in Construction Technology and Management from the Indian Institute of Technology Delhi, India and a Bachelor of Technology (Honors) degree in Civil Engineering from Aligarh Muslim University, India. Prior to studying for the PhD, he worked in a Fortune 500 and Forbes 2000 company for over four years.

Dr Hasan teaches both undergraduate and postgraduate construction project management courses at Deakin. His research interests include project success factors, occupational health and safety, construction productivity and human-technology interactions. He can be reached at abid.hasan@deakin.edu.au

Ron Watermeyer is a Director of Infrastructure Options Pty(Ltd), a Visiting Adjunct Professor at the School of Construction Economics and Management, University of the Witwatersrand, South Africa, the Chair of the ISO Subcommittee for Construction Procurement, a Board Member of Engineers Against Poverty, and a Board Member of FIDIC Credentialing Ltd. He graduated with a civil engineering degree in 1978 and functioned as a site engineer on a mega project and as a structural engineer in a specialist design office for the first decade of his career. He worked as a consulting civil and structural engineer for the next two decades. Over the last decade, he has worked with public-sector clients in the delivery of infrastructure projects. He was awarded a Doctor of Engineering degree by the University of Witwatersrand in 2009, and the 2010 Institution of Civil Engineers' International Medal for his contributions over time to the delivery of infrastructure. He can be reached at watermeyer@ioptions.co.za

Ezekiel Chinyio is a Reader in Construction Management in the Faculty of Science and Engineering, University of Wolverhampton, UK. He has undertaken research on many aspects of construction including stakeholder management, the needs of construction clients, and risk, stress and knowledge management. He has won research funding as a principal investigator. He pioneered the "Psychology in Construction" (Psycon) initiative to reinforce the versatility and wealth of tools and principles in the built environment. Ezekiel has over 110 refereed publications. He is a Member of the Chartered Institute of Building, UK. He can be reached at E.Chinyio@wlv.ac.uk

Eric-Kingkof Kofi Opoku-Ohemeng is the Managing Director of KIS Plus. He is an independent consultant and expert adviser specializing in infrastructure asset management and infrastructure development (project management and engineering) with over 22 years of experience in the construction and engineering industry. He has been instrumental in the development, implementation and delivery of major and mega infrastructure projects around the world. He is a chartered engineer, a chartered construction manager, a registered asset management professional, a Certified Asset Management Assessor, and a Lead Asset Management Auditor (PASS55 and IS055000). He is a Fellow of the Institute of Asset Management (IAM) and the Chartered Institution of Highways and Transportation (CIHT), and a Member of the Chartered Institute of Building. He also holds double Masters degrees and a Bachelor's degree with honors from Edinburgh Napier University, UK. He is a professional qualifications reviewer and assessor for the IAM, co-author of IAM's Leadership and Competence Guidelines, and a reviewer and contributor to the CIHT *Asset Management Journal*. He can be reached at kingkof@outlook.com

Abimbola Windapo is a Professor of Construction Management at the Department of Construction Economics and Management, University of Cape Town, South Africa, with more than 34 years of experience in practice, teaching, and research on the construction industry and its projects. She has held various teaching and administrative positions at the University of Cape Town and the University of Lagos, Nigeria, and worked as a construction professional at Bouygues Nigeria Ltd and in private consulting. She is a C2 rated researcher with the National Research Foundation of South Africa and a Professional Construction Project Manager and Mentor registered with the South African Council for the Project and Construction Management Professions and also with the Council of Registered Builders of Nigeria. She is also a Fellow of the Nigerian Institute of Building. Her research is interdisciplinary and focuses on construction industry development, construction business, and project management from a performance and practice perspective. She can be reached at Abimbola.windapo@uct.ac.za

Emmanuel Adinyira, PhD, is an Associate Professor of Construction Project Management and the Vice Dean of the Faculty of Built Environment at Kwame Nkrumah University of Science and Technology, Ghana. He is also a Visiting Professor at the CIDB Centre of Excellence, University of Johannesburg, South Africa. His areas of specialization include construction project management, safety, health and environment; and construction education and training. He has served as a guest editor, editor, sectional editor, and editorial board member for several national and international journals. His global experience in construction education and training includes working as a visiting scholar at Loughborough University, UK; the University of West of England, UK and the University of Johannesburg, South Africa. He has also served as a placement coach (local supervisor) for the Saxion University of Applied Science, Netherlands and Hochschule Fur Technik Stuttgart University of Applied Sciences, Germany. He can be reached at rasadii@yahoo.com; eadinyira.cap@knust.edu.gh

Kofi Agyekum, PhD, is a Senior Lecturer of Construction Technology and Management in the Department of Construction Technology and Management, Kwame Nkrumah University of Science and Technology, Ghana. His areas of specialization include Circular Economics in Construction, Building Pathology, Sustainable and Lean Construction, and Construction Project Management. He has served as a guest editor and editorial board member for several national and international journals. He is a Commonwealth Academic Fellow. He is also a Professional Peer Reviewer and holds a recognized peer review certificate from the Publons Academy in the UK (since 2018). Due to his dedication to reviewing articles, he was promoted to a mentor position and is currently a Certified Publons Academy Mentor. He can be reached at agyekum.kofi1@gmail.com

Nayanthara De Silva is a professor in Facilities Management in the Department of Building Economics at the University of Moratuwa, Sri Lanka. She has been an academic for over 17 years, authoring many highly cited research papers. She is currently the director of the MSc in Occupational Safety and Health Management programme at the University of Moratuwa. She is also a Fellow of the Institute of Facilities Management Sri Lanka, a Chartered Engineer and a member of the Institute of Engineers Sri Lanka. Her research interests are the performance of the facilities management industry; maintainability; safety of buildings; risk analysis; and facilities management procurement. She can be reached at endds@uom.lk

Ashan Senel Asmone is a Senior Lecturer at the Department of Building Economics, University of Moratuwa, Sri Lanka. He obtained his doctoral degree in Building Science from the National University of Singapore. He majored in facilities management at the undergraduate level and holds a Master's degree in environmental management. He has many years of experience in the built environment both as a researcher in safety, sustainability, and maintainability with several publications under his name, and as a practitioner and a project consultant in building project delivery. He can be reached at ashana@uom.lk

Roshani Palliyaguru is a Senior Lecturer at the Department of Quantity Surveying at the University of Vocational Technology, Sri Lanka. She obtained her BSc degree with First Class Honors from the University of Moratuwa, Sri Lanka in 2004. She completed her PhD at the School of the Built Environment, the University of Salford, UK in 2010. She has over 17 years of experience in teaching, research, and professional services in academic institutions in the UK, Australia and Sri Lanka. She has also been involved in a number of funded research projects, collaborating with international partners. Her research interests include resilience building in the built environment, protection of critical infrastructure, governance in public–private partnership projects, collaboration in Building Information Management based construction, and climate mitigation and adaptation in the built environment. Her research excellence is further demonstrated through the authoring of a number of papers in journals and proceedings of international conferences, as well as previous book chapters. She can be reached at rpalliyaguru@uovt.ac.lk

Dilanthi Amaratunga holds the chair of Disaster Risk Management at the University of Huddersfield, UK. She is a leading international expert in disaster resilience who has had an extensive academic career. She provides expert advice to national and local governments and international agencies including the United Nations Office for Disaster Risk Reduction (UNDRR). She is engaged in many significant research projects around the world, in partnership with key academics and other organizational stakeholders. To date, she has produced over 500 publications, mainly refereed papers and reports, and has delivered over 100 keynote speeches in around 30 countries. Among many leadership roles, she is the joint chief editor of the *International Journal of Disaster Resilience in the Built Environment*, a member of the UNDRR's European Science and Technology Advisory Group representing the UK, and a Steering Committee Member of the UK's Frontiers of Development programme. She is a Fellow of the Royal Institution of Chartered Surveyors, Fellow of The Royal Geographical Society, and a Fellow and a Chartered Manager of the Chartered Management Institute, UK. She can be reached at d.amaratunga@hud.ac.uk

Aravindi Samarakkodi is a PhD researcher at the Global Disaster Resilience Centre, University of Huddersfield, UK. In 2018, she obtained her BSc (first-class honors) degree in Quantity Surveying from the University of Moratuwa, Sri Lanka. She completed her MSc in 2020 and has worked as a Research Assistant on several European Commission funded projects. Her current research interests include performance measurement in smart cities, risk management in the built environment, novel applications of advanced data tools, and building delivery concepts that support informed decision-making at all levels of the infrastructure lifecycle and urban disaster resilience. While doing her PhD, she is making a contribution as a Research Assistant on the Erasmus+ funded INClusive Disaster Education (INCLUDE) project, which aims to reimagine online distance learning education so that it better supports the diverse disaster risk reduction community. She can be reached at Aravindi.Samarakkody@hud.ac.uk

Shavindree Nissanka is a full-time researcher affiliated to the Global Disaster Resilience Centre, at the University of Huddersfield, UK. She holds a Bachelor of Science degree course in Quantity Surveying. She is an Associate Member of the Chartered Institute of Management Accountants (ACMA, CGMA) and also a member of the Association of Chartered Certified Accountants (ACCA) UK. She is currently undertaking research for her PhD on utilizing financial incentives for disaster resilient housing. She also contributes to research projects on areas such as built environment learning for climate adaptation, rethinking construction to reduce disaster risks, disaster resilient building codes, disaster resilience in smart cities, and infrastructure resilience. She can be reached at Shavindree.Nissanka@hud.ac.uk

Shubham Bajaj hails from a small town called Vidisha located in the central part of India. He graduated in Civil Engineering and post graduated in Infrastructural Civil Engineering from the Indian Institute of Technology Madras, India. His research interests include Cost Estimation, Behavioral Economics and Cost Management. During his post-graduate degree, he produced a research paper in the proceedings of the Engineering Project Organization Society conference 2020 on the topic, "Cost estimation and cost overruns in the construction industry." Having developed a passion for Management Principles and Administration, he has joined the Indian Civil Services. He has served as a government official in the Indian Railway Management Service and is currently a government official in the Indian Police Service. He can be reached at shubhambajaj2002@gmail.com

Ashwin Mahalingam joined the faculty in the Division of Building Technology and Construction Management of the Department of Civil Engineering at the Indian Institute of Technology, Madras (IIT-Madras) in 2006. He received his BTech degree in Civil Engineering from IIT-Madras and then proceeded to Stanford University in the USA for a Masters in Construction Engineering and Management. He then helped start up an internet-based company in the USA called All Star Fleet, aimed at providing asset management services for construction companies. Following this, he returned to Stanford University to pursue a PhD programme in the area of Infrastructure Project Management. Ashwin's research interests are in the areas of public–private partnerships (PPP) in infrastructure planning and management, the management and governance of large engineering projects, and the use of technology in infrastructure development. Ashwin is also a co-founder of Okapi Advisory Services Pvt. Ltd and serves as a Director on the Board. He is the Editor of the *Engineering Project Organization Journal* (EPOJ) and has served on many national committees. He can be reached at mash@civil.iitm.ac.in

Gangadhar Mahesh, PhD, is an Associate Professor at the National Institute of Technology Karnataka, India. He has been an Assistant Professor at the National Institute of Construction Management and Research, India and a Post-Doctoral Fellow at The University of Hong Kong, Hong Kong, SAR. He also has extensive experience in the industry, having worked as an architect in India and as a contracts manager in Thailand. His teaching and research interests are in contract management, risk management, and construction industry development frameworks. He can be reached at gangadhar.mahesh@gmail.com

Desalegn Girma Mengistu is an Assistant Professor at Hawassa University Institute of Technology, Ethiopia. He holds a PhD degree from the National Institute of Technology Karnataka, India and has experience in the industry, having worked as a project manager and project coordinator. His teaching and research interests are in construction project management, contracts management and construction industry development. He can be reached at m.g.desalegn@gmail.com

Mohan M. Kumaraswamy was previously in industry in Sri Lanka and Nigeria, then in full-time academia for 21 years at the University of Hong Kong (HKU). He is now an Honorary Professor at HKU and also at the University of Moratuwa, Sri Lanka. Mohan was, and remains active in professional institutions, industry link bodies and international research bodies and journal editorial boards, for example, as one of three Joint Co-ordinators of the CIB Working Commission W122 on Public–Private Partnerships; being on the Editorial Board of the ASCE *Journal of Construction Engineering and Management*; and being the Editor-in-Chief of the *Journal of Built Environment Project and Asset Management* (BEPAM) which he launched in 2011. He has led many research projects including some funded by the World Bank. His works are published widely in international journals and conferences; and they have covered themes including project procurement, contract administration, claims and dispute minimization, technology exchange, built asset management, and construction industry development. He can be reached at mohan@hku.hk

Shamas-ur-Rehman Toor received his PhD degree from the National University of Singapore. He is an international development practitioner and currently works at the Asian Infrastructure Investment Bank, Beijing, China. Previously, he worked at the Islamic Development Bank Group, Saudi Arabia, and University of New South Wales, Australia. He has authored over 30 international refereed journal papers, one book, three book chapters and 38 peer-reviewed papers presented at international conferences. His research is on the areas of leadership development, organizational behavior and project management. He can be reached at shamastoor@gmail.com

Silvio Melhado is a Professor of Project and Design Management. He holds a PhD degree in Civil Engineering from the University of Sao Paulo, Brazil. He is currently acting as an Associate Professor at ÉTS, University of Québec, Montréal, Canada, and also a Senior Professor at *Escola Politécnica*, University of Sao Paulo, Brazil, and Visiting Professor at University of Pernambuco, Recife, Brazil. He teaches mostly MSc courses related to project and design management. He has supervised 45 MSc candidates, 10 PhD candidates and 3 Post-Doctoral Researchers to completion. He is the coordinator of a Master's degree programme in construction project management; he has also supervised 63 monographs. He has written articles and books on construction management, building design and management, performance and innovation in construction projects, risk management, sustainable construction, and management of the design office. He is the Co-ordinator of Working Commission W096 on Architectural Design and Management of the International Council for Research and Innovation in Building and Construction (CIB). He can be reached at silvio.melhado@etsmtl.ca

Flavia de Souza is a Lecturer in Project and Design Management; and a Risk Consultant. She is a civil engineer from Fundação Armando Alvares Penteado, and has a PhD degree from the University of Sao Paulo, Brazil. Her experience in civil engineering includes work on risk management, project management and design management. As an academic, she is certified as a supervisor for the professional Masters Programme Construinova at *Escola Politécnica*, University of São Paulo and on this programme, she has supervised master's research on risk management, design management, and building information modelling (BIM). She has written articles on construction management, building design and management, performance and innovation in construction projects, risk management, sustainable construction, and management of design offices. She can be reached at flavia.souza@usp.br

Fernanda Borges is a PhD candidate in Civil Engineering at the University of Sao Paulo, Brazil (since 2021). She holds a Master's degree in Civil Engineering from the University of Sao Paulo (2016–2019); and a bachelor's degree in Architecture and Urbanism from University of Sao Paulo with a complementary degree in Civil Engineering (2004–2011). She is currently a project management consultant for sanitation infrastructure projects in Sao Paulo, Brazil. She is also a researcher on topics related to project management, infrastructure management, public–private partnership (PPP) projects, risk management, change management, and building information modelling (BIM). She can be reached at fernanda.varella.borges@usp.br

Mariana Wyse holds a Master's degree in Civil Engineering from the University of Sao Paulo (2010–2013). She had her bachelor's degree in Architecture and Urbanism from University of Sao Paulo with a complementary degree in Civil Engineering (2002–2009). She has also recently completed a bachelor's degree in law from the University of Sao Paulo (2017–2022). She is currently a project manager for sanitation infrastructure projects in Sao Paulo and a lecturer on the programme of specialization on construction project management at *Escola Politécnica*, University of Sao Paulo. She has authored articles on building design and management, and design office management, and is a researcher on topics related to project management, infrastructure management, business strategy and governance. She can be reached at marianawyse@usp.br

Tiely Mognhol has a Master's degree in Civil Engineering from the University of Sao Paulo, Brazil (2016–2019); and a Bachelor's degree in Civil Engineering from University of Ouro Preto, Brazil (2004–2009). Her experience as a civil engineer has mainly been in the project management of infrastructure projects. She is currently a lecturer on the civil engineering and architecture programs. She is also a researcher on topics related to project management, infrastructure management, design management, project success factors and international construction. She can be reached at tielyzm@alumni.usp.br

Kumar Neeraj Jha is a Professor with the Department of Civil Engineering, Indian Institute of Technology Delhi. He researches in the area of construction project management, project success factors, asset management, schedule, cost, quality, and safety. He started his career with Larsen and Toubro Ltd and was instrumental in the successful completion of a number of construction projects of national importance. He has authored 4 books and about 140 papers in international and national journals and conference proceedings. He has supervised 15 PhD scholars and more than 100 MTech students. He can be reached at knjha@civil.iitd.ac.in

Ajit Kumar Sinha has worked as a Superintendent Engineer at Prasar Bharti, Civil Construction Wing, CGO Complex, New Delhi. He earned his PhD degree in construction management from the Indian Institute of Technology Delhi. He was working in risk management, PPP construction, dispute resolution, environmental clearance, project financing, and litigation in construction. He has managed and delivered many prestigious government projects. He can be reached at ajitgaya@rediffmail.com

Satish Kumar Viswanathan is a practicing construction management professional with more than 18 years of experience in the construction industry. He obtained his bachelor's degree in Civil Engineering with Distinction from Bharathiyar University, India. He has also completed his Master's degree in Construction Management and Post-Graduate Diploma in Project Management. He has a doctoral degree from the Indian Institute of Technology Delhi in the area of risk management and entry strategies for international construction projects. He has authored a number of papers which have been published in journals and conference proceedings. He has been involved in the execution of various nationally important and award-winning projects. He can be reached at satish.dae@gmail.com

Santu Kar is an Assistant Professor in the Department of Civil Engineering at the Indian Institute of Technology Guwahati, India. He earned his MTech and PhD degrees from IIT Delhi, and a BE degree from Jadavpur University, India. His research interests include materials management, automation in construction, green building, smart cities, resource optimization, and sustainable construction. He has more than five years industry experience at Larsen & Toubro (L&T) Construction. He also has more than two years teaching experience. He has delivered lectures on software applications on project management in several training programs for professionals. He was a member of the panel which prepared the Draft of IS code on Procurement Management. He has 10 publications including six papers published in ASCE journals of which one was selected and included in the Editor's choice collection. He has also written two chapters in books released by international publishers. He is a reviewer of papers for several international journals. He can be reached at santu.iitd.11@gmail.com

Sparsh Johari is an Assistant Professor in the Department of Civil Engineering in Indian Institute of Technology (IIT) Guwahati, India. He obtained his PhD degree in Construction Management from IIT Delhi. He has expertise in workforce management; productivity, quality, and safety in construction; project management; capacity building; project evaluation; and performance appraisal. He has conducted technical and financial audits of various government and non-government agencies. He has also worked with the Construction Skills Development Council of India to develop national-level standards for construction workers. Currently, he is working in the area of digitalization in training systems. He can be reached at sparshjo@gmail.com

Luciani Somensi Lorenzi is a Senior Lecturer in the Department of Civil Engineering at Federal University of Rio Grande do Sul (UFRGS), Brazil. She has a Masters and PhD degrees in Engineering. She is also the Coordinator and Research Leader of the Building Performance Institute (IDUFRGS). She is a member of the Technical Committee for Innovative Products of the National System for Technical Assessment of Innovative Products (CT-SINAT Inovadores) of the Ministry of Regional Development of Brazil. She is the Joint Coordinator of the Building Performance Group: Management and Innovation, a research group at the Brazilian National Council for Scientific and Technological Development. She is also a researcher at NORIE (Center for Innovation in Building) and LEME (Structural Modeling and Tests Laboratory). She is a Founding Member of the Brazilian Association of Construction Pathology. She can be reached at 00178889@ufrgs.br

Paulo Roberto Pereira Andery is an engineer. He holds a masters and PhD degrees in Engineering. He is a Senior Lecturer in the Department of

Materials Engineering and Construction at Universidade Federal de Minas Gerais (UFMG), Brazil. He is a Joint Coordinator of the Minas Gerais Project Management Group, a research group at UFMG. He is an Associate Editor of *Revista Gestão & Tecnologia de Projetos*. He is a member of Working Groups and the Technical Committee of the PBQP-H — Programa Brasileiro de Qualidade e Produtividade do Habitat (Brazilian Program of Quality and Productivity in the Habitat). He is a member of the graduate program in Construction Materials and Management at UFMG, as well as a coordinator of consulting projects. He can be reached at pauloandery@gmail.com

Patrícia Elizabeth Ferreira Gomes Barbosa is an architect and urban planner. She is a specialist in civil production engineering. She has a Master's degree in Civil Construction from Universidade Federal de Minas Gerais (UFMG), Brazil. She is the Managing Partner of PGB Arquitetura, Engenharia e Negócios, a design and construction firm. He is a Joint Coordinator of the Minas Gerais Project Management Group, a research group at UFMG. She is a Senior Lecturer on the MBA in Civil Construction program of the UFMG, and on graduate and undergraduate programs in engineering and architecture and urbanism at DOM HELDER, UNI-BH, UNA and Izabela Hendrix Methodist Institute. She has an association with ANTAC, a Brazilian National Association of Built Environment Technology. She was a Counselor of the Regional Council of Architecture and Urbanism CAU/MG in 2018–2020. She was also a member of the National Materials Commission (SIMAC) at the PBQP-H — *Programa Brasileiro de Qualidade e Produtividade do Habitat* (Brazilian Programme of Quality and Productivity in the Habitat) in 2018–2021 and 2021–2023. She can be reached at patricia@pgbengenharia.com.br

Yan Ning is a professor at Nanjing University, China. He obtained his PhD degree from the National University of Singapore, and conducted post-doctoral research at the University of Hong Kong. His research interests cover project governance and public project management. He was the recipient of the IPMA Young Researcher Award and his papers have been published in the *International Journal of Project Management* and some other high quality journals. He can be reached at ny@nju.edu.cn

Shang Gao is a Senior Lecturer in Construction Management at the University of Melbourne, Australia. He has a diverse range of research interests in construction management with a focus relating to Lean Construction. He is the author of *Lean Construction Management — the Toyota Way*, which is the first book that addresses the application of the practices of the Toyota Way practices in the construction industry to achieve lean construction management. He has also served as a consultant to large construction firms in China, Singapore, Indonesia and Australia. He can be reached at Shang.gao@unimelb.edu.au

Clinton Aigbavboa is a Professor at the Department of Construction Management and Quantity Surveying, University of Johannesburg, South Africa. Before joining the academic field, he was a quantity surveyor on several infrastructure projects in Nigeria and South Africa. He is the immediate past Vice Dean of the Faculty of Engineering and Built Environment, University of Johannesburg. He has extensive knowledge on practice, research, training, and teaching. He is currently the Director of the Construction Industry Development Board Centre of Excellence and the Sustainable Human Settlement and Construction Research Centre at the University of Johannesburg. He is also an author of 12 research books that were published with Springer Nature and CRC Press. He is Editor-in-Chief of the *Journal of Construction Project Management and Innovation* and has received national and international recognition in his field of research. He is rated by the South Africa National Research Foundation. He can be reached at caigbavboa@uj.ac.za

John Aliu is a Research Associate with the Institute for Resilient Infrastructure Systems, College of Engineering, University of Georgia, USA. Before that, he was a Postdoctoral Research Fellow at the Construction Industry Development Board Centre of Excellence, University of Johannesburg, South Africa. He holds a PhD in Civil Engineering and has research interests in construction and engineering education, skills development, construction technologies, digital construction, project management, technological innovation and learning in the era of the Fourth Industrial Revolution. He has extensive knowledge in conducting high-quality multi-disciplinary research, training, and teaching. He also serves as a regular reviewer for various ASCE, Elsevier, Emerald,

Springer and Taylor & Francis built environment journals. He is a member of Project Management South Africa and the South African Institution of Civil Engineering. He has co-authored a research book published by CRC Press and has authored several book chapters, and papers in peer-reviewed journals and conference proceedings. He can be reached at john.aliu@uga.edu

Wellington Didibhuku Thwala is a Research Professor at the College of Science, Engineering and Technology (CSET), Department of Civil Engineering at the University of South Africa. He has extensive experience in providing service as a consultant for project leadership and management of construction projects and in teaching project management subjects at the postgraduate level. In addition, he has extensive industry experience. His research focuses on Industry 4.0, sustainable construction, leadership and project management. He is a National Research Foundation rated researcher. He is the Editor-in-Chief of the *Journal of Construction Project Management and Innovation*. He also serves as an editorial board member for many reputable international journals. He can be reached at thwaladw@unisa.ac.za

https://doi.org/10.1142/9789811224720_fmatter

Contents

https://doi.org/10.1142/9789811224720_fmatter

List of Figures

https://doi.org/10.1142/9789811224720_fmatter

List of Tables

https://doi.org/10.1142/9789811224720_fmatter

List of Boxes

https://doi.org/10.1142/9789811224720_fmatter

List of Abbreviations

AACE	Association for the Advancement of Cost Engineering
ABDIB	Brazilian Association of Infrastructure and Base Industries
ABNT	Brazilian Association of Technical Standards
ADB	Asian Development Bank
AEC	Architecture, Engineering and Construction
AIPM	Australian Institute of Project Management
ANN	Artificial Neural Networks
AOSIS	Alliance of Small Island States
APM	Association for Project Management
BCA	Building and Construction Authority
BIM	Building Information Modelling
BNDES	Brazilian National Economic and Social Development Bank
BOCWA	Building and Other Construction Workers Act
BOK	Body of Knowledge
BoQ	Bills of Quantities
BREEAM	Building Research Establishment Environmental Assessment Method

Ci3	Construction Industry Improvement Initiative India
CBIC	Brazilian Chamber of the Construction Industry
CCPM	Critical Chain Project Management
CDM	Construction Design and Management Regulations
CIB	International Council for Research and Innovation in Building and Construction
CIC	Construction Industry Council
CIDA	Construction Industry Development Authority
CIDB	Construction Industry Development Board
CIDC	Construction Industry Development Corporation
CII	Construction Industry Institute
CIIP	Construction Industry Improvement Programs
CIOB	Chartered Institute of Building
CIRC	Construction Industry Review Committee
CITP	Construction Industry Transformation Programme
CONQUAS	Construction Quality Assessment Scheme
CoST	Infrastructure Transparency Initiative
CPD	Continuing Professional Development
CPI	Consumer Price Index
CPM	Critical Path Method
C-PMBOK	China-PMBOK
CPWD	Central Public Works Department
DCCPMBOK	Developing-Countries Construction Project Management Body of Knowledge
DCPMBOK	Project Management Body of Knowledge for Developing Countries
DPR	Detailed Project Report
DRR	Disaster Risk Reduction
ERP	Enterprise Resource Planning
EVA	Earned Value Analysis
EVM	Earned Value Management
FIDIC	International Federation of Consulting Engineers
FMKT	Facilities Management Knowledge Transfer
FTE	Full-Time Equivalent

GBC	Green Building Certification
GDP	Gross Domestic Product
GMPI	Global Multidimensional Poverty Index
GNI	Gross National Income
GVA	Gross Value Added
HIPC	Heavily Indebted Poor Countries
HIS	Housing of Social Interest (HSI)
IAPPM	International Association of Project and Program Management
ICB	International Competence Baseline
ICLEI	Local Governments for Sustainability
ICMS	International Cost Management Standards
ICT	Information and Communications Technology
ICTAD	Institute for Construction, Training and Development
IDB	Inter-American Development Bank
IDMS	Infrastructure Delivery Management System
IEG	Independent Evaluation Group
IES	International Ethics Standards
IFC	International Finance Corporation
IFM	Integrated Facilities Management
IFMA	International Facilities Management Association
IMF	International Monetary Fund
INBoK	Indian Infrastructure Body of Knowledge
IOT	Internet of Things
IPD	Integrated Project Delivery
IPMA	International Project Management Association
4IR	Fourth Industrial Revolution
ISO	International Organization for Standardization
KPI	Key Performance Indicator
LDC	Least Developed Country
LEED	Leadership in Energy and Environmental Design
LLDC	Landlocked Developing Countries

MCMV	*Programa Minha Casa, Minha Vida* (which means, "My House, My Life Program)
MFI	Microfinance Institutions
MSME	Micro, Small and Medium-sized Enterprises
MUDC	Ministry of Urban Development and Construction
NASA	National Aeronautics and Space Administration
NEC	The New Engineering Contract
NGO	Non-Government Organization
NQF	National Qualification Framework
NSPE	National Society of Professional Engineers
O&M	Operation and Maintenance
OECD	Organization for Economic Cooperation and Development
OH&S	Occupational Health and Safety
OPHI	Oxford Poverty and Human Development Initiative
P2P	Possible to Profitable
PDCA	Plan-Do-Check-Act
PDRM	Project Management Methodology for Post-Disaster Reconstruction
PERT	Program Evaluation Review Technique
PM	Project Management
PMBOK	Project Management Body of Knowledge
PMCDF	Project Managers Competency Development Framework
PMI	Project Management Institute
PMP	Project Management Professional
PPI	Project Performance Indicators
PPP	Public–Private Partnerships
PROMPT	Projects Resource Organisation Management Planning Technique
PRINCE	PRojects In Controlled Environments
QCBS	Quality and Cost Based Selection
RAMP	Risk Analysis and Management for Projects

R&D	Research and Development
RICS	Royal Institution of Chartered Surveyors
RIVANS	Relationally Integrated Value Networks
ROCKS	Roads Cost Knowledge System
ROM	Rough Order of Magnitude
RoR	Rate of Return
SACPCMP	South African Council for the Project and Construction Management Professions
SADC	Southern Africa Development Community
SAP	Systems Application Products
SAQA	South African Qualifications Authority
SDG	Sustainable Development Goal
SHE	Safety, Health and Environment
SIDS	Small Island Developing States
SME	Small and Medium Enterprise
TFM	Total Facilities Management
TMO	Temporary Multi-Organization
TQM	Total Quality Management
TVET	Technical and Vocational Education and Training
UNDP	United Nations Development Program
UNDRR	United Nations Office for Disaster Risk Reduction
UNHDI	United Nations Human Development Index
UN-Habitat	United Nations Human Settlements Programme
UN-OHRLLS	United Nations Office of the High Representative for the Least Developed Countries, Landlocked Developing Countries and the Small Island Developing States
VfM	Value for Money
VR	Virtual Reality
VUCA	Volatile, Uncertain, Complex, and Ambiguous
WASH	Water, Sanitation and Hygiene
WBS	Work Breakdown Structure
WEF	World Economic Forum

Part 1

Introducing the Book, and the Need for such a Body of Knowledge

https://doi.org/10.1142/9789811224720_0001

Chapter 1

Introducing *Building a Body of Knowledge in Project Management in Developing Countries*

George Ofori

London South Bank University, UK

Abstract

The aim of this chapter is to introduce this book. It begins with a rationale for the book, wherein it briefly presents the current state of project management from the perspective of the developing countries. It then sets out the aim and objectives of the book. The nature of the chapters is then outlined. This information had been provided to the authors to guide them in preparing the chapters. This is followed by the synopses of the chapters prepared by the Book Editor. Finally, in the conclusion, the Book Editor assesses the extent to which the book meets the rationale which inspired the launch of its compilation, and the aim and objectives which were set out for the book.

Keywords: Project management, body of knowledge, developing country context, lack of fit, proposals for change, the future

Introduction

The rationale for the book is presented in this section. The current state of project management is briefly presented, as is the set of circumstances that projects face in developing countries. The previous calls for action to address the gap between the existing frameworks for project management and the situation on the ground in the developing countries are next discussed. Then the aim and objectives of the book and the nature of the chapters are presented.

Present state of project management

Project management is broadly defined as the application of the art and science of management to the execution of all kinds of projects. As a subject, project management has a large volume of literature and an established body of knowledge, although the components of this body of knowledge are categorized and presented in a number of different ways. Some professional institutions and national standards agencies have conceptualizations of project management. The *Guide to the Project Management Body of Knowledge* (PMBOK) of the Project Management Institute (PMI) (2017) is arguably the most well-known. The international standard, ISO 21500, also presents components of project management.

The concepts of project management can be applied on all projects in all sectors of the economy. However, projects differ in many respects. Moreover, the situations in which they are undertaken are also different. Thus, the universal framework is not likely to be appropriate on all projects. Recognizing the unique features of construction activity and projects, the PMI (2016) has produced the Construction Extension, which provides construction-specific guidance for the project management practitioner. The developing countries have an operating environment presenting a set of factors influencing the project which are different from those in industrialized countries where the existing bodies of knowledge were compiled.

Since the 1960s, it has been suggested that it is necessary to make changes to the way project management is practiced in order for it to work in the developing countries (Hirschman, 1967). This call has been repeated on many occasions (Russell-Hodge and Hunnam, 1998; Youker, 2007), and it continues to be made (Ika *et al.*, 2021). Ofori (2016) highlights aspects that should be considered when seeking to improve the performance of the construction industry in developing countries. For example, he suggests that the 10 *knowledge areas* outlined in the PMI PMBOK (Sixth Edition) (Project Integration Management; Project Scope Management; Project Schedule Management; Project Cost Management; Project Quality Management; Project Resource Management; Project Communications Management; Project Risk Management; Project Procurement Management; and Project Stakeholder Management), each of which is considered to contain all or some of the project management processes and activities, do not consider all the areas which are critical in developing countries.

It is also necessary for the existing field of project management to pay greater, more specific attention to some other issues that are particularly relevant to developing countries, such as land acquisition (Zoomers *et al.*, 2017); the management of the operation of the built item (Rogage *et al.*, 2020); and the management of post-disaster reconstruction projects (Mannakkara and Wilkinson, 2013; Sospeter *et al.*, 2022). Moreover, it is pertinent to note that the framework should facilitate the introduction of new technology such as Building Information Modelling (BIM) (Ilter and Ergen, 2015) and robotics (De Soto *et al.*, 2019); new project performance parameters such as sustainability (Stanitsas and Kirytopoulos, 2022); and worker welfare (Kamardeen, 2022) in the context of the developing countries. Thus, it is evident that *A Body of Knowledge in Project Management in Developing Countries* is a book that is the need of the moment.

Aim and objectives

The aim of this book is to present a state-of-the art account of the field of project management and propose a body of knowledge of the field for the developing countries.

The book has the following objectives:

1. Present the current state of knowledge on project management by considering the trends, and how they widen the content and scope of the field;
2. Explore the need for a special body of knowledge of project management for the developing countries;

3. Determine the nature of the field of project management in the developing countries, consider the contents of the field, and discuss the relationships between the proposed new field and the established bodies of knowledge; and
4. Consider the future prospects of the field of project management in developing countries and how the development of the body of knowledge for those countries might influence mainstream project management.

Focus of chapters

Most of the chapters in this book cover each of the areas of the body of knowledge of project management. Each of these chapters considers the subject from the perspective of developing countries. It highlights ways in which what is proposed by the authors differs from what pertains in the industrialized countries and presents approaches which will work in the special context of the developing countries. Some of the other chapters present case studies of project management in construction from a number of developing countries; and others discuss directly the contribution they make to the development of the overall project management body of knowledge for developing countries (DCPMBOK).

Nature of each chapter

Each chapter of this book presents and discusses the main concepts relating to its topic in mainstream project management and considers the issues that are of direct relevance to the developing countries; discusses likely future development of the relevant concepts; and proposes aspects for further research on, and development of, the field of knowledge as it relates to the developing countries.

Each chapter of the book is based on a Knowledge Area(s) of project management (where relevant). However, the chapter discusses the principles in the particular area rather than considering the individual processes and activities into detail. It covers the nature of, and rationale for, the relevant aspects of construction project management.

Each chapter is designed and written to form part of an important reference book for practitioners, students, researchers and administrators. Thus, it is based on a strong review of the literature. Each chapter is intended to be an authoritative and enduring piece on the topic it covers.

Structure of the book

The chapters in this book are categorized under the following headings:

- Introduction — chapters which introduce the book, and its main subject;
- Project management in developing countries;
- Project management knowledge areas with developing country perspectives and considerations;
- (Adding to knowledge): necessary areas of project management, especially in a developing country context;
- Project management in various developing countries; and
- The future: project management body of knowledge for developing countries.

Synopses of chapters

The synopses of the chapters are now presented, adopting as subheadings, the categories in the structure outlined above.

Introduction

Ofori writes on "Introducing *Building a Body of Knowledge in Project Management in Developing Countries*" in this chapter (Chapter 1). In this introduction, he gives the initial explanation of the need for considering the developing-country perspective in project studies. He showcases the book by presenting a summary of the contents of the chapters.

In the chapter entitled: "Need for a *Body of Knowledge* on Project Management in Developing Countries" (Chapter 2), Ofori notes that the project is now ubiquitous in business and in life in general, and it is necessary to manage each project to ensure that it results in the desired outcomes. Noting that there have been attempts to conceptualize projects and project management and to compile a body of knowledge for project management, he considers the nature and importance of a project and the current state of project management and its body of knowledge. He discusses the results from the application of project management in general, and in the developing countries in particular. He suggests that it is necessary to further develop project management and consider the circumstances of developing countries in doing so. He briefly presents a way forward to attain these objectives.

Project management in developing countries

Lizarralde, Páez and Herazo write on: "Imported Project Management Practices in Developing Countries: The Problem of Insufficient Adaptation to Local Project Governance Systems in the Construction Sector" (Chapter 3). They observe that there is a call in the developing countries for the application of new ideas, methods and tools in construction such as standardized project management "Bodies of knowledge," Building Information Modelling (BIM) and green building certification. There is a rush to adopt procedures and practices from the industrialized countries without questioning their validity and pertinence in local contexts, but these practices often fail to respond to the fragmented and dynamic character of the local construction industry. Lizarralde, Páez and Herazo argue that there are mismatches between governance approaches in the Global South and the imported project management practices. The project management practices in developed countries face greater challenges when they are adopted in developing countries without sufficient adaptation and customization. They conclude that while there is a need to improve practices in developing countries, these should emerge from culturally relevant best practices, be rooted in local project governance conditions and have the characteristics of the local construction industry.

In the chapter, "Project Management and International Development: The Nexus and the Future of Project Management in Developing Countries" (Chapter 4), Ofori notes that developing countries need a range of projects to engender their long-term national progress in every sphere: economic, social, environmental, institutional and physical. Thus, the efficient management of projects is of particular importance to the countries. However, the results of performance on projects in the developing countries are poorer than in their industrialized counterparts. Ofori shows that the context of the developing countries makes the application of the existing approach to project management inappropriate. He explores possible synergies between international development and project management. This shows that the body of knowledge on, and the practice of, project management should be decolonized. Ofori makes a tentative attempt to lay out what the nature of the decolonized project management field of knowledge would look like.

Project management knowledge areas with developing country perspectives and considerations

In the chapter entitled: "Project Scope Management in Developing Countries" (Chapter 5), Tuuli, Adaku, Banye, and Tettey note that project scope defines the end result or mission of the project in specific, tangible and measurable terms. Thus, project scope management is a critical success factor in project delivery. New scope addition has been identified as one of the causes of project delay and cost escalation. In the developing country context, the prevalence of issues such as ill-defined scope, scope creep and scope change is further compounded by factors including politics, budget constraints, lack of expertise and lack of stakeholder engagement. Tuuli, Adaku, Banye, and Tettey analyze two case studies highlighting the typical Scope Management approach on a social intervention project and a private-sector residential development project in Ghana. The case studies show that inadequate, ill-defined or incomplete scope definition leads to significant scope changes, with consequential cost and schedule implications.

Doloi's chapter is titled: "Project Schedule Management in Developing Countries" (Chapter 6). He notes that schedule management comprises key project functions but the efficiency derived through a schedule depends on context-specific lead up activities in relation to the project environment. The evidence from the literature shows that projects in developing countries are managed without much of the lead up work and often without appropriate definition of scope. Due to unique issues in their contexts, a project in a developed country poses different sets of challenges from that in a developing country. The project management body of knowledge is found to be inadequate for dealing with the long and unstructured project phases in the developing country context. However, there is not much work on producing a body of knowledge encompassing these issues. Doloi uses research at the Smart Villages Lab at the University of Melbourne, Australia, a review of the literature and a case study from India to discuss the development and delivery practices of projects using an enhanced schedule management framework. He shows that the framework can help to achieve enhancements in schedule management practice in similar economies around the world.

Ankrah and Manu write on "Project Cost Management" (Chapter 7). They note that projects consume costly resources that need to be managed to ensure that their outturn costs are within the budget. However, the literature reports that projects across the globe overrun their cost and that factors that cause cost overruns are a prevalent problem in developing countries. Project cost management comprises four steps: cost planning, cost estimating, budgeting and cost control. Factors that explain the project environment in developing countries may necessitate a different approach to project cost management and should be considered when managing project costs in these countries. They include: project and organization forces (procurement arrangements, project management competencies and productivity); sector/industry forces (availability of country-level cost benchmarking indices and construction industry standards and policies); country/economic forces (strength of public institutions, corruption and inflation rate); and global forces (international cost and ethics standards, and global initiatives and policies). Ankrah and Manu discuss future trends in project cost management in developing countries, including the influence of construction industry 4.0 transformations, and carbon accounting and costing practices. They propose some directions for future research in project cost management in developing countries.

Rwelamila writes on "Quality Management in Construction Projects in Developing Countries — Where To, From Current Body of Knowledge?"

(Chapter 8). He notes that construction industries, like other industries across the world, consider quality as one of the primary project parameters. Thus, the various generic project management bodies of knowledge consider project quality management as one of the central knowledge areas. The frameworks are for managing project quality in all industries (except the PMI publication which has a construction extension) and also do not distinguish between issues in industrialized countries and those in developing countries. However, project management dynamics in industrialized countries differ significantly from those in developing countries. Rwelamila adopts existing BoK project quality management frameworks as the baseline with variants of developing country quality management approach as additions or improvers to propose an appropriate developing country quality management approach. Rwelamila revisits the quality management BoK and highlights its shortfalls and present approaches that will work in the special context of developing countries; presents and discusses mainstream project management; considers quality management issues that are of direct relevance to developing countries; discusses likely future development in project quality management in developing countries; and finally, proposes further research on, and further development of, project quality management as it relates to developing countries.

In their chapter on "Curbing Communication Challenges in Construction Project Management in Developing Countries" (Chapter 9), Emuze, Mollo, and Awuzie note that whereas there has been increasing emphasis on dealing with challenges in construction project management relating to cost, time, quality, and safety and health, inadequate attention has been paid to project communication management. They explore practical measures that will engender effective project communication management in construction in developing countries. They propose that project success is endangered when the planning, collection, sharing and management of information are ineffective. They examine issues relating to behavior, culture, diversity and platform that affect communication and project outcomes. They stress that communication management has played a vital, but under-recognized, role in the realization of good project performance in construction in developing countries. They suggest that an effective approach to managing communication in construction in developing countries would be to mitigate barriers relating to language and cultural diversity in tandem with the use of digital technologies. The conceptual argument is that enabling social interaction and use of technologies curbs project communication management challenges in construction in developing countries.

Hasan and Kamardeen write on "Construction Project Risk Management in Developing Countries" (Chapter 10). They note that the construction industry is criticized for poor performance on its projects due to schedule delays, cost overruns, poor quality and high rates of accidents. In construction projects, the ability to identify, assess and manage risks has a direct impact on the achievement of various project objectives. As construction projects are exposed to an uncertain environment, they require effective risk management throughout their lifecycle for their successful completion. However, despite several advances in risk management, project risk management in construction in developing countries has remained inadequate. Studies on construction risks and risk management frameworks have mainly focused on developed nations, which have significantly different socio-political, economic and legal systems. Hence, the suggestions and risk management frameworks need to be customized to suit the unique context of the developing countries. Hasan and Kamardeen discuss the main risks encountered in construction projects and the risk management strategies and frameworks applied in developing countries. They utilize a socio-ecological theory to develop a holistic risk management framework and apply the framework to analyze occupational health and safety risks in construction projects in developing countries.

In the chapter titled "Project Procurement Management in Developing Countries" (Chapter 11), Watermeyer outlines three phases of procurement: planning, acquisition and contract management. The existing project management standards provide generic guidance on concepts, processes and practices applicable to all types of projects. Watermeyer identifies the specificities of the construction industry and articulates the differentiators in practices between the construction industry and what is catered for in the generic body of knowledge for project procurement management. He identifies the procurement challenges and needs faced in developing countries. The underlying environment within which construction projects are delivered and the resources available to undertake projects are the major differentiators between developed and developing countries. Strategic and tactical choices and the manner and extent of their application differ. The level of maturity in performing the client "buying" function can also differ. Watermeyer identifies the need for, and nature of, a construction-specific body of knowledge for project procurement management and indicates the knowledge, skills and attitudes required of practitioners in this field. He suggests that more research be undertaken to establish the client "buying" function body of knowledge and to broaden the understanding of the linkage between client maturity in the "client" buying function and project outcomes.

The title of the chapter Chinyio and Opoku-Ohemeng write is: "Project Stakeholder Management in Developing Countries" (Chapter 12). They outline some problems encountered while implementing stakeholder management in developing countries, formulate solutions to these problems and offer guidance on the implementation of stakeholder management in developing countries. Semi-structured virtual interviews with practitioners in some developing countries informed the study. The content analysis of the interview data showed that, apart from the internal stakeholders, another set of project stakeholders include community organizations, trade unions, non-government organizations and various individuals or groups — these many stakeholders present high chances of conflicting stakes. Power influences the prioritization of stakes in developing countries; i.e., the interests of more powerful stakeholders (such as government and public establishments) are accorded higher priority. Moreover, some traditions and cultures are strong in communities, regions or nations, and stakeholder engagements follow these norms. Another major influence in some developing countries is land ownership, which tends to be a leveraging factor on which some external stakeholders either bargain for compensation and concessions or attempt to disrupt a project. They conclude that there is scope for increasing the awareness and thus, the power, of external stakeholders in developing countries.

(Adding to Knowledge): Necessary areas of project management, especially in a developing country context

Windapo writes on "Project Performance Indicators and their Management in Developing Countries" (Chapter 13). She notes that what makes the concept of project success difficult and complicated in practice is that there is no consensus on how it should be measured, and this complicates the management of projects. She suggests that scholars view the many ways of measuring success as being dependent on the interest and business goals of each project stakeholder. In developing countries, construction project environments are dynamic due to the involvement of many stakeholders, with different interpretations and prioritization of project performance indicators. Windapo examines project performance indicators in the context of developing countries with the view to establishing the important indicators common to project stakeholders and where there are usually quite clear differences. She develops a conceptual model of project performance indicators common to developing countries and discusses the implications of the model for theory and practice.

Adinyirah, Agyekum, and Ofori write on "Managing the Operating Environment of Projects in Developing Countries" (Chapter 14). They note that any project's operating environment has an impact on project management decisions. They suggest that projects in developing countries are more sensitive to their operating environments than those in industrialized countries, mainly because of the varied and, often, changing nature of projects' environmental factors such as the cultural, economic, political, social, physical, institutional and technological. They note that failure to properly manage the unstable operating environment of projects is arguably the chief cause of the less-than-optimum project outcomes often recorded in developing countries. They examine the operating environment in the context of developing countries and the differences and similarities with those in developed countries. They suggest approaches for the context of developing countries by discussing aspects of the project environment and suggesting ways in which it may be influenced to increase the probability of a successful outcome; and they recommend topics for future research on this area of knowledge related to developing countries.

The topic for De Silva and Asmone is "Embedding Facilities Management Knowledge into Project Management in Developing Countries" (Chapter 15). They suggest that an important goal of project management is to achieve value for money (VfM) for the clients throughout the lifecycle of the project. Proper project management enables facilities management to reach this goal through appropriate procurement strategies and value management practices, considering the facility's operational requirements to realize minimum operational cost. De Silva and Asmone note that the need for project management to incorporate facilities management is more critical in developing countries as the operational budgets of facilities are usually insufficient to maintain optimum facility performance. In this context, in developing countries, project management is important for the success of facilities management. Similarly, facilities management has the potential to improve project management. De Silva and Asmone attempt to build a body of knowledge for developing countries in terms of how project management and facilities management relate to, and affect, each other. They establish and operationalize the integration of these fields to attain the untapped value of Integrated Facilities Management. They suggest that developing countries should embrace technological advancements, apply procurement methods favorable to facilities management, apply facilities management benchmarks and employ value-driven knowledge-based facility managers.

The title of the chapter by Palliyaguru, Amaratunga, Samarakkodi, and Nissanka is: "Distinct Project Management for Post-disaster Reconstruction Projects in Developing Countries" (Chapter 16). They note that while there is a large volume of literature on post-disaster reconstruction, particularly in developing countries, knowledge on the differences in project management concepts, processes, activities and practices adopted for routine construction and those specific to post-disaster reconstruction projects is fragmented and needs to be established. They explore the need for a specialized body of knowledge of project management for disaster reconstruction in developing countries. They analyze the challenges, conditions and factors encountered on past disaster reconstruction projects in developing countries such as Sri Lanka. They study the extent to which traditional project management concepts, processes, practices and activities are appropriate in dealing with the challenges that confront disaster reconstruction projects in developing countries and propose changes required in the current generic project management approach to make it suitable for disaster reconstruction projects in developing countries.

Bajaj and Mahalingam write on: "How Cost Estimators Develop Estimates: Experiences From the Indian Context" (Chapter 17). They note that cost estimates in construction projects are often incorrect, leading to cost overruns. The literature suggests that estimation is mildly chaotic and random. While a number of behavioral, cognitive and structural explanations are given for cost estimates differing from final project costs, the voice of estimators is rarely heard. Bajaj and Mahalingam seek to understand and explain the dynamics of construction cost estimating in the developing country context and how estimating can be restructured and bias eliminated. They describe how project costs are estimated in the context of construction projects in India through studying the experiences of the people involved in the estimating. They find that several practices of estimating are pursued by different stakeholders in various positions in the project value chain. They did not find evidence of strategic misrepresentation, but found some evidence of optimism bias. They recommend the creation of separate standards and practices for different types of firms and different levels of estimates.

Mahesh, Mengistu, and Kumaraswamy write on: "BoK in Developing and Implementing Construction Industry Improvement Programs" (Chapter 18). They note that construction project performance is influenced by industry-wide issues such as the business environment, sector-specific drivers and challenges, and various country-specific issues. The imperatives for addressing such industry issues have led to the formulation and implementation of industry improvement programs in both industrialized and developing countries. However, the performance and image of the industry has not yet been significantly improved. They seek to identify common core components and critical elements of a body of knowledge for developing and implementing Construction Industry Improvement Programmes (CIIPs), especially in developing countries. They review previous CIIPs in Hong Kong, Singapore and the UK to identify key themes, lessons and challenges from their implementation. They compare these with improvement programs and requirements of developing countries with examples from Ethiopia, India and Sri Lanka, to initiate the development of the body of knowledge to guide the planning and implementation of construction industry reform programs in developing countries. They identified these knowledge areas of CIIPs: Manpower

Development; Enhancing Capacity; Institution Building; Improving Practices; and Planning for Smoother Demand. They conclude that enabling optimal project performance at the national level calls for holistic industry-level improvements rather than piecemeal developments.

Toor and Ofori write on "Project Leadership in Construction in Developing Countries" (Chapter 19). They note that leadership plays an important role in social settings: in the political arena, social environment or business organization. The nature of construction projects makes leadership essential. They are technically complex and involve many stakeholders with diverse backgrounds and often competing needs. Project managers tend to focus on managing the technical tasks, conscious about the budget, schedule and other project parameters, and often pay less attention to the importance of the human element. This leads to poor team and project performance, underlining the point that the need for effective leadership in construction is acute owing to problems of the construction industry and poor performance on its projects. Studies further indicate that the developing countries face even more severe problems in these regards and that hinders their efforts to establish the physical foundation for the socio-economic development of those countries. Toor and Ofori highlight the importance of effective project leadership and its development in construction in the developing countries. They explain leadership and its relevance to projects, consider the special requirement of project leadership in construction, discuss the need for project leadership in construction in the developing countries and provide suggestions for project leadership development in the construction industries in the developing countries.

Project management in various developing countries

Souza, Borges, Wyse, Mognhol, and Melhado write on: "Infrastructure Projects and Project Management in Brazil: Challenges and Trends" (Chapter 20). They note that the Brazilian infrastructure scene has changed in recent years, with growing participation of the private sector and falling public investments, since the constraints on federal public expenditure from 2016; the *Lava Jato* operation; and reduction in availability of loans. This led most Brazilian infrastructure corporations to rethink their processes and fostered the entry of new national and international companies. Project management has been sensitive to the changes made, improving risk management in the corporations and efficient cost management. Integrated management solutions and obtaining licenses and authorizations also became essential to efforts to attain efficiency in the use of resources. They discuss the infrastructure projects in Brazil, the market and internationalization trends in infrastructure projects and the current state of project management knowledge to explain procurement, risk, cost and stakeholder management as well as the use of technology such as BIM to address the industry challenges. They consider ethics and governance as pillars for infrastructure project management. They offer proposals on new management areas that are relevant to infrastructure project management in developing countries.

Jha, Sinha, Vishwanathan, Kar, and Johari write on: "Project Management in Developing Countries — A Case of Indian Construction Industry" (Chapter 21). They present an overview of the Indian construction industry, covering the status of construction workers, the state of Indian project performance and the efforts made to improve them. They note that the Indian construction industry is estimated to be worth about US$640 billion in 2022; the construction industry is the second largest employer, being responsible for the participation of 16 percent of the country's working population. The industry in India is fragmented; the large-sized firms work in all the construction segments, medium-sized firms in niche activities and small firms as subcontractors. In comparison with the developed countries, the Indian construction industry is labor-intensive and the deployment of modern machinery and techniques is limited. Moreover, most Indian construction firms are reluctant to follow the regulations. These aspects influence the project management approach of Indian construction firms. Jha, Sinha, Vishwanathan, Kar and Johari set out the practices of the Indian construction industry in the key project management knowledge areas such as integration management, scope management, resource management, communication management, risk management, procurement management, stakeholder management and leadership.

Lorenzi, Andery, and Barbosa write on "Project Management in Brazil: A Reflection About the Brazilian Context and Its Impact on Social Housing Projects" (Chapter 22). They note that social housing projects have recently stood out in the Brazilian construction industry, owing to the great social impact in a country with a large housing deficit. These projects were less affected by the substantial economic downturn that had an impact on the industry. The management systems of these projects were conditioned by financial, regulatory and managerial systems based on ISO 9001 and other performance-based standards. Lorenzi, Andery and Barbosa describe circumstances that had an impact on project management processes, including public financing mechanisms for housing projects, which was conditional upon the provisions of a quality management system developed specifically for construction companies, which is a component of the Brazilian Habitat Quality and Productivity Programme. Another important initiative is the Brazilian Standard on Performance-Based Buildings which has been promoting changes in project management processes including better definition of design scope and design management processes, improvement in the integration of design and construction phases and improvement of procurement processes. In the final section of the chapter, how some of these processes have been used in both public and corporate projects is discussed.

Ning and Gao write on "Rules First or Practice First? The Paradox of Quality Management in Innovative Projects in Developing Countries: The Case of China" (Chapter 23). They note that project quality management is undertaken through the plan-do-check-act (PDCA) method, which assumes that formal rules (such as regulations and codes) work as the guidelines. However, these formal rules appear to be less systematic in developing countries. This might lead to a practical paradox, while the absence of formal rules may hinder the adoption of innovative quality management. In such a context, the development of rules should be prioritized. On the other hand, innovative projects often give rise to the emerging formal rules. They note that addressing this paradox may have implications for quality management in innovative projects in developing countries. They examine how stakeholders manage the paradox of quality management in innovative projects in China. They studied one precast project to delineate the trajectory of quality management and development of formal rules. Their key findings are: it is necessary to undertake experimentation before full-scale application; during the experimentation and implementation, it is important to formalize quality management plans and it is important to engage a wide range of stakeholders who can contribute their knowledge to the development of the new technology and increase the legitimacy of innovative quality management methods.

In "A Review of the Evolution of Project Management in South Africa" (Chapter 24), Aigbavboa, Aliu, and Thwala note that there is a shortage of skilled project managers in the country as the demand for project management skills in South Africa has increased across a wide variety of industries. This shortage is exacerbated by the significant volumes of investment in infrastructure and services. The advent of the Fourth Industrial Revolution (4IR) has initiated a digital transformation across industries, including the project management profession. Through a bibliometric approach, they examine the evolution of the project management concept in South Africa over a 26-year period in works indexed in the Scopus database. They examine the implications of the 4IR on the project management profession and how project managers can leverage on this wave of digitalization. They predict the skills that project managers will be required to have in order to thrive in the digital era and offer suggestions to higher education institutions as they restructure their curricula and research agenda to align them with the requirements of "Project Management 4.0."

The future

In the chapter entitled: "Developing the Field of Knowledge of Project Management: The Perspective of the Developing Countries" (Chapter 25), Ofori addresses these questions: at what stage is this body of knowledge in its development? How relevant is it to the developing countries? What is its future? How can the needs, concerns and attributes of the developing countries be appropriately reflected in it? He notes that the body of knowledge of the field of project studies is growing, receiving contributions from many disciplines. He considers the current misconceptions in the practice of project management and research in project studies such as the tendency to consider all projects to be the same, and the low level of attention paid to the context of projects. He then discusses the theoretical development of project management and the level of development of the field and notes that there are disagreements on the extent to which the lack of progress in the field is responsible for the poor performance on projects. He considers the future of project management, starting with the challenges facing the field, and setting out suggestions by some authors for further research. He then adopts a developing country perspective and takes up the subject of decolonizing project studies.

In the final chapter of the book entitled "Future of Project Management in Developing Countries" (Chapter 26), Ofori discusses the nature of the construction industry and process, in order to highlight the peculiar nature of construction activity and the need for special actions in managing it, which cannot be adequately covered by generic frameworks. He then considers the importance of projects in developing countries and the problems of the construction industry in these countries. He presents a brief summary of the discussion in the book and considers the possible implications of a developing country body of knowledge for project studies in general. Ofori discusses the future of project management, including the need for its improvement and the challenges facing it and presents an agenda for research in the future. He makes a case for the decolonization of project management. Finally, he presents an action plan to bring about the body of knowledge of project management for developing countries, and makes initial proposals on what a PMBOK for the developing countries should look like.

Conclusion

The summary of the chapters provided here in the introduction of the book shows that the chapters provide a comprehensive coverage of the subject of project management and its practice in developing countries. The aim and objectives of the book have been met. The chapters, together, present a state-of-the art account of the field of project management, and show the need for changes in content and approach to reflect the perspectives of the developing countries. They present possible areas and topics of a body of knowledge of that field specifically for the developing countries.

The book shows that project management is an important set of skills that is critical for effectively undertaking and completing projects which are now common in almost all sectors of the economy. Project management has many areas to address, and there is much progress to make in filling gaps and dealing with misconceptions in its own body of knowledge. The book also makes a strong case for the development of a body of knowledge particularly to guide research on, and practice of, project management in developing countries. Researchers, practitioners and students of project management in developing countries construction economics will find this book a very useful resource.

References

De Soto, B.J., Agosto-Juan, I., Joss, S. and Hunhevicz, J. (2019). Implications of Construction 4.0 to the workforce and organizational structures. *International Journal of Construction Management*. https://doi.org/10.1080/15623599.2019.1616414.

Hirschman, A.O. (1967). *Development Projects Observed*. The Brookings Institute Press, Washington, DC.

Ika, L.A., Keeys, L.A., Tuuli, M.M., Sané, S. and Ssegawa, J.K. (2021). Call for papers special collection: Managing and leading projects in Africa. *Project Leadership and Society*. 2. https://doi.org/10.1016/j.plas.2021.100023.

Ilter, D. and Ergen, E. (2015). BIM for building refurbishment and maintenance: Current status and research directions. *Structural Survey*, 33(3), 228–256. https://doi.org/10.1108/SS-02-2015-0008.

Jaysawal, N. and Sudeshna Saha, S. (2018). Impact of displacement on livelihood: A case study of Odisha. *Community Development Journal*, 53(1), 136–154. https://doi.org/10.1093/cdj/bsw026.

Kamardeen, I. (2022). Work stress related cardiovascular diseases among construction professionals. *Built Environment Project and Asset Management*, 12(2), 223–242. https://doi.org/10.1108/BEPAM-06-2021-0081.

Mannakkara, S. and Wilkinson, S. (2013). Build Back Better principles for post-disaster structural improvements. *Structural Survey*, 31(4), 314–327. https://doi.org/10.1108/SS-12-2012-0044.

Ofori, G. (2016). Construction in developing countries: Current imperatives and potential. In K. Kahkonen and M. Keinanen (Eds.), *CIB World Building Congress 2016 on Intelligent Built Environment for Lives*. 30 May–3 June, Tampere University of Technology, Tampere.

PMI (2016). *Construction Extension to the PMBOK® Guide*. Upper Darby, PA.

PMI (2017). *A Guide to the Project Management Body of Knowledge*, 6th Edition. Upper Darby, PA.

Rogage, K., Clear, A., Alwan, Z., Lawrence, T. and Kelly, G. (2020). Assessing building performance in residential buildings using BIM and sensor data. *International Journal of Building Pathology and Adaptation*, 38(1), 176–191. https://doi.org/10.1108/IJBPA-01-2019-001.

Russell-Hodge, J. and Hunnam, P. (1998). Learning about culture through projects in aid programmes. In R. Lundin and C. Midler (Eds.), *Projects as Arenas for Renewal and Learning Processes*. Kluwer, Boston, MA, pp. 47–58.

Sospeter, N.G., Rwelamila, P.D. and Gimbi, J.J. (2022). A conceptual framework for managing post-disaster reconstruction projects in emerging economies: The case of Angola. *Built Environment Project and Asset Management*, 12(2), 205–222. https://doi.org/10.1108/BEPAM-03-2021-0040.

Stanitsas, M. and Kirytopoulos, K. (2022). Underlying factors for successful project management to construct sustainable built assets. *Built Environment Project and Asset Management*, 12(2), 129–146. https://doi.org/10.1108/BEPAM-10-2020-0166.

Youker, R. (2007). Managing projects financed by international lending agencies. In D.I. Cleland and L.R. Ireland (Eds.), *Project Manager's Handbook: Applying Best Practices Across Global Industries*. McGraw Hill, New York, pp. 97–105.

Zoomers, A., van Noorloos, F., Otsuki, K., Steel, G. and van Westen, G. (2017). The rush for land in an urbanizing world: From land grabbing toward developing safe, resilient, and sustainable cities and landscapes. *World Development*, 92, 242–252. https://doi.org/10.1016/j.worlddev.2016.11.016.

https://doi.org/10.1142/9789811224720_0002

Chapter 2

Need for a *Body of Knowledge* on Project Management in Developing Countries

George Ofori

London South Bank University, UK

Abstract

Projects have become ubiquitous in business and in life in general. It is necessary to manage projects to ensure that they result in the desired outcomes. There have been attempts to conceptualize projects and project management and to compile a body of knowledge for project management. What is the history of project management? What is the current state of project management? How appropriate is the existing body of knowledge to developing countries? How can it be further developed, taking the context of these countries into consideration?

This chapter begins by discussing the nature and importance of a project. This is followed by consideration of why it is necessary to manage projects, the nature of project management, and the attempts made to conceptualize it and to build a body of knowledge on it. The results from the application of project management in general, and in the developing countries in particular, are discussed. It is suggested that it is necessary to further develop project management and consider the circumstances of developing countries. A way forward is presented.

Keywords: Project, project management, importance and history, body of knowledge, developing countries, the future

Introduction

The aim of this chapter is to begin the argument for the need for a body of knowledge for project management in developing countries. The objectives of the chapter are: to explain the nature of a project and the need to manage projects; to discuss project management including its origins, importance, benefits and demerits, and its body of knowledge; to consider the developing countries and their needs for projects; and to discuss the development of the field of project management.

What is a project?

The Association for Project Management (APM) describes a project as "a unique, transient endeavour, undertaken to achieve planned objectives, which could be defined in terms of outputs, outcomes or benefits."[1] The Project Management Institute (PMI) considers a project as "a temporary endeavor undertaken to create a unique product, service or result."[2] International Project Management Association's (IPMA) International Competence Baseline (ICB) version 4.0 (2015, p. 27) defines a project as "a unique, transient endeavour undertaken to bring about change and to achieve planned objectives." The US Bureau of Reclamation (2012, p. 7) offers this definition: "A project is temporary, unique, and the product of a multifaceted and progressively elaborated process that produces a solution for a specific objective." The international non-governmental organization, PM4NGOs (2020, p. 209), defines a project as: "A set of activities meeting agreed objectives in a specific period of time with an agreed set of resources." A project is unique because it is a specific set of operations designed to accomplish a singular goal (International Organization for Standardization (ISO), 2017).

From the many definitions, it can be deduced that a project is a series of non-routine and unique activities that are undertaken to accomplish specific, definable objectives, stated in terms of time, cost, and other

[1] https://www.apm.org.uk/resources/what-is-project-management/

[2] https://www.pmi.org/about/learn-about-pmi/what-is-project-management

relevant performance requirements. Thus, projects differ from continuous or repetitive operational systems although the achievement of specific objectives of a project entails a process. A project requires a team of people, often cross-functional and multi-disciplinary or from different organizations, who come together temporarily to focus on specific objectives.[3] Thus, on a project, many activities have to be coordinated, often across organizational or geographical boundaries. Projects consume resources, some of which are in short supply, finite or non-renewable. Projects constitute a dynamic response to both internal developments and external incidents and complexities, and they involve risks and uncertainties. From Nicholas (1990), Pinto (1996), and Kor and Wijner (2007), the following features can be added. A project can be controlled from one point. It is oriented toward a deliverable, a result, or a product; it is essential to those concerned; and the failure of a project can be fatal to at least some of the parties involved in it, or which have an interest in it. With these attributes, projects require to be systematically, effectively, and efficiently managed.

Projects differ in their nature and characteristics. They may be categorized in terms of: size; complexity (expressed by the unfamiliarity, magnitude, or diversity of effort); type of client; industry or sector; and level of certainty (expressed by the difficulty in predicting the measure of success of the final outcome). Binder (2007) categorizes projects into: Traditional project, where "a large majority of team members work for the same organisation"; Distributed project, which "involves team members working in many locations"; International project, which is "when a distributed project includes people located across country borders"; Virtual project, which "is composed of team members dispersed geographically and working in different organisations"; and Global project, which is "a combination of virtual and international projects, which includes people from different organisations working in various countries across the globe." Nicholas and Steyn (2008) present a typology of projects which they plot in terms of the cost-time (in man hours) against uncertainty (in time-cost-performance), and ranges from a student's term paper through a nuclear plant to a manned mission to Mars, and beyond. An often-referred-to

[3] https://www.apm.org.uk/resources/what-is-project-management/

example of a large and complex infrastructure project illustrating the application of project management tools and practices is the England–France Channel project (1988–1994), involving two arrays of government agencies; many financial institutions; engineering, construction and other organizations of various sizes from many countries; applying two main traditions of construction practices; involving many necessary adjustments to the goal and performance factors; and language, use of standard metrics, and other communication differences (Lemley, 1992; Winch *et al.*, 2002; Anderson and Roskrow, 2020).

What makes projects important, and what makes them useful?

Projects are found in all sectors of the economy, including those sectors such as construction and shipbuilding where projects are the norm ("project-based" sectors), and others such as information technology (IT), manufacturing, financial services, retail, hospitality, law and transport, where projects exist side-by-side with the non-project routine activities. Projects have become important to even these organizations because of the benefits they bring. A project enables the organization to tackle transient tasks as they arise. Thus, Gemünden *et al.* (2018, p. 147) conceptualize the project-oriented organization as "an entrepreneurial, future- and stakeholder-oriented innovating organisation, which uses projects as temporary, task-focused organisations, to define, develop, and implement its strategies, to transform its structure, culture and behavior, and to define and develop new products, services, and business models."

Projects are becoming increasingly common. There is said to be a "projectification" of society, as discussed below. Clegg and Courpasson (2004) and Lindgren and Packendorff (2006) are among authors who consider project-based work as one of the many new "post-bureaucratic" organizational forms that have entered most industries in the last few decades. This development toward project-based structures has been seen in many industries and organizations as inevitable and, indeed, desirable (Söderlund and Tell, 2009). In their paper entitled, "The projectification of everything," Jensen *et al.* (2016, p. 21) consider projectification to be "omnipresent not only in the economy but also in our society and our lives," and conceptualize it as "a human condition." Gareis (2002) notes that projects and programs are undertaken in the economy and also in social groups such as municipalities, associations, schools, churches, and even families. He suggests that competence in project management is key to the competitiveness of companies and countries. As a consequence of projectification, the ability to organize operations in the form of projects in an effective manner is considered to be a core competence in many organizations today (Gareis and Huemann, 2001; Söderlund and Tell, 2009). In the context of this book, projects are necessary activities for realizing most of the outputs and outcomes that lead to improvements in the quality of life.

What is project management?

There are many definitions of "project management," but they highlight common features of projects, aspects of the process, and similar objectives. Project management involves managing discrete packages of work which comprise a particular task, to achieve specific objectives. APM (n.d.) defines it as "…the application of processes, methods, skills, knowledge and experience to achieve specific project objectives according to the project acceptance criteria within agreed parameters. Project management has final deliverables that are constrained to a finite timescale and budget."

The "objectives" in this definition may be expressed in terms of: outputs (such as a new item of infrastructure); outcomes (such as the community in an area being provided with improved transport services); benefits (such as increased incomes of farmers in a district); or strategic objectives (such as improving the quality of life of the population in two years).

The PMI defines project management as "the application of knowledge, skills, tools, and techniques to project activities to meet the project requirements."[4] Some other definitions of project management are:

a. The ISO 21500:2021 series of project management standards defines it as: "coordinated activities to direct and control the accomplishment

[4] https://www.pmi.org/about/learn-about-pmi/what-is-project-management

of agreed objectives" (ISO, 2021, clause 3.4); and ISO 10006, a standard for quality in project management, defines it as a "unique process consisting of a set of coordinated and controlled activities with start and finish dates, undertaken to achieve an objective conforming to specific requirements, including constraints of time, cost and resources" (ISO, 2017);

b. PRINCE2, the UK standard for project management, offers this definition: "a temporary organization that is needed to produce a unique and predefined outcome or result at a pre-specified time using predetermined resources";
c. The IPMA (2015) defines project management as "a time and cost constrained operation to realize a set of defined deliverables up to quality standards and requirements"; and
d. PM4NGOs defines project management as: "Planning, organizing and managing resources to bring about the successful completion of specific project goals, outcomes and outputs" (PM4NGOs, 2020, p. 209).

After reviewing several definitions, Siles (n.d.) suggested that "project management is 'the planning, implementing, and monitoring of project activities to meet project objectives, achieved by effectively controlling and balancing the constraint of time, cost, and scope in producing quality deliverables that meet or exceed the expectations of the project stakeholders.'" Nicholas and Steyn (2008) provide this summary of project management. A person, designated as the project manager, heads the project organization and operates independently of the organization's normal chain-of-command. This project organization reflects the cross-functional, goal-oriented, and temporary nature of the project. The project manager is responsible for integrating the contributions of people from different disciplines and overseeing the start and completion of their activities to achieve the project objectives and negotiating with functional managers for support as necessary. Decision-making, accountability, outcomes, and rewards are shared among members of the project team and the supporting functional units. When a project ends, the project organization is disbanded, and the members of the team return to their functional units or are reassigned to new projects. As noted by Byrne (2010), project management is a life skill for all.

Project, program, and portfolio and their management

"Project" is often used in relation to "project," "program," and "portfolio." It is necessary to explain the differences among them. IPMA's definitions of these terms show the differences. IPMA (2015, p. 27) defines a project as "a unique, temporary, multi-disciplinary and organised endeavour to realise agreed deliverables within predefined requirements and constraints"; and it considers a program as being "set up to achieve a strategic goal. A programme is a temporary organisation of interrelated programme components managed in a coordinated way to enable the implementation of change and the realisation of benefits." Finally, a portfolio "is a set of projects and/or programmes, which are not necessarily related, brought together to provide optimum use of the organisation's resources and to achieve the organisation's strategic goals while minimising portfolio risk." Table 2.1 presents the APM's definitions of a project, program, and portfolio, and the management of each of them.

Table 2.1: Definitions of project, program, and portfolio.

Level	Item	Definition
Project	A project	A unique, transient endeavor undertaken to bring about change and to achieve planned objectives.
	Project management	The application of processes, methods, knowledge, skills, and experience to achieve specific objectives for change.
Program	A program	A unique, transient, strategic endeavor undertaken to achieve beneficial change and incorporating a group of related projects and business-as-usual (steady-state) activities.
	Program management	The coordinated management of projects and business-as-usual (steady state) activities to achieve beneficial change.
Portfolio	A portfolio	A collection of projects and/or programs used to structure and manage investments at an organizational or functional level to optimize strategic benefits or operational efficiency.
	Portfolio management	The selection, prioritization, and control of an organization's projects and programs in line with its strategic objectives and capacity to deliver.

Source: APM (2019b)

Why is it necessary to manage projects?

As a project has particular features and constraints, as well as an operating environment and thus, many dependencies, it is necessary to adopt a structured approach to the management of the activities involved in it. APM (2015) notes that trillions of pounds are invested in projects, programs, and portfolios every year. The cost of failure can have a catastrophic effect on the economy, the environment, and society. Watermeyer and Philips (2020) give an example of two power projects that had been planned to relieve a power crunch in South Africa, delays to which caused stress in the national economy. The set constraints of the project need to be aimed at; targets set; and plans, schedules, and budgets prepared to guide performance to attain them. The operating environment of the project might also bring about obstacles that need to be tackled with a systematic approach. Moreover, a project involves many persons, and in some cases, several companies, and their roles and activities need to be assigned and coordinated. The stages of each project should be related to each other toward attaining the common project aims and objectives. Finally, each project has many stakeholders with different aspirations and expectations who need to be consulted and their aspirations aligned and satisfied.

Project management is aimed at producing an output or outcome which will effect some change for the benefit of the organization that initiated the project. Projects that require more formal management are those that have a finite timespan, are complex in terms of work or groups involved, and require the management of change and/or management of risks.[5] Wideman (1991) argues that the application of the traditional management principles and approaches to project-type work is invalid because the nature of a project implies that a different management philosophy, strategy, and relationships are required.

There are both internal and external pressures on organizations to adopt a strategic approach to, and excel in, managing projects. Kerzner (2008) suggests that the external pressures include: *Competition*, stemming from the customers' expectations and actions taken by other firms; *Quality standards* required by customers — increasingly, they require high quality, with fewer failures; *Financial outcomes* — clients and users expect service

[5] https://www.apm.org.uk/resources/what-is-project-management/

providers to accept lower profit margins, while providing value for money; *Legal concerns* — clients and society expect adherence to the generally widening and increasingly more stringent laws and regulations; *Technological factors* — customers expect the application of state-of-the-art technology at reasonable prices; *Social concerns* — employees want a system that allows them to do more work in less time; *Political factors* — these influence competition among firms in a global economy; *Economic pressures* — these include the impact of exchange rates and cost of borrowing; and *Stockholders' concerns* — stockholders want internal growth and external expansion through cost-effective operations.

A project environment features the following (Wideman, 2006): temporary teamwork and informal relationships, complex management arrangement, specific time constraints, limited and/or shared resources, measurable progress against plans, and rapid change. This uncertain environment calls for adaptability and rapid response to change and should enable the application of high-level technical and managerial competence and decentralization in decision-making (Nicholas and Steyn, 2008). Kerzner (2017) lists these challenges to the management of projects: project complexity; risks; special, often changing requirements of customers; changes in technology; and a need for forward planning and pricing. Gemünden *et al.* (2018) model the project-oriented organization as consisting of three core segments: values, structures, and people. They empirically found that these segments increase project success, innovation and business success.

Importance, advantages and disadvantages of project management

Importance of project management

As noted above, it is suggested that there is a "projectification" of society and especially in the industrialized countries (Ekstedt, 2009; Schoper *et al.*, 2018), while Ika *et al.* (2021) note that projectification is gathering pace in the developing countries. Increasingly, there are people undertaking a formal role in many sectors, using the tools and techniques of project management. Box 2.1 presents a review of the current situation of project management in India.

Box 2.1: Project management in India.

PMI India commissioned a study on the state of project management in the country. The objective was to develop an understanding and evaluate the importance given to the application of project management principles in the private and public sectors.

The Indian economy is on a high-growth trajectory; GDP grew by 6–10 percent during the past few years. With the effects of the global slowdown on India, infrastructure investment has been identified as the most important element in bringing the country back to the 8–9 percent growth trajectory. Therefore, India's growth over the next five years leans on the effective management of its big infrastructure agenda. However, time and cost overruns have been a major problem on several projects, especially government projects. The implementation status of these projects underscores the critical gaps in the application of proper professional management, in accordance with established international models and guiding principles. Therefore, learning and using project management is becoming crucial for the continued growth of India.

Despite sufficient awareness of the benefits of project management, "lack of client-led demand" and "lack of clarity of benefits" are the major factors influencing adoption of project management practices.

What are the key benefits actualized/expected?
In India, the industry perceives project management as a "time management tool." The major benefits achieved include timely completion of projects within the original budget and business impacts, indicated by revenue growth following the successful project implementation.

What are the challenges in adopting project management?
There is a low level of understanding of project management. Many respondents in the study identified it as more of an execution and monitoring tool rather than a planning tool. Most of the companies do not feel the need to apply its practices to simpler projects. Most respondents who have undergone project management certification felt that they would not invest in the training on their own, and that it was the company's responsibility to invest in project management skills and certification. Inadequacy of skilled and semi-skilled personnel often limits productivity and causes a divergence of the results from what was intended.

What causes resistance to project management?
The most basic form of resistance discovered by the research is the formal definition and classification of the discipline of project management on

Box 2.1: (*Continued*)

grounds of identity. Many respondents mentioned the existence of project management, but were unable to provide or accept a standard definition of it. The quantification of costs and benefits through project management in most organizations is only in terms of time and cost; qualitative improvement is hardly conceived as a benefit. Most of the companies associate the performance of their project management teams first with aspects of project completion. There are few carrots and fewer sticks; most companies felt incentives for better performance or penalties for poor performance were not sufficiently strong to engender acquisition of project management practices.

Growth drivers

The drivers of the growth of project management included: the infrastructure boom and development of more complex projects; client-led demand in the IT sector, with increasing share of the Indian IT sector in the global IT market; procurement practices and guidelines needing to be upscaled in project management practices; and projects implemented under public–private partnership (PPP), as guidelines for monitoring of PPP projects have been issued by the Planning Commission and with new regulations affixing accountability for delays and overruns within the administrative ministry for each project.

Key action areas and priorities

The study identifies a number of actions by various stakeholders. The important ones to be addressed are:

- Government: Demonstrate the relevance of project management principles in planning and appraisal stages; raise the profile of project management institutions; and develop and deliver appropriate courseware for agencies.
- The industry: Obtain endorsement for project management through demonstration and documentation; and promote project management certification beginning with including it in construction contracts.
- Academic institutions: Develop project management courseware matching international standards; obtain recognition for project management as a profession; and build awareness among organizations and incentivize certification.

Source: Indicus Analytics and Ace Global (2010).

Many claims are made concerning the extent of projectification. Shenhar and Dvir (2004) claimed that projects form half of today's organizational activity. However, Schoper *et al.* (2018) empirically estimate the degree of projectification (measured as the share of project work in total work) of three European economies, considering all sectors of the economy and all project types. They found that projectification comprises 34.7 percent of economic activities in Germany, 32.6 percent in Norway, and 27.7 percent in Iceland. They conclude that, in advanced economies, about one-third of all economic activities is project work, but there are major differences among the individual sectors.

A study commissioned by the APM (PwC, 2018) examined projectification in the UK and its economic impact. Its key findings were:

- The project management profession makes a significant contribution to the UK economy — 2.13 million full-time equivalent workers (FTEs) are employed in the UK project management sector (7.96 percent of employed FTEs)
- The profession generates £156.5bn of annual gross value added (GVA) (8.9 percent of UK GVA) (in contrast, the construction industry's GVA is £113bn, and the financial services sector, £115bn)
- Recognition of the importance of good project management has been growing; organizations in all sectors are optimistic about the future of project management — 40 percent predict a growth in project size, and 34 percent expect project budgets to grow over the next three years
- Challenges include more than half of organizations expressing concern over the impact of political uncertainty in the UK and skills and capability shortages.

Advantages of project management

To the APM, effective project management has many benefits, including: providing a greater likelihood of achieving the desired result; ensuring efficient and best value use of resources; and satisfying the differing needs of the project's stakeholders.[6] PMI notes that the value of project management

[6] *Ibid.*

is underlined by its rapid, worldwide growth as a strategic organizational competence; as a subject for training and education; and as a career path.[7] PMI further suggests that projects are critical drivers of business success.[8] The rationale for following the project management approach is that it helps in handling complex, costly, and risky assignments by enabling an interdisciplinary, task-oriented approach. Gemünden *et al.* (2018) note that the project-oriented organization makes a major contribution to innovation and success in business.

Wideman (2006) and Kerzner (2017) identify the following advantages of the application of project management: improved scope definition with a results orientation; optimization in the allocation and use of resources; greater quality conformance and reliability; reduced cost and time; improved risk management and better control; and enhanced morale and ability to develop greater team spirit and mission orientation for the personnel. The project and its goals can be shared with participants and other stakeholders to explain roles, responsibilities, and authority structure and to engender support. Kerzner (2017) suggests the following potential benefits from project management: functional responsibilities are identified to ensure that every activity is accounted for and can be assigned; time limits for individual activities are determined and scheduled; a method for trade-off analysis is identified; progress and accomplishment against plans is measured; problems are identified, and corrective actions can be taken; estimating and monitoring capabilities can be applied and enhanced for future application; and lessons can be learned for improving performance in future.

Disadvantages of project management

Project management has its limitations and demerits. Kerzner (2017) presents some of these disadvantages, from the perspective of the organization: organizational policies might not be applied consistently on different projects; there might be lower effectiveness of the utilization of personnel by deploying staff members on projects as functional activities and skills

[7] https://www.pmi.org/about/learn-about-pmi/what-is-project-management

[8] https://www.pmi.org/pmbok-guide-standards/foundational/pmbok

may be duplicated on each project; as project participants' line management is not consistent, their career development might suffer; and support from "central" functional groups might not be optimal.

It should also be noted that the possible lack of continuity in employment in project-based work has an impact on the commitment, productivity, and wellbeing of individual workers. The complexity of the matrix organizations that needs to be formed in the organization housing the project and its human resource implications are well studied (see some of the early works: Davis and Lawrence (1978) and Stuckenbruck (1979)). Another issue is the possible difficulty in attracting the best talent into project-based firms. Berglund *et al.* (2020) explore the consequences of the projectification of society for individuals. Based on the concepts of *entrepreneurial selves* and *prosumption*, they propose the concept of the *projectified self.* They call for emancipatory studies in future that can explore and express the consequences of the projectification of society.

It is suggested that more work should be done to understand projectification and its impact. Henning and Wald (2019) note that while several studies have investigated projectification and its effects at the firm level, the macroeconomic implications of project work have not been well studied. They analyze such effects of firm-level projectification, studying the interlinkages between different sectors by extending input–output modelling. The results indicate that projectification can have positive macroeconomic implications for production and innovativeness, employment, and income that differ across economic sectors, but it can also have negative impacts. They concluded that the appropriateness of the use of temporary forms of organizing depends on the economic sector and sectoral interdependencies.

A brief history of project management

Early history

Many authors offer different opinions as to how and when project management started. Some note that projects have been managed for centuries (Morris, 2010); authors usually refer to the Pyramids in Egypt around 2500 BC, the Hanging Gardens of Babylon, the Great Wall of China, and the Roman and Greek buildings and infrastructure (Nicholas and Steyn, 2017). However, it should be evident that civilized society had been undertaking projects even before then (Morris, 2012). Kozak-Holland (2011) covers some large projects of the last 4,500 years, including the Giza Pyramid, the Parthenon, the Colosseum, the Gothic Cathedrals of Europe, the Taj Mahal, and the Transcontinental Railway. He suggests that they were delivered in a systematic way with similar characteristics to today's projects. Typically, they had a project charter, a business justification, and a project sponsor, followed a similar life-cycle of phases to that used today, and followed all the PMBOK knowledge areas. He refutes these misperceptions: that the projects had unlimited budgets with no economic return, used predominantly a slave workforce, had unlimited timelines, and did not use project management concepts.

Why are the 1950s adopted as the start?

Many authors such as Chiu (2010) consider Henri Fayol (1841–1925), who identified five functions of management every manager performed, and Henry Gantt (1861–1919), credited with devising the Gantt chart, which recognizes the benefits of breaking up projects into small manageable tasks, and that some tasks may depend on each other, as the founders of project management. Many other authors suggest that only in the 1950s did organizations start to apply systematic management tools and techniques to projects (Heagney, 2018). PMI notes that project management "has always been practised informally, but began to emerge as a distinct profession in the mid-20th century."[9] Some, such as Kwak (2003), consider the modern project management era to have started in 1958 with the development of the Program Evaluation Review Technique (PERT) on the US Navy's Polaris project on submarine-launched ballistic missiles and Critical Path Method (CPM) by E.I. du Pont de Nemours Company, in building a major chemical plant for which accurate estimates of cost and time were needed (although it is acknowledged that in 1896, Karol Adamiecki had developed the Theory of Work Harmonisation). Similarly, Shenhar and Dvir (2004) note that projects as an organized activity could

[9] https://www.pmi.org/about/learn-about-pmi/what-is-project-management

be found in every civilization and the roots of project management can be traced to the second half of the 19th century, but as a formal discipline, project management started only when the first PERT charts marked the beginning of a new discipline. Many also consider the earlier Manhattan project to have marked the beginning of modern project management (Shenhar, 2007). In a seminal article, Gaddis (1959, p. 1) considered project management to be of strategic importance, noting:

> "The United States today faces the enormous problem of how to regain undisputed technological leadership. The character of American technological advancement during the next five years will shape our future and determine our survival or extinction. The role to be played by project management in these years ahead will be challenging, exciting, and crucial. Truly it will be the acid test of the project manager and the project concept, but it will be much more than that. It will be a momentous trial of free enterprise, business administration, and progressive industrial management as we know them today."

Milestones in modern project management

Kwak (2003) identified four periods in the history of "modern project management" (see also Seymour and Hussein, 2014):

- Prior to 1958 — better transportation and telecommunication systems allowed for greater mobility and more speedy communication; Gantt charts, developed in 1917, were in use; the concept of job specification (setting out knowledge, skills and abilities needed for a job) was being applied
- 1958 to 1979 — there was significant technological advancement. Project management tools such as PERT (1957) and CPM (1958) were developed; Polaris and Apollo were major projects; the use of the Work Breakdown Structure (WBS) approach was mandated by the US Department of Defense for any large and complex project in 1962. The first project management institution, now IPMA, was formed in 1965; and the PMI in 1969. In the 1970s, availability of affordable mini-computers facilitated emergence of project management software and tools

- 1980 to 1994 — in the 1980s, software programs were mostly based on the Projects Resource Organisation Management Planning Technique II (PROMPT II), which was later refined into the PRojects In Controlled Environments (PRINCE) model. Another major development was the Theory of Constraints, aimed at helping organizations to achieve their goals using the premise that the rate of goal achievement by a system is limited by at least one constraint (Cox and Goldratt, 1986). In 1986, Scrum, an agile software development model encouraging software development by multiple small teams, was developed (Takeuchi and Nonaka, 1986). In 1987, PMBOK® was published by PMI, based on a 1983 White Paper. In 1994, the first CHAOS report of the Standish Group (which reviewed IT project performance and environments and provided advice) was published
- 1995 to 2003 — technology continued to have an impact on the management of projects; in 1996, PRINCE was upgraded to PRINCE2, and in 1997 an alternative method of planning and managing projects, the Critical Chain Project Management (CCPM), was introduced. CCPM emphasized the resources required to complete the project rather than the specific tasks (Goldratt, 1997). In 1998, the PMI's PMBOK became an American standard. In 2001, The Agile Manifesto was produced, founded on core values aimed at enabling software developing teams to perform well.

Similarly, Shenhar and Dvir (2004) considered 1960 to the 2000s as representing distinct "generations," according to the styles that dominated project management attitudes.

1. 1960s: this was the scheduling era; it started with the introduction of PERT and CPM to the construction, space, and aeronautics industries. Focus was on coordination of sequential or parallel activities and control of performance. This was done through IT and planning
2. 1970s: organizations needed to manage complex projects involving participants from different disciplines. The challenge was to ensure integration and teamwork on many complex operations. This was done through process facilitation and role definition

3. 1980s: the main consideration was uncertainty reduction; to make stable decisions that stand the test of time and protect against uncertainties. This was done through a search for information, selective redundancy and risk management
4. 1990s: with the accelerated pace of business, time-to-market was the driving factor in many industries. The main management style was "simultaneity" (integrating tasks and people while differentiating between them at the same time, and dealing with competing demands) (Laufer *et al.*, 1996). This was done through responsiveness and collaboration
5. 2000s: the views and trends are — adaptation (projects differ, "one size does not fit all"); strategic thinking (project management practices must be connected with business strategy); and globalization (projects are increasingly being carried out with teams in different parts of the world and there was a need for global virtual coordination).

On the theoretical development of the field of project management, Lindgren and Packendorff (2009) note that it gradually became a distinct area of scientific inquiry, and more specialized researchers were publishing in its dedicated journals. The two main journals are the *Project Management Journal* (published from 1969 by PMI) and the *International Journal of Project Management* (published from 1983 in collaboration with IPMA). Some authors, such as Seymour and Hussein (2014), suggest that academic degree programs were first offered around 2008. However, many programs had started earlier, such as the M.Sc. (Construction Project Management) program at the National University of Singapore (started in 1993). In the 2000s, communications technology was making it increasingly easier to work from home or other places. Some construction companies, such as Bechtel Corporation, have been thriving on the 24-hour project development approach.[10] While working from home is said to have started in 1973 in the light of the fuel crisis (Baruch and Yuen, 2000), the virtual worker has become mainstream, especially following the COVID-19 pandemic (Vyas and Butakhieo, 2021). As more businesses adopt a more collaborative virtual workspace, challenges in aspects

[10] https://www.bechtel.com/services/

such as leadership, trust, control, and communication emerge. These issues have come to the fore in project management research, as discussed below. In 2012, the ISO 21500:2012 Standard for Project, Programme and Portfolio Management was released. In the UK, in 2017, the APM attained chartered status, a mark of quality and esteem as an institution. In 2021, the Seventh Edition of *PMBOK Guide* was released.

What does project management involve?

The main components of project management, developed from an outline provided by APM,[11] are now presented.

a. Identifying and setting out reasons why the project is necessary;
b. Determining project requirements, specifying the quality of the deliverables, evaluating the viability of the proposed project, and estimating the resources that will be needed and the timescales for activities;
c. Preparing a business case to justify the investment;
d. Obtaining statutory approval, if necessary;
e. Securing the agreement of the client and main stakeholders, and funding and other necessary support for the project;
f. Developing, and getting approval for, a management plan for the project;
g. Managing the procurement process and advising the client on the selection of the main project executing organization;
h. Implementing the project plan and leading and motivating the project delivery team;
i. Managing the project budget; other performance criteria; and risks, issues, and changes on the project;
j. Monitoring progress on the project against the plan and ensuring necessary action is taken to address possible issues;
k. Maintaining communications with stakeholders and the project organization;

[11] https://www.apm.org.uk/resources/what-is-project-management/

l. Managing the providers in the value chain of the project;
m. Coordinating the statutory inspection of the completed item and/or its formal registration; and
n. Closing the project in a controlled manner upon completion, or when appropriate, after arranging the handing over to the sponsor(s) and subsequent management of the facility, if necessary.

Performance on projects

Performance on projects, including on large ones where elaborate project management frameworks and resources are used, has been poor. Morris (2010, p. 21) reviews studies on project success and failure over many decades. He notes that studies of World-Bank–funded projects between 1945 and 1985 concluded that more attention should be paid to technological adequacy, project design, and institution building. International development projects had earlier been analyzed (Hirschman, 1967). Morris and Hough (1988) reviewed 34 studies covering 1,536 projects and programs of the 1960s and 1970s. Typical sources of difficulties were: unclear success criteria; changing sponsor strategy; poor project definition; fascination with, and uncertainty of, technology; concurrency; poor quality assurance; poor linkage with sales and marketing; inappropriate contracting strategy; unsupportive political environment; lack of top management support; inflation; funding difficulties; poor control; inadequate manpower; and geophysical conditions. They also noted that most of these factors fell outside the standard project management guidelines of the time. Morris (2010, p. 21) continues:

> "Later studies of project success and failure, such as those by Miller and Lessard (2000) on very large engineering projects, Flyvberg, Buzelius and Rothengatter on road and rail projects, and Meier (2008) on US defence and intelligence projects as well as the … CHAOS Reports by Standish (1994 and later) emphasised similar factors, namely:
>
> - the importance of managing the front-end project definition stages of a project;
> - the pivotal role of the owner (or sponsor); and
> - the need to manage in some way, project 'externalities.'"

A study by APM (2015), which involved responses from over 860 practitioners, found that whereas over 90 percent of respondents considered their projects to be successful to some degree, just 22 percent of projects wholly met their original objectives. About one in eight projects failed to meet their budget, and about one in six failed to meet their schedule. However, overall, only 6 percent of projects proved wholly unsuccessful. This appeared to show that knowledge of the key to success is often not applied. The study revealed that the environment in which the projects operate, which influences the conditions for project success, is at the heart of improving project outcomes.

Another study by KPMG, Australian Institute of Project Management, and IPMA (2019) involving over 500 respondents in 57 countries provides perspectives on trends in project and program management globally, and the challenges the project management community faces. Project performance was found to be unsatisfactory in all the countries. About 19 percent of organizations deliver successful projects, at least most of the time; and 44 percent are likely to deliver projects that meet original goal and business intent. About 30 percent of organizations are likely to deliver projects on time; 36 percent are likely to deliver projects on budget; and 46 percent of projects are delivered with stakeholder satisfaction. Firms globally face difficulties in delivering projects that meet all objectives around the time, cost, scope, and stakeholder satisfaction parameters. The challenges include: the application of consistent governance oversight; a focus on managing benefits; and managing change through the project lifecycle.

McKinsey Global Institute (Agarwal *et al.*, 2016) found that large infrastructure projects across asset classes typically take 20 percent longer to finish than scheduled and are up to 80 percent over budget. Denicol *et al.* (2020) explore the megaproject management literature to help improve understanding of the causes and solutions of poor megaproject performance. They analyze 6,007 titles and abstracts and 86 full papers and identify 18 causes and 54 cures to address poor megaproject performance. Cantarelli *et al.* (2012, p. 324) note that, "Cost overruns in transport infrastructure projects know no geographical limits; overruns are a global phenomenon." Flyvberg (2019) notes that capital project overruns are one of life's certainties. While the size and number of "megaprojects" (those costing over US$1billion) is growing, such projects consistently fail to be delivered on time or to budget, and often fail to yield the financial returns targeted. In a study of 3,022 projects, only 0.2 percent were on budget, on time, and on benefits. Some 27 percent were within the budget, while 2.8 percent were on budget and on time. Flyvberg (2019) adds that analysis by the Saïd Business School suggests that megaprojects are often commissioned for the wrong reason and due to their size and complexity, are pre-determined to systemic failure. Some recent attempts to reduce the effects of the failure factors were leading to improvement.

There has been a search for factors that influence performance and success on projects (see, for example, Chileshe and Haupt, 2005). Box 2.2 presents the APM framework for project management success. Although in the study, APM's success framework was overwhelmingly supported by survey respondents, it was evident that it is often not applied in practice.

Box 2.2: APM's project success framework.

APM's (2015, p. 4) 12 project success factors identified in a major research study involving 860 respondents from around the world, "provide a framework for project success that defines the environment in which projects can be delivered successfully." Each factor was identified as playing a crucial role in the formation and delivery of the project. They are:

1. Effective governance — leadership, responsibilities, reporting lines, and communications among the parties
2. Goals and objectives — these are clearly specified and recognized by all stakeholders, and project leaders have a clear vision of the project outcomes
3. Commitment to project success — all parties involved in the project are committed to the project's success and project leadership inspires commitment in others
4. Capable sponsors — they assume ultimate responsibility and accountability for the project outcomes
5. Secure funding — contingency funding is recognized from the start and tight control of budgets is in place to ensure maximum value is realized
6. Project planning and review — pre-project planning is thorough with realistic time schedules, there is regular progress monitoring, active risk management, and a post-project review

Box 2.2: (*Continued*)

7. Supportive organizations — the environment in which the project operates is project-friendly; the organization provides support and resourcing and access to stakeholders
8. End-users and operators — are engaged in the design of the project and are able to take on what the project has produced effectively and efficiently
9. Competent project teams — project professionals and other team members are fully competent and engage in positive behaviors, which encourage success
10. Aligned supply chain — all suppliers are aware of project needs, schedules, and quality standards, all tiers of supply chains are coordinated
11. Proven methods and tools — good practice project management tools, methods, and techniques are applied in a way that maintains an effective balance between flexibility and robustness
12. Appropriate standards — quality standards are used to drive the quality of the outputs, and adherence to other standards is monitored to ensure delivery in accordance with best practice.

From this framework, five factors were found to have "the strongest and most consistent relationship" with the traditional measures of project success: time, cost, and quality, and were viewed by APM as "the formula for success" (APM, 2015, p. 15). These were: project planning and review; goals and objectives; effective governance; competent project teams; and commitment to success.

Source: APM (2015).

Body of knowledge of project management

Main bodies of knowledge

Project management has a large volume of literature and an established body of knowledge although its components are categorized and presented in many different ways. The Project Management Body of Knowledge (PMBOK) of the PMI (2017) is arguably the most well-known; the APM (2019a) and some other professional institutions and national standards such as that of Australia, also have conceptualizations (see the Australian National Competency Standards).[12] The ISO 21500:2021 series of standards (ISO, 2021) also presents components of project management.

The *APM Body of Knowledge 7th Edition* provides "the concepts, functions and activities that make up professional project management." It reflects the nature of the profession, recognizing project-based working at all levels, and across all sectors for decision-makers, project professionals, and the teams in which they work.[13] APM describes the seventh edition as "collaborating with the project community to create a foundation for the successful delivery of projects, programmes and portfolios."[14]

PMI notes that *A Guide to the Project Management Body of Knowledge (PMBOK® Guide) Seventh Edition* has been updated to meet current challenges, "better align to how people work today and help you be more proactive, innovative and nimble."[15] This edition of the *PMBOK® Guide*:[16] covers the range of development approaches (predictive, traditional, adaptive, agile, hybrid, and so on); provides a section devoted to tailoring the development approach and processes; expands the list of tools and techniques; focuses on project outcomes in addition to deliverables; and is integrated with PMIstandards+™ for access to content that helps the user to apply the *PMBOK® Guide*. The new edition presents 12 principles of project management and 8 project performance domains critical for the effective delivery of project outcomes.

How did the PMBOK emerge? Allen (1995) noted that the US PMI began the development of its body of knowledge in 1980 with the objective of defining the scope and structure of project management as a prerequisite for developing a distinct project management profession. The PMBOK document was later being presented as the authority in areas including: defining generally accepted practices of project management;

---

[12] https://www.yumpu.com/en/document/view/9558724/australian-national-competency-standards-for-project-management

[13] https://www.apm.org.uk/book-shop/apm-body-of-knowledge-7th-edition/

[14] https://www.apm.org.uk/resources/what-is-project-management/

[15] https://www.pmi.org/pmbok-guide-standards/foundational/pmbok

[16] *Ibid.*

defining the basis of certification testing for project management professionals; and defining the basis for the accreditation of degree-granting education programs. After 1992, the PMBOK development activities shifted from the creation of an "information-structure reference" to a "professionalism-authority reference." Allen (1995) studied the need for a body of knowledge and proposed these basic PMBOK concepts: the definition of basic objectives that address both practitioner and professional needs and the international realities of the project management community; the definition of the major elements of a PMBOK document structure; the definition of a universal project-management classification structure to be used to organize and codify the increasing quality of PMBOK material; and the definition of the management and administrative infrastructure needed to develop, implement and maintain an international PMBOK system. Wideman (1995) considers why there is the need for a project management body of knowledge, and why the knowledge gained over time must be more effectively transferred in future, and also sets out criteria for the development of such a body of knowledge.

Other bodies of knowledge

PM4NGOs, which was founded in 2010, is "an international NGO that promotes and sustains the professionalism of program and project management in the international development sector." Its vision is: "An equitable and sustainable world where social investment achieves the greatest impact."[17] Its mission is: "To promote and sustain the professionalism of program and project management in the international development sector."[18] Its aim is to reach donor organizations and NGOs, as well as community-based organizations and individuals on the ground, often working "against the odds and with minimal resources." PM4NGOs develops best practice guides, methodologies, tools, and techniques to help project managers in the development sector to attain excellence and to improve the impact of their social investment projects and programs. PM4NGOs owns Project DPro and Program DPro, which are guides for project and program management.

---

[17] https://www.pm4ngos.org/about-us/

[18] *Ibid.*

Some of the international development agencies have their own guides for project management for use on the projects they sponsor in the developing countries. An example is that of the Japan International Cooperation Agency (2006), which the agency claimed to be the first in the world to also relate to program management.

Project management in construction

Table 2.2 presents the main features of the construction process, its product and the organizations and industry involved. These features

Table 2.2: A primer on construction.

Questions on aspects	Features of construction
Why construction is needed; what is the purpose of construction?	Construction creates the buildings and infrastructure required for economic activity and for improvement in living standards; it plays a key role in national economies, and in sustainable long-term development.
What is the goal in construction?	Construction work is undertaken to meet set performance requirements, including budget over the long term, time, health and safety, environmental considerations, efficient operation, durability over time, and sustainable management of the disposal of the debris upon demolition.
What is the approach taken; how is it done?	Construction is undertaken in projects commissioned by public or private clients and increasingly in PPPs in any part of the country. The planning, design, construction, and operation and facilities management are undertaken by separate specialist organizations. The materials and techniques are from both local and foreign sources. The government is involved in the process as a regulator and manager of the development of industry capability.
What is the operating environment?	Constructed items are location-specific. Thus, the process is subject to the features of the location including the regulatory and administrative systems; the financial and legal systems; and the social and cultural systems.
Who are the stakeholders?	Construction has a wide range of stakeholders. They include the internal players directly involved in delivering the built item including the client; and external stakeholders including the government, the users and beneficiaries, the residents in the environs of the project, and the natural environment and posterity.

show the need for the process, the participating individuals, and the organizations to be effectively managed in order to obtain the desired output (the built item) and outcomes (improvement in efficiency of the operations in the item, or improvement in the quality of life). It is also important to develop the industry to continuously enhance its capacity and capability to complete its tasks (Rwelamila and Abdul-Aziz, 2020; Ofori, 2021).

Recognizing the unique features of construction, the PMI (2016) has produced the *Construction Extension to the PMBOK® Guide*, which provides construction-specific guidance for each of the *PMBOK® Guide* Knowledge Areas, and guidance in these additional areas which are not found in the *PMBOK® Guide*:[19]

- All project resources, rather than just human resources;
- Project health, safety, security, and environmental management;
- Project financial management, in addition to cost; and
- Management of claims in construction.

The latest edition of the *Construction Extension* also follows the new PMBOK structure, discussing the principles in each of the Knowledge Areas rather than the individual processes. This approach broadens the applicability of the *Construction Extension* by increasing the focus on the "what" and "why" of construction project management.[20] This edition also includes discussion of emerging trends and developments in the construction industry that affect the application of project management to construction projects.

The discussion now turns to the developing countries to consider briefly the nature of these countries and the application of project management in their context.

[19] https://www.pmi.org/pmbok-guide-standards/foundational/pmbok/construction-extension
[20] *Ibid.*

Developing countries

What is a developing country?

What is a "developing country"? The common definition is an economic indicator based on gross national income (GNI) per capita as determined by the World Bank, which adopts this classification of countries (Serajuddin and Hamadeh, 2020):

a. Low-income countries: per capita GNI of US$1,036 and below in July 2019;
b. Lower-middle-income countries: per capita GNI between US$1,036 and US$4,045;
c. Upper-middle-income countries: per capita GNI between US$4,046 and US$12,535;
d. High-income countries: per capita GNI of US$12,535 and above.

"Low-income" and "Lower-middle-income" nations are referred to as "developing countries."

Many authors disagree with the use of one economic indicator to "measure" "development." There is a large volume of literature in the field of Development Economics on the subject of measuring development (see, for example, Sen (1999), Stiglitz *et al.* (2010)), and various alternative indicators of "development," such as the UN Human Development Index (HDI) and the Global Multidimensional Poverty Index (GMPI) have been developed. These are discussed in Chapter 3. While there is a debate on the appropriate definition of development, the GNI per capita definition is widely used, and other indicators, such as HDI and GMPI, are applied to moderate and refine the results of the economic measure.

Among those who disagree with the notion of "developing countries," Meikle (2019) suggests that developing countries differ significantly, and their situations can change. It is worth noting that the classification of "developing countries" by the World Bank is undertaken every year; in 2020, seven countries moved to higher categories, and three countries to lower categories. Developing countries are also dissimilar in many regards, including their prospects for development, their natural and human capital, and their infrastructure base. Finally, some countries with high GNI per capita have poverty, malnutrition, and other human and infrastructure indicators similar to those of a typical developing country.

Construction project performance in developing countries

Many studies show that the majority of projects in developing countries fail, or at least fall short of the plans and expectations (see, for example, Ahsan and Gunawan, 2010; Aibinu and Jagboro, 2012; Ahmadzai and Paracha, 2016). Ofori (2016) suggests that performance on projects in such contexts is unsatisfactory, by using many yardsticks: performance on similar projects in industrialized countries; comparison with the targets of the projects; and ability to meet the expectations of clients and other stakeholders. Damoah *et al.* (2015) studied the causes of project failure on government projects in Ghana in a survey of practitioners and the general public. The top 10 causes in order of importance were: monitoring, corruption, political interference, changes in government, bureaucracy, lack of continuity, fluctuation in prices, planning, delays in payments, and release of funds. In a study in Nigeria, Alao and Jagboro (2017) assessed the tendency of public projects in the country to be abandoned. Hawkins and Prado (2020) examined infrastructure data from 10 member countries of CoST, the Infrastructure Transparency Initiative (almost all of which are developing countries) and found that many of them faced challenges, with difficulties keeping to time and budget and problems with procurement being the most common problems.

In the research roadmap for Working Commission 107 on Construction in Developing Countries of the International Council for Research and Innovation in Building and Construction (CIB), it is noted that "current assessments of various projects in developing countries … paint a picture of project failures across public and private sectors)" (Rwelamila and Ogunlana, 2015, p. 7). The majority of failed projects depict these "umbrella dimensions":

- Inefficient projects — projects failing to meet budget and schedule expectations;

- Weak impact on customers/stakeholders — projects unable to meet technical specifications, address customer/stakeholders needs, and satisfy them;
- Unsuccessful business/or unsuccessful development strategy — projects not achieving significant commercial success (private sector) or development programs/projects unable to achieve developmental goals (public sector); and
- Unsustainable potential — projects unable to contribute toward improving the standard of living, provide better infrastructure, or help to create a conducive environment for investment.

Eja and Ramegowda (2020) investigated the causes, effects, and consequences of project failure in developing countries with particular reference to Nigeria and found that project failure is frequent in such countries. Some of the causes were: poor financial capacity, inaccurate costing and corruption, incompetence and lack of knowledge, poor planning and estimation, poor communication, poor contracting and contractor practices, frequent design scope changes and errors, socio-cultural and political interference, and poor leadership and corruption. The effects of project failure were: loss of revenue to the state, loss of revenue to citizens, substandard infrastructure, and low empowerment of the community. The consequences were: low rates of economic growth, sector-centric underdevelopment, loss of foreign aid or tougher donor guidelines, loss of elections by leaders, and lack of confidence in the state from financial institutions.

Need for a PMBOK for developing countries

Culture and context

It is argued that project management is culturally bound and that the notion of the project itself is a Western one (Koster, 2010). Thus, it is suggested that it is necessary to make changes to the way project management is practiced in order for it to work in developing countries (Russell-Hodge and Hunnam, 1998). Al-Sedairy and Rutland (1994) are among many authors who have highlighted the unique nature of project management in a typical developing country. Dinsmore and Coddas (1993) and Cleland and Gareis (2007) discuss the challenges of working on international projects. Youker (2007) has written several works about the difficulties of managing projects in developing countries, focusing on those funded by the World Bank. Ofori (2016) highlights aspects that should be considered when seeking to improve the performance of the construction industry in developing countries, and they include actions on how projects are managed.

Authors outline the contexts of developing countries and their implications for projects. Roohnavaz (2018) notes that the oil and gas and extractive industries face the challenge of locating new resources in remote parts of developing countries. These projects face skills shortages, inhospitable locations, outdated engineering practices and technology, and logistical issues. The construction of the civil engineering infrastructure is often on the critical path owing to the fixed-period concessions. Roohnavaz (2018) suggests that overcoming these challenges calls for a critical rethink in traditional civil engineering construction practice. Using case studies from Central Asia, the Middle East, and Africa, he shows that innovative solutions that maximize the use of the local workforce, materials, and technology should be designed in line with project timelines.

Frameworks that work in developing countries

Some existing frameworks for project management appear to be able to consider the circumstances in developing countries. Golini and Landoni (2014) show the distinctive characteristics of international development projects of non-governmental organizations and analyze the state-of-the-art of project management processes and tools for such projects. They study the differences between standard project management methodologies (i.e., PMBOK® Guide and IPMA) and the methodologies for non-government organizations (i.e., PM4NGOs and PM4DEV). They found that there is the need for specific managerial approaches and tools for international development projects, and that standard project management methodologies could be complemented by specific tools (such as the logical framework) in order to increase the likelihood that high social impact is the outcome of the project. Similarly, Munro and Ika (2020) compare project management standards from two non-profit, one parastatal, and two governmental organizations in international development with the APM and PMI standards to identify their different knowledge areas, concepts, tools, and emphases. They find that the former standards have different ideas of what project management entails. While APM and PMI standards have strengths in scoping and scheduling, the international development standards emphasize beneficiary participation, environmental impact, gender, unintended consequences of projects, soft objectives, evaluation techniques, and cross-cultural issues.

Many governments have frameworks and guidelines for project management seeking to improve the effectiveness of the management of projects. An example is *The Indian Infrastructure Body of Knowledge* (INBoK), which includes areas not covered in the PMI and APM bodies of knowledge such as: Interface and Integration Management; Change Management; Concessionaire/Contractor Compensation Management; Supply Chain Management; and Value Creation and Benefits improvement.

Another example is South Africa, where the Infrastructure Delivery Management System (IDMS), a project procurement and management system for public infrastructure, was developed (National Treasury, 2012). The main objectives are: to be a best practice guide, setting guidelines and acting as a benchmark to public-sector infrastructure delivery; support improved delivery of infrastructure; address apparent deficiencies in the availability of a skilled and competent workforce; curb the challenges of poor planning that have faced public-sector infrastructure delivery; seek to ensure value for money during infrastructure delivery; and seek to reduce the infrastructure gap in the country and make quality infrastructure affordable. However, the IDMS has faced challenges including (Chingangacha *et al.*, 2021): poor interdepartmental relationships and unclear communication channels; poor leadership and management structures; limited technical capacity; and governance issues and collusion within the industry. Thus, the local context presents obstacles even to frameworks formulated with knowledge of the indigenous situation.

Conclusion

The project is an important means for accomplishing tasks in all sectors of the economy. Project management is a critical concept that is important for ensuring the delivery of projects which meet the set performance parameters. Success in project management is a key contributor to national development and enhancement of the quality of life of the populace. Efforts have been made to conceptualize project management and to draw up a body of knowledge. While project management as a field has been developing, the results on projects have been disappointing. In developing countries, the results are even worse. It would appear that the current concepts and techniques of project management are not appropriate for those countries.

The many "guidelines" or "frameworks" of project management shows that there is no single blueprint; and there are competing proposals of "methods" or "best practices." If projects are common and are the routine in some sectors such as construction, then there can be no cultural exclusivity in project management. As projects are undertaken in different geographical, organizational, and social environments, it is necessary to introduce local contexts and circumstances into the determination of best approaches to particular issues. It is necessary to develop a body of knowledge of project management for developing countries. It is pertinent that some of these countries, such as India, have developed their own project management bodies of knowledge. Researchers on project management should start to decolonize project management.

References

Agarwal, R., Chandrasekaran, S. and Sridhar, M. (2016). Imagining Construction's Digital Future, 24 June. https://www.mckinsey.com/business-functions/operations/our-insights/imagining-constructions-digital-future

Ahmadzai, N. and Paracha, S. (2016). Why do projects crash and burn in fragile countries? *Review of Integrative Business Economics Research*, 5(1), 315–328.

Ahsan, K. and Gunawan, I. (2010). Analysis of cost and schedule performance of international development projects. *International Journal of Project Management*, 28(1), 68–78.

Aibinu, A.A. and Jagboro, G.O. (2002). The effects of construction delays on project delivery in Nigerian construction industry. *International Journal of Project Management*, 20, 593–599.

Al-Sedairy, S.T. and Rutland, P. (1994). Project management as a way forward in a developing country. In D.I. Cleland and R. Gareis (Eds.), *Global Project Management Handbook*. McGraw Hill, New York, pp. 5-3–5-23.

Alao, O.O. and Jagboro, G.O. (2017) Assessment of causative factors for project abandonment in Nigerian public tertiary educational institutions. *International Journal of Building Pathology and Adaptation*, 35(1), 41–62.

Allen, W.E. (1995). Establishing some basic project-management body-of-knowledge concepts. *International Journal of Project Management*, 13(2), April, 77–82. https://doi.org/10.1016/0263-7863(94)00020-D.

Anderson, G. and Roskrow, B. (Eds.) (2020). *The Channel Tunnel Story*. Taylor & Francis, London.

APM (n.d.). What is project management? https://www.apm.org.uk/resources/what-is-project-management/

APM (2015). *Conditions for Project Success*. Princes Risborough. https://www.apm.org.uk/media/1621/conditions-for-project-success_web_final_0.pdf

APM (2019a). *APM Body of Knowledge,* 7th Edition. Princes Risborough.

APM (2019b). *APM Glossary*. Princes Risborough.

Axelos (2017). *Managing Successful Projects with PRINCE2*, 6th Edition. The Stationery Office, London.

Baruch, Y. and Yuen, K.J. (2000). Inclination to opt for teleworking: A comparative analysis of United Kingdom versus Hong Kong employees. *International Journal of Manpower*, 21(7), 521–539.

Berglund, K., Lindgren, M. and Packendorff, J. (2020). The worthy human being as prosuming subject: 'Projectified selves' in emancipatory project studies. *Project Management Journal*, 51(4), 367–377. https://doi.org/10.1177/8756972820930534.

Binder, J. (2007). *Global Project Management: Communication, Collaboration and Management Across Borders*. Gower, Aldershot.

Byrne, J.J. (2010). Project management as a twenty-first century life skill. Paper presented at PMI® Global Congress 2010 — North America, Washington, DC. Project Management Institute, Newtown Square, PA. https://www.pmi.org/learning/library/project-management-life-skills-knowledge-6540

Cantarelli, C.C., Flyvberg, B. and Buhl, S.L. (2012). Geographical variation in project cost performance: The Netherlands versus worldwide. *Journal of Transport Geography*, 24, 324–331. https://doi.org/10.1016/j.jtrangeo.2012.03.014.

Chigangacha, P., Haupt, T. and Awuzie, B. (2021). Examining the maturity of South Africa's government departments to implement the Infrastructure Delivery Management System (IDMS). *Acta Structilia*, 28(2), 108–142.

Chileshe, N. and Haupt, T.C. (2005). Modelling critical success factors of construction project management (CPM), *Journal of Engineering, Design and Technology*, 3(2), 140–154. https://doi.org/10.1108/172605.

Chiu, Y.C. (2010). *An Introduction to the History of Project Management: From the Earliest Times to A.D.1900*. Eburon, Delft.

Chiu, Y.C. (2011). *A History of Ancient Project Management: From Mesopotamia to the Roman Empire*. Eburon, Delft.

Clegg, S. and Courpasson, D. (2004). Political hybrids: Tocquevillean views on project organizations. *Journal of Management Studies*, 41(4), 525–547.

Cleland, D.I. and Gareis, R. (Eds.) (2007). *Global Project Management Handbook*. McGraw Hill, New York, pp. 1-3–1-15.

Construction Industry Institute (2014). *Project Management Skills of the Future*, RS281-1. Austin, TX.

Cox, J. and Goldratt, E.M. (1986). *The Goal: A Process of Ongoing Improvement*. North River Press, Great Barrington.

Crawford, L., Hobbs, J.B. and Turner, J.R. (2002). Investigation of potential classification systems for projects. *Proceedings of PMI Research Conference 2002*, Seattle, WA, pp. 181–190.

Damoah, I., Akwei, C. and Mouzughi, Y. (2015). Causes of government project failure in developing countries — Focus on Ghana. *British Academy of Management (BAM) Conference*, September, 8–10 September, Portsmouth, UK.

Davis, S.M. and Lawrence, P.R. (1978). Problems of matrix organizations. *Harvard Business Review*, 56(3), 131–142.

Denicol, J., Davies, A. and Krystallis, I. (2020). What are the causes and cures of poor megaproject performance? A systematic literature review and research agenda. *Project Management Journal,* 51(3), 328–345. https://doi.org/10.1177/8756972819896113.

Dinsmore, P.C. and Codas, M.M.B. (1993). Challenges in managing international projects. In P.C. Dinsmore (Ed.), *The AMA Handbook of Project Management*. American Management Association, New York, pp. 457–464.

Eja, K.M. and Ramegowda, M. (2020). Government project failure in developing countries: A review with particular reference to Nigeria. *Global Journal of Social Sciences*, 19, 35–47. https://dx.doi.org/10.4314/gjss.v19i1.4.

Ekstedt, E. (2009). A new division of labour: The "projectification" of working and industrial life. *Building Anticipation of Restructuring in Europe*, 65, 31–53.

Flyvberg, B. (2019). Why megaprojects systemically fail — And what can be done about it? Said Business School. https://www.sbs.ox.ac.uk/oxford-answers/why-megaprojects-systemically-fail-and-what-can-be-done-about-it

Gaddis, P.O. (1959). The project manager. *Harvard Business Review*, May–June, pp. 89–97.

Gareis, R. (2002). Management in the project-oriented society. Paper presented at *PMI® Research Conference 2002: Frontiers of Project Management Research and Applications*, Seattle, Washington. Project Management Institute, Newtown Square, PA. https://www.pmi.org/learning/library/management-project-oriented-society-1937

Gareis, R. and Huemann, M. (2001). Assessing and benchmarking project-oriented societies. *Project Management — International Project Management Journal, Project Management Association Finland, Norwegian Project Management Forum*, 7(1), 14–25.

Gemünden, H.G., Lehner, P. and Kock, A. (2018). The project-oriented organization and its contribution to innovation. *International Journal of Project Management*, 36(1), 147–160. https://doi.org/10.1016/j.ijproman.2017.07.009

Goldratt, E. (1997). *Critical Chain*. North River Press, Great Barrington.

Golini, R. and Landoni, P. (2014). International development projects by non-governmental organizations: An evaluation of the need for specific project management and appraisal tools. *Impact Assessment and Project Appraisal*, 32(2), 121–135. https://doi.org/10.1080/14615517.2014.894088.

Hawkins, J. and Prado, M.G.F.A (2020). CoST — The Infrastructure Transparency Initiative: From disclosed data to sector reform. *Proceedings of the Institution of Civil Engineers — Civil Engineering*, 173(1), pp. 39–47. https://doi.org/10.1680/jcien.19.00024.

Heagney, J. (2018). *Fundamentals of Project Management*, 5th Edition. American Management Association, New York.

Henning, C.H.C.A. and Wald, A. (2019). Toward a wiser projectification: Macroeconomic effects of firm-level project work. *International Journal of Project Management*, 37(6), 807–819. https://doi.org/10.1016/j.ijproman.2019.04.002.

Hirschman, A. O. (2015 [1967]). *Development Projects Observed*. The Brookings Institute Press, Washington, DC.

Ika, L.A., Keeys, L.A., Tuuli, M.M., Sané, S. and Ssegawa, J.K. (2021). Call for papers special collection: Managing and leading projects in Africa. *Project Leadership and Society*, Vol. 2, December. https://doi.org/10.1016/j.plas.2021.100023.

Indicus Analytics and Ace Global (2010). *Project Management Practices in India*. PMI Organisation Centre, Delhi. https://www.pmi.org.in/pdfs/white_paper/PMI_WhitePaper__301120171225_project-management-practices-india.pdf

International Organisation for Standardisation (2017). ISO 10006:2017 — Quality management — Guidelines for quality management in projects. Geneva.

International Organisation for Standardisation (2021). ISO 21500:2021 Project, Programme and Portfolio Management — Context and concepts. Geneva.

IPMA (2015). *Individual Competence Baseline for Project, Programme and Portfolio Management*, Version 4.0. Zurich.

Japan International Cooperation Agency (JICA) (2006). Program Management Guide from the Application of P2M to JICA Activities. Tokyo.

Jensen, A., Thuesen, C. and Geraldi, J. (2016). The projectification of everything: Projects as a human condition. *Project Management Journal*, 47(3), 21–34. https://doi.org/10.1177/875697281604700303.

Kerzner, H. (2008). *Advanced Project Management: Best Practices on Implementation*, 2nd Edition. Wiley, Hoboken, NJ.

Kerzner, H. (2017). *Project Management: A Systems Approach to Planning, Scheduling and Controlling*, 11th Edition. Wiley, Hoboken, NJ.

Kor, R. and Wijnen, G. (2007). *59 Checklists for Project and Programme Managers*. Gower, Aldershot.

Koster, K. (2010). *International Project Management*. Sage, London.

Kozak-Holland, M. (2011). *The History of Project Management: Lessons from History*. Multi-Media Publications, Lakefield, Ontario.

KPMG, Australian Institute of Project Management and International Project Management Association (2019). *The Future of Project Management: Global outlook 2019 — Summary report*. https://home.kpmg/content/dam/kpmg/au/pdf/2019/future-of-project-management-global-outlook-2019-summary-report.pdf

Kwak, Y.H. (2003). Brief history of project management. In K.A. Carayannis (Ed.), *The Story of Managing Projects*. Quorum Books, Westport, CT.

Laufer, A., Denker, G.R. and Shenhar, A.J. (1996). Simultaneous management: The key to excellence in capital projects. *International Journal of Project Management*, 14(4), 189–199.

Lemley, J.K. (1992). The Channel Tunnel: Creating a modern wonder-of-the-world. *PM Network*, 6(5), 14–32.

Lindgren, M. and Packendorff, J. (2006). 'What's new in new forms of organizing?' On the construction of gender in project-based work. *Journal of Management Studies*, 43(4), 841–866.

Lindgren, M. and Packendorff, J. (2009) Project Leadership as a Research Field: Antecedents, current research and a critique. Unpublished paper, KTH Royal Institute of Technology, Stockholm, Sweden. https://www.diva-portal.org/smash/get/diva2:1354244/FULLTEXT01.pdf [Accessed 15 January 2022].

Loch, C., DeMeyer, A. and Pich, M. (2006). Managing the unknown: A new approach to managing high uncertainty and risks in projects. Wiley, Hoboken, NJ.

Meikle, J. (2019). A response to George Ofori's special note. *Journal of Construction in Developing Countries*, 24(2), 207–208.

Morris, P.W.G. (2012). A brief history of project management. In P.W.G. Morris, J.K. Pinto and J. Söderlund (Eds.), *The Oxford Handbook of Project Management*. Oxford University Press, Oxford, pp. 15–36.

Morris, P.W.G. and Hough, G.H. (1987). *The Anatomy of Major Projects: A Study of the Reality of Project Management*. Wiley, Chichester.

Munro, L.T. and Ika, L. (2020). Guided by the beauty of our weapons: Comparing project management standards inside and outside international development. *Development in Practice*, 30(7), 934–952. https://doi.org/10.1080/09614524.2020.1766421.

National Institution for Transforming India and Quality Council of India (2020). *The Indian Infrastructure Body of Knowledge (INBoK): A Technical Baseline to the Practice of Program and Project Management in India*. Delhi.

National Treasury (2012). *Standard for an Infrastructure Delivery Management System*. Pretoria.

Nicholas, J.M. (1990). *Managing Business and Engineering Projects: Concepts and Implementation*. Prentice Hall, Englewood Cliffs, NJ.

Nicholas, J.M. and Steyn, H. (2008) *Project Management for Business, Engineering, and Technology: Principles and Practice*, 3rd Edition. Butterworth-Heinemann, Oxford.

Ofori, G. (2012) Reflections on the great divide: Strategic review of the book. In G. Ofori (Ed.), *Contemporary Issues in Construction in Developing Countries*, Spon Press, Abingdon, pp. 1–19. https://doi.org/10.4324/9780203847350.

Ofori, G. (2016). Construction in developing countries: Current imperatives and potential. In K. Kahkonen and M. Keinanen (Eds.), *CIB World Building Congress 2016 on Intelligent Built Environment for Lives*, 30 May–3 June, Tampere University of Technology, Tampere.

Ofori, G. (2021). Construction in developing countries: Need for new concepts and theorising of contextual specificities to the global corpus of knowledge. *Proceedings, West Africa Built Environment Research (WABER) Conference*, 9–10 August, Accra, Ghana.

Pinto, J.K. (1996). *Power and Politics in Project Management.* Project Management Institute, Sylva, NC.

PM4NGOs (2020). *Project DPro: Project Management for Development Professionals Guide — PMD Pro*, 2nd Edition. Arlington.

PMI (2016). *Construction Extension to the PMBOK® Guide 2016.* Upper Darby, PA.

PMI (2017). *A Guide to the Project Management Body of Knowledge,* 6th Edition. Upper Darby, PA.

PwC (2018). *The Golden Thread: A Study of the Contribution of Project Management and Projects to the UK's Economy and Society.* APM, Princes Risborough.

Roohnavaz, C. (2018). Infrastructure construction in developing countries: A shared approach to sustainability. *Proceedings of the Institution of Civil Engineers — Engineering Sustainability*, 171(5), 223–237. https://doi.org/10.1680/jensu.17.00006.

Russell-Hodge, J. and Hunnam, P. (1998). Learning about culture through projects in aid programmes. In R. Lundin and C. Midler (Eds.), *Projects as Arenas for Renewal and Learning Processes.* Kluwer, Boston, MA, pp. 47–58.

Rwelamila, P.D. and Abdul-Aziz, A.A. (2020). *Improving the Performance of Construction Industries for Developing Countries: Programmes, Initiatives, Achievements and Challenges.* Routledge, Abingdon.

Rwelamila, P.D. and Ogunlana, S. (2015). W107 Construction in Developing Countries — Research roadmap for consultation. CIB, Rotterdam. https://www.irbnet.de/daten/iconda/CIB_DC30745.pdf

Schoper, Y., Wald, A., Ingason, H.T. and Fridgeirsson, T.V. (2018). Projectification in Western economies: A comparative study of Germany, Norway and Iceland. *International Journal of Project Management*, 36(1), 71–82. https://doi.org/10.1016/j.ijproman.2017.07.008.

Sen, A. (1999). *Development as Freedom.* Oxford University Press, Oxford.

Serajuddin, U. and Hamadeh, N. (2020). New World Bank country classifications by income level: 2020–2021. https://blogs.worldbank.org/opendata/new-world-bank-country-classifications-income-level-2020-2021

Seymour, T. and Hussein, S. (2014). The history of project management. *International Journal of Management and Information Systems*, 233–240. https://doi.org/10.19030/ijmis.v18i4.8820.

Shenhar, A.D.D. (2007). *Reinventing Project Management.* Harvard Business School Press, Boston.

Shenhar, A.J. (1992). Project management style and the space shuttle program: A retrospective look. *Project Management Journal*, 23(1), 32–37.

Shenhar, A.J. (2001). One size does not fit all projects: Exploring classical contingency domains. *Management Science*, 47(3), 394–414.

Shenhar, A.J. and Dvir, D. (1996). Toward a typological theory of project management. *Research Policy*, 25, 607–632.

Shenhar, A. and Dvir, D. (2004). Project management evolution: Past history and future research directions. Paper presented at *PMI® Research Conference: Innovations*. London, England, 11–14 July. Project Management Institute, Newtown Square, PA.

Shenhar, A. and Dvir, D. (2007). *Reinventing Project Management: The Diamond Approach to Successful Growth and Innovation*. Harvard Business School Press, Cambridge.

Siles, R. (n.d.). Definitions of project and project management. https://www.pm4dev.com/pm4dev-blog/entry/definitions-of-project-and-project-management.html

Söderlund, J. and Tell, F. (2009). The P-form organization and the dynamics of project competence: Project epochs in Asea/ABB, 1950–2000. *International Journal of Project Management*, 27(2), 101–112. https://doi.org/10.1016/j.ijproman.2008.10.010.

Stanleigh, M. (2010). *The Future of Quality and Project Management*. Business Improvement Architects, Toronto. https://bia.ca/the-future-of-quality-and-project-management/

Stiglitz, J.E., Sen, A. and Fitoussi, J.-P. (2010). *Mismeasuring Our Lives: Why GDP Doesn't Add Up*. New Press, New York.

Stingl, V. and Geraldi, J. (2017). Errors, lies and misunderstandings: Framing the literature on decision bchaviour in projects. *International Journal of Project Management*, 35(2), 121–135.

Stuckenbruck, L.C. (1979). The matrix organization. *Project Management Quarterly*, 10(3), 21–33.

Takeuchi, H. and Nonaka, I. (1986). New product development game. *Harvard Business Review*, January. https://hbr.org/1986/01/the-new-new-product-development-game

US Bureau of Reclamation (2012). *Reclamation: Managing Water in the West — An Introduction to Project Management*. Department of Interior, Washington, DC.

Vyas, L. and Butakhieo, N. (2021). The impact of working from home during COVID-19 on work and life domains: An exploratory study on Hong Kong.

Policy Design and Practice, 4(1), 59–76. https://doi.org/10.1080/25741292.2020.1863560.

Watermeyer, R. and Philips, S. (2020). *Public Infrastructure Delivery and Construction Sector Dynamism in the South African Economy*. National Planning Commission and GIZ, Pretoria.

Wideman, R.M. (Ed.) (1991). *A Framework for Project and Program Management*. Project Management Institute, Newtown Square, PA.

Wideman, R.M. (1995). Criteria for a project-management body of knowledge. *International Journal of Project Management*, 13(2), 71–75. https://doi.org/10.1016/0263-7863(95)00004-A.

Wideman, R.M. (2006). *A Management Framework for Project, Program and Portfolio Integration*. Trafford, Vancouver, BC.

Winch, G.M., Clifton, N. and Millar, C. (2002). Organization and management in an Anglo-French consortium: The case of Transmanche-Link. *Journal of Management Studies*, 37(5), 663–685. https://doi.org/10.1111/1467-6486.00198.

Youker, R. (2007). Managing projects financed by international lending agencies. In D.I. Cleland and L.R. Ireland (Eds.), *Project Manager's Handbook: Applying Best Practices Across Global Industries*. McGraw Hill, New York, pp. 97–105.

Part 2

Project Management in Developing Countries

https://doi.org/10.1142/9789811224720_0003

Chapter 3

Imported Project Management Practices in Developing Countries: The Problem of Insufficient Adaptation to Local Project Governance Systems in the Construction Sector

Gonzalo Lizarralde*, Holmes Páez† and Benjamin Herazo‡

*School of Architecture Université de Montréal
†School of Engineering, Pontificia Universidad Javeriana
‡Faculty of Environmental Design Université de Montréal

Abstract

Few professionals in developing countries want to "miss the boat." There is a growing call in the Global South for standardized project management "Bodies of knowledge" (BoK), Building Information Modelling (BIM) practices, green building certifications, and other imported methods and tools. There is a constant rush to rapidly integrate procedures and practices that come from the North (or the West), without questioning their validity and pertinence in local contexts. It is clear that imported practices contribute to consolidating a consistent language and to project protocols, but quite often, they fail to respond to the fragmented and dynamic character of the construction industry and are a poor fit when it comes to improving project quality.

In this chapter, we focus on the characteristics of project governance in the construction industry in the global North and South. We argue that there are several mismatches between governance approaches in the Global South and the importation of project management BoK, BIM practices, and green certification methods. We argue that the challenges related to implementing project management practices in developed countries are exacerbated when methods are adopted in developing countries without sufficient adaptation and customization. We conclude that there is a need to highlight project management practices that truly respond to the characteristics of construction project governance in the Global South. There is a need to improve practices in low-income countries, but these should not be based on the introduction of methods from the North or the West. Instead, they must emerge from culturally relevant best practices and be rooted in local project governance conditions and the characteristics of the local building sector.

Keywords: Construction, building sector, project management, Global South, BIM practices, green certification, adaptation in building methods

Introduction: The houses that were never built, and those that were

After a mighty earthquake destroyed Port-au-Prince, Haiti, in 2010, dozens of Canadian construction entrepreneurs wanted to contribute to the reconstruction process. Canadians had donated millions of dollars to Haiti, and there was a potential to use those funds in housing reconstruction projects. Patrice Gagnon[1] was one of those entrepreneurs, and, given our research work in construction in the Global South, he wanted to meet us. Gagnon was well intentioned, and we could see early on that he was a clever businessperson.

He had been planning to build a residential project in the periphery of Port-au-Prince. During our meeting in Montreal, he got straight to the point: "I have significant experience in wood construction," he said. "I can ship a hundred prefab houses to Haiti and have them built in two months.

[1]The name has been changed to protect the confidentiality of the participant.

Wood construction will solve many of the problems that led to this destruction in the first place."

We explained several of the challenges ahead and raised questions about the availability of land, labor, and other issues, such as obtaining construction permits and the bureaucracy required to clear customs for imported materials in the Haitian port. Yet, he seemed convinced he would be moving forward with his residential project.

Gagnon was not alone. Between 2010 and 2015, there were hundreds of projects, plans, and ideas launched to reinforce the Haitian building sector, boost the construction industry, and design residential units to "build back better." A common idea shared by non-government organizations (NGOs) and development agencies was that the construction industry in Haiti was weak and inefficient. Better construction practices, regulations, and standards were required. Many believed that there was a real potential to export not only construction technology but also better construction practices and methods.

One of the most prominent residential initiatives brought together some of the best architecture and construction companies in the world. The idea was to build a settlement in an area called Zoranjé, in the periphery of Port-au-Prince, using the best standards of construction and management (Figure 3.1). The project was funded by The Clinton Foundation and benefited from the project management experience of Malcom Reading Consultants, a London-based firm. The initiative, called "Building Back Better Communities," was also supported by an academic consortium comprising the Massachusetts Institute of Technology and the Harvard School of Architecture, and received significant attention in Haiti and abroad — including the leadership of former US President Bill Clinton and the former President of Haiti, Michel Martelly. Malcom Reading Consultants organized an international competition to select the best designers and constructors. A housing exhibition was built in Zoranjé, so that Haitians could see the housing prototypes and invest in the new solutions.

However, neither Gagnon nor the Clinton Foundation managed to conduct successful projects in Haiti. Gagnon did not build a single house, and the Clinton Foundation, Malcom Reading Consultants, and the Ivy League universities eventually abandoned the Zoranjé project. The "Building Back Better Communities" housing exhibition became a ghost town.

Figure 3.1: A pre-fabricated housing unit designed by an international architectural firm, located in the abandoned area of Zoranjé, where the Clinton Foundation and several international organizations attempted to build reconstruction projects.

To be sure, these two cases were not totally rare during the reconstruction period. In reality, very few foreign construction companies managed to build houses in Haiti after the disaster, and very little was achieved in terms of reinforcing the local construction industry. As well, it is not because foreign stakeholders did not try, or because they lacked experience in project management or construction. Professional associations, philanthropies, design firms, and contractors tried to build houses and hospitals, published project guidelines, set up new protocols, and established construction standards. However, very little was achieved in terms of improvements in the built environment.

One case was different, though. After the disaster, the *Corporación Antioquia Presente*, a Colombian NGO with about 10 permanent staff members, built 72 residential units in one of the most notorious areas of Port-au-Prince. The funds came from Colombian donors, and the houses were delivered on time, using disaster-resistant solutions. In a relatively short period of time, 72 low-income families enjoyed not only new homes but also a livable neighborhood, as well as a beautiful landscape with edible plants and productive gardens (see Figures 3.2(a) and 3.2(b)).

Figure 3.2(a): A residential project in Haiti, built by a Colombian NGO.

Figure 3.2(b): A residential project in Haiti, built by a Colombian NGO.

Why did successful construction companies from Canada, the US, the UK, and many countries in Europe fail to operate in the Haitian context? Why did one small NGO manage to do more than many other specialized construction companies?

There are perhaps many reasons for why the international construction companies failed in Haiti, ranging from the foreigners' insufficient knowledge of local law and regulations, to their limited attention span and lack of interest in remaining in the country throughout the implementation process. However, our research also showed something else: the Colombian NGO *Corporación Antioquia Presente* had a certain knowledge of "how things work" in the building sector in developing countries, knowledge that Canadian, European, and American construction companies did not have. Its expertise was not so much about project management practices but about project governance and the social, economic, and political conditions in which construction operates. Officers of the Colombian NGO knew that obtaining land and permits was cumbersome, that politicians could get in the way, that construction supplies were hard to obtain, that local entrepreneurs were not always reliable, and that qualified labor was difficult to find. They neither battled against these problems nor did they ignore them. Instead, they understood that this was part of the context in which the work had to be done, and they devised partnerships, alliances, and contingency measures to deal with these and other common challenges. Was it about implementing more rigorous project management practices? Or was it about deploying strict protocols and measures to guarantee budget, time, and quality management?

Only to a certain extent. More importantly, officers of the NGO understood that the success of the project implied building and maintaining trust among stakeholders (including the beneficiaries themselves) in order to overcome these barriers. Partnering with the local church became crucial, and local nuns were involved in planning activities. The NGO also realized that it was key to involve the beneficiaries in the decision-making process and to have a plan B, and a plan C, in case the local entrepreneur failed to meet targets. Adaptation to local conditions also proved to be vital, including making several changes to the original design, modifications to the original sequence of activities, and events that included and integrated local partners.

These cases of residential (re)construction in Haiti help us understand the impact of differences in the way the construction project governance operates in developed and developing nations. They also help us to illustrate the overarching argument of this chapter: Standardized project management practices originated in the North are not useful if stakeholders do not have a thorough understanding of the social, cultural, political, and economic conditions in which projects evolve in the Global South.

However, in order to develop this argument, we must first answer the following questions: Can we actually assume that there are two distinct forms of functioning in construction in developed and developing countries? Is there, for instance, a clean-cut difference between construction in, say, Canada and Haiti?

Fifty shades of gray: Formality and informality in the building industry

The answers to these questions are complex. First, the construction industry in developing nations is far from homogeneous. Construction practices, methods, and standards in Brazil are different from those in Cameroun or Haiti (incidentally, the same can be said about construction in wealthier nations: construction in, say, Singapore, is different from construction in Canada). Second, there are perhaps several countries that would be difficult to classify in one side or the other of a developed/developing divide. Is the construction sector in China equivalent to that of Nigeria or Cuba? What about wealthy economies in the Middle East, which import Western practices but also labor from poor countries? Third, most developing nations have a construction sector that combines two forms of economy and production: formal and informal. In many cases, such as Haiti and in many African countries, the informal construction sector accounts for more than half of the economic activity in construction and more than half of housing production (Lizarralde, 2014). Fourth, it is naïve to pretend that construction in developed countries does not have a certain influence of informality. Do-It-Yourself construction and home improvements, for instance, are sometimes conducted at the margins of registered permits and procedures. Yet they are a multi-million-dollar component of construction in Australia, Canada and in the US.[2] Fifth, black markets, unregistered labor and work, collusion, and other forms of informality (and dubious legitimacy) also happen in developed nations. Finally, vernacular forms of construction — often related to forms of craftsmanship and artisan work — exist in almost all nations, and often operate in ways that are different from those of professional, industrialized, and commercial construction.

So, can we say that the construction industries in developed and developing nations are different? Several authors (Ofori, 2019; Rwelamila, 2012a; Toor *et al.*, 2012) and the contributors to this book assume that they are. The argument is that, despite the previous caveats, there are sufficient differences to justify such a division. However, here, we argue that this is not a black-or-white distinction. Instead, we sustain the argument that there is a continuum of differences between a highly industrialized, standardized, regulated, and specialized form of construction (which tends to be more common in wealthier countries) and a labor-intensive, and less regulated, standardized, and specialized form of construction that we call "informal," and which tends to be more common in the Global South. Figure 3.3 illustrates how this continuum exists in both developed

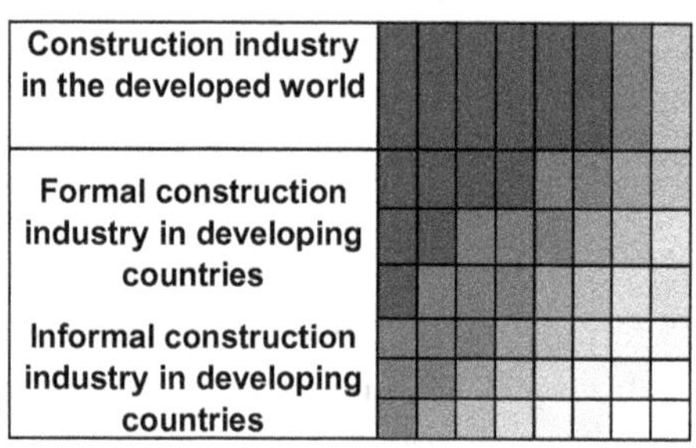

Figure 3.3: Representation of levels of formality-informality in construction in developed and developing nations.

[2]Find the full figure here: https://www.statista.com/statistics/239753/total-sales-of-home-improvement-retailers-in-the-us/. See the figure at: https://www.statista.com/statistics/809304/average-annual-home-improvement-spend-us/

Highly Regulated	Technology intensive	Highly specialized labor	Highly litigious	Highly standardized	Highly influenced by prefabrication	Significant presence of highly qualified labor	Significant impact of formal communication	Highly influenced by TI and digital technology	Highly influenced by professional decision making
Barely regulated	Labor intensive	Barely specialized labor	Barely litigious	Barely standardized	Not much influenced by prefabrication	Significant presence of low qualified labor	Significant impact of informal communication	Barely influenced by TI and digital technology	Barely influenced by professional decision making

Figure 3.4: Representation of levels of formality-informality in construction sectors.

and developing nations too. The model illustrates that a certain form of informality does exists in construction in wealthier nations. It also shows that construction in developing nations tends to have a combination of: (a) a sector that resembles that of wealthy nations; and (b) another sector that tends to be dominated by informal practices and the informal economy.

Figure 3.4 lays out (albeit in an over-simplified manner) what these shades of gray often mean. On one side of the spectrum, we find a sector that is highly regulated, technology-intensive, litigious, and significantly influenced by specialized and highly qualified labor, standardization, prefabrication, formal forms of communication, information technology, digital technology and professional decision-making. On the opposite end, we find the characteristics that we often associate with informal construction.

Is informality a difference in legality? It is not. Some forms of informality can be legal. For example, in informal settlements in the Global North, construction labor is hired at the margins of legal contracts and fiscal rules. Yet, informal construction is not necessarily considered a criminal activity. Besides, formality and informality are not only characteristics of the economy, neighborhoods, and means of production. These terms are also used to characterize ways of functioning in project governance in construction.

Formality and informality in project governance

Since the early works of Cherns and Bryant (1984), scholars have studied the formal structure of the temporary group of organizations (often called the temporary multi-organization or TMO) that undertake projects. Those interested in formality often explore governance from three angles. First, procurement strategies and legal approaches, focusing on contractual relationships between firms (Rowlinson and McDermott, 1999; Walker *et al.*, 2008; Walker and Hampson, 2003) and economic transactions between clients and organizations that are part of the production chain (Reve and Levitt, 1984; Ruuska *et al.*, 2010). Second, the structure of the client organization (Green, 1996; Nahapiet and Nahapiet, 1985), which is known to have a key impact on the functioning of the TMO (Cherns and Bryant, 1984). Finally, formal authority and power relations between stakeholders or project team members. Here, several authors have focused, for instance, on the authority delegated by the client to the project team manager (Walker, 2007).

Projects can be influenced by other forms of interaction between stakeholders, notably informal communication and structuring — an approach that is often referred to as the coactivational view (Dainty *et al.*, 2006). Scholars interested in this view often focus on non-contractual relations between project participants. These mechanisms include relations between units and departments *within* organizations (notably within the client organization) and *between* organizations (Reve and Levitt, 1984). These researchers have found that non-contractual relations, federative mechanisms, and soft managerial skills contribute to creating the appropriate conditions for project governance (Emmitt and Gorse, 2007; Pietroforte, 1997). Cooperation between participants helps reduce adversarial relationships and improves project performance (Anvuur and Kumaraswamy, 2008; Kvan, 2000). Leadership, established formally and informally, influences relationships between team members (Emmitt and Gorse, 2007). Informal communication (i.e., communication that is not necessarily documented in permanent form) is key in determining the relationships between project actors (Pietroforte, 1997) and project governance mechanisms (Chan and Raisanen, 2009). In situations of greater uncertainty, which characterize some construction projects (Koskela and Howell, 2002; Williams, 1999), informal meetings and personal contacts are useful means of communication that help develop trust and shared meanings (Pietroforte, 1997).

To be fair, informality in construction is not always regarded positively (Chan and Raisanen, 2009). For example, scholars have found that informal groups or clans within organizations can create conflicts and tensions (Naoum, 2001). However, there is a consensus that a certain form of informality in project governance is required for project success.

Imported ideas, methods, and practices

Our previous research has shown that, in the continuum from formality to informality (from the dark gray to a pale gray, in Figures 3.3 and 3.4), absolute formality and informality only exist as abstract notions (Lizarralde, *et al.*, 2008; Lizarralde and Root, 2008; Lizarralde *et al.*, 2013). Here we argue that, when it comes to differences between countries, this continuum operates in parallel with the transfer of ideas, practices, methods, and approaches from developed to developing countries — or, to put it differently, from North to South or from Western countries to the rest.

To be sure, various forms of South-to-South and South-to-North influences also exist. For example, European and American professionals have been inspired by the work of celebrated architects, masons, artisans, and designers from Africa, Asia, Latin America, and the Caribbean (Karagiannis and Wagner, 2007). Construction materials and technologies have also traveled from colonized to dominant nations and between countries from the Global South. Celebrated buildings and urban solutions from the South have influenced practices at the frontiers of wealthy nations (Lall, 1982). However, the history of colonialism, imperialism, and neoliberalism teaches us that the big chunk of transfer between wealthy and poor nations has consisted in extraction practices from dominated cultures and imports and technology transfer from the dominant ones (Schandl *et al.*, 2018).

Standardized project management "Bodies of Knowledge" (BoK), Building Information Modelling (BIM) practices, Green Building Certification (GBC), digital technologies, and other imported methods and tools are the latest forms of transfer in construction from the Global North to the Global South, and these practices are rapidly influencing project management approaches in the latter (Zhang *et al.*, 2019). BoK are introducing a new set of languages and proposing new protocols and procedures. BIM practices are modifying flows of information, changing communication practices, and creating new interfaces. Building certifications are adding additional project processes, modifying monitoring activities, and helping to introduce new protocols and checklists that need to be considered during decision-making (He *et al.*, 2018).

Currently (in 2021), there are over 600,000 members of the Project Management Institute (PMI) in 214 countries and territories around the world, with 306 chapters (98 in developing countries) and 10,000 volunteers serving local members in over 80 countries. The PMBOK has sold an unknown (but perhaps very high) number of copies in countries of the Global South. PMI local associations exist in Angola, Botswana, Rwanda, Guatemala, Honduras, Nicaragua, in the Philippines, and in more than 50 other countries (Anderson *et al.*, 2021).

Now take the case of BIM. There are thousands of members of BIM professional associations in developing nations. BIM awards are given in many countries of the Global South. BIM local associations exist in South America, Africa, and Asia (McAuley *et al.*, 2017). In 2019, 500,000 Revit licenses ("Revit" is an Autodesk software used in BIM practices) were sold around the world, including 2 million legal licenses in the world, apart from subscription contracts (4 million) and illegal copies (12 million), for a total of 18 million users worldwide (Autodesk Forum, 2020). The common notion is that "some of the developing countries are sharing a majority of the same challenges within their construction industries as those in developed countries relating to cost and time overruns" (Sahil, 2016). As a consequence of this, "industries in developing countries, to some extent, are using BIM to address these problems" (Sahil, 2016). This adoption is not homogeneous: "The level of implementation of BIM and its maturity differs from country to country. Definitely, the biggest driver to BIM implementation in different countries is due to government-led initiatives" (Gómez Sánchez, 2016).

A similar pattern exists regarding building certifications. Today, hundreds of labels exist in both developed and developing countries to certify buildings, infrastructure, neighborhoods, and even cities. These include "Leadership in Energy and Environmental Design" (LEED) and the "Building Research Establishment Environmental Assessment Method"

(BREEAM), two of the most popular green certifications for buildings in the US and UK, respectively. This industry of building certifications is growing rapidly. In the early 2000s, there were only about 40 LEED-certified buildings in the US. In 2018, there were more than 67,000 LEED-registered buildings[3] and more than 95,000 projects using LEED worldwide.[4] Today, there are more than 2.2 million BREEAM-registered buildings in more than 80 countries. It is estimated that there are over 600 different green certification systems for buildings and neighborhoods alone (Vierra, 2016). It is fair to say that building certification is now a multi-million-dollar industry of consulting services, grants, books, courses, graduate programs, industry fairs, and conferences (Dodge Data & Analytics, 2018).

In the light of all of this, we can raise three additional questions: Why do people in the Global South adopt these foreign practices? Is this form of transfer a positive one? What are the unintended consequences of the rapid adoption of foreign practices in construction? Let us start with the first question.

The push factors

A common argument is that stakeholders in developing countries lack the proper skills, techniques, and protocols to achieve both quality and efficiency on projects (Bui *et al.*, 2016; Ekundayo *et al.*, 2013) — notably on megaprojects or complex projects of infrastructure or urban transformation (Othman and Ahmed, 2013). Lack of expertise often justifies hiring foreign construction companies and professionals, who bring with them new practices, methods, and protocols (Imbert, 1990). Another common argument is that urban and real estate initiatives in developing countries are sometimes aspirational. Ideas of the type of "progress" that exists in wealthy nations inspire clients and developers to import solutions and design ideas. These two arguments have been used to justify, for instance, the participation of foreign construction companies and developers in

[3] See the graph at: https://www.statista.com/statistics/323383/leed-registered-projects-in-the-united-states/

[4] See full article at: https://www.usgbc.org/articles/green-building-accelerates-around-world-poised-strong-growth-2021

Vietnam. Many suburban and peri-urban developments in Hanoi and in other Vietnamese cities reject traditional urban forms and adopt, instead, ideas and models from Singapore and Taiwan (Labbé, 2014, 2015, 2018; Labbé *et al.*, 2010; Labbé and Musil, 2013). Foreign companies originating from these countries bring with them not only alien urban and architectural forms but also their own construction and managerial practices. There are two additional ways to facilitate the transfer of ideas. One is through young professionals from the Global South who study in the universities in the Global North bringing new practices back home. The other is through alliances, joint ventures, and consortiums between international construction firms and local firms where both parties share knowledge, practices, and expertise (Bröchner *et al.*, 2004).

Our research shows that there are at least five additional factors that facilitate or encourage this transfer of ideas and methods from the North to the South. We now discuss these factors.

1. **Orchestration and lobbying by international agencies:** International consulting agencies have played a critical role in both determining standards and implementing practices aimed at achieving them. After the 2010 earthquake in Haiti, the United Nations Human Settlements Programme (UN-Habitat) pushed for the implementation of urban standards in a self-made settlement called Canaan, in the outskirts of Port-au-Prince (Petter *et al.*, 2020). These standards were accompanied by project management principles and guidelines. Several other projects in Haiti had to be conducted through the project management guidelines set by United Nations Development Program (UNDP) or the United Nations Office for the Coordination of Humanitarian Affairs. Even countries that have, for several years, resisted the implementation of international standards have recently adopted them. For example, Cuba has now widely adopted the urban agenda dictated by UN agencies (Aragón *et al.*, 2020).

   Several urban consulting agencies currently act as orchestrators of municipalities in the Global South. Orchestration here means a mode of indirect governance whereby an institution attempts to influence policy and practices through intermediaries using non-coercive means (Abbott *et al.*, 2011). Local Governments for Sustainability (ICLEI) is a common orchestrator of urban practices in more than 1,750 local governments in over 100 countries, including Bogotá, Nairobi, and Bangkok. There are more than 35 cities in developing countries that are part of the Rockefeller Foundation's 100 resilient cities program. Standards set by the Organization for Economic Cooperation and Development (OECD) are now applied to members from the Global South, such as Colombia and Mexico. In most cases, these organizations conduct constant lobbying to promote the adoption of project management and urban management practices among municipalities and other public institutions. One of these intermediaries, C40, is present in Kenya, the Philippines, Ecuador, and other countries of the Global South.

2. **Conditions by donor organizations:** Donor and development agencies sometimes also promote the adoption of project management practices in the Global South. For example, Canadian development agencies have insisted for many decades that projects that are undertaken with Canadian funds implement The Logical Framework, a project management technique derived from goal-oriented management (Golini *et al.*, 2015). The World Bank has also pushed for the implementation of minimum standards in construction in poor nations (The World Bank, 2015). In Haiti, the *Agence française de développement*, France's international development agency, requested the use of project management protocols for the construction of the University Hospital in Port-au-Prince. In Colombia, the National Planning Department and other development agencies have pushed for the adoption of standardized processes, in many cases under pressure from international funding bodies.
3. **Trade agreements:** Bilateral and multi-lateral trade agreements often specify not only standards but also practices that must be implemented to achieve them (such as the ISO standards). These agreements often create the conditions to facilitate the importation of technology and expertise (Hoekman *et al.*, 2005).
4. **Academic lobbying:** Universities have played a crucial role in the implementation of project management standards, BIM practices, building certifications, and digital technologies in construction in the Global South. Research laboratories and groups in the Global North

have benefited from both public and private funding toward the development of research to enhance the implementation of their results in the construction industry. Most often, these laboratories have cashed in on the widely popular idea that innovation is required to boost the economy. Rather than critically exploring these practices, several scholars and their teams have effectively acted as lobbyists to promote their adoption (Bogenschneider, 2020).

Universities, think-tanks, and research groups in the Global South have also recently started to follow this trend. By incorporating innovative practices in curricula and research agendas, scholars are contributing to the promotion and implementation of foreign practices and methods. In the Global South, innovation in this regard has been less about developing new local practices and more about importing "innovative" solutions from more industrialized countries (Silva Ardila, 2020).

5. **Competitive advantage and reputation:** Companies in developing nations have joined the approach adopted by their counterparts in the Global North to support the adoption of innovative practices in an attempt to create competitive advantage. Several companies in developing nations see the adoption of project management standards, BIM practices, and expertise in building certifications as ways of boosting their reputation, presenting new "products" to their clients, showing an innovative edge, and consolidating market niches (Aghimien *et al.*, 2018; Gómez Sánchez, 2016). For large companies, the adoption of these innovative practices serves to marginalize small companies and win over business rivals (Klein Woolthuis *et al.*, 2013). Foreign practices in Colombia, for instance, are often seen to be more efficient than local practices; their adoption provides prestige to these larger companies (Campos *et al.*, 2021). Some have even adopted BoK and BIM terms in English, with little adaptation to local contexts.

The pull factors

The enthusiasm with new project process methods among professionals and academics does not mean that implementation is easy. A study by members of our team in Colombia (Beltrán *et al.*, 2020) shows that, despite lobbying efforts, the principal factors that hinder the implementation of PMI-sanctioned practices are the lack of:

- A "culture of projects" among government agencies
- Political will to implement "best practices"
- Support and leadership in the implementation of new methods
- A single entity responsible for project management implementation
- Knowledge about "best" practices
- Organizational "maturity"
- Training in project management
- Interest in the use of best practices
- Human, physical, and/or technological resources for implementation.

Researchers also highlight difficulties in the implementation of BIM practices in the Global South. According to several authors (such as Abubakar *et al.*, 2014; Bui *et al.*, 2016) common barriers include: (a) social resistance to change; (b) legal and contractual constraints; (c) the high cost of training; (d) the lack of an enabling environment in government policies and legislation; (e) the lack of trained professionals to handle the tools; (f) the lack of clients requesting the use of BIM on projects; (g) lack of proof of financial benefits; (h) high cost of integrated software and models; and (i) paradoxically, the lack of standards to guide implementation, coupled with the lack of awareness of such standards among industry stakeholders.

The implementation of GBCs in developing countries also faces several challenges. A study in Ghana (Darko, *et al.*, 2018) found that the most significant barriers are related to the role of government, including lack of the following: government incentives, policies, and regulations; promotion by government; local institutes and facilities; green building rating systems and labeling programs; demonstration projects; and training for project personnel. Other barriers found by Darko *et al.* (2018) include resistance to change, lack of importance attached to GBCs by senior management, and unfamiliarity with GBCs among construction professionals.

It is pertinent to note that several authors have found that "resistance to change" is a common barrier to the implementation of new project practices (Häkkinen and Belloni, 2011). However, most authors writing on this subject imply that this is a problem to be overcome, as if the resistance to change is somehow illegitimate or unjustified (Marefat *et al.*, 2019). Very few authors have dwelt on the reasons for this resistance to change or have shown interest in exploring whether the claims of resistance have a certain value and legitimacy.

One pressing question, then, is: if implementation is difficult, is it justified by sufficient benefits for the building sector and society?

The advantages and disadvantages of imported practices

In order to tackle potential benefits in the Global South, we must first ask: Are standardized project management BoK, BIM practices, and GBCs a good thing in *developed* nations?

The benefits of these practices are controversial. Several scholars and experts have argued that standardized project management practices fail to respond to the complexity and dynamic character of construction (Koskela and Ballard, 2006; Koskela and Howell, 2002). They deplore the situation that most standardized practices are mechanical — often assuming that managers have the control over most variables (Saunders, 1992). These critics claim that different approaches, based on soft systems analysis or design thinking, for instance, are required in the construction process. In these new approaches, stakeholders must recognize the importance of uncertainty and learn to navigate complexity (de Blois and De Coninck, 2008). Project leaders must not only establish procedures for tackling problems but also redefine the problem and adapt solutions throughout the project process (Boutinet, 1990), as new information is available and changes are addressed. Here, testing, learning, and problem redefinition are crucial to achieve project quality (de Blois *et al.*, 2011).

Other authors have criticized the way in which BIM and other technologies have modified project management practices. They deplore the concentration of information in the hands of a few people (often those in charge of the BIM model) and the limited success in knowledge and information integration (Alreshidi *et al.*, 2017). For example, critics have found that integrated design practices are often seen by some stakeholders as a waste of time (Leoto and Lizarralde, 2019a; 2019b; Suermann and Issa, 2009). Other critics have noticed that sophisticated BIM technologies are often underused. As one expert put it in a seminar we organized in 2018: "BIM technology is like a Ferrari. It is hardly exploited to its full capacity if you run at 30 km per hour" (Lizarralde *et al.*, 2018).

GBCs have recently been accused of having a negative effect on project management practices (Herazo and Lizarralde, 2015). Critics argue that they have become rhetoric exercises, wherein stakeholders make efforts to check boxes on a list of objectives, without a genuine interest in reducing the impact of the buildings on the environment (Yudelson, 2016). Many certification methods, they argue, lead project leaders to focus on individual targets, missing the objective of developing innovative solutions to effectively reduce pollution or energy consumption (Newsham *et al.*, 2009). Practitioners have learned to get around the difficult decisions required to truly reduce environmental impacts — that is by building less, not building greener (Power, 2010). In this way, project management practices have become mechanical exercises to reach a certain target and obtain the certification, rather than a tool that provides the space to rethink the objective of the project or challenge its very pertinence (Levée, 2019). "The only truly sustainable building is the one that is never built," said one of these critics in a seminar we organized on this issue in 2019. "But now you see all these international bodies proudly showing that they have certified thousands of buildings worldwide, without questioning whether it was actually necessary to build them in the first place" (Lizarralde *et al.*, 2019).

Defenders of these new practices often claim, in sum, that the baby should not be thrown out with the bathwater. Most of them recognize that there are problems in the way these practices are often adopted (He *et al.*, 2020), but, for these defenders, the real problem lies in poor implementation, often due to an inappropriate interpretation of new practices. If anything, the tools need to be improved, not discarded (Shan and Hwang, 2018). They argue that standardized practices contribute to set objective targets and benchmarks, produce a common language that all stakeholders can understand, and serve to monitor change in measurable ways (Doan *et al.*, 2017). Defenders also contend that project performance measurement requires a certain level of standardization, and thus, homogeneity, among practices in different countries.

These arguments are, perhaps, all valid. However, the emphasis of the defenders on the importance of implementing new protocols and methods often denotes their real objective: having the method implemented, not reaching a better outcome. Therefore, if the pertinence of these approaches is contested in developed nations, what about their pertinence in the Global South? In order to explore this, we must understand the differences in project governance between developed and developing nations. A research project we reported on in *Construction Management and Economics* did exactly that (Lizarralde *et al.*, 2013).

Governance differences between developed and developing nations

In 2012, our team wanted to know whether project governance in construction in wealthier nations differs from that in the poorer nations. We conducted a research project that included three main steps. First, we compared several projects and eventually analyzed in detail the process of two similar buildings in the tourism sector: one in Canada and one in Ecuador. Second, we conducted an international survey containing 17 multiple-choice questions. Our final sample included 110 respondents of which 47 were located in developing countries: 23 in Latin America, 10 in Northern Africa and the Middle East, three in Asia, seven in Eastern Europe, and four in Sub-Saharan Africa. There were also 63 respondents in developed countries: 45 in North America, 15 in Europe, and three in other industrialized countries. In total, we had answers from 68 architects, 23 engineers, 11 project managers, six urban planners, and two participants with a non-identified profession. In the final step, we conducted detailed interviews with respondents who had experience only in developing nations or in both developed and developing nations.

The results, with respect to governance mechanisms, were definitive. We found differences in at least six different areas; these are now outlined.

1. **Hierarchy:** Hierarchy within organizations and in the TMO tends to be different in developed and developing nations. Take the case of

construction clients. Whereas in the Global South projects are more likely to be initiated as a result of the interests and pressure of middle management, they tend to be initiated by top management in developing countries. This top management entity in developing nations also tends to have fewer intermediaries than in developed nations and tends to be more hierarchical and to concentrate more decision-making power in the hands of those in the upper echelons. The role played by top management in the Global South is often played by the procurement units in industrialized nations.

Procurement units exercise their power within projects in three ways. First, by commissioning and managing the project, acting as project champions within the TMO. Second, by leading communications between the client organization and professionals and contractors. And finally, by assuming responsibility for project development. Clients in wealthy countries often delegate more responsibilities and decision-making power to management units or professionals who do not necessarily occupy top management positions. It is important to note that this difference applies to both mature and immature organizations. This means that it is not the size or structure of the client organization that determines the concentration of power, but the intrinsic organizational culture that tends to value hierarchies that determine the concentration of power.

2. **Trust:** Trust plays a significant role in project governance in both the Global North and the Global South. It is crucial for the establishment of constructive relationships between stakeholders (Smyth, 2006), notably in an industry that is characterized by adversarial relationships between firms. Winch (2001) identifies two types of trust: self-interested trust, "future orientated in terms of the expectation that one's transaction partner is trustworthy and will not behave opportunistically in future transactions;" and socially orientated trust, that Winch describes as "past orientated" and the result of "obligations generated through social and family networks."

   In the Global South, trust between professionals and clients is key in the establishment of healthy governance. Informality, notably in the form of informal communication, social interaction, and constant and direct exchanges between individuals, helps in building this trust. In this context, informal communication is key to comfort, in convincing and informing stakeholders, and in building cooperation and reliance. A study in Colombia (Carreño Sánchez *et al.*, 2017) shows that women working in project management consider that they are better than men in creating a climate of trust. For Carreño Sanchez, this capacity to generate trust is one of the most important managerial skills, only after leadership, decision-making capacity, communication, and negotiation (incidentally, the same study found that more men are assigned to larger and more complex projects than women).

3. **Regulations:** In the Global North, professional and civil responsibility (enforced by laws, professional associations, and regulations) is taken more seriously than in the Global South. As one respondent put it during our study: "Rules exist, but there is often a way around." There are consequences of this capacity to maneuver around regulations, notably in terms of the perception of uncertainty. For example, greater corruption in the Global South hinders approval and inspection processes. Informality plays a role here: it is typically viewed as a mechanism to avoid bureaucracy and red tape and to accommodate things when variables change (Campos *et al.*, 2021).
4. **Informal structuring:** When we started the project, we expected to find more informal communications in projects in the Global South than in industrialized nations. But this was not the case; we found a similar relative frequency of informal communications among participants as well as perceptions of informal communications in all the countries we studied. However, there is a difference in the reasons for, and the uses of, informality in construction in the Global North and the Global South. Informality is useful in contexts where corruption and bureaucracy are common, notably because such informality increases efficiency by avoiding lengthy procedures and red tape. Our respondents in the Global South had an ambivalent view of informality: they perceived it as both risky and necessary. In the Global North, respondents argued that informality is not an alternative to formal procedures but rather supports contractual relations between participants.

Our respondents in all the countries covered in the study recognized that informal communication can be a source of conflict.

Formalized communication helps prevent conflicts caused by interpretations of information or misunderstandings, but in the Global South, informal communication serves as a management and coordination tool to move forward. Verbal agreements and exchanges between participants allow more rapid decision-making and problem solving. Arrangements are sometimes made informally and official documents come after.

5. **Stakeholders' roles:** Interviewees argued that municipalities have greater influence on projects in developed than developing nations. Professional institutions and trade associations and external stakeholders also have more influence in the Global North; they often put pressure on developers and professionals to respect rules and standards. Therefore, there are more possibilities to have checks and balances in governance structures in the Global North.
6. **Management style:** Several studies (Rwelamila, 2012a, 2012b; Shiferaw *et al.*, 2012) confirm that project management practices in developing nations are less structured and formalized than in industrialized countries. Our study showed that there is also a difference in management styles in developed and developing nations. In the former, project management is often based on (or copied from) the models developed in the Global North. Most often, management is conducted loosely in developing countries. Stakeholders' roles are less defined, compared to more wealthy countries, where strict formal protocols regulate professional conduct. Instead, respondents in the Global South considered human interactions and social relations to be more important than those in the Global North. These interactions are crucial for adapting the process to changes and constraints. In this way, problems are addressed in a more organic manner, based on personal interactions between participants. In the Global North, respondents argued, efficiency and respect of deadlines and budgets are more important than human interactions.

How to understand differences in project governance

Some scholars have assumed that project governance in developing countries has deficiencies that need to be corrected with more rigorous project management practices. Aghimien *et al.* (2018), for instance, note that Value Management, an idea originating from corporate America, is not fully implemented in Nigeria or in other developing nations, but they do not argue that the concept perhaps makes little sense in Nigeria and other African countries. Instead, they deplore the situation that there is an "unwillingness to entertain new ideas and concepts" (Aghimien *et al.*, p. 829). Similarly paternalistic approaches have been found in other studies on the barriers in BIM implementation in developing nations (Saka and Chan, 2020). According to this approach, standardized methods can be a "remedy" to construction problems in the Global South, only if stakeholders see their true value and are willing to accept new ideas.

Our studies lead us in a different direction, one in which we see these differences in project development as natural outcomes arising from the different responses to the environment. In our approach, these differences are not necessarily problems to be fixed, but part of the solutions that have emerged in less industrialized nations to cope with hostile political and economic environments. Informality in project governance has emerged as a response mechanism to avoid complications caused by bureaucracy and red tape, and as an effective tool to facilitate flexibility and adaptability in dynamic contexts. Similarly, strong leadership by top management has emerged as an approach to address unclear rules, hierarchical business structures, and changing environments. Finally, flexible and adaptive management can be viewed as part of the solution to hostile business contexts.

There is a lot of space for improvement in construction in the Global South. Additional managerial skills can benefit professionals in developing nations. However, implementing imported project practices without a thorough understanding of local conditions is rarely the right answer. A deeper understanding of the characteristics of project governance and why these characteristics exist in the first place are both required in order to work effectively in the Global South. What we must avoid is a prescriptive approach to what we may perceive from the outside as "problems." There are unintended consequences of the rapid adoption of foreign practices.

The unintended consequences of foreign practices

Already in the 1980s, some scholars noticed the risk of importing project management practices from wealthy nations. Stuckenburg and Zomorrodian (1987) argued that in the Global South, "the application of project management is recommended only when certain technical, political, and environmental conditions are met." "Even then," they added, "it will only work when it is incorporated into an indigenous framework based on local values, beliefs, and behavioural patterns" (p. 167). Decades later, this principle is still valid in many cases. We argue here that the challenges in implementation that already exist in developed countries are exacerbated when standardized practices are adopted in the Global South without proper adaptation to project governance conditions. We now discuss some of the risks we associate with uncritical adoption of foreign practices.

Lack of pertinence: A strong emphasis on detailed planning, without recognizing the existence of uncertainty and its possible impact on the project, might reduce the capacity of stakeholders to adapt to the reality of the project (Rodríguez-Rivero *et al.*, 2020). Planning and anticipation are required to be able to manage resources, but adaptation to changes that occur within and outside the project is also key. In contexts of high uncertainty, or where there are frequent changes within the project environment, such as those that characterize construction in the Global South, stakeholders' capacity to react, modify plans, find new solutions, and implement these solutions are all of crucial importance.

Mechanistic approaches that assume that performance is the result of applying rigorous protocols, yet ignore the dynamic character of uncertainty, represent a challenge in the construction industry in the Global South. Yet, foreign practices sometimes disregard the need for, and value of, changes in project plans. For example, the Logical Framework Analysis measures performance according to pre-established goals. In this evaluation, achieving goals that were not initially proposed has a reduced value when compared to the rigorous achievement of the original plan.

Lack of contextualization: Indiscriminate adoption of foreign practices can also prevent stakeholders from finding local solutions that have cultural, social, and economic value. Take the case of specialization. The lower level of specialization among professionals in the Global South might actually reduce industry and process fragmentation. Professionals with a wide spectrum of skills (for instance, ranging from urban planning, to architecture, to landscape architecture and interior design) can perhaps more easily adapt to sudden changes in projects and the environment. As they have relatively large "toolkits," these professionals can also better navigate uncertainty and respond to fluctuations in both the market and the overall economy. Take also the case of informal communication and relationships. Protocols that reduce informality and favor the rigorous implementation of formal procedures limit the possibilities among stakeholders to establish trust through informal mechanisms. Such protocols also increase bureaucracy and erode the value attached to interpersonal exchanges.

According to Cole (2010), when it comes to building certifications in the Global South, there is often "a risk of standards' homogenization, mainly affecting consciousness, recognition and promotion of design strategies." Besides, Cole argues, the inappropriate cross-cultural "importation" of specific technical strategies may prove potentially detrimental to environmental progress. Similarly, writes Sev (2010), "the adaptability of any existing tool of a developed nation is mostly a problematic issue in a developing country." The author argues that "when adapting the performance criteria of a current tool, regional/cultural differences and priorities must be considered to make the system feasible and applicable, and accurately reflect the real conditions" (p. 853). In fact, it has been shown that many certification methods on performance and sustainable development concentrate on international standards dealing with energy efficiency and reduction of water consumption, as well as focus on technical requirements related to climate control and materials selection (Shan and Hwang, 2018). These methods underestimate other contextual factors related to climate, geography, and culture, as well as factors related to basic human needs, such as availability of services and housing conditions.

Professionals in the Global South are increasingly adopting the project management language developed in the North. "Scope management," "project integration management," "scope validation techniques," and other terms are now part of the construction jargon in the Global South. Some of this jargon is difficult to transfer to other languages. Project management, for instance, can be translated in different ways in Spanish, masking or highlighting nuances: *administración de proyectos*, *gerencia de proyectos*, *gestión de proyectos*, and *dirección de proyectos*. However, in many cases, stakeholders adopt the language, but not necessarily the culture of planning, anticipation, organization, project monitoring, and evaluation. In other words, they adopt the "form" but not the "essence" required for effective project planning, design, and execution. In several countries in the Global South, institutions have adopted terms for project phases that hardly describe the real activities that actually take place.

If trust among stakeholders is important in the Global South, why not focus on project management practices that reinforce the creation of trust? If adaptation is both required and desirable, why not adopt practices that fully value change in response to contextual characteristics? Similarly, there are better ways in which project management practices can account for cultural differences in hierarchy and management styles.

Distraction from structural changes: The quest to implement foreign practices also distracts us from noticing the real changes that are required in the construction sector in the Global South. Corruption is one of the most significant problems affecting project processes in developing nations (Damoah *et al*., 2018; Owusu *et al*., 2019). Quite often, it is not additional protocols, checklists, and documents that are required, but more ethical approaches, and more democratic and transparent institutions. Corruption, greed, and partisan interests can be pursued with or without rigorous project management techniques. What is needed to prevent such problems is the establishment or consolidation of institutions committed to social and environmental justice. In this regard, mechanistic project management practices that fail to challenge the moral value of decisions do little to improve society and the built environment. We should not forget the differences between men and women in the built environment sector. Huge gender gaps still exist in the construction industry in all countries, but particularly in the Global South. It is still hard to see how BoK of project management of foreign origin are contributing to fill this gap.

The principles and language of management might be useful in improving efficiency and attaining benchmarks. However, they do not always address the ethical challenges that exist in public administrations and in the private sector in the Global South. Decision making should not only be measured against performance and efficiency benchmarks but also with respect to values and moral worth. Only in this way can the construction industry fully contribute to the enhancement of the quality of the built environment and to society.

Perpetuating second-class solutions: Project management and industry practices that ignore the existence of the informal sector do little to improve the built environment and living conditions in the Global South. The informal sector cannot be ignored; it needs to be included in policies and practices that attempt to elevate quality, accountability, and business responsibility. Ignoring the existence of the informal sector only perpetuates its problems. Training and measures aimed at improving business practices must also target informal entrepreneurs, contractors, and developers.

Paradoxically, more sophisticated project management practices (for example, those that encourage standardization and industrialization) can affect the number of jobs in the construction industry in the Global South. The trade-off between jobs and technology should not prevent improvements in the industry, but it has an impact on the type of adaptations that are required in practices coming from the Global North.

Local ideas, methods, and practices

We are not arguing here that all foreign practices must be dismissed in the Global South. Several countries in the Global South have already embarked on a transition toward practices more focused on project management. This transition can be seen as a "natural" process of change. Besides, some improvements through project management procedures are still required; but, as we have argued in this chapter, foreign ideas must be confronted with local project governance practices, and a critical analysis of their pertinence is increasingly required.

Champions of change are, and will be, required. Researchers must assume a more critical stance. They must challenge the pertinence of foreign practices rather than lobby uncritically for their adoption. Governments can promote the development of effective solutions, focusing on local realities and designing policies and programs that reinforce skills and practices among developers, contractors, professionals and informal entrepreneurs. Public institutions can better integrate the informal sector into the industry, facilitating credit, training and regularization of firms that operate in it. NGOs and actors in the non-profit sector can also promote the adoption of local practices, involve the informal sector, and contribute to establishing protocols and practices that reflect cultural values and have social significance.

There is a need to identify, promote, and disseminate project management practices that truly respond to the characteristics of project governance in the Global South. Practices in developing nations need to be improved and reinforced, but changes should not be based on the indiscriminate introduction of methods from the North, or the West. Instead, they must emerge from culturally relevant practices, rooted in project governance characteristics and in the conditions of the local building sector. This is the most significant challenge for creating new bodies of knowledge.

References

Abbott, K.W., Genschel, P., Snidal, D. and Zangl, B. (2011, September). *International organizations as orchestrators*. Conference presented at the International Studies Association Annual Meeting.

Abubakar, M., Ibrahim, Y.M., Kado, D. and Bala, K. (2014). Contractors' perception of the factors affecting building information modelling (BIM) adoption in the Nigerian construction industry. Paper presented at the *Computing in Civil and Building Engineering*, ASCE, Orlando, Florida. https://ascelibrary.org/doi/abs/10.1061/9780784413616.022.

Aghimien, D.O., Oke, A.E. and Aigbavboa, C.O. (2018). Barriers to the adoption of value management in developing countries. *Engineering, Construction and Architectural Management*, 25(7), 818–834.

Alreshidi, E., Mourshed, M. and Rezgui, Y. (2017). Factors for effective BIM governance. *Journal of Building Engineering*, 10, 89–101.

Anderson, M., Whitby, K., Schofield, L. and McLarnon, H. (2021, May). January 2021 PMI Fact File Stats. https://www.projectmanagement.com/blog-post/68280/January-2021-PMI-Fact-File-Stats

Anvuur, A.M. and Kumaraswamy, M. (2008). Better collaboration through cooperation. In H. Smyth and S. Pryke (Eds.), *Collaborative Relationships in Construction: Developing Frameworks*, pp. 107–128.

Aragón, E., Lizarralde, G., González, G., Olivera, A., Bornstein, L., Herazo, B. and Labbé, D. (2020). The language of risk and the risk of language: Social struggles in coastal communities in Cuba. *International Journal of Disaster Risk Reduction*, 50(101712).

Autodesk Forum (2020). Autodesk Knowledge Network. https://forums.autodesk.com [Accessed 16 November 2020].

Beltrán, A., Rincón, M. and Páez-Martínez, H.-J. (2020). *Emprendimiento institucional en la decisión de implementar dos planes de desarrollo: La Operación Colombia (1960–61) y el Plan de las Cuatro Estrategias (1971–72).* MSc. Trabajo de grado, Universidad Javeriana, Bogota.

Bogenschneider, K. (2020). Positioning universities as honest knowledge brokers: Best practices for communicating research to policymakers. *Family Research*, 69(3), 628–643.

Boutinet, J.P. (1990). *Anthropologie du projet* (1 ed.). Presses universitaires de France, Paris.

Bröchner, J., Rosander, S. and Waara, F. (2004). Cross-border post-acquisition knowledge transfer among construction consultants. *Construction Management and Economics,* 22(4), 421–427.

Bui, N., Merschbrock, C. and Munkvold, B.E. (2016). A review of building information modelling for construction in developing countries. *Procedia Engineering*, 164, 487–494.

Campos, N., Engel, E., Fischer, R.D. and Galetovic, A. (2021). The ways of corruption in infrastructure: Lessons from the Odebrecht case. *Journal of Economic Perspectives*, 35(2), 171–190.

Carreño Sánchez, F., Vargas Marín, Á.C. and Giraldo, G.E. (2017). Caracterización del rol actual de la mujer en la gerencia de proyectos en Colombia. *Revista EAN*, 83, 93–117.

Chan, P. and Raisanen, C. (2009). Informality and emergence in construction. *Construction Management and Economics*, 27(10), 907–912.

Cherns, A. and Bryant, D. (1984). Studying the client's role in construction management. *Construction Management and Economics*, 2(2), 177–184.

Cole, R.J. (2010). Building environmental assessment methods: redefining intentions and roles. *Building Research & Information*, 33(5), 455–467.

Dainty, A., Moore, D. and Murray, M. (2006). *Communication in Construction: Theory and Practice*. Taylor & Francis, London; New York.

Damoah, I.S., Akwei, C.A., Amoako, I.O. and Botchie, D. (2018). Corruption as a source of government project failure in developing countries: Evidence from Ghana. *Project Management Journal*, 49(3), 17–33.

Darko, A., Chan, A.P.C., Yang, Y., Shan, M., He, B.-J. and Gou, Z. (2018). Influences of barriers, drivers, and promotion strategies on green building technologies adoption in developing countries: The Ghanaian case. *Journal of Cleaner Production*, 200, 687–703.

de Blois, M. and De Coninck, P. (2008). The dynamics of actors and stakeholders participation: An approach of management by design. *Architectural Engineering and Design Management*, 4, 176–188.

de Blois, M., Herazo, B., Latunova, I. and Lizarralde, G. (2011). Relationships between construction clients and participants of the building industry: Structures and mechanisms of coordination and communication. *International Journal of Architectural Engineering and Design Management*, 7(1), 3–22.

Doan, D.T., Ghaffarianhoseini, A., Naismith, N., Zhang, T., Ghaffarianhoseini, A. and Tookey, J. (2017). A critical comparison of green building rating systems. *Building and Environment*, 123, 243–260.

Dodge Data and Analytics (2018). *World Green Building Trends 2018.* Dodge Data & Analytics, Bedford.

Ekundayo, D., Jewell, C. and Awodele, O. (2013). Executive project management structure and the challenges facing its adoption in the Nigerian construction industry. *International Journal of Architecture, Engineering Construction and Building Materials*, 2(3), 158–169.

Emmitt, S. and Gorse, C.A. (2007). *Communication in Construction Teams.* Taylor & Francis, London.

Golini, R., Kalchschmidt, M. and Landoni, P. (2015). Adoption of project management practices: The impact on international development projects of non-governmental organizations. *International Journal of Project Management*, 33(3), 650–663.

Gómez Sánchez, J.M. (2016). The status of BIM adoption and implementation experiences of construction companies in Colombia. Paper presented at the *Proceedings of the VII Elagec*, Bogotá, Colombia.

Green, S. (1996). A metaphorical analysis of client organizations and the briefing process. *Construction Management and Economics*, 14(2), 155–164.

Häkkinen, T. and Belloni, K. (2011). Barriers and drivers for sustainable building. *Building Research & Information*, 39(3), 239–255.

He, Q., Wang, Z., Wang, G., Zuo, J., Wu, G. and Liu, B. (2020). To be green or not to be: How environmental regulations shape contractor greenwashing behaviors in construction projects. *Sustainable Cities and Society*, 63, 102462.

He, Y., Kvan, T., Liu, M. and Li, B. (2018). How green building rating systems affect designing green. *Building and Environment*, 133, 19–31.

Herazo, B. and Lizarralde, G. (2015). The influence of green building certifications in collaboration and innovation processes. *Construction Management and Economics*, 33(4), 279–298.

Hoekman, B.M., Maskus, K.E. and Saggi, K. (2005). Transfer of technology to developing countries: Unilateral and multilateral policy options. *World Development*, 33(10), 1587–1602.

Imbert, D.C.I. (1990). Human issues affecting construction in developing countries. *Construction Management and Economics*, 8(2), 219–228.

Karagiannis, N. and Wagner, P. (2007). *Varieties of World-making: Beyond Globalization* (Vol. 14). Liverpool University Press.

Klein Woolthuis, R., Hooimeijer, F., Bossink, B., Mulder, G. and Brouwer, J. (2013). Institutional entrepreneurship in sustainable urban development: Dutch successes as inspiration for transformation. *Journal of Cleaner Production,* 50, 91–100.

Koskela, L. and Ballard, A. (2006). Should project management be based on theories of economics or production? *Building Research and Information*, 34(2), 154–163.

Koskela, L. and Howell, G. (2002). The underlying theory of project management is obsolete. Paper presented at the *Proceedings of the Project Management Institute Research Conference*, Seattle, WA.

Kvan, T. (2000). Collaborative design: What is it? *Automation in Construction*, 9(4), 409–415.

Labbé, D. (2014). *Land Politics and Livelihoods on the Margins of Hanoi, 1920–2010*. UBC Press, Vancouver.

Labbé, D. (2015). Chapter five once the land is gone: Land redevelopment and livelihood adaptations on the outskirts of Hanoi, Vietnam. *Balanced Growth for an Inclusive and Equitable ASEAN Community*, 148.

Labbé, D., Collin, J.-P. and Boudreau, J.-A. (2010). *Facing the Urban Transition in Hanoi: Recent Urban Planning Issues and Initiatives*. INRS Centre-Urbanisation Culture Société, Montréal, QC.

Labbé, D. (Ed.) (2018). *Bridging the Gap: Towards a Better Integration of Masterplanned New Urban Areas and Urbanised Villages*. The Giới Publishers.

Labbé, D. and Musil, C. (2013). Periurban land redevelopment in Vietnam under market socialism. *Urban Studies,* 51(6), 1146–1161.

Lall, S. (1982). *Developing Countries as Exporters of Technology*. Springer, London.

Leoto, R. and Lizarralde, G. (2019a). Challenges for integrated design (ID) in sustainable buildings. *Construction Management and Economics*, 1–18.

Leoto, R. and Lizarralde, G. (2019b). Challenges in evaluating strategies for reducing a building's environmental impact through integrated design. *Building and Environment*, 155, 34–46.

Levée, V. (2019). La certification Passivhaus au Québec. *Formes*, 15(2020), 37–38.

Lizarralde, G. (2014). *The Invisible Houses: Rethinking and Designing Low-cost Housing in Developing Countries*. Routledge, London.

Lizarralde, G., Davidson, C., Pukteris, A. and de Blois, M. (Eds.) (2008). *Building Abroad: Procurement of Construction and Reconstruction Projects in the International Context: Colloque-atelier, 25–28 Octobre 2008*. Groupe de

Recherche IF, grif, Faculté de l'aménagement, Université de Montréal, Montréal.

Lizarralde, G. and Root, D. (2008). The informal construction sector and the inefficiency of low cost housing markets. *Construction Management and Economics*, 26(2), 103–113.

Lizarralde, G., Tomiyoshi, S., Bourgault, M., Malo, J. and Cardosi, G. (2013). Understanding differences in construction project governance between developed and developing countries. *Construction Management and Economics*, 31(7), 711–730.

Lizarralde, G., Leoto, R., Silva, D., Bernier, P. and Helal, B. (2018, 27 April). *Au delà de Revit. Les opportunités et les limites de la méthodologie BIM et ses relations avec la gestion de projets.* Conference presented at the *Séminaires Interfaces*, Montréal, Canada.

Lizarralde, G., Pearl, D., Langlois, L., Courchesne, J., Chayer, J.-A., Frenette, M., Bourassa, A. and Abraham, Y.-M. (2019, 26 April). *Architecture et urbanisme : Les certifications vertes. Mythes et réalités* Conference presented at the Séminaires Interfaces, Montréal, Canada.

Marefat, A., Toosi, H. and Hasankhanlo, R.M. (2019). A BIM approach for construction safety: Applications, barriers and solutions. *Engineering, Construction and Architectural Management*, 26(9), 1855–1877.

McAuley, B., Hore, A., and West, R. (2017). *BICP Global BIM Study — Lessons for Ireland's BIM Programme*. Technological University Dublin, Dublin, IR.

Nahapiet, H. and Nahapiet, J. (1985). A comparison of contractual arrangements for building projects. *Construction Management and Economics*, 3(3), 217–231.

Naoum, S. (2001). *People and Organizational Management in Construction*. Thomas Telford Books, London.

Newsham, G.R., Mancini, S. and Birt, B.J. (2009). Do LEED-certified buildings save energy? Yes, but.... *Energy and Buildings*, 41(8), 897–905.

Ofori, G. (2019). Construction in developing countries: Need for new concepts. *Journal of Construction in Developing Countries*, 23(2), 1–6.

Othman, E. and Ahmed, A. (2013). Challenges of mega construction projects in developing countries. *Organization, Technology & Management in Construction: An International Journal*, 5(1), 730–746.

Owusu, E.K., Chan, A.P.C. and Ameyaw, E. (2019). Toward a cleaner project procurement: Evaluation of construction projects' vulnerability to corruption in developing countries. *Journal of Cleaner Production*, 216, 394–407.

Petter, A.-M., Labbé, D., Lizarralde, G. and Goulet, J. (2020). City profile: Canaan, Haiti — A new post disaster city. *Cities*, 104(102805).

Pietroforte, R. (1997). Communication and governance in the building process. *Construction Management and Economics*, 15, 71–82.

Power, A. (2010). Housing and sustainability: Demolition or refurbishment? 163(4), 205–216.

Reve, T. and Levitt, R.E. (1984). Organization and governance in construction. *International Journal of Project Management*, 2(1), 17–25.

Rodríguez-Rivero, R., Ortiz-Marcos, I., Díaz-Barcos, V. and Lozano, S.A. (2020). Applying the strategic prospective approach to project management in a development project in Colombia. *International Journal of Project Management*, 38(8), 534–547.

Rowlinson, S.M. and McDermott, P. (1999). *Procurement Systems: A Guide to Best Practice in Construction*. Routledge, New York.

Ruuska, I., Ahola, T., Artto, K., Locatelli, G. and Mancini, M. (2011). A new governance approach for multi-firm projects: Lessons from Olkiluoto 3 and Flamanville 3 nuclear power plant projects. *International Journal of Project Management*, 29(6), 647–660.

Rwelamila, P.D. (2012a). Construction project performance in developing countries. In G. Ofori (Ed.), *Contemporary Issues in Construction in Developing Countries*. Spon Press, Abingdon, pp. 318–346.

Rwelamila, P.D. (2012b). Project management trilogy challenges in Africa: Where to from here? *Project Management Journal*, 43(4), 5–13.

Sahil, A.Q. (2016). *Adoption of Building Information Modeling in Developing Countries: A Phenomenological Perspective.* Unpublished Theses, Colorado State University.

Saka, A.B. and Chan, D.W.M. (2020). Profound barriers to building information modelling (BIM) adoption in construction small and medium-sized enterprises (SMEs): An interpretive structural modelling approach. *Construction Innovation*, 20(2), 261–284.

Saunders, G. (1992). Project management: A systems perspective. *International Journal of Project Management*, 10(3), 153–159.

Schandl, H., Fischer-Kowalski, M., West, J., Giljum, S., Dittrich, M., Eisenmenger, N., Geschke, A., Lieber, M., Wieland, H., Schaffartzik, A., Krausmann, F., Gierlinger, S., Hosking, K., Lenzen, M., Tanikawa, H., Miatto, A. and Fishman, T. (2018). Global material flows and resource productivity: Forty years of evidence. *Journal of Industrial Ecology*, 22(4), 827–838.

Sev, A. (2010). Comparative review of widely used building environmental assessment tools and suggestions for developing countries. In E. Dikbas (Ed.), *Managing IT in Construction/Managing Construction for Tomorrow*. Taylor & Francis, London, pp. 845–854.

Shan, M. and Hwang, B.-G. (2018). Green building rating systems: Global reviews of practices and research efforts. *Sustainable Cities and Society*, 39, 172–180.

Shiferaw, A.T., Klakegg, O.J. and Haavaldsen, T. (2012). Governance of public investment projects in Ethiopia. *Project Management Journal*, 43(4), 52–69.

Silva Ardila, D. (2020). Global policies for moving cities: The role of think tanks in the proliferation of Bus Rapid Transit systems in Latin America and worldwide. *Policy and Society*, 39(1), 70–90.

Smyth, H. (2006). Measuring, developing and managing trust in relationships. In S. Pryke and H. Smyth (Eds.), *The Management of Complex Projects: A Relationship Approach*. Blackwell Publishing, Oxford, pp. 97–120.

Stuckenbruck, L.C. and Zomorrodian, A. (1987). Project management: The promise for developing countries. *International Journal of Project Management*, 5(3), 167–175.

Suermann, P.C. and Issa, R.R.A. (2009). Evaluating industry perceptions of building information modelling (BIM) impact on construction. *Journal of Information Technology in Construction (ITcon)*, 14.

The World Bank (2015). *Building Regulation for Resilience: Managing Risks for Safer Cities*. The World Bank, Washington.

Toor, S. and Ogulana, S. (2012). Leadership and its development in construction in developing countries. In G. Ofori (Ed.), *Contemporary Issues in Construction in Developing Countries*. Spoon Press, Taylor & Francis, New York, pp. 242–267.

Vierra, S. (2016). Green Building Standards and Certification Systems. Whole Building Design Guide. https://www.wbdg.org/resources/green-building-standards-and-certification-systems, National Institute of Building Sciences.

Walker, A. (2007). *Project Management in Construction* (5th ed.). Blackwell, Oxford, UK.

Walker, D. and Rowlinson, S. (2008). *Procurement Systems: A Cross-industry Project Management Perspective*. Taylor & Francis, London, New York.

Walker, D.H.T. and Hampson, K. (2003). *Procurement Strategies: A Relationship-based Approach*. Malden, MA: Blackwell Pub.

Williams, T.M. (1999). The need for new paradigms for complex projects. *International Journal of Project Management*, 17(5), 269–273.

Winch, G.M. (2001). Governing the project process: A conceptual framework. *Construction Management and Economics*, 19(8), 799–808.

Yudelson, J. (2016). *Reinventing Green Building: Why Certification Systems Aren't Working and What We Can Do About It*. Canada: New Society Publishers.

Zhang, Q., Oo, B.L. and Lim, B.T.H. (2019). Drivers, motivations, and barriers to the implementation of corporate social responsibility practices by construction enterprises: A review. *Journal of Cleaner Production*, 210, 563–584.

https://doi.org/10.1142/9789811224720_0004

Chapter 4

Project Management and International Development: The Nexus and the Future of Project Management in Developing Countries

George Ofori

London South Bank University, UK

Abstract

Developing countries need a range of projects to foster their long-term national progress in every sphere: economic, social, environmental, institutional, and physical. Thus, the efficient management of projects is of particular importance to these countries. This is underscored by the fact that these countries lack the financial capacity and managerial and technological capability to bear the consequences of poor performance in the management of projects. However, as discussed in Chapter 2 of this book, the results of projects in the developing countries are poorer than those in their industrialized counterparts. Whereas there are gaps in provision of all types of buildings and infrastructure in developing countries, a great deal has been built. What are the lessons from the projects that have been completed? In particular, what does the well-documented experience on international projects teach researchers and practitioners about the traditional approach to project management?

This chapter explores project management performance in the developing countries using, in particular, international development projects on which there is a good volume of literature. It is shown that many factors in the context of the developing countries make the application of the existing approach to project management inappropriate. The possible synergies between international development and project management are explored. This shows that the body of knowledge on, and the practice of, project management should be decolonized. A tentative attempt is made to lay out what the nature of the decolonized project management field of knowledge would look like.

Keywords: Development gap, international development, project management approach, context, operating environment, decolonization

Introduction

A development gap persists in the developing countries, and it is necessary to find the best ways and means of filling this gap. The aim of this chapter is to examine the appropriateness of the current approach to project management to developing countries. The objectives are to: discuss what a developing country is; why it is important that project management is effective and efficient in these countries; how appropriate the existing approach is, in the context of these countries; and what can be done to bring about change. First, the definition of a "developing country" is explored. Second, the critical need for projects in developing countries is used to demonstrate the reason for good project management performance. Third, the experience from project management on international projects is discussed. Finally, the need for a new approach to project management in developing countries is considered, and possible options discussed.

The discussion of the nature of developing countries, which was started in Chapter 2, is continued here, and covered in more detail.

What is a developing country?

The income indicator

As noted in Chapter 2, the common definition of a "developing country" is an economic indicator based on gross national income (GNI) per capita as determined by the World Bank, which adopts this classification of countries (Serajuddin and Hamadeh, 2020):

- Low-income countries: per capita GNI of US$1,036 and below in July 2019
- Lower-middle-income countries: per capita GNI of between US$1,036 and US$4,045
- Upper-middle-income countries: per capita GNI of between US$4,046 and US$12,535
- High-income countries: per capita GNI of US$12,535 and above.

"Low-income" and "Lower-middle-income" nations are referred to as "developing countries."

Alternative measures of development

As noted in Chapter 2, many authors disagree with the use of one economic indicator (GNI per capita) to "measure development." There is a large and growing volume of literature in the field of Development Economics on the subject of measuring development (see, for example, Sen, 1999; Stiglitz *et al.*, 2010) which has led to the formulation of various alternative indicators of "development," such as the UN Human Development Index (HDI) and the Global Multidimensional Poverty Index (GMPI).

It is pertinent to briefly discuss the HDI. It was created to stress the point that people and their capabilities should be the criteria for assessing the development of a country and not economic growth alone. For example, the HDI can be used to ask how a country with a high GNI per capita can have a relatively low human development outcome (UNDP, 2020). HDI "is a summary measure of average achievement in key dimensions of human development: a long and healthy life, being knowledgeable and have a decent standard of living. HDI is the geometric mean of normalised indices for each of the three dimensions" (UNDP, 2020, 2021). HDI is used as an index to rank countries; it places countries on a scale of 0–1 and categorizes them into one of four levels of human development: low human development (0–0.55), medium human development (0.55–0.70), high human development (0.70–0.80), and very high human development (0.80–1.0).

Another indicator, GMPI, complements traditional monetary poverty measures by capturing the acute deprivations in health, education, and living standards that a person faces simultaneously (Oxford Poverty and Human Development Initiative (OPHI), 2020, 2021).

Distinguishing developing countries considering construction

With respect to construction, Ofori (2012) noted differences between developed and developing countries by considering: features of the construction industry, projects, and products; performance of the construction industries; and aspects of the driving forces of construction in the two groups of countries — including environmental issues and climate change, construction safety and health, poverty alleviation, globalization, technology development and innovation, information and communications technology (ICT), quality and productivity, and disaster prevention and reconstruction. The analysis showed that there is a difference between the construction industry in the developing and those in developed countries; Ofori (2012) called this "developing country exceptionalism."

Groupings of developing countries

It is pertinent to note that there are other designations and groupings of countries, with reference to their state of development. Some of these are now considered.

Least Developed Countries[1]

According to the United Nations Office of the High Representative for the Least Developed Countries, Landlocked Developing Countries and the

[1] https://worldpopulationreview.com/country-rankings/least-developed-countries

Small Island Developing States (UN-OHRLLS) (2021a), Least Developed Countries (LDCs) are low-income countries facing severe structural setbacks to sustainable development. LDCs have low levels of human assets and are highly vulnerable to economic and environmental shocks. The classification is undertaken every three years by a United Nations (UN) committee which assesses three criteria: human assets, economic vulnerability, and GNI per capita (UN-OHRLLS, 2021a):

a. *Income criterion*, the inclusion threshold is set at the three-year average of the level of GNI per capita, which the World Bank defines for identifying low-income countries; at the 2021 review, it is $1,018. The graduation threshold is set at 20 percent above the inclusion threshold; at the 2021 review it is $ 1,222;[2]
b. *Human Assets Index (HAI)*, based on indicators of: (a) nutrition — percentage of population undernourished; (b) health — mortality rate for children aged five years or under; (c) education — the gross secondary school enrollment ratio; and (d) adult literacy rate; and
c. *Economic Vulnerability Index (EVI)*, based on indicators of: (a) population size; (b) remoteness; (c) merchandise export concentration; (d) share of agriculture, forestry, and fisheries; (e) share of population in low elevated coastal zones; (f) instability of exports of goods and services; (g) victims of natural disasters; and (h) instability of agricultural production.

It is evident that the LDCs are generally the poorest by per capita income. There are now 47 LDCs; the first of them were added to the list in 1971.[3] Six countries have been upgraded from the list between 1994 and 2021. They are Botswana, Cape Verde, Equatorial Guinea, the Maldives, Samoa and Vanuatu. The goal of the UN is that half of the current LDCs should progress out of the category by 2022. A UN General Assembly resolution (A/RES/76/8 adopted on November 24, 2021),

---

[2] https://www.un.org/development/desa/dpad/least-developed-country-category/ldc-criteria.html

[3] https://www.un.org/development/desa/dpad/wp-content/uploads/sites/45/publication/ldc_list.pdf

decided that Bangladesh, the Lao People's Democratic Republic, and Nepal will graduate five years after the adoption of the resolution, i.e., on November 24, 2026.[4]

Highly Indebted Poor Countries

The multi-lateral, bilateral, and commercial creditors began the Heavily Indebted Poor Countries (HIPC) Initiative in 1996 (World Bank, 2018a). It was designed to ensure that the poorest countries in the world are not overwhelmed by unmanageable or unsustainable debt burdens. It reduces the debt of countries meeting strict criteria. To be eligible for the HIPC initiative, a country must: face an unsustainable debt situation after the full application of the traditional debt relief mechanisms; be only eligible for highly concessional assistance from the International Development Association and from the IMF's Poverty Reduction and Growth Trust; have established a track record of reform and sound policies through IMF and World Bank supported programs; and establish a track record of reform and develop a Poverty Reduction Strategy Paper that involves civil society participation. It is beneficial for countries to belong to the program. It is noted that the HIPC and related Multilateral Debt Relief Initiative programs have relieved 37 countries (31 of them in Africa) of more than US$100 billion in debt.[5]

Small Island Developing States

Small Island Developing States (SIDS) were recognized as a distinct group of developing countries facing specific social, economic, and environmental vulnerabilities at the UN Conference on Environment and Development in 1992. The UN recognizes 38 of its member states as belonging to the Alliance of Small Island States (AOSIS), an ad hoc negotiating body at the UN. AOSIS includes other island entities that are non–UN member states or are not self-governing or non-independent territories.

---

[4] *Ibid*

[5] https://www.worldbank.org/en/topic/debt/brief/hipc

These countries have similar economic characteristics. UN-OHRLLS (2021b) notes that:

> SIDS tend to confront similar constraints in their sustainable development efforts, such as a narrow resource base depriving them of the benefits of economies of scale; small domestic markets and heavy dependence on a few external and remote markets; high costs for energy, infrastructure, transportation, communication and servicing; long distances from export markets and import resources; low and irregular international traffic volumes; little resilience to natural disasters; growing populations; high volatility of economic growth; limited opportunities for the private sector and a proportionately large reliance of their economies on their public sector; and fragile natural environments.

The UN has been assisting the SIDS in their development efforts, starting with the Programme of Action for the Sustainable Development of Small Island Developing States finalized in Barbados in 1994.

Landlocked developing countries

UN-OHRLLS (2021c) notes that lack of access to the sea, remoteness and isolation from world markets, and high transit costs impose constraints on the socio-economic development of Landlocked Developing Countries (LLDC). Additional border crossings of their sea-borne trade and long distance from the market increase their costs of transport services. LLDCs are among the poorest of the developing countries, and they tend to heavily depend on a limited number of commodities for their export earnings. Of 32 LLDCs, 17 are classified as LDCs. The LLDCs are more remote from major world markets than landlocked countries in Europe which tend to export mainly high-value-added products and are surrounded by major developed markets; thus, they are able to successfully mitigate the consequences of their geographical handicap.

Why are projects necessary in developing countries?

The developing countries require a large volume of construction work to meet their development needs by closing the gap between their current levels and attainments and the relevant Sustainable Development Goal

(SDG) targets, along the path to attaining the aspirations for all countries encapsulated in the 2030 Agenda for Sustainable Development signed by the world's leaders in September 2015 which aims to realize 17 SDGs by 2030 (UN, 2015). The preamble to the declaration is (p. 1):

> This Agenda is a plan of action for people, planet and prosperity. It also seeks to strengthen universal peace in larger freedom. We recognize that eradicating poverty in all its forms and dimensions, including extreme poverty, is the greatest global challenge and an indispensable requirement for sustainable development.
>
> All countries and all stakeholders, acting in collaborative partnership, will implement this plan. We are resolved to free the human race from the tyranny of poverty and want and to heal and secure our planet. We are determined to take the bold and transformative steps which are urgently needed to shift the world on to a sustainable and resilient path. As we embark on this collective journey, we pledge that no one will be left behind.
>
> The 17 Sustainable Development Goals and 169 targets which we are announcing today demonstrate the scale and ambition of this new universal Agenda. … They seek to realize the human rights of all and to achieve gender equality and the empowerment of all women and girls. They are integrated and indivisible and balance the three dimensions of sustainable development: the economic, social and environmental.
>
> The Goals and targets will stimulate action over the next 15 years in areas of critical importance for humanity and the planet.

The developing countries need to improve their infrastructure base to support economic activities toward long-term growth and to improve the investment climate in order to attract local and foreign investment (UNCTAD, 2020), such as by improving the ranking in such lists as the World Economic Forum rankings; infrastructure is a major pillar in many of these rankings (World Economic Forum, 2021). It is also necessary to improve the quality of life of the people in these countries in terms of housing, sanitation, and leisure, as set out in their national planning documents (see, in Uganda, National Development Authority, 2015) and SDG reports (see, Department of Economic and Social Affairs 2018) as well as in global strategy documents such as the *New Urban Agenda* (United Nations, 2017), the global declaration at United Nations Conference on

Housing and Sustainable Urban Development (Habitat III) in Quito, Ecuador in 2016. Through efficiently and effectively managed projects, the developing countries can meet their needs.

The need is both large and urgent. An extract from the foreword to the SDG 2021 report by the UN Secretary-General, Mr. António Gutteres (UN, 2021, p. 2) outlines the current need for projects in the developing countries:

> Regrettably, the SDGs were already off track even before COVID-19 emerged. Progress had been made in poverty reduction, maternal and child health, access to electricity, and gender equality, but not enough to achieve the Goals by 2030. In other vital areas, including reducing inequality, lowering carbon emissions and tackling hunger, progress had either stalled or reversed. As the pandemic continues to unfold, … some significant impacts in many areas … are already apparent. The global extreme poverty rate rose for the first time in over 20 years, and 119 to 124 million people were pushed back into extreme poverty in 2020. There is a risk of a generational catastrophe regarding schooling, where an additional 101 million children have fallen below the minimum reading proficiency level, potentially wiping out two decades of education gains. … A brighter future is possible. We must use the crisis to transform our world, deliver on the 2030 Agenda and keep our promise to current and future generations.

Box 4.1 presents a summary of the latest SDG report to highlight the size and urgency of the needs of the developing countries in terms of projects (UN, 2021).

Box 4.1: What needs to be done in the developing countries.

SDG 1

The share of the world's population living in extreme poverty (people living on less than \$1.90 per day) fell from 741 million or 10.1 percent in 2015 to 689 million or 9.3 percent in 2017. However, the rate of reduction slowed to less than 0.5 percent annually between 2015 and 2017, compared with one percent annually between 1990 and 2015. The COVID-19 pandemic

Box 4.1: (*Continued*)

compounded threats to progress from conflict and climate change. Estimates suggest that in 2020, there was an increase of between 119 million and 124 million global poor, the first annual rise in the extreme poverty rate since 1998, from 8.4 percent in 2019 to 9.5 percent in 2020. Based on current projections, the global poverty rate is expected to be 7 percent (around 600 million people) in 2030, missing the target of eradicating poverty.

SDG 2
Between 720 and 811 million people in the world faced hunger in 2020, an increase of 161 million from 2019. The prevalence of undernourishment increased from 8.4 percent in 2019 to 9.9 percent in 2020. Hunger affects 21.0 percent of the population in Africa, compared with 9.0 per cent in Asia and 9.1 percent in Latin America and the Caribbean. More than half of the world's undernourished live in Asia (418 million) and over one-third in Africa (282 million). Nearly one in three people in the world (2.37 billion) were affected by moderate or severe food insecurity in 2020, an increase of almost 320 million from 2019. The highest levels of food insecurity were found in sub-Saharan Africa (66.2 percent), while prevalence rose fastest in Latin America and Caribbean — from 24.9 percent in 2014 to 40.9 percent in 2020.

SDG 4
It is necessary to improve basic school infrastructure. Data from 2016 to 2019 show that, globally, more than one-fifth of primary schools lacked access to basic drinking water or single-sex toilets, more than one-third lacked basic handwashing facilities, and one in four did not have electricity. This means that 818 million children lacked basic handwashing facilities at their schools at the start of the COVID-19 pandemic. Internet service and computers in schools are even more scarce. Almost half of primary schools in LDCs lack single-sex toilets — an important factor in girls' attendance — and over two-thirds lack electricity. The pandemic is spotlighting the importance of sanitation facilities; the need for ICT infrastructure to support remote learning; and adequate classroom space, air filtration in school buildings, and access to the Internet and computers at home.

SDG 6
Between 2015 and 2020, the proportion of the global population using safely managed drinking water services increased from 70.2 percent to 74.3 percent. However, another two billion people still lacked safely managed drinking

Box 4.1: (*Continued*)

water in 2020, including 771 million who were without basic drinking water, half of them (387 million) in sub-Saharan Africa.

The proportion of the global population using safely managed sanitation services increased from 47.1 percent in 2015 to 54 percent in 2020, but 3.6 billion people still lacked safely managed sanitation in 2020, including 1.7 billion who were without even basic sanitation. Achieving universal access to safely managed sanitation by 2030 will require a quadrupling of current rates of progress.

The proportion of the global population with basic hygiene rose from 67.3 percent in 2015 to 70.7 per cent in 2020. Thus, at the start of the COVID-19 pandemic, 2.3 billion people worldwide (one in three) lacked a basic hand-washing facility at home, and 670 million had no handwashing facility at all. In the LDCs, only one in two health-care facilities had basic water services, two in five had basic sanitation services, and three in four had basic hygiene services in 2019.

SDG 7

The global electricity access rate improved from 83 percent in 2010 to 90 percent in 2019; 1.1 billion people received electricity for the first time. However, 759 million people were still without access in 2019, three-quarters of them in sub-Saharan Africa. At the current pace, 660 million people will still be without electricity in 2030 (555 million in sub-Saharan Africa). In Africa, the number of people with access to electricity increased from 33 percent in 2010 to 46 percent in 2019; in Central and Southern Asia, the corresponding figures were 75 percent and 95 percent, respectively. However, in developing countries in Africa and Asia, basic electricity services are now unaffordable for more than 25 million people who had previously gained access, due to population growth and increasing levels of poverty.

SDG 9

Rural road connectivity helps reduce poverty by raising agricultural productivity, business profitability, and employment. Rural access index data — measuring the proportion of people within two kilometers of an all-season road — from 25 mostly developing countries for 2018–2019 indicate that almost 300 million out of 520 million rural dwellers lack good access to roads.

In 2020, almost the entire world population lived within range of mobile networks, with 85 percent covered by a fourth-generation (4G) network (between 2015 and 2020, global 4G coverage doubled). However, only 51 percent of the

Box 4.1: (*Continued*)

population used the Internet in 2019, leaving 3.7 billion people without Internet access. In LDCs, only one in five people were online in 2020, indicating failure to achieve the target of universal and affordable Internet access.

SDG 11
Between 2014 and 2018, the proportion of the urban population living in slums worldwide increased from 23 percent to 24 percent, translating to over one billion slum dwellers: Eastern and South-Eastern Asia (370 million or 27 percent of the urban population in 2018), sub-Saharan Africa (238 million or 56 percent of the urban population in 2018), and Central and Southern Asia (226 million or 31 percent of the urban population in 2018). The needs of these people are rarely taken into account in conventional urban planning, financing, and policy-making. The pandemic has disproportionately affected low-income households and those working in the informal sector.

Poorly planned and managed urbanization results in a disconnect between the provision of infrastructure and residential concentrations, leading to inadequate networks of streets and a lack of reliable transport systems. This diminishes the potential of cities to leverage economies of scale and agglomeration. Only about half of the world's population live within 500 meters walking distance of low-capacity transport systems (such as buses or trams) and within 1,000 meters of high-capacity systems (such as trains and ferries), according to 2019 data from 610 cities in 95 countries.

SDG 12
Globally, new renewable electricity capacity installations developed significantly over the past decade, outpacing installations in non-renewable electricity capacity since 2012. In 2018, the majority of new renewable electricity capacity was installed in developing countries, primarily owing to the uptake of new solar and wind capacity, which increased by a compound annual growth rate of 72 percent and 22 percent, respectively, from 2010 to 2019. In 2019, developing countries had 219 watts per capita of renewable energy capacity. However, renewable energy capacity was 880 watts per capita in developed countries; thus, there is room for growth.

SDG 15
Forests are repositories for most of the world's biodiversity, covering 4.1 billion hectares of land. They help regulate the water cycle; mitigate climate change; and are a direct source of food, income, shelter, and energy for some 1.6 billion people. There was progress toward the sustainable management of

Box 4.1: (*Continued*)

the world's forest from 2000–2010 to 2010–2020. The area of forest under certification increased or remained stable at the global level and in most regions, as did the proportion of forests in protected areas or under long-term management plans, and the above-ground forest biomass per hectare. Although the rate of decline has slowed, the loss of forests globally remains alarming. The proportion of forest area fell from 31.9 percent of the world's total land area in 2000 to 31.2 percent in 2020, a net loss of almost 100 million hectares. The rate of forest loss has increased in South-Eastern Asia and Africa, and also in LDCs, LLDCs, and SIDS, mostly due to the conversion of forest to agricultural land.

SDG 16
Corruption is antithetical to sustainable development, aggravating income inequality, reducing domestic and foreign investment, and lowering the quality of public sector services. Yet it is common in many countries to have to pay bribes to access essential public services related to health care, education, water, electricity, and the justice system. In more than 120 countries and territories over 2011–2020, the average prevalence rate of bribery in low-income countries is 37.6 per cent, compared to 7.2 percent in high-income countries. COVID-19 has brought unprecedented opportunities for corruption.

SDG 17
The pandemic is testing multi-lateral and global partnerships. Although official development assistance (ODA) increased and remittance flows declined less than expected in 2020, foreign direct investment (FDI) dropped by 40 percent. The impacts of the pandemic are leading to debt distress in many countries, and also limiting countries' fiscal and policy space for critical investments in recovery (including access to vaccines), climate action and attaining the SDGs.

Net ODA flows by member countries of the Development Assistance Committee of the OECD reached $161 billion in 2020, an increase of 7 percent in real terms from 2019. Net ODA flows represented 0.32 percent of donors' combined GNI in 2020, falling short of the 0.7 percent target.

In 2020, FDI dropped below $1 trillion (from $1.5 trillion in 2019) for the first time since 2005. Lockdown measures slowed existing investment projects, and the prospect of a deep recession led multi-national enterprises to reassess new projects. International FDI flows to developing and transition economies in sectors relevant to the SDGs fell by about one third in 2020.

Source: UN (2021).

Why is it necessary to get project management right in developing countries?

By considering the nature and features, and the characteristics and circumstances of the developing countries, heterogeneous as they are, it can be concluded that it is critical to get project management right in the developing countries. The need for projects that is common to the LDCs, HIPCs, SIDS, and LLDCs is to meet the basic needs of the citizenry as well as to set up the physical foundation for their development and improve the quality of life.

It is necessary to meet the targets of projects and obviate the constraints of the projects undertaken in developing countries because, for example, meeting cost targets on projects will enable the countries to have more project output and better outcomes for the budget available. It will also enhance affordability of the built items or the services provided in them to the citizenry. The countries lack the resources to undertake rework during construction or repair of defective work in operation or to maintain the items. Thus, quality, which affords the built items durability, is important in these countries. Meeting the schedule or early completion will enable the built item to be put to productive use early. Finally, environmental performance will limit the damage to the ecosystems. An extract from Watermeyer and Philips (2020, pp. vi to vii) on two power projects that were intended to ease a critical national power shortage illustrates how critical project management can be for a developing country:

> The time and cost-over-runs on the Kusile and Medupi coal power plants provide an indication of the degree to which mismanaged mega projects can damage the economy. The two projects have:
>
> - failed to resolve the energy shortfall that they were planned to address;
> - caused severe damage to the South African economy and to economic growth due to the resultant rolling blackouts;
> - left ESKOM (the national power utility) reliant on a three-year, R128-billion government bailout to remain solvent; and
> - put the sovereign balance sheet at risk, and was a major contributor to the downgrades of South Africa's investment gradings by international grading agencies.

An extract from the Project DPro presented in Box 4.2 outlines why project management matters in the context of developing countries.

Box 4.2: Why does project management matter?

Agents of Change

The development and humanitarian sectors have experienced substantial growth in the past few decades… our responsibility as professionals within these sectors is to provide the maximum benefit for the targeted individuals, groups, and communities in which the interventions take place. *Projects are the foundation for the sectors. If teams fail to provide the intended outputs at the project level, a domino effect will occur, making it less likely that the contextual, behavioral, and situational changes we seek at the outcome, program, and portfolio levels actually occur. Essentially, projects are the vehicle through which changes can occur. It is vital that the management of projects is effective and efficient so that a foundation is created that enables change.* Project management must be approached intentionally, with processes, procedures, tools, and techniques …that contribute to the maximum change possible for communities and beneficiaries.

Context

The focus of the Project DPro is to provide adaptable tools and processes to help those implementing projects on the ground, increasing the likelihood of success. In 2018, PM4NGOs launched the Program Guide for Development Professionals (Program DPro) to complement the Project DPro Guide and showcase the differences and provide guidance on the ways we approach and manage projects and programs. Often in practice within organizations, there is little differentiation between the two, the terms are frequently used interchangeably. The Project DPro and Program DPro aim to ensure these differences are clear.

Accountability

There is an increased demand for accountability in the development and humanitarian sector, but …there are different levels of accountability: upward, downward, and horizontal accountability.

Downward Accountability: We are also accountable to the communities and people we are serving with our interventions, ensuring that we are providing high quality services and products in the most cost-effective way possible. An intervention that is operating within a conflict context may require more

Box 4.2: (*Continued*)

thought and analysis when it comes to downward accountability. Conflict sensitive frameworks that include the principle of "do no harm" are important to take into consideration.

Upward Accountability: When we are working with donor and taxpayer funding, we have an obligation to use those funds in a responsible manner, providing the maximum benefit possible. We also have an obligation to the program and portfolio levels in our organization, ensuring that the projects we are implementing align with the strategy of the organization as a whole …

Horizontal Accountability: Projects … are part of a network of interventions being implemented by various organizations … within a geographical region. Horizontal accountability takes into [consideration] the partnerships, relationships, and collaboration efforts we have with our peers and other organizations. We need to consider how our intervention fits into the development and humanitarian picture within a given context and … how these partnerships and collaboration efforts can bring about that higher level change we are seeking.

Source: PM4NGOs (2020, pp. 18–19)

PM4NGOs (2020) notes that all projects share similar challenges, including: designing and delivering project results in the context of time, budget, quality, scope, risk, and constraints; developing comprehensive and detailed project plans and managing them through the entire life of the project; managing projects that are often implemented via partners, consortia, contractors, subcontractors, and suppliers; and identifying potential risks and establishing processes to avoid and address these risks and ensuring that the intended project benefits are delivered. However, there are some characteristics that make managing projects in the development sector unique and especially challenging:

- development and humanitarian projects are responsible for delivering tangible outputs and also for delivering less tangible outcomes related to promoting social change and/or behavioral change;
- development projects are less likely to focus on delivering concrete products as the ultimate goal of the project and are often service

oriented, intended to bring about improvements in the well-being of the target populations;

- development projects aim to address complex problems of poverty, inequality, and injustice;
- development projects tend to operate in exceptionally challenging contexts (limited resources, high risks, complex procurement networks, unstable political and financial environments and unsafe conditions);
- project implementation is often managed through a complex array of stakeholder relationships (partner agencies, government ministries, community-based organizations, contractors, global consortia) that have different compliance requirements, perspectives, and expectations;
- the project approach is often as important as the outcomes themselves (high priority is placed on participation and rights-based approaches);
- transferring knowledge and learning to the target population is a priority during each phase of the project; and
- projects in the development and humanitarian sectors can be subject to changing and challenging funding environments.

Project performance in developing countries

As discussed in Chapter 2, many studies show that the majority of projects in developing countries fail, or at least, fall short of the plans and expectations (see, for example, Aibinu and Jagboro, 2002; Ahmadzai and Paracha, 2016). Thus, the group of countries that most need projects face many challenges in project performance. Ofori (2016) suggests that performance on projects in such contexts is unsatisfactory using many yardsticks including: performance on similar projects in industrialized countries; comparison with the targets of the projects; and ability to meet the expectations of clients and other internal and external stakeholders. Ahmadzai and Paracha (2016) note that, in developing, fragile, and conflict-affected countries, improving the success rate of projects is one of management's greatest challenges. Again, as outlined in Chapter 2, Damoah *et al.* (2015) studied the causes of project failure on government projects in Ghana, and the top 10 overall rankings for the causes in the order of importance were:

monitoring; corruption; political interference; change in government; bureaucracy; lack of continuity; fluctuation of prices; planning; delays in payments; and release of funds.

In a wide-ranging study, Ika (2012) discusses project management problems on international development projects in Africa and suggests that they may fall into one or more of four traps: the *one-size-fits-all* technical trap; the *accountability-for-results* trap; the *lack-of-project-management-capacity* trap; and the *cultural* trap. He suggests actions to help international development to move away from the prevailing *one-size-fits-all* project management approach; to focus the attention of project management for international development on managing objectives for long-term development results; to increase the supervision efforts of the aid agencies in countries where project results are poor; and to tailor project management to cultures in the countries concerned. Ika also proposes an agenda for research on ways in which the project management literature can support the design and implementation of international development projects in Africa.

Another study in Ghana by Amponsah (2012) sheds light on reasons why projects fail. The reasons found are interdependent and intertwined. For example, 59 percent of the respondents cited the lack of project pre-financing (which is likely to cause delays) as a cause of project failure. Some 54 percent of respondents blamed cumbersome procurement processes as a major cause of project delays and hence project failure; and 35 percent of respondents considered delayed commencement of implementation as contributing to project failure. Some 60 percent of respondents did not apply any monitoring and evaluation methods; these respondents cited lack of adequate planning, delays in the release of funds, and interference by policymakers as the main causes of delays. Some 70 percent of interviewees indicated that their projects were not competitively bid for, whereas 77 percent of respondents reported that the stakeholders' participation was in the form of assistance; only on rare occasions did they play key roles in the planning and design stages of the project.

In one of the two of the papers in the special issue of the *Journal of African Business* on the theme, "Why do projects fail in Africa" edited by Ika and Saint-Macary (2014) which were on construction, Ofori (2014) notes that project outcomes in Ghana have been adjudged to be poor as a result of how projects are managed, the form project management takes, and the project management approaches used; and low project management expertise has been identified as a contributory factor to how projects have been managed in Ghana. He investigated project management competency levels in Ghana. The results showed that Ghanaian managers possess varying degrees of project integration, human resource, communication, quality, risk, and scope management competencies. The study recommends the systematic and deliberate improvement of project management competencies in order to increase the rate of project success. In the second paper, Rwelamila and Ssegawa (2014) assess the adequacy of the content of current graduate programs in project management offered in the Southern Africa Development Community (SADC) countries for training competent project managers. They found that, of the seven programs they analyzed, only one could be considered to be moderately adequate with respect to the defined measurement. Most of the programs were lacking in the coverage of the "soft issues" relating to project management.

Assessing the readiness of the construction industries in Africa to deliver the continent's priority projects, Ochungo and Odinga (2019) note that many studies have found that Africa's infrastructure construction firms often do not meet project objectives of time, budget, and functionality. This has often caused delays, abandonment, or disillusionment on the part of investors. They note that while several contributing factors to these failures have been identified, very little seems to have been done on the project management readiness of African construction firms. They found that: "Africa has a huge technical skills gap which is the main reason for the dismal performance in construction projects' delivery" (p. 64). They propose a "readiness training model for policy planners and educational practitioners to help build Africa's human capacity in infrastructure project management" (p. 64).

In more recent studies on project performance in developing countries, Olowa and Ibrahim (2021) investigate how professionals adapt the use of project management tools and, in particular, planning, monitoring, and control techniques within the context of the Nigerian construction industry to manage schedule performance for positive project outcomes. Ebiega-Oselebe *et al.* (2021) found that, in Nigeria, the perceptions of community stakeholder groups are often neglected when ascertaining the success or failure of a construction project. As what the community views as project success and failure do not align with the views of the client, consultants, and contractors, for the construction industry, allowing the voices of all stakeholders to be heard would enhance the chances of a wider range of stakeholders considering the project as successful. They suggest that meaningful community engagement should be viewed with the same level of importance as time, cost, and quality. Abbasi and Al-Mharmah (2000) argue that planning, monitoring, and control tools and techniques are not as prominent in project management in developing countries as is evident in developed countries. They claimed that the use of these tools and techniques usually reflect the social, economic, and political values upheld by the stakeholders.

The discussion now proceeds to consider international development projects.

Project management and international development

International development involves the undertaking of a large volume and wide variety of projects. Thus, there is much scope for these projects to be studied as the process of development proceeds. Ika *et al.* (2020a, p. 469) use the term "international development" to mean "the process and the conscious promotion of the goals of the sustainable and equitable reduction of poverty and the improvement of living standards in low- and middle-income countries." They are among authors who note that the conversation between the domains of project management and international development has been "narrow and shallow" (see also, Davies *et al.*, 2018); there has not been much interaction between researchers in the two fields of study although much has been written on each of the two fields.

Discussing the relationship between the two fields, Ika *et al.* (2020a) note that while little has been written on the contribution of project management to international development (Heeks and Stanforth, 2014; Ika, 2012), the project management literature has also not explored the ways in which international development projects can provide inspiration and opportunities for project management research (Ika and Hodgson, 2014).

Ika *et al.* (2020a) note that projects have long been instruments of choice for driving business, organizational, and national change — this has given rise to the process of projectification of activities discussed in Chapter 2. They cite the works of many authors, including Heeks and Stanforth (2014) and Schoper *et al.* (2018), and observe that projects play a central role in addressing many of those challenges in developing countries. These call for new forms of international development and collaboration (Morris, 2013). Thus, there is the need for greater understanding in both fields of knowledge and for appreciating their interlinkages.

The lack of research linking the two areas belies the historical interrelationship between them. Ika *et al.* (2020b) note that although some of the foundations of project management grew out of the challenges associated with international development (see, for example, Hirschman, 1967; Rondinelli, 1983; Morris, 1994; Youker, 2007), there is little cross-fertilization between the project management and international development fields of knowledge. They argue that the impetus for project management to tackle not only the traditional tasks of international development but also emerging global challenges such as COVID-19 and climate change makes this cross-learning significant, beneficial, and timely.

Project management in developing countries: A new movement

Project management in context: Projects as experiments

What does the literature on the experience on international development projects teach about the management of projects? Characteristics of international development projects which make them "different" include (Youker, 2007): a "very large array of stakeholders whose views must be considered" (p. 99); the role of the project sponsor is often unclear; environments in developing countries vary, and there is often a lack of infrastructure; resources are in short supply, especially trained human resources; local citizens may have unique concepts of time and value structures; each country and donor has its own systems; the financing agency often leads project identification and administration in line with its own objectives; involving local beneficiaries in project discussions is difficult because of language, volume, distance, and communication problems; corruption is often a problem — monitoring systems are required to ensure transparency; and project success often requires an entrepreneurial project manager and a champion.

It is suggested that the features of developing countries call for a different approach to project management. Picciotto (2020), a former Director General of the Independent Evaluation Group (IEG) of the World Bank Group, which evaluates the development effectiveness of the Group, drawing on his 40-year-long career at the Bank, explores the intersection of project management and international development and stresses that projects be considered to be experiments (Rondinelli, 1983) where processes must always be adaptable. He suggests that the development experience contrasts with "the inward looking, results-obsessed, metrics-driven, and value-free approach" that prevails in mainstream project management practice. Picciotto (2020) referred to a "New Project Management Movement" that challenges the core principles of mainstream project management thinking (such as Shenhar and Dvir, 2007). He suggests that project management thinkers should abandon a narrow, goal-oriented approach and rigid focus and instead embrace adaptable processes, systems thinking, and experimental approaches where appropriate.

Similarly, Rodriguez-Rivero *et al.* (2020) note that because international development projects take place in a developing world where the uncertainty surrounding their environment is high (such as country risks), this makes them fail often. Yet, the existing methodologies fall short in addressing these risks and uncertainties. They discuss "la prospective" (Berger, 1957), an approach which offers a way to foresee possible futures, and to embrace uncertainty and convert it into risks and opportunities through stakeholder participation, to improve the odds of success in projects. They find that this approach works where stakeholders, including the project team, envision the future of their project, consider its uncertainties and risks, and explore, through a scenario analysis, the best ways to deal with them and attain success on the project in a participatory manner. It also improves the project's effectiveness and impact. Li *et al.* (2020) explore what defines a competent international project manager in emerging and developing countries. Their results indicate that international project manager competences can be understood from an efficiency-effectiveness–oriented perspective and an input-output–focused perspective. Four competence sets are identified: fundamental knowledge and skills, goals-oriented competences, uncertainty and change management competences, and stakeholder management competences.

Going further, Goldini *et al.* (2020) note that the international development enterprise offers many "hard-won" lessons for project management scholarship, especially in complex and uncertain settings. In such settings, project management thinkers should broaden their connections with the social sciences. Goldini *et al.* (2020) suggest that project scholars should learn from the peculiar governance, delivery, institutional analysis, (external) stakeholder engagement, complexity, strategic alignment, and adaptation of international development projects as interorganizational projects with high levels of collaboration and coordination, which tackle global challenges in different contexts.

The black box of project management in national development

Estimates show that more than US$250 billion is spent on international development projects every year (even considering only those funded by official development assistance), often with less than the expected impact (Honig, 2018). Thus, there is a strong debate on the effectiveness of international aid (see for example, Easterly, 2006; Sachs, 2005; Calderisi, 2007; Moyo, 2009). Many authors in this debate adopt a macro-economic perspective in examining whether aid contributes to economic growth or poverty reduction (Mekasha and Tarp, 2018) and others from a micro-economic perspective, studying whether the projects achieve their specified objectives (such as Feeny and Vuong, 2017; Mishra and Newhouse, 2009).

The study of development projects tends to be narrow. For example, Ika (2015) notes that economists usually ignore the inner workings of the project management "black box"; and there is no discussion of how project management contributes to project outcomes in either the international development economics literature or the broader economics literature. Therefore, there is not much knowledge, in both the project management and the international development literature, about how international development projects are carried out, why they fail, how they can succeed better, and what role project management processes can play in their delivery (Ika, 2015).

Andrews (2018) examines World-Bank–funded public policy reform projects and reveals that while 25 percent are project *management* failures (not on time, scope, and budget), 50 percent are international *development* failures (little or no impact). Andrews *et al.* (2012) suggest that the "top-down and best-practices" should be replaced by a "muddling through" approach for managing projects such as the Problem Driven Iterative Adaptation model. Drawing from contingency theory, Ramalingam *et al.* (2014) suggest that "best practices" should be replaced with "best fit" to context, actors, and issue. Similarly, Ika (2018) analyzes World-Bank–funded projects and finds that the Hiding Hand prevails over the Planning Fallacy, contrary to Flyvbjerg's (2016) claims.

In Box 4.3, Hekala (2012) advises donor agencies to take an interest in project management to ensure the success of their projects.

Box 4.3: Donors should care about project management.

Hekala (2012) suggested that, to him, the fact that the 2011 McKinsey and Devex Development Agency Effectiveness Survey of 1,210 respondents (Lovegrove *et al.*, 2011) reported that "only 36 percent of those surveyed said that most aid projects achieve their intended impact … is not at all surprising, having worked in the field of international development for the last 14 years. In fact, a 36 percent success rate may even be optimistic." This is because international development projects are inherently high risk; they have many factors that are beyond the control of the project implementer, even if they are employing project management best-practices. He notes that "International development projects' inherent risks … can be better managed and controlled because two principal causes of project failure are 1) poor project planning and 2) inadequately skilled project managers."

Hekala (2012) noted that, for donors, a "project" is the most common method for assistance delivery. Businesses and governments have followed PMI standards to ensure the effective execution of projects from modifications to human resource policies to building a dam. Donors and international

Box 4.3: (*Continued*)

development professionals are typically "accidental project managers," professionals with project, program, or portfolio management responsibilities yet without any formal education, background, skills, or certifications in the discipline. He suggested that donors funding international development projects "must take advantage of the cascade of formal project, program and portfolio management standards maintained by PMI and consider 'project management' as distinct a discipline as economics"... "Donors need more people to move beyond their academic disciplines towards the project management discipline. Daily work references for international development professionals should include 'A Guide to the Project Management Body of Knowledge', the ... ISO standard for project management, and the PMI standards for program and portfolio management." He gave examples from his experience of the usefulness of project management skills on projects.

Finally, Hekala (2012) noted that: "Hopefully, in the future, donors will incorporate the collective knowledge of decades of practice, millions of projects, and hundreds of thousands of professionals in project management into their work, and then demand that those implementing projects they fund do the same."

Source: Hekala (2012).

It would appear that some existing project management frameworks (which are less common in usage) are more appropriate for application in the developing countries. As discussed in Chapter 2, Munro and Ika (2020) compare project management standards used for international development with those used on other projects, and conclude that, while international development standards put more emphasis on beneficiary participation, environmental impact, human rights, gender, unintended consequences of projects, soft objectives, and evaluation techniques, conventional project management standards are stronger when considering scoping and scheduling. Landoni and Corti (2011) compare five international development project management standards issued by government aid agencies in Australia, Canada, the European Commission, Japan, and the US. They conclude that these standards have both similarities and differences, and they underline the need for a new international standard for project management.

Recent experience from World Bank projects

Reports on World Bank projects yield a useful array of lessons for project management in the developing countries. Youker (2007) summarized these problems in managing international development projects from World Bank evaluation reports: lack of shared perception and agreement on project objectives by donor, government personnel and other stakeholders; lack of commitment to project by team, management, and stakeholders; lack of detailed, realistic, current project plans (schedule, budget, responsibility); unclear lines of authority and responsibility; lack of adequate resources, especially from government; poor feedback and control mechanisms for early detection of problems; poor or no analysis of major risk factors; and delays caused by bureaucratic administrative systems (approvals, procurement, personnel, land acquisition, and release of funds).

Similarly, Ika (2015) empirically demonstrates that success in international development projects funded by the World Bank is a two-dimensional construct and that projcct supervision significantly influences project *management* success (on time, scope, and budget) but not international *development* success (such as impact on poverty, income, and health). Ika and Donnely (2017), in their comparative case study of four capacity building projects in Ghana, Indonesia, Sri Lanka, and Vietnam, highlight structural, institutional, and managerial success conditions and suggest that international development projects thrive when multi-stakeholder commitment, collaboration, alignment, and adaptation are high. In another study, Yalegama *et al.* (2016) studied community-driven international development projects in Sri Lanka and identified three critical success factors: an enabling community environment, measurable project management outcomes, and community project management engagement. Julian (2016) finds that the mismatch between actual and reported results in international development projects is due to the differing and changing stakeholder interests and perceptions in reporting stakeholder activities, outputs, and outcomes.

Finally, the IEG of the World Bank Group asserts that its work "provides evaluative evidence to help the World Bank Group deliver better services and results to its clients."[6] The IEG seeks to generate lessons from

[6] https://ieg.worldbankgroup.org/about-us

past experience and accountability to shareholders and stakeholders. Langley *et al.* (2018) of the IEG sought to answer this question: "Why do some World Bank projects succeed, while others fail?" They undertook a structured literature review and identified factors under these three broad categories:

1. **Country-level factors:** Elements of a country's economic and socio-political environment that may influence project outcomes. Examples of these factors are: economic conditions, human development measures, conflict and fragility, environment, and macroeconomic management and policies.
2. **Political economy-level factors:** Elements related to the incentives and interactions between borrowers and donors in selecting and executing successful projects. Examples of these are: alignment of donor and recipient objectives, a conducive policy environment, and natural resource dependence.
3. **Project-level factors:** Characteristics or elements of project preparation and supervision that are plausibly within the control of the World Bank. Examples of these factors are: quality of design, supervision effort, monitoring and evaluation (M&E) capacity, task team leader, and team characteristics.

In the IEG's 2017 report (World Bank, 2018b), the political-economy factors that had a positive influence on project performance were identified as: alignment of donor and borrower interests; World Bank team leader's track record; incorporation of lessons learned and analytical work; results chain quality; collaboration with local stakeholders; design/analysis quality; selectivity of projects; and supervision quality. Other relevant studies by World Bank personnel include: Blum (2014), Denizer *et al.* (2011), and Ralston (2014). For example, Ralston (2014) studied factors which lead to success in the difficult environments of fragile and conflict-affected states.

The discussion now considers project management as an area of knowledge and discusses how it can be developed with the context of developing countries in mind. It takes the first steps in making suggestions on the decolonization of the field. This subject is further considered in Chapter 25 of this book.

Decolonizing project management: The first steps

Importance of culture in project management

The issue of culture in project management is even more relevant in the developing countries. Rwelamila *et al.* (1999) note that the lack of "ubuntu" (African group solidarity) among project stakeholders in the SADC public building industry has generated strong opinions. In their study, they sought to indicate some issues affecting the relationships among project stakeholders. They addressed two propositions: *(1) that the lack of "ubuntu" between project stakeholders is primarily due to an inappropriate project organizational structure; and (2) that a default traditional construction procurement system provides a poor relationship management system.* They conclude that the procurement system in use on public building projects in the SADC countries is inappropriate and differs significantly from that recommended in the theory, resulting in poor relationships among project stakeholders. This has led to a situation where project management is a "firefighting" activity, where group solidarity among project stakeholders is non-existent. They suggest that the SADC public building industry should establish appropriate methods of selecting building procurement systems as a prerequisite in formulating appropriate project organizational structures that will bring about a spirit of real cooperation between project stakeholders toward project success.

In discussing factors leading to project failure in Ghana, Amponsah (2012) notes that: "A deep and careful analysis of these factors exposes a layer of thread that runs through almost all the reasons tabled by the respondents as [being] the cause of project failure. This layer of thread could be referred to as the collective programming … of the mind … which informs the attitudes and behaviours of members of an organisation or business unit. This layer of thread is called culture" (p. 70). For example, in Ghana, a project leader would be reluctant to accept his/her faults. In that context, there is the attitude that the "leader is either an expert or always right." Team members cannot question decisions and seek clarifications; they are not consulted on, and are not involved in, key decision-making. Finally, in Ghana and most of Africa, the values of non-confrontation and harmony with nature would usually cause a project participant to withdraw from a conflict or avoid it altogether.

The importance of giving due consideration to culture in project studies is often highlighted. Geraldi *et al.* (2020) note that engineering tends to undervalue the social aspect; thus, engineers see the cultural aspect as a separate domain, as something that has nothing to do with actual work on, or relating to, the project. Sveningsson and Alvesson (2016) refer to this as an "anti-culture," in which people do not see the value of culture and do not want to participate in (project) culture shaping through reflexive practices. Therefore, they argue that there should be progressive movement away from the technocratic roots that had entrapped the project studies field of knowledge. Similarly, Kreiner (2020) notes that, in project studies, there is: "the awkward body of knowledge in which the field is currently entrapped, philosophically, theoretically, and practically." Instead, this cultural background should be integrated with the diversity of relevant knowledge areas.

Towards decolonization

In project research, it is suggested that a multi-centric approach should be adopted. Geraldi *et al.* (2021) observe that the limited geographic spread of project scholars they found in their study may be the result of cultural differences between Western and non-Western scholars and of historic developments in the field. They note that the imposing of one's values and worldview upon others, also conceptualized as ethnocentrism (Adler and Ghadar, 1993), is a risk in project studies. Finally, as Geraldi *et al.* (2021) note, a more regiocentric approach, which allows for local interpretation and situations, would give space to more indigenous project management topics and debates (such as mindfulness, which has emerged as an important project philosophy of Chinese megaproject management (Wang and Zhu, 2021)).

The discussion in this chapter points to a need to decolonize project management. This is further discussed in Chapter 25.

Concluding remarks and the way forward

There has been an argument on how best to determine the level of development of a country, and several possible measures have been proposed. There are differences among the developing countries, and many groupings and categorizations have emerged. That these groupings are based on particular inadequacies or hindrances to development indicates that there are countries which have some way to go in terms of social development and the quality of life of their citizens. These developing countries have a great need for projects of all types in order to meet their developmental requirements. They need the delivery of these projects to be efficient and effective.

The results of projects around the world indicates that the effectiveness of the practice of project management is less than desirable. Experience also shows that not all projects are the same, and there is a fallacy in the thought that a standard set of practices and tools will be universally applicable and successful on all projects. Moreover, from the experience obtained from international development projects and the work of international non-government organizations and their umbrella organization, it is evident that the conventional, generic PMBOKs are not fully helpful in the management of projects in the developing countries. There is a need to develop an appropriate body of knowledge for developing countries. This should be less rigid and prescriptive, and recognize the particular context of these countries. There is a need for project management to be decolonized, and for guides for applying it in practice in the developing countries to be formulated.

References

Abbasi, G.Y. and Al-Mharmah, H. (2000). Project management practice by the public sector in a developing country. *International Journal of Project Management*, 18(2), 105–109. https://doi.org/10.1016/S0263-7863(98)00074-X.

Adler, N. and Ghadar, F. (1993). A strategic phase approach to international human resource management. In D. Wong-Rieger and F. Rieger (Eds.), *International Management Research: Looking to the Future*, Walter De Gruyter, Berlin, pp. 136–161.

Ahmadzai, N. and Paracha, S. (2016). Why do projects crash and burn in fragile countries? *Review of Integrative Business Economics Research*, 5(1), 315–328.

Aibinu, A.A. and Jagboro, G.O. (2002). The effects of construction delays on project delivery in Nigerian construction industry. *International Journal of Project Management*, 20, 593–599.

Ameh, O.J., Soyingbe, A.A. and Odusami, K.T. (2010). Significant factors causing cost overruns in telecommunication projects in Nigeria. *Journal of Construction in Developing Countries*, 15(2), 49–67.

Amponsah, R. (2012) The Real Project Failure Factors and the Effect of Culture on Project Management in Ghana. Investment Climate and Business Environment Research Fund (ICBE-RF) Research Report No. 45/12. Dakar. https://media.africaportal.org/documents/The_Real_Project_Failure_Factors_and_the_Effect_of_Culture_on_Project_Manageme_LFNzOro.pdf

Andrews, M. (2018). Public policy failure: 'How often' and 'what is failure, anyway'? A study of World Bank project performance. Harvard University Center for International Development Paper No. 344, Cambridge, MA.

Andrews, M., Pritchett, L. and Woolcock, M. (2012). Escaping capability traps through problem-driven iterative adaptation. Harvard Kennedy School Faculty Research Working Paper Series No. 12-036, Cambridge, MA.

Berger, G. (1957). Sciences humaines et prévision. *La Revue des Deux Mondes*, 3, 417–426.

Biesenthal, C., Clegg, S., Mahalingam, A. and Sankaran, S. (2018). Applying institutional theories to managing megaprojects. *International Journal of Project Management*, 36(1), 43–54. https://doi.org/10.1016/j.ijproman.2017.06.006.

Blum, J.R. (2014). What Factors Predict How Public Sector Projects Perform? Policy Research Working Paper 6798. World Bank, Washington, DC.

Calderisi, R. (2007). *The Trouble with Africa: Why Foreign Aid Isn't Working*. Palgrave-Macmillan, New York, NY.

Damoah, I., Akwei, C. and Mouzughi, Y. (2015). Causes of government project failure in developing countries — Focus on Ghana. *British Academy of Management Conference*, September, Portsmouth.

Delisle, J. (2018). Uncovering temporal underpinnings of project management standards. *International Journal of Project Management*, 37(8), 968–978. https://doi.org/10.1016/j.ijproman.2019.09.005.

Department of Economic and Social Affairs (2018). *Voluntary National Reviews: Synthesis report — Synthesis of Voluntary National Reviews 2018*. United Nations, New York.

Easterly, W. (2006). *The White Man's Burden: Why the West's Efforts to Aid the Rest Have Done So Much Ill and So Little Good*. Penguin Press, New York.

Ebiega-Oselebe, O., Watts, G. and Higham, A. (2021). Construction project success as a wicked problem: The role of the local community in Ebonyi, Nigeria. *Construction and Human Settlements Management Journal*, 1(2), 49–66.

Feeny, S. and Vuong, V. (2017). Explaining aid project and program success: Findings from Asian Development Bank interventions. *World Development*, 90, 329–343.

Flyvbjerg, B. (2014). What you should know about megaprojects and why: An overview. *Project Management Journal*, 45(2), 6–19. https://doi.org/10.1002/pmj.21409.

Flyvbjerg, B. (2016). The fallacy of beneficial ignorance: A test of Hirschman's Hiding Hand. *World Development*, 84(1), 176–189.

Heeks, R. and Stanforth, C. (2014). Understanding development project implementation: An actor-network perspective. *Public Administration and Development*, 34(1), 14–31.

Hekala, W. (2012). Why donors should care more about project management. *Devex*, 27 February. https://www.devex.com/news/why-donors-should-care-more-about-project-management-77595

Hirschman, A.O. (1967). *Development Projects Observed.* Brookings Institution, Washington, DC.

Honig, D. (2018). *Navigation by Judgment. Why and When Top-down Management of Foreign Aid Doesn't Work.* Oxford University Press, New York.

Horsey, S., Taylor, J.E. and De la Garza, J.M. (2014). Deploying Best Practices in Unfamiliar Countries, RT-294. Construction Industry Institute, Austin, TX.

Ika, L.A. (2012). Project management for development in Africa: Why projects are failing and what can be done about it. *Project Management Journal*, 43(4), 27–41. https://doi.org/10.1002/pmj.21281.

Ika, L.A. (2015). Opening the black box of project management: Does project supervision influence project impact? *International Journal of Project Management*, 33, 1111–1123.

Ika, L.A. (2018). Beneficial or detrimental ignorance: The straw man fallacy of Flyvbjerg's test of Hirschman's Hiding Hand. *World Development*, 103(1), 369–382.

Ika, L.A. and Donnelly, J. (2017). Success conditions for international development capacity building projects. *International Journal of Project Management*, 35(1), 44–63.

Ika, L.A. and Hodgson, D. (2014). Learning from international development projects: Blending critical project studies and critical development studies. *International Journal of Project Management*, 32(7), 1182–1196.

Ika, L. and Saint-Macary, J. (2014). Why do projects fail in Africa? *Journal of African Business*, 15(3), 151–155. https://doi.org/10.1080/15228916.2014.956635.

Ika, L.A., Söderlund, J., Munro, L.T. and Landoni, P. (2020a). When project management meets international development, what can we learn? *International Journal of Project Management*, 38(8), 469–473. https://doi.org/10.1016/j.ijproman.2020.10.004.

Ika, L.A., Söderlund, J., Munro, L.T. and Landoni, P. (2020b). Cross-learning between project management and international development: Analysis and research agenda. *International Journal of Project Management*, 38(8), 548–558. https://doi.org/10.1016/j.ijproman.2020.10.005.

Julian, R. (2016). Is it for donors or locals? The relationship between stakeholder interests and demonstrating results in international development. *International Journal of Managing Projects in Business*, 9(3), 505–527.

Kreiner, K. (2020). Conflicting notions of a project: The battle between Albert O. Hirschman and Bent Flyvbjerg. *Project Management Journal*, 51(4), 400–410. https://doi.org/10.1177/8756972820930535.

Landoni, P. and Corti, B. (2011). The management of international development projects: Moving toward a standard approach or differentiation? *Project Management Journal*, 42(3), 45–61.

Langley, W., Peng, X. and Behrens, J. (2018). Uncovering factors of project success: A literature review, July 24. https://ieg.worldbankgroup.org/blog/uncovering-factors-project-success-literature-review

Li, Y., Sun, T., Shou, Y. and Sun, H. (2020). What makes a competent international project manager in emerging and developing countries? *Project Management Journal,* 51(2), 181–198. https://doi.org/10.1177/8756972820901387.

Lovegrove, N., Gebre, B., Lee, T. and Kumar, R. (2011). McKinsey-Devex survey results: Practitioners see need for new approaches to system-wide reform, 19 December. https://www.devex.com/news/mckinsey-devex-survey-results-practitioners-see-need-for-new-approaches-to-system-wide-reform-77026

Mekasha, T.J. and Tarp, F. (2018). A meta-analysis of aid effectiveness: Revisiting the evidence. United Nations University World Institute for Development Economics Research (WIDER) Working Paper 2018/44.

Mishra, P. and Newhouse, D. (2009). Does health aid matter? *Journal of Health Economics*, 28, 855–872.

Morris, P.W.G. (1994). *The Management of Projects*. Thomas Telford, London.

Morris, P.W.G. (2013). *Reconstructing Project Management*. Wiley-Blackwell, Chichester.

Morris, P.W.G and Geraldi, J. (2011). Managing the institutional context for projects. *Project Management Journal*, 42(6), 20–32. https://doi.org/10.1002/pmj.20271.

Moyo, D. (2009). *Dead Aid: Why Aid is Not Working and How There is a Better Way for Africa.* D&M Publishers, Vancouver, BC.

Muianga, E.A.D., Granja, A.D. and Ruiz, J.A. (2014). Influence factors on cost and time overruns in Mozambican construction projects: Preliminary findings. *Proceedings of the 5th International Conference on Engineering, Project and Production Management.* Port Elizabeth, South Africa: Nelson Mandela Metropolitan University, pp. 10–21.

Müller, R. and Klein, G. (2020). The COVID-19 pandemic and project management research. *Project Management Journal*, 51(6), 579–581. https://doi.org/10.1177/8756972820963316.

Munro, L.T. and Ika, L.A. (2020). Guided by the beauty of our weapons: Comparing project management standards inside and outside international development. *Development in Practice*, https://doi.org/10.1080/09614524.2020.1766421.

Narayanan, V.K. and Huemann, M. (2021). Engaging the organizational field: The case of project practices in a construction firm to contribute to an emerging economy. *International Journal of Project Management*, 39(5), 449–462.

National Development Authority (2015). *Second National Development Plan 2015/16 — 2019/20: Uganda Vision 2010.* Kampala.

Ochungo, E.A. and Odinga, R.A. (2019). Project management readiness: A glimpse into the troubled rhetoric and the expected delivery of 2020 Priority Action Projects in Africa. *Journal of Business and Management Sciences,* 7(2), 64–71. https://doi.org/10.12691/jbms-7-2-2.

Ofori, D. (2014). An exploratory study of project management competency in Ghana. *Journal of African Business*, 15(3), 197–210. https://doi.org/10.1080/15228916.2014.956644.

Ofori, G. (2012). Reflections on the great divide: Strategic review of the book. In G. Ofori (Ed.), *Contemporary Issues in Construction in Developing Countries.* Spon Press, Abingdon, pp. 1–19. https://doi.org/10.4324/9780203847350.

Ofori, G. (2021). Construction in developing countries: Need for new concepts and theorising of contextual specificities to the global corpus of knowledge. *Proceedings, West Africa Built Environment Research (WABER) Conference*, 9–10 August, Accra, Ghana.

Olowa, T. and Ibrahim, D. (2021). Appraisal of planning, monitoring, and controlling tools and techniques on time schedule performance of construction projects in Nigeria. *Construction and Human Settlements Management Journal*, 1–16.

OPHI (2020). Charting pathways out of multidimensional poverty: Achieving the SDGs. Oxford Poverty and Human Development Initiative and United Nations Development Programme, Oxford. https://ophi.org.uk/wp-content/uploads/G-MPI_Report_2020_Charting_Pathways.pdf

OPHI (2021). Policy — A multidimensional approach. Oxford Poverty and Human Development Initiative and Department of International Development, Oxford. ophi.org.uk/policy/multidimensional-poverty-index/

Picciotto, R. (2020). Towards a 'new project management' movement? An international development perspective. *International Journal of Project Management*, 38(8), 474–485.

PM4NGOs (2020). *Project DPro: Project Management for Development Professionals Guide — PMD Pro*, 2nd Edition. Arlington.

Prokopy, L.S. (2005). The relationship between participation and project outcomes: Evidence from rural water supply projects in India. *World Development*, 33(11), 1801–1819.

Ramalingam, B., Laric, M. and Primrose, J. (2014). *From Best Practice to Best Fit: Understanding and navigating wicked problems in international development*. Overseas Development Institute, London.

Rodriguez-Rivero, R., Ortiz-Marcos, I., Diaz-Barcos, V. and Lozano, S.A. (2020). Applying the strategic prospective to project management in a development project in Columbia. *International Journal of Project Management*, 38(8), 534–547.

Rondinelli, D.A. (1983). *Development Projects as Policy Experiments: An Adaptive Approach to Development Administration*. Methuen and Co., New York.

Rwelamila, P.D. and Ssegawa, J.K. (2014). The African project failure syndrome: The conundrum of project management knowledge base — The case of SADC. *Journal of African Business*, 15(3), 211–224. https://doi.org/10.1080/15228916.2014.956645.

Rwelamila, P.D., Talukhaba, A.A. and Ngowi, A.B. (1999). Tracing the African project failure syndrome: The significance of "ubuntu." *Engineering, Construction and Architectural Management*, 6(4), 335–346.

Sachs, J.D. (2005). *The End of Poverty: Economic Possibilities For Our Time*. Penguin Books, New York.

Schoper, Y.-.G., Wald, A., Ingason, H.T. and Fridgeirsson, T.V. (2018). Projectification in Western economies: a comparative study of Germany, Norway and Iceland. *International Journal of Project Management*, 36, 71–82.

Schwab, K. and Zahidi, S. (2020). *The Global Competitiveness Report Special Edition 2020: How Countries Are Performing on the Road to Recovery.* World Economic Forum, Geneva.

Sen, A. (1999). *Development as Freedom.* Oxford University Press, Oxford.

Serajuddin, U. and Hamadeh, N. (2020). New World Bank country classifications by income level: 2020–2021. https://blogs.worldbank.org/opendata/new-world-bank-country-classifications-income-level-2020-2021

Shenhar, A. and Dvir, D. (2007) *Reinventing Project Management: The Diamond Approach to Successful Growth and Innovation.* Harvard Business School Press, Cambridge.

Simushi, S. and Wium, J. (2020). Time and cost overruns on large projects: Understanding the root cause. *Journal of Construction in Developing Countries*, 25(1), 129–146. https://doi.org/10.21315/jcdc2020.25.1.7.

Stiglitz, J.E., Sen, A. and Fitoussi, J.-P. (2010). *Mismeasuring our Lives: Why GDP Doesn't Add Up.* New Press, New York.

Styhre, A. (2020). Thinly and thickly capitalized projects: Theorizing the role of the finance markets and capital supply in project management studies. *Project Management Journal,* 51(4), 378–388. https://doi.org/10.1177/8756972820931278.

Sveningsson, S. and Alvesson, M. (2016). *Managerial Lives: Leadership and Identity In An Imperfect World.* Cambridge University Press, Cambridge.

United Nations (2015). *Resolution adopted by the General Assembly on 25 September 2015 — Transforming Our World: The 2030 Agenda for Sustainable Development.* New York.

United Nations (2017). *New Urban Agenda.* New York.

United Nations (2021). *Sustainable Development Goals Report 2021.* New York.

United Nations Conference on Trade and Development (2021). *World Investment Report 2021: Investing in Sustainable Recovery.* United Nations, Geneva.

United Nations Development Programme (UNDP) (2020). *Human Development Report 2020: The Next Frontier — Human Development and the Anthropocene.* New York.

UNDP (2021). *Human Development Reports — Human Development Index (HDI),* United Nations Development Programme. http://hdr.undp.org/en/content/human-development-index-hdi

United Nations Office of the High Representative for the Least Developed Countries, Landlocked Developing Countries and the Small Island Developing States (UN-OHRLLS) (2021a). Criteria for Identification and Graduation of LDCs. http://unohrlls.org/about-ldcs/criteria-for-ldcs/

UN-OHRLLS (2021b). About the Small Island Developing States. http://unohrlls.org/about-sids/

UN-OHRLLS (2021c). About the Landlocked Developing Countries (LLDCs). http://unohrlls.org/about-lldcs/

Wang, L. and Zhu, F. (2021). Attention and mindfulness: A tale of two megaprojects. In N. Drouin, S. Shankaran and A.H. van Marrewijk (Eds.), *Megaproject Leaders: Reflections on Personal Life Stories*. Edward Elgar Publishing, Cheltenham.

Watermeyer, R. and Philips, S. (2020). *Public Infrastructure Delivery and Construction Sector Dynamism in the South African Economy*. National Planning Commission and GIZ, Pretoria.

World Bank (2018a). Heavily Indebted Poor Countries (HIPC) Initiative, January 11. https://www.worldbank.org/en/topic/debt/brief/hipc

World Bank (2018b). Results and Performance of the World Bank Group 2017: An Independent Evaluation. Washington, DC.

Yalegama, S., Chileshe, N. and Ma, T. (2016). Critical success factors for community-driven development projects: A Sri Lankan community perspective. *International Journal of Project Management*, 34(1), 643–659.

Youker, R. (2007). Managing projects financed by international lending agencies. In D.I. Cleland and L.R. Ireland (Eds.), *Project Manager's Handbook: Applying Best Practices Across Global Industries*. McGraw Hill, New York, pp. 97–105.

Part 3

Project Management Knowledge Areas: Developing Country Perspectives and Considerations

https://doi.org/10.1142/9789811224720_0005

Chapter 5

Project Scope Management in Developing Countries

Martin Morgan Tuuli*, Ebenezer Adaku*,
Eric Z. Banye* and Annette S. Tettey†

**GIMPA Business School*
Ghana Institute of Management and
Public Administration (GIMPA), Ghana
†SKOL Consult Ltd, Accra, Ghana

Abstract

Project scope defines the end result or mission or functionality of the project — a product or service for the client/customer — in specific, tangible, and measurable terms. Thus, project scope management has been identified as a critical success factor in project delivery. When scope is not properly defined at the beginning of the project and managed effectively across the project phases, the likelihood of failure is high, with new scope addition identified as one of the causes of project delay and cost escalation. Issues of ill-defined scope, scope creep, and scope change are particularly compounded in the developing country context by politics, budget constraints, lack of expertise, lack of stakeholder engagement, and other factors. Therefore, this chapter examines scope management from the perspective of developing countries. The chapter covers key topics such as: Scope Initiation, Scope Definition,

Scope Planning, Verification and Control of the Project Scope, Scope Creep and the Politics of Project Scope, and Approaches to Effective Project Scope Management. The chapter concludes with two case studies highlighting the typical Scope Management approach on a Social Intervention Project and a Private-sector Residential Development Project in Ghana. The case studies show that inadequate, ill-defined, or incomplete scope definition is a recipe for significant scope changes, with consequential cost and schedule implications.

Keywords: Project scope, work breakdown structure, scope creep, project performance, scope verification

Introduction

Scope is one of the "triple constraints" of project management, with time and cost being the other two (Kerzner and Saladis, 2009; Shirazi *et al.*, 2017). Unlike cost and time, scope is often described as being fuzzy because it is usually expressed in qualitative terms, and that leaves room for interpretation and misunderstanding, creating the biggest source of conflicts on a project (Bigelow, 2012). Project scope management has been identified as a critical success factor in project delivery. This is because project scope defines the end result or mission or functionality of the project — a product or service for the client/customer — in specific, tangible, and measurable terms (Larson and Gray, 2018). When scope is not properly defined at the beginning of the project and managed effectively across the project phases, the likelihood of failure is high (Ogunberu *et al.*, 2018). Scope change is identified as one of the causes of project delay and cost escalation (Kaliba *et al.*, 2009). A Project Management Institute (PMI) report revealed that while 19 percent of all projects are unsuccessful, more than 50 percent of projects suffer scope creep (Project Management Institute, 2017). For example, scope creep costs about four times the initial development costs, including deferred benefits and reduced return on investment (ROI), increased maintenance costs, and additional loss (Gurlen, 2003).

Issues of ill-defined scope, scope creep and scope change are particularly compounded in the developing country context by politics, budget constraints, lack of expertise, lack of stakeholder engagement, and so on (Asiedu and Adaku, 2019). These impacts are possible because there are opportunities for the project scope to be progressively elaborated upon throughout the project life cycle (PMI, 2017). Although project scope definition is regarded as a key element in successful project management, particularly in the developing country context, research on scope management is sparse (Kagogo and Steyn, 2019). Due to the pressure on financial resources to fund infrastructure, for example, in the developing country context (Kaliba *et al.*, 2009), the effects of scope change is detrimental (Senouci *et al.*, 2017) and scope creep remains a major problem (Shirazi *et al.*, 2017). Indeed, Hilali *et al.* (2019), in a study in Afghanistan, found that the leading contributory cause of project failure is poor contractual scope management.

Yap and Skitmore (2018) found many root causes of scope change in the developing country context, and grouped them into: client-induced, contractor-induced, and consultant-induced changes. Five factors were found to affect scope change: lack of coordination among the professional consultants, change of requirement or specification, addition or omission of scope, errors or discrepancies in design documents, and unforeseen ground conditions. Hilali *et al.* (2019) also found that one of the notable reasons for poor management of scope in the developing country context is uncertainty, which is compounded by country-specific constraints caused by harsh terrain, gap in the project knowledge, and so on. In particular, project professionals often exhibit ignorance about the requirements necessary for an adequately defined scope of work (Hilali *et al.*, 2019). Amoatey and Anson (2017) also found that the most critical causes of scope creep in developing countries were changes by the client, unforeseen risk, and unclear scope, which cause overruns in the project completion time and increases in project cost.

Therefore, this chapter examines scope management from the perspective of developing countries with the view to identifying effective strategies for scope management. In the rest of the chapter, first, Project Scope Initiation is explained, and then Defining the Project Scope is explored. Scope Planning is also examined, followed by a discussion of Verification and Control of the Project Scope. The foregoing provides the background for discussing Scope Creep and the Politics of Project Scope. This leads to an examination of Approaches to Effective Project Scope Management. The chapter concludes with a presentation of a case study of scope management on a social intervention as well as a private residential development project in Ghana.

Project scope initiation

Project scope initiation is an integral part of project initiation and is the first step in project scope management. Project initiation itself is the first phase in the project life cycle and normally follows the birth of the project through a decision of the management to execute a specific project (Yemini *et al.*, 2018). Project initiation enables the initiators to begin to create the project charter, scope statement, and the business case for the project. Thus, the initiation phase of any project can be considered as the best time to add value during the project life cycle as it is the phase where the highest number of options exist for modifying the project with minimal expenditure (Verzuh, 2016). Therefore, project success largely depends on the project initiation phase as it has the potential to minimize risks and uncertainty during the project, although very few project tasks are actually undertaken in this phase (Yemini *et al.*, 2018).

A draft scope statement is the primary outcome of scope initiation and it formally defines the scope of the project. The scope statement evolves as the project unfolds through negotiation with key stakeholders and as project initiators and contributors learn. Therefore, Bigelow (2012) notes that "no project's scope can ever be entirely free of fuzziness — free from subjectivity and imperfect definitions — as long as human beings are involved. On the other hand, it's also highly improbable that any project will ever survive initiation if its scope is entirely vague, undefined, and subject to unpredictable expectations" (p. 4). *Scope evolution* captures the agreed changes to the project scope as a result of taking into account stakeholder needs, learning from end-user needs, regulations, and the market with consequential effect on the proposed budget and schedule for the project (Russell *et al.*, 2018).

In a developing country context, challenges of scope initiation and definition of scope statement are compounded by political maneuvering. As Yemini *et al.* (2018) point out, it is at the project initiation phase that institutional politics and internal and external environment imperatives need to be fully accounted for. Therefore, it is important at this scope initiation stage to begin to identify all the relevant stakeholders and inputs into the scope definition.

Defining the project scope

Scope definition is one of the early activities undertaken under project scope management. Essentially, it aims to articulate the end results of the project when it is completed. This aspect of scope management is usually not engaged with properly, and, invariably, it lays the foundation for poor scope management on most projects in developing countries. For instance, a common scenario in the development of projects is where the consultants (i.e., designers) are handed old plans of similar projects as their scope definition for further development. Often, the consultants, not convinced about the needs and scope of clients, will then proceed to seek further information to clarify the project needs.

Although scope definition is one of the critical stages of project scope management, the opportunity available at this stage to point the project in the right direction is often missed in most developing countries, partly because there is little or no stakeholder involvement. To ensure the scope definition stage is effective in most developing countries, certain components are proposed to be considered (see Figure 5.1) to contribute to advancing the draft scope statement that emerges from the scope initiation stage. These are:

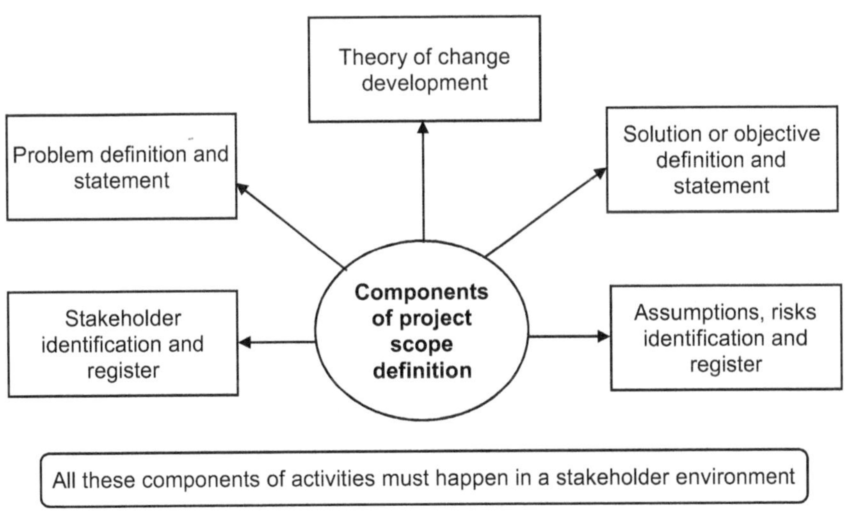

Figure 5.1: Components of project scope definition.

- Stakeholder identification and preparation of a register
- Problem definition and statement
- Theory of change development
- Solution or objective definition and statement
- Assumptions, risks identification, and register.

Stakeholder identification and preparation of a register: The project stakeholders are individuals or organizations that either affect or are affected by the project (Freeman, 1984; PMI, 2017). They are required to be identified as early as possible, and a register of them be kept. They are then to be engaged to contribute to further development of the project, particularly in respect of scope definition. In some developing countries, such as Ghana, local authorities, often acting as project-implementing agencies, rarely ensure effective stakeholder identification and engagement during project implementation. This phenomenon has led to instances where project users (such as shopkeepers or market traders) have rejected or abandoned newly constructed structures (such as modernized markets) as a result of their inputs not having been sought, and the structures not delivered in accordance with their preferences. This component is important to ensure that a proper definition of the project scope that is acceptable to all the relevant stakeholders is realized. This potentially reduces any disagreement at the end of the project in terms of the project success.

Problem definition and statement: Often, the justification for a project is the existence of a problem. Thus, a proper definition of the problem makes a case for the development of a good project. Stakeholders normally live with the undesirable conditions or problems and will be the appropriate parties to be around the table to define the problem as a basis for the project. The selection of the right stakeholders ensures a proper definition of the project scope. Wrong selection of the stakeholders could lead to wrong problem definition and ultimately wrong scope definition. In most developing countries, whether it is the cultural background where there is power distance or politics, public authorities often maintain a weak connection with stakeholders regarding problem definitions. For example, in Southern Ethiopia, as reported in a study by Wondirad *et al.* (2020), the exclusion of the local community in an eco-tourism initiative was met with planning and implementation challenges, culminating in natural resource destruction by the local communities.

Theory of change development: The definition of the problem sets the stage for thinking about the strategy to address the problem. Thus, a clear path of ideas is articulated that, when followed, will ensure an effective solution to the problem via the project. Often, the theory of change serves as a communication tool that describes the "story" and logical coherence of planned interventions (i.e., projects) (Archibald, *et al.*, 2016). Specifically, it indicates what needs to be available for interventions or projects to succeed. Further, it establishes "if… then…" relationships, with clear assumptions, between project components or actions to explain how problems can be addressed through projects. For instance, in designing a small educational project in a local community in Ghana where the theory of change tool was used and presented at a project stakeholder meeting, local stakeholders were able to make a connection to the need for a simple and low-cost teachers' residence, as part of the project, to attract teachers to, and retain them in, the locality. In most developing countries, this component regarding project scope definition is usually missing, and this reduces the chance that the project scope will adequately meet the project goals.

Solution or objective definition and statement: Following the project theory of change, the nature of the solution, via the project, becomes evident. Hence, the solution or project objective statement can be formulated. In other words, the theory of change serves as an input for the project objective definition and statement. A clear and precise project objective provides vivid boundaries and focuses project stakeholders, particularly in developing countries, on the relevant components needed for a successful project.

Assumptions, risks identification, and register: Most projects in developing countries fail or are ill-designed as a result of poor assumptions or improper risk identification and management (McFarlan, 1981; Baccarini *et al.*, 2004). In the presence of project stakeholders, relevant assumptions and risks can be identified and a register for them kept to support their proper management during the project development process. As indicated earlier, in most developing countries, stakeholders' engagement with project scope development is poor, and this undermines the effectiveness of project assumptions and risks identification. However, in very uncertain and unpredictable project environments, like in most developing countries, a comprehensive listing and understanding of the risks helps to minimize rampant changes in the scope.

For optimal results of the scope definition stage of project scope management, all these components of activities must happen in a stakeholder environment or setting to help the project scope statement to evolve.

Scope planning

Following the definition of the project scope captured in the form of a scope statement, the scope needs to be further planned and developed. The PMBOK, Sixth edition, considers scope planning as the process of developing a written scope statement or plan which lays the foundation for future project decisions regarding the validation and control of project components required for the successful completion of a project. The scope statement or plan provides pointers to components of the project that project participants must keep an eye on and how essentially these ought to be managed during the life span of the project. The scope statement or plan, an output of the scope planning process, primarily benefits the project by:

- Clearly delineating the limits and exclusions of the project and thereby establishing a common understanding of the project remit among project participants.
- Providing a picture ahead of time what success, at least in the immediate term, would look like as far as the project is concerned.
- Offering a meaningful and effective basis of agreement between the client and the supplier regarding the delivery of the project.
- Establishing a reasonable baseline for changes in project requirements and features throughout the project life span.

Effective scope planning requires a checklist of what needs to be done and what needs to be available at the end of the process in the form of key components a scope statement or plan. Some project management researchers (for example, Larson and Gray, 2018) indicate the following checklist as key components of a scope statement or plan:

- Project objectives
- Deliverables
- Milestones
- Technical requirements
- Limits and exclusions
- Reviews with the customer.

However, Bigelow (2012) suggests that the above list is just the starting point and needs to be augmented and expanded to define other components of the project as the project evolves, decisions are made, and project initiators learn.

Very often, the mechanisms utilized for planning project scope are expert judgment and meetings. Under expert judgment, one or a few experts, perhaps based on their prior experience with similar projects, are given the privilege to scope out the project. Otherwise, meetings among relevant project stakeholders are relied upon to develop the project scope. Ideally, the latter is considered an optimal approach as it offers the opportunity to confirm the project aim by the project participants and how that filters into the development of the project components to realize the ultimate goal of the project. In that sense, the project scope is developed in context and enhances the chance that the project will be accepted by the end users or customers. In some cases, an iterative process can be used. Either the experts scope out the project and this is subsequently validated by the larger group of project participants/stakeholders, or vice versa. Figure 5.2 indicates a process for project scope planning.

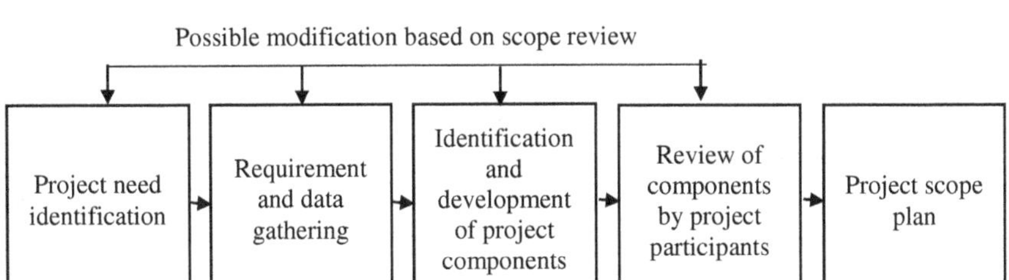

Figure 5.2: Scope planning process.

For optimal scope planning, some project management capacity, either internal or external, is required to manage the process from project need identification to project scope plan. An individual or a firm with such project management capability is key at this point. However, in most developing countries, there are often no such arrangements, resulting in a poor project scope plan (Asiedu and Adaku, 2019). Clients who may have no, or very little, project management capabilities, often come up with a brief supposedly indicating the project needs as a basis for engaging consultants (mostly designers), in the case of construction projects, who are required to assist to develop the project scope further. The assumption often made here by clients is that the consultants or designers have the requisite project management capabilities to support effective project scope planning but this is usually not the case, and this undermines the effective planning of project scope in developing countries' environments.

Work breakdown structure

One of the specific tools for clarifying and planning the scope of projects is the work breakdown structure (WBS). The essence of the WBS is to sub-divide the scope of the project into manageable components for realistic assignment of resources for their execution or completion (Burke, 1999). It is normally a hierarchical structure which assists project managers and project participants to identify components of the project required to successfully complete it (Larson and Gray, 2018). Essentially, it is an outline of the project with different levels of details. It establishes the relationship between the project, the ultimate deliverable, and its components. With the help of the WBS tool, the major deliverables of the project are first identified, then subsequently the sub-deliverables until the lowest level of the project activity. Every item in the WBS requires time and cost estimates (Larson and Gray, 2018). Thus, the WBS supports the development of the project schedule and cost.

There are normally two approaches to illustrating the WBS of projects. They are either:

- Presented graphically in rectangular boxes, or
- Indicated as coded text indents (table content format).

These two approaches of WBS are illustrated in Figures 5.3 and 5.4, respectively, for a simple three-bedroom residential project. Any of these approaches is considered best practice in a developed country context. Generally, in most developing countries, these approaches are also adopted. Nonetheless, the difference here is with respect to the capability of the relevant project team members to fully deploy them in an integrated manner with other project management practices and processes such as scheduling and cost development. This highlights the challenge of "resource void" — regarding the lack of adequate human resources — in carrying out projects in developing countries' environments (Asiedu and Adaku, 2019). For instance, in Ghana, from the authors' many years of experience regarding the project planning process, the development of schedules and cost, particularly for construction projects', is rarely

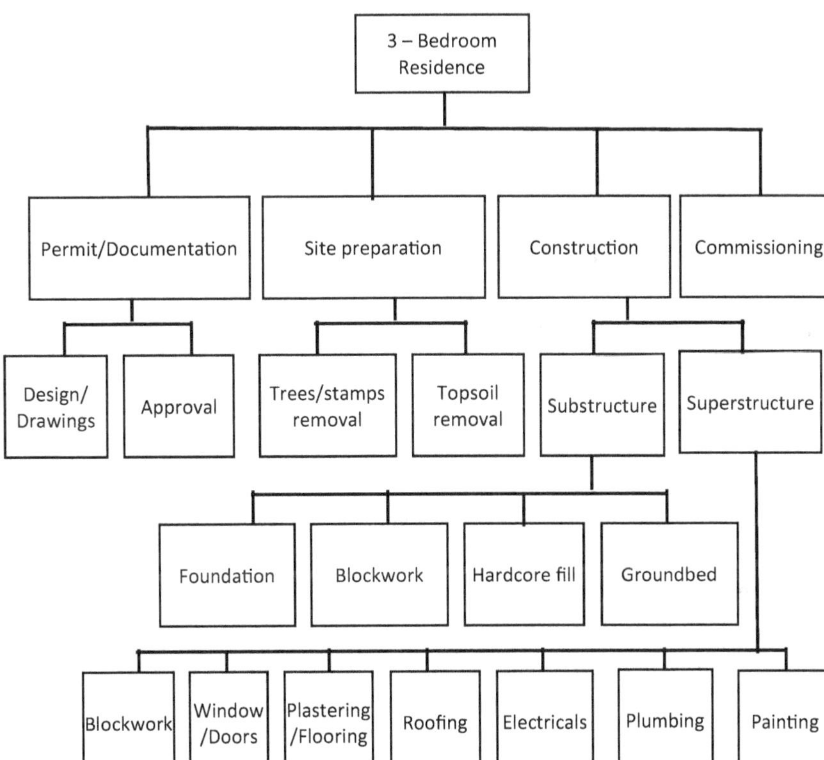

Figure 5.3: WBS for a simple three-bedroom residential project.

1.0.0 Three-bedroom residence
- **1.1.0 Permit/Documentation**
  - 1.1.1 Design/Drawings
  - 1.1.2 Approval
- **1.2.0 Site preparation**
  - 1.2.1 Trees/stamps removal
  - 1.2.2 Topsoil removal
- **1.3.0 Construction**
  - 1.3.1 Substructure
    - *1.3.1.1 Foundation*
    - *1.3.1.2 Blockwork*
    - *1.3.1.3 Hardcore fill*
    - *1.3.1.4 Groundbed*
  - 1.3.2 Superstructure
    - *1.3.2.1 Blockwork*
    - *1.3.2.2 Window/Door*
    - *1.3.2.3 Plastering/Flooring*
    - *1.3.2.4 Roofing*
    - *1.3.2.5 Electricals*
    - *1.3.2.6 Plumbing*
    - *1.3.2.7 Painting*
- **1.4.0 Commissioning**

Figure 5.4: Text indents WBS for a simple three-bedroom residential project.

informed by the WBS. This is often so, because the schedule and cost developments of construction projects are carried out by professionals such as Quantity Surveyors (QSs) who normally develop projects' cost and schedules directly from design drawings. Over-reliance on their technical abilities and the speed required to deliver project cost documents (i.e., Bills of Quantities (BOQs)) and schedules explain their omission of certain critical steps, such as WBS, in the development of construction project schedules and cost. It is clear that such a quick fix approach to construction project cost and schedule developments is at the root of the common cost and schedule development inaccuracies and attendant cost and time overruns in developing countries' environments. Additionally, the rare use of the WBS structure in the definition of project cost and schedules reveals the weak embeddedness of project management practices in the delivery of projects in developing countries' environments, particularly construction projects. This is similar in social intervention projects where, in most cases, the lack of a detailed activity plan, clear schedule, and cost often results in over-budgeting or under-budgeting of projects, with consequential effects on project scope.

Verification and control of project scope

Normally, the developed scope statement or plan serves as the baseline document for verification and control of the project deliverables upon their completion. The PMBOK, Sixth edition, describes scope verification as the process of formalizing acceptance of project deliverables by the project participants. Generally, if the scope planning exercise was done well by ensuring that all the items on the scope checklist were duly addressed, the relevant components of the project needed to successfully complete it would have been identified, reviewed, approved, and agreed upon by the project participants at an early stage of the project. This will then set the stage for smooth project scope verification and control. The value in this process is the enhanced probability of acceptance of the final project by project participants, particularly the client and end-users, upon its completion. Project scope verification, and control should be aligned with the various major stages of the project life span — definition, planning, execution, and closure — to ensure a systematic approach to scope verification and control.

Normally, project meetings and inspections are the common mechanisms adopted by project participants for verifying and controlling project scope. This happens in Ghana. Often, the project manager, where one is involved, or mostly the project designers or consultants, call for project meetings with subsequent site inspections, at the instance of the client, to verify and control for all the initially agreed-upon components of the project. In such fora, scope discrepancies are discussed and the relevant project party assigned or tasked to address the anomaly identified prior to project acceptance.

In practice, one of the challenges undermining the effectiveness of the project scope verification and control exercise, particularly in developing countries, is poor scope planning (Gurlen, 2013; Amoatey and Anson, 2017). Hence, it is at such project meetings and inspections for scope verification and control that avenues are provided for further scope planning. This phenomenon does not only undermine the quality of the scope verification and control stage by ensuring that the project participants keep their eyes on the ball, regarding the end results of the project, but also, as Gurlen (2013) indicates, this sows the seeds for project scope creep.

Scope change control

Varying project requirements or features are almost inevitable on most projects (Amoatey and Anson, 2017). This is so because assumptions and environmental factors, both internal and external, based on which earlier scope decisions were made, may change. Scope changes may emanate from various sources such as the project client, end-users, team members, or the project manager. Changes to project scope may fall into either of the following categories:

- Changes that were expected such as sub-structure works variations, in the case of a construction project, and could be accommodated by the implementation of the contingency funds on the project. In social intervention, this takes the form of varying activities as a strategy to achieve results.
- Changes that fall out of the project development framework. This may be due to some drastic changes in the client's priorities and requirements and hence a significant variation to the project design and delivery. Owing to the nature of such changes, approaches beyond using the contingency fund in the implementation are required. It might also be necessary to look for additional funding and possible extension of time. In social intervention projects, this could be due to the emergence of a livelihood crisis that may require the rechanneling of project funds into addressing the crisis to enable beneficiaries to cope, adapt, and become resilient.

Since changes are unavoidable on projects, the establishment of a proper system for change management and control at an early stage of the project will be necessary. Russell *et al.* (2018) described managed scope change, which is normally agreed or approved as scope evolution, in contrast to unmanaged change, which is characterized as scope creep. Larson and Gray (2018) indicate that any project scope change control system is often designed to ensure the following:

- Indicate the proposed changes
- Identify the expected impacts of the proposed change(s) on the project time and cost
- Review, assess, and approve or disapprove changes formally
- Negotiate and resolve conflicts of change, conditions, and costs
- Inform project participants affected by the proposed change
- Revise the baseline schedule and budget
- Trace all changes that are to be implemented.

In most developing countries, with Ghana being a typical example, and considering the many projects on which the authors have worked, there are often inadequate standardized toolkits or templates for managing scope changes, particularly on public projects. In many instances, project scope changes are initiated verbally either during project inspections or at project review meetings by project participants. Such orally suggested changes, for example at project review meetings, are at best captured in minutes while, in the case of project inspections, many of such orally suggested changes are lost in the absence of a meticulous recorder. The effective management of scope changes and control in developing country environments will require availability of toolkits or templates that will ensure a shift from mostly oral and informal practices to written and formal approaches. Considering the aim of a project change control system, templates needed to effectively manage and control the scope of projects in developing countries must consider the components indicated in Figure 5.5. First, the template must provide for an indication of the date and specific number of the change request to aid easy referencing. Second, the template must make a provision for a description of the change request, specifically, providing further details and explanation of the particular change being requested. Third, the template must allow for an indication of the assessment and impact of the requested change. This provides the information needed for the scope change requester, as well as

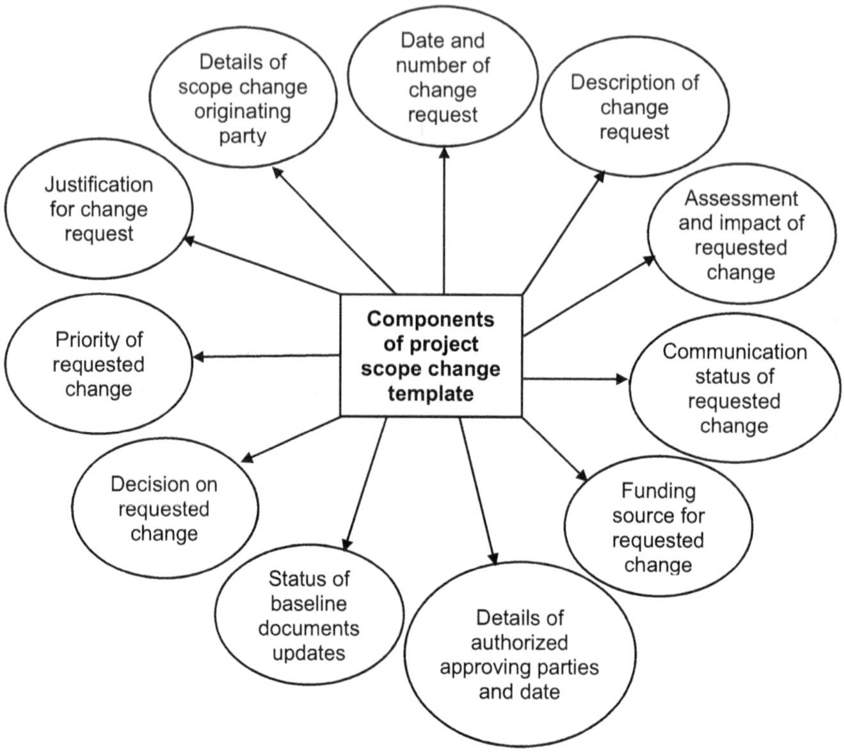

Figure 5.5: Components of project scope change template.

relevant project parties, to make informed decisions as to whether or not to accept the change.

Fourth, there should be details of the scope change originating party to ensure scope changes can be properly traced to their sources. Fifth, the template should include a justification for the requested scope change. This ensures that only relevant and value-adding changes are suggested and accepted by project parties in other to avoid the phenomenon of scope creep. Sixth, the priority of the requested change must be indicated; whether it is an *emergency*, *urgent*, or *low-priority* change request. Such information will guide the project manager to make optimal decisions on the project, at all times, in order to avoid any potential adverse effect of the requested change that could have been avoided as a result of early execution of the requested change. Seventh, there should be an indication of the funding source(s) for the requested change. Often, in developing country environments, project parties suggest changes to project scope without regard to specific funding sources for such changes (Amoatey and Anson, 2017). Hence, such information does not only engender confidence in a requested change among project parties but also forces financial discipline on the project to avoid potential cost overruns. Eighth, a decision on the requested change must be indicated on the template. The decision could be *approve, disapprove, defer*, or any other decision response having regard to the peculiar nature of the project. Ninth, there should be an indication of the details of the authorized approving parties and dates. Such information can provide an appropriate reference where doubts and misunderstanding occur in the future in respect of a change request. Tenth, the template must indicate the communication status of the requested change. This component clarifies project parties who are affected by the requested change. A simple *Yes* or *No* can be indicated as a response to whether or not they have been informed about the requested change and decision. In this way, relevant project parties are brought to the same level of information in respect of project scope.

Essentially, the view regarding the suggested components is to move away from prescriptions and to allow room for flexibility considering the nuances of environmental factors surrounding project delivery in developing countries. This means that, depending on the scale of the project, and on grounds of proportionality, a scope change template can adapt the proposed components in respect of the items that must be indicated on it. In addition, a pragmatic scope change control process, as indicated in Figure 5.6, appears to be necessary to enhance the overall scope management of projects in developing countries.

Scope creep

There is often a misconception between project scope changes and scope creep (Amoatey and Anson, 2017). Russell *et al.* (2018) attempt to differentiate the two by describing managed scope change as scope evolution in contrast to unmanaged change, characterized as scope creep. Generally,

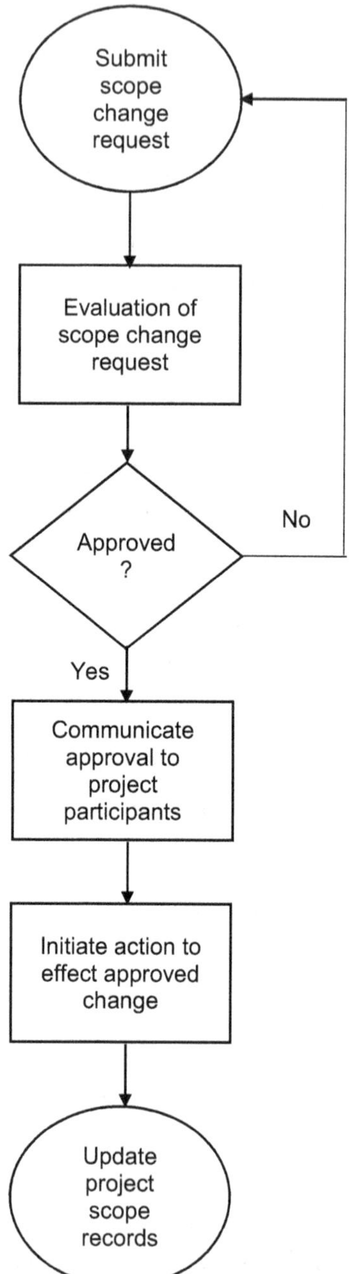

Figure 5.6: Scope change control process.

scope changes occur when suggested changes to the project scope are formally submitted, evaluated, approved, and communicated to all relevant project participants, i.e., scope evolution. On the other hand, scope creep is considered as a phenomenon where many little or minor changes are suggested to the project scope unofficially, without the knowledge of relevant project participants. These minor changes often culminate in bigger scope changes with sometimes severe impacts on project schedules and budgets (Hussain, 2012; Larson and Gray, 2018). Some researchers, such as Helms (2002), indicate that scope creep is a rather derogatory label given to the organic process in which project clients identify their needs in procuring projects. Although Helm (2002) appears to argue for a more natural approach for project clients to clarify their needs regarding the procurement of projects via the phenomenon of scope creep, this view undermines the need to ensure a reasonable definition of problems and their consequent targeting with appropriate project designs in order to ensure efficiency in project delivery.

Scope creep in developing countries

In developing countries, where there are limited resources as opposed to developed countries, emphasis on efficiency in respect of project delivery cannot be over-emphasized. However, in most developing countries, there are often weaker structures and mechanisms, for instance in public institutions, for results definition (i.e., projects) and most importantly how those results can be realized via scope planning (Asiedu and Adaku, 2019; Amoako-Gyampah *et al.*, 2021). This is often so because projects are normally initiated by units in organizations which may not have the requisite project management capability. Where support is received by such smaller units from other competent units, individuals involved from such competent units do not usually commit sufficient time to meetings scheduled, at an early stage of the project, to define the project results. These developments sow the seeds of project scope creep as such competent individuals later or intermittently pop up at project implementation review meetings to suggest changes to the project scope.

Further, in most developing countries the level of accountability, particularly within the public space, is low. Thus, most political leaders with their civil servant assistants initiate projects on the grounds of populism without any firm funding arrangements (Amoatey and Anson, 2017; Asiedu and Adaku, 2019). This, coupled with weak contract enforcement mechanisms (Asiedu and Adaku, 2019), provides fertile grounds for scope creep as the political leaders, often for political expediency, keep expanding project requirements and features with little or no regard to budgets and schedules. In social intervention projects, scope creep is often the result of poor management skills, lack of a detailed workplan, lack of regular project reviews with the key partners, and, on rare occasions, budget limitations. However, managed project changes often emanate from the implementer based on field experience and are then approved by the donor (Russell *et al.*, 2018).

In some cases, change in the donor priorities could also lead to managed change in the scope. The degree of change depends on the extent to which the project has already been implemented and the time left to project completion. Yet, Bigelow (2012) notes that a project's ability to change could be its most significant advantage given the fuzzy nature of project scope, a view that questions the traditional assumption that changes in scope that affect time and cost should be avoided. Indeed, the tensions between the traditional view and that suggested by researchers such as Bigelow (2012) has given rise to the development of contemporary methodologies for project management, such as agile project management. Thus, change can make a crucial difference in a project's ultimate value to the organization — "after all, the project's objectives are subordinate to those of the organization — not vice-versa" (Bigelow, 2012, p. 8).

Approaches to effective project scope management

There may be some similarities regarding effective approaches to the management of project scope in both developing and developing countries. However, considering the unique environments within which projects are carried out in developing countries, as discussed earlier, the approaches required for effective management of scope will need to reflect the peculiar nature of such environments. Thus, the following approach is suggested:

- *Focus on mechanisms and capabilities for results definition:* projects are considered solutions to undesirable situations. The ability to properly articulate the undesirable situation and subsequently address it with an effective solution via a project lays a foundation for meaningful scope definition, planning, and development. Specifically, attention should be paid to, and capacity built among, project parties, particularly project implementing agencies, around the use of a *theory of change* to clarify expected project results. The output of this tool will provide inputs to the project objective statement; scope definition, planning, and development; and ensure a meaningful alignment of thoughts in project scope management.
- *Early involvement of relevant project participants:* as indicated earlier, the engagement and involvement of stakeholders in projects, particularly users and beneficiaries, are weak in developing countries. It is necessary to get this right in order to put project results definition in its proper perspective and ensure that the project scope definition, planning, and development processes benefit from the collective wisdom of relevant project participants. In this way, a foundation is laid for a common understanding of what is expected and how it is going to be delivered, right from the outset. This can minimize project scope changes and potentially avoid scope creep.
- *Establishment of project support units, especially for public projects:* for medium to large public projects, project support units (PSUs) will be required to be set up to boost the project management capabilities of the procurement entities, particularly in scope management. This is to make up for the absence, or inadequacy, of project management capabilities in the public procurement entities. Private project procuring organizations can also consider doing this. The PSUs can be viewed as special-purpose vehicles that may be dissolved upon the completion of the projects.
- *Strengthening of public accountability systems:* political leaders and civil servants should be held accountable for the projects they initiate to curb the problem of scope creep.
- *Strengthening of contract enforcing mechanisms:* in most developing countries, public projects are often delayed in their implementation

owing to delays in payments to contractors. Such delayed payments are mostly reimbursed without the payment of any interest to the contractors. This practice relaxes the pressure on the public project procuring entities to expedite processes to arrange funding for the completion of public projects. On such prolonged projects, there are significant scope changes, and ultimately, scope creep. Strengthening contract-enforcing mechanisms and ensuring the fulfillment of the obligations of all parties will provide the incentive, particularly to public clients, to manage project scope appropriately to ensure project success.

Case study 1: Scope management on a social intervention project in Ghana

Background

Micro, Small and Medium-sized Enterprises (MSMEs) play an important role in the provision of water, sanitation and hygiene (WASH) products and services in Ghana. However, these enterprises face obstacles arising from difficulty in gaining access to financing. The traditional financial institutions, including banks and non-bank financial institutions, are unwilling to lend to the sector. Moreover, the high interest rates and tough collateral requirements of the financial institutions make sourcing loans a problem for WASH MSMEs, institutions, and households. Following an increase in government investment in rural sanitation as part of the National Environmental and Sanitation Policy, and implementation of sanitation by-laws at the district assembly level, there has been a huge increase in household demand for WASH services. However, access to appropriate and affordable products still remains a challenge, with wide disparities between geographical locations (broadly between rural and urban areas), as well as among people of different gender and income status.

Catalyzing WASH from Possible to Profitable (P2P) was a five-year (2016–2019) project funded by the Embassy of the Kingdom of the Netherlands and jointly implemented by SNV Netherlands Development Organisation (as the project coordinator) and Fidelity Bank Ghana Limited (as custodian and Fund Manager of the revolving fund). P2P was a private-sector–led social intervention program that sought to improve access to finance and technical assistance for households, house owners, and MSMEs for WASH investments and services. The goal of P2P was to increase access to WASH services at the household level by scaling up access to finance and capacity development services by MSMEs. P2P was a nationwide project covering households, MSMEs and Microfinance Institutions (MFIs) in Ghana.[1]

Given the constraints in private-sector participation regarding access to finance, the P2P was designed with the following objectives;

- Bridging the gap between the WASH demand and supply
- Providing affordable on-lending loans to trigger financial institutions lending to WASH
- Providing opportunities for MFIs to increase their WASH client base
- Providing relatively lower interest rates and collateral requirements for borrowers
- Building governance structures and improving technical knowledge of MSMEs
- Stimulating the financial services sector in Ghana to lend to the WASH sector and initiate similar socially-oriented lending schemes for WASH and other socio-economically inclined sectors
- Building the capacities of MSMEs in business strategies for sustainable purposes and financial institutions in identifying WASH-related business opportunities.

The project was expected to reach different categories of WASH beneficiaries. The targets were:

- 1,200 households to receive loans to access WASH services in urban areas
- 180 micro businesses to receive loans
- 30 small businesses to receive loans
- 30 medium businesses to receive loans.

---

[1] https://snv.org/project/p2p-catalysing-wash-possible-profitable

P2P was using a private-sector development approach to maximize value for money in the WASH sector. The project was tailored to provide access to finance at both the household and MSME levels through a revolving fund managed by Fidelity Bank. Fidelity Bank on-lends to WASH MSMEs and MFIs at an attractive interest rate. Thus, the MFIs served as the financial intermediary between Fidelity Bank and the households and were the conduit in reaching households with the WASH loans. P2P also aimed to provide technical assistance required by MSMEs to enable them to establish the structures required to obtain loans from financial institutions and be able to adequately respond to the growing demand for WASH services by households.

Scope initiation

The project was conceived as a novel pilot private-sector–led project for addressing social intervention, specifically in the WASH sector. The scope at the inception was developed by the WASH sector experts and was targeted at the identified financial gaps in the sector. The project design, approach, objectives, results, and targets were informed by:

- the sector assessment report commissioned by the donor to understand the financial challenges in the sector; and
- the joint consultation with the sector experts, MSMEs in the sector and the various district assemblies.

The sector assessment report showed that there was a need for finance by WASH enterprises, and that about 53 percent of Ghanaian enterprises in the WASH space were willing to seek loans from the commercial banks and MFIs but the financial products were not suitable for the WASH value chain.

The strategic focus of the donor and the expertise of the implementation partners also played a role in defining the scope. Based on these stakeholder consultations, the partners developed a scope statement. As a novel pilot project, the scope statement was regularly reviewed based on lessons learned during the implementation to ensure that the project served the needs of the beneficiaries.

Defining and planning the project scope

As characteristic of any well-developed project, the scope was defined and refined based on the strategic objective of stakeholders (i.e., including the donor, the government of Ghana, MSMEs, households, and Fidelity Bank). These stakeholders defined the problem; determined the geographical coverage for the project; and agreed on the objectives of the project, the risks underlying the project, the partners' responsibilities, and the implementation strategy. During the project inception phase, baselines were developed for the key indicators to help track progress. A detailed work plan was developed jointly by SNV and Fidelity Bank with clear activities under each component.

Verification and control of the project scope

The value of project verification and control is to enhance tracking of the achievement of the results by matching actuals with plan as well as baseline. The Project Manager of the WASH intervention project noted in an interview that:

"The project results verification was so important for us on the project. We had a full-time staff in charge and the system put in place helped to regularly check progress of deliverables."

The project verification and control tasks were jointly done by the implementing partners, with SNV leading in the technical verification. The loan monitoring and verification were done by the financial institutions which provided the on-lending service to the households and MSMEs. In the first two years of the project, monitoring and verification were done physically by engaging with the beneficiaries through the usage of monitoring forms and one-on-one interviews, as well as physically inspecting the facilities which the loan was used for. From 2018, the P2P adopted AKVO Flow (Field Level Operation Watch) tool. It is a reliable and smart technology used to collect, manage, analyze, and display geographically referenced monitoring and evaluation data through the use of mobile phones and Internet connectivity. It offered rapid data collection, survey flexibility, and analytical tools so that decisions can be made on reliable data and visual evidence. The quantitative analytical indicators were prepared in the dashboard. It captures responses in texts, numbers, photographs, GPS locations, or even bar codes.

The AKVO flow made use of three main components:

- An Android smartphone application that allowed the data collection team on the ground to do surveys directly on their telephones including taking photographs of the facilities.
- An Internet-based management tool that made it possible to design survey questionnaires and manage how they were distributed to people through their telephones.
- Maps and dashboards that provided opportunity for survey results to be accessed online. The GPS coordinates that were recorded on the telephones were visually mapped as well.

Again, partners set up quarterly project reviews to discuss the approach and progress of achieving results. Since the project was a pilot, new ideas and approaches were always considered during each review. After one year of implementation, the scope was significantly changed.

Scope changes

As a pilot project, the project scope was changed a number of times by the project team. These changes were formally discussed, evaluated, and approved by relevant project participants. Some of these changes were as a result of the wrong assumptions. The Project Manager in an interview averred:

"The beauty of this project was the flexibility in the project scope. Although the purpose of the project remained the same, the approach and targets were intermittently adjusted. The flexibility allowed for greater learning and documentation of what works in such a private-sector led intervention in the WASH space."

For example, it was envisaged that the processing of the loan for the MSMEs would take a few days but in reality, it took more than the expected number of days. This delayed the disbursement of the amount to be provided as loans within the period. Further, prospective borrowers were assumed to have all the necessary documentation and capacity. However, during the loan evaluation, it was noticed that the clients did not have the required capacity. Hence, a capacity development component was introduced into the project known as a business academy. The flexibility in managing the scope was key in the project success since it was a pilot with virtually no existing model to follow. One major change in the project scope was the methodology to increase access to knowledge and awareness. Although initially different tools were planned for implementation, the team chose a more cost-effective strategy (in the form of the business academy) in building the capacities and creating a networking cycle for the MSMEs and MFIs. The changes in the scope were principally influenced by the political terrain. The policies of government in the WASH sector and the assumptions at the beginning of the project kept changing. For example, the project was designed to ensure that 2,600 households received loans to access WASH services in urban areas while 200 micro businesses, 350 small businesses, and 300 medium-sized and seven large businesses would receive business loans. Based on the lessons learnt during implementation and in consultation with the key stakeholders, the project partners collectively agreed and revised the targets downward to 1,200 households, 180 micro business, 30 small businesses, and 30 medium businesses. This scope change was successful because of the extensive consultation among the project participants.

Managing scope changes

To ensure the project was managed effectively, a number of meetings were held with the project participants. Explaining how the scope changes were made, the Project Manager indicated:

"On this project, we had a team that regularly reviewed the scope and made the necessary adjustment to ensure that the project achieved the best results; the donor equally participated in these reviews."

During project meetings, the scope change recommendations from participants were scrutinized by all stakeholders, and the impact on cost and time assessed before the change was made. This helped to clearly define the project results and also ensured that the project scope planning process benefited from the collective expertise of relevant project stakeholders. This approach helped to minimize scope changes and avoid project scope creep.

Due to the novelty of the project, there was great interest in the implementation of the project within the WASH development partners and the Ministry of Sanitation and Water Resources of Ghana. The team used various national platforms, including the National Community-Led Total Sanitation (CLTS) stock taking forum, the Mole conference (organized by the Coalition of NGOs in Water and Sanitation (CONIWAS)), and Water Engineering and Development Centre of Loughborough University, UK, to update and receive feedback from, WASH sector players on the implementation of the project.

The President of Ghana's initiative in 2017 of moving Ghana Beyond Aid also brought to the fore the importance of public–private partnerships in achieving results. These policy directions also played a role in the changes to the initial scope, resulting in a focus on the private sector (through the MSME) other than the households. Changes in the scope also meant changes in the initial targets developed with the donor.

Key lessons learnt

The P2P project is a novel private-sector-led approach to maximize value for money in the WASH sector. The project was designed to be completed in 2019, but it ended in 2020 with a lot of useful lessons for effective project scope management which entails scope initiation, scope definition, scope planning, verification, and control.

First, the project had a clear definition of the key stakeholders. The stakeholders were identified at the beginning of the project. These were the donor, the government of Ghana, WASH MSMEs, the associations of WASH actors, households/beneficiaries, the project implementer (SNV), partners (Fidelity Bank), and the MFIs. For successful project scope management, it is necessary to identify the stakeholders who will help frame the problem, define objectives, and identify realistic risks with respect to the project.

Second, the scope initiation process was systematic, and it helped to develop a participatory scope statement. This helped to reduce the risk of cost overrun and scope creep. When scope is not properly defined at the beginning of projects and managed effectively across the project phases, the likelihood of failure is high; scope additions are identified as one of the causes of project delays and cost escalation. Issues of ill-defined scope, scope creep, and scope change are particularly compounded in the developing country context by politics, budget constraints, lack of expertise, and lack of stakeholder engagement. In the P2P project, although cost was not an issue, the many changes in the scope ultimately resulted in the achievement of an entirely different set of targets as compared to what was originally conceived. However, this was acceptable due to the broader stakeholder engagement from the inception phase.

Third, the objectives of the project kept changing from inception to about halfway through the implementation, after which there was clarity and focus. The lessons learned during the implementation were used as a basis to realign the project objective to ensure a successful project. Therefore, it is important to allow and expect some level of flexibility in project designs, particularly social intervention projects in the developing country context. As societies are dynamic and subject to a plethora of unforeseen risks, rigidities in project objectives and scope, particularly social intervention ones, could potentially lead to frustrations among project participants and eventually undermine project success.

Case study 2: Scope management on a commercial residential development project in Ghana

Background

The second case is on a commercial residential development project located in a high-end residential area in Accra, Ghana. This project involved the construction of a five-storey, 31 apartments development for sale. It was a joint venture initiative involving a local real estate developer, a bank, and the original owners of the land who supported the local development.

The project followed the traditional procurement route and the initially planned duration was 14 months. However, the project was actually completed in 36 months. The contract sum initially proposed for the project was GHS 9.5 million (approximately US$1.6 million), but the final project cost was GHS 17 million (approximately US$2.9 million). The project design was not fully detailed at the start; and thus, there were a lot of provisional sum packages included in the tender and contract documents. As construction works progressed, designs for the provisional sum work packages had to be further detailed and the costs estimated. In addition to the provisional sums, there were also provisions for prime cost sums for nominated subcontractors to be appointed to carry-out some work packages. This approach to procurement created some major scope issues that had an adverse impact on the success of the project, including significant escalations in cost and time.

Scope initiation

This residential development was identified by the client's management team as a commercially viable business venture in that location to meet the acute housing needs in the Ghanaian capital. This was also a high-end residential area, and the project was designed to meet the needs of customers at the upper end of the residential market.

Scope definition

The project scope definition process for this residential development project continued deep into the construction stage as more relevant stakeholders were identified and engaged with. The primary stakeholders included: the project sponsors (the real estate company, the bank, and the owners of the land); the project team (comprising the contractor and consultants); and the end-users who had already paid a deposit for the property. Secondary stakeholders included the neighbors whose properties were affected during the project development process. The project team also had to engage with some public and regulatory organizations such as the Department of Urban Roads, Ghana National Fire Service, and Environmental Protection Agency. All these stakeholders engaged with the scope management on the project in diverse ways. Changes to the scope were effected by taking into account stakeholders' needs. Some end-user demands were also accommodated, such as first-hand inspection of the project during construction, resulting in change requests that had a cost and time impact.

There was limited secondary stakeholder involvement at the pre-construction phase of the project. Most of the project management team's engagement with secondary stakeholders on the project was routed through the developer. Where these stakeholders had a request, these were first presented to the developer, who then notified the project manager. The project management office then deliberated on the requests in relation to implications on the project and its requirements. Some stakeholder requests disrupted construction activities. Secondary stakeholders such as statutory bodies (for example, Ghana National Fire Service) also had an impact on the project scope as they requested for certain changes to the spatial arrangements in the project design during their regular checks for fitness to their requirements.

Scope planning

In this project, although the project managers were engaged from the pre-contract stage and helped in defining the scope of the works, the scope for some provisional sum works could still not be defined as the developer was uncertain of the details at that stage. Thus, the clients relied on the designers and project managers for the early management of the project, particularly scope planning. Many provisional sums and prime cost sums were left for subsequent detailing. The main contractor also had some works taken away from them and assigned to subcontractors because the main contractor was not delivering on the project as expected.

Verification and control of the scope

On this project, inspection and testing were the tools of choice for verification and control of scope activities, because the project was executed through the use of a staggered program of works. Inspections and testing were set out in the project execution plan and undertaken at periodic intervals. A checklist approach was employed such that any defects or non-compliance with requirements were flagged for rectification.

There were challenges in managing and controlling scope, especially as there were many subcontractors involved in the project. This was compounded by the numerous provisional and prime cost sums allowed on the project. The subsequent finalization of the details of the provisional and prime cost sums presented scope management challenges, particularly dealing with confirming designs and details against fixed budgets. The Project Manager shared:

"So in terms of the design and the exact cost there wasn't any certainty at that time. So while work was going on, designs were still being completed. And because the client also hadn't defined it properly and it hadn't been captured so at the point where you are ready to execute the work that's when you know the extent of it and you already have a fixed budget to work with."

There was also an arrangement where the client supplied some materials due to their access to credit and bulk purchases and this presented challenges leading to wastage of materials, poor quality, delays, and cost escalation. The challenges mainly stemmed from the poor coordination between the client and the contractor in this arrangement.

Scope changes

The project underwent a lot of scope changes as there was a considerable difference between the initial scope and the scope at completion. The Project Manager noted:

"There were enormous changes to the project scope and this was attributable to too many provisional sums, a lot of variations…uncertainty…variations at some points."

On the nature of the actual changes, the Project Manager stated:

"The changes involved spatial re–arrangement, specification changes or upgrade in specifications. For other changes, it was purely add-ons, so they weren't there to begin with but at some point, the client was like, it would be good to have this here, so those came as additional works."

Generally, the happenings on the project indicated poor scope management from the outset of the project development process.

Managing scope changes

Proper scope change management is paramount. Among other objectives, it ensures that the client is aware of the impact of scope changes in order to make informed decisions. On this project, attempts were made at this during the project through reports submitted to the client, particularly on schedule and cost impacts of proposed changes prior to change approvals. However, this did not help much due to the incomplete design as well as the use of provisional and prime cost sums. Such arrangements made the project scope vulnerable to changes.

Key lessons learnt

A number of insights can be drawn from this case, which could benefit the management of scope on future projects.

First, although relevant stakeholders were identified and made inputs into the project scope, many of these activities happened quite late in the scope development process. Specifically, the late and limited engagement with a key group of secondary stakeholders (the local residents affected by the project) was not helpful. This reflects a phenomenon in developing countries where stakeholders who are adversely affected by projects are often taken for granted or ignored. With economic development and growing social awareness, stakeholders are becoming conscious of their rights and possible avenues for redress in circumstances where projects affect them adversely. Hence, project proponents and implementing organizations in developing countries should pay attention to effective and timely project stakeholder engagements to avoid the potential of project scope changes from having to consider the interests of stakeholders later in the project development process.

Second, the limited involvement of project end-users, particularly at the scope initiation stage, sowed the seed for changes in the scope of the project when opportunities were offered to them during the project execution stage. Future proponents of commercial projects should consider arrangements that would allow end-users to be identified as early as possible and their inputs considered in the project scope development process to avoid later significant changes to the scope.

Third, the use of numerous prime cost and provisional sums undermined effective scope management. This made the verification and scope control process difficult. Efforts should be made to ensure that reasonable details are provided, particularly at the pre-tender stages of construction projects, to minimize the inclusion of prime cost and provisional sums, which often are triggers of scope changes.

Finally, an adequate risk management framework is necessary during the scope development process. For instance, the risks associated with quality and waste that were introduced by the client's arrangement to supply some materials to the site could have been identified and mitigated, if a proper risk management framework had been in place during the scope management process.

Conclusion

This chapter set out to examine scope management in the developing country context. It has highlighted the peculiar issues in that context as they relate to Project Scope Initiation, Defining the Project Scope, Scope Planning and Verification, and Control of the Project Scope.

There are several key takeaways from this chapter. First, as project scope initiation is the first phase in the project scope management life cycle, it is the best time to add value during the project because it is the phase with the highest number of options to modify the project with minimal expenditure (Verzuh, 2016); to minimize risks and uncertainty during the project (Yemin *et al.*, 2018); and to enhance the potential of project success. To maximize this value-added potential in the developing country context, institutional politics and internal and external environment imperatives need to be considered, and relevant stakeholders need to be identified and their inputs factored into the scope definition at the project scope initiation stage.

Second, scope definition articulates the end product of the project for the customer at project completion. Therefore, the importance of the link between project scope definition and project performance cannot be overemphasized. In the developing country context, ensuring that scope definition leads to project success requires that stakeholder identification, problem definition and statement, theory of change development, objective definition and statement and assumptions, and risks identification and register all play a key role in defining the project.

Third, the scope planning process ensures that project need identification, gathering of requirements and data, identification and development of project components, reviewing of components by project participants (and stakeholders), and development of project scope plan proceed appropriately. In the developing country context, scope planning can be made more effective by employing expert judgment and engaging an individual or a firm with project management capabilities.

Fourth, in developing countries, scope change control is mostly done verbally and informally. Informality plays a fundamental role in contexts where corruption and bureaucracy are common to facilitate project efficiency and avoid lengthy procedures (Lizarralde *et al.*, 2013). Yet, to be effective, scope change control and verification should be systematic and proactive. As such, a project control template as well as a pragmatic scope change control process has been outlined to effectively manage, control, and enhance the overall scope management of projects in developing countries.

Finally, through two cases studies, Scope Creep and the Politics of Project Scope issues are examined by considering how scope changes were initiated and managed within the context of two different types of projects: one involving a social intervention and the other a commercial residential project. The case studies show that, inadequate, ill-defined, or incomplete scope definition is a recipe for significant scope changes with consequential cost, schedule, and other adverse implications on projects. This is also the case for projects with a fuzzy scope as a result of uncertainties. Yet, there is a distinction between project scope changes and scope creep (Amoatey and Anson, 2017) and this distinction is important in the developing country context. Russell *et al.* (2018) differentiate between: (a) managed scope change as scope evolution, which is made up of changes formally submitted, evaluated, approved, and communicated to all relevant project participants; and (b) unmanaged change as scope creep, which is formed from many minor changes which are suggested to the project scope unofficially or informally without the knowledge of the relevant project participants. Managed scope change can make a crucial difference in the ultimate value of the project to the organization since the project's objectives are aligned to the objectives of the organization but not vice versa (Bigelow, 2012). To deal with the issues of scope creep in the developing country context, greater accountability and strong contract enforcement mechanisms, especially within the public space, are needed to prevent political leaders with their civil servant assistants from initiating projects to appeal to the ordinary people without considering the funding implications, or to keep expanding project requirements and features with little or no regard to budget or schedule (Asiedu and Adaku, 2019).

Evidently, both the conceptual examination of scope management and the case studies presented offer some lessons, guidance, and methods for not only defining project scope but also managing project scope changes to prevent scope creep. There is a clear role for research on scope management in the developing country context to shed light on some of the issues highlighted in this chapter. For example, the role of stakeholders in scope initiation and scope definition is apparent. Yet, the political, administrative, economic, and social context of developing countries results in little or no stakeholder involvement or engagement in projects, leading to ill-defined project scope. The power relationships between some stakeholders may also be unbalanced, resulting in a situation where powerful stakeholders often dominate the mobilization of specific interests on project effects and "sustainable" alternatives. The persistence of project failures in developing countries and the role of scope management also requires further examination. More research is needed to enhance scope management in the developing country context.

References

Amoako-Gyampah, K., Acquaah, M., Adaku, E. and Famiyeh, S. (2021). Social capital and project management success in a developing country environment: Mediating role of knowledge management. *Africa Journal of Management*, 7(3), 339–374. https://doi.org/10.1080/23322373.2021.1927450.

Amoatey, C.T. and Anson, B.A. (2017). Investigating the major causes of scope creep in real estate construction projects in Ghana. *Journal of Facilities Management*, 15(4), 393–408. https://doi.org/10.1108/JFM-11-2016-0052.

Archibald, T., Sharrock, G., Buckley, J. and Cook, N. (2016). Assumptions, conjectures, and other miracles: The application of evaluative thinking to theory of change models in community development. *Evaluation and Program Planning*, 59, 119–127.

Asiedu, R.O. and Adaku, E. (2019). Cost overruns of public sector construction projects: A developing country perspective. *International Journal of Managing Projects in Business*, 13(1), 66–84.

Baccarini, D., Salm, G. and Love, P.E.D. (2004). Management of risks in information technology projects. *Industrial Management & Data Systems*, 104(4), 286–295. https://doi.org/10.1108/02635570410530702.

Bigelow, B. (2012). Scope — Mastering the fuzzy constraint. Paper presented at PMI® Global Congress 2012 — EMEA, Marseilles, France. Project Management Institute, Newtown Square, PA.

Bigelow, K.E. (2012). Designing for success: Developing engineers who consider universal design principles. *Journal of Postsecondary Education and Disability*, 25(3), 211–225.

Burke, R. (1999). *Project Management: Planning and Control*, 3rd Edition. John Wiley & Sons Ltd, Chichester, England.

Freeman, R.E. (1984). *Strategic Management: A Stakeholder Approach.* Pitman, Boston, MA.

Gurlen, S. (2003). Scope creep. www.umsl.edu/~sauterv/analysis/ 6840_f03_papers/gurlen/ [Accessed 27 April 2021].

Helms, H. (2002). In defense of scope creep. https://alistapart.com/article/scopecreep/ [Accessed 22 October 2020].

Hilali, A., Charoenngam, C. and Barman, A. (2019). Barriers in contractual scope management of international development projects in Afghanistan. *Engineering, Construction and Architectural Management*, 26(8), 1574–1592.

Hussain, O. (2012). Direct cost of scope creep in governmental construction projects in Qatar. *Global Journal of Management and Business Research*, 12(14), 73–84.

Kagogo, T.S. and Steyn, H. (2019). Effect of scope readiness on capital projects in mining: A Namibian case study. *South African Journal of Industrial Engineering*, 30(1), 257–269.

Kaliba, C., Muya, M. and Mumba, K. (2009). Cost escalation and schedule delays in road construction projects in Zambia. *International Journal of Project Management*, 27, 522–531.

Kerzner, H. and Saladis, F.P. (2009). *Value-driven Project Management.* Wiley, Hoboken, NJ.

Larson, E.W. and Gray, C.F. (2018). *Project Management: The Managerial Process*, 7th Edition. McGraw Hill, New York.

Lizarralde, G., Tomiyoshi, S., Bourgault, M., Malo, J. and Cardosi, G. (2013). Understanding differences in construction project governance between developed and developing countries. *Construction Management and Economics*, 31(7), 711–730.

McFarlan, F.W. (1981). Portfolio approach to information systems. *Harvard Business Review*, 142, September–October, pp. 142–150.

Ogunberu, A.O., Akintelu, S.O. and Olaposi, T.O. (2018). Application of project scope management practices on project success among telecommunication organizations in Nigeria. *International Journal of Development and Sustainability*, 7(2), 518–532.

Project Management Institute (PMI) (2017). *A Guide to the Project Management Body of Knowledge, PMBOK*, 6th Edition. Project Management Institute, Newtown Square, PA.

Russell, J., Pferdehirt, W. and Nelson, J. (2018). *Technical Project Management in Living and Geometric Order: A Practical Perspective*, 3rd Edition. University of Wisconsin Press books, Madison.

Senouci, A., Alsarraj, A., Gunduz, M. and Eldin, N. (2017). Analysis of change orders in Qatari construction projects. *International Journal of Construction Management*, 17(4), 280–292.

Shirazi, F., Kazemipoor, H. and Tavakkoli-Moghaddam, R. (2017). Fuzzy decision analysis for project scope change management. *Decision Science Letters*, 6, 395–406.

Verzuh, E. (2016). *The Fast Forward MBA in Project Management*, 5th Edition. Wiley, Hoboken, NJ.

Wondirad, A., Tolkach, D. and King, B. (2020). Stakeholder collaboration as a major factor for sustainable ecotourism development in developing countries. *Tourism Management*, 78, 104024. https://doi.org/10.1016/j.tourman.2019.104024.

Yap, J.B.H. and Skitmore, M. (2018). Investigating design changes in Malaysian building projects. *Architectural Engineering and Design Management*, 14(3), 218–238.

Yemini, M., Oplatka, I. and Sagie, N. (2018). Project Initiation. In M. Yemini, I. Oplatka and N. Sagie (Eds.), *Project Management in Schools*. Palgrave Pivot, Cham, pp. 23–42. https://doi.org/10.1007/978-3-319-78608-7_2.

https://doi.org/10.1142/9789811224720_0006

Chapter 6

Project Schedule Management in Developing Countries

Hemanta Doloi

University of Melbourne, Australia

Abstract

Schedule management is one of the core project management knowledge areas. While schedule management comprises the sequence of some of the key functions undertaken in the project processes, the efficiency derived through a schedule depends on significant lead up activities in relation to the project scope management and project development environment. The lead up work required in order to realize an accurate project schedule is highly context specific. Variability in the practice, which comes not only from the type, size, and nature of projects but also from the operating environment, plays a significant role. Unlike the developed economies, both empirical and anecdotal evidence shows that projects in developing countries are managed without much of the lead up work and often without appropriate definition of scope. Due to some unique issues ranging from external funding agencies to complexity in stakeholder composition, a project in a developed economy poses different sets of challenges from a project being undertaken in a developing economy. There is a large volume of literature, including a significant body of knowledge, for guiding and supporting the implementation of projects generally. Yet, such literature is found to be inadequate for dealing with the issues associated mainly with the long and unstructured project phases in the developing country context. Over the past decades, there have been many reports about the issues involved in managing projects in developing countries. However, there is not much work on producing any reference with a specific body of knowledge encompassing these issues.

Focusing on best practice processes in project schedule management, this chapter puts forward a logical analysis of the extent of the best practice processes being applicable in managing projects in the context of developing countries. Based on research undertaken at the Smart Villages Lab (SVL) at the University of Melbourne, Australia, a review of the mainstream literature and the author's observations over many years, theoretical underpinnings along with comparison and contrast associated with the development and delivery practices of projects are discussed using an enhanced schedule management framework. The framework, developed from the current schedule management body of knowledge (PMI, 2017), aims to reflect the key issues associated with the time management processes across the project phases. In order to rationalize the framework with respect to the developing countries, a case study from the context of India, one of the rapidly emerging developing economies, is used. The chapter then highlights the key processes of the framework from a practice perspective and shows that it can help to achieve potential enhancements in schedule management practice across similar economies around the world.

Keywords: Schedule management framework, front-end effort, theoretical underpinning, best practice, context specificity, developing countries

Introduction

Projects are the backbone of any society, and when it comes to developing countries, projects act as lifelines for supporting the growth trajectory of the economy and the community. Before a project is developed, appropriate front-end effort is crucial. It is necessary for successful identification of the need for the project, setting-up the priorities, and the management of the processes and required resources, including the implementation and operations strategy. Projects are subsets of programs. In developing countries, programs and projects are used by the administrations for advancing both economic and social development (Adams, 2017). A prevailing practice in developing countries is that the projects and programs are used for securing credits and other financial assistance from international funding agencies. Due to specific requirements on the granting of credits for administrative tasks, often necessary front-end planning for initiating projects gets compromised (Rondinelli, 1976). Due to high administrative control at both program and project levels, the nature of the problems associated with the delivery of projects is quite common across the developing countries.

Despite the availability of project management best practice, the variations in successful project delivery in developing countries is quite substantial. As asserted in a World Bank report many decades ago (Waterston, 1965), the issues in poor management practices are not due to the complexity in the project itself but lack of institutional capacities in project delivery. In most situations, there is no demarcation between the professional competencies and institutional maturity required in managing program and projects. Poor planning is often due to numerous internal agencies being involved in approval processes. Lack of understanding of the lead time required in each approval process results in the establishment of sub-standard baseline plans. With such faulty baseline planning, successful delivery of projects is compromised and the target performance set at the outset is impossible to achieve.

Project schedule is contingent on clear definition of the project scope and accurate estimation of effort and duration with respect to the limited availability and underlying efficiencies of some of the relevant resources. Ambiguity in the lead up planning and approval processes creates uncertainty in the schedule development process. If the project schedule is nested within the program schedule and the disbursement of program funds, as is often the case, is dependent on approvals being obtained from external funding agencies, the complexity in the project substantially increases. Therefore, before developing any meaningful schedule management process, the intrinsic issues over the lead up processes should be analyzed and appropriately considered.

Figure 6.1 depicts some of the broad issues associated with the three intrinsically related factors in a typical project: project, ownership, and finance. As shown in the figure, while each of these factors comprises a range of independent issues, there are many common issues, and this shows

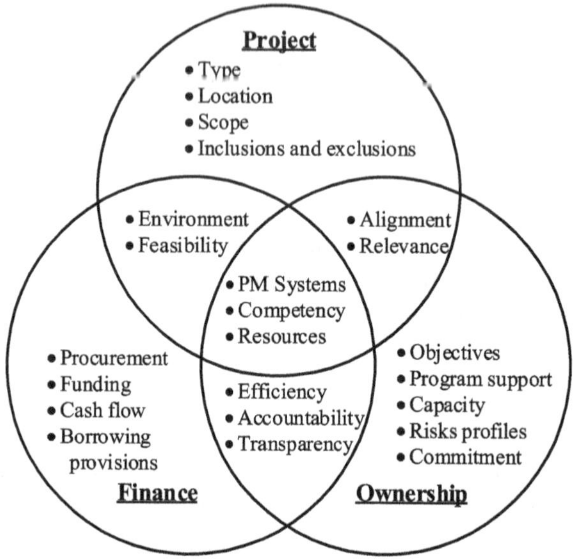

Figure 6.1: Relationships between Project, Ownership, and Finance.

the interdependence between the factors. The issues such as type, location, scope, and inclusion and exclusions have to be defined from a project-specific context. As far as the ownership is concerned, it is crucial to define at the outset, objectives, program support, capacity for undertaking project work, risk profiles, and commitments. From the finance perspective, procurement routes, funding arrangement, cash flow requirement, and borrowing terms and conditions should be evaluated and assessed before the project journey is embarked upon. While environmental issues and feasibility analysis are to be evaluated from the project and financial perspectives, the alignment and relevance of the selected project need to be rationalized with respect to the project and the ownership. The common issues such as project management systems, underlying competencies of relevant organizations, and project team and available resources, should be assessed, taking into consideration the project, ownership, and finance factors.

In the following section, some of the common issues are discussed. They are then incorporated into the practice framework in the subsequent sections.

Role of the key stakeholders and project delivery

While a large volume of literature on project management concerning projects in developed countries is available, there are few published references on projects undertaken in developing countries. Contrasting the relationships depicted in Figure 6.1, in developing countries, most of the projects are commissioned by the public agencies and most of the time reporting on performance and efficiencies is not an expectation within the stipulated project development framework. Within the typical sphere of the stakeholders, both promoters and financiers are usually government owned entities, and thus contractors responsible for delivering the projects are the only parties exposed to scrutiny in the underlying performance analysis. A good understanding of the roles and obligations of the contractors in planning and management of projects is crucial. This section highlights some of the key issues concerning the planning and development of projects from contractors' perspectives (Nguyen *et al.*, 2013).

In developing countries, projects are often developed without undertaking rigorous due diligence processes at the front end. As a result, the mapping of professional capabilities and competencies of the key stakeholders with respect to the underlying challenge and technical requirements in project delivery is compromised. Contractors' reliability and commitment, coupled with technical competencies in people management and organizational capability, play crucial roles in successful project delivery (Klein and Park, 2015). The technical competence of contractors is one of the prevailing factors, especially in the projects done either in private or semi-private arrangements. Yet, due to the nature of government-funded projects and with the centralized governance approach, evaluation of contractors' competencies in relation to the projects' scope and delivery challenges is often not carried out objectively. Contractors are usually selected based on relationships and financial capabilities. Financial capability of the contractors is usually one of the significant considerations in the selection process because contractors are often expected to carry out the work from their own funds even without getting timely access to the project funds. This is common due to the regimented budgetary and transaction cycles of public agencies, where project contracts often lack necessary planning in cashflow regimes commensurate with the construction schedule (Ssebanakitta, 2013; Singh and Gupta, 2015; Zachary, 2015). Thus, fallacies in the planning and delivery of projects become the burden of the contractors, yet their continuous involvement and commitment is not solely driven by profit margin alone but depends on a range of other factors (Emejeit *et al.*, 2021).

As suggested by Allen and Meyer (1990), contractors' engagement and capacity in developing countries needs to be viewed in relation to these three key perspectives: *affective commitment*, *continuance commitment*, and *normative commitment*. In affective commitment, emotional affiliation is one of the key elements in contractors' engagements in projects. In continuance commitment, contractors are usually driven by the costs and profits analysis whereas the cashflow in projects is usually non-uniform throughout the project stages. Through normative commitment, contractors are morally obliged to, somehow, complete the project although the delivery process might be affected by the inefficiencies throughout the project.

Although the role of the contractor is crucial in successful project delivery, there is usually no system of checks and balances for scrutinizing the contractors' performance in the context of the stipulated project management practices (Aluonzi *et al.*, 2016). In these circumstances, contractors are not bound by any particular standards or performance benchmarks and thus, the planning and performance measures across the project knowledge areas become less prevalent. The contractor's involvement and success in a particular project is based not only on qualifications and experience but also on a number of factors such as the support of the top management, political parties, and parts of the bureaucracy, including underlying resources, interests, commitments, and a conducive project environment. While contractors are expected to complete projects following the stipulated timeframe as in the contract schedule, the contractor's continuous commitment and interest throughout the construction phase is perhaps the most important driver for achieving success. Types of projects and frequencies of occurrence are also important for contractors to stay motivated, meaning one-off projects usually do not provide necessary stimulus and incentives for maximizing contractor's efficiency and schedule management (Doloi *et al.*, 2012).

As the role of the design team is closely linked to the sponsor or project owner, this further hinders the potential for contractors in driving efficiency in planning and construction (Santoso *et al.*, 2003). Given the intrinsic relationships between the owners and designers, there is a power imbalance between the key internal stakeholders in most projects. As a result, contractors' commitment to technical planning and programming at the early stage of project is affected. Due to lack of a clear framework defining responsibilities and timely deliverables by the design team, often, the contractor's schedules do not reflect the accurate work plan, which eventually affects the progress and delivery of the project. Lack of clarity in scope and owner's tendency of making frequent changes to the project also make the planning process for contractors quite inefficient.

The above section highlights the fact that contractors in developing countries are not necessarily in a position to take full responsibility for schedule performance on projects. Due to a complex network of stakeholders, coupled with lack of clear demarcation of roles, responsibilities, and commitments, contractors are unable to execute projects following the stipulated standards and practices. Rather, contractors' relationships, commitment, interests, and obligations in relation to the project development environment prevail over the best practice processes, and the underlying technical and professional competencies required for driving efficiencies in schedule management become less prevalent in most projects.

Time planning issues in developing countries

The chronic delay in construction projects in developing countries is the result of poor definition of project scope and unrealistic time planning without appropriate consideration of the lead time required from initial estimation to the start of construction. Rondinelli (1976) reported seven broad issues associated with poor project management practices in most developing countries: ineffective project planning and preparation; faulty appraisal and selection processes; defective project design; problems with start-up and activation; inadequate project execution, operation, and supervision; and ineffective external coordination and poor control of project activities. A study by Arditi *et al.* (1985) focusing on Turkish public-sector construction projects reported a range of factors associated with national economic policies and public agencies causing delays. Faridi and El-Sayegh (2006) reported that the process of approving drawings and poor pre-planning are the two root causes of construction delay in the United Arab Emirates. Based on research in Saudi Arabia, Al-Khalil and Al-Ghafly (1999) reported that lack of stakeholders' agreement is one of the key causes of construction delay. El-Razek *et al.* (2008) identified the main causes of delay in construction projects in Egypt as lack of a team spirit and disagreements on priorities within the project development environment.

Focusing on Indian construction projects, Iyer and Jha (2005) reported seven key issues associated with delay: conflict among project participants, ignorance and lack of knowledge, poor cooperation among the authorities concerned, hostile socio-economic and climatic conditions, reluctance in making decisions in a timely manner, aggressive market competition, and short bid preparation time. Odeyinka and Yusif (1997) asserted that client-requested design variations were among the main causes of delay on Nigerian construction projects. Doloi *et. al.* (2012) reported seven key factors causing delays on Indian construction projects. They are lack of commitment, inefficient site management, poor site coordination, improper planning, lack of clarity in project scope, lack of communication, and substandard construction contracts. From the above reviews, it is clear that issues affecting poor schedule performance in projects in developing countries span the entire project development lifecycle, with particular concern on a lack of comprehensive project plans.

Brief review of best practices in schedule management

For decades, the popularity, adoption, and adaptation of project management standards have been growing across organizations globally. Within the project management standards, three clear dimensions are: Projects, People, and Organizations (Crawford, 2004). Figure 6.2 depicts some of the key global standards in relation to the three project management dimensions. While the focus in this section is on project schedule management, applications of underlying processes for managing schedule cannot be discussed in isolation from any of the three dimensions. As much as the project standards are important for evaluating, assessing, and planning the

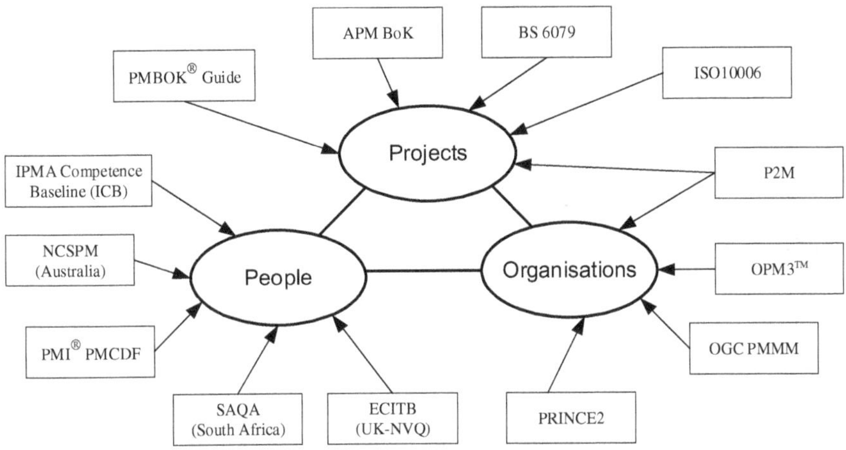

Figure 6.2: Key global standards in three key dimensions of project management.

project schedule from the project scope perspective, without due reference to the organizational and people capabilities, schedule execution and control processes cannot be undertaken effectively. As projects are carried out by the people within a structured organizational setup, lack of efficacy in any of the three dimensions affect the execution of project plans, which eventually leads to not only schedule overrun but also failures across all aspects of the projects.

In project management practice, the performance-based standards are quite common in countries such as Australia, Japan, New Zealand, South Africa, and UK. Performance-based standards refer to the competency framework where stipulated competencies in projects, people, and organizations form the backbone in delivering projects. As most of the leading organizations have clear performance thresholds expected in projects, the behavioral standards required for the people in the project organizations are important performance measures in most projects. Detailed discussion of these standards is beyond the scope of this chapter; thus, only a brief coverage is presented here.

One of the key standards, "PMBOK Guide," was developed by the Project Management Institute (PMI) in the US (PMI, 2017). PMBOK presents the key project management knowledge areas where processes, tools, and techniques and inputs-outputs are clearly laid out from a project planning perspective. The nine knowledge areas in that edition of the guide were Integration, Scope, Time, Cost, Risk, Quality, Procurement, Human Resources, and Communication management. For construction projects, there were three additional knowledge areas included in the construction extension of the standard document. The knowledge areas were Stakeholder Management; Financial Management; and Health, Safety, Security, and Environment management.

The APM BoK of the Association for Project Management Body of Knowledge is described as providing the foundation for the successful delivery of projects, programs, and portfolios across all sectors and industries (APM, 2021). The key reference point of the APM BoK is the five key dimensions of professionalism required for managing projects effectively. These dimensions are: Breadth, Depth, Commitment, Achievements, and Accountability (APM, 2021).

BS6079 is the British Standard for providing guidance on projects; it focuses on the entirety of the project lifecycle phases. The phases include the executing and delivering project management activities, commissioning, operating, decommissioning, and recycling phases (BSI, 2021). ISO10006 was developed by the International Organization for Standardization, and it provides guidelines for quality management in projects. It provides the guidance for executing and managing stipulated quality specifications in projects (ISO, 2021).

The Project and Program Management guidebook developed for Japanese project management (P2M) focuses on both project standards and organizational capabilities in project management contexts (PMAJ, 2021). OPM3, the Organizational Project Management Maturity Model, was developed by the PMI for highlighting the performance standards of the project organizations in relation to the projects. OPM3 is a globally acknowledged standard that provides tools and techniques for measuring organizational maturity against a comprehensive set of organizational best practice processes (PMI, 2017).

The "OGC PMMM" is the project management maturity model developed and adopted by the then Office of Government Commerce in the UK to assist projects organizations to equip themselves with the fundamental organizational capabilities in managing projects. Appropriate organizational capabilities are required for effective implementation of the stipulated PRINCE2 methodologies in projects and thereby improve the likelihood of success in projects (OGC, 2006)

On the people dimension, the Engineering Construction Industry Training Board — National Vocational Qualification (ECITB) refers to the skills required in the project management workforce and for meeting the challenges in complex project environments under the jurisdiction of the UK. Addressing the issues around the identified significant market failures, the organization was established to impart relevant training to the workforce for meeting the needs of the engineering construction industry and thereby improving the professional competencies of the project management professionals (ECITB, 2021).

The South African Qualifications Authority (SAQA) oversees the implementation of the National Qualification Framework (NQF) for providing the workforce with enhanced understanding on a range of competency measures. The competency measures include: Economic Transformation, Integration, High Energy and Corporate Vibrancy, Quality Service, Integrity, Quality, Professional Qualifications, and Environmental Sustainability (SAQA, 2021).

"PMI PMCDF" is the Project Managers Competency Development Framework developed by the PMI as a measure of the standards within the project management team (PMI, 2017). The key principles of the PMCDF are based on the premise that competencies have a direct effect on performance and qualified project managers must possess a minimum level of competencies to be able to perform effectively in the project management role.

NCSPM stands for the National Competency Standards for Project Management developed by the Australian Institute of Project Management (AIPM). The NCSPM depicts a range of competency units being established against three formal qualifications, namely, Certificate IV, Diploma, and Advanced Diploma. The NCSPMS-based professional qualification levels are closely aligned to the government accredited Australian Qualifications Framework (AQF) (AIPM, 2021).

Individual Competence Baseline (ICB) is a global standard developed by the International Association of Project Management (IPMA), which considers the competence of project managers in the distinct roles of project, program, and portfolio managers. The standard articulates the competency standards for "People" in relation to soft and behavioral aspects;

"Practice" in relation to understanding of Projects, Programs, and Portfolios; and "Perspective" in terms of the project's contexts and viewpoints (IPMA, 2021).

As shown above, among many standards providing guidance in project schedule management, the two major standards are the PMBOK (PMI, 2017) and Project in Controlled Environment — PRINCE2 (OGC, 2017). A third standard, Scrum (2017) is also available but as far as schedule management is concerned, this standard does not specify any process-based planning in managing schedule in projects. Most of the location-specific standards across the countries have been derived from the first two standards and thus, the review here is limited to the first two documents in the context of schedule management.

The *PMBOK 5th Edition* (PMBOK, 2017) contains six key processes within the schedule management knowledge area. The six processes are now briefly discussed.

1. Plan schedule management

The process of planning schedule management encompasses the policies, procedures, and underlying documentation for the planning and management of the project schedule. The assumptions in this process include the established project documentation, detailed scope statements, and the methodology for executing the project. The execution stage entails monitoring and controlling of the schedule to ensure the delivery and completion of the project as stipulated in the set targets.

2. Define activities

Based on the detailed project scope of the project, a hierarchical work breakdown structure (WBS) is developed by breaking down the large scope of deliverables into smaller trade packages, activities, or sub-activities so that effort at the lowest level of activities in the hierarchy is measurable. In defining activities, assessment of the risk profiles from the execution perspective plays a critical role in the context of managing, controlling, and completing the activities as outlined in the baseline plans.

3. Sequence activities

Focusing on the dependency relationships of the activities, relational links are established ensuring a seamless workflow in the project. Four different types of relations are used for sequencing the activities. They are finish-to-start, start-to-finish, start-to-start, and finish-to-finish. Lead and lag times are used for introducing the overlapping of, or delays in, activities, respectively. The nested schedule is developed following the logical sequencing of the activities or trade packages focusing on various levels of hierarchy in the WBS.

4. Estimate activity durations

The effort of an activity represents the work-period required to complete the activity following a calendar time. The effort in activities is usually measured in terms of the required materials, labor, equipment, and overheads so that an accurate estimate of duration and cost can be worked out before the schedule is developed. Both productivity and availability factors associated with the resources are considered as well.

5. Develop schedule

The schedule is developed following the sequencing of the activities and by incorporating the constraints. The outcomes of the process of developing the schedule is the determination of the total amount of time required to complete the project. By applying any of the widely used methods such as precedence diagramming method, the critical path is computed, which assists in establishing the schedule baseline plan. Schedule compression and schedule risk assessments are performed as part of the process of developing the schedule process.

6. Control schedule

Control schedule entails monitoring progress and reviewing the status as the project proceeds through the execution stage. Real-time progress data is collected from the execution stage and compared against the baseline plans to see how the project is progressing and whether or not there is any variation that requires corrections or mitigation in order to deliver the project as set out in the stipulated objectives.

Unlike PMBOK, the PRINCE2 (OGC, 2017) does not have a separate part that directly refers to schedule management. Rather, in PRINCE2, the emphasis is on the stage-based management, where the schedule is managed in stages under a broad or high-level plan of the project. Thus, themes and processes with a particular reference to project products are the prevailing concepts in the PRINCE2-based project delivery method.

While discussing schedule management from a developing countries perspective, the rest of the chapter focuses on the relevant knowledge areas and processes with reference to PMBOK (PMI, 2017).

The above discussion highlights the fact that efficiency in project management is not simply based on how a project is managed but also depends on the competence of the project management team along with the maturity levels of the project organization in relation to the project development environment.

While the above is a summary of the existing best practices within the mainstream literature, the evidence of project failure across multiple aspects should lead to some rethinking of whether or not such best practice knowledge applies in the context of developing countries (Emejeit *et al.*, 2021). Evidently, standards and best practices are somehow followed in an effort to drive efficiency in most projects in developed countries, yet the gap is quite substantial in the prevailing practices in developing countries. The consensus among researchers, practitioners, and policymakers suggests that global standards and processes used in projects undertaken in developed countries do not quite deliver the stipulated performance in the projects in the context of developing countries (Doloi *et al.* 2019). This could be due to the complexity of the composition of the stakeholders; unique project circumstances; and power imbalances between the owners, financiers and delivery crews. There is a need for a contextual reinvigoration of the best practice knowledge that requires careful assessment and empirical exploration as presented in the rest of the chapter (Emejeit *et al.*, 2021).

Issues in schedule management practices — A case study

Having reviewed the root causes of poor project time management in developing countries and the good practice processes of schedule management, the mismatch between the industry practices and the good ones is clearly visible. Although project management best practices are available, the poor track record of schedule management in developing countries is due to many issues within the project development environment. In most of the cases, while the bureaucratic and advisory institutional mechanism is one of the dominating factors, lack of capacity and competition in the market place is also one of the key causes of poor schedule performance, especially in the public projects. As discussed earlier, for large capital projects, developing countries usually rely on funds from external agencies. As the funds are externally borrowed using the government machinery, a significant proportion of the ownership, if not all, stays with the government during the implementation of the projects. For projects funded by internal revenue, the responsibility for management lies with the multiple government departments, but they are overseen by the relevant ministries.

Meaningful discussion of, and derivation of insights into, the schedule management practices constitute an important first step before establishing the best practice framework for potential improvement. While the literature highlights the underlying shortcomings of the practices, empirical evidence provides a compelling depiction of the situation, which in turn assists in deriving a workable framework. The following sections present a public-sector case study project from an Indian city located in the state of Assam.

Description of the case project

The case project is an in-ground reinforced concrete storm water drain, 3.4 km long, which runs through a busy part of a small town located in the state of Assam, India. Figure 6.3 shows the approximate location and

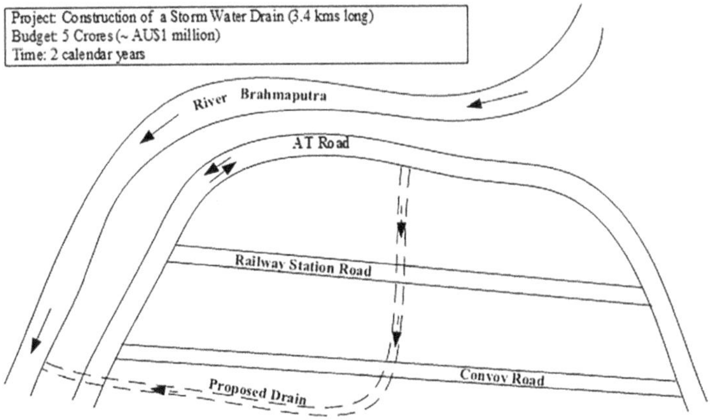

Figure 6.3: A storm water drain project in an urban area.

alignment of the drain project that cuts through three major roads before connecting the outlet to the river. The project had a budget of approximately AU$1 million (about 5 Crores Indian Rupees) and the allocated time was two calendar years. The calendar year usually includes all the local and national holidays. The size of the drain is about 2.4 × 2.4 square meters built as a box construction through a trench in the ground.

Dependency relations in the project

Figure 6.4 shows the relevant authorities and stakeholders involved in the project. This being a public sector project, there are many departments involved across the project phases. The owner of the project, which is the authority in the local jurisdiction, is the Department of Drainage (Town and Country Planning) (DDT&CP). However, DDT&CP is not the sole

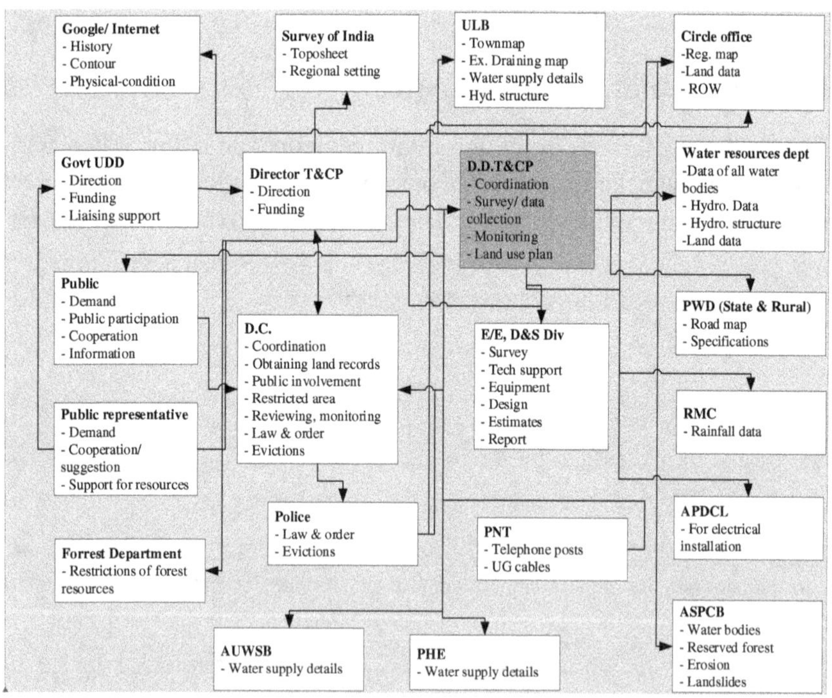

Figure 6.4: Relevant authorities and stakeholders involved in the project.

authority in funding decisions as the funds are allocated and approved by the Directorate of Town and Country Planning. Once the project is initiated, the District Commissioner's (DC) office gets involved for some of the key activities in relation to the project site. The activities of the DC office include coordination, obtaining land records, public involvement, restricted area access, reviewing, monitoring progress, law and order, and evictions for clearing the site and right of ways. The DC office then becomes one of the core agencies for engaging with other relevant departments in relation to liaising with the public, land issues, and law and order and environmental issues.

For the technical information and support, the departments such as Water Authority, Electrical and Mechanical Authority, Public Works Departments, Telecommunications Department, and Weather Department are engaged by the owner organization. There are 21 organizations involved in this project. With the dependencies around each organization, the scheduled time of two calendar years is an optimistic estimate. The same situation applies in cost planning and budgeting.

Figure 6.5 shows 22 key activities in the project. While these activities are related to the construction phase only, the lead up work leading to construction also takes a large chunk of time in addition to the construction timeframe. Due to the dependencies of multiple departments, most of the activities are scheduled with finish-to-end relationships, with the

Activities

1. Preparation of drawing and specifications (3 days)
2. Tendering (2 days)
3. Work order (5 days)
4. Site allocation (7 days)
5. Site exploration (7 days)
6. Site setting up (10 days)
7. Levels (7 days)
8. Earthworks (13 months)
9. Gradation (7 days)
10. Shuttering (1 month)
11. Steel work (12 months)
12. Brickwork (9 months)
13. RCC walls (13 months)
14. RCC conduits (13 months)
15. RCC top slabs (6 months)
16. Curing (6 months)
17. Removal of shuttering (3 months)
18. Casing (6 months)
19. Plastering walls (4 months)
20. Plastering top slabs (3 months)
21. Landscaping (2 months)
22. Final inspection (1 month)

Total estimate: 5 Crores (~ $1 million), **Est. Actual time:** 730 working days (3.5 yrs)

Figure 6.5: Preliminary activities in the project.

exception of a few activities with minimal overlaps. The schedule thus shows a total time of 720 working days, which equates to approximately three and half calendar years. The required time as per the schedule is more than the original target of two years.

While this is a typical scenario of most public sector projects in developing countries, private sector projects are also not different in relation to governance structure and development environment. As discussed above, due to the involvement of numerous interdependent agencies, the project development environment is highly complex. The agencies are usually burdened with large project portfolios and significant workload. In such a situation, the assignment of responsibility and a sense of urgency in decision-making at the local level are not very clear. A small delay in each agency during the upstream processes eventually results in longer delays downstream. In undertaking these projects, best practice processes are neither followed nor referred to in both project and organizational settings. One of the key reasons perhaps is the lack of any structured project management team with the sole responsibility to deliver the project with stipulated targets.

Tailoring the best practice in schedule management

Having reviewed the above case study, the nature and characteristics of the underlying issues associated with schedule management can be generalized across the developing countries. While scale and type of project may present different context-specific scenarios, due to the similarities in governance and funding arrangements for projects, overall practices across the developing countries are quite similar. As discussed above, despite the existence of the body of knowledge in managing projects using best practice methodology, the practice is not followed in the developing country context. As asserted by Rondinelli (1976), the reason for deviating practices is not simply about the ill-intentions of the participants but mainly due to lack of both institutional and organizational capacities. While a proactive training program is considered to be one of the potential mitigating initiatives, a tailored or customized body of knowledge reflecting the project development environment in the developing countries context is desirable. The remainder of the chapter focuses on establishing such a body of knowledge in the context of schedule management.

Project scope and activities definition chain diagram

Before discussing the schedule management practices in developing countries, it is prudent to revisit the best practice body of knowledge and decipher the underlying processes and steps within the relevant knowledge areas from a project development perspective. While the mainstream literature depicts project development processes, environmental, strategic, and business objectives are seldom explored (PMI, 2017). Due to the interconnected nature of the project development environment, these cannot be marginalized (Doloi, 2008). An integrated approach must be devised for appropriate realization of the interdependencies of these entities so that logical sequencing of processes can be drawn aligning the project objectives in relation to the project development environment. Figure 6.6 shows the scope and activities definition pyramid with respect to the formulation of projects over the initial phases of the project lifecycle leading to the schedule development. At the top of the pyramid are the business needs of the project. Typically, the business needs of projects are

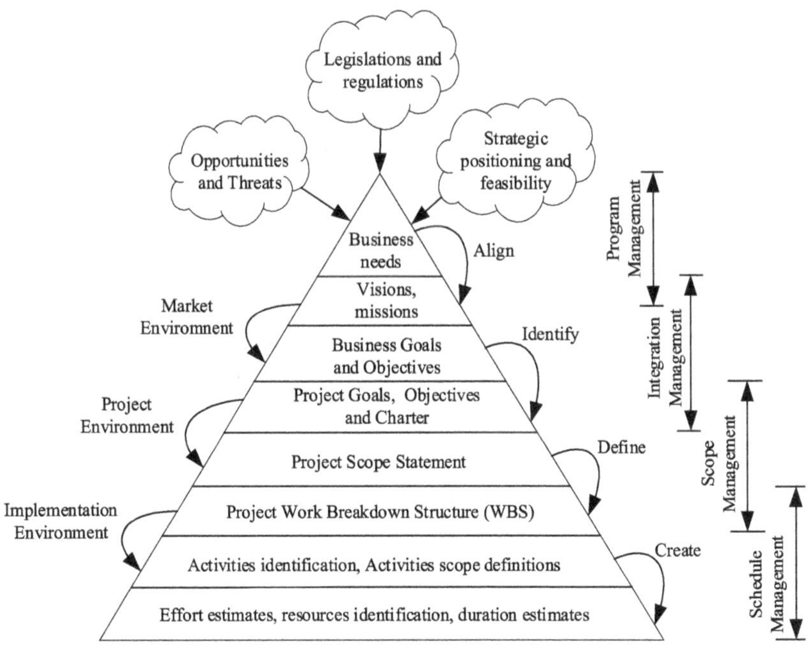

Figure 6.6: Project scope and activities definition chain diagram.

driven by three key elements: *legislation and regulations*, *opportunities and threats*, and *strategic positioning and feasibility*. Necessary considerations need to take place at this level before selecting the project, and this is more so in projects in the context of developing countries due to the scarce resources and limited opportunities for carrying out capital projects. Once the business needs are identified, a vision and mission are established by closely aligning the project to the program or corporate management strategies of the organization. The project business case may need multiple iterations until and unless it is closely aligned with the strategic organizational position.

Integration management, being one of the key knowledge areas, facilitates the transformation of the project business case into an executable plan by combining all the relevant knowledge areas. One of the most important outputs of integration management is the project charter that clearly articulates the key management processes, terms of reference, organizational capacities and responsibilities, and governance mechanisms, including agreements and conditions associated with the target project. The majority of the information contained in a project charter is of a high level, such as high-level definition of the project with strategic requirements, alignment, goals, and objectives. The contents of the project charter are neither measurable nor tangible but highly significant for steering the project on the right course. Once the project charter is established, the required scope management plan facilitates a clear scope statement, including inclusions, exclusions, and constraints associated with the project. The scope definition plan should reflect on the clarity of the scope with a well-established demarcation of the project's work boundaries. In other words, no less or no more work will be undertaken but only what has been stipulated in the scope plan. In the case of scope changes or variations required on the project, a clear scope change control process should be established with delegations of approval authorities including roles and responsibilities for the implications and availability of supporting resources.

Following the scope definition, the WBS becomes the most critical input into the schedule management plan. The WBS entails the scope of the project in relation to logical grouping of the trade packages from the constructability perspective. The trade packages include all the work to be done within the project by both the main contracting party as well as all the subcontractors. The trade packages are broken down into activities and sub-activities or tasks to a level where accurate estimation of the required effort, resources and control are possible to ascertain. While there is usually no specific rule around the level of hierarchy in the WBS, appropriate risk assessment of the activities, including containment mechanisms, should be used to determine the tasks leading to the highest level of estimation accuracy of both cost and time.

Activity definition and estimation errors

The key to success in schedule management is the level of accuracy with which the tasks level of the WBS is accomplished. However, in the project management practices in developing countries, such accuracy is a rare phenomenon and small errors made in each step potentially accumulate to become big issues as the project proceeds. It is important to identify and address the consequential and phase-based errors before they accumulate to an unmanageable level as the project progresses (Doloi, 2008). Figure 6.7 shows various types of errors that can potentially occur in the scope and activities definition chain leading to the schedule development. These errors are categorized into seven different types as discussed below.

- Error Type 1: Inconsistency between business needs and vision statements at the corporate level
- Error Type 2: Inconsistency between project vision and business goals and objectives
- Error Type 3: Inconsistency between business objectives and project objectives
- Error Type 4: Inconsistency between project objectives and charter and project scope definition
- Error Type 5: Inconsistency between project scope and WBS
- Error Type 6: Inconsistency between project WBS and trade packages
- Error Type 7: Inconsistency between project trade packages and activities definition and effort estimates.

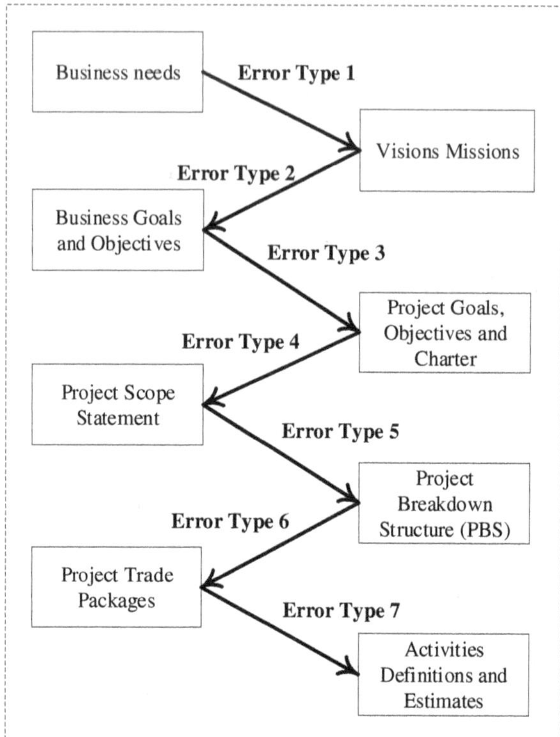

Figure 6.7: Activity definition and estimation errors.

The errors in each process are unique in nature, and they have differing degrees of significance with relatively higher intensity at the top and lower intensity at the bottom. To achieve the desired efficiency in schedule management practice, it is necessary to mitigate these errors, adopting a methodical approach. The focus should be on maintaining consistency of information across the respective processes.

Error Type 1 occurs when the business needs of the project do not align well with the vision and mission of the project organization at the corporate or program level. This is a common type of error in most countries, and more so in developing countries, when the projects are contingent on the external funding being received and the support and willingness of the political parties which are influenced by the timing of the project in relation to the term of the government. Once Error Type 1 is committed, Error Type 2 will be triggered. Having misaligned the vision statement at the corporate level, the chances of correctly setting the business goals and objectives become thin, which eventually triggers the occurrence of Error Type 3, leading to a compromised project goal and objectives including the contents of the project charter. Once the project charter is affected at this important level of the project development phase, Error Type 5 with ill-definition of the project scope then has an impact on the sub-standard WBS, which eventually triggers Error Type 6, leading to inadequate groupings of the trade packages, and this undermines the contracting process for engaging subcontractors in the project. Once Error Type 6 occurs, ripples with Error Type 7 will impact the accuracy of the activities definitions and estimation of effort and durations. Activities definition and duration estimates, being the core input in the schedule development process, such errors will undermine the schedule management process and lead to a faulty time baseline plan for the project.

The above discussion shows the significance of not only realizing the series of errors in the lead up activities for schedule development but also the importance of mitigating errors at the outset of the project development process. While the project development process starts at the corporate or program level with a requirement of a clear business case, the errors due to lack of institutional capacity, coupled with inherent dependencies across multiple organizations, make the projects inefficient from the schedule management perspective.

Benefits mapping

Benefits mapping is one of the best ways to rationalize the project decisions in the context of both strategic investments and measurable impacts on the community. Figure 6.8 shows an example of a project benefits map covering all key facets of the project development. In the figure, the benefits of a project are defined across four key areas: *strategic needs*, *business objectives*, *product demand and utilization*, and *changes and adaptations*.

Under the strategic needs, four areas of considerations with respective weights are used to assess the project options at the corporate or program level. The next level of benefits analysis involves business objectives to be

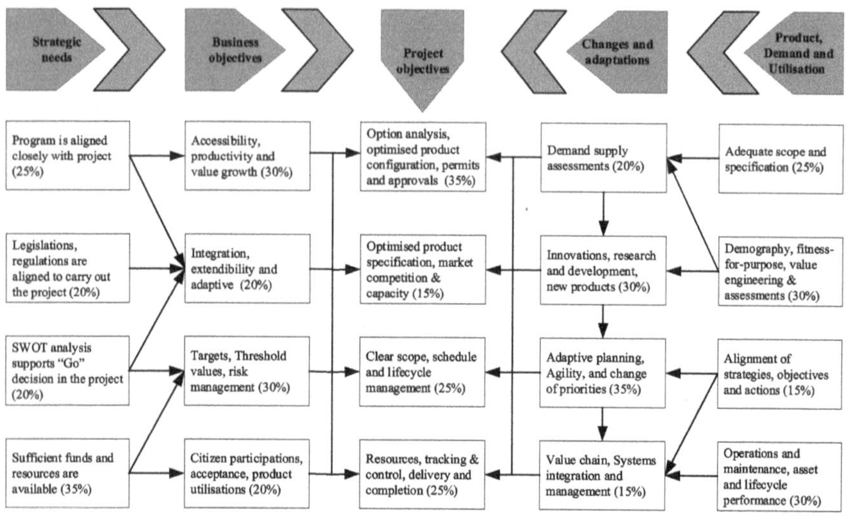

Figure 6.8: Sample benefits map.

assessed under four key considerations. Each consideration is assessed against the assigned weights of the benefits and by linking it to the respective considerations of the previous areas. The weights allocated under each area are based on the general assessments of how much effort typically goes into a standard project under each of the project phases. The percentage of weights in individual areas sums up to an overall effort being 100% (Doloi, 2008). For instance, program alignment with a 25% weight under the "strategic needs" should be analyzed in relation to its potential contribution to two areas of considerations, *accessibility, productivity, and value* growth (30%) and *integration, extendibility, and being adaptive* (20%) under "business objectives."

As much as it is important to ensure that strategic needs and business objectives are aligned with the project objectives, similar emphasis is also required for ensuring close alignment of project demands and utilization and changes and adaptations. Under project demands and utilization, four areas of considerations with individual weights are presented. For instance, adequate scope and specifications, with 25% weight, refers to the required size and quality of the end facility for meeting the demand in the community. Similarly, the consideration, demography, fitness-for-purpose, value engineering, and assessments, with 30% weight, refers to the necessity of the purpose-built end facility that meets the need and impacts positively on growth and support of the community in the long run.

These considerations collectively contribute to four others under the changes and adaptation before the project goes through the development cycles. Demand and supply, with a weight of 20%, is one of the first considerations to make sure that the market-driven variability and underlying parameters support the project's intended objectives and justifies the development.

Once the project objectives are rationalized through the benefits mapping process, the project's objectives are then further refined in terms of options analysis (weight 35%), market competition and capacity (weight 15%), scope and schedule management (weight 25%), and resources, tracking, and delivery plans (weight 25%). These considerations not only provide clarity in project scope definition but also support the development of an accurate baseline plan for ensuring the efficient delivery of the project.

From the above discussion, the mapping of the benefits in multiple considerations provides a foundation for effective project planning with accurate definitions of project scope and specifications with respect to the development environment. With such an approach, the underlying time planning processes in developing countries should significantly enhance the practice of schedule management.

Comprehensive schedule management and underlying processes

The efficiency in schedule management depends on the realistic establishment of the time baseline plan, including a monitoring and tracking mechanism. This is even more so for the projects in developing countries due to the fact that projects often lack clarity in macro-planning approaches where the project development lifecycle is typically longer than the projects undertaken in developed economics. As discussed earlier, due to the nature of interrelated budgetary constraints depicted by the financial cycle of the public agencies, the planning of projects needs to be done by integrating relevant and circumstantial sets of input parameters, including necessary course of time in each phase. Thus, while the measure of efficiency in projects could still be based on the typical cost and time milestones, the plan itself needs necessary contextualization commensurate with the development environment. The following sections discuss methodical steps of schedule management practices under the three key processes, *schedule planning*, *schedule development*, and *schedule control.*

Schedule planning

Figure 6.8 depicts the processes leading to the establishment of an accurate and comprehensive time schedule in projects. Schedule planning processes entail clear articulation of policies and procedures, including the development of relevant planning documentation required in schedule development. Leading to the schedule planning processes, accurate and relevant input from both program or corporate management and project integration management are crucial.

Program or corporate management being the very first knowledge area, the outputs from need analysis, benefits analysis, options analysis, and strategies and priorities form the key inputs for setting out the best course in the project. The outcome of this knowledge area results in an accurate establishment of the project's business case and objectives, which becomes the key input for the next important knowledge area, project integration management. In integration management, formal agreements with all the key stakeholders, including funding arrangements, are set out in relation to the final business case of the project. The outcomes of the integration management activity that results in project goals and objectives and project charter form the key input for in the schedule planning phase.

Figure 6.9 depicts the key enablers in the schedule planning process. As discussed above, project charter, project management plan, and inclusions and exclusions provisions are important input for the scope management knowledge area. At this stage, relevant legislation and regulations in relation to the project need to be referred to, to ensure the legitimacy of the scope of works being undertaken in the project. While the scope baseline, along with a WBS, forms a good basis, external inputs such as the approvals of the relevant authorities and task dependencies, including logistical considerations, are crucial in the schedule management plan.

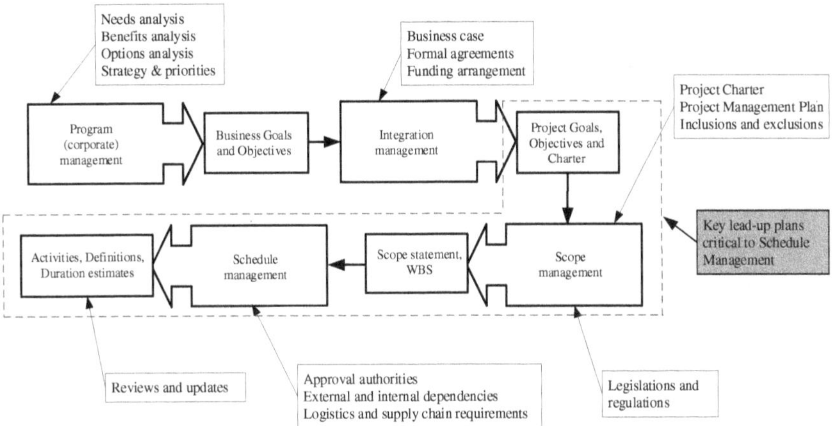

Figure 6.9: Approach to prepare an accurate and comprehensive time schedule.

In the developing countries context, accuracy in the outputs from program management and integration management is important for undertaking an accurate schedule planning processes so that the outputs support the establishment of a realistic time baseline plan required for the construction phase of projects. Commitment to timely approval of the external authorities, including legislative and regulatory support in relation to the project, should be sought before developing the schedule plans. Proper understanding of both external and internal dependencies from the implementation perspective is important during the activities estimation process. Reviews and updates of all the information at this stage of planning assist in increasing the level of accuracy in the succeeding schedule development process.

Schedule development

Schedule development is an iterative process. While it entails activities' sequencing following logical links and dependencies, it is important to consider different levels of abstraction in schedule development. This consideration is relevant in the developing countries contexts due to the scarce resources and conflicting stakeholder priorities on projects.

Figure 6.10 shows a five-level abstraction framework comprising both program and project hierarchies required in schedule development. The first level of abstraction is about a program network where many areas of programs are listed. In developing countries, it is important to draw a logical sequence of project networks under each of the program areas from both resource and institutional capacity perspectives. The project network is the starting point of the project hierarchy where the WBS is derived.

The list of activities and duration estimates identified in the schedule planning process provides the input into schedule development, focusing on the project-level network. Taking into consideration the longer lead time in projects, especially in the developing countries, the project network plans act as a true indication of the overall time a project may require from start of concept to the end of construction. Thus, project network planning preceding the activities network is an important first step in establishing the time baseline on projects.

Following the nested network structure, the network of trade packages is then derived from the project network by grouping the trades according

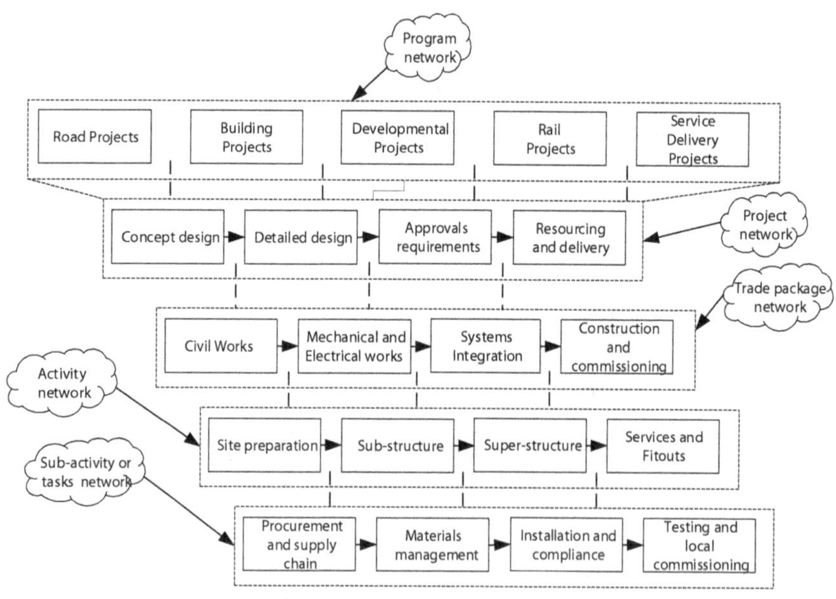

Figure 6.10: Relations between master schedule and sub-schedules.

to the classifications of work. The advantage of nested scheduling practice is that it allows adjustment of the schedule at multiple levels, reflecting the dependency relations between the program and project network structures.

Under the trade package network, the nested activities schedule is generated to establish the time baseline plan that governs the implementation of the project. Before establishing the relations among the dependencies and sequencing the tasks, dependencies associated with sub-activities, including lead time for sub-contracting and other logistical considerations, are required to be ascertained at the lowest level of the network hierarchy.

Once the nested networks of activities at various levels of abstractions are established; the schedule is then verified and analyzed for ascertaining the critical path in the project. Depending on the project location, the project calendar, including resources calendars, is adjusted to reflect the actual calendar time required to complete the project.

As stated earlier, the project schedule needs to undergo multiple iterations with respect to factors such as resources availability; risk profiles of activities and contingencies; alternative construction methodology, including value engineering initiatives; and underlying project constraints. Once a reasonable schedule is developed and accepted by all the agencies concerned and other stakeholders, the baseline plan is established as a final project schedule. The final schedule is then used for guiding the implementation phase of the project. In the implementation stage, appropriate processes and procedures must be in place for recording of progress, controlling, monitoring, tracking, and production of status reports of the project. Upon establishing the schedule baseline plan, the entire project management plans are then updated.

Schedule control

Schedule control is arguably one of the most critical processes for driving efficiencies encompassing the three core project management knowledge areas of scope, time, and cost. Adequate control measures of the baseline schedule result in containing scope and cost variances. Owing to the high dependencies of multiple agencies in the developing countries, schedule control is poor and as a result both scope and cost variations increase considerably in most projects.

Figure 6.11 depicts the schedule control process, and monitoring and reporting are shown as enablers for achieving the required control. While control is important for managing time, processes and procedures for effective progress recording, monitoring and reporting are equally important in projects.

Efficiency in schedule monitoring and reporting is contingent on project baseline plans being executed effectively during the implementation phase. The project baseline plans are categorized in two parts, *technical* and *ancillary*. Under the technical category, the baseline plans comprise scope plan, resources plan, cost plan, schedule risk plan, quality plan, and procurement plan. The ancillary category comprises change requests and control plan, site management plan, work performance plan, communication plan, organizational process assets, subcontractors management plan, and stakeholder management plan.

Both technical and ancillary plans form inputs in the schedule control process. As far as monitoring is concerned, the collection of accurate real-time data on each of these plans as the project progresses through the

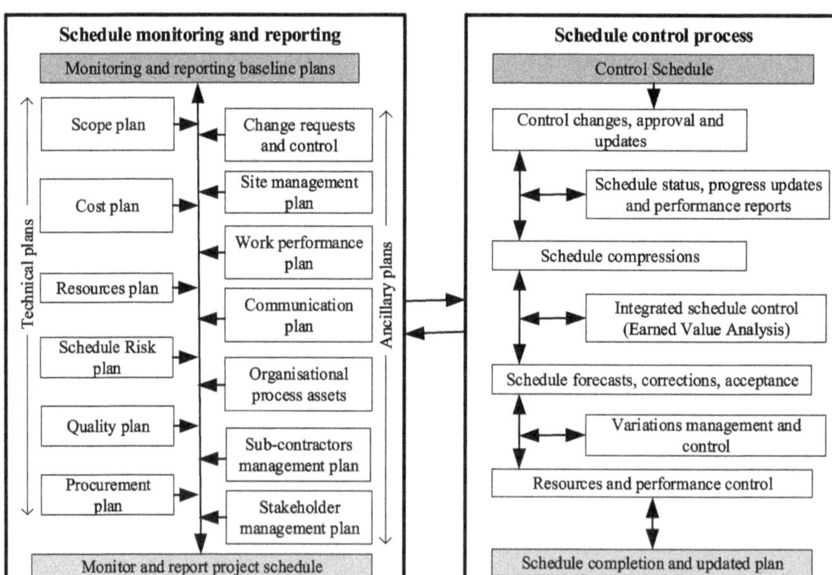

Figure 6.11: Schedule control process.

implementation phase is the most important aspect. While the project managers are responsible for setting up data collection and reporting practices, due to the absence of a dedicated project team, projects in developing countries would require all authorities concerned to record the progress data on a timely basis and in the stipulated format in order to report on the status of the project.

On the reporting process, one of the commonly used techniques is Earned Value Analysis (EVA), where actual progress data in terms of work carried out is placed against the planned work over cost and time ordinates during the specified reporting periods. The planned progress of work is a function of all the ancillary plans being managed following the baseline plans. Change requests and control is a function that needs to be managed efficiently so that the legitimacy on scope changes is reflected in respective scope, time, and cost baseline plans. Similarly, efficient implementation of the site management plan or communication plan supports the planned management of the scope baseline plan and thereby the control and management of scope changes. Performance measurement of the organizational process assets and subcontractors also plays a significant role in keeping the scope baseline intact.

Once the reporting and monitoring of the project progress is underway, the control process kicks in where planned progress is measured against the actual progress in an integrated cost-time space. This integrated controlling tool, known as EVA, results in a series of performance indicators which not only shows the variations but also provides a roadmap for taking corrective actions in the project (PMBOK, 2017).

In the event of any new constraints being imposed such as early completion, scope or budget reductions, change of owner or owner's organization, change of financial division or cashflow regimes, or change of contractors or contractual provisions, including change of project development environment, the baseline plans need to be updated and the status reporting is then recalibrated on the new baseline plans. Progress monitoring, reporting, and control measures are adjusted as stipulated in the updated baseline plans.

In the developing countries contexts, monitoring, reporting, and controlling of projects do not follow any standard process, and this is because variations are considered to be quite obvious, especially in the public sector projects. Due to the lack of coordination, awareness, and commitment of the multitude of agencies involved in the project development lifecycle, any short delay in a localized context results in a longer delay at the project implementation stage. The segregated schedule control process with independent monitoring and reporting should assist in effective coordination among the authorities concerned and achieve better control in schedule management for timely delivery of projects.

Conclusion

Despite the existence of a significant body of knowledge in the mainstream literature, the difference in schedule management practice in projects between developing countries and developed economies is quite stark. While multiple factors are responsible for such differences, funding arrangement, budgetary provisions, and institutional capacities are considered to be the primary factors affecting schedule performance in most projects. Within the developing countries, differences in practice also exist between the public and private sector projects. Based on the published information and also having reviewed a case study from India, the key issues in terms of project development lifecycle, governance, and organizational settings are discussed. Referring to the best practice schedule management, a brief discussion on the processes, tools and techniques, and outputs is undertaken.

In an attempt to establish a tailored practice for managing project schedule in the contexts of developing countries, a methodical and rationalized approach has been put forward by taking into consideration a whole lifecycle approach, starting from the project development to schedule management and control. In the tailored practice, three key areas have been emphasized: activities definition chains, errors estimates, and benefit mapping. Under the activities definition chain approach, the processes of project development from concept stage to schedule development stage have been established. Causal relationships and interdependencies in relation to four key project management knowledge areas, program management, integration management, scope management, and schedule management are discussed. The importance of the project development environment and underlying factors associated with the target projects is highlighted for ensuring clarity in scope definitions including inclusions, exclusions, and constraints.

Referring to the prevailing practices in developing countries, cascading impacts of poor upstream decisions and ripples of errors that affect the accuracy of sequential processes across multiple knowledge areas are discussed using an errors estimation diagram. Estimation of errors in processes as the project proceeds from one stage to the next is an important tool for driving efficiency in schedule management, especially in the projects with poor track records in meeting the targets.

Benefits mapping provides the opportunity for realizing the cause and effects of the actions being taken in developing selected options at an early stage. Once the selected option proceeds toward developing as a project, the scrutiny of the benefits become intense and meaningful for establishing the best course of action leading to setting up the specific project objectives. The process of benefits mapping assists in defining project scope, specifications, value realizations, and innovations, ensuring complete alignments across financial, social, and environmental dimensions.

Schedule planning, schedule development, and schedule control processes have been discussed from the perspective of potential improvement of schedule management in projects in developing countries. Nested scheduling integrating program network with project and activities networks at different levels of abstraction is one of the most effective approaches in effective schedule management of projects, especially the projects without a clearly defined boundary at the early stages. The importance and efficiency of complete individual project plans as a project passes through one knowledge area to the next have been highlighted in schedule development practice. Clarity and completeness of information play critical roles in accurate establishment of the schedule baseline so that monitoring and reporting at the implementation stage result in variations within the acceptable range. In the context of controlling the schedule, the segregated approach between monitoring and reporting and control assists not only in focusing control of individual projects' plans but also in taking corrective actions at localized settings. From the monitoring and reporting perspective, the project plans are categorized as technical plans and ancillary plans. While technical plans provide the road map toward completing the activities onsite, ancillary plans facilitate overall development processes being successfully executed. Onsite progress data assists in implementing stipulated controlling tools such as

EVA so that the outcomes as in status reports and variance analysis contribute toward the controlling and mitigation processes, ensuring effective schedule management in the project.

References

Adams, A.B. (2017). Project management for developing countries: Back to basics. *Dama International Journal of Researchers*, April, 5–9.

Allen, N.J. and Meyer, J.P. (1990). The measurement and antecedents of affective, continuance and normative commitment to the organization. *Journal of Occupational Psychology*, 11(25), 135–143.

Aluonzi, G., Oluka, P.N. and Nduhura, A. (2016). Contract management and performance of road maintenance projects: The case of Arua municipality. *Universal Journal of Management*, 4(10), 550–558.

APM (2021). *APM Body of Knowledge,* 7th Edition | Project Management. www.apm.org.uk [Accessed August 2021].

Al-Khalil M.I. and Al-Ghafly M.A. (1999). Important causes of delay in public utility projects in Saudi Arabia. *Construction Management and Economics*, 17(5), 647–655.

AIPM (2021). Australian Institute of Project Management. www.aipm.com.au [Accessed August 2021].

Arditi, D., Akan, G.T. and Gurdamar, S. (1985). Reasons for delays in public projects in Turkey. *Construction Management and Economics*, 3(2), 171–181.

BSI (2021). BS 6079 Project Management Blog — BSI. www.bsigroup.com [Accessed August 2021].

Crawford, L.H. (2004). Global body of project management knowledge and standards. In P.W.G Morris and J.K. Pinto (Eds.), *The Wiley Guide to Managing Projects*. John Wiley & Sons, Hoboken, NJ, pp. 1150–1196

Doloi, H. (2008). *Life Cycle Project Management — A Systems Based Approach to Managing Complex Projects*. VDM Verlag, Saarbrucken, Germany.

Doloi, H. Iyer, K.C., Sawhney, A. and Rentala, S. (2012). Analysing factors affecting delays in Indian construction projects. *International Journal of Project Management*, 30, 479–489.

Doloi, H., Sawhney, A. and Iyer, K.C. (2012). Structural equation modelling approach for investigating factors affecting delay in Indian construction projects. *Construction Management and Economics*, 30(10), 869–884.

Doloi, H., Green, R. and Donovan, S. (2019). *Planning, Housing and Infrastructure for Smart Villages*. Routledge, Abingdon.

El-Razek, A.M.E., Bassioni, H.A. and Mobarak, A.M. (2008). Causes of delay in building construction projects in Egypt. *Journal of Construction Engineering Management*, 134, 831–841.

Emejeit, A., Nagitta, O.P., Okoche, M. and Mkansi, M. (2021). Contractor commitment and the delivery of road infrastructure projects in Uganda: A practitioner perspective. *African Journal of Management*. https://doi.org/10.1080/23322373.2021.1930695.

ECITB (2021). Engineering qualifications — ECITB. www.ecitb.org.uk [Accessed August 2021].

Faridi, A. and El-Sayegh, S. (2006). Significant factors causing delay in the UAE construction industry. *Construction Management and Economics*, 24, 1167–1176.

Iyer, K.C. and Jha, K.N. (2005). Factors affecting cost performance: Evidence from Indian construction projects. *International Journal of Project Management*, 23, 283–295.

Islam, M.S. (2017). Construction delays in developing countries: A review. *KICEM Journal of Construction Engineering and Project Management*, March, 1–12.

IPMA (2021). International Project Management Association. https://www.ipma.world/individuals/standard/ [Accessed August 2021].

ISO (2021). ISO 10006:2017 — Guidelines for quality management in projects. www.iso.org [Accessed August 2021].

Klein, H.J. and Park, H. (2015). Organisational commitment. In *International Encyclopedia of the Social & Behavioural Sciences*, 2nd Edition (e-book). https://doi.org/10.1016/B978-0-08-097086-8.22032-1.

Nguyen, T.A., Chovichien, V. and Takano, S.E. (2013). Project evaluation, weight assessment, construction project evaluation indexes, project success. *International Journal of Construction Engineering and Management*, 2013(3), 70–84.

Odeyinka, H.A. and Yusif, A. (1997). The causes and effects of construction delays on completion cost of housing projects in Nigeria. *Journal of Financial Management of Property and Construction*, 2, 31–44.

OGC (2017). *PRINCE 2 (PRojects IN Controlled Environments)*, 6th Edition. Office of the Government Commerce (OGC), London.

OGC (February 2006). *Portfolio, Programme & Project Management Maturity Model (P3M3) (Version 1.0)*. Office of Government Commerce (OGC). Crown, pp. 1–77.

PMI (2017). *Guide to the Project Management Body of Knowledge — PMBOK*. PMI, Newtown Square, PA.

PMAJ (2021). Project Management Association of Japan (PMAJ). www.pmaj.or.jp [Accessed August 2021].

Rondinelli, D.A. (1976). Why development projects fail. Problems of project management in developing countries. *Project Management Quarterly*, 7(1), 10–15.

SAQA (2021). South African Qualifications Authority (SAQA) — Overview. https://nationalgovernment.co.za [Accessed August 2021].

Santoso, D.S., Ogunlana, S.O. and Minato, T. (2003). Assessment of risks in high rise building construction in Jakarta. *Engineering, Construction and Architectural Management*, 10(1), 43–55.

Ssebanakitta, P. (2013). Impact of procurement reforms on procurement of works in Uganda. *Journal of Public Procurement and Contract Management*, 2(1). 105–110.

Singh, A. and Gupta, B. (2015). Job involvement, organisational commitment, professional commitment, team commitment. *Benchmarking: An International Journal*, 22(6), 1191–1211.

Schwaber, K. and Sutherland, J. (2017). The Scrum Guide. https://www.scrumguides.org/docs/scrumguide/v2017/2017-Scrum-Guide-US.pdf [Accessed 8 October 2020].

Waterston, A. (1965). *Development Planning: Lessons and Experience*. The Johns Hopkins University Press, Baltimore, p. 249.

Zachary, A.M. (2015). Affective commitment as a core essence of organisational commitment. *Human Resource Development Review*, 14(4), 389–414.

https://doi.org/10.1142/9789811224720_0007

Chapter 7

Project Cost Management

Nii A. Ankrah* and Emmanuel Manu†

Aston University, UK
†Nottingham Trent University, UK

Abstract

Projects consume costly resources that need to be managed to ensure that their outturn costs are within the intended budget. It is common to find references in the literature to projects across the globe that overrun their costs. Project cost management involves the costing of resources needed to complete project activities and developing an understanding of the factors that affect these costs. In this chapter, project cost management is deemed to comprise four steps: cost planning, cost estimating, budgeting, and cost control. A review of the literature found that factors that cause cost overruns are prevalent in developing countries. Developing country factors that may necessitate a different approach to project cost management have been evaluated as comprising project and organization forces (procurement arrangements, project management competencies, and productivity), sector/industry forces (country-level cost benchmarking indices and construction industry standards and policies), country/economic forces (public institutions, corruption, and inflation rate), and global forces (international cost and ethics standards, global initiatives, and conventions). These forces and their associated factors help to explain the project environment in developing countries and what should be considered when managing project costs in those countries. Future trends in project cost management in developing countries are considered as comprising the influence of Construction Industry 4.0 transformations, and carbon accounting and costing practices on project cost management. Some directions for future research in project cost management in developing countries are proposed.

Keywords: Carbon costing, cost management, cost variance, inflation, institutional weaknesses, standards and policies

Introduction

Projects require commitment of limited and costly resources. Given the competing demands for these resources, decisions to undertake projects must be analyzed from a cost and value perspective. Effective management is required to secure successful project outcomes. However, the track record of project delivery across the globe suggests significant failures in some of these processes leading to cost overruns on most construction projects as the following examples demonstrate.

- The Sydney Opera House in Australia, an iconic building, should have cost AUS$7 million. The costs escalated to over AUS $100 million and it was delivered nine years later than planned (from 1959–1973) (Reichold and Graf, 1999).
- The cost overrun for the US$5 billion international airport in Denver, USA, opened in 1995,was close to 200 percent (Flyvbjerg *et al.*, 2003).
- The Channel Tunnel link between the UK and Continental Europe, which was planned to cost £2.7 billion (at 1985 prices) was delivered at £4.568 billion (at 1985 prices) (Winch, 2013), representing a cost overrun of roughly 64% on the capital works (Goldsmith and Boeuf, 2019). Including financing and corporate costs, the overrun ballooned to 122%.
- The City of Boston's Central Artery project in the US (referred to as the Big Dig) was to cost US$2.6 billion (based on 1982 prices), but was completed at US$14.8 billion (or $8.08 billion in 1982 dollars, meaning a cost overrun of about 190%) and seven years late (National Academy of Sciences, 2003; Ahiaga-Dagbui *et al.*, 2017).
- The Edinburgh Trams project in Scotland was initially expected to cost £375 million (US$462 million), but was completed three years

late at a reported £776 million (US$956 million) (Ahiaga-Dagbui *et al.*, 2017), even with significant scope reduction to curtail the growing cost.

- The HS2 project, planned to add extra capacity to the rail network in the UK by building a high-speed rail line to connect London and Southeast UK to the north, was forecast to cost £33.4 billion (capital cost). This figure had risen to £55 billion by 2016 (Elgot, 2016). Following a review in 2019, the cost escalated to between £65 billion and £88 billion (at 2015 prices), more than the funding of £55.7 billion (2015 prices) previously agreed with HM Treasury (NAO, 2020); and some independent reviews suggest that the final costs of HS2 would rise again to £110 billion (2015 prices) (Berkeley, 2020).

These high-profile examples are matched in the developing world where there is even less capacity to accommodate such cost overruns (Ofori, 2007). A few examples illustrate the prevalence of this cost management problem.

- The Bandra–Worli Sea Link (Rajiv Gandhi Sea Link) in Mumbai, India, is a cable-stayed bridge, aimed at decongesting traffic between two of Mumbai's suburbs. Construction began in 1999 with a budget of US$100 million, and was to be completed by 2004. However, the project was delayed by six years and was completed in 2010 at US$250 million, a cost overrun of 150%.
- The Ryugyong Hotel in Pyongyang, North Korea, a 105-storey skyscraper whose construction began in 1987 with a budget of US$750 million, was externally completed in 2012 at an alleged cost of US$2 billion (167% more) (Designing Buildings Ltd, 2021), and the internal works are still not completed.
- The Three Gorges Dam in China planned at US$10 billion, was delivered for US$26 billion (Construction Global, 2020).

As the litany of examples above shows, it is not uncommon to find references to projects that overrun their estimated costs around the world. Flyvbjerg *et al.* (2004) report that nine out of 10 infrastructure projects overrun their budgets (see also Aljohani *et al.*, 2017). A KPMG (2015) report suggested that only 25 percent of projects are delivered within budget. In the developing countries, project delivery with high cost overruns appears to be the norm (Roachanakanan, 2005; Amoa-Abban and Allotey, 2014). The point is made by Ofori (2007) that developing countries have a poorer level of performance in project delivery, and yet, for such countries, the consequences of failure are more serious. Given that cost represents one of the indicators of project success, this represents a failure of cost management and indeed of project management generally across the majority of construction projects. This is a concern, given the huge pipeline of infrastructure projects that is expected to be delivered by 2030 globally to ensure the expected levels of economic growth (see, for example, Garemo *et al.*, 2015) as the world seeks to attain the Sustainable Development Goals (SDGs) and transition to climate-sensitive economic models.

An introduction to project cost management

Projects consume resources that have associated costs. As observed by PMI (2016), scope, design, constructability, and performance changes can occur throughout the project lifecycle. Therefore, a lifecycle approach to the management of costs is warranted. This is critical as project decisions at different stages have the potential of defining the subsequent recurring cost of using and maintaining the result of the project. For example, limiting the number of design reviews can reduce the cost of the project but increase the resulting product's operating costs (PMI, 2017).

As a starting point, it is useful to examine the principles and principal requirements of this cost management function, as defined by the main standards governing project management practice.

The management of costs

Project cost management deals with the cost of the resources required for projects and the factors affecting such costs. Cost management is defined in the PMBOK (PMI, 2017) as the combination of "processes involved in planning, estimating, budgeting, financing, funding, managing and

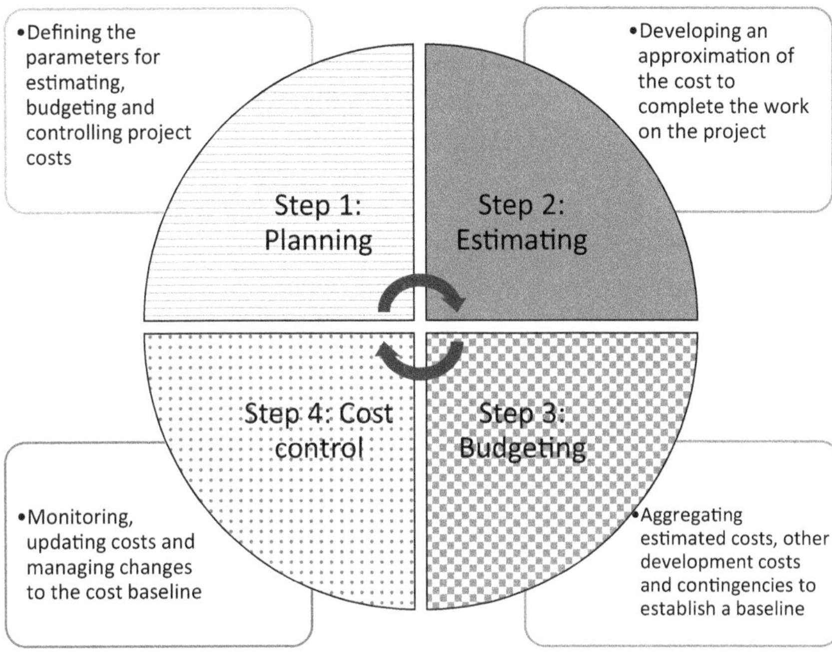

Figure 7.1: The project cost management process.

controlling costs so that the project can be completed within the approved budget." PMI (2016) states that it "entails managing the day-to-day project costs." Its purpose, as observed by BS ISO 21502:2020, is to establish the financial controls required to facilitate the delivery of projects within approved budgets. Therefore, its importance to the success of construction projects and, by extension, an organisation's profitability cannot be overstated. The PMBOK offers a four-stage process for project cost management (Figure 7.1).

BS ISO 21502:2020 also highlights the key activities as: estimating, budgeting, acquiring funds and cost control. It is important to note that these stages or activities are not sequential. In practice, there is extensive overlap, interaction and iteration between these stages, and with activities required in other project management domains (PMI, 2017). Cost management starts at the early stages of projects during scope definition where critical decisions impacting on cost are made and there is the greatest opportunity to influence cost by optimizing project decisions (PMI, 2016).

Cost management planning

According to the PMI (2017), this activity that occurs as part of early project planning defines the approach for each of the subsequent stages in the cost management process shown in Figure 7.1. The output of this stage is a cost management plan which forms part of the project management plan.

This stage requires firm decisions to be made about financial data to underpin project costing (such as exchange rates, cost databases and productivity factors), project approval requirements that will influence the management of the project costs, the risk management strategy, and how cost control documents such as bills of quantities (BoQs) will be prepared. Decisions also extend to when costs are accounted for (accounting codes), variance thresholds, reporting periods and formats, information systems to be used, tracking methodologies, the earned value management (EVM) techniques and any relevant requirements defined by applicable codes of practice or forms of contract. PMI (2016) suggests that the plan should be customized for the needs of the owner/sponsor with due consideration to other stakeholders' needs.

PMI (2017) recommends that planning meetings should be attended by "the project manager, the project sponsor, selected project team members, selected stakeholders, anyone with responsibility for project costs, and others as needed."

The key benefit of the planning process is that it helps to clarify how emerging factors should be incorporated into the cost management process.

Estimating

Estimating is the process of developing a quantitative assessment of the probable cost of a project (BS ISO 21502:2020; PMI, 2017). It occurs throughout the project as needed (PMI, 2017). Depending on the stage of the project, estimating may adopt basic techniques such as rough order magnitude (ROM) estimates, referred to as order of cost estimate in the UK, or the more sophisticated bottom-up analytical estimating techniques such as unit rate estimating or operational estimating.

Estimating should account for market conditions, published or researched information, exchange and inflation rates (particularly for multi-currency multi-year projects), as well as uncertainty and risk. There is also now a requirement to consider the lifecycle cost of a project, which may include operating costs (PMI, 2016).

This stage determines the monetary resources required for a project which may inform the decision to proceed with the project or lead to value engineering and constructability analysis to improve the business case, facilitate design-to-cost function, and optimize the decision-making process (PMI, 2016).

Budgeting

Budgeting is the baselining of the cost estimate. It is the "process of aggregating the estimated costs of individual activities or work packages to establish an authorised cost baseline" (PMI, 2017). BS ISO 21502:2020 refers to a schedule-based budget identifying when funds are needed and when costs will be incurred. The benefit of budgeting is that it provides a basis for monitoring and controlling project performance.

A key component of budgeting is the inclusion of management reserves to fund unforeseen work within the scope, referred to in PMI (2017) as "unknown unknowns." The budget, once established, forms the basis for project funding requirements.

Cost control

Cost control involves monitoring the status of the project in relation to consumption of project funds and the work being accomplished for such expenditure, updating project costs, and managing changes to the cost baseline (BS ISO 21502:2020; PMI, 2016, 2017). Many projects suffer cost overruns due to inadequacies in the cost control regime which according to the PMBOK (PMI, 2017) should include:

- "Influencing the factors that create changes to the authorized cost baseline;
- ensuring that all change requests are acted on in a timely manner;
- managing the actual changes when and as they occur;
- ensuring that cost expenditures do not exceed the authorized funding by period, by Work Breakdown Structure component, by activity, and in total for the project;
- monitoring cost performance to isolate and understand variances from the approved cost baseline;
- monitoring work performance against funds expended;
- preventing unapproved changes from being included in the reported cost or resource usage;
- informing appropriate stakeholders of all approved changes and associated cost; and
- bringing expected cost overruns within acceptable limits."

As can be seen from the list above, a critical success factor in cost control is having an integrated change management plan (PMI, 2016, 2017).

Earned value analysis (EVA) is used to compare the performance measurement baseline to actual results to determine if a change, corrective action, or preventive action is necessary. It is performed throughout the project. PMI (2017) sets out a detailed approach to the application of this technique. An emerging trend is the inclusion of the concept of earned schedule (ES), which replaces the schedule variance measures used in traditional EVA (earned value – planned value) with ES and actual time (AT).

A key benefit of cost control is that the cost baseline is maintained throughout the project, and where adjustments are required, it helps make a case for additional funding (BS ISO 21502:2020).

It is remarkable that, with such a well-defined framework for cost management, cost variance is still pervasive across the construction industry. This could be because the framework does not prescribe the actual techniques or specify the standards of data to be used. There is an absence of literature to fully map out the cost management practices of developing countries in a way that allows for comparison with the standard framework of the professional institutions. Cost overruns are attributable to many factors, some of which are legitimate reasons for the cost variance. To provide some context for the review of cost management in construction, the next section examines these common causes of cost variance.

Causes of cost variance

A rich body of literature covers cost variance on construction projects. Seminal works include Flyvbjerg *et al.* (2014, 2016), Ahiaga-Dagbui *et al.* (2015, 2017), Love and Ahiaga-Dagbui (2018) and Love *et al.* (2016, 2019). There are disagreements on the causal factors. However, these studies have established that cost variance is multi-causal and the causes arise throughout the project lifecycle. Love *et al.* (2016) signpost inaccurate comparisons, long periods between setting of initial budgets and commencement of projects with resultant inflationary effects, and scope change. Flvybjerg *et al.* (2014) points to optimism bias, planning fallacy or, even worse, strategic misrepresentation, a euphemism for outright deception, as lying at the heart of this pervasive phenomenon. Love *et al.* (2019) question the planning fallacy theory as an explanation of cost overruns. Other reasons found include lack of leadership and maturity among project owners, lack of trust and collaboration, and poor contractor performance (KPMG, 2015).

Love *et al.* (2015) classify the causes of cost overruns into political, economic, psychological, and managerial factors. Aljohani *et al.* (2017) catalog 173 causal factors, the main factors being: "frequent design change, contractors' financing, payment delay for completed work, lack of contractor experience, poor cost estimation, poor tendering documentation, and poor material management." Aljohani *et al.* (2017) highlighted the important point that such global findings are not always applicable for individual countries. As the variations in the levels of cost overrun could also be related to factors such as project size, project type, and project location, it is logical to review what the literature reveals about projects in developing countries.

Several studies have been undertaken from a developing country perspective. Prominent among these are those that examine the situation in Nigeria (such as, Ikechukwu *et al.*, 2017; Nwokenkwo, 2019), Pakistan (such as, Ahmed *et al.*, 2018), India (such as, Subramani *et al.*, 2014), Malaysia (such as, Memom *et al.*, 2012), South Africa (such as, Mulalo *et al.*, 2018), Ghana (such as, Amoa-Abban and Allotey, 2014), and Jordan (such as, Faten Albtoush *et al.*, 2021). Subramani *et al.* (2014) studied the causes of cost overruns in India and found that slow decision-making, poor schedule management, increase in material/machine prices, poor contract management, poor design or delay in providing design information, rework due to wrong work, problems in land acquisition, wrong estimation or estimation method, and long period between design and time of tendering were the principal causes of cost overruns. Although questions can be raised about the research design and quality of data generated, these findings resonate with those reported elsewhere.

The studies in developing countries can be placed into two categories; those that focus on establishing the level of overrun in a particular jurisdiction (see for example, Memom *et al.*, 2012), and those that identify the causal factors and their degree of importance (see for example, Memom *et al.*, 2012; Ejaz *et al.*, 2011; Mbachu and Nkado, 2007). Many of these studies rely on survey data of varying degrees of quality with calculations of relative importance as the basis for establishing the rank order of the factors and calculations of agreement such as Kendall's Coefficient of Concordance (W) to test the degree of convergence of opinions of different groups of project participants (see for example, Ejaz *et al.*, 2011; Frimpong *et al.*, 2003).

Among studies in the first category, Memom *et al.* (2012) investigated the time and cost performance of projects in Malaysia. The survey data only confirmed already established knowledge that cost overruns are common. This was complemented by qualitative information that provided good insight into measures that could improve cost performance on projects.

The majority of studies have been in the second stream. In a study of groundwater projects in Ghana, Frimpong *et al.* (2003) used data from owners, consultants, and contractors to rank 26 factors. This appears to have been emulated by other researchers such as Ejaz *et al.* (2011), who also ranked 26 factors based on which they made recommendations concerning aspects that should receive most attention during project development. Albtoush *et al.* (2021) also produced a rank order list of factors causing cost overrun and used factor analysis to produce a parsimonious set of underlying factors affecting projects in Jordan comprising financial difficulties, material costs, design issues, and additional works. The foregoing examples illustrate a longstanding problem that has been the subject of extensive research over many years, but there is no evidence of sustained improvements to show that the research has yielded meaningful and useful insights. Further examples include the survey of the South African construction industry by Mbachu and Nkado (2007) and Ramabodu and Verster (2010), the survey of project participants in Nigeria by Fagbenle and Owolabi (2014) and the survey of cost escalation factors in Pakistan by Ahmed *et al.* (2018).

A few studies have adopted alternative approaches to survey research methods. Amoa-Abban and Allotey (2014) documented a case study of a renovation project to identify factors contributing to the high cost overrun of building projects which is common in Ghana. Whilst there are inconsistencies in the data presented, this study provided evidence of fraudulent claims by contractors, scope creep, change, and fluctuations. Another case study was undertaken by Roachanakanan (2005) on the Thai construction industry; it highlighted factors similar to those outlined above.

Table 7.1 presents a summary of the principal causes of poor cost performance in developing countries as established by extant research. Some studies classify these causal factors as internal or external (see, for example, Aljohani *et al.*, 2017; Mbachu and Nkado, 2007), indicating factors within the direct control of project teams that are a consequence of decisions made by them (internal factors), and those that they have no control over but need to respond to in their planning. Very few studies have undertaken in-depth research into the cost management process, mechanisms, techniques, and tools to establish why they have failed to respond effectively to the factors that are now well-established as contributors to poor construction project cost performance. For example, Nwokenkwo (2019) attempted to empirically determine the impact of budgeting and budget control on project performance in Nigeria. Arguably, a better design of this study would have been to examine the nature and quality of budgeting and budget control procedures as this would have delivered insights and identified measures and tools that could be used to improve the poor performance of construction projects. Thus, the extant research is a lost opportunity to forensically review current practice in developing countries.

To appreciate how the various factors influence or relate to current cost management practice, these factors are mapped onto the cost management cycle in Table 7.1 to provide a framework for considering appropriate strategies for addressing these. The next section explores the more significant of these developing world factors in more detail, then critically evaluates how current cost management practice responds to these matters, and proposes adaptations of current cost management practice required to effectively respond to these challenges as well as future research that can underpin the evolution and adaptation of cost management practice in developing countries in order to secure improvements in the cost management process and, ultimately, performance of projects.

Developing country factors affecting cost management

There are many contributors to cost increases, some of which are unique to developing countries such as inordinate payment delays, inflation, and absence of national cost norms and data. Issues around fraud and political interference have also come up. As Table 7.1 shows, many of these causes of cost overruns in developing countries are linked to the complexity of the environment within which projects are executed. According to Rwelamila (2007), complexity of the project environment is dictated by forces that originate from the project itself, the organization sponsoring the project and organizations involved in project implementation; the industry; forces from the country/economy; and forces emanating from the global environment in terms of economics, politics, and other social factors. These four forces are used in the rest of this chapter to evaluate the project environment in developing countries:

- Project and organizational forces, such as unforeseen ground conditions, inappropriate procurement, contracting and pricing strategies,

Table 7.1: Factors that cause construction cost overruns in developing countries.

	Amoa-Abban & Allotey (2014)[a]	Venter (2015)[b]	Mbachu & Nkado (2007)[b]	Albtoush *et al.* (2021)[c]	Frimpong *et al.* (2003)[a]	Ahmed *et al.* (2018)[d]	Ejaz *et al.* (2011)[d]	Subramani *et al.* (2014)[e]	Roachanakanan (2005)[f]	Ikechukwu *et al.* (2017)[g]	Nwokenkwo (2019)[g]	Gbate *et al.* (2019)[g]	Fagbenle & Owolabi (2012)[g]	Memon *et al.* (2012)[h]	El-Ahwal *et al.* (2016)[i]	Naveenkumar & Prabhu (2016)[e]	Park & Papadopoulou (2012)[j]	Abusafiya & Suliman (2017)[k]	Nurafiqah (2017)[h]	Le-Hoai (2008)[l]	Al Adawi & Yahia (2021)[m]	Meampol & Ogunlana (2006)[f]	Heravi & Mohammadian (2021)[n]	Mansur *et al.* (2019)[o]	Enshassi *et al.* (2010)[p]	Zou *et al.* (2007)[o]	Andrić *et al.* (2019)[j]
Planning stage factors																											
Inadequate control procedures					✓		✓							✓													
Inappropriate estimating methods								✓							✓								✓			✓	
Failure to plan budgeting and budgetary control strategy											✓		✓										✓		✓		
Estimating stage factors																											
Inadequate allowances for uncertain work/Uncertainty	✓			✓																							
Fluctuations	✓			✓	✓	✓						✓		✓	✓		✓			✓					✓	✓	✓
Errors, omissions and misinterpretations			✓	✓					✓			✓						✓	✓	✓	✓			✓			
Poor quality service			✓																								✓
Poor scope definition (incomplete design and poor documentation)			✓	✓		✓			✓			✓		✓				✓	✓		✓				✓	✓	
Poor estimating	✓				✓	✓	✓	✓				✓		✓	✓		✓	✓	✓	✓	✓		✓		✓	✓	
Excessive tolerance of uncertain scope	✓								✓					✓													
Planning and scheduling deficiencies					✓	✓	✓	✓								✓	✓	✓	✓		✓		✓	✓	✓	✓	
Delays in land acquisition						✓		✓													✓						✓
Lack of (or unreliable) cost benchmarking data						✓						✓															
Interest rates						✓																					

(*Continued*)

Table 7.1: (*Continued*)

	Amoa-Abban & Allotey (2014)[a]	Venter (2015)[b]	Mbachu & Nkado (2007)[b]	Albtoush *et al.* (2021)[c]	Frimpong *et al.* (2003)[a]	Ahmed *et al.* (2018)[d]	Ejaz *et al.* (2011)[d]	Subramani *et al.* (2014)[e]	Roachanakanan (2005)[f]	Ikechukwu *et al.* (2017)[g]	Nwokenkwo (2019)[g]	Gbate *et al.* (2019)[g]	Fagbenle & Owolabi (2012)[g]	Memon *et al.* (2012)[h]	El-Ahwal *et al.* (2016)[i]	Naveenkumar & Prabhu (2016)[e]	Park & Papadopoulou (2012)[j]	Abusafiya & Suliman (2017)[k]	Nurafiqah (2017)[h]	Le-Hoai (2008)[l]	Al Adawi & Yahia (2021)[m]	Meeampol & Ogunlana (2006)[f]	Heravi & Mohammadian (2021)[n]	Mansur *et al.* (2019)[o]	Enshassi *et al.* (2010)[p]	Zou *et al.* (2007)[o]	Andrić *et al.* (2019)[j]
Forex rate fluctuations																	✓								✓		✓
Budgeting stage factors																											
Inefficient budgeting											✓	✓	✓														
Cost control stage factors																											
Construction delays (for example due to non-payment)	✓			✓								✓		✓	✓			✓				✓		✓	✓		
Additional work	✓			✓											✓				✓	✓					✓		
Change/Variations	✓			✓		✓			✓			✓	✓	✓	✓	✓	✓	✓	✓	✓	✓				✓	✓	✓
Valuation errors	✓																								✓		
Productivity		✓				✓								✓		✓		✓						✓			
Poor contractor (and/or consultant) performance		✓										✓				✓			✓	✓							✓
Adversarial client/contractor relationships		✓																									
Claims			✓											✓				✓							✓		
Undue interference by client			✓						✓					✓		✓			✓								
Payment delays			✓	✓	✓	✓	✓							✓		✓	✓	✓		✓	✓					✓	
Slow decision-making				✓		✓	✓	✓						✓		✓			✓		✓		✓				
Fraud	✓																		✓								
Inflation					✓	✓	✓	✓	✓			✓					✓		✓						✓	✓	
Cash flow issues					✓	✓	✓						✓	✓				✓	✓					✓			

(*Continued*)

Non-application of relevant budgetary control								✓		✓	✓				✓				✓			✓		
General/Unclassified factors																								
Skills gap/Skills shortage	✓	✓	✓	✓	✓		✓		✓	✓	✓	✓	✓	✓	✓	✓	✓		✓		✓			✓
Leadership	✓	✓		✓																				
Inappropriate procurement, contracting & pricing strategies	✓	✓	✓						✓			✓		✓			✓					✓		
Poor contractor management (supply chain issues)			✓	✓	✓	✓					✓	✓	✓	✓	✓		✓				✓		✓	
Material and plant procurement			✓	✓	✓				✓	✓	✓	✓	✓	✓	✓	✓	✓		✓		✓	✓		✓
Poor technical performance			✓											✓	✓				✓		✓	✓		✓
Contractor's financial difficulties			✓		✓					✓	✓				✓	✓	✓	✓			✓			
Owner's financial difficulties											✓	✓			✓		✓	✓		✓		✓	✓	
Inclement weather			✓	✓	✓							✓		✓			✓					✓		
Unforeseen ground conditions			✓	✓	✓									✓			✓	✓			✓	✓		✓
Delays in work approval			✓	✓	✓								✓	✓		✓	✓					✓		
Delays in supply of information (and decision-making)/Communication issues			✓	✓	✓	✓			✓		✓			✓	✓	✓	✓	✓	✓		✓	✓		
Unreliable plant			✓		✓						✓		✓	✓		✓					✓			
Government policies and political instability				✓					✓					✓			✓					✓	✓	
Influence of local government (bureaucracy or political interference)				✓	✓				✓														✓	
Poor site and project management				✓							✓		✓	✓	✓	✓	✓				✓			
Defects and rework				✓	✓	✓			✓		✓				✓		✓				✓			
Corruption					✓							✓		✓		✓								
Bidding strategy			✓		✓				✓					✓								✓		
Terrorism					✓																			
Lag between design and tender						✓																		
Project location and market conditions									✓			✓	✓									✓		✓
Third-party problems (for example neighbors)													✓											
COVID-19 related																		✓						

Note: [a]Ghana, [b]S. Africa, [c]Jordan, [d]Pakistan, [e]India, [f]Thailand, [g]Nigeria, [h]Malaysia, [i]Developing Countries, [j]Asia, [k]Bahrain, [l]Vietnam, [m]Oman, [n]Iran, [o]China, [p]Gaza Strip.

contractor's financial difficulties, and poor site and project management and competencies and abilities of organizations that play key roles in the management of projects.

- Sector/industry forces, such as availability of national-level cost benchmarking indices, and construction industry standards and policies.
- Country/economic forces, such as inflation, government policies and political instability, bureaucracy, or political interference that affect the wider environment within which projects are undertaken.
- Global forces, such as global standards and policies, and initiatives that have an influence on project management in developing countries.

It is important to understand how these forces necessitate a different approach to project cost management in developing countries since they can help to explain the unique project environment in developing countries.

Project and organizational forces

Project and organizational forces here are those that originate from the project itself and the organizations that are sponsoring the project or are involved in its delivery. The forces here that need to be considered when managing project costs include the differences in procurement arrangements, project management competencies, and productivity, compared to developed countries.

Procurement arrangements

The procurement arrangements that are adopted have an influence on the outturn cost of projects. These arrangements include the procurement method or routes (such as traditional, design and build, and management), the tendering approach (such as competitive and negotiated), the adopted contract strategy (such as priced contracts, target contracts, cost reimbursement contracts, and remeasurement contracts), and the contract forms used, be they standard or bespoke. The procurement arrangements in use in many developing countries were inherited from Western countries (Ofori, 2000). A common strand within them is the propagation of a transactional (such as lowest price competitive tendering, and traditional design-bid-build arrangements) rather than a collaborative approach. Most of these procurement arrangements also tend not to treat cost management and site production as collaborative processes that need to be managed jointly by clients, contractors, and their supply chain. On the other hand, the Western originators have continued to reform and adopt more collaborative procurement arrangements that promote such features as early supply chain engagements; joint planning, risk management, and problem solving; and shared risks and reward mechanisms. The use of enterprise-based procurement models such as alliancing for public projects (Mills *et al.*, 2020, Lehto and Aaltonen, 2021) is evidence of this trend in developed countries.

The challenge posed by transactional procurement arrangements is that they promote adversarialism, contract administration inefficiencies, claims, disputes, and litigation. This increases the transaction costs of projects. Transaction costs are additional costs that arise from regulating transactions between parties rather than the direct costs of production. These include contract set-up costs, costs of finding and selecting a suitable partner, and engaging in exchange and contracting activities (Farajian, 2010). For construction projects, these include bidding costs, costs of estimating and drawing up a contract, contract administration costs, costs of dealing with variations or changes to the original contract and contractual claims, and cost of disputes (Li *et al.*, 2013). Whilst problems that arise from transactional procurement arrangements are not unique to developing countries, they may have more implications for cost management practice as they tend to cause variations between early project cost estimates and outturn costs.

In many developing countries, public-sector projects dominate due to high infrastructure deficits as compared to developed nations (Tyson, 2018; Colonnelli and Ntungire, 2020; Kirchberger, 2020). Infrastructure projects in developing countries are also initiated through Public–Private Partnerships (PPPs) that involve some government facilitation (Gurara *et al.*, 2017; Kirchberger, 2020). Infrastructure projects in developing countries are either funded directly by host governments, through private-sector financiers, grants, loan facilities, and grants from Multilateral Development Banks (such as the World Bank, Asian Development Bank, and African Development Bank) and donor support from bilateral institutions (Leigland, 2018). In 2015, 57 percent of PPP funding in developing countries came from governments, multi-laterals, and bilateral institutions, with the balance coming from commercial sources (Leigland, 2018). PPP projects generally involve higher procurement costs including the costs of negotiating and arranging finance, and legal and technical costs of developing the PPP (Leigland, 2018). These PPP costs are much higher in developing countries; Bhattacharya *et al.* (2012) found that PPP procurement costs in developing countries can constitute up to 10 percent of overall investment costs. It is common for infrastructure projects in developing countries to be affected by political interference, adding to project uncertainties.

Project management competencies

The prominence of the public sector in the delivery of projects in developing countries suggests that the project management competencies (the ability to perform the project management process efficiently (Gareis and Huemann, 2000)) of public-sector client organizations will have an influence on the management of project costs. Based on a case study in South Africa, Rwelamila (2007) argued that public-sector infrastructure clients in developing countries that are responsible for infrastructure delivery do not always possess the necessary project management competencies. This can translate into inadequate project planning, poor budgeting and poor risk and contract management, which have an impact on the management of project costs. Ahadzie *et al.* (2009a, 2009b) argued for promoting competency-based training programs that can foster continuous skills acquisition and professional development of project managers in developing countries, and developed competency-based measures that could support professional development of project managers in mass house building projects. Such efforts to strengthen project management competencies in developing countries will help impart project cost management expertise.

Productivity

Construction productivity has an influence on the cost of projects and thus, cost management, in developing countries. Indeed, poor productivity translates into "high prices, leading to low levels of output for a given level of expenditure" (Kirchberger, 2020). The construction industry in the developing world continues to suffer from low productivity, particularly among small and medium-sized enterprises (SMEs). This has been attributed to skills gaps, inadequate training, rework, management style and incentives to labor by Adebowale and Agumba (2021) who undertook a metadata analysis of research on productivity growth in developing countries.

A McKinsey report on productivity in construction provides further evidence of the low and uncertain productivity levels that characterize developing countries (McKinsey Global Institute, 2017). Productivity in this report is defined as the "value added by construction workers (output in terms of structures created minus purchased materials) per hour of work." This is corroborated by World Bank construction productivity data modelled in Figure 7.2 which shows developing countries such as India, Brazil, Colombia, Egypt, India, Malaysia, Nigeria and Thailand, lagging at the bottom of the productivity scale (vertical axis). This implies that infrastructure is delivered at higher cost for owners and lower profitability for contractors which ultimately leads to a squeeze on wages for workers. According to McKinsey Global Institute (2017), high labor productivity often also goes hand in hand with shorter and more reliable project schedules.

Hassan *et al.* (2018) and Kaming *et al.* (1997) blame the low productivity on the non-availability of materials, inadequate supervision, skills shortage, lack of proper tools and equipment and incomplete drawings and specifications.

Sector/industry forces

Country-level cost benchmarking indices

The absence of cost indices is a major barrier to the development of reliable forecasts and budgets for cost control purposes. Unlike the situation in countries such as the UK, where benchmarking data and indices are

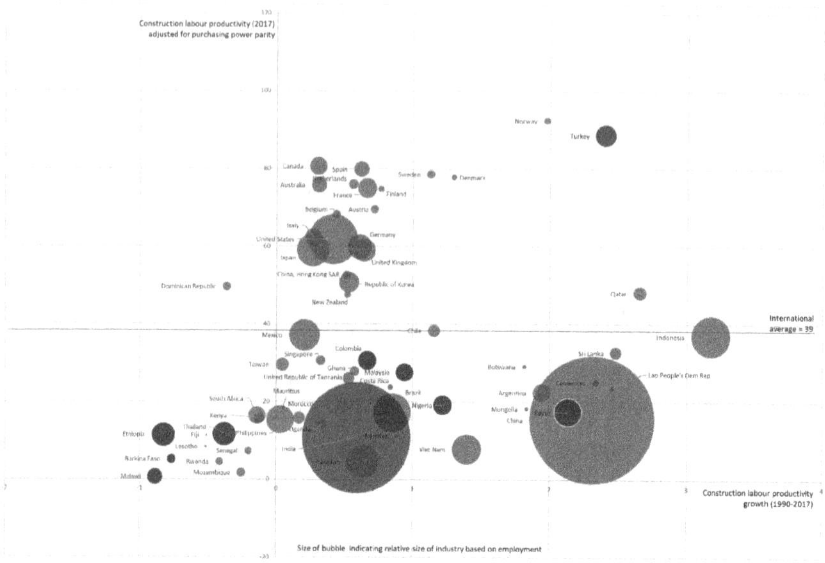

Figure 7.2: Construction productivity and productivity growth.

Source: McKinsey Global Institute, 2017.

available and facilitate the use of estimating techniques like reference class forecasting and systems dynamics, such resources are generally non-existent in the developing world. Fagbenle and Owolabi (2012) suggested, following a study of budgeting practices in Nigeria, that there was a need to have "up-to-date data of current and forecast of future requirements as well as the cost of major building materials and components"; and that a reliable and universal system would allow for more effective cost benchmarking. There is still no evidence of the development and maintenance of any such cost databases in developing countries. Kirchberger (2020) observed that cost data are rarely held centrally in developing countries, making benchmarking activities challenging. Organizations such as AECOM, recognizing this gap, have developed their own cost database tools. AECOM's Global Unite system is designed to capture and benchmark cost data from all the AECOM key geographies into one central database (AECOM, 2020) to facilitate their project cost management processes around the world. The availability of these cost databases in developing countries can help to advance cost estimating practice from a bottom-up technique toward the use of parametric cost estimating techniques that require cost datasets for statistical modelling.

Construction industry standards and policies

Cost management practices are usually driven by standards and practice norms promoted by professional institutions, including those for quantity surveying, cost management, and cost engineering. The cost management standards being used in some developing countries date back to practices from their colonial past. As in procurement, some of the developed countries from which these practices originate have advanced their practices. In many developing Commonwealth countries, the professional institutions continue to promote the preparation of BoQs based on standards drawn from earlier editions of the Royal Institution of Chartered Surveyors (RICS) Standard Methods of Measurement (Nani *et al.*, 2012; Smith, 2016), although the use of BoQs has arguably been in decline over the years in the UK. This BoQ approach has promoted a bottom-up approach to preparing project cost estimates across developing Commonwealth countries — a culture that undermines the application of more advanced parametric cost estimating techniques based on statistical models.

Many other laws and policies have an influence on project cost management; they include procurement laws and planning and building control regulations. Therefore, regulations and policies that apply to the construction industries in developing countries should be reviewed in terms of their implications for the cost of delivering construction projects.

Country/economic forces

The challenges facing most developing countries include unstable political systems, lack of transparency and enforcement of rules and regulations, weak economic systems typified by lack of diversification in the economy, and weak investment in human capital (Arayssi, 2020). Economic challenges in developing countries, such as rising inflation, have been worsened by the COVID-19 crisis (Anand and Shreya, 2021). These challenges influence the cost of projects in these countries and should be considered when estimating and budgeting project costs. Public institutions, bribery and corruption, and inflation are evaluated below to explain how they influence the cost of projects in developing countries.

Public institutions

The national context within which construction projects are executed has an impact on project cost management. Effective institutions minimize uncertainty in the project environment, which influences transaction costs on projects (Alonso and Garcimartín, 2013). Ofori (2000) acknowledged that institutional weakness is a key challenge facing the construction industry in developing countries. The public institutions that are meant to enforce laws and regulations are relatively weaker and more bureaucratic in developing and emerging economies. The rule of law estimates from the World Bank's Worldwide Governance Indicators Database captures perceptions of the extent to which agents have confidence in, and abide by, the rules of society, and in particular, the quality of contract enforcement, property rights, the police, and the courts, and the likelihood of crime and violence. Figure 7.3 shows how a sample of developing countries lag behind their developed country counterparts.

The government effectiveness estimate captures perceptions on the quality of public services, the quality of the civil service and the degree of its independence from political pressures, the quality of policy formulation and implementation, and the credibility of the government's commitment to such policies. Figure 7.4 shows that, generally, developing countries lag behind developed countries and have poorer and less stable governance estimates over time. This problem is further complicated by the cultural, economic, and political heterogeneity that can exist across developing countries (Barasa *et al.*, 2017), and even within-country variations in the performance of formal institutions in some large developing countries (Shi *et al.*, 2012). The strength or weakness of public institutions can vary across different regions in the same country, making it

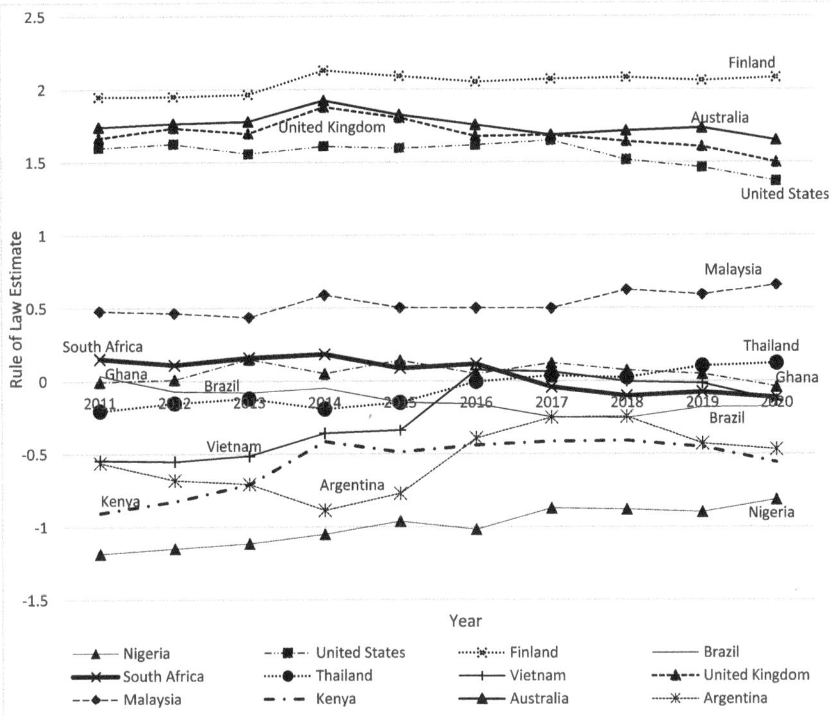

Figure 7.3: Rule of law estimate.

Source: Worldwide Governance Indicators Database [Last updated September 27, 2021].

difficult to predict the impact that public institutions can have on project delivery costs. Yet, the high levels of uncertainty from a lack of faith in strong public institutions make it harder to predict and control the transaction cost of projects in developing countries.

Collier *et al.* (2016) found that unit costs of road works were much higher in countries that had weakened institutions because of security conflicts. Abdel-Galil *et al.* (2020) argued that the ability to quantify the transaction cost of construction projects across different locations will enhance the ability to predict project costs accurately. They sought to model transaction costs of construction projects in Egypt and predicted an average pre-contract transaction cost of 3.64% and a post-contract transaction cost of 8.48%. Further research of this nature is needed to model

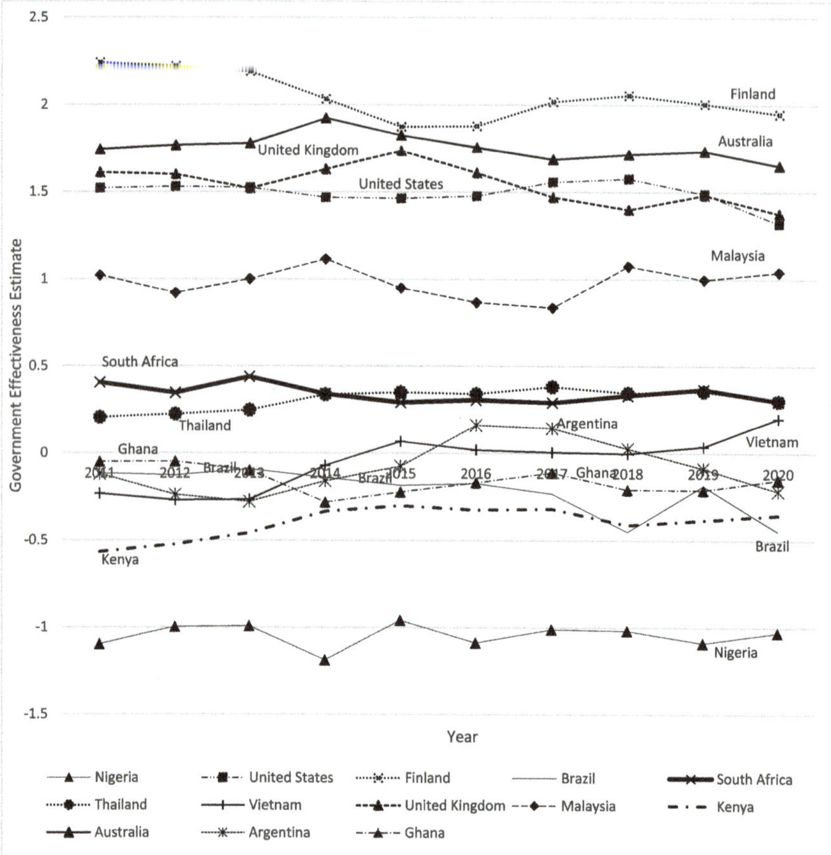

Figure 7.4: Government effectiveness estimate.

Source: Worldwide Governance Indicators Database [Last updated September 27, 2021].

transaction costs of projects in different developing countries to produce percentage adjustment factors, which can then be used to predict, plan, budget, and control transaction costs on projects.

For the public sector, these institutional weaknesses can also manifest themselves as political interference on infrastructure projects, introducing such issues as scope creep, budget uncertainties, delays in decision making, and inflated cost estimates. Weak national institutions are also linked to a higher likelihood of occurrence of bribery and corruption, with the impact on project cost management being more prevalent in developing countries. All these factors make it difficult to estimate and budget for project cost accurately.

Bribery and corruption

Corruption has been defined by Transparency International (2021) as "the abuse of entrusted power for private gain" and poses a major problem for the management of public construction projects (Locatelli *et al.*, 2017; Kirchberger, 2020). A correlation has been established between corruption on projects and the quality and cost of infrastructure that is delivered (Tanzi and Davoodi, 1998; Kirchberger, 2020). Corruption results in higher-than-usual public infrastructure investment and spending, suggesting that project cost estimates will have to be inflated to conceal these project costs. According to Locatelli *et al.* (2017), large, unique, and complex publicly administered projects tend to be more prone to corruption because of the relative ease and opportunity they provide to hide bribes and inflated claims. Whilst corruption remains a global challenge, it tends to be more prevalent in emerging and developing countries due to weaker institutions and the lack of transparency. Colonnelli and Ntungire (2020) argue that the dependence, in developing countries, of the construction industry on public procurement, coupled with the sizeable nature of the contracts, provide public officials and politicians with opportunities for rent-seeking.

Data on corruption from the World Bank's Worldwide Governance Indicators Database indicates in Figure 7.5 that most developing countries lag behind their developed country counterparts. The World Bank Control of Corruption estimate captures perceptions of the extent to which public power is exercised for private gain, including both petty and grand forms of corruption, as well as "capture" of the state by the elite and private interests. This data indicates that projects executed in developing countries are more likely to be affected by corrupt practices, which poses a challenge in the management of the cost of these projects.

This trend is affirmed by many studies on the impact of bribery and corruption on construction projects in developing countries. Collier *et al.* (2016) found that unit costs per km of 40–59 mm asphalt overlays in road works are 30 percent higher in countries with higher levels of corruption such that a country moving from the 75th percentile of corruption to the

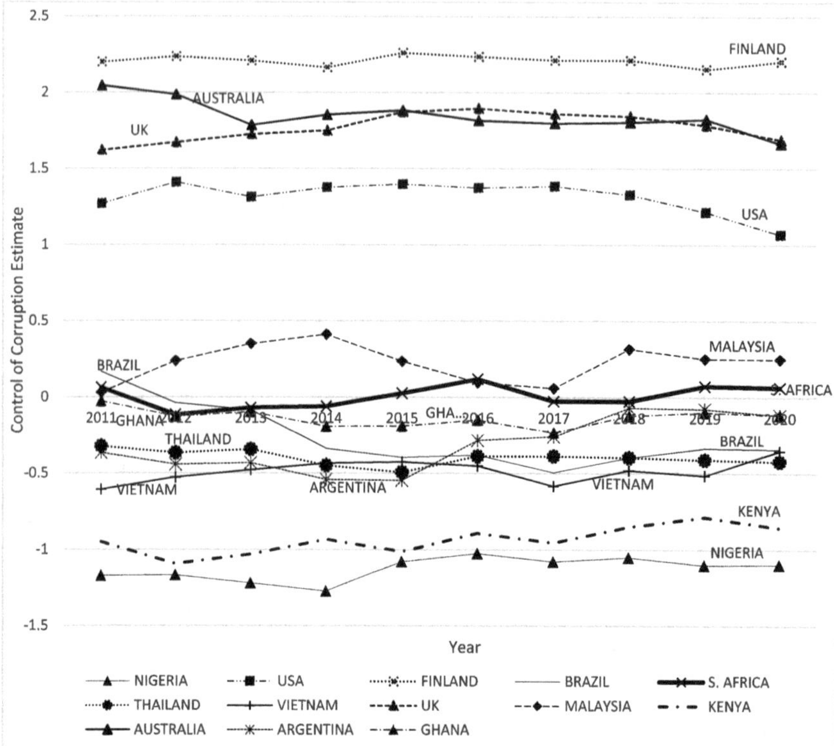

Figure 7.5: Control of corruption estimate.

Source: Worldwide Governance Indicators Database [Last updated September 27, 2021].

20th percentile was associated with a 6.8 percent reduction in unit costs. This has implications for project cost estimation and budgeting practices in developing countries as these will be inaccurate if costs from bribery and corruption are not considered. There is a greater need for implementation of anti-corruption measures to address this problem in developing countries. These are realistic, systematic, and strategic measures that are developed, applied, and enforced to mitigate or expunge corruption and its detrimental effects (Owusu *et al.*, 2019). There is a need for further research on the effectiveness of measures to tackle bribery and corruption and their effects on projects. Efforts should also be made to raise standards of professional ethics in developing countries, implement robust governance systems, and increase transparency of infrastructure project costs.

Inflation rate

A critical factor that accounts for poor project cost management and cost overruns is inflation (Musarat *et al.*, 2020). The inflation rate in the economy is a quantitative measure of the rate at which prices of goods and services increase consistently over time. The standardized measure of inflation is computed by tracking price changes for specified consumer items in an inflation basket, resulting in an inflation metric known as the consumer price index (CPI). Similar measures are computed to track changes in tender prices and construction inputs (materials, labor, and equipment). Thus, the estimation of inflation is a crucial part of project cost management, especially for projects with longer durations. Inflation accounts for changes in construction material prices (Musarat *et al.*, 2020), labor wages (Alaloul *et al.*, 2021), and machinery hire rates (Musarat *et al.*, 2021a). Labor wage increases are also correlated with the rate of inflation. Inflation can have an impact on the reliability of project cost estimates if it is not accurately factored into project budgets (Musarat *et al.*, 2021b).

The usual practice is to estimate additional inflation costs that occur from the date estimates are prepared (estimate base date) using inflation indices. These estimates cater for price increases that occur after the base date, to some point during the construction period. In the UK, there are guidelines in the New Rules of Measurement for Cost Estimating and Cost Planning that inflation should be estimated from the estimate base date through to the mid-point of the estimated construction duration (RICS, 2012). These estimates are based on indices that track increases in construction costs and tender prices in the UK. In the developing countries, there are not always clear and standardized guidelines on how inflation should be factored into cost estimates, making the practice more arbitrary. Also, in most developing countries, inflation indices that track construction cost and tender price increases are not readily available. Thus, inflation estimates are based on standard CPI indices. Therefore, there is a need to track and maintain construction-specific inflation data within developing countries. This will help to improve the accuracy of cost estimates and comparison of differences in inflation rates in construction markets across countries. At present, data on costs in various countries is provided by global consultancy firms (see AECOM, 2020; Arcadis, 2021).

The rate of inflation in developing countries tends to be more erratic and unstable as compared to developed countries, making it more challenging to forecast, as illustrated by the World Bank CPI for selected developed and developing countries in Figure 7.6. This erratic nature of inflation can affect the reliability of project cost estimates in developing countries and, together with the higher likelihood that forecast inflation figures will be inaccurate, makes it challenging to estimate project cost in developing countries.

The unreliability of project budgeting and forecasting is exacerbated by late payments and project delays in developing countries due to poor project management. It is prudent that project cost estimates and cost plans are revised and updated at regular intervals to cater for inflation.

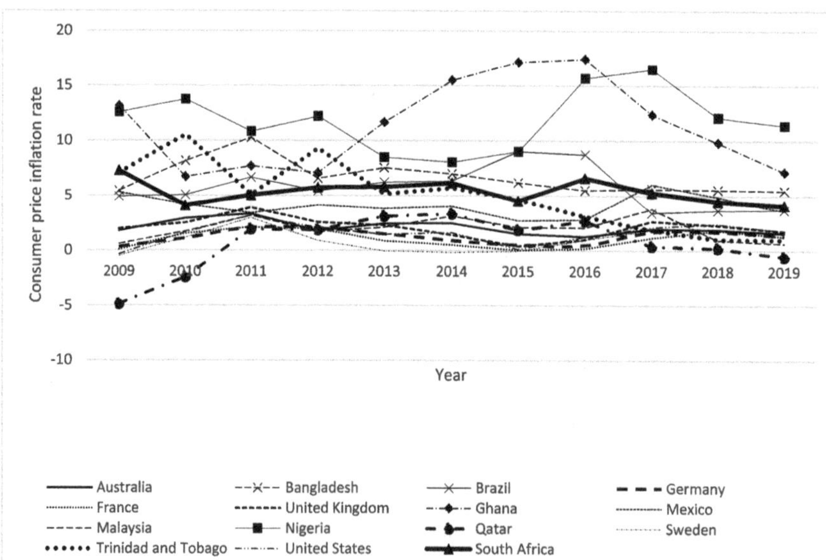

Figure 7.6: Inflation comparison between selected developing and developed countries.

Source: Ha *et al*. (2021).

There should also be standardized guidance for estimating inflation as part of cost management in developing countries.

Global forces

Cost management practices in developing countries are also affected by global forces. These include global standards that have a direct influence on cost management such as the International Cost Management Standards (ICMS) (see Smith, 2016; ICMSC, 2021), the International Ethics Standards (IES) (see Gäbele, 2015; IES, 2021), international initiatives such as the Infrastructure Transparency Initiative (CoST) (see CoST, 2012), and other global policies such as the 2016 Paris Climate Change Agreement (United Nations, 2015) and the 2021 Glasgow Climate Pact (see UN Climate Change Conference, 2021).

International standards

Developing a global dataset of construction costs is a challenge for several reasons, including the highly differentiated nature of construction projects (for example, roads, buildings and bridges), and the different types of costs (for example, estimated costs, contracted costs, and outturn cost) (Kirchberger, 2020). Any success on this front will require a global standard to ensure consistency in the reporting of project costs across countries. The ICMS is a standard being promoted across the coalition of countries that contributed to drafting it (ICMSC 2021). The vision is for the ICMS to provide a single method for grouping, classifying, and reporting construction project costs, eliminating inconsistencies and discrepancies in global cost datasets when benchmarking and predicting project finances (Smith, 2016). Cost data generated in accordance with the ICMS standards allows clients to establish a robust cost envelope in the early project stages, so that design and other developments can take place within those set parameters (Muse, 2019). Of the 49 professional institutions that contributed to the Third Edition of the ICMS, 14 are from developing countries (Botswana, Brazil, China, Fiji, Ghana, India, Indonesia, Kenya, Malaysia, Nigeria, the Philippines, South Africa, Sri Lanka, and Uganda).

The IES was drafted by the International Ethics Standards Coalition (IESC) (2021), which comprises professional institutions from around the world that aim to produce a unified set of shared high-level ethical principles that should be promoted across property, construction, infrastructure, and related professions (Gäbele, 2015). The coalition includes professional institutions from developing countries such as Botswana, Ghana, India, Indonesia, Malaysia, Nigeria, the Philippines, Senegal, South Africa, Thailand, and Uganda. Successful implementation of these universal ethics principles can help to stem the impact of bribery and corruption on project cost management in all countries.

International initiatives and conventions

A number of international initiatives have an influence on cost management practices in some developing countries. An example is CoST, an international initiative aimed at improving transparency and accountability in public infrastructure projects (CoST, 2011, 2012; Hawkins *et al.*, 2015). CoST works with government agencies, and private sector and civil society organizations to promote the disclosure, validation, and interpretation of infrastructure project data in the hope that this transparency informs and empowers citizens to hold decision makers to account. Such an initiative is aimed at helping to minimize mismanagement, cost inefficiencies, and corruption in the management of public projects, hence improving the cost management outcomes. Currently, 18 countries participate in CoST, most of which are developing countries (Argentina, Colombia, Costa Rica, Ecuador, Ethiopia, El Salvador, Ghana, Guatemala, Honduras, Indonesia, Malawi, Mexico, Mozambique, Panama, Thailand, Timor-Leste, and Uganda). Research could be undertaken on the impact of CoST on the management of infrastructure project costs in these developing countries, and how wider participation can be achieved.

The climate emergency and its associated global conventions such as the Glasgow Climate Pact (UN Climate Change Conference, 2021) aim at keeping alive the Paris Agreement to maintain global temperature rise at 1.5°C (United Nations, 2015). These conventions will continue to intensify the emphasis on carbon accounting and carbon costing of construction projects in all countries.

Future trends in project cost management

The future trends influencing project cost management globally include the impact of Construction Industry 4.0 transformations on the ability to analyze and predict project costs more accurately and the integration of carbon accounting and costing into the traditional cost management process. These developments will influence cost management practices in developing countries.

Project cost management and Construction Industry 4.0

Cost management practices are increasingly being influenced by the digital transformations that are having an impact on the management of construction projects. These transformations, which are driving change in every industry, are referred to as Industry 4.0. Moshood *et al.* (2020) described Industry 4.0 as the digital conversion of production and manufacturing, which enables the use of third-stage technologies, such as analytics, big data, and the Internet of Things (IoT). Construction Industry 4.0 is described by Sawhney *et al.* (2020) as "a framework that encompasses industrial production (prefabrication, 3D printing and assembly, offsite manufacture), cyber-physical systems (actuators, sensors, IoT, robots, cobots, drones), and digital and computing technologies (Building Information Modelling (BIM), video and laser scanning, AI and cloud computing, big data and data analytics, reality capture, Blockchain, simulation, augmented reality, data standards and interoperability, and vertical and horizontal integration)." Some of these Construction Industry 4.0 tools and processes have begun to have an impact on project delivery and hence cost management practices in developing countries.

Projects such as the Capitec Bank's 21,500 m^2 headquarters in Stellenbosch, South Africa; 36,700 m^2 premium-grade office development; 144 Oxford Road project in Johannesburg, South Africa; and the Blackbell Shopping Mall, Ikota, Lagos State, Nigeria, are examples of BIM-enabled projects in African countries (BIM Africa Initiative, 2020). The long-term implication of BIM on cost management includes faster, more reliable, and accurate quantity take-off and cost estimating; automated computations that minimize calculation errors; the ability to quickly categorize cost reports and estimates into zones/locations; improved visualization of the elements for measurement and costing purposes; and enhanced communication and collaboration amongst the project team that can help identify and resolve design and construction problems (AECOM, 2020).

The availability of big data analytics tools and the efforts to improve and standardize the collation and reporting of project cost data is likely to transform cost management processes toward cost intelligence. Analytic tools and machine learning algorithms can be applied to large volumes of data to predict the cost of projects or its constituent elements. Managing the cost of refurbishment projects can also be facilitated by the application of video and 3D laser scanning techniques in gathering data on the state of existing assets. Also, virtual and augmented reality devices can enhance the visualization of cost data, which can be applied together with other digital asset data as projects progress on site — as part of digital control rooms that are set-up for projects. The live nature of visualizing costs against progress on site can help make cost control a more proactive process. This way, intelligent data driven cost projections can enable corrective action to be taken as part of cost control measures rather than reacting to and reporting cost overruns.

Project cost management and carbon costing and accounting

The climate emergency and the global drive to achieve the carbon reduction target are also influencing cost management practices. The global ambition to limit temperature rise to 1.5°C has resulted in increasing pressure from funders, regulators, and international agencies to demonstrate efforts being taken to limit carbon impacts of construction projects (IFC, 2019). To evidence carbon reduction efforts at the project level, measurement of the carbon impact of projects (carbon accounting) and the costing of carbon (carbon pricing) is becoming normal practice in most developed countries (RICS, 2017; IFC, 2019) and will extend to many developing countries (Lu *et al.*, 2019). This was a feature of the addition made to the Third Edition of the ICMS, which integrated carbon costing, reporting, and benchmarking into cost management practice (ICMSC, 2021). The developing countries that are members of the

ICMS coalition will have to engage in the accounting and reporting of project carbon data for benchmarking purposes. The integration of carbon costing into traditional costing functions in developing countries is a potential research topic.

Conclusion and further research directions

In the PMI framework, project cost management comprises planning for cost management, estimating project costs, determining the budget, and controlling the project cost. Despite this well-defined framework, it has been established that cost overruns are pervasive on construction projects, particularly in developing countries. The factors that are likely to influence project cost management in developing countries are categorized into project and organizational forces (procurement arrangements, project management competencies, and productivity), sector/industry forces (availability of country-level cost benchmarking indices, and construction industry standards and policies), country/economic forces (the public institutions, bribery and corruption, inflation rate), and global forces (international cost and ethics standards, global initiatives, and policies). These forces and their associated factors have helped to explain how the project environment in developing countries can differ from what prevails in developed countries and how this influences project costs.

Actions for improving project cost management in developing countries include continuing training and development of professionals in project management competencies that are responsive to local cost management challenges; the development of reliable cost data for estimating and benchmarking project costs; and the implementation of anti-corruption measures that can help minimize the impact of bribery and corruption on project costs. Professional institutions in developing countries, whose responsibilities includes cost management, can promote and embed professional standards, policies, and initiatives that can help to improve practices.

Much of the existing literature focuses on factors that cause cost overruns rather than the practices in planning for cost management, cost estimating, budgeting, and cost control, including how they differ across developing and developed countries. Similarly, Olawale and Sun (2010) suggested that the literature is dominated by studies that identify causes of cost and time overruns rather than practices that can help to effectively control the cost of projects. Further research directions could include evaluating cost management practices across developing countries, including how these can be improved, particularly in uncertain and unpredictable project environments. Studies could also examine the application of digital technologies for cost estimating and cost control. There could also be further research on Construction Industry 4.0 transformations and how these are influencing cost estimating, budgeting, and cost control practices, such as BIM implementation and improvements in the reliability of cost estimates and the client's budgeting, use of drone surveys to monitor progress and control the cost of projects, and the shift toward cost analytics and cost intelligence from the developing country perspective.

Project cost management related to Construction Industry 4.0 transformations will require accurate and reliable cost data. Thus, the development of a cost database for projects in developing countries will be another area for future research and development. The World Bank's Roads Cost Knowledge System (ROCKS) represents such an effort. This database on road work costs in developing countries can be used to obtain average and range unit costs, which will help to improve the reliability of cost estimates and reduce the risks generated by cost overruns (World Bank, 2006). Further research, development, and investment is needed to develop and maintain a reliable cost database that has a wider coverage in terms of project types. There is also a need for further research on enhancing ethics in the management of infrastructure project costs in developing countries. Such research could focus on the commercial realities of promoting universal ethics principles across countries despite differences in customs, culture, business practices, and socio-economic circumstances.

References

Abdel-Galil, E., Ibrahim, A.H. and Ahmed Alborkan, A. (2020) Assessment of transaction costs for construction projects. *International Journal of Construction Management*. https://doi.org/10.1080/15623599.2020.1738204.

Abusafiya, H.A.M. and Suliman, Saad M.A. (2017). Causes and effects of cost overrun on construction project in Bahrain: Part I (Ranking of Cost Overrun Factors and Risk Mapping). *Modern Applied Science*, 11(7), 20–27. https://doi.org/10.5539/mas.v11n7p20.

Adebowale, O.J. and Agumba, J.N. (2021). A meta-analysis of factors affecting labour productivity of construction SMEs in developing countries. *Journal of Engineering, Design and Technology* [ahead-of-print]. https://doi.org/10.1108/JEDT-05-2021-0277.

AECOM (2020). *Africa Property & Construction Cost Guide 2020/2021*, 31st Edition, AECOM SA (Pty) Limited. https://communications.aecom.com/Africa_Property_Construction_Cost_Guide_2020-21 [Accessed 12 December 2021].

Ahadzie, D.K., Proverbs, D.G., Olomolaiye, P.O. and Ankrah, N.A. (2009a). Competencies required by project managers for housing construction in Ghana: Implications for CPD agenda. *Engineering, Construction and Architectural Management*, 16(4), 353–375. https://doi.org/10.1108/09699980910970842.

Ahadzie, D.K., Proverbs, D.G., Olomolaiye, P.O. and Ankrah, N.A. (2009b). Towards developing competency-based measures for project managers in mass house building projects in developing countries. *Construction Management and Economics*, 27(1), 89–102. https://doi.org/10.1080/01446190802621028.

Ahiaga-Dagbui, D.D., Smith, S.D., Love, P.E.D. and Ackermann, F. (2015). Spotlight on construction cost overrun research: superficial, replicative and Stagnated. In A. Raiden and E. Aboagye-Nimo (Eds.), *Proceedings of 31st Annual ARCOM Conference, Association of Researchers in Construction Management*, 7–9 September, 2015, Lincoln, UK.

Ahiaga-Dagbui, D., Love, P.E.D., Smith, S.D. and Achermann, F. (2017) Toward a systemic view to cost overrun causation in infrastructure projects: A review and implications for research. *Project Management Journal [online]*, 48(2), 88–98. http://www.pmi.org/learning/library/systemic-view-cost-overrun-causation-infrastructure-projects-10703

Ahmed, S., Memon, A., Memon, N.A., Laghari, A., Akhund, M.A. and Imad, H.U. (2018). Common factors of cost escalation in construction industry of Pakistan. *Engineering, Technology & Applied Science Research*, 8(6), 3508–3511. https://doi.org/10.48084/etasr.2278.

Al Adawi, O.S. and Yahia, H.A. (2021). Causes of costs overrun in road construction project in Oman. *Journal of Student Research*. https://pdfs.

semanticscholar.org/fb0a/ff884d8c7a823c1d20cb4a0ec531599e5e12.pdf?_ga=2.211578141.960335390.1640617253-679570770.1637543267 [Accessed 28 December 2021].

Alaloul, W.S., Musarat, M.A., Liew, M.S., Qureshi, A.H. and Maqsoom, A. (2021). Investigating the impact of inflation on labour wages in Construction Industry of Malaysia. *Ain Shams Engineering Journal*, 12(2), 1575–1582.

Albtoush, A.M. Faten, Doh, S.I. and Rahman, R.A. (2021). Underlying factors of cost overruns in developing countries: Multivariate analysis of Jordanian projects. *4th National Conference on Wind & Earthquake Engineering, IOP Conf. Series: Earth and Environmental Science*, 682 (2021) 012019. https://doi.org/10.1088/1755-1315/682/1/012019.

Aljohani, A., Ahiaga-Dagbui, D. and Moore, D. (2017). Construction projects cost overrun: What does the literature tell us? *International Journal of Innovation, Management and Technology*, 8(2), 137–143. https://doi.org/10.18178/IJIMT.2017.8.2.717.

Alonso, J.A. and Garcimartín, C. (2013). The determinants of institutional quality. More on the debate. *Journal of International Development*, 25(2), 206–226. https://doi.org/10.1002/jid.1710.

Amoa-Abban, K. and Allotey, S. (2014). Cost overruns in building construction projects: A case study of a Government of Ghana Project in Accra. *Developing Country Studies*, 4(24), 54–64. https://www.iiste.org/Journals/index.php/DCS/article/viewFile/17118/17478 [Accessed 28 December 2021].

Anand, B. and Shreya, G. (2021). Pandemic inflation: A menace to tame for developing countries? https://blogs.lse.ac.uk/southasia/2021/10/25/pandemic-inflation-a-menace-to-tame-for-developing-countries/ [Accessed 28 December 2021].

Andrić, J.M., Mahamadu, A.-M., Wang, J., Zou, P.X.W. and Zhong, R. (2019). The cost performance and causes of overruns in infrastructure development projects in Asia. *Journal of Civil Engineering and Management*, 25(3), 203–214. https://doi.org/10.3846/jcem.2019.8646.

APM (2019). *APM Body of Knowledge*, 7th Edition. Association for Project Management, Princes Risborough, UK.

Arayssi, D. (2020). The developing countries: Challenges in the global economy. https://ssrn.com/abstract=3589489 or http://dx.doi.org/10.2139/ssrn.3589489 [Accessed 27 December 2021].

Arcadis (2021). Investing for a sustainable recovery: International-Construction-Cost-Index-2021. https://www.arcadis.com/en/knowledge-hub/perspectives/global/2021/international-construction-costs-2021 [Accessed 16 December 2021].

Barasa, L., Knoben, J., Vermeulen, P., Kimuyu, P. and Kinyanjui, B. (2017). Institutions, resources, and innovation in East Africa: A firm level approach. *Research Policy*, 46(1), 280–291. https://doi.org/10.1016/j.respol.2016.11.008.

Barbosa, F., Woetzel, J., Mischke, J., Ribeirinho, M.J., Sridhar, M., Parsons, M., Bertram, N. and Brown, S. (2017). *Reinventing Construction: A Route To Higher Productivity*. McKinsey Global Institute.

Berkeley, T. (2020). A Review of High Speed 2, Dissenting Report by Lord Tony Berkeley House of Lords. https://documentcloud.adobe.com/link/review?uri=urn%3Aaaid%3Ascds%3AUS%3A8e9c8f87-2650-4aa0-8e0f-0eaf6e709640#pageNum=71 [Accessed 23 March 2021].

Bhattacharya, A., Romani, M. and Stern, N. (2012). Infrastructure for Development: Meeting the Challenge. Policy paper sponsored by The Centre for Climate Change Economics and Policy, the Grantham Research Institute on Climate Change and the Environment, in collaboration with the Intergovernmental Group of Twenty-Four on International Monetary Affairs and Development (G-24) (June). http://www.lse.ac.uk/GranthamInstitute/wp-content/uploads/2014/03/PP-infrastructure-for-development-meeting-the-challenge.pdf [Accessed 20 December 2021].

BIM Africa Initiative (2020). African BIM Report 2020, Research and Development Committee. https://bimafrica.org/download/african-bim-report-2020/?wpdmdl=5000&masterkey=5f4ad4978fde2 [Accessed 15 December 2021].

BSI (2020). *BS ISO 21502:2020 Project, Programme and Portfolio Management — Guidance on Project Management,* 1st Edition. Geneva, Switzerland.

Collier, P., Kirchberger, M. and Söderbom, M. (2016). The cost of road infrastructure in low- and middle-income countries. *The World Bank Economic Review*, 30(3), 522–48. https://doi.org/10.1093/wber/lhv037.

Colonnelli, E. and Ntungire, N. (2020). Construction and public procurement in Uganda. In J. Page and F. Tarp (Eds.), *Mining for Change: Natural Resources and Industry in Africa*. Oxford University Press, Oxford, UK, pp. 326–348. https://doi.org/10.1093/oso/9780198851172.003.0015.

Construction Global (2020). Major construction projects that went billions over budget. https://www.constructionglobal.com/construction-projects/info-graphic-major-construction-projects-that-went-billions-over-budget [Accessed 12 December 2021].

CoST (2011). Report on baseline studies: International comparison. Technical Report. Construction Sector Transparency Initiative, London.

CoST (2012). Construction sector transparency initiative information pack. CoST International Secretariat, London, UK. https://infrastructuretransparency.org/wp-content/uploads/2018/06/37_CoST_Information_Pack.pdf [Accessed 28 December 2021].

Designing Buildings Ltd (2021). Ryugyong Hotel, North Korea. https://www.designingbuildings.co.uk/wiki/Ryugyong_Hotel,_North_Korea [Accessed 22 April 2021].

Ejaz, N., Ali, I. and Tahir, M. (2011). Assessment of delays and cost overruns during construction projects in Pakistan. *International Conference on Structural Engineering Construction and Management*. http://dl.lib.uom.lk/handle/123/9431 [Accessed 15 May 2021].

El-Ahwal, M., El-Attar, S.S. and Abdel-Hafez, W.A. (2016). Factors leading to cost overrun occurrence in construction projects. *Port Said Engineering Research Journal*, 20(1), 71–77. https://doi.org/10.21608/pserj.2016.33641.

Elgot, J. (2016). Urgent clarity needed on HS2 costs and timescale, MPs warn. *The Guardian*. https://www.theguardian.com/uk-news/2016/sep/14/hs2-high-speed-rail-project-commons-public-accounts-committee-report [Accessed 22 April 2021].

Enshassi, A., Kumaraswamy, M. and Al-Najjar, J. (2010). Significant factors causing time and cost overruns in construction projects in the Gaza Strip: Contractors' perspective. *International Journal of Construction Management*, 10(1), 35–60. https://doi.org/10.1080/15623599.2010.10773137.

Fagbenle, O.I. and Owolabi, J.D. (2012). Developing a realistic budget for construction projects: Lessons from Nigeria. *International Review of Business and Social Sciences*, 1(3), 17–23.

Farajian, M. (2010). Transaction cost estimation model for US infrastructure Public Private Partnerships, Doctoral dissertation, University of Maryland. University Library. http://hdl.handle.net/1903/10494.

Flyvbjerg, B., Bruzelius, N. and Rothengatter, W. (2003). *Megaprojects and Risk: An Anatomy of Ambition*. Cambridge University Press, Cambridge.

Flyvbjerg, B., Garbuio, M. and Lovallo, D. (2014). Better forecasting for large capital projects. *McKinsey on Finance*, Number 52, Autumn 2014, pp. 9–13.

Flyvbjerg, B., Hon, C.-K. and Fok, W.H. (2016). Reference class forecasting for Hong Kong's major roadworks projects. *Proceedings of the Institution of Civil Engineers, Civil Engineering*. http://dx.doi.org/10.1680/jcien.15.00075.

Gäbele, F. (2015). CLGE part of the International Ethics Standards Coalition established at the United Nations in New York. *GeoInformatics*, 18(2), 40.

https://www.proquest.com/openview/d247ae7b800189b43764532346339cfb/1/advanced [Accessed 28 December 2021].

Gareis, R. and Huemann, M. (2000). Project management competences in the project-oriented organization. In J.R. Turner and S.J. Simister (Eds.), *Gower Handbook of Project Management*. Gower Publishing, Hampshire, pp. 709–721.

Garemo, N., Matzinger, S. and Palter, R. (2015). Building big infrastructure projects is always risky, but there are ways to improve the odds of a smooth landing. McKinsey & Company. https://www.mckinsey.com/business-functions/operations/our-insights/megaprojects-the-good-the-bad-and-the-better [Accessed 23 April 2021].

Goldsmith, H. and Boeuf, P. (2019). Digging beneath the iron triangle: The Chunnel with 2020 hindsight. *Journal of Mega Infrastructure & Sustainable Development*, 1(1), 79–93. https://doi.org/10.1080/24724718.2019.1597407.

Gurara, D., Klyuev, V., Mwase, N., Presbitero, A., Xu, X.C. and Bannister, G. (2017). Trends and challenges in infrastructure investment in low-income developing countries. IMF Working Paper WP/17/233, International Monetary Fund. https://www.imf.org/-/media/Files/Publications/WP/2017/wp17233.ashx [Accessed 23 December 2021].

Ha, J., Kose, M.A. and Ohnsorge, F. (2021). One-stop source: A global database of inflation. *Policy Research Working Paper 9737*. World Bank, Washington, DC.

Hasan, A., Baroudi, B., Elmualim, A. and Rameezdeen, R. (2018). Factors affecting construction productivity: A 30 year systematic review. *Engineering, Construction and Architectural Management*, 25(7), 916–937. https://doi.org/10.1108/ECAM-02-2017-0035.

Hawkins, J., Fernz, B., Matthews, P., Prado, M. and Wells, J. (2015). *Engineers against poverty — The Construction Sector Transparency (CoST) Initiative: Final Report for the World Bank Development Grant Facility*. https://infrastructuretransparency.org/wp-content/uploads/2018/06/156_CoST-Final-Report-for-the-World-Bank-Development-Grant-Facility-EAP.pdf [Accessed 28 December 2021].

Heravi, G. and Mohammadian, M. (2021). Investigating cost overruns and delay in urban construction projects in Iran. *International Journal of Construction Management*, 21(9), 958–968. https://doi.org/10.1080/15623599.2019.1601394.

ICMSC (2021). *ICMS: Global Consistency in Presenting Construction Life Cycle Costs and Carbon Emissions*, 3rd Edition. International Cost Management Standard Coalition, https://icmscblog.files.wordpress.com/2021/11/icms_3rd_edition_final.pdf.

IES (2021). *International Ethics Standards: An ethical framework for the global property market.* https://ies-coalition.org/wp-content/uploads/2021/05/International-Ethics-Standards-May-1st-2021.pdf [Accessed 25 December 2021].

IFC (2019). *Greening construction: The role of carbon pricing*. https://www.ifc.org/wps/wcm/connect/4a3fce61-a95b-4944-8059-62b9f9f450ea/201905-Greening-Construction-Full-Report.pdf?MOD=AJPERES&CVID=mH6grRT [Accessed 28 December 2021].

Ikechukwu, A.C., Emoh, F.I. and Kelvin, O.A. (2017). Causes and effects of cost overruns in public building construction projects delivery, in Imo State, Nigeria. *IOSR Journal of Business and Management*, 19(7), 13–20. https://doi.org/10.9790/487X-1907021320.

Islam, M.S. and Trigunarsyah, B. (2017). Construction delays in developing countries: A review. *Journal of Construction Engineering and Project Management*, 7(1), 1–12. https://doi.org/10.6106/JCEPM.2017.3.30.001.

Kaming, P.F., Olomolaiye, P.O., Holt, G.D. and Harris, F.C. (1997). Factors influencing craftsmen's productivity in Indonesia. *International Journal of Project Management*, 15(1), 21–30. https://doi.org/10.1016/S0263-7863(96)00019-1.

Kirchberger, M. (2020). Construction sector in developing countries: Some key issues. In J. Page and F. Tarp (Eds.), *Mining for Change: Natural Resources and Industry in Africa*. Oxford University Press. https://doi.org/10.1093/oso/9780198851172.003.0003.

KPMG (2015). *Climbing the curve: 2015 Global Construction Project Owner's Survey*. KPMG International, Global construction survey 2015. https://assets.kpmg/content/dam/kpmg/pdf/2015/04/global-construction-survey-2015.pdf [Accessed 23 August 2022].

Le-Hoai, L., Lee, Y.D. and Lee, J.Y. (2008). Delay and cost overruns in Vietnam large construction projects: A comparison with other selected countries. *KSCE Journal of Civil Engineering*, 12, 367–377. https://doi.org/10.1007/s12205-008-0367-7.

Lehto, A.M. and Aaltonen, K. (2021). Cultural change in the construction industry: The role of project alliance organizational culture. *The Journal of Modern Project Management*, 8(3), 100–111. https://doi.org/10.19255/JMPM02509.

Leigland, J. (2018). Public–private partnerships in developing countries: The emerging evidence-based critique. *The World Bank Research Observer*, 33(1), 103–134. https://doi.org/10.1093/wbro/lkx008.

Li, H., Arditi, D. and Wang, Z. (2013). Factors that affect transaction costs in construction projects. *Journal of Construction Engineering and Management*, 139(1), 60–68. https://doi.org/10.1061/(ASCE)CO.1943-7862.0000573.

Liu, L., Wehbe, G. and Sisovic, J. (2010). The accuracy of hybrid estimating approaches. A case study of an Australian State road and traffic authority. *The Engineering Economist,* 55(3), 225–245. https://doi.org/10.1080/0013791X.2010.502962.

Locatelli, G., Mariani, G., Sainati, T. and Greco, M. (2017). Corruption in public projects and megaprojects: There is an elephant in the room! *International Journal of Project Management*, 35(3), 252–268. https://doi.org/10.1016/j.ijproman.2016.09.010.

Love, P.E.D. and Ahiaga-Dagbui, D.D. (2018). Debunking fake news in a post-truth era: The plausible untruths of cost underestimation in transport infrastructure projects. *Transportation Research Part A: Policy and Practice*, 113, 357–368. https://doi.org/10.1016/j.tra.2018.04.019.

Love, P.E.D., Smith, J., Simpson, I., Regan, M. and Olatunji, O. (2015). Understanding the landscape of overruns in transportation infrastructure projects. *Environment and Planning B: Planning and Design,* 42(3), 490–509. https://doi.org/10.1068/b130102p.

Love, P.E.D., Ahiaga-Dagbui, D.D. and Irani, Z. (2016). Cost overruns in transportation infrastructure projects: Sowing the seeds for a probabilistic theory of causation, *Transportation Research Part A: Policy and Practice*, 92, 184–194. https://doi.org/10.1016/j.tra.2016.08.007.

Love, P.E.D., Sing, M.C.P., Ika, L.A. and Newton, S. (2019). The cost performance of transportation projects: The fallacy of the Planning Fallacy account. *Transportation Research Part A: Policy and Practice*, 122, 1–20. https://doi.org/10.1016/j.tra.2019.02.004.

Lu, K., Jiang, X., Tam, V.W.Y., Li, M., Wang, H, Xia, B. and Chen, Q. (2019). Development of a carbon emissions analysis framework using building information modelling and life cycle assessment for the construction of hospital projects. *Sustainability*, 11(22), 6274. https://doi.org/10.3390/su11226274.

Mansur, S.A., Zin, R.M. and Linbo, L. (2019). Components of cost overrun in China construction projects. *IOP Conference Series: Materials Science and Engineering*, 620. https://doi.org/10.1088/1757-899X/620/1/012081.

Mbachu, J. and Nkado, R. (2007). Factors constraining successful building project implementation in South Africa. *Construction Management and Economics*, 25(1), 39–54. https://doi.org/10.1080/01446190600601297.

Meeampol, S and Ogunlana, S.O. (2006). Factors affecting cost and time performance on highway construction projects: Evidence from Thailand. *Journal of Financial Management of Property and Construction*, 11(1), 3–20.

Memon, A.H., Rahman, I.A. and Azis, A.A.A. (2012). Time and cost performance in construction projects in southern and central regions of Peninsular Malaysia. *International Journal of Advances in Applied Sciences*, 1(1), 45–52. http://doi.org/10.11591/ijaas.v1.i1.pp45-52.

Memon, A.H., Rahman, I.A. and Abdul Aziz, A.A. (2012). The cause factors of large project's cost overrun: A survey in the southern part of Peninsular Malaysia. *International Journal of Real Estate Studies*, 7(2). https://www.utm.my/intrest/files/2013/08/THE-CAUSE-FACTORS-OF-LARGE-PROJECT%E2%80%99S-COST-OVERRUN-A-SURVEY-IN-THE-SOUTHERN-PART-OF-PENINSULAR-MALAYSIA.pdf [Accessed 23 August 2022].

Michaelis, A.R. (1996). The great channel tunnel. *Interdisciplinary Science Reviews*, 21(1), 1–5. https://doi.org/10.1179/isr.1996.21.1.1.

Mills, G., Evans, D. and Candlish, C. (2020). Anglian Water@ one Alliance: A new approach to supply chain management. In S. Pryke (Ed.), *Successful Construction Supply Chain Management: Concepts and Case Studies*. John Wiley & Sons Ltd., Chichester, UK, pp. 237–249.

Moshood, T.D., Adeleke, A.Q., Nawanir, G., Ajibike, W.A. and Shittu, R.A. (2020). Emerging challenges and sustainability of Industry 4.0 Era in the Malaysian construction industry. *International Journal of Recent Technology and Engineering*, 9(1), 1627–1634. https://doi.org/10.35940/ijrte.A2564.059120. SSRN: https://ssrn.com/abstract=3599053

Mrityunjay, B. (2010). Bandra–Worli Sea Link: An engineering marvel. *Science Reporter*, March. http://nopr.niscair.res.in/bitstream/123456789/7515/1/SR%2047%283%29%2029-33.pdf [Accessed 22 April 2021].

Mulalo, R., Ibrahimu, K. and Nwobodo-Anyadiegwu, E. (2018). Project cost overrun in the South African construction sector: A case study of Johannesburg metropolis. *Proceedings of the International Conference on Industrial Engineering and Operations Management*, Pretoria, Johannesburg, South Africa, October 29–November 1, 2018, ©IEOM Society International.

Musarat, M.A., Alaloul, W.S. and Liew, M.S. (2021a). Impact of inflation rate on construction projects budget: A review. *Ain Shams Engineering Journal*, 12(1), 407–414. https://www.scopus.com/inward/record.uri?eid=2-s2.0-85086455403&doi=10.1016%2fj.asej.2020.04.009&partnerID=40&md5=1d4757b9a332d03bd4b28f2855dff723

Musarat, M.A., Alaloul, W.S. and Liew, M.S. (2021b). Inflation rate and labours' wages in construction projects: economic relation investigation, *Engineering, Construction and Architectural Management* [ahead-of-print]. https://doi.org/10.1108/ECAM-07-2020-0478.

Musarat, M.A., Alaloul, W.S., Liew, M.S., Maqsoom, A. and Qureshi, A.H. (2020). Investigating the impact of inflation on building materials prices in construction industry. *Journal of Building Engineering*, 32, 101485.

Muse, A. (2019). We now have a truly global structure in place for growing the project and cost management professions internationally, *RICS Construction Journal*. https://www.proquest.com/openview/84d27830b93fbdf24aa4de5f175b2566/1?pq-origsite=gscholar&cbl=2028822 [Accessed 28 December 2021].

Nani, G., Edwards, P., Adjei-Kumi, T., Badu, E. and Amoah, P. (2012). Customisation and desirable characteristics of a standard method of measurement for building works in Ghana. *The Australasian Journal of Construction Economics and Building*, 8(2), 30–40. https://doi.org/10.5130/ajceb.v8i2.3004.

NAO (2020). High Speed Two: A progress update. Report by the Comptroller and Auditor General, HC 40 SESSION 2019–20 24 January. NAO, London, UK.

National Academy of Sciences (2003). *Completing the "Big Dig": Managing the Final Stages of Boston's Central Artery/Tunnel Project*. National Academy of Engineering, National Research Council, and Transportation Research Board. Washington, DC: The National Academies Press. https://doi.org/10.17226/10629.

Naveenkumar, G.V. and Prabhu, V. (2016). Factors influencing time and cost overruns in construction projects. *International Journal of Innovative Research in Science, Engineering and Technology*, 5(4), 6468–6473. https://doi.org/10.15680/IJIRSET.2016.0504254.

Nurafiqah, A.H. (2017). Cost overrun of construction project in Pahang: Causes and solution. Unpublished project paper, Faculty of Civil Engineering and Earth Resources, Universiti Malaysia Pahang. http://umpir.ump.edu.my/id/eprint/21388/ [Accessed 28 December 2021].

Ofori, G. (2000). Challenges of construction industries in developing countries: Lessons from various countries. In *2nd International Conference on Construction in Developing Countries: Challenges Facing the Construction Industry in Developing Countries*, Gaborone, Botswana, November.

Olawale, Y.A. and Sun, M. (2010). Cost and time control of construction projects: Inhibiting factors and mitigating measures in practice, *Construction*

Management and Economics, 28(5), 509–526. https://doi.org/10.1080/01446191003674519.

Owusu, E.K., Chan, A.P., DeGraft, O.-M., Ameyaw, E.E. and Osei-Kyei, R. (2019). Contemporary review of anti-corruption measures in construction project management. *Project Management Journal*, 50(1), 40–56. https://doi.org/10.1177/8756972818808983.

Park, Y.-I. and Papadopoulou, T.C. (2012). Causes of cost overruns in transport infrastructure projects in Asia: Their significance and relationship with project size. *Built Environment Project and Asset Management*, 2(2), 195–216. https://doi.org/10.1108/20441241211280873.

PMI (2016). *The Construction Extension to the PMBOK® Guide*. Project Management Institute, Newtown Square, PA.

PMI (2017). *A Guide to the Project Management Body of Knowledge (PMBOK Guide),* 6th Edition. Project Management Institute, Newtown Square, PA.

Ramabodu, M.S. and Verster, J.J.P. (2010). Factors contributing to cost overruns of construction projects. *Proceedings of 5th Built Environment Conference*, 18–20 July 2010, Durban, South Africa.

Regan, M., Smith, J. and Love, P.E.D. (2015). Better infrastructure procurement for public private partnerships: An Australian perspective. In T.M. Froese, L. Newton, F. Sadeghpour and D.J. Vanier (Eds.), *Proceedings of ICSC15: The Canadian Society for Civil Engineering 5th International/11th Construction Specialty Conference*, University of British Columbia, Vancouver, Canada, June 7–10.

Reichold, K. and Graf, B. (1999). *Buildings that Changed the World.* Prestel Publishing, Munich, New York.

RICS (2012). *NRM 1 — Order of Cost Estimating and Cost Planning for Capital Building Works*, 2nd Edition. RICS Books, Coventry.

RICS (2017). Whole life carbon assessment for the built environment, 1st Edition. https://www.rics.org/globalassets/rics-website/media/news/whole-life-carbon-assessment-for-the--built-environment-november-2017.pdf [Accessed 25 December 2021].

Roachanakanan, K. (2005, May). A case study of cost overruns in a Thai Condominium Project. Unpublished PhD thesis, Texas A&M University.

Rwelamila, P.M.D. (2007). Project management competence in public sector infrastructure organisations, *Construction Management and Economics*, 25(1), 55–66. https://doi.org/10.1080/01446190601099210.

Sawhney, A., Riley, M. and Irizarry, J. (2020). *Construction 4.0: An Innovation Platform for the Built Environment*, 1st Edition. Routledge. https://doi.org/10.1201/9780429398100.

Shah, R. K. (2016). An exploration of causes for delay and cost overruns in construction projects: Case study of Australia, Malaysia & Ghana. *Journal of Advanced College of Engineering and Management*, 2(1), 1–15. https://doi.org/10.3126/jacem.v2i0.16097.

Shi, W.S., Sun, S.L. and Peng, M.W. (2012). Sub-National institutional contingencies, network positions, and IJV partner selection, *Journal of Management Studies*, 49(7), 1221–1245. https://doi.org/10.1111/j.1467-6486.2012.01058.x.

Smith, P. (2016). Global professional standards for project cost management. *Procedia — Social and Behavioral Sciences*, 226, 124–131. https://doi.org/10.1016/j.sbspro.2016.06.170.

Subramani, T., Sruthi, P.S. and Kavitha, M. (2014). Causes of cost overrun in construction. *IOSR Journal of Engineering (IOSRJEN)*, 4(6), 1–7. https://doi.org/10.9790/3021-04640107.

Tanzi, V. and Davoodi, H. (1998). *Roads to Nowhere: How Corruption in Public Investment Hurts Growth*. International Monetary Fund. https://www.imf.org/external/pubs/ft/issues12/index.htm [Accessed 6 October 2021].

Transparency International (2021). *What is Corruption*. https://www.transparency.org/en/what-is-corruption [Accessed 6 October 2021].

Tyson, J. (2018). Partnering with private finance for developing country infrastructure: Five challenges, five solutions. ODI Working Paper. London: Overseas Development Institute. https://odi.org/en/publications/private-infrastructure-finance-in-developing-countries-five-challenges-five-solutions/ [Accessed 25 December 2021].

UN Climate Change Conference (2021). COP26: The Glasgow climate pact. https://ukcop26.org/wp-content/uploads/2021/11/COP26-Presidency-Outcomes-The-Climate-Pact.pdf [Accessed 28 December 2021].

United Nations (2015). Paris agreement. https://unfccc.int/sites/default/files/english_paris_agreement.pdf [Accessed 28 December 2021].

Wikipedia (2021). Bandra–Worli Sea Link. https://en.wikipedia.org/wiki/Bandra%E2%80%93Worli_Sea_Link#cite_note-dna-https://www.youtube.com/watch?v-14 [Accessed 22 April 2021].

Winch, G.M. (2013). Escalation in major projects: Lessons from the channel fixed link. *International Journal of Project Management*, 31(5), 724–734. https://doi.org/10.1016/j.ijproman.2013.01.012.

World Bank (2006). *Road Costs Knowledge System (ROCKS) Version 2.3 User's Guide*. Transport and Urban Development Department, The World Bank, Washington, DC.

Zou, P.X.W., Zhang, G. and Wang, J. (2007). Understanding the key risks in construction projects in China. *International Journal of Project Management*, 25, 601–614. https://doi.org/10.1016/j.ijproman.2007.03.001.

https://doi.org/10.1142/9789811224720_0008

Chapter 8

Quality Management in Construction Projects in Developing Countries — Where To, From Current Body of Knowledge?

Pantaleo D. Rwelamila

University of South Africa

Abstract

Construction industries, like other industries across the world, consider Quality as one of the primary project parameters. Thus, generic project management bodies of knowledge (BoK) published by different project management profession voluntary organizations, such as the Association for Project Management (APM), Project Management Institute (PMI), and International Association of Project and Program Management (IAPPM), consider project quality management (PQM) as one of the central knowledge areas. These organizations provide generic frameworks for managing project quality across all industries; they do not deal with specific industries (except the PMI publication, which has a Construction extension). Furthermore, they do not seem to distinguish between PQM issues in industrialized and developing countries. There are strong indications to suggest that project management dynamics in industrialized countries differ significantly from those in developing countries. Hence, these differences are manifested in the management of construction project parameters. This chapter takes a leaf from the theme of this book where existing BoK PQM frameworks are primarily adapted as baseline approaches and developing country quality management approach variants are embraced as additions or improvers to propose an appropriate developing country quality management approach. In order to present an appropriate PQM body of knowledge for developing countries, the chapter covers the following: revisit quality management BoK as it exists and highlight its shortfalls and present approaches which will work in the special context of developing countries; present and discuss mainstream project management; consider quality management issues that are of direct relevance to developing countries; discuss likely future developments in PQM in developing countries; and finally, propose further research and further development of PQM as it relates to developing countries.

Keywords: Quality management, construction projects, body of knowledge, developing countries, the future

Introduction

A construction project is considered successful when it is completed on time, within budget, following specifications (Quality Management), meeting health and safety and environmental requirements, meeting utility requirements, and to stakeholders' satisfaction (Ofori, 2000; Windapo and Rotimi 2012; Rwelamila *et al.*, 2015; Abdullahi *et al.*, 2019). However, levels of project performance and project success are significantly low in the construction industry, especially in developing countries (Odediran *et al.*, 2013; Isa *et al.*, 2013). One of the significant reasons for owners' dissatisfaction with construction projects is their poor quality (Abdulrahman *et al.*, 2010; Achi *et al.*, 2007). Every customer wants a quality product that meets its needs and is worth the value of the money it has invested in the product (Achi *et al.*, 2007). Therefore, customers tend to be satisfied when quality products and services are delivered to them. Project executors need to understand the customers' needs and requirements so that both their stated and implied quality levels can always be met. Understanding the customers' needs and requirements could enable organizations to implement quality management practices and imbibe cultures which guarantee their customers' satisfaction.

A strong commitment to quality and continuous company-wide quality improvement will lead to improvement in quality performance and increased profit margins for any construction organization. Poor performance has adverse effects that transcend the industry to have an impact on national growth and sustainable development (Windapo, 2006). For example, structural failure seems to abound in developing countries (Taiwo and Afolami, 2010) with worst cases resulting in building collapse, often with major causalities (Windapo and Rotimi, 2012). In a nutshell, quality management practices have a direct impact on quality enhancement, elimination of rework, and the enabling of synergy between different project parameters, and resulting in client satisfaction (Smallwood and Rossouw, 2008; Alwi *et al.*, 1999).

Construction (building, civil engineering, and other types of work) has become more complex, partly due to project owners' increasing demands and expectations. Hoonakker (2006) reported that the construction industry's clients are demanding improved quality of service, quicker construction of buildings, and innovations in technology. As a result, construction products and systems have had to become more innovative to meet the owners' demands. However, newer and innovative procurement processes bring about challenges that contractors need to manage effectively while delivering value to the project owner. Also, with the advent of globalization, construction firms are striving to achieve internationally accepted quality levels to ensure their leading position in emerging international markets. Hence the need for a proper system that provides more quality when compared to other project objectives (Abdulrahman *et al.*, 2010). There are strong indications to suggest that there is a need for a global collection of processes, best practices, terminologies, and guidelines that are accepted as quality management standards across construction industries. The global collection should be able to provide a framework for quality management across countries for clients, contractors, consultants, materials suppliers, plant suppliers, and construction industry policymakers. Contemporary umbrella global collections of processes, best practices, terminologies, and guidelines on project management are known as Project Management Bodies of Knowledge (PMBOK), where quality management (QM) in projects is one of the PMBOK units. Because the body of knowledge is constantly growing as practitioners discover new methods or best practices, it must be updated and effectively disseminated.

Contemporary examples of well-established PMBOK include:

- International Project Management Association (IPMA) Individual Competence Baseline (IPMA ICB) — version 4.0; IPMA Project Excellence Baseline (IPMA PEB) — version 1.0; and IPMA Organisational Competence Baseline (IPMA OCB) — version 1.1 (IPMA, 2016);
- International Association of Project and Program Management (IAPPM) — IAPPM Project and Portfolio Model (IAPPM, 2003);
- Association for Project Management (APM) — Body of Knowledge, 7th Edition (APM, 2019);
- Project Management Institute (PMI) — A Guide to the Project Management Body of Knowledge (6th Edition) (PMI, 2017); and
- International Organization for Standardization (ISO): 21500: Guidance on Project Management (ISO, 2012).

The amount of detail in each of the above documents differs significantly. The documents are not specific for particular industries. They provide generic information that can be adopted for different projects in different industries or sectors by clients, contractors, consultants, materials suppliers, plant suppliers, and policymakers.

It is important to note that *most of the PMBOK documents are* intended to be subsets of what could be referred to as a universal set project management (as a discipline) body of knowledge that is generally recognized as a good practice project management theory and practice by practicing project managers. Being generally recognized means the knowledge and practices described are applicable to most projects most of the time and there is a consensus about their value and usefulness. Thus, "good practice" means there is a general agreement that the application of the knowledge, skills, tools, and techniques can enhance the chances of success over many projects. This means that sometimes the "latest" project management trends may not be part of the latest version of what is found in a particular *PMBOK document*. This chapter is written with this baseline understanding which is accepted as a lesson in addressing the theme of this chapter and consequently the theme of the book.

Quality management BoK documents as they exist — Their shortfalls in context of construction projects in developing countries

A close look at all the PMBOK documents, especially those published by APM (2019), PMI (2017), IAPPM (2003), and other related documents such as the Project Excellence Baseline by IPMA (2016) and guidance on project management by ISO (2012) shows that they seem to deal with project parameters at a generic level. They address fundamentals of project parameters from a position of generality without dealing with contextual matters within particular region or country set-ups. Thus, challenges of developing countries are not reflected directly in these documents. It is expected that those managing construction projects or those becoming project core team members will adapt what is provided in these documents to suit the challenges facing projects in developing countries.

There is evidence to suggest that developing countries have been facing a myriad of social, political, and economic problems, which influence the way in which project parameters are managed in these countries (Rwelamila and Abdul-Rashid 2021; Rwelamila and Ogunlana, 2019). That these problems have resulted in an exacerbation of poverty, inadequate infrastructure, higher rates of unemployment, and so forth, and occasional outbursts of civil unrest should condition construction project management lenses when managing project quality in developing countries. Consequently, the execution of roads, dams, water supply systems, schools, houses, hospitals, factories, and other projects that support development within acceptable levels of quality has become imperative. According to Morris *et al.* (2000), this is because the initiation of these projects is considered to drive development and contribute toward the alleviation of the effects of most social, political, and economic problems. To guarantee the actualization of such projects, especially within the limits of the resources available and quality constraints in such countries, project management practice must be enriched with appropriate developing country lenses as described above.

This section undertakes a critical review of contemporary PMBOK documents and considers the possibility of adapting their PQM frameworks to formulate appropriate construction PQM approaches suitable for developing countries. The subsequent sections are organized to provide an overview of project quality management practice in developing countries — primarily guided by the question: "How generic are quality management BoK documents as they exist in the eyes of a developing country construction industry?" The literature review on PQM is based on the works of adherents of contemporary PMBOK documents (specifically Burke (2006); Juran (1995), International Organization for Standardization (2013); Nicholas and Steyn (2017: Chapter 9); Evans and William (2011); Ireland (2006)).

Contemporary PMBOK documents use different approaches to deal with PQM. As described above, PQM fundamentals are articulated across various industries for both goods and services. For example, Nicholas and Steyn (2017) and Burke (2006) take a leaf from some PMBOK documents (such as, APM (2019) and PMI (2017)) and argue that the project manager has the ultimate responsibility for quality management on the project. They further suggest that quality management has equal priority with other project parameters. However, they strongly suggest that direct measurement of quality may be the responsibility of the quality assurance department or a dedicated person in the project providing such oversight.

Contemporary PMBOK documents seem to stand on project management practices across sectors, and quality management is approached as a broad subject matter when one traces its history and development. In the interest of brevity owing to lack of space, this chapter does not address issues of quality management history and organization or firm-wide quality management issues. These could be found in other sources, for example, in Juran (1995), International Organization for Standardization (2013), Nicholas and Steyn (2017: Chapter 9) and Evans and William (2011). Thus, this chapter focuses on construction PQM fundamentals and principles in practice.

There is evidence from a range of contemporary PMBOK documents to suggest that the definition of quality lies between various borders and it could be broadly defined as a basic tool for a natural property of any good or service that allows it to be compared with any other good or service of its kind. Thus, the word "quality" has many meanings, but basically, it refers to the set of inherent properties of an object that allows the satisfaction of stated or implied needs.

Therefore, PQM, when one interprets what is discussed in contemporary PMBOK documents, could be defined as the process for ensuring that all project activities necessary to design, plan, and implement a project are effective and efficient with respect to the purpose and objective, and its performance. With projects becoming more expensive, larger, more complex, and more technically advanced, Burke (2006), a conformist of contemporary PMBOK documents, emphasizes the need to assure that the service will meet stringent requirements, thus the focus of quality management.

PQM fundamentals in practice through PMBOK documents lenses

Quality definitions

Burke (2006) provides the following "Quality Definitions" as a basis for understanding the fundamentals of PQM:

- **Quality management philosophy:** the involvement of all project participants to ensure the goals and objectives of the project and resulting product, facility, or service meet the needs of the client, project team, and other stakeholders.
- **Quality planning:** the process of identifying the quality standards the project needs to comply with, to achieve the required condition and satisfy the terms of the contract.
- **Quality control:** the method of inspection, in process inspection and final inspection to confirm that the product or service has met the required condition. The required condition should be laid down in the scope statement, specifications, and the project quality plan.
- **Quality assurance:** a systematic process of defining, planning, implementing, and reviewing the management processes, in order to provide adequate confidence that the product or service will be consistently completed to the required condition.
- **Quality control plan:** it integrates the project schedule with quality control, by listing the sequence of work, performance requirements, inspection requirements and hold points.

Project quality characteristics

Linking the organization leading the project quality practices and the PQM approaches, Ireland (2006) contends that quality practices may vary from those of the organization leading the project and can pose some significant challenges to a project manager who is trying to design, develop, and deliver a project's product or service in such a manner that it gives value to the client. Thus, caution should be exercised in the selection of project partners or vendors.

Different organizations' quality practices are typically based on the needs of their clients. Some organizations have lower expectations for the capabilities and features of products or services that include reliability, utility, and maintainability. These expectations may result from the inability of an organization to produce a high-grade product or high-standard service for such reasons as poor inputs, low-skilled workers, lack of modern tools, and unsophisticated designs. When services are conceived in a project environment and finally provided to meet the client requirements, the levels of service being offered and the features of the service must match or exceed the client expectations.

Planning for quality

In project management practice, it is important to note that modern quality management is a prevention-oriented function that calls for anticipating requirements, thus, planning is a major consideration. According to Ireland (2006), planning requires that a person define the future service to be developed and how its framework will be put together. He further argues that the project manager, as the primary quality leader, must set the standards for quality and ensure they are met through both comprehensive plans and follow-through on the actual service development framework and testing of the service.

Learning from various PQM practices, it is important to note that planning for quality takes on many aspects of defining the service in terms that are understood by the performing parties and that these parties have the capability to meet specified levels of skills (Ireland, 2006). Some examples and areas for consideration in project quality are now outlined:

- **Specifications:** for precision of measurements, they should consider the difference between the owner's organization of the project and those of all the participants.
- **Measures used in putting together specifications and contracts:** one system may be used to convert specifications and respective contracts to the general practice of the organization undertaking the project. Conversions are problematic and can lead to confusion and error. The project manager should be aware of this and manage the conversion process as closely as possible.

Specifications practices

In developing the requirements and service framework design, it is vital that the specifications accurately communicate what is needed in a precise language that cannot be misunderstood. Specifications should state what is to be accomplished and how it is to be accomplished. Under certain circumstances, the specifications may also state how something is not to be accomplished, for example, that a specific procedure or process should not be used.

Well-communicated specifications are essential if a quality service is to be designed, formulated, and delivered to the client. The method of formulating the specifications and details included in it will be supportive of working under different project environments and conditions. It is essential to communicate the requirements for the service, and a combination of media should be used, ranging from words and notations through mathematics and numbers, to graphics and illustrations.

Quality costs

Burke (2006) asserts that it costs less to get the job right the first time. He argues that some project managers never seem to have the time to get it right the first time, yet seem to have the time to rework the job. In most situations, the cost of this rework often costs much more than the original item of work in terms of manhours and other consumables. Therefore, it is fundamental, that the PM should emphasize the need for "right first time" and make sure that the project quality plan is sound and easy to understand by project implementors and implementors have sufficient knowledge and skills in areas of their expertise.

Quality costs are a combination of management costs, which include: prevention costs (expenses associated with steps taken to make sure the service will be configured to required conditions), appraisal costs (expenses incurred while checking and inspecting the work to confirm that it has achieved the required condition), failure costs (internal, i.e., costs related to expenses incurred within the project due to service failure and inefficiencies; and external, i.e., expenses incurred outside the project, usually motivated by the client).

Conclusion — From contemporary PMBOK documents to construction PQM in developing countries

The PQM fundamentals covered in contemporary PMBOK documents discussed above hinge on the centrality of project management across sectors. Thus, when a project manager performs quality management planning, the first thing they need to do is either adopt the quality policy of their parent organization or supplement it. The policy should guide the project manager's efforts. The quality plan should include the quality baseline defining performance expectations. It should also include instructions for how the project quality assurance and quality control will be handled. Quality, costs, schedule, utility, human resources, risk, and communication may have been planned somewhat independently on a project, and now is the time to make sure they all work well together.

It is important to note that the fundamentals covered under contemporary PMBOK documents above are relevant to PQM in developing countries in terms of the QM knowledge base, tools, and techniques. For those responsible for construction projects in developing countries, there is a need to interpret the quality management knowledge base, tools in the context of quality management issues which are of direct relevance to developing countries as described in in the next section.

In order to interpret the quality management knowledge base and tools in the context of PQM practice issues which are of direct relevance to developing countries, there is a need to have a concerted effort from government ministries and other construction industry organizations in the developing countries. These initiatives could be through policy and other undertakings, which could be supported through construction industry development agendas by statutory agencies responsible for construction industry development. Establishing a Developing-Countries Construction PMBOK (DCCPMBOK) should be the ultimate milestone toward strengthening construction project management regimes in developing countries. The way forward is discussed below, in the section after next.

Construction project management — Quality management issues of direct relevance to developing countries

The issues of construction quality have always existed across the world (Gitlow *et al.*, 2005). In a construction project scenario, quality can be defined as meeting the legal, aesthetic (Arditi and Gunaydin, 1997) and functional requirements of a construction project (Berawi, 2006). Clients, from both the public and private sectors, nowadays place more emphasis on the quality of items rather than the price which was the major concern in the past. Hence, there has been a rapid expansion of international competition in construction quality (Abdul-Rahman and Berawi, 2002; Kostas, 2010; Tsiotras and Gotzamani, 1996).

According to Abdul-Rahman *et al.* (2004), Turk (2006), and Arditi and Gunaydin (1997), high quality of construction projects includes factors such as the design being easily understandable and applicable, conformity of design with specifications, economics of construction, ease of operation, ease of maintenance, and energy efficiency. Zantanidis and Tsiotras (1998) and Abdul-Rahman and Berawi (2002) noted that expectations for quality construction projects will continue to grow rapidly as the number of affluent, educated, and quality-conscious customers is increasing. With the globalization of the economy, construction firms worldwide are actively engaged in achieving internationally accepted quality levels to ensure their leading position in the international market, especially in developing economies. Thus, there arises the need to have a proper system that ensures that quality is considered to be critical, coupled with a high level of attention paid to quality management in the construction industry (Abdul Rahman *et al.*, 2006; Hiyassat, 2000). Scholars indicate that quality management has been adopted by many countries in their respective construction industries. The countries include South Africa (Rwelamila, 1995); Malaysia (Chew and Chai, 1996); Hong Kong (Au and Yu, 1999; Leung *et al.*, 1999; Tang and Kam, 1999); Singapore (Low and Omar, 1997; Low and Yeo, 1997); Greece (Tsiotras and Gotzamani, 1996; Zantanidis and Tsiotras, 1998); Turkey (Turk, 2006); Jordan (Hiyassat, 2000); Saudi Arabia (Bubshait and Al-Atiq, 1999); Sweden (Landin, 2000); and the US (Chini and Valdez, 2003).

Quality management is a complex effort that may not be fruitful if only technical aspects are focused upon, and this has led to the modern concept of total quality management (TQM) (Tan and Abdul Rahman, 2005). Besterfield *et al.* (2003) define TQM as both a philosophy and a set of guiding principles that represent the foundation for continuously improving an organization, which in most situations is a project-based organization. Many tools, methods, and techniques have been developed worldwide to give substance to the concept of TQM (Berawi, 2004; Geraedts *et al.*, 2001). Many companies obtained the ISO 9000 standards certification as a first step toward TQM (Hiyassat, 2000; Peter *et al.*, 2010). However, if people are not serious in implementing quality management, no matter how good the system is, there are strong indications that it will fail eventually. It is due to this human element that there is a strong perception that the majority of the quality-related problems are caused by human-related factors, especially professionalism and ethics (Peter *et al.*, 2010).

While the foregoing summary review of quality management in construction is a mixed bag covering industrialized and developing countries, it is important to note that developing countries seem to face more, and complex, challenges and the appropriate solutions to quality management issues need different approaches. The current status of quality management in construction projects in developing countries needs to be scrutinized if this chapter is going to contribute toward meeting the objectives of this book of producing a PMBOK document rooted in the realities of the construction industries in developing countries.

Bawane (2017) provided a balanced reflection on the current status of quality management in construction in the developing countries. He argued that the construction industry in developing countries is often characterized by low productivity, lack of standards and poor quality. Furthermore, but using an argument applied to construction industries across the globe, that it is also criticized for not learning from the manufacturing industry that has successfully implemented the philosophy of quality in all spheres of its activities. However, before making any attempt to draw parallels between the two industries, he examined the kind of environment under which each of them operates. The manufacturing industry, he argued, operates under a closely monitored environment where it is possible to control all variables that have a bearing on product quality. On the other hand, construction on site, he affirmed, is not an automated process and, unlike engineering goods, it is the people rather than the machines and technology that influence the project outcome. According to Bawane (2017), construction is a very complex process that involves multiple parties and interests, including the client, engineer, architect, other consultants, contractors, and vendors. Thus, the very nature of construction, he suggested, appears to be the real barrier to quality management success (Lowshine, *et al.*, 2002). Based on several studies on the construction industry (such as Love and Li, 1998), he concluded that the industry's fragmented nature, lack of effective coordination and communication among the parties, adversarial contractual relationships, and lack of customer focus inhibit the its performance.

Bawane (2017) reflected on the quality management system (QMS) within construction industries in developing countries and argued for the need for QMS to evolve around the specific characteristics of the construction project and its environment. He supported the observation of Thomas *et al.* (2002) that traditional QMSs are often unrepresentative of the workface and are usually preoccupied with instruments of control and their administration rather than the outputs that are important to the client. He further argued that the ISO-based generic approaches to quality management are bureaucratic in nature and generally abstract and more concerned with the management system than with the control of the work process. Thus, the construction industries of developing countries are confronted by these international quality organization dynamics over and above their positions of immaturity, when compared with construction industries in industrialized countries.

Factors affecting construction quality management in developing countries

There are several factors that impede the management of construction quality in developing countries (Ofori, 2016; Sospeter and Rwelamila, 2021; Rwelamila, 2021; Rwelamila and Abdul-Rashid, 2021; Bawane 2017). These factors can be classified under internal factors and external factors (Rwelamila and Abdul-Rashid 2021; Bawane 2017).

Internal factors

Managing and ensuring that construction quality is attained faces many critical factors that stem from the internal shortcomings of the industry (Rwelamila and Abdul-Rashid 2021; Bawane 2017; Rwelamila and Ogunlana, 2019). These include:

(a) Contractual provisions — the decades-old tendering and contracting procedures prevailing in most developing countries do not focus on quality;

(b) Organizational structure — except for few corporate firms, most of the construction companies lack a well-defined organizational setup. Most contractors operate with a skeletal workforce and have ad-hoc approaches towards resource mobilization. Quality management through sound organizational setup is still not a familiar concept to most firms;

(c) Lack of technical expertise — the construction industries need to equip themselves with technical capabilities, both human and non-human, to ensure effective quality assurance on and off the construction sites. Most contractors lack the financial capabilities to support such an in-house facility. Staff responsible for implementation of quality are inadequately trained, and in most construction projects, on-site quality checks are carried out by relatively less experienced supervisory personnel;

(d) Slow pace of mechanization — construction in developing countries is a labor-intensive activity that provides employment with little investment. Like any other labor-intensive industry, the construction industry is also characterized by low productivity and poor quality. Mechanization of construction activities could be a solution to overcome the limitations of the workers who are involved in onsite operations. The level of mechanization of the construction industry in industrialized countries is about 60–70 percent, compared to 15–20 percent in developing countries (Bawane, 2017). The slow pace of mechanization of the construction industry in developing countries can be attributed to the high investment required and the low turnover of firms. The smaller firms, which execute up to 90 percent of the total volume of work, usually opt for hiring the equipment they require, as owning the expensive machineries is not a viable proposition (Bawane, 2017). Mechanization has an influence on the quality of construction as it eliminates human error;

(e) Lack of training and skills — the construction sector provides employment to those with little education or skill. For example, in China and India, which could be described as "towards graduating from developing countries status," 50 percent and 73 percent of the workforce, respectively, did not have much schooling (ILO, 2001). The objective of improving construction quality can be realized by upgrading the skills of the workforce. Hence, training becomes vital in meeting the skill requirements of the construction industry. Unlike the manufacturing industry, which meets its requirement of skilled workforce through a large number of vocational training institutes, the construction industries in most developing countries rely on informal and traditional apprenticeship arrangements where laborers learn the trade skills from master craftsmen. However, such training may not satisfy the demand for higher quality. Thus, the need for an institutional framework to provide quality-oriented training to construction industries; and

(f) Limited financial capabilities — to match the requirements of the prevailing competitive environment, it is crucial for the construction industries to enhance their capabilities in human and non-human resources. The available capital is not adequate to meet the resource requirements. To address this, the industry and governments need to develop a mechanism to enable the flow of funds to the construction industry. For example, the banking sector may be encouraged to adopt lending norms that could address the requirements of the construction industry.

External factors

Internal reforms within the construction industry alone will not yield the desired results regarding construction quality unless the issues stemming from the other fronts are also addressed through public–private partnership initiatives (such as formulation of a construction industry policy with the involvement of the private sector). These factors are external to the construction industry, yet critical to construction project quality and its management. The following are salient initiatives:

(a) *Technological developments in allied industries* — the construction industry has major linkages with the building materials industry since materials account for 58 to 60 percent of construction costs (Elkhalifa and Shaddad, 2008). These materials include cement, steel, building blocks, roofing material, fittings/fixtures, glass, paints, and other chemicals. Much of these materials is manufactured in the unorganized sector using low-grade technology. The quality of materials is critical in ensuring the construction quality; ironically, the locally produced materials are characterized by lack of quality and standards. The building materials industry in developing countries requires technological upgrading. The industry needs to have sound research and development facilities and programs to equip itself with the state-of-the-art technology. As this requires a huge investment that most developing countries may not be able to afford, imaginative initiatives, such as a regional approach to this investment could alleviate the burden of funding technological advancement by the countries.

(b) *Globalization* — the emergence of globalization provided the multinational organizations with opportunities of extending their business operations in the developing countries. Construction is one sector where globalization has made a significant impact; one can see a good number of foreign construction firms in developing countries. While investigating the implications of globalization on the Asian construction industry, Raftery *et al.* (1998) identified three trends: (a) greater private sector participation in infrastructure projects; (b) increased vertical integration in the packaging of construction projects; and (c) increased foreign participation in domestic construction. Equipped with superior technical and managerial capabilities, the international firms can deliver the projects within the stipulated time, cost and quality. The dominance of foreign firms will continue until the local industry acquires the capabilities and expertise to handle large and complex projects without compromising the quality. On the positive side, globalization can be seen as an opportunity to upgrade the local industry through technology transfer and enhancement of the skills of the construction workforce. This initiative is possible when there is a statutory entity responsible for construction industry development (Sospeter and Rwelamila, 2021; Rwelamila, 2021; Rwelamila and Abdul-Rashid, 2021; Ofori, 2016).

(c) *Quality certification* — with the emergence of new trade regimes under the World Trade Organization (WTO), companies are being persuaded to adopt QMSs to meet the demands of customers in a globalized market (Bawane, 2017). During the last two decades, ISO 9000, a series of international quality standards, has emerged as a system that can be applied to different types of business organizations to obtain improvements in quality procedures and products. The appropriateness of ISO 9000 to the construction industry is still a matter of debate since the end product of the construction process is not a repetitive unit but an item that may be unique in its design and composition. According to Bawane (2017), international construction firms operating in developing countries are pursuing ISO certification as it is increasingly becoming mandatory for bidding in projects funded by national and international agencies.

Which way for construction industries?

As discussed above, the construction industries in developing countries face several inherent challenges. Resolving the issues of construction project quality and their management lies in seeking long-lasting solutions to the problems facing construction industries in these countries. That current generic PMBOK documents are falling short of becoming the only direct base documents for construction management professionals, and other professionals making up the core teams in developing countries needs a critical eye. The focus of any construction industry over and above PQM fundamentals should be on capacity building, both the human and non-human, through a strategically devised approach. It is imperative for the construction industries in developing countries to bring about radical changes in their outdated contractual provisions and technical specifications. At the organizational level, every action must be guided by a well-defined quality policy. The concept of TQM as the base of culture for every construction firm (contractors and consultants) can be suitably modified to meet the requirements of the developing countries' construction industries.

The section below takes a paradigm-shift road — from the generic models to specific issues of developing countries.

Project quality management practice — From generic to developing countries' specifics

PQM issues covered in PMBOK documents seem to come from a position of viewing quality as a process of inspecting constructed items to separate the good ones from the bad. However, in the contemporary environment in developing countries, defects and failures should be prevented in the first place, rather than inspect for them, i.e., "You cannot right a wrong by inspection." It is necessary to build in processes to ensure that things are done right the first time, every time, and develop a culture where everybody is quality-focused.

A closer assessment of contemporary PMBOK documents suggests that any project-management mature construction industry should be able to digest the generic PQM knowledge base, tools, and techniques based on contemporary PMBOK documents and apply them at a project level to achieve quality levels to clients' satisfaction. That construction industries in most industrialized countries have reached acceptable levels of project management maturity (Cain, 2003), embracing contemporary PMBOK documents as a foundation in managing project quality is a norm. Reaching project management maturity by industrialized countries construction industries means that they are not being challenged by quality management issues similar to those facing developing countries as discussed above.

If contemporary PMBOK documents are going to make sense in developing countries, it is important that additional documentation and initiatives are in place to bridge the gap between current construction quality management capabilities in developing countries and what contemporary PMBOK documents are providing to those countries. The contents of proposed additional documentation and initiatives are discussed below. Over and above the provisions on construction project quality management in contemporary PMBOK documents as indicated above, the following should form part of a Developing-Countries Construction PMBOK (DCCPMBOK).

Addressing internal factors

A specific section within a DCCPMBOK should address the need for best practice contractual provisions — this provision should take a leaf from the Chartered Institute of Building (CIOB) (2019) Code of Quality Management and emphasize the need to embed quality into contracts — quality management plans to be incorporated within the contract; and the emphasis on the responsibility of the "Employer" to provide contract documents (drawings, bills of quantities specifications, and schedules) to define both quantity and quality. The section should also address the issue of risk related to different types of procurement systems and the need for the contractor to institute a quality assurance system to demonstrate compliance with the contract requirements. Furthermore, it should be a requirement for the QMS (see Figure 8.1) to ensure coordination and management of interfaces between the specialty contractors and the submission of documents to the client for review.

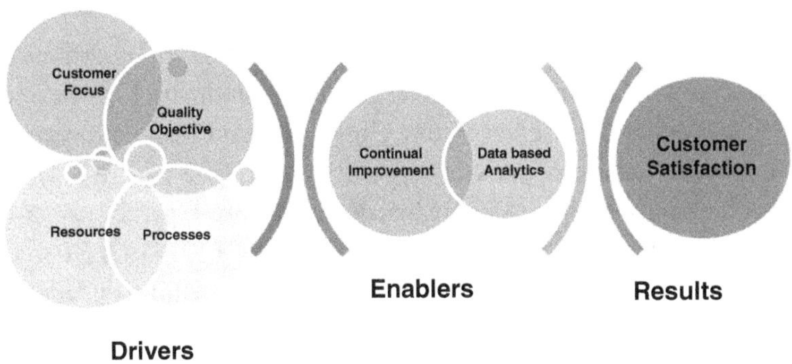

Figure 8.1: Quality management system.
Source: Anon. (2018).

The QMS, as illustrated in Figure 8.1, should be able to provide guidance and set out requirements for establishing an appropriate quality management procedure to lower cost, increase productivity, meet the customer's satisfaction, and gain market share by construction organizations (Neyestani, 2016). The system should assist construction companies in developing countries to successfully achieve their quality objectives and ensure that all phases of the construction project consistently meet client's requirements.

The following activities (based on ISO 9001:2008) should be considered when construction companies and other built environment organizations in developing countries implement the QMS (Neyestani, 2016):

- Overall requirements for the QMS and documentation;
- Management responsibility, focus, policy, planning, and objectives;
- Resource management and allocation;
- Product realization and process management; and
- Measurement, monitoring, analysis, and improvement.

Another specific section of the DCCPMBOK should focus on construction firms (both specialist and general contractors). A national register of contractors should be established and one of the major requirements of a fully-fledged construction firm is to adhere to what Rwelamila and Ssegawa (2014) refer to as "Creating an environment for successful projects (CESP)" requirements — becoming typical project-based organizations. In this way, they will have a sound organizational setup and consequently be able to manage quality appropriately.

A specific section addresses the need for across the board technical expertise — that is, the need for construction industries in developing countries to equip themselves with technical capabilities, both human and non-human, to ensure effective quality assurance (see Figure 8.2) on and off the construction sites. As construction firms are typical project-based organizations, within Rwelamila and Ssegawa's (2014) CESP requirements, they should address issues of financial capabilities, adequately trained staff, and having experienced supervisory personnel on construction sites.

Figure 8.2: Quality assurance.

According to the MEASURE Evaluation (2001) (Figure 8.2), each core function represents a constellation of activities. The figure indicates that rather than a unique sequence of steps that initiate quality assurance activities, all core functions need to take place in a balanced manner for a quality assurance strategy to be effective.

There is always risk involved in any construction project, more so in developing countries, and quality assurance is essential in preventing problems during construction and reducing risk. If quality issues are only identified after an activity has been completed, the result is re-work and program delays (Neyestani, 2016). When quality issues are not identified at all during the construction process, it can lead to difficult and costly defects liability periods, buildings that are inefficient to operate, or structures that fail a few years after practical completion. Therefore, quality assurance should focus on the procedures that the construction company has implemented to ensure that the design meets quality standards and the highest industry standards are applied every step of the way (Neyestani, 2016).

As part of addressing internal factors, there is a need to have industry-wide initiatives addressing issues of low productivity and poor quality. With all project-based organizations meeting Rwelamila and Ssegawa's (2014) CESP requirements, issues of low productivity and poor quality will be addressed. There is also the need for construction industries in developing countries to have a culture of training their workforce. There is the need for an institutional framework to provide quality-oriented training in the construction industries. The CIOB (2019) addresses this aspect by emphasizing that culture and attitude are vital in achieving success in quality, and it argues that culture and attitude should begin at the tender stage with effective quality planning (see Figure 8.3). The CIOB (2019) is convinced that this should come from training and education, backed by a commitment from the stakeholders to deliver good-quality construction.

Project quality planning should follow the activities embedded in the project quality plan as illustrated in Figure 8.3. According to the Construction Forum Myanmar (2018), project quality is mainly a management responsibility because management undertakes the controlling and monitoring function for the project.

Documents are the main method of communication in project management. Therefore, the project quality plan should describe a way to manage and control the documents used in the project. Usually, there can be a common documentation repository with controlled access to store the documents (Construction Forum Myanmar 2018).

The correct requirements to be implemented are listed in the requirement scope document. This is an abstraction of the requirements sign-off document. Having requirements noted in the project quality plan helps the quality assurance team to correctly validate them. In this way, the quality

Figure 8.3: Project quality plan.

assurance function should help the project team to know exactly what to test and what to leave out from the scope.

Design control should specify the controls and procedures used for the design phase of the project (Construction Forum Myanmar, 2018). Usually, there should be design reviews to analyze the proposed technical design and assess its correctness. For fruitful design reviews, senior designers or the engineers/architects of the respective domains should get involved. Once the designs are reviewed and agreed, they are signed-off with the client. With time, the client may come up with changes to the requirements, or new requirements. In such cases, design may be changed. Every time the design is changed, the changes should be reviewed and signed-off.

Once construction on the project starts, all the processes, procedures, and activities should be closely monitored and measured. Through this type of control, the project management team can make sure that the project is progressing along the correct path. These are covered under the development control and rigor component (Construction Forum Myanmar, 2018).

The testing and quality assurance component takes precedence over other components. This is the element that describes the main quality assurance functions of the project. This section should clearly identify the quality objectives for the project and the approach to be taken to achieve them.

Finally, the risks and mitigation component includes identification of project quality risks. It is important that the project management team should come up with appropriate mitigation plans to address each quality risk.

Addressing external factors

Construction-industry–wide initiatives are needed to deal with technological developments in allied industries. It is imperative that investments are made in a technology upgrade of the construction materials industry, as discussed above. It requires a huge investment that most developing countries cannot afford and can only be attained through innovative approaches between the public and private sectors. Public–private partnerships should be encouraged where, for example, primarily private-sector organizations should jointly agree on contributing to research, for example, from a proportion of their profits, and these contributions could be tax deductible. The logistics of these arrangements should be articulated in the proposed DCCPMBOK document.

There is a need for appropriate initiatives to address the dynamics of globalization and benefit from the process. In dealing with the dynamics of globalization by capitalizing on what Raftery *et al.* (1998) referred to as implications of globalization, each developing country should have a blueprint to encourage alliances between local firms and international firms, specifically for capacity-building initiatives as the international firms with superior technical and managerial capabilities can facilitate skills transfer to local firms. Hence, globalization can be seen as an opportunity to upgrade the local industry through technology transfer and skill enhancement of the construction workforce. The issues raised by Raftery *et al.* (1998) above should guide appropriate provisions in the proposed DCCPMBOK document.

As an industry-wide initiative through a public–private coalition, quality certification could become an industry program with clear milestones. Through the World Trade Organization (WTO) trade regime, companies will be persuaded to adopt quality management systems in order to meet the demands of clients in a globalized market, and secondly, with ISO 9000 certification as one of the requirements for construction firms, the industry will realize improvements in quality procedures and completed products (Figure 8.4). Lessons can be learnt from the CIOB (2019) covered under what they refer to as "Quality Standards" — other additions (in context) in the proposed DCCPMBOK document.

The "bridge" built by addressing the internal and external factors described above will create a sustainable environment in developing countries and put in practice "Actions on Quality" as proposed in the CIOB (2019) Code of Quality Management. As a construction industry norm in any developing country, it will be possible to embrace prevention activities, assurance activities, remedial activities, and understanding implications of poor quality and embrace PQM best practices with high levels of commitment.

In addition to what has been described above as the "bridge" built by addressing internal and external factors, the DCCPMBOK should have

Figure 8.4: ISO 9000 Quality management principles.

another section addressing the need for any developing country to have a construction-industry–wide conducive environment necessary for quality management best practices to take place in construction projects. The environment necessary for such best practices is based on the UK's three best practice standards and their six goals, which are described in detail by Cain (2003). A summary of the three best practice standards and their six goals is now provided.

The three best practice standards are (Cain 2003):

(a) ***The need for better public buildings (targeting functional performance of the completed buildings)*** Well-designed buildings should enhance the quality of life for the end-users. Hence, the following practices should stop: regarding good design as an optional extra; treating lowest cost as best value; valuing initial capital cost as more important than whole-life cost; and imagining that effectiveness and efficiency are divorced from design. Moreover, the following approaches should be embraced: measuring efficiency and waste in construction; appointing integrated teams focusing on the whole-life impact and performance of a development; encouraging longer-term relationships with integrated project teams as part of long-term programs, always subject to rigorous performance review; and using whole-life costing in the value-for-money assessment of buildings.

(b) ***The obligations that define a best practice client (based on "rethinking construction era" emphasis***) According to Cain (2003), the obligations of a Charter Client are: preparing a program of cultural change with targets for its achievement over a period of at least three, but preferably five years or more; measuring their own performance in achieving their cultural change program; monitoring the effects of implementing the program of cultural change, by calculating the national key performance indicators that apply to their project; and annually reviewing and amending as necessary the cultural change program in the light of what has been achieved. The best practice standard requires clients to have procurement processes that deliver (using measurement as the basis of proof) the following key improvements to the constructed products of the industry: major reductions in whole-life costs; substantial improvements in functional efficiency; a quality environment for end-users; reduced construction time; improved predictability on budgets and time; reduced defects on hand-over and during use; and elimination of inefficiency and waste in the design and construction process.

(c) ***The need to modernize construction (addressing the poor performance of the construction industry and the consequence for the public purse)*** As articulated by Cain (2003, pp. 19–20), a series of questions need to be considered by public procurers seeking to improve quality and value for money. The key questions are:
   (i) Is supply chain integration achieved from the outset of the design process?
   (ii) Has the whole design and construction team been assembled before the design is well developed?
   (iii) What are the likely whole-life (running, maintenance, and other support) costs?
   (iv) Have appropriate techniques, such as value management and value engineering, been used to determine whether the potential for waste and inefficiency has been minimized in the method of construction?
   (v) Have efficiency improvements, to be delivered by the construction process, been quantified?

Best practice (c) above includes those areas where measurement of construction performance is essential and priority areas to be measured are outlined in Cain (2003, p. 20).

The six primary goals of construction best practice (Cain, 2003, p. 22) include:

(i) The finished building should deliver maximum functionality, which includes delighted end-users;
(ii) End-users should benefit from the lowest optimum cost of ownership;
(iii) Inefficiency and waste in the utilization of labor and materials should be eliminated;
(iv) Specialist suppliers should be involved in design from the outset to achieve integration and buildability;
(v) Design and construction of the buildings should be achieved through a single point of contact for the most effective coordination and clarity of responsibility; and
(vi) Performance and improvement achievements should be established by measurement.

The proposed DCCPMBOK should embrace fully Cain's (2003) best practice standards as discussed above.

Further research on, and further development of, PQM as it relates to developing countries

Clients in developing countries, like their counterparts in industrialized countries, want good quality, reliability, and consistency with construction project outputs and outcomes that meet their expectations and requirements. Thus, quality matters to everyone in the construction business in developing countries. However, construction industries in developing countries, as discussed in the preceding sections of this chapter, face several factors that impede the management of construction quality.

Contemporary PMBOK documents are designed for mature construction industries in industrialized countries which are not facing the quality management issues that confront the developing countries. Hence, there is a significant gap of preparedness between project management mature construction industries in industrialized countries and non-project management mature industries in developing countries. In order to address the PQM gap, it has been suggested above that a hybrid construction PMBOK document should be designed to form an appropriate PMBOK for construction industries in developing countries. This hybrid document (DCCPMBOK) should have three building blocks: (a) contemporary generic PMBOK documents (any of the existing documents); (b) a "bridge" built by addressing internal and external factors in a document; and (c) a document on a conducive environment for implementing quality management best practices.

Strengthening this DCCPMBOK and making sure that it is used by all stakeholders involved in construction projects in developing countries is fundamental. For what is contained in the DCCPMBOK to make sense, it is expected that all three DCCPMBOK building blocks should constitute a seamless body of knowledge and be easy to understand by various stakeholders involved in managing projects in developing countries. Experience from those who will use the hybrid document should lead to further improvement on the DCCPMBOK. Furthermore, that the first two building blocks described above are addressing the PQM gap between the two blocks of construction industries described above, suggests the need for continuous improvement of the two blocks. Hence, future research should focus on strengthening the two buildings blocks and consequently strengthening the DCCPMBOK.

Future research should cover topics including the following:

(a) The feasibility of establishing independent entities within developing countries to provide a standard assessment system on the quality of construction projects. The research should focus on the possibility of benchmarking the Singapore Construction Quality Assessment Scheme (CONQUAS), which was introduced in 1989. As a de facto national yardstick, CONQUAS has been periodically fine-tuned to keep pace with changes in technology and quality demands of an increasingly more sophisticated population. The introduction of a similar scheme into any developing country could provide a good standardization tool and mark the institution of a level of benchmarking/competition and a backbone of building blocks (a) and (b).

(b) Research on formalizing efforts of learning from other industries about PQM and how this should be done. According to CIOB (2019), the construction industry must learn from other industries. There is a need to discard the idea that construction is different from other industries; every industry has a set of challenges.

(c) Research on the status of various construction-related academic programs that include quality management in their curriculums. The inclusion of quality in a curriculum, either at a college, or on site, should be seen as important.

(d) Within developing countries, are current quality management approaches adequate in three areas: (i) supervision, (ii) sign-off, and (iii) workmanship? If not, what is to be done to enhance the level professional/specialist skills?

References

Abdullahi, U., Bustani, S.A., Hassan, A. and Rotimi, F.E. (2019). Assessing quality management practice in Nigerian construction. *Journal of Construction Business and Management*, 3(2), 17–25.

Abdul-Rahman, H., Hanid, M. and Yap, X.W. (2004). Does professional ethics affect quality of construction — A case in a developing economy? *Total Quality Management*, 25(3), 235–248.

Abdulrahman, H., Wang, C. and Wen, Y.X. (2010). How professional ethics impacts construction quality. *Scientific Research and Essays*, 5(23), 3742–3749.

Abdul-Rahman, H. and Berawi, M.A. (2002). Power quality system, a new system for quality management in globalization — Towards innovation and competitive advantages. *Quality Assurance: Best Practice, Regulation, and Law*, 9(1), 5–30.

Abdul-Rahman, H., Berawi, M.A., Berawi, A.R., Mohamed, O., Othman, M. and Yahya, I.A. (2006). Delay mitigation in the Malaysian construction industry. *Journal of Construction Engineering and Management*, 132(2), 125–133.

Achi, O.F., Onukwube, H.N. and Ajayi, O.M. (2007). An assessment of quality management of building projects in Nigeria. *Proceedings: Construction and Building Research Conference*. Royal Institute of Surveyors (COBRA). Georgia Tech., Atlanta, GA, 6–7 September.

American Society for Quality (2021). Learn About Quality. https://asq.org/quality-resources/iso-9000 [Accessed 31 May 2021].

Anon (2018). Good Quality Management Systems, Techno FAQ (December). https://technofaq.org/posts/2018/12/good-quality-management-systems [Accessed 8 June 2021].

Arditi, D. and Gunaydin, H.M. (1997). Total quality management in the construction process. *International Journal of Project Management*, 15(4), 235–243.

Association for Project Management (APM) (2019). *Body of Knowledge*, 7th Edition. https://www.apm.org.uk/resources/what-is-project-management/ [Accessed 5 July 2020].

Au, J.C.W. and Yu, W.W.M. (1999). Quality management for an infrastructure construction project in Hong Kong. *Logistics Information Management*, 12(4), 309–314.

Bawane, P. (2017). Construction quality management: Issues and challenges before construction industry in developing countries. *International Journal of Engineering Development and Research*, 5(3), 1208–1211.

Berawi, M.A. (2004). Quality revolution: Leading the innovation and competitive advantages. *International Journal of Quality & Reliability Management*, 21(4), 425–438.

Berawi, M.A. (2006). Distinguishing concept types in function models during the act of innovation (PhD thesis). Oxford Brookes University, Oxford.

Besterfield, D.H., Michna, C.B., Besterfield, G.H. and Sacre, M.B. (2003). *Total Quality Management*, 3rd Edition. Upper Saddle River, NJ: Prentice Hall.

Bubshait, A.A. and Al-Atiq, T.H. (1999). ISO 9000 Quality standards in construction. *Journal of Management in Engineering*, 15(2), 43–53.

Burke, R. (2006). *Project Management Techniques* (Paperback, 3rd College Edition). Burke Publishing, Cape Town, South Africa.

Cain, C.T. (2003). *Building Down Barriers — A Guide to Construction Best Practice*. Spon Press, London, UK.

Chartered Institute of Building (CIOB) (2019). Code of Quality Management, Chartered Institute of Building, Bracknell, UK.

Chew, Y.S. and Chai, L.N. (1996). *ISO 9002 in Malaysian Construction Industry*. McGraw Hill, London.

Chini, A.R. and Valdez, H.E. (2003). ISO 9000 and the US construction industry. *Journal of Management in Engineering*, 19(2), 69–77.

Cleland, D.I. and Ireland, L.R. (2007). *Project Management-Strategic Design and Implementation*. McGraw-Hill International Edition, Singapore.

Construction Forum Myanmar (2018). https://www.constructionforum-myanmar.com/2016/03/project-quality-plan.html [Accessed 8 June 2021].

Elkhalifa, A. and Shaddad, M.Y. (2008). The Building Materials Industry and Housing Sector in Sudan. *Architects' Third Scientific Conference on Urban Housing in Sudan*, 28–30 April, Khartoum, Sudan.

Evans, J.R. and William, M.L. (2011). *The Management and Control of Quality*, 8th Edition. Cengage Learning South-Western, Mason, OH.

Geraedts, H.P.A., Montenarie, R. and Rijk, P.P.V. (2001). The benefits of TQM. *Computerized Medical Imaging and Graphics*, 25, 217–220.

Gitlow, H.S., Oppenheim, A.J., Oppenheim, R. and Levine, D.O. (2005). *Quality Management*, 3rd Edition. McGraw-Hill, Boston, MA.

Hiyassat, M.A.S. (2000). Applying the ISO standards to a construction company: A case study. *International Journal of Project Management*, 18, 275–280.

Hoonakker, P. (2006). Quality management in construction industry. *Proceedings of the ASQ World Conference on Quality and Improvement*, Milwaukee, WI, 1–3 May.

International Labour Organisation (ILO) (2001). The construction industry in the 21st century: Its images, employment prospects and skill requirements. Report for the 2001 ILO Tripartite Meeting on the Construction Industry, Geneva.

International Organization for Standardization (ISO) (2013). Quality Management Principles http://www.iso.org/iso/iso_9000 [Accessed 12 February 2020].

International Project Management Association (IPMA) (2016). IPMA Individual Competence Baseline (IPMA ICB) — Version 4.0; IPMA Project Excellence Baseline (IPMA PEB) — Version 1.0; and IPMA Organisational Competence Baseline (IPMA OCB) — Version 1.1 https://www.ipma.world/new-ipma-icb-peb-and-ocb-ready-for-download/ [Accessed 5 July 2020].

International Association of Project & Program Management (IAPPM) (2003). IAPPM Project & Portfolio Model https://www.slideshare.net/IAPPM?utm_campaign=profiletracking&utm_medium=sssite&utm_source=ssslideview [Accessed 5 July 2020].

International Organisation for Standardization (2012). ISO 21500:2012 Guidance On Project Management. https://www.iso.org/standard/50003.html [Accessed 5 July 2020].

Ireland, L.R. (2006). Project quality management in international projects. In D.I. Cleland and R. Garies (Eds.), *Global Project Management Handbook: Planning and Controlling International Projects*, 2nd Edition. McGraw-Hill, New York, pp. 15-1–15-11.

Isa, R.B., Jimoh, R.A. and Achuenu, E. (2013). An overview of the contribution of construction sector to sustainable development in Nigeria. *Net Journal of Business Management*, 1(1), 1–6.

Juran, J.M. (1995). *A History of Managing for Quality: The Evolution, Trends, and Future Directions of Managing for Quality*. ASQC Quality Press, Madison, WI.

Kostas, N.D. (2010). Developing full-spectrum innovation capability for survival and success in the global economy. *Total Quality Management & Business Excellence*, 21(2), 159–170.

Landin, A. (2000). ISO 9001 within the Swedish construction sector. *Construction Management and Economics*, 18(5), 509–518.

Leung, H.K.N., Chan, K.C.C. and Lee, T.Y. (1999). Costs and benefits of ISO 9000 series: A practical study. *International Journal of Quality & Reliability Management*, 16(7), 675–690.

Low, S.P. and Omar, H.F. (1997). The effective maintenance of quality management systems in the construction industry. *International Journal of Quality & Reliability Management*, 14(8), 768–790.

Low, S.P. and Yeo, H.K.C. (1997). ISO 9000 Quality assurance in Singapore's construction industry: An update. *Structural Survey*, 15(3), 113–117.

MEASURE Evaluation (2001). Quality Assurance Approach, The MEASURE Evaluation project. https://www.measureevaluation.org/prh/rh_indicators/service-delivery/quality-of-care/quality-assurance-approach.html [Accessed 10 June 2021].

Morris, P.W.G., Patel, M.B. and Wearne, S.H. (2000). Research into revising the APM project management body of knowledge. *International Journal of Project Management*, 18, 155–164.

Neyestani, B. (2016, December). Effectiveness of Quality Management System (QMS) on construction projects. https://doi.org/10.5281/zenodo.290272.

Nicholas, J.M. and Steyn, H. (2017). *Project Management for Engineering, Business and Technology*. Routledge, London, UK.

Odediran, S.J., Babalola, M.O. and Adebiyi, H.A. (2013). Assessment of business development strategies in the Nigerian construction industry. *Journal of Business & Management*, 2(1), 34–45.

Ofori, G. (2000). Challenges of construction industries in developing countries: lessons from various countries'. In A.B. Ngowi and J. Ssegawa (Eds.), *Refereed Proceedings of the 2nd International Conference Facing the Construction Industry in Developing Countries, Challenges Facing the construction industry in developing countries*, National Construction Industry

Council, University of Botswana, and CIB. Proceedings, Second International Conference of CIB Task Group 29, 15–17 November, Gaborone, pp. 1–11.

Ofori, G. (2016). Construction in Developing Countries: Current imperatives and potential. In K. Kahkonen and Keinanen (Eds.), *CIB World Building Congress 2016 on Intelligent Built Environment for Life.* Tampere 30 May–3 July 2016, Tampere Department of Civil Engineering, Construction Management and Economics, Tampere University of Technology.

Peter, H., Pascale, C. and Todd, L. (2010). Barriers and benefits of quality management in the construction industry: An empirical study. *Total Quality Management & Business Excellence*, 21(9), 953–969.

Project Management Institute (PMI) (2017). *A Guide to the Project Management Body of Knowledge*, 6th Edition. Project Management Institute, Newtown Square, PA.

Raftery, J., Pasadilla, B., Chiang, Y.H., Hui, E.C.M. and Tang, B.S. (1998). Globalization and construction industry development: Implications of recent development in the construction sector in Asia. *Construction Management and Economics*, 16, 729–737.

Rwelamila, P.D. (1995). Quality management in the SADC construction industries. *International Journal of Quality & Reliability Management*, 12(8), 23–31.

Rwelamila, P.D. (2021). Improving the performance of the South African construction industry. In P.D. Rwelamila and A.R.A. Aziz (Eds.), *Improving the Performance of Construction Industries in Developing Countries: Programmes, Initiatives, Achievements and Challenges*. Taylor & Francis, Abingdon, UK.

Rwelamila, P.D. and Abdul-Rashid, A.A. (2021). Construction industry development — General introduction. In P.D. Rwelamila and A.R.A. Aziz (Eds.), *Improving the Performance of Construction Industries in Developing Countries: Programmes, Initiatives, Achievements and Challenges*, Taylor & Francis, Abingdon, UK.

Rwelamila, P., Fewings, P. and Henjewele, C. (2015). Addressing the missing link in PPP Projects: What constitutes the public? *Journal of Management in Engineering*, 31(5). https://doi.org/10.1061/(ASCE)ME.1943-5479.0000330.

Rwelamila, P.D. and Ogunlana, S. (2019). W107 — Construction in developing countries research roadmap — Final Report, CIB, Rotterdam.

Rwelamila, P.D. and Ssegawa, J.K. (2014). The African Project Failure Syndrome: The conundrum of project management knowledge base — The case of SADC. *Journal of African Business*, 15(3), 211–224.

Smallwood, J. and Rossouw, J.H. (2008). The implementation of quality management systems in South African construction. *Proceedings of RICS/COBRA Construction and Building Research Conference*, Dublin, Ireland.

Sospeter, N.G. and Rwelamila, P.D. (2021). The case of Tanzania. In P.D. Rwelamila and A.R.A. Aziz (Eds.), *Improving the Performance of Construction Industries in Developing Countries: Programmes, Initiatives, Achievements and Challenges*, Taylor & Francis, Abingdon, UK.

Taiwo, A.A. and Afolami, J.A. (2010). Incessant building collapse: A case of a hotel in Akure, Nigeria. *Journal of Building Appraisal*, 6(3–4), 241.

Tan, C.K. and Abdul Rahman, H. (2005, May 4–5). Preliminary research into overcoming implementation problems of quality management in construction projects. In M.N. Daud, Y. Ahmad, F.A. Mohd Rahim and R. Sulaiman (Eds.), *Proceedings of the 4th MICRA Conference*, University of Malaya, Kuala Lumpur, pp. 08(15)–08(27).

Tang, S.L. and Kam, C.W. (1999). A survey of ISO 9001 implementation in engineering consultancies in Hong Kong. *The International Journal of Quality & Reliability Management*, 16(6), 562–574.

Tsiotras, G. and Gotzamani, K. (1996). ISO 9000 as an entry key to TQM: The case of Greek industry. *The International Journal of Quality & Reliability Management*, 13(4), 64–76.

Turk, A.M. (2006). ISO 9000 in construction: An examination of its application in Turkey. *Building and Environment*, 41, 501–511.

Windapo, A. (2006). The threat of building collapse on sustainable development in the built environment in Nigeria. *Proceedings: National Conference on Sustainable Development and the Built Environment*, Nigerian Institute of Building, Jos, 9–12 August, 59–65.

Windapo, A.O. and Rotimi, J.O. (2012). Contemporary issues in building collapse and its implications for sustainable development. *Buildings*, 2(3), 283–299.

Zantanidis, S. and Tsiotras, G. (1998). Quality management: A new challenge for the Greek construction industry. *Total Quality Management*, 9(7), 619–653.

https://doi.org/10.1142/9789811224720_0009

Chapter 9

Curbing Communication Challenges in Construction Project Management in Developing Countries

Fidelis Emuze, L.G. Mollo and Bankole Awuzie

Central University of Technology, Bloemfontein, South Africa

Abstract

While there has been increasing emphasis on reducing challenges in construction project management linked to cost, time, quality, and safety, limited attention has been paid to project communication management (PCM). The aim of this chapter is to fill this gap by addressing the question: What practical measures will engender effective PCM in construction in developing countries? Drawing on examples of construction project practices, it is proposed, in this chapter, that project success is endangered when the planning, collection, sharing, and management of information are ineffective. The behavior-, culture-, diversity-, and platform-related issues that affect communication and project outcomes are examined. In the chapter, overall, emphasis has been placed on the notion that communication management has played a vital, but under-recognized, role in the realization of project performance in construction in developing countries. It is suggested that an effective practical approach to managing communication in construction in developing countries would be to mitigate language- and cultural diversity-related barriers in tandem with the use of digital technologies. The conceptual argument is that enabling social interaction and use of technologies curbs PCM challenges in construction in developing countries.

Keywords: Collaboration, communication, construction, developing countries, project management, social interaction

Background

Communication is defined as the process of acquiring all relevant information, interpreting this information, and effectively disseminating the information to persons who might need it (Emmitt and Gorse, 2006). According to Taleb *et al.* (2017), communication remains the foundation of every human interaction between different parts of the dialog, and it gives meaning and solidity to the conducted activities. Communication entails individuals having the ability to interact effectively with clients and other professionals (Zulch, 2014). As such, project communication management (PCM) is a critical success factor for engendering improved construction project performance in all countries. Communication, regardless of project type, is a fundamental indicator of superior performance of a team.

Thus, PCM is a major factor that influences project outcomes and, as such, it can be one of the major problems that leads to failures. The intention in this chapter is not to analyze the tools or techniques of PCM, whether in oral, written, or behavioral (gesture) forms, but to emphasize the efficacy of PCM because how people communicate is as important as what people communicate (Saiedian and Dale, 2000). Many reasons for this are given in the relevant literature, of which a few are cited in this chapter. PCM is vital as it brings individuals, teams, organizations, and ideas together to construct meanings that establish ways to act. To communicate is to act, which implies that communication is a product, and producer, of a social reality (Ferreira, 2011). PCM is also a representation of the thoughts and paradigms of the collective involved in delivering a project.

The execution of a construction project activity is a collective endeavor, involving people with diverse skills, expertise, and aptitudes working together (Dainty *et al.*, 2007). For example, projects comprise a community of practice (CoP) within which people need to share ideas and be understood, in diverse situations, through communication. Members of the CoP have to transmit and receive information. After receiving and working on the information, the receiver transmits feedback to the original sender or to a new receiver. In effect, the trajectory of information sharing in the CoP is not linear, but is a cyclical process to affirm that communication has taken place (Almeida *et al.*, 2010). Construction work thus involves communication and collaboration between project actors in the form of architects, engineers, site agents, foremen, tradespeople, and general workers (Dainty *et al.*, 2007).

Accordingly, communication planning pulls the project together (Burke, 2013). For example, in the construction industry, project actors are responsible for not only developing the project organizational structure but also establishing communication lines required for pulling the project together. Burke (2013) defined a line of communication as a formal or informal link between two or more people, departments, companies, suppliers, contractors, or stakeholders. It should be acknowledged that the line of communication tends to follow the organizational chart, which not only outlines the stakeholders or project actors' positions but also implies responsibility, authority, and hierarchy.

The cyclical nature of communication and the diversity of actors on construction project worksites can result in PCM being bedeviled with problems either in terms of realizing project goals or in the development of collaborative, respectful, and trusting relationships within a CoP (Molena and Rovai, 2016). In the construction sector, for instance, project teams concluded that the regularity with which meetings were held affected how well a team accomplished its goals (Ammeter and Dukerich, 2002). Meetings have been identified as communication tools that facilitate the attainment of a common ontology concerning project progress within the project team (Gorse and Emmitt, 2009).

Given that effective communication is a significant element of project management (Zuo *et al.*, 2018), it is necessary always to improve PCM. The effectiveness of PCM in a developing country depends on a range of factors which include: clarity, trust, conciseness, agility, formality, feedback, completeness, transparency, storage, language, regularity (periodicity), security, and accessibility, as described in Table 9.1, compiled from

Table 9.1: Factors affecting project communication.

Factor	Description
Accessibility	Availability of information to everyone when required and necessary
Agility	Allowing sufficient time for response and action
Clarity	Adequate organization of content to facilitate understanding
Completeness	Having all required information to prevent ambiguity
Conciseness	The information presents the objective with ease
Feedback	Receiving answers to suggestions, criticisms, and new ideas
Formality	Using official templates and channels to convey information
Language	Using plain language without jargon to share information
Regularity	Sharing information consistently as and when due
Transparency	Ease of reaching/knowing everyone involved
Trust	Providing reliable and believable information from sources
Security	Ensuring privacy and confidentiality when required
Storage	Archiving information in an ordered way for future use

Adapted from Molena and Rovai (2016, p. 685).

a study in Brazil. The descriptions of these factors, derived from the work of several authors, show that they extend beyond the construction site. According to Dow and Taylor (2010), the major components of PCM include: communicating in a timely manner; generating the right information; and collecting, distributing, and storing information. These elements are also mentioned in Table 9.1.

It is notable that the professionals who worked in project operations in Brazil (the Sao Paulo PMI Chapter) gave greater importance to clarity, trust, agility, and complete information (Molena and Rovai, 2016). The preference of the professionals is understandable as they had to address several problems attributed to communication on their projects. Such problems included: lack of data storage, documents with incomplete information, technical issues with communication channels, lack of trust between interlocutors, and different languages, to mention a few. However, these problems are not peculiar to Brazil, as studies show that they pervade construction in developing countries. Ejohwomu *et al.* (2017) used a questionnaire survey to identify the significant barriers to effective communication in the Nigerian construction industry. They contended that unclear objectives, an ineffective reporting system, unclear channels of communication, and lack of trust hindered effective information sharing in the Nigerian construction industry. After an investigation into the link between project performance, trust, and communication in Hong Kong, it was suggested that improving information flow enhances project performance, which engenders trust between the team members (Cheung *et al.*, 2013). The insights gained from the studies carried out in Brazil and Nigeria indicate that all is not well with PCM in developing countries, where solutions must take cognizance of the techniques and tools required to engender an effective communication protocol in projects.

In addition, one of the most important skills required by project managers (PMs), whether in construction or any other industry, is the ability to communicate effectively. The ability of a PM to influence work teams is associated with effective ways of sharing information. For instance, communication skills help a PM to influence the tasks and conditions of projects positively (Ziek and Anderson, 2015). In two highly cited PCM studies by Henderson (2004; 2008), it was posited that encoding and decoding communication by a PM is related to satisfaction and productivity. Using data collected from cross-functional project teams from multiple disciplines, Henderson (2004) showed that there is a link between communication and performance. In a follow-up study, published in 2008, Henderson found that the competence of PMs to transmit information contributes significantly to team member satisfaction and productivity.

This chapter focuses on how to reduce PCM challenges among work teams in construction in developing countries. To achieve this, it was necessary to identify what practical measures will engender effective PCM in construction in developing countries. The dynamics of PCM relating to project performance are presented in the next section, followed by suggestions of a path for progress.

PCM and construction project outcomes

The construction industry, involving project team members, is regarded as being complex. It is necessary for project team members to achieve a high degree of communication and mutual understanding to deliver a project successfully (Khlaifat *et al.*, 2019). Performance in construction project management is measured according to various parameters. PCM is viewed as an essential factor (Khanyile *et al.*, 2019). Furthermore, recent developments around the globe have resulted in the inclusion of parameters such as material and resource efficiency, health and safety, and social value, apart from the conventional parameters of time, cost, and quality (Kibert, 2016; Raiden *et al.*, 2018; Manu *et al.*, 2020). Accordingly, it is necessary for a PM to understand the dynamics associated with managing communication to be able to manage the construction process to deliver a project. Challenges in communication management experienced by project teams, which have the potential to affect any of the project performance parameters, include: language and cultural diversity within the project team, nature of communication behavior prevalent within project teams, and the completeness or clarity of the project brief.

These communication challenges culminate in an increase in rework, reduction of product quality, low employee morale, low levels of client satisfaction, end-user apathy, and lack of safety (Manu *et al.*, 2020). These issues represent facets of project, and project management, failure. Thus, effective communication management remains a salient contributor to project management and project success. In Table 9.2, communication challenges that impede construction project success in various countries are shown. The challenges occur in both developed and developing countries.

These challenges, and their impact on various aspects of project management performance, are presented using vignettes in the following sections. The vignettes were derived by juxtaposing excerpts from the

Table 9.2: Examples of PCM challenges in construction projects in developing countries.

Challenges	Sources
Language and cultural diversity	Emuze and James (2013); Oswald *et al.* (2019)
Behavior-related issues	Gorse and Emmitt (2007), Sun *et al.* (2015); Jiang and Pretorius (2010); Olanrewaju *et al.* (2017)
Platforms of information shared	Yaser *et al.* (2019); Alsamadani *et al.* (2013); Vahabi *et al.* (2020)

Table 9.3: Overview of student residence project.

Project team	Description
Client	South African University of Technology (SAUoT)
Project team	Clients, Consultants, Contractor, and Subcontractors
Project duration	24 months
Project Value	R 90,000,000.00 ($5,272,194.79)*
Project Size	50-room

Note: *USD converted on xe.com on September 23, 2020.

literature (Table 9.2) and relevant data from observations made during a case study. The case study contained details of issues, relating to communication management, witnessed during the construction of new, on-campus student accommodation at the South African University of Technology (SAUoT). This project is referred to as *Student Residence*. Project characteristics of *Student Residence* are provided in Table 9.3.

The purpose of the vignettes below is to facilitate in-depth understanding of the implications of communication challenges for the success parameters of project management, namely: cost, time, quality, and health and safety outcomes, in the context of a developing country. The dynamics of communication challenges in a project environment are real. As can be deduced from the vignettes, when the dynamics of these challenges are mitigated, an improvement in project performance and project management outcomes is likely. However, when the dynamics of these challenges are allowed to proliferate, the potential for conflicts and unpleasant project situations is high. The dynamics affirm that communication is a factor that determines the success or failure of projects and project management (Söderlund, 2011) because communication not only involves the exchange of information but also has consequences for the outcomes of projects (Ziek and Anderson, 2015). The dynamics show that communication is a process of constructing and disputing meanings, where dispute indicates a need amongst the project actors. The vignettes illustrate the notion that communication is the mutual triggering of coordinated behavior that occurs between members of a social unit.

Vignette 1: Impact of cultural diversity-related communication challenges on project management outcomes

The temporary multi-organizational and fragmented nature of a construction project has been highlighted (Emuze and James, 2013; Awuzie and McDermott, 2015; Oswald *et al.*, 2019). This characteristic implies the collaboration of representatives from different organizations and backgrounds in the delivery of a construction project. As such, the construction process entails the presence of a culturally diverse workforce. Cultural diversity has several benefits, including the variety of perspectives, skills, and personal attributes that individuals within a multi-cultural team can contribute (Ochieng and Price, 2010). Cultural diversity comprises any, or a combination of, the following: age, gender, ethnicity, religion, personality, social status, and sexual orientation. However, the levels of diversity witnessed in construction project sites have been noted as having a direct impact on the effectiveness of project communication and an indirect impact on project management outcomes.

In a study by Emuze and James (2013), the contribution of language and cultural diversity to ineffective communication on construction sites within the South African context was investigated. The study acknowledged the culturally diverse nature of the workforce that is present on construction sites in the country. A culturally diverse workforce is to be expected in the South African construction industry because of the different ethnic groups present in the country. This is further compounded by the influx of migrant workers from a number of the neighboring countries. Findings deduced from Emuze and James (2013) highlighted the significant contribution of the diversity in culture to the plethora of misunderstandings experienced within the project teams working on the surveyed projects.

Similarly, the findings from data obtained from *Student Residence* showed the same challenges. In this instance, the contractor and the project manager were sourced from the Gauteng Province in South Africa and had recruited most of the subcontractors and artisans from across the country. The contractor's project manager (C-PM) on the site alluded to instances where the artisans, who had been sourced locally and from neighboring Lesotho, had to take instructions from him, using the English Language, on how to carry out trench excavations, among other activities. This led to several cases of misinterpretation and subsequent rework. This prompted the recruitment of a site manager who was bilingual, with proficiency in the English and Sesotho languages. The recruitment of this site manager contributed to improved communication and negotiations on the construction site.

The C-PM explained that they had experienced protests by the artisans because of the misunderstanding of the cultural diversity among the workforce. One such protest was attributed to the inability of one of the subcontractors to approve leave applications for some workers who wanted to travel to Lesotho to attend a traditional (ritual) ceremony. During deliberations to resolve the impasse, the affected workers had argued that their culture was not being respected by management, hence they decided to embark on the protest and abandon site activities. This disagreement resulted in project delays, poor work quality, cost increase, and low morale among workers. The C-PM responded to these issues of cultural diversity by closing the project sites for three days, to allow the workers to travel to Lesotho to attend the traditional ceremony. This exemplar situation is evidence of the potential of ineffectual communication to result in avoidable conflicts which, in turn, affect productivity.

Issues were raised also concerning the health and safety communication on the *Student Residence* site. Most of the artisans (especially migrant workers) found it difficult to comprehend the notices on site concerning the health and safety protocol. It was observed also that the attitude and perception of these workers toward the health and safety protocol were influenced by their culture and belief systems.

Based on the foregoing, the need for the development and sustenance of a project culture which all project actors must subscribe to has become imperative. Such a project culture will seek to absorb all individual belief systems which might hinder effective PCM (Loosemore and Muslmani, 1990; Zheng *et al.*, 2017).

Vignette 2: Impact of language-related communication challenges on project management outcomes

Language-related communication challenges are not peculiar to construction sites in the developing world, as illustrated by Oswald *et al.* (2019), who drew evidence from a construction site in the UK. In their study, Oswald *et al.* (2019) chronicled the inability of most of the artisans recruited for the project from Eastern Europe (where there are emergent countries with developing economies) to communicate with the rest of the workforce because of language barriers. According to the study, this had major implications for health and safety performance on the project as it was difficult for these migrant workers to comprehend the health and safety protocols that existed on site. This problem was resolved with the recruitment of a bilingual translator to work with the health and safety advisor on the project. However, the inadequacy of the arrangement, and in particular, in terms of the number of translators, was pointed out by the health and safety advisor (Oswald *et al.*, 2019, p. 1):

> There are clearly problems with this one-in-six translator policy [one English speaker to every six non-English workers in a team]. What happens when half the team is on site, and the other half is in the office? The English speakers are usually the office guys, the project managers, or the engineers, or even the foreman — we could be looking in completely the wrong place. And what if they are away training, or ill or on their jollies [holidays], or just not wearing their black band? Then they aren't much help if you are trying to communicate with the guys out on the park [the construction site].

Corroborating the views elucidated in Oswald *et al.* (2019), Emuze and James (2013) further chronicled burgeoning incidences of miscommunication and misunderstanding among project team members, particularly between site managers and workers, because of language differences on construction sites. It was observed in the conclusion of the study that misunderstanding by workers of assigned tasks and miscommunication of relevant information by project stewards (managers) continually undermined the attainment of successful project outcomes.

These ineffective communication tendencies relating to language and cultural barriers result in rework and other construction problems on site when they are not addressed adequately (Emuze and James, 2013). Sharing a common culture and/or language between site managers and site workers is sometimes important for effective communication, morale, and productivity (Emuze and James, 2013). However, this is seldom the case in construction projects in developing countries, so there is a need to mitigate unsatisfactory situations (Molena and Rovai, 2016).

Vignette 3: Impact of communication behavior-related challenges on project management outcomes

The nature of interaction between project team members has an impact on communication effectiveness (Jiang and Pretorius, 2010; Gorse and Emmitt, 2007). Such interactions are described as communication behavior and are classified into: monitoring, managing, challenging, and negotiating behaviors (Sun *et al.*, 2015). The exhibition of any, or a combination, of these communication behaviors by the project manager toward the project team members tends to have a significant influence on their level of willingness to participate toward the attainment of the deliverables and outcomes of the project. In a study by Jiang and Pretorius (2010), the impact of the communication behaviors exhibited by Chinese and South African PMs on different project activities was examined. The study considered: project communication, negotiation, conflict resolution, contract processes, and team-building, all of which contribute to the efforts to attain successful project outcomes. According to the findings of the study, the significant effect of communication behaviors on four of the project activities was established, except for contract practices. This implied that the impact of communication behaviors was mostly on the social plane of group interactions and not the task-based plane.

In another study, Gorse and Emmitt (2007) delineated group interactions along two cardinal planes: social and task-based. The former is concerned with socio-emotional communication leading to the evolution and maintenance of relationships between group members; and the latter is concerned with communication relating to the completion of assigned tasks. However, both communication genres are relevant for successful project management outcomes.

In another research, Sun *et al.* (2015) corroborated the criticality of certain communication behaviors (monitoring, managing, challenging, and negotiating) in improving team performance directly, thereby facilitating successful project outcomes from an innovation perspective within Architecture, Engineering and Construction (AEC) project teams. Sun *et al.* (2015) sought to identify and define the communication behaviors of interorganizational project teams, which had the potential to influence performance in innovative implementation within the context of integrated project delivery (IPD) systems. The effective adoption and implementation of innovative practices is becoming increasingly important to the attainment of successful construction project outcomes due to complexity, pace, and uncertainty (Morris *et al.*, 2012) and pervasive overruns in time and cost (Patty and Denton, 2010). However, for such innovations to be successful in contributing toward the success of the project, the buy-in of most members of the project team is required. This can be achieved through effective communication. Accordingly, there is a need for advocates for the adoption and implementation of innovation within construction project teams to ensure that appropriate communication behavior is deployed to secure the necessary level of buy-in.

In their study mentioned above, Gorse and Emmitt (2007) made the case for better understanding of communication mechanisms within construction project teams and groups, as well as at the level of interpersonal relationships. It is pertinent to discuss how they proceeded to achieve the objective of the study in some detail. Gorse and Emmitt (2007) set out to model the nature of team interactions from a communication behavior perspective, relying on data sourced from 36 live project meetings from 10 construction projects. Based on the findings from the study, the researchers established the predominant use of task-based interaction by project teams during the exchange of project-related information at site meetings and related platforms, to the detriment of social interaction. Accordingly, they maintained that this low level of social interaction among participants negated the ability of most of them to comment on or challenge instructions or information provided by the PM in a constructive manner.

To buttress the significance of achieving the right mix of social and task-based interactions, Gorse and Emmitt (2007) submitted that, whereas project teams shared task-based information through ideas, information, opinions, and suggestions for the attainment of project goals, the formation of relationships between them was dependent largely on their show of support, establishment of values, and amicable resolution of differences. Whilst highlighting the essential role of the latter (forming inter-team relationships) in enabling project success, Gorse and Emmitt (2007) inferred that such relationships can be achieved only through interaction that has social and emotional content. However, the low levels of social and emotional content observed were attributed readily to the temporality of the construction project, team and the continued influx and exit of different team members upon completion of their tasks at different stages of the project.

In conclusion, Gorse and Emmitt (2007) admitted to the utility of socio-emotional interaction in emphasizing the importance of the information conveyed, but maintained that the perception of the communicator's communication behavior by the recipients would influence their willingness to use the information received. Suffice it to say that the communication behavior exhibited will contribute to the level of trust in the information communicated. This is a salient point to note in the quest to evolve an effective communication management platform for construction projects because the lack of trust, lack of honesty, selective listening, reluctance to communicate, misunderstanding of body language between workers and their supervisors, and workers' fear of authority, all of which emanate from perceptions of communication behavior, have been identified as communication barriers in construction projects.

On site at *Student Residence*, challenges associated with communication behaviors of the workers and their supervisors (the site agent and C-PM) were noticed. The artisans disclosed that they would gauge the body language of their supervisors before making suggestions to improve certain practices on site. Also, site meetings were mostly conducted in a uni-directional manner, whereby information was mostly conveyed to the workers by their supervisors, and most of the reservations which the workers had were not voiced at this time. An example of this could be related to the attendance of the traditional festival (referred to in Vignette 1) by a work-gang from the site. Whereas the workers ought to have informed the site agent formally concerning their intention to attend the event, they presumed, most likely judging by the body language of the site agent, and his supposed understanding of the cultural affinities of the workers, that he would not oppose their attending the event. Their fear of authority discouraged them from bringing the issue to the attention of the C-PM in a timely manner, hence the resort to a protest.

Based on the foregoing discussion under this vignette, the communication behaviors exhibited by members of the project team influenced the manner of interactions (communication) in the team and also their level of performance which, in turn, had an impact on project performance and outcomes.

Vignette 4: Communication platforms

Evidence has shown that the choice of an appropriate platform for disseminating various types of information within the project team, and the frequency with which this is done, plays a critical role in engendering effective communication management (Project Management Institute (PMI), 2017; Muller, 2015). Different platforms exist for the dissemination of information to a diverse range of project actors. For example, site meetings are considered to be an important communication platform between the contractor, consultants and site workers as they provide opportunities for face-to-face interactions among these parties to review activities on the site over a particular period. The advent of different digital platforms has also opened a vista of communication channels for the dissemination of project-based information.

The choice of communication platform is influenced mostly by the nature of the information being shared and the composition of the intended audience. For example, during the execution of a project, if wrong technical information is delivered to the workforce, the work will be executed wrongly and will have to be demolished and correction measures applied; these processes are associated with extra costs and waste generation. The nexus between choosing the right communication platform to share the right information and the desired influence was articulated in a study by Yaser *et al.* (2019).

In another study, Alsamadani *et al.* (2013) investigated communication between workers and supervisors in construction work-crews in the US. In the research, Alsamadani *et al.* (2013) considered the health and safety performance of nine work-crews based on the frequency of health and safety communication between workers and their supervisors. Findings from the study indicated that the crews that posted the highest health and safety performance were those that had received formal safety communication from their supervisors on a weekly basis, whereas three crews that received infrequent or no communication at all performed very poorly in those regards.

In a study to examine communication management in construction projects in Sri Lanka, Senaratne and Ruwanpura (2016) agreed that attaining the right fit between the medium (tools) of communication and the nature of the information had a significant influence on construction project outcomes. Adapting the communication management protocol, as provided for in the *A Guide to the Project Management Body of Knowledge (PMBOK Guide)* (Sixth Edition) (PMI, 2008), Senaratne and Ruwanpura (2016) outlined the relevant tools for achieving this fit within the contexts of construction projects.

Another issue relating to communication platforms and the nature of communication is the completeness of the shared information. Evidence abounds concerning the severe implications of incomplete information on project outcomes. For example, rework that is a persistent problem in construction (Zhang *et al.*, 2012), may occur due to incomplete information that often leads to cost (Hwang *et al.*, 2009) and time overruns (Love *et al.*, 2016), apart from quality (Arashpour *et al.*, 2014) issues on projects. This is also the case with the lack of appropriate levels of clarity required for a project brief.

In one scenario, the receipt of an incomplete version of updated support materials resulted in the collapse of a building that caused injury to workers on site (Emuze *et al.*, 2017). The collapse, which occurred while a mall was still under construction, resulted in two fatalities and 29 injuries as immediate consequences. The cause-and-effect diagrams compiled by Emuze *et al.* (2017) showed that the major factors responsible for the accident pertained to the method, materials, man, and measurement involved during construction. In other words, failures mushroomed in the project because the method of construction was executed incorrectly, and the material use and handling was suspect. Inadequate information was a common causal factor, apart from poor construction work and its supervision, structural design, and regulatory control.

Path to progress in PCM

Lack of effective communication hinders coordination, with negative implications for project performance (Arditi *et al.*, 2017). This is why Senaratne and Ruwanpura (2016) discovered that effective communication leads to a full comprehension of what is required to achieve project deliverables. In a model for enhancing project performance, Anantatmula (2015) showed that communication is an essential factor for unified team dynamics and decision-making. In essence, effective communication is vital to control time and cost in construction projects. For example, in a Malaysian study, the interviewees agreed that effective communication within the project team was necessary for project time and cost control (Yap and Skitmore, 2020). This is consistent with previous findings, from which it was contended that effective communication is a prerequisite for superior project performance (Zuo *et al.*, 2018). Clarity in communication is vital to avoid rework, which is detrimental to project time- and cost-performance, owing to the additional effort involved in rectifying the defects (Yap *et al.*, 2017). Some extracts from the interview data cited by Yap and Skitmore (2020) emphasize the need to find a pathway forward. The insightful comments by the interviewees in Yap and Skitmore (2020, pp. 11–12) included:

> ...communicate well...fewer disputes, fewer discrepancies would arise.
>
> ...in any project development, teamwork (not individual) is required to come out with the most effective design to meet client's need ...within the time frame and budget requirements.

> ...project meetings provide a platform for resolving coordination issues thru weekly fixed time to highlight the discrepancy in drawings.
>
> ...architectural visual experience is important. Seeing is believing in space creation.
>
> ...out-of-office session, such as a casual dinner, to destress and know each other better.
>
> ...WhatsApp's chat group provides day and night communication.
>
> ...photographs can be transmitted via mobile phones.

The above quotes and the discussed vignettes highlight a need to chart a path to progress in PCM, especially in relation to construction in developing countries. In the path to progress in PCM, communication is regarded as a skill and a factor. As a factor, the focus of PCM is on the relationship between communication (information flow) and progress to determine the success or failure of projects and project management (Söderlund, 2011). While poor communication affects team performance negatively (Katz, 1982), effective communication affects performance positively. Past studies showed that the amount of communication among team members is a strong predictor of project outcomes (Ziek and Anderson, 2015). High-performing teams exchanged more messages and had increased communication frequency to predict team task performance (Chiocchio *et al.*, 2012).

The path to progress in PCM which is illustrated in Figure 9.1, should be underpinned by a common purpose, which should bring together the means of achieving cost, time, safety, and quality targets of a project. One key attribute of having a common purpose is the ability of a team to overcome the negative aspects of diversity and other challenges, as shown in Figure 9.2. Such a focus ensures that everyone involved in a project is in agreement about why they must communicate as they work together.

Furthermore, the efforts to achieve progress in PCM requires practices that go beyond the individual, project, and the proverbial "email" to ensure collective commitment is evident in how people act during the project. Supportive inputs from stakeholders, with the use of an applicable domain and devices, helps to ensure that relevant project information is used in a timely and correct manner. From site management to general

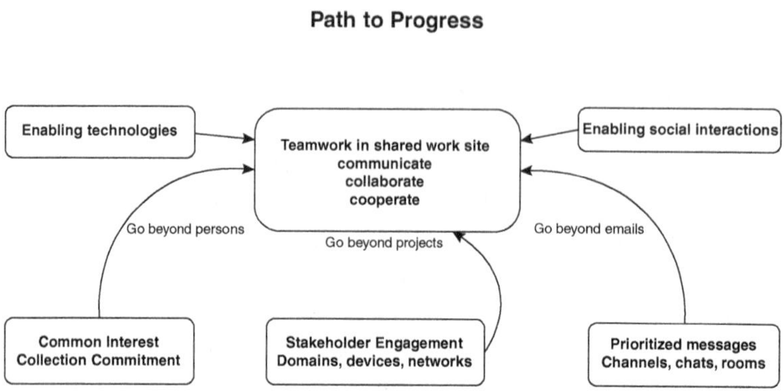

Figure 9.1: Inputs into the path to progress in project communication management.

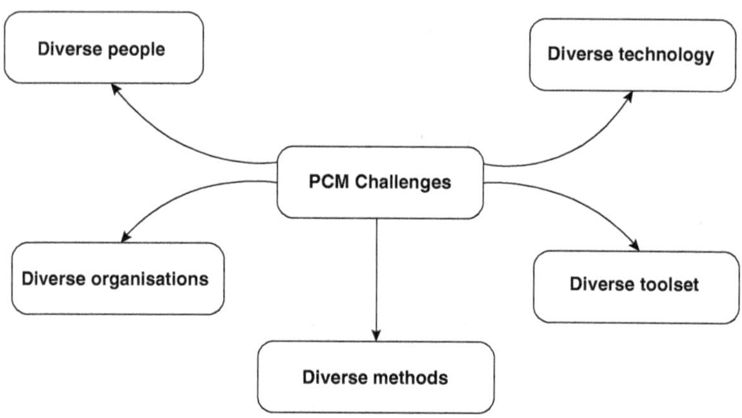

Figure 9.2: Illustration of PCM challenges.

workers on a site, the use of relevant channels for communication should be permitted to enable agility. With the proper social interaction and technologies, superior teamwork can be engendered in projects. As confirmed by the findings of studies in the literature, teamwork must be supported with two-way communication, members with diverse backgrounds, a common purpose (motivated by a shared vision), and common goals that are measurable (Rubrich, 2012).

There are many tools for, and approaches to, communication in projects (i.e., telephone, MS Teams, ZOOM, Skype, Cisco WebEx, dashboard, email, video-conferences, collaborative design tools, and face-to-face). In the PMBOK (PMI, 2017), methods for sharing information are specified. These include interactive communication (meetings, phone calls, instant messaging, and video-conferencing), push communication (letters, memos, reports, emails, faxes, blogs, and press releases), and pull communication (intranet sites, e-learning, lessons learned databases, and knowledge repositories). These methods mentioned above are applicable to PMs practicing in construction in developing countries.

It is suggested that, in general, the more tools used by PMs, the more successful a project team will be (PMI, 2017; Henderson and Stackman, 2010). When Henderson and Stackman (2010) studied project communication to determine to what extent the teams relied on mediated communications rather than face-to-face interactions, they discovered that project size was a factor. From their results, teams working on projects of US$1 million or less tended to be co-located and reliant on face-to-face interactions, while teams working on large projects relied on mediated platforms. Given that project sizes in developing countries mostly tend to be less than US$1 million, it can be argued that the use of face-to-face communication will be more frequent than alternative methods. By implication, the path to progress should enhance elements of social interaction among project teams.

The contribution of positive social interaction to the enhancement of PCM is vital because teamwork in construction involves multiple organizations working together on a project. In effect, working as a team in construction involves managing human relationships to promote collaboration (Anantatmula, 2015). The importance of social interaction is best explained in terms of human nature and reactions to change. When a change is discovered unannounced in a project or an enterprise, it gives rise to rumors to fill a communication void. Rumors ensue when project leaders fail to share information with the team effectively. If site management fails to communicate with the work team effectively, confusion and rumors will ensue (Rubrich, 2012). However, PMs can avoid the confusion, fear, insecurity and resistance loop by announcing change in a timely and effective manner. Effective communication thus engenders common interest, enthusiasm, and excitement within a working team.

Summary

In this chapter, the underlying theme about communication as a factor was the perception that improving PCM would have a positive impact on project performance. While not discounting technologies for accumulating and transmitting information, the emphasis in this chapter was on social interaction as a way to improve PCM in construction in developing countries. In the chapter, the argument is reiterated that it is through communication that projects are created, directions and decisions transmitted, and outcomes determined. Essentially, communication is the source of the dialog between project actors that shapes the outcome of projects.

In this chapter, practical measures have been highlighted that should engender an effective PCM in developing countries. Drawing on examples from vignettes and past studies, it has been suggested that project success is endangered when the planning, collection, sharing, and management of information is ineffective because communication is a determinant of performance. Working in teams requires participants to communicate, in order to cooperate and collaborate to realize the project outcomes. The path to progress in PCM is a practical approach suggested here to improve communication in construction projects in developing countries.

In developing countries, PMs should pay attention to concepts, techniques, and tools that focus on social interaction among people in construction. Site managers should understand the flow of events and human actions that frame task completion in projects within an array of social agendas, practices, and stakeholder relations. It could be said that:

> *If project management is the engine of superior performance in the delivery of construction assets in developing countries, then communication is the fuel.*
>
> (Fidelis Emuze, 2022)

This statement underscores the importance of PCM in the delivery of construction projects in developing countries.

References

Almeida, L.M.D.S., Souza, L.G.M.D. and Mello, C.H.P. (2010). Internal communication as a marketing tool to quality promotion: Case study in a global communication company. *Gestão & Produção*, 17, 19–34.

Alsamadani, R., Hallowell, M. and Javernick-Will, A.N. (2013). Measuring and modelling safety communication in small work crews in the US using social network analysis. *Construction Management and Economics*, 31(6), 568–579.

Ammeter, A.P. and Dukerich, J.M. (2002). Leadership, team building, and team member characteristics in high performance project teams. *Engineering Management Journal*, 14, 3–10.

Anantatmula, V.S. (2015). Strategies for enhancing project performance. *Journal of Management in Engineering*, 31, 04015013.

Arashpour. M., Wakefield, R., Blismas, N. and Lee, E.W.M. (2014). Analysis of disruptions caused by construction field rework on productivity in residential projects. *Journal of Construction Engineering and Management*, 140(2), 1–12.

Arditi, D., Nayak, S. and Damci, A. (2017). Effect of organizational culture on delay in construction. *International Journal of Project Management*, 35, 136–147.

Awuzie, B.O. and McDermott, P. (2015). A conceptual model for evaluating infrastructure-based temporary multi-organisations. *Built Environment Project and Asset Management*, 5(1), 103–120.

Burke, R. (2013). *Project Management Techniques*, 2nd Edition. Burke Publishing, Hong Kong.

Cheung, S.O., Yiu, T.W. and Lam, M.C. (2013). Interweaving trust and communication with project performance. *Journal of Construction Engineering and Management*, 139, 941–950.

Chiocchio, F., Grenier, S., O'neill, T.A., Savaria, K. and Williams, J.D. (2012). The effects of collaboration on performance: A multilevel validation in project teams. *International Journal of Project Organisation and Management*, 4, 1–37.

Dainty, A., Moore, D. and Murray, M. (2007). *Communication in Construction: Theory and Practice*. Routledge, London.

Dow, W. and Taylor, B. (2010). *Project Management Communications Bible*. John Wiley & Sons, Indianapolis, IN.

Ejohwomu, O.A., Oshodi, O.S. and Lam, K.C. (2017). Nigeria's construction industry: Barriers to effective communication. *Engineering, Construction and Architectural Management*, 24(4), 652–667.

Emmitt, S. and Gorse, C. (2006). *Communication in Construction Teams*, 1st Edition. Routledge, London.

Emuze, F. and James, M. (2013). Exploring communication challenges due to language and cultural diversity on South African construction sites. *Acta Structilia*, 20(1), 44–65.

Emuze, F.A., van Eeden, L. and Geminiani, F. (2017) A South African case study on the causes of building collapse. *Journal of Construction*, 10(4), 11–28.

Ferreira, E.G.M. (2011). Social dialogue: Communication in building relationships between organizations and neighboring communities — The case Ampla (Tese de Doutorado). Universidade de São Paulo, São Paulo. www.teses.usp.br/teses/disponiveis/27/27154/tde-23092011-182224/ [Accessed 20 August 2021].

Gamil, Y. and Rahman, I.A. (2017). Identification of causes and effects of poor communication in construction industry: A theoretical review. *Emerging Science Journal*, 1(4), 239–247.

Gorse, C.A. and Emmitt, S. (2009). Informal interaction in construction progress meetings. *Construction Management and Economics*, 27(10), 983–993.

Gorse, C.A. and Emmitt, S. (2007). Communication behaviour during management and design team meetings: A comparison of group interaction. *Construction Management and Economics*, 25(11), 1197–1213.

Henderson, L.S. (2004). Encoding and decoding communication competencies in project management — An exploratory study. *International Journal of Project Management*, 22, 469–476.

Henderson, L.S. (2008). The impact of project managers' communication competencies: Validation and extension of a research model for virtuality, satisfaction, and productivity on project teams. *Project Management Journal*, 39, 48–59.

Henderson, L.S. and Stackman, R.W. (2010). An exploratory study of gender in project management: Interrelationships with role, location, technology, and project cost. *Project Management Journal*, 41(5), 37–55.

Hwang, B-G., Thomas, S.R., Haas, C.T. and Caldas, C.H. (2009). Measuring the impact of rework on construction cost performance. *Journal of Construction Engineering and Management*, 135(3), 187–198.

Jiang, D. and Pretorius, L. (2010). Communication behaviour in international engineering projects: An empirical and comparative study between South Africa and China. *Technology Management for Global Economic Growth PICMET 2010*, pp. 1–8. Phuket, Thailand.

Katz, R. (1982). The effects of group longevity on project communication and performance. *Administrative Science Quarterly*, 27(1), 81–104.

Khlaifat, D.M., Alyagoub, R.E., Sweis, R.J. and Sweis, G.J. (2019). Factors leading to construction projects' failure in Jordon. *Journal of Construction Management*, 19(1), 65–78. https://doi.org/10.1080/15623599.2017.1382092.

Kibert, C.J. (2016) *Sustainable Construction: Green Building Design and Delivery*, 4th Edition. Wiley, Chichester, UK.

Kines, P., Andersen, L.P., Spangenberg, S., Mikkelsen, K. L., Dyreborg, J. and Zohar, D. (2010). Improving construction site safety through leader-based verbal safety communication. *Journal of Safety Research*, 41, 399–406.

Love, P.E.D., Ackermann, F., Smith, J., Irani, Z. and Edwards, D.J. (2016). Making sense of rework causation in offshore hydrocarbon projects. *Project Management Journal*, 47(4), 16–13.

Loosemore, M. and Muslmani, H.A. (1999). Construction project management in the Persian Gulf: Inter-cultural communication. *International Journal of Project Management*, 17(2), 95–100.

Manu, P., Emuze, F.A., Saurin, T.A. and Hadikusumo, H.W. (Eds.) (2020). *Construction Health and Safety in Developing Countries*. Routledge, Abingdon, UK.

Molena, A. and Rovai, R.L. (2016). Reference model for improved communicability in projects. *International Journal of Managing Projects in Business*, 9(3), 682–706.

Morris, P.W.G., Pinto, J.K and Soderlund, J. (2012). *The Oxford Handbook of Project Management*. Oxford University Press, Oxford, UK.

Mueller, J. (2015). Formal and informal practices of knowledge sharing between project teams and enacted cultural characteristics, *Project Management Journal*, 46(1), 5368.

Ochieng, E.G. and Price, A. (2010). Managing cross-cultural communication in multicultural construction project teams: The case of Kenya and UK. *International Journal of Project Management*, 28, 449–460.

Olanrewaju, A., Tan, S.Y. and Kwan, L.F. (2017). Roles of communication on performance of the construction sector. *Procedia Engineering*, 193, 763–770.

Oswald, D., Wade, F., Sherratt, F. and Smith, S. (2019). Communicating health and safety on a multinational construction project: Challenges and strategies. *Journal of Construction Engineering and Management*, 145(4), 1–34. https://doi.org/10.1061/(ASCE)CO.1943-7862.0001634.

Patty, R.M. and Denton, M.A. (2010). *The End of Project Overruns: Lean and Beyond for Engineering, Procurement and Construction*. Universal Publishers, Boca Raton, FL.

Project Management Institute (2017). *A Guide to the Project Management Body of Knowledge (PMBOK Guide)*, 6th Edition. Project Management Institute, Inc, Newtown Square, PA.

Raiden, A., Loosemore, M., King, A. and Gorse, C. (2018). *Social Value in Construction*. Routledge, Abingdon, UK.

Rubrich, L. (2012). *An Introduction to Lean Construction: Applying Lean to Construction Organisations and Processes*. WCM Associates, Fort Wayne, IN.

Saiedian, H. and Dale, R. (2000). Requirements engineering: Making the connection between the software developer and customer. *Information and Software Technology*, 42, 419–428.

Senaratne, S. and Ruwanpura, M. (2016). Communication in construction: A management perspective through case studies in Sri Lanka. *Architectural Engineering and Design Management*, 12(1), 3–18.

Söderlund, J. (2011). Pluralism in project management: Navigating the crossroads of specialization and fragmentation. *International Journal of Management Reviews*, 13, 153–176.

Sun, W., Mollaoglu, S., Miller, V. and Manata, B. (2015). Communication behaviours to implement innovations: How do AEC teams communicate in IPD projects? *Project Management Journal*, 46(1), 84–96.

Taleb, H., Ismail, S., Wahab, M.H., Rani, W.N. and Amat, R.C. (2017). An overview of project communication management in construction industry projects. *Journal of Management, Economics, and Industrial Organization*, 1(1), 1–8.

Vahabi, A., Nasirzadeh, F. & Mills, A. (2020): Impact of project briefing clarity on construction project performance. *International Journal of Construction Management*. https://doi.org/10.1080/15623599.2020.1802681.

Yap, J.B.H., Abdul-Rahman, H. and Chen, W. (2017). Collaborative model: Managing design changes with reusable project experiences through project learning and effective communication. *International Journal of Project Management*, 35, 1253–1271.

Yap, J.B.H. and Skitmore, M. (2020). Ameliorating time and cost control with project learning and communication management: Leveraging on reusable knowledge assets. *International Journal of Managing Projects in Business*. https://doi.org/10.1108/IJMPB-02-2019-0034.

Yaser, G., Ismail, A.R. and Sasitharan, N. (2019). Investigating the effect of poor communication in terms of cost and time overruns in the construction industry. *International Journal of Construction Supply Chain Management*, 9(2), 94–106.

Zamani, V., Banihashemi, S.Y. and Abbasi, A. (2020). How can communication networks among excavator crew members in construction projects affect the relationship between safety climate and safety outcomes? *Safety Science*, 128, 1–12.

Zhang, D., Haas, C.T., Goodrum, P.M., Caldas, C.H. and Granger, R. (2012). Construction small-projects rework reduction for capital facilities. *Journal of Construction Engineering and Management*, 138(12), 1377–1385.

Zheng, J., Wu, G., Xie, H. and Xu, H. (2017). Ambidextrous leadership and sustainability-based project performance: The role of project culture. *Sustainability*, 9(12), 2336.

Ziek, P. and Anderson, J.D. (2015). Communication, dialogue and project management. *International Journal of Managing Projects in Business*, 8(4), 788–803.

Zulch, B. (2014). Leadership communication in project management. *Procedia — Social and Behavioral Sciences*, 119, 172–181.

Zuo, J., Zhao, X., Nguyen, Q.B.M., Ma, T. and Gao, S. (2018). Soft skills of construction project management professionals and project success factors. *Engineering, Construction and Architectural Management*, 25(3), 425–442.

https://doi.org/10.1142/9789811224720_0010

Chapter 10

Construction Project Risk Management in Developing Countries

Abid Hasan and Imriyas Kamardeen

Deakin University, Australia

Abstract

The construction industry is a significant contributor to both the economy and employment in developing countries. However, the industry is criticized for the poor performance of construction projects due to schedule delays, cost overruns, poor quality, and high rates of accidents. In construction projects, the ability to identify, assess, and manage risks directly impacts the achievement of various project objectives. Construction projects are exposed to an uncertain environment and, as a result, require effective risk management throughout the project lifecycle for their successful completion. However, despite several advances in risk management, project risk management in construction projects in developing countries has remained inadequate. Studies about construction risks and risk management frameworks have mainly focused on developed nations with significantly different socio-political, economic, and legal systems. Hence, the suggestions and risk management frameworks need to be revisited and customized to suit the unique context of the developing countries. Although risk management principles and processes apply to various organizations and contexts, this chapter covers project risk management only. Specifically, this chapter first discusses the main risks encountered in construction projects and the risk management strategies and frameworks applied in developing countries. Next, it takes a distinct approach in which a socio-ecological theory is used to develop a holistic risk management framework. Finally, as an example, the framework is applied to analyze occupational health and safety risks in construction projects in developing countries.

Keywords: Construction, developing countries, project success criteria, project risks, risk management, socio-ecological model

Introduction

Risk is a widely used term in different contexts. Hertz and Thomas (1983) defined risk as a variety of situations involving many unknown, unexpected, frequently undesirable, and often unpredictable factors. The ISO 31000 standard (ISO 2018) defines risk as the effect of uncertainty on an organization's ability to meet its objectives. The standard further explains that the effect of an uncertainty could be both positive and negative. Furthermore, the objectives can be financial, occupational health and safety, and sustainability goals applied at different strategic and operational levels within a profit-based organization, not-for-profit organization, or a public-sector entity. The probability of the occurrence of undesirable events and their possible impact vary, depending on the nature of the business and industry.

Various researchers have classified risks differently — for example, internal and external risks or political risk, market risk, and financial risk (El-Sayegh, 2008; Perera *et al.*, 2009). Many other researchers have focused on risks affecting project performance parameters such as schedule/time, cost, quality, and safety (Zou *et al.*, 2007; Choudhry *et al.*, 2014). Similarly, previous studies have examined risk and risk management in different types of projects, based on procurement methods (for example, design-build projects or public–private partnership projects), size of the project (such as small projects or mega projects), type of the project (for example, building projects or infrastructure projects), location of the project (such as remote projects or international projects), project lifecycle phases (for example, feasibility stage or design stage), and viewpoints of stakeholders (such as contractors or consultants) (El-Sayegh, 2008; Rebeiz, 2012; Goh and

Abdul-Rahman, 2013; Vu *et al.*, 2017; Wu *et al.*, 2017; Santoso and Gallage, 2020). Therefore, risks in construction projects are contextual by nature. The external risk factors related to in-country economic risks, political risks, and Force Majeure risks are beyond the control of construction organizations, as opposed to internal risks, where stakeholders can exercise more control to manage the risks. Similarly, the complexity encountered in mega construction projects could add unique challenges to predicting risks compared to assessing the risks in small projects (Erol *et al.*, 2020). For example, the prominent risk factors in the build–operate–transfer of mega transportation projects in developing countries are financial issues related to design changes, occupational safety and health, insolvency of one of the private partners, currency risk, and fluctuations in the interest or inflation rates (Aladağ and Işik, 2017).

Perera *et al.* (2014) found that construction and design phases are prone to risks such as design errors by the consultant, delays in payment by the client, and delays in the client's decision-making process. Wu *et al.* (2017) identified five critical risk categories for project management success in the Chinese construction industry: those related to the designer, those concerning the contractor, those related to the subcontractor, those concerning the client, and those related to the government. They further found that of the five risks, the client-related risks, such as project funding problems and variations, have the most important relationship with project success, followed by risks related to the contractor. Regardless of the risk typology, a systematic approach to risk management in a construction project is essential for its successful completion.

Research shows a high degree of correlation between effective risk management and project success (Nawaz *et al.*, 2019). Since construction organizations are project-based, both project- and enterprise-level risks affect their ability to meet organizational goals and objectives. Risks are integral to any construction project, regardless of its size and nature, due to uncertainties and unknowns associated with it (Wu *et al.*, 2017). While many risks remain common in construction projects in developed and developing countries, previous studies show that the consequences and likelihood of risk occurrence could be higher in developing countries, often due to poor risk management. For instance, Zou *et al.* (2007) compared risks in construction projects in China with those in Australia. They found that contractors face more risks in China due to project funding problems, contractors' poor management competency, poor skills of the workers, inadequate safety measures or unsafe operations, and suppliers' inability to deliver materials on time.

Previous studies show that poor quality of work, premature failure of the facility, poor safety, inadequate or incorrect design, financial risk, payment delays, stakeholder issues, delays in permits or approval of the project, exchange rate fluctuations, inflation, and insufficient contingency reserves/plans are the most critical risks in construction projects in developing countries (Tang *et al.*, 2007; Amoah and Pretorius, 2020; Owusu-Manu *et al.*, 2020). Many construction projects in developing countries fail to meet the project completion date (Iyer and Jha, 2006; Assaf and Al-Hejji, 2006; Islam and Trigunarsyah, 2017; Wang *et al.*, 2018). The occurrence of cost overrun in construction projects are also common in developing countries (Shehu *et al.*, 2014; Derakhshanalavijeh and Teixeira, 2017; Kamal *et al.*, 2022; Coffie and Aigbavboa, 2020). Similarly, the construction industry in developing countries has poor safety and quality performance (Cheng *et al.*, 2012; Zahoor *et al.*, 2017; Umar and Egbu, 2018; Kamal *et al.*, 2019, Santoso and Gallage, 2020). Still, not all contractors in developing countries implement proper risk management in their construction projects (Mohamed *et al.*, 2015).

The present chapter on project risk management in construction projects in developing countries seeks to provide insights into the main project risks and reasons behind poor project performance in these countries. A robust understanding of risk management processes could help researchers and practitioners devise better risk management strategies. First, the chapter discusses project performance risks in construction projects in developing countries. While there could be several types of risks, the discussion is limited to risks related to crucial project performance indicators such as time, cost, quality, safety, and environment or sustainability. Next, we discuss the latent causes of construction project risks to explain poor risk management in developing countries. Then, the socio-ecological theory is used to derive a project risk management framework for developing countries. Lastly, the conclusion section presents key insights along with limitations of the study and suggestions for future research.

Key project performance risks in construction projects in developing countries

Key performance indicators of construction projects include duration, budget, quality, safety, and sustainability (Cox *et al.*, 2003). As a result, risk management efforts are primarily directed toward managing risks that may lead to higher costs, schedule delays, poor-quality work, safety incidents, and damage to the environment. Risk management is prioritized in accordance with the significance of influences on the key project performance indicators (Sohrabinejad and Rahimi, 2015). Typical project performance risks encountered in construction projects in developing countries are discussed briefly in the following sections.

Delay risk

Delays in construction project completion constitute a chronic problem in many developing countries. For instance, Iyer and Jha (2006) reported delays in 260 out of 646 central sector projects in the Indian construction industry. The delay ranged from one to 252 months and the combined time overrun was reported to be around 40 percent. Similarly, Assaf and Al-Hejji (2006) found 10 and 30 percent of time overruns in almost 70 percent of large projects in Saudi Arabia. Delays in project completion could result in significant additional costs to the client, contractor, or both (Trauner *et al.,* 2009). Delays can disturb the project cash flow and lead to cost overruns and penalties, or disincentives in construction projects (Hasan and Jha, 2016).

Since delays in project completion are common in the construction industry in developing countries, much research has been conducted to identify the risk factors in different types of projects in particular country contexts. The most critical factors affecting schedule performance in construction projects in Malaysia are financial and coordination problems (Alaghbari *et al.*, 2007); construction progress, owner management, staff competency, and the external environment in Vietnam (Thi and Swierczek 2010); safety, financial risk, operational risk, relationships among key stakeholders, and political risks in China (Wu *et al.,* 2017); and resource availability, the project manager's competence, inadequate planning, monitoring and control, and the project being in the public interest in Afghanistan (Kakar *et al.*, 2020). Wang *et al.* (2018) found the causes of variations, delays in progress payments, exceptionally low bids, and subcontractors' poor performance and communication issues as the most important causes of construction project delays in China. Chen *et al.* (2020) identified four key challenges leading to delays of infrastructure projects in China: (1) shortage of funding and delayed payment; (2) disruptions the project causes to the public, community, and environment; (3) poor construction planning and management; and (4) low productivity and work quality. Kamal *et al.* (2019) also identified inadequate project management as the most critical risk factor affecting schedule performance on construction projects in Pakistan. The main sources of delays in construction projects can be categorized into four main groups (or the 4P concept) — project related, practices, participants, and procurement (Ansah and Sorooshian, 2018). Islam and Trigunarsyah (2017) identified 53 frequent causes of construction delays in developing countries and categorized them into eight major groups. They found contractor's cash flow problems, poor site management, delays in progress payment by the owner, improper planning and scheduling, and frequent change orders during construction as the most critical and frequent factors causing schedule delays all over the developing world.

Cost overrun risk

Completing a construction project within the stipulated budget is one of the vital project success criteria. However, construction projects in developing countries face various risk factors that contribute to increases in the project cost. For instance, Shehu *et al.* (2014) found that more than 50 percent of Malaysian construction projects were prone to cost overruns. Coffie and Aigbavboa (2020) examined the cost overrun of building construction projects completed between 2011 and 2016 in Ghana and found that 96 percent of the projects experienced cost overruns.

Several studies have identified rework and change orders as leading causes of cost overruns in construction projects in developing countries. Al-Janabi *et al.* (2020) claimed that rework is the prime cause of cost overruns in the Egyptian construction industry. Rework due to unacceptable quality of work, insufficient budget from the government, and lack of technical knowledge among supervisors were the most crucial factors responsible for cost overruns in mega-hospital construction projects in Iran (Balali *et al.*, 2020). Kamal *et al.* (2019) also found rework as the most critical factor affecting cost performance on construction projects in Pakistan. Senouci *et al.* (2017) examined the influence of change orders on cost. They found that design errors, significant changes in the quantum of work, change of brief or scope by the owner, and differing site conditions lead to change orders and cost overruns in Qatari construction projects. In many developing countries, a weak economic environment and unstable policies significantly affect the project's final cost and schedule (Kassem *et al.*, 2020). Risks related to inflation, and variations in the interest and foreign exchange rates impact the project cost and profitability when material, plant, and equipment are purchased in foreign currencies (Mazher *et al.*, 2018). Asiedu and Adaku (2020) found that poor contract planning and supervision, change orders, weak institutional and economic environment of projects, and lack of effective coordination among the contracting parties are the primary causes of cost overruns in public-sector construction projects in Ghana. Musarat *et al.* (2020) found the inflation rate as the most critical factor influencing cost overrun in Malaysian construction projects due to significant deviations in the prices of construction materials during the project lifecycle.

Previous studies have also identified a lack of project management skills and poor stakeholder management as leading causes of cost overruns in construction projects in developing countries. Johnson and Babu (2020) found these top five causes of cost overruns in the UAE construction industry: design variation, poor cost estimation, delay in client's decision-making process, client's financial constraints, and inappropriate procurement methods. Durdyev *et al.* (2017) identified three main contributors to cost overruns in Cambodia's residential building industry as project and cost management, project finance, and project risk factors. Sinesilassie *et al.* (2018) argued that conflict among project participants and project manager's ignorance and lack of knowledge negatively impacted Ethiopian public construction projects' cost performance. Derakhshanalavijeh and Teixeira (2017) found that inaccurate estimates, improper planning, frequent design changes, inadequate labor/skills, inflation of machinery, labor, raw material and transportation costs were the leading causes of cost overrun in oil and gas construction projects in Iran.

Quality risk

Clients want good quality, reliability, and consistency with projects. Failure to meet the client's expectations and requirements of quality is a risk prevalent in many construction projects in developing countries. The construction industry in developing countries shows reluctance in adopting new techniques and is over-reliant on traditional approaches to quality management (Ullah *et al.*, 2017). Construction defects often lead to rework, which can have a negative impact on the project. Defective work, rework, remedial work, and poor-quality work in construction projects lead to schedule and cost overruns, conflicts, and disputes. The direct rework cost ranges from 5 to 20 percent of the contract value, whereas indirect costs due to schedule delays and disputes between stakeholders could be significant (Love and Edwards, 2004; Ye *et al.*, 2014).

Balouchi *et al.* (2019) argued that the leading cause of rework with the most impact on project cost is inadequate site supervision and inspection. The lack of experience, use of low-standard work procedures, and inadequate site monitoring and inspection have been identified as the primary contributors to poor-quality construction work in developing countries (Santoso and Gallage, 2020). Kamal *et al.* (2019) also found inadequate supervision as the most critical factor affecting the quality of construction projects in Pakistan. Additionally, changes in the scope of work and requests to accelerate completion could significantly affect the project's quality if the contractor places more emphasis on speeding up the project (Santoso and Gallage, 2020). Abdul-Rahman *et al.* (2014) claimed that lack of ethical standards and unethical acts by different stakeholders directly affect the quality of construction projects.

Occupational health and safety risk

The construction industry is one of the riskiest industries in terms of workplace accidents in both developed and developing economies. For instance, in Australia, 417 construction workers were killed between

2002–2003 and 2013–2014 (a rate of 2.24 fatalities per 100,000 workers) (Safe Work Australia, 2015). In the UK, 35 construction fatalities occurred in 2014–2015 (1.62 per 100,000 workers) (HSE, 2015), and it was 874 fatalities (9.5 per 100,000 workers) in the US in 2014 (BLS, 2015). Construction fatality rates in developing countries are much worse; they are three to six times higher than that of developed nations (Umar and Egbu, 2018). For instance, Ghana recorded a fatality rate of 77.6 per 100,000 workers (Kheni *et al.*, 2010). The Korean construction industry had a fatality rate range of 18.9 to 39.7 per 100,000 workers (Yoon *et al.*, 2013), and it was 13 fatalities per 100,000 workers in the Taiwanese construction industry (Cheng *et al.*, 2012). The Turkish construction industry accounted for 33.5 percent (570 out of 1,700) of total fatalities for all industries in 2011 (Gürcanli and Müngen, 2013). Patel and Jha (2016) revealed that 11,614 workers died annually in the Indian construction industry between 2008 and 2012, which is equivalent to 38 fatalities per day, and a fatal accident rate of 22 per 100,000 workers. Likewise, the Pakistani construction industry employed 7.3 percent of the total labor force but accounted for 14.1 percent of all accidents (Zahoor *et al.*, 2017).

Several factors are responsible for the high rates of construction fatalities in developing countries. The deployment of unskilled workers and a lack of standards for equipment used on construction sites in those countries present health and safety risks in construction projects. Besides, workers might be injured traveling to the site or do not receive timely care in the event of an accident due to slow emergency response and inadequate infrastructure (Gibb and Bust, 2006). Zahoor *et al.* (2017) identified the three most substantial contributors in the Pakistani construction industry: lack of enforcement of safety regulations and rules by government agencies, inadequate safety budget and lack of provision of safety incentives by the client, and unsatisfactory provision of safety training and resources by the contractor.

Wells and Hawkins (2015) argued that awarding construction contracts based on the lowest tender price in developing countries forces contractors to reduce the tender price by cutting the cost associated with safety management. Kheni *et al.* (2010) claimed that low literacy levels of workers, owner's/managers' ignorance of Occupational Health and Safety (OH&S) responsibilities, and ineffective OH&S administration were critical factors for poor safety in the Ghanaian construction industry. Gibb and Bust (2006) reported that poor safety management infrastructure, communication challenges due to language and literacy barriers, unregulated work practices, using traditional work methods, non-availability of construction equipment, extreme weather conditions, and corruption negatively affect safety management in developing countries. Similarly, research shows a lack of commitment to, and implementation of, safety management systems by contractors in countries such as Tanzania and South Africa (Mwombeki, 2005; Haupt and Smallwood, 2005). In brief, reasons for poor OH&S and higher fatality rates in developing countries are attributable to the government, project owners/clients, procurement methods, workers, and contractors.

Environmental risk

Sustainability is a critical consideration in construction projects due to their links with environmental risks such as soil or groundwater contamination; geological instability; proximity of projects to environmentally distressed areas; and handling, transport and disposal issues of hazardous construction materials and wastes. Rahman and Esa (2014) defined environmental risk as any risk or potential risk to the environment (of whatever degree or duration) and includes all types of impacts. Construction projects have considerable environmental and ecological effects (Yusof *et al.*, 2017). Construction activities contribute significantly to carbon emissions. According to Huang *et al.* (2018), the construction industry creates 315 million tons of direct carbon dioxide emission annually. Construction projects also contribute significantly to particulate matters, which can affect the air quality and cause diseases such as silicosis, lung cancer, cardiovascular disorders, chronic obstructive pulmonary diseases, and even premature death (Yang *et al.*, 2020; Wang *et al.*, 2020).

Environmental risk management and sustainable development demand the adoption of proper methods to improve environmental performance in construction projects (Rahman and Esa, 2014). However, lack of awareness of, and focus on, environmental sustainability has been noted in construction organizations in developing countries such as India (Tripathi *et al.*, 2021). Similarly, in Malaysia, Rahman and Esa (2014) noted an inadequate focus on environmental sustainability and poor handling of environmental risks, which are characterized by inadequate planning, lack of environmental management plans, poor enforcement of regulations, and low awareness and commitment among construction stakeholders to protecting the environment (Rahman and Esa, 2014).

Risk management in construction projects in developing countries

An overview of project risk management

Risk management is an integral part of project management. In the words of Nicholas and Steyn (2008), "project management is risk management." While it is impossible to eliminate various uncertainties inherent in a construction project, risk management aims to minimize the adverse effect of risks when elimination is not possible (Maylor, 2010). Risk management is an iterative process, and the project performance usually depends on appropriate risk management over the project lifecycle. The effectiveness of risk management directly relates to the achievement of project success factors and project objectives (Baloi and Price, 2003).

Risk management is one of the 10 knowledge areas in the sixth edition of the *Project Management Body of Knowledge* (PMBOK) Guide (Project Management Institute, 2017). The PMBOK's Project Risk Management knowledge area contains seven processes: plan risk management, identify risks, perform qualitative risk analysis, perform quantitative risk analysis, plan risk responses, implement risk responses, and monitor risks, which allow risk mitigation to achieve performance objectives. The APM Body of Knowledge (7th edition) defines risk management as a process that allows individual risk events and overall risk to be understood and managed proactively, optimizing success by minimizing threats and maximizing opportunities and outcomes (Association for Project Management, 2019). According to ISO 31000 (ISO 2018), risk management is a set of coordinated activities and methods that direct an organization to control risks that can affect its ability to achieve business objectives. It includes risk management principles, frameworks, and programs. Additionally, there are other guidelines, standards, and frameworks, providing a step-by-step process to risk management, such as RAMP (Risk Analysis and Management for Projects) developed by the Institution of Civil Engineers and the Institute and Faculty of Actuaries (2014).

Risk management in construction projects in developing countries

Risk assessment is a vital part of risk management. Previous studies and risk management standards prescribe several risk assessment techniques and tools. Both qualitative techniques (for example, risk probability and impact assessment, risk matrix, Delphi, and risk data quality assessment) and quantitative techniques based on statistical methods (such as decision tree analysis, sensitivity analysis, multi-criteria decision-making, artificial neural networks, and fuzzy set theory) have been used for risk assessment in construction projects in developing countries (Zayed *et al.*, 2008; Mahamid, 2013; El-Sayegh, 2014; Patel and Jha, 2015; Mazher *et al.*, 2018; Nawaz *et al.,* 2019). Previous studies show that qualitative risk assessment methods are used much more frequently than quantitative techniques in construction projects in developing countries.

The standard qualitative techniques used in risk management are checklists, expert interviews, experience, and brainstorming (Choudhry and Iqbal, 2013; Goh and Abdul-Rahman, 2013; Smith *et al.*, 2014). However, a high level of subjectivity is often involved in qualitative risk assessment practices due to their reliance solely on individuals' intuition, judgment, or experience. These checklists ignore interdependencies among risk factors and neglect the emergence of new risks over the project lifecycle (Yildiz *et al.*, 2014). Project participants in the Chinese construction industry apply techniques such as: (a) brainstorming for risk identification, (b) joint evaluation by key participants for risk analysis and developing risk response strategies, and (c) periodic document reviews for risk monitoring (Tang *et al.*, 2007). Mohamed *et al.* (2015) also found that the common method of risk identification in the Malaysian construction industry is brainstorming and analyzing historical data from previous projects. In Pakistan, Nawaz *et al.* (2019) noted that lessons learned from past projects were the most frequently used risk identification technique, followed by risk review meetings and interviews.

While qualitative risk management techniques could provide an accurate assessment of risk in a predictable project environment, different perceptions of risk, attitudes, and judgments could bring in subjectivity and errors (Akintoye and Macleod, 1997; Loosemore *et al.*, 2006). In contrast, statistical algorithms and simulations could provide more accurate risk assessment in noisy environments (Choudhry *et al.*, 2014; Gondia *et al.*, 2020). It is also crucial to recognize the cause-effect relationship and risk paths of a combination of various interdependent risk factors (Yildiz *et al.*, 2014).

Latent causes of poor risk management in construction projects in developing countries

Several factors lead to poor risk management in construction projects; they include a tick-the-box approach, misinterpretations or poor conceptualization of risks, disintegrated approaches to risk management, deficiencies in risk management practices, and lack of organizational support (Erol *et al.*, 2020). In practice, most organizations in developing countries employ an informal risk management process. Often, risk assessment practices include only risk identification, without further analysis of the probability or impact of risk (Tang *et al.*, 2007; Goh and Abdul-Rahman, 2013; Serpell *et al.*, 2017). The risk management approach is often reactive. Most small construction companies in developing countries do not follow a standard or well-established risk management framework (Amoah and Pretorius, 2019). Tadayon *et al.* (2012) claimed that Iranian construction companies do not focus on risk management in their projects. Tang *et al.* (2007) concluded that the risk management systems applied in the Chinese construction industry tend to be informal and inadequate to manage project risks. Similarly, Serpell *et al.* (2017) reported the reactive, sporadic, and unstructured risk management practices in the Chilean construction industry, resulting in insufficient capacity to manage project risks appropriately. Besides, contractors are unwilling to apply risk management to reduce the operational cost of projects. Consequently, inadequate risk management practices due to the lack of risk management capabilities and knowledge, and the ineffectiveness of risk identification strategy, lead to delays and cost overruns in many construction projects in developing countries (Tang *et al.*, 2007; Mohamed *et al.*, 2015; Serpell *et al.*, 2017; Nawaz *et al.*, 2019).

Incomplete information in construction projects is the root cause of risk, and as the amount of information increases, uncertainty and risk are likely to reduce (Xiang *et al.*, 2012). Lu and Yan (2013) argued that many contractors in developing countries depend on their gut feelings to deal with risk due to incomplete information and lack of risk management skills. They often ignore risks with a high probability of occurrence compared to risks with potentially serious effects. Risk decisions in small companies rely on the owners' traits and, therefore, are influenced by the psychological and demographic traits, risk perception, and risk appetite of the owner, along with a set of organizational variables (Acar and Göç, 2011). Construction project managers who score higher in extroversion tend to perceive risk as low and are more likely to be risk-seeking. In comparison, those who score higher in agreeableness and conscientiousness tend to perceive higher levels of risk and be more risk-avoiding (Wang *et al.*, 2016). Also, the award of contracts to local contractors lacking the necessary competence results in poor risk management. Iyer *et al.* (2020) posited that risks are not considered during contractor pre-qualification in developing countries; they suggested the incorporation of future risk scenarios for a project in the prequalification criteria.

Corruption and lack of accountability have remained major underlying causes of risks in construction projects in developing countries. Economic instability and institutional failures lead to risks in construction projects in these countries (Ogbu and Adindu, 2020). Owners sometimes intentionally do not reveal some of the risks in the contract documents comprehensively and explicitly and, therefore, contractors become exposed to such risks during the construction phase (Andi, 2006). In most developing countries, complex construction projects involve major international construction firms that may not possess any practical experience or knowledge of the local construction industry (Viswanathan and Jha, 2020). The political uncertainty and culturally different environment pose additional risks (Ashley and Bonner, 1987; Vu *et al.*, 2017).

In summary, previous studies on risk management in developing countries have consistently raised the issues of lack of project management and risk management skills, poor stakeholder management, corruption, and less attention to formal risk management as the underlying causes leading to poor risk management and, consequently, poor performance on construction projects. Therefore, a new risk management framework should consider broader aspects in developing countries in addition to the traditional considerations.

Project risk management framework for developing countries: Socio-ecological model

Construction projects in developing countries face various types of risks related to cost, time, quality, safety, and sustainability, as explained above. Departing from the traditional approach, this chapter now adopts the socio-ecological theory to analyze the sources of project risks in developing countries and then develop a framework of interventions for minimizing risk. Bronfenbrenner (1977) first introduced the socio-ecological theory, which continued to be developed until 2005, as a framework for understanding the multi-faceted and interactive effects of individual and environmental factors that influence outcomes as well as to identify effective interventions for modifying the outcomes. The theory has been applied in many fields owing to its broad and in-depth approach to preventive interventions (May *et al.*, 2008; Allegrante *et al.*, 2010; Al-rasheed and Kamardeen, 2017). Figure 10.1 illustrates a modified version of the

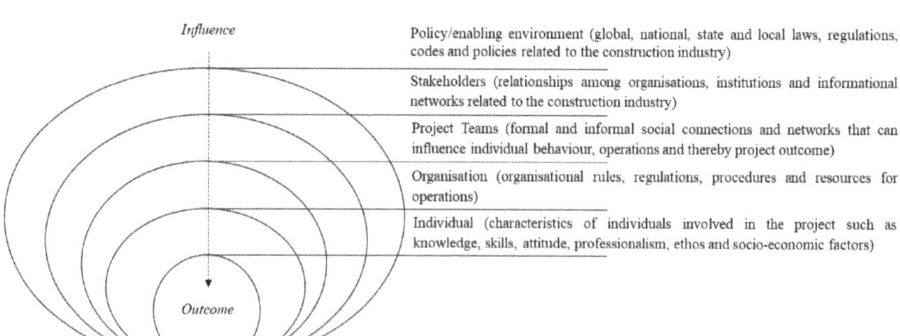

Figure 10.1: Modified socio-ecological model.

socio-ecological theory, with its five nested, hierarchical layers of influence on project outcomes. Although the layers in the figure appear separate from each other, they exert nested, top-down influences.

The modified model postulates that project outcomes are determined by influence from five levels:

- Individual — characteristics of project personnel (for example, knowledge, skills, attitude, behavior, professionalism, ethos, and socio-economic factors).
- Organization — organizational rules, regulations, and operational procedures affecting how well services are provided to clients.
- Project Teams — formal and informal social connections and networks influencing individual behavior, operations, and thereby project outcome; they include individuals from multiple organizations.
- Stakeholders — relationships among organizations, institutions, and informational networks related to business operations; this concerns largely external stakeholders.
- Policy/enabling environment — global, national, state, and local laws, regulations, codes, and policies related to the business concerned.

The socio-ecological theory is used to develop a holistic risk management framework for construction projects in developing countries, as

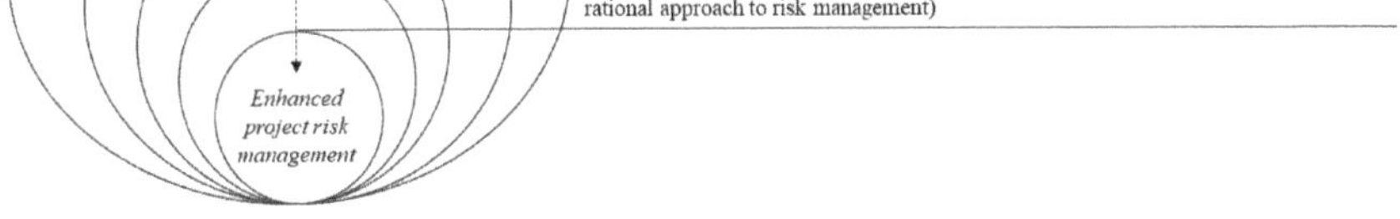

Figure 10.2: Socio-ecological model of project risk management for developing countries.

shown in Figure 10.2. The model in Figure 10.2 can be applied to mitigate the root causes of risks in construction projects in developing countries.

The risk management framework suggests the application of a hierarchy of risk control activities, including six stages: elimination, substitution, isolation, engineering control, administrative control, and behavior. The effectiveness of risk control diminishes as the process moves from elimination through substitution to behavior. Hence, the latent risk factors discussed in the previous sections and synthesized in Figure 10.2 need to be controlled, and specifically eliminated, to minimize project risks in developing countries. However, of the six typical risk responses in the form of retention, reduction, control, sharing, transfer, and avoidance (Kerzner, 2003; Loosemore *et al.*, 2006), Bahamid and Doh (2017) found that the risk management approach in construction projects in developing countries generally attempts to transfer or avoid risks. The risk management practices in developing countries need to shift from risk transfer to risk reduction and elimination through an objective assessment of risk and subsequent risk control. Table 10.1 shows the different levels of the socio-ecological model of latent causes of project risks in construction projects in developing countries. Next, some of the measures for addressing these latent causes at different socio-ecological levels are discussed.

At the policy level, local and central governments in developing countries can play an essential role in addressing some of the prevalent project risks with appropriate standards and detailed guidelines. Taofeeq *et al.* (2020a) found that government policies, rules, and regulations strengthen the relationship between personal factors affecting contractors' risk attitudes in the construction industry in Malaysia. Consequently, government policy could play an important role in the management of risks in the construction industry. For instance, contractors often show low willingness to purchase construction insurance in developing countries. Akinradewo *et al.* (2020) found that few contractors in developing countries have adopted insurance as a primary means of risk management in their construction projects despite insurance being efficient in managing external risks. However, social pressure from the environment (such as local laws and regulations and contract requirements) was seen to positively impact contractors' willingness to purchase construction insurance (Liu *et al.*, 2018). Deng *et al.* (2014) concluded that the top five ranked

Table 10.1: Socio-ecological analysis of latent causes of project risks in developing countries.

Level of influence	Construction industry relevance	Examples of latent risk factors
Individual	Construction professionals and workers	• Negligent behavior and poor attitude towards risk • Biased decision-making • Lack of risk management knowledge and skills • Lack of professional ethics • Unskilled workers
Organization	Construction and consultancy organizations	• Improper or inadequate operational procedures and methods • Informal approach to risk management • Poor governance • Poor allocation of resources for risk management • Corrupt organizational practices
Project teams	Work relations and project contracts	• Flawed assumptions and poor design • Poor project stakeholder management • Deficiencies in bidding and contract documents • Contractual and informal work relations and groups • Poor implementation of risk management
Stakeholders	Broader construction industry, education sector, regulatory institutions, professional institutions, corporate bodies, workers unions	• Poor stakeholder management • Lack of trust and cooperation • Inconsistent approach to risk management • Lack of up-to-date project management knowledge base • Lack of comprehensive risk management curriculum and professional development opportunities
Policy/ enabling environment	Laws, regulations, codes related to construction	• Inadequate government policy measures • Unpredictable economic and political environments • Lack of standards and guidelines • Poor enforcement of building codes, safety regulations, business laws, law of tort and anti-corruption laws and other workplace laws • Procedural unfairness

variables for political risk management for international construction enterprises are: relationship with governments, misconduct of contractors, experiential knowledge of political risks, relations with power groups, and localization. Therefore, government policies, along with stable political and economic environments, could positively influence risk management in construction projects in developing countries.

Many researchers have regarded stakeholders as the primary risk source causing schedule delays in construction projects and, therefore, give priority to recommendations on mitigating stakeholder-related risks (Mok *et al.*, 2017; Chen *et al.*, 2020). However, Xia *et al.* (2018) found that stakeholders could be the main actors in managing risks and their risk management ability should be enhanced through the improvement in the management of stakeholders. Goh *et al.* (2013) recommend conducting workshops involving project participants and stakeholders for managing project risk, particularly for risk identification and analysis by reaching a consensus and common understanding on project risks. These workshops are also likely to raise awareness to workshop participants about the importance of proper risk management systems. Understanding the critical factors that affect various stakeholders' risk attitudes in construction projects could result in better decision-making and risk management. For instance, Chan *et al.* (2011) examined risk assessment and allocation in public–private partnerships in China. They found that the major risks that the public sector preferred to accept are within the systematic risk category, especially political, legal, and social risks. They also found that construction, operation, and relationship risks, in addition to economic risks, were preferred to be retained by the private sector. The remaining risk is preferred to be shared between the two sectors. Wang and Yuan (2011) found that the critical factors affecting the risk attitudes of contractors are: (1) knowledge and experience; (2) contractors' character; (3) personal perceptions; and (4) the economic environment. Clients can use this information to select contractors with risk attitudes that align with the corresponding requirements of different construction projects. Zou *et al.* (2007) recommended that clients, designers, and government bodies should take the responsibility to manage their relevant risks and work cooperatively throughout the project lifecycle. Therefore, it is crucial that both internal and external stakeholders in developing countries work together to deliver a construction project successfully.

At the project level, project teams need to implement risk management throughout the lifecycle of the project. Mazher *et al.* (2018) recommend that project uncertainties be reduced by conducting project feasibility studies; selecting strong private sponsors for the project; and acquiring land, permits, and approvals early. It is suggested that contractors undertake a holistic review of risk using an objective benchmark for risk assessment. Iyer *et al.* (2020) found that including risk assessment of projects while deciding the criteria for prequalification increases the chance of project success. Perera *et al.* (2014) suggested an integrated approach incorporating the early involvement of contractors in conceptual and design stages, outsourcing designing and estimation stages to specialized service providers, and enhancing the implementation of risk management as an essential element of bidding documents, alongside close cooperation among project participants. Also, contractors and subcontractors with robust construction and management knowledge should be employed to minimize construction risks and carry out safe, efficient, and quality construction activities (Zou *et al.*, 2007).

Standard contract terms and conditions should demand that contractors take insurance cover to indemnify all works and the people associated with a project (Akinradewo *et al.*, 2020). However, the insurable and non-insurable construction project risks and technical exclusions, along with cost-benefit analysis of insurance cover, demand further investigation. Nonetheless, construction insurance could play an integral role in guaranteeing a project's success, with insurers sharing losses resulting from natural disasters and other contingencies (Owusu-Manu *et al.*, 2020). Specifically, Owusu-Manu *et al.* (2020) identified risks such as injury to persons, damage to properties during construction, fire, earthquake, and heavy rain as insurable risks. Also, project risks are perceived and managed differently in different national cultures. Risks are fewer and easier to manage where the host culture is similar to the contractor's culture than when the host culture is different (Liu *et al.*, 2015). Therefore, cultural awareness, cooperation among project team members, awareness of project-specific risks, and sound risk management knowledge and capabilities could help project teams to manage risks in construction projects in developing countries.

At the organization level, construction companies need to adopt a formal risk management process and allocate sufficient resources to facilitate the process. Construction organizations can cultivate a risk-focused culture, set up a risk management department, develop a risk management procedure, and get aid from external services to improve project risk management. Chileshe and Kikwasi (2014) assumed that critical success factors for implementing risk assessment and management practices are awareness of risk management processes, teamwork and communications, and management style. Proper risk assessment should be of critical importance to contractors, whereas deciding whether to undertake a particular project or participate in a partnership is the decision of the client. Liu *et al.* (2013) reinforced this by stating that enterprise-level risk management could positively influence risk management in construction projects.

Lastly, at the individual level, previous studies have shown that personal factors such as educational background, experience, professional competence, and emotional intelligence influence the risk management approach in construction projects (Kim and Reinschmidt, 2011; Adeleke *et al.*, 2018). Similarly, leadership and communication styles also influence how project risks are managed (Adeleke *et al.*, 2018). An individual's risk attitude could have positive or negative effects on decision-making (Lee and Foo, 2020). For example, an extroverted project professional tends to be willing to take more risks and views risk as a positive matter as opposed to an introverted professional. Karimi and Taghaddos (2020) found that higher experience and educational attainment of craft workers significantly mitigates the level of accident risks in young and middle-aged craft workers. Taofeeq *et al.* (2020b) suggest recruiting employees with similar values and beliefs to reduce risk in construction projects. Measures such as appropriate employee recruitment, training, and motivational practices could improve construction workers' risk attitudes (Taofeeq *et al.*, 2020b). Therefore, it is essential to identify and manage human risk factors in construction projects.

The socio-ecological model for risk management implies the need for a much broader policy and industry-wide change in developing countries than just the sporadic implementation of risk management by a few large organizations in construction projects. A holistic risk management paradigm is associated with strengthening risks inhibitors at each level of the socio-ecological model using top-down industry-wide initiatives. The policy measures in the form of laws and regulations, along with awareness among the stakeholders through standards, education, and training, are likely to bring more sustainable changes to how organizations and individuals manage risks in construction projects in developing countries. The multi-faceted interactive levels of the model demand interventions from all levels within the construction industry to improve risk management in construction projects, as discussed in this chapter. While actions at different levels appear to be distinct, they also influence each other as different levels overlap. Without coordinated actions at multiple levels of the socio-ecological model of risk management, it would be challenging to attain long-term improvements in risk management and, thereby, project performance in developing countries.

Example of the application of the proposed risk management framework

The socio-ecological model of project risk management could be used to identify and manage risks present at different functional and operational levels. While the framework can be used for managing different types of construction project risks such as delays, cost overruns, poor quality, and safety, this section demonstrates the application of the socio-ecological model for OH&S risk management. Figure 10.3 illustrates the application of the model to reduce the OH&S risks in construction projects in developing countries.

At the policy level, the governments in developing countries need to formulate and implement OH&S laws, regulations, and standards specific to the construction industry. Moreover, regulatory bodies (for example, those similar to the Occupational Safety and Health Administration or OSHA in the US and WorkSafe in different states and territories of Australia) could ensure the application of OH&S in construction projects. At the project level, OH&S risks could be reduced by implementing safe design to assess and eliminate or minimize risks early in the design process. Next, involvement of both external and internal stakeholders would be crucial for the success of OH&S risk management plan in construction projects. At the organizational level, contractors in developing countries need to stress the development of a positive safety culture by placing a

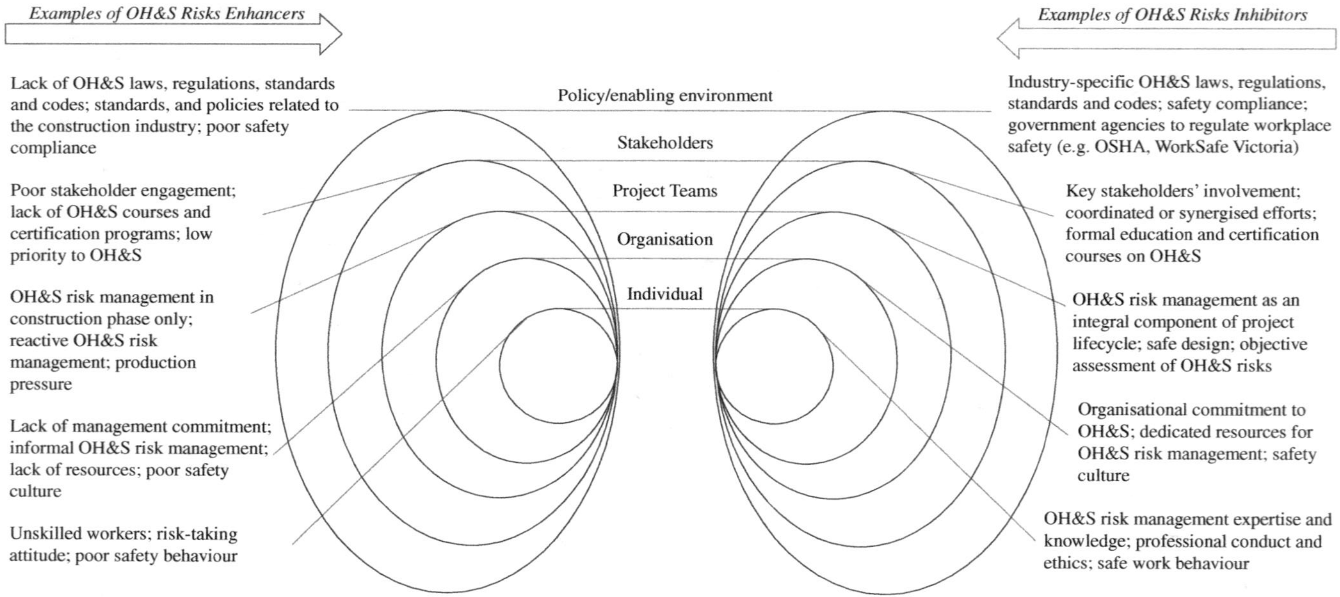

Figure 10.3: An example of socio-ecological model for OH&S risk management in construction projects in developing countries.

high level of importance on safety beliefs, values, and attitudes within the company or workplace. This will involve developing a safety climate and safe work behavior through rules and procedures, safety commitment, training and compliance, teamwork and communication, and safety culture. Finally, the poor attitude toward OH&S risks in construction projects in developing countries needs to be changed through education, training, communication, and incentives.

When approaching OH&S risks, the actions taken at the policy level of the socio-ecological model would prove crucial for triggering industry-wide changes in developing countries concerning how OH&S risks are managed in construction projects. While such changes will drive OH&S reforms within construction organizations, more actions will need to be taken at organizational levels in the form of management commitment, behavioral and cultural change, and training of construction workers to sustain OH&S risk prevention efforts. In addition to specific actions to be taken at each level, coordinated efforts at different levels of the socio-ecological model are likely to bring about improvements in OH&S performance in construction projects in developing countries.

Conclusion

Construction projects in developing countries are characterized by higher risks than those in developed nations. The most common risks are project completion delays, cost overruns, poor quality, high rates of accidents, and environmental damages. These risks have many immediate interwoven causes. However, these immediate causes are the result of several underlying factors at various levels of the construction industry in developing countries. The chapter applied the socio-ecological theory to dissect the problem and identify those latent factors for identifying appropriate risk mitigation measures. It is posited that managing risks in construction projects in developing countries requires concerted efforts by multiple players. The government and authorities should invest adequate resources and efforts to develop and enforce policies, standards, codes, and regulations related to construction operations. The wider construction industry, which includes clients, contractors, consultants, and professional bodies, should change its culture to be risk and project success conscious and implement better contractual methods, continued professional development programs, and innovative design and construction methods. Organizations in the construction industry should have regulated work procedures and policies that minimize risks in all their operations. At the project level, where different organizations interface to deliver a project, it is important to maintain complete design and documentation, clear communications, a collaborative working culture, and a win-win attitude among parties. At the individual level, professionalism, commitment, responsibility and accountability beyond contractual terms, ethical and conscientious conduct, and continued learning and professional development should be adopted. These are elements of a broad risk management framework and should be contextualized to the application context.

The major limitation of this chapter is the lack of real-world application of the proposed risk management framework. Future research can study ways and means of implementing the framework in developing countries and evaluating its benefits and challenges.

References

Abdul-Rahman, H., Hanid, M. and Yap, X.W. (2014). Does professional ethics affect quality of construction — A case in a developing economy? *Total Quality Management & Business Excellence*, 25(3–4), 235–248.

Acar, E. and Göç, Y. (2011). Prediction of risk perception by owners' psychological traits in small building contractors. *Construction Management and Economics*, 29(8), 841–852.

Adeleke, A.Q., Windapo, A.O., Khan, M.W.A., Bamgbade, J.A., Salimon, M.G. and Nawanir, G. (2018). Validating the influence of effective communication, team competency and skills, active leadership on construction risk management practices of Nigerian construction companies. *The Journal of Social Sciences Research*, 6, 460–465.

Akinradewo, O., Aghimien, D., Aigbavboa, C. and Onyia, M. (2020). Factors influencing the adoption of insurance as a risk treatment tool by contractors in the construction industry. *International Journal of Construction Management*, 1–9.

Akintoye, A.S. and Macleod, M.J. (1997). Risk analysis and management in construction. *International Journal of Project Management*, 15(1), 31–38.

Aladağ, H. and Işik, Z. (2017). Role of financial risks in BOT mega transportation projects in developing countries. *Journal of Management in Engineering*, 33(4), 04017007.

Alaghbari, W.E., Kadir, M.R.A., Salim, A. and Ernawati (2007). The significant factors causing delay of building construction projects in Malaysia. *Engineering Construction & Architectural Management*, 14(2), 192–206.

Al-Janabi, A.M., Abdel-Monem, M.S. and El-Dash, K.M. (2020). Factors causing rework and their impact on projects' performance in Egypt. *Journal of Civil Engineering and Management*, 26(7), 666–689.

Al-Rasheed, H. and Kamardeen, I. (2017). *Improving the Psychological Health of Foreign Workers in Developing Countries: A Socio-Ecological Analysis of the Saudi Construction Industry*. Nova Science Publishers, Inc., New York.

Allegrante, J.P., Hanson, D.W., Sleet, D.A. and Marks, R. (2010). Ecological approaches to the prevention of unintentional injuries. *Italian Journal of Public Health,* 7, 24–31.

Amoah, C. and Pretorius, L. (2020). Evaluation of the impact of risk management on project performance in small construction firms in South Africa. *Journal of Engineering, Design and Technology*, 18(3), 611–634.

Andi (2006). The importance and allocation of risks in Indonesian construction projects. *Construction Management and Economics*, 24(1), 69–80.

Ansah, R.H. and Sorooshian, S. (2018). 4P delays in project management. *Engineering, Construction and Architectural Management,* 25(1), 62–76.

Ashley, D.B. and Bonner, J.J. (1987). Political risks in international business. *Journal of Construction Engineering and Management*, 113(3), 447–467.

Asiedu, R.O. and Adaku, E. (2020). Cost overruns of public sector construction projects: A developing country perspective. *International Journal of Managing Projects in Business*, 13(1), 66–84.

Assaf, S.A. and Al-Hejji, S. (2006). Causes of delay in large construction projects. *International Journal of Project Management*, 24(4), 349–357.

Association for Project Management (2019). *PM Body of Knowledge*, 7th Edition. APM, Princes Risborough, UK.

Bahamid, R.A. and Doh, S.I. (2017). November. A review of risk management process in construction projects of developing countries. In *IOP Conference Series: Materials Science and Engineering*, Vol. 271, No. 1.

Balali, A., Moehler, R.C. and Valipour, A. (2020). Ranking cost overrun factors in the mega hospital construction projects using Delphi-SWARA method: An Iranian case study. *International Journal of Construction Management*, 1–9.

Baloi, D. and Price, A.D. (2003). Modelling global risk factors affecting construction cost performance. *International Journal of Project Management*, 21(4), 261–269.

Balouchi, M., Gholhaki, M. and Niousha, A. (2019). Reworks causes and related costs in construction: Case of Parand mass housing project in Iran. *International Journal of Quality & Reliability Management*, 36(8), 1392–1408.

Bronfenbrenner, U. (1977). Toward an experimental ecology of human development. *American Psychologist*, 32(7), 513–531.

Bureau of Labor Statistics (BLS) (2015). National census of fatal occupational injuries in 2014 (preliminary results). http://www.bls.gov/news.release/pdf/cfoi.pdf [Accessed 18 April 2020].

Chan, A.P., Yeung, J.F., Yu, C.C., Wang, S.Q. and Ke, Y. (2011). Empirical study of risk assessment and allocation of public–private partnership projects in China. *Journal of Management in Engineering*, 27(3), 136–148.

Chen, L., Lu, Q. and Zhao, X. (2020). Rethinking the construction schedule risk of infrastructure projects based on dialectical systems and network theory. *Journal of Management in Engineering*, 36(5), 4020066.

Cheng, C., Leu, S., Cheng, Y., Wu, T. and Lin, C. (2012). Applying data mining techniques to explore factors contributing to occupational injuries in Taiwan's construction industry. *Accident Analysis and Prevention*, 48, 214–222.

Chileshe, N. and Kikwasi, G.J. (2014). Critical success factors for implementation of risk assessment and management practices within the Tanzanian construction industry. *Engineering, Construction and Architectural Management*, 21(3), 291–319.

Choudhry, R.M., Aslam, M.A., Hinze, J.W. and Arain, F.M. (2014). Cost and schedule risk analysis of bridge construction in Pakistan: Establishing risk guidelines. *Journal of Construction Engineering and Management*, 140(7), 04014020.

Choudhry, R.M. and Iqbal, K. (2013). Identification of risk management system in construction industry in Pakistan. *Journal of Management in Engineering*, 29(1), 42–49.

Coffie, G.H. and Aigbavboa, C.O. (2020). Comparative assessment of construction cost overruns: A case study of regional distribution in Ghana. *African Journal of Science, Technology, Innovation and Development*, 12(1), 123–126.

Cox, R.F., Issa, R.R. and Ahrens, D. (2003). Management's perception of key performance indicators for construction. *Journal of Construction Engineering and Management*, 129(2), 142–151.

Deng, X., Low, S.P., Li, Q. and Zhao, X. (2014). Developing competitive advantages in political risk management for international construction enterprises. *Journal of Construction Engineering and Management*, 140(9), 04014040.

Derakhshanalavijeh, R. and Teixeira, J.M.C. (2017). Cost overrun in construction projects in developing countries, gas-oil industry of Iran as a case study. *Journal of Civil Engineering and Management*, 23(1), 125–136.

Durdyev, S., Omarov, M., Ismail, S. and Lim, M. (2017). Significant contributors to cost overruns in construction projects of Cambodia. *Cogent Engineering*, 4(1), 1383638.

El-Sayegh, S.M. (2008). Risk assessment and allocation in the UAE construction industry. *International Journal of Project Management*, 26(4), 431–438.

El-Sayegh, S.M. (2014). Project risk management practices in the UAE construction industry. *International Journal of Project Organisation and Management*, 6(1–2), 121–137.

Erol, H., Dikmen, I., Atasoy, G. and Birgonul, M.T. (2020). Exploring the relationship between complexity and risk in megaconstruction projects. *Journal of Construction Engineering and Management*, 146(12), 04020138.

Gibb, A. and Bust, P. (2006). *Construction Health and Safety in Developing Countries*. European Construction Institute, Loughborough, UK.

Goh, C.S. and Abdul-Rahman, H. (2013). The identification and management of major risks in the Malaysian construction industry. *Journal of Construction in Developing Countries*, 18(1), 19–32.

Goh, C.S., Abdul-Rahman, H. and Abdul Samad, Z. (2013). Applying risk management workshop for a public construction project: Case study. *Journal of Construction Engineering and Management*, 139(5), 572–580.

Gondia, A., Siam, A., El-Dakhakhni, W. and Nassar, A.H. (2020). Machine learning algorithms for construction projects delay risk prediction. *Journal of Construction Engineering and Management*, 146(1), 04019085.

Gürcanli, G.E. and Müngen, U. (2013). Analysis of construction accidents in Turkey and responsible parties. *Industrial Health*, 51(6), 581–595.

Hasan, A. and Jha, K.N. (2016). Acceptance of the incentive/disincentive contracting strategy in developing construction markets: Empirical study from India. *Journal of Construction Engineering and Management*, 142(2), 04015064.

Haupt, T.C. and Smallwood, J.J. (2005). The need for construction health and safety (H&S) and the construction regulations: Engineers' perception. *Journal of the South African Institution of Civil Engineering*, 47(2), 2–8.

Health and Safety Executive, UK (2015). Health and safety in construction sector in Great Britain, 2014/15. http://www.hse.gov.uk/statistics/industry/construction/construction.pdf [Accessed 12 April 2020].

Hertz, D. and Thomas, H. (1983). *Risk Analysis and its Application*. John Wiley & Sons, New York.

Huang, L., Krigsvoll, G., Johansen, F., Liu, Y. and Zhang, X. (2018). Carbon emission of global construction sector. *Renewable and Sustainable Energy Reviews*, 81(P2), 1906–1916.

Institution of Civil Engineers and the Institute and Faculty of Actuaries (2014). *Risk Analysis and Management for Projects*, 3rd Edition. ICE Publishing, London.

Islam, M.S. and Trigunarsyah, B. (2017). Construction delays in developing countries: A review, *KICEM Journal of Construction Engineering and Project Management*, 7(1), 1–12.

Iyer, K.C. and Jha, K.N. (2006). Critical factors affecting schedule performance: Evidence from Indian construction projects. *Journal of Construction Engineering Management*, 132(6), 871–881.

Iyer, K.C., Kumar, R. and Singh, S.P. (2020). Understanding the role of contractor capability in risk management: A comparative case study of two similar projects. *Construction Management and Economics*, 38(3), 223–238.

Johnson, R.M. and Babu, R.I.I. (2020). Time and cost overruns in the UAE construction industry: A critical analysis. *International Journal of Construction Management*, 20(5), 402–411.

Kakar, A.S., Hasan, A. and Jha, K.N. (2020). Schedule success factors in construction projects in a war-affected region. *Journal of Legal Affairs and Dispute Resolution in Engineering and Construction*, 12(3), 1–10.

Kamal, A., Abas, M., Khan, D. and Azfar, R.W. (2022). Risk factors influencing the building projects in Pakistan: From perspective of contractors, clients and consultants. *International Journal of Construction Management*, 22(6), 1141–1157.

Karimi, H. and Taghaddos, H. (2020). Impact of age on the strength of experience and education role in fatal injuries prevention in Iranian construction craft workers. *Journal of Construction Engineering and Management*, 146(7), 04020070.

Kassem, M.A., Khoiry, M.A. and Hamzah, N. (2020). Assessment of the effect of external risk factors on the success of an oil and gas construction project. *Engineering, Construction and Architectural Management*, 27(9), 2767–2793.

Kerzner, H. (2003). *Project Management: A System Approach to Planning, Scheduling and Controlling*, 8th Edition. John Wiley & Sons, New Jersey.

Kheni, N.A., Gibb, A.G.F. and Dainty, A.R.J. (2010). Health and safety management within small and medium-sized enterprises (SMEs) in developing countries: Study of contextualised influences. *Journal of Construction Engineering and Management*, 136(10), 1104–1115.

Kim, H.J. and Reinschmidt, K.F. (2011). Effects of contractors' risk attitude on competition in construction. *Journal of Construction Engineering and Management*, 137(4), 275–283.

Lee, C.K. and Foo, M.Y. (2020). Risk attitudes and the big five personality traits: A study on construction project practitioners in Malaysia. *International Journal of Construction Management*, 1–11. https://doi.org/10.1080/15623599.2020.1793506.

Liu, J., Lin, S. and Feng, Y. (2018). Understanding why Chinese contractors are not willing to purchase construction insurance. *Engineering, Construction and Architectural Management*, 25(2), 257–272.

Liu, J., Meng, F. and Fellows, R. (2015). An exploratory study of understanding project risk management from the perspective of national culture. *International Journal of Project Management*, 33(3), 564–575.

Liu, J.Y., Zou, P.X. and Gong, W. (2013). Managing project risk at the enterprise level: Exploratory case studies in China. *Journal of Construction Engineering and Management*, 139(9), 1268–1274.

Loosemore, M., Raftery, J., Reilly, C. and Higgon, D. (2006). *Risk Management in Projects*, 2nd Edition. Taylor & Francis, Abingdon, UK.

Love, P.E. and Edwards, D.J. (2004). Determinants of rework in building construction projects. *Engineering, Construction and Architectural Management*, 11(4), 259–274. https://doi.org/10.1108/09699980410547612.

Lu, S. and Yan, H. (2013). A comparative study of the measurements of perceived risk among contractors in China. *International Journal of Project Management*, 31(2), 307–312.

Mahamid, I. (2013). Common risks affecting time overrun in road construction projects in Palestine: Contractors' perspective. *Australasian Journal of Construction Economics and Building*, 13(2), 45–53.

May, M., Tranter, P.J. and Warn, J.R. (2008). Towards a holistic framework for road safety in Australia. *Journal of Transport Geography*, 16, 395–405.

Maylor, H. (2010). *Project Management*, 4th Edition. Prentice Hall, London.

Mazher, K.M., Chan, A.P., Zahoor, H., Khan, M.I. and Ameyaw, E.E. (2018). Fuzzy integral–based risk-assessment approach for public–private partnership infrastructure projects. *Journal of Construction Engineering and Management*, 144(12), 04018111.

Mohamed, O., Abd-Karim, S.B., Roslan, N.H., Mohd Danuri, M.S. and Zakaria, N. (2015). Risk management: Looming the modus operandi among construction contractors in Malaysia. *International Journal of Construction Management*, 15(1), 82–93.

Mok, K.Y., Shen, G.Q., Yang, R.J. and Li, C.Z. (2017). Investigating key challenges in major public engineering projects by a network-theory based analysis of stakeholder concerns: A case study. *International Journal of Project Management*, 35(1), 78–94.

Musarat, M.A., Alaloul, W.S., Liew, M.S., Maqsoom, A. and Qureshi, A.H. (2020). Investigating the impact of inflation on building materials prices in construction industry. *Journal of Building Engineering*, 32, 101485.

Mwombeki, F.K. (2005). Occupational health and safety challenges in construction sites in Tanzania. *Proceedings of W99 Triennial International Conference: Rethinking and Revitalizing Construction Safety, Health, Environment and Quality*, Construction Research Education and Training Enterprises, Port Elizabeth, South Africa, pp. 778–789.

Nawaz, A., Waqar, A., Shah, S.A.R., Sajid, M. and Khalid, M.I. (2019). An innovative framework for risk management in construction projects in developing countries: Evidence from Pakistan. *Risks*, 7(1), 24.

Nicholas, J.M. and Steyn, H. (2008). *Project Management for Business, Engineering, and Technology: Principles and Practice*. Elsevier Butterworth-Heinemann, Burlington, MA.

Ogbu, C.P. and Adindu, C.C. (2020). Direct risk factors and cost performance of road projects in developing countries: Contractors' perspective. *Journal of Engineering, Design and Technology*, 18(2), 326–342.

Owusu-Manu, D.G., Ghansah, F.A., Darko, A., Asiedu, R.O. and Edwards, D.J. (2020). Insurable and non-insurable risks in complex project deals: Case of the Ghanaian construction industry. *Journal of Engineering, Design and Technology*, 18(6), 1971–1995.

Patel, D.A. and Jha, K.N. (2015). Neural network model for the prediction of safe work behavior in construction projects. *Journal of Construction Engineering and Management*, 141(1), 04014066.

Patel, D.A. and Jha, K.N. (2016). An estimate of fatal accidents in Indian construction. In P.W. Chan, C.J. Neilson (Eds.), *Proceedings of the 32nd Annual ARCOM Conference*, 5–7 September, Manchester, UK, Vol. 1, pp. 577–586.

Perera, B.A.K.S., Dhanasinghe, I. and Rameezdeen, R. (2009). Risk management in road construction: The case of Sri Lanka. *International Journal of Strategic Property Management*, 13(2), 87–102.

Perera, B.A.K.S., Rameezdeen, R., Chileshe, N. and Hosseini, M.R. (2014). Enhancing the effectiveness of risk management practices in Sri Lankan road construction projects: A Delphi approach. *International Journal of Construction Management*, 14(1), 1–14.

Project Management Institute (2017). *A Guide to the Project Management Body of Knowledge (PMBOK Guide)*, 6th Edition. Project Management Institute, Newtown Square, PA.

Rahman, N.N.N.A. and Esa, N. (2014). Managing construction development risks to the environment. In N. Kaneko, S. Yoshiura and M. Kobayashi (Eds.), *Sustainable Living with Environmental Risks*. Springer, Tokyo. https://doi.org/10.1007/978-4-431-54804-1_16.

Rebeiz, K.S. (2012). Public–private partnership risk factors in emerging countries: BOOT illustrative case study. *Journal of Management in Engineering*, 28(4), 421–428.

Safe Work Australia (2015). Construction Industry Profile. http://www.safeworkaustralia.gov.au/sites/SWA/about/Publications/Documents/911/construction-industry-profile.pdf [Accessed 13 October 2020].

Santoso, D.S. and Gallage, P.G.M.P. (2020). Critical factors affecting the performance of large construction projects in developing countries: A case study of Sri Lanka. *Journal of Engineering, Design and Technology*, 18(3), 531–556.

Senouci, A., Alsarraj, A., Gunduz, M. and Eldin, N. (2017). Analysis of change orders in Qatari construction projects. *International Journal of Construction Management*, 17(4), 280–292.

Serpell, A., Ferrada, X. and Rubio, N.L. (2017). Fostering the effective usage of risk management in construction. *Journal of Civil Engineering and Management*, 23(7), 858–867.

Shehu, Z., Endut, I.R., Akintoye, A. and Holt, G.D. (2014). Cost overrun in the Malaysian construction industry projects: A deeper insight. *International Journal of Project Management*, 32(8), 1471–1480.

Sinesilassie, E.G., Tabish, S.Z.S. and Jha, K.N. (2018). Critical factors affecting cost performance: A case of Ethiopian public construction projects. *International Journal of Construction Management*, 18(2), 108–119.

Smith, N.J., Merna, T. and Jobling P. (2014). *Managing Risk in Construction Projects*, 3rd Edition. Wiley Blackwell, UK.

Sohrabinejad, A. and Rahimi, M. (2015). Risk determination, prioritization, and classifying in construction project case study: Gharb Tehran commercial-administrative complex. *Journal of Construction Engineering*, 2015, Article ID 203468, 1–10. https://doi.org/10.1155/2015/203468.

Tadayon, M., Jaafar, M. and Nasri, E. (2012). An assessment of risk identification in large construction projects in Iran. *Journal of Construction in Developing Countries,* 17(1), 57–69.

Tang, W., Qiang, M., Duffield, C.F., Young, D.M. and Lu, Y. (2007). Risk management in the Chinese construction industry. *Journal of Construction Engineering and Management*, 133(12), 944–956.

Taofeeq, M.D., Adeleke, A.Q. and Chia-Kuang, L.E.E. (2020a). Government policy as a key moderator to contractors' risk attitudes among Malaysian construction companies. *Journal of Engineering, Design and Technology*, 18(6), 1543–1569.

Taofeeq, D.M., Adeleke, A.Q. and Ajibike, W.A. (2020b). Human factors influencing contractors' risk attitudes: A case study of the Malaysian construction industry. *Construction Economics and Building*, 20(1), 96–116.

Thi, C.H. and Swierczek, F.W. (2010). Critical success factors in project management: implication from Vietnam. *Asia Pacific Business Review*, 16(4), 567–589.

Trauner, T. Jr, Manginelli, W., Lowe, J., Nagata, M. and Furniss, B. (2009). *Construction Delays: Understanding Them Clearly, Analyzing Them Correctly*. Elsevier, Philadelphia, PA.

Tripathi, K.K., Hasan, A. and Neeraj Jha, K. (2021). Evaluating performance of construction organizations using fuzzy preference relation technique. *International Journal of Construction Management*, 21(12), 1287–1300.

Wang, C.M., Xu, B.B., Zhang, S.J. and Chen, Y.Q. (2016). Influence of personality and risk propensity on risk perception of Chinese construction project managers. *International Journal of Project Management*, 34(7), 1294–1304.

Wang, T.K., Ford, D.N., Chong, H.Y. and Zhang, W. (2018). Causes of delays in the construction phase of Chinese building projects. *Engineering, Construction and Architectural Management*, 25(11), 1534–1551.

Wang, J. and Yuan, H. (2011). Factors affecting contractors' risk attitudes in construction projects: Case study from China. *International Journal of Project Management*, 29(2), 209–219.

Wang, N., Mengersen, K., Tong, S., Kimlin, M., Zhou, M., Liu, Y. and Hu, W. (2020). County-level variation in the long-term association between PM2. 5 and lung cancer mortality in China. *Science of the Total Environment*, 738, 140195.

Wells, J. and Hawkins, J. (2015). Promoting construction health and safety through procurement: A briefing note for developing countries. http://engineersagainstpoverty.org/wp-content/uploads/2018/07/EAP-ICE_HS_Briefing_Note.pdf [Accessed 3 November 2020].

Wu, Z., Nisar, T., Kapletia, D. and Prabhakar, G. (2017). Risk factors for project success in the Chinese construction industry. *Journal of Manufacturing Technology Management*, 28(7), 850–866.

Xia, N., Zou, P.X., Griffin, M.A., Wang, X. and Zhong, R. (2018). Towards integrating construction risk management and stakeholder management: A systematic literature review and future research agendas. *International Journal of Project Management*, 36(5), 701–715.

Xiang, P., Zhou, J., Zhou, X. and Ye, K. (2012). Construction project risk management based on the view of asymmetric information. *Journal of Construction Engineering and Management*, 138(11), 1303–1311.

Ullah, F., Thaheem, M.J., Siddiqui, S.Q. and Khurshid, M.B. (2017). Influence of Six Sigma on project success in construction industry of Pakistan. *The TQM Journal*, 29(2), 276–309.

Umar, T. and Egbu, C. (2018). Causes of construction accidents in Oman. *Middle East Journal of Management*, 5(1), 21–33.

Viswanathan, S.K. and Jha, K.N. (2020). Risk mitigation modelling of international construction projects executed by Indian firms: A structural equation modelling approach. *Engineering, Construction and Architectural Management,* 27(9), 2687–2713.

Vu, H.A., Cu, V.H., Min, L.X. and Wang, J.Q. (2017). Risk analysis of schedule delays in international highway projects in Vietnam using a structural equation model. *Engineering, Construction and Architectural Management*, 24(6), 1018–1039.

Wu, Z., Nisar, T., Kapletia, D. and Prabhakar, G. (2017). Risk factors for project success in the Chinese construction industry. *Journal of Manufacturing Technology Management*, 28(7), 850–866.

Yang, H., Song, X. and Zhang, Q. (2020). RS&GIS based PM emission inventories of dust sources over a provincial scale: A case study of Henan province, central China. *Atmospheric Environment*, 225, 117361.

Ye, G., Jin, Z., Xia, B. and Skitmore, M. (2014). Analyzing causes for reworks in construction projects in China. *Journal of Management in Engineering*, 31(6), 04014097. https://doi.org/10.1061/(ASCE)ME.1943-5479.0000347.

Yildiz, A.E., Dikmen, I., Birgonul, M.T., Ercoskun, K. and Alten, S. (2014). A knowledge-based risk mapping tool for cost estimation of international construction projects. *Automation in Construction*, 43, 144–155.

Yoon, S.J., Lin, H.K., Chen, G., Yi, S., Choi, J. and Rui, Z. (2013). Effect of occupational health and safety management system on work-related accident rate and differences of occupational health and safety management system awareness between managers in South Korea's construction industry. *Safety and Health at Work*, 4(4), 201–209.

Yusof, N., Awang, H. and Iranmanesh, M. (2017). Determinants and outcomes of environmental practices in Malaysian construction projects. *Journal of Cleaner Production*, 156, 345–354.

Zahoor, H., Chan, A.P.C., Gao, R. and Utama, W.P. (2017). The factors contributing to construction accidents in Pakistan. *Engineering, Construction and Architectural Management*, 24(3), 463–485.

Zayed, T., Amer, M. and Pan, J. (2008). Assessing risk and uncertainty inherent in Chinese highway projects using AHP. *International Journal of Project Management*, 26(4), 408–419.

Zou, P.X., Zhang, G. and Wang, J. (2007). Understanding the key risks in construction projects in China. *International Journal of Project Management*, 25(6), 601–614.

https://doi.org/10.1142/9789811224720_0011

Chapter 11

Project Procurement Management in Developing Countries

Ron Watermeyer

School of Construction Economics and Management, University of the Witwatersrand, Johannesburg

Abstract

Procurement includes a planning, acquisition, and contract management phase. Project procurement management, which embraces these three phases, is one of the 10 knowledge areas identified in the PMBOK@ Guide (2016) and one of the 17 practices described in ISO 21502. These standards provide generic guidance on concepts, processes, and practices applicable to all types of projects that may be located within any industry and do not provide industry-specific adaptations. This chapter identifies the specificities of the construction industry and articulates the differentiators in practices between the construction industry and what is catered for in the generic body of knowledge for project procurement management. It identifies the need for and nature of a construction-specific body of knowledge for project procurement management and indicates the knowledge, skills, and attitudes required of practitioners in this field. The procurement challenges and needs faced in developing countries are identified. The underlying environment within which construction works projects are delivered and the resources available to deliver projects are the major differentiators between developed and developing countries. Strategic and tactical choices and the manner and extent of their application will differ. The level of maturity in performing the client "buying" function can also differ. More research is required to establish the client "buying" function body of knowledge. Research is also required to broaden the understanding of the linkage between client maturity in the "client" buying function and project outcomes. Evidence-based research is also required to inform strategic and tactical decisions.

Keywords: Delivery management, procurement, procurement strategy, procurement system, sustainable development, targeted procurement

Introduction

Procurement can be narrowly or broadly defined. ISO 20400:2017, defines procurement narrowly as "the activity of acquiring goods or services from suppliers." ISO 6707-2:2017 defines procurement more broadly as: "the process which creates, manages and fulfills contracts relating to the provision of goods, services and construction works or disposals, or any combination thereof." This latter definition recognizes that there are three phases to the procurement process, namely (Watermeyer, 2018):

- a planning phase during which decisions are made as to what, where, and when goods and services are required; how the market is to be approached; and what is the number, type, nature, and timing of the required contracts;
- an acquisition phase during which contracts are entered into following the execution of a selection procedure; and
- a contract management phase during which compliance with requirements, changes in requirements and risk events which manifest themselves during the execution of contracts are managed.

ISO 10845-1, which embraces a broad definition for procurement, identifies six principal procurement activities, which establish actions and deliverables or milestones associated with the procurement process, i.e., a "buying" and "supply" function in the delivery of construction works. Table 11.1 indicates the alignment between the ISO 10845-1 activities and the three phases to procurement.

Table 11.1: Purpose of procurement-related processes identified in the PMBOK®Guide and ISO 21502.

Procurement phases	ISO 10854-1 principal activities No	Description	PMBOK®Guide's purpose for process (6th Edition)	ISO 21502 purpose of practice
Planning	1 2	Establish what is to be procured Decide on procurement strategies	**Plan procurement management** To: • document project procurement decisions, specify the approach, and identify potential sellers; and • determine whether or not to acquire goods and services from outside the project and, if so, what to acquire as well as how and when to acquire it.	**Planning procurement** Define a procurement strategy, taking into account: • the project's "make or buy" decisions; • the delivery practices; • the type of legally binding agreements; • the procurement process to be used.
Acquisition	3 4 5	Solicit tender offers Evaluate tender offers Award the contract	**Conduct procurements** To obtain seller responses, select a qualified seller to implement the legal agreement for delivery and award a contract.	**Evaluating and selecting suppliers** To select suppliers. based on selection activities in accordance with stated evaluation criteria.
Contract management	6	Administer the contract and confirm compliance with requirements	**Control procurements** To manage procurement relationships, monitor contract performance to meet the project's requirements according to the terms of the legal agreement, make changes and corrections as appropriate, and close out contracts.	**Administering contracts** To administer contracts by monitoring contract performance, managing. contract changes and corrections, dealing with claims and ending contracts thereby enabling the contracted parties' performance to meet the project's requirements according to the terms of the legal agreement. **Closing contracts** To close out contracts when: • the contract obligations of the parties have been met; or • the contract is closed early, in accordance with the contract's termination clauses.

The establishment of what is to be procured (Activity 1) initiates the procurement process. Procurement strategy (Activity 2) is all about the choices made in determining which of the required goods and services or combinations thereof are to be delivered through a particular contract, the contracting arrangements, how procurement is to be used to promote secondary procurement objectives, if any, and the selection methods used to solicit tender offers. Conditions for the calling for expressions of interest to prequalify respondents to participate in a specific contract, project, or program and conditions of tender govern Activity 3 to 5. Conditions of contract (i.e., terms that collectively describe the rights and obligations of contracting parties and the agreed procedures for the administration of their contract) govern Activity 6 (Watermeyer, 2018).

Project procurement management is one of the 10 knowledge areas identified in the PMBOK®Guide (Sixth edition, 2016). Procurement is also one of 17 practices described in ISO 21502:2020. These international publications recognize that there are three phases in the procurement processes. Whilst the terms used in these publications are different, there is common purpose in the intent of the identified processes. Furthermore, they also align with the principal activities identified in ISO 10845-1 as indicated in Table 11.2.

Table 11.2: Significant differences commonly encountered between the procurement of general goods and services for consumption and the procurement of construction works.

Characteristic / consideration	General goods and services for consumption	Provision of construction works
Satisfying the business need	Commonly achieved through the production of a specification, which then forms a requisition for goods or services	Satisfied though multiple contracts which need to be procured and managed in such a way that the anticipated benefits are progressively realized
Demand management	The demand is usually determined and managed through inventory/ bin levels or the frequency of the required service	Managed through service life plans, based on an assessment of current performance against desired levels of service or functionality and strategic infrastructure plans Demand also needs to be proactively managed through the delivery process to prevent scope creep

Table 11.2: (*Continued*)

Characteristic / consideration	General goods and services for consumption	Provision of construction works
Risks	Risks are relatively low. The consequences of late/non-delivery of • goods are typically low as bin levels generally have a reserve level • services are typically low as it usually impacts only on the productivity of staff in a specific area	Risks are high due to uncertainties at the start of a contract. Consequences of late/non-delivery are high
Interdependencies and interfaces between contracts	Interdependencies and interfaces between contracts are rare. Single contracts with no interdependencies are commonly required to satisfy needs	Several interfaces and interdependencies between contracts as works (products) are developed or maintained on a site. A supply chain needs to be contracted and mobilized
Final contract price of contract	The final contract price typically equates to the quantum of goods or services which are consumed multiplied by the agreed rate	Final contract price is the sum of the initial contract price, price adjustment for inflation, and the cost of risk events for which the client is at risk
Budget, contract price and purchase order value	The contract price is commonly adjusted to fit the budget or the budget reduced to the contract amount when it is known. The purchase order (financial control) amount typically equals the contract price which in turn equals the budget	The budget needs to include contingencies to fund price adjustment for inflation (if any) and risk events for which the client is at risk. Purchase order amount may also need to be adjusted to access contingencies to fund contractual commitments
Conditions of contract	Frequently a contract or a service level agreement is negotiated after the evaluation of tenders, based on the tender submission. This is possible as the contractor carries all risks and change management is not provided for	Standard conditions of contract include the procedures for the administration of the contract. They also allocate risks to the parties to the contract and enable risks to be priced, tenders to be compared on a comparative basis and change management to be effected
Value for money (cost effectiveness)	Reducing the cost of resources, increasing output for a given input or minimizing input for a given output while maintaining quality	Optimal use of resources or the effective, efficient, and economic use of resources to achieve intended project outcomes

The PMBOK®Guide (2016) suggests that a body of knowledge is "a term that describes the knowledge within the profession of project management." The American Society of Civil Engineers (ASCE, 2008) regards a body of knowledge "as the necessary depth and breadth of knowledge, skills, and attitudes required of an individual entering the practice of civil engineering at the professional level in the 21st century." ISO 24773-1:2019 defines this term as "a collection of knowledge items or areas generally agreed to be essential to understanding a particular subject."

The PMBOK®Guide considers project management to be "the application of knowledge, skills, tools, and techniques to project activities to meet the project requirements" and suggests that project management is "accomplished through the appropriate application and integration of the project management processes identified for the project." The Association of Project Managers, the chartered body for the project management profession, regards project management as the "application of processes, methods, skills, knowledge and experience to achieve specific project objectives according to the project acceptance criteria within agreed parameters." ISO 21502:2020 defines project management as "coordinated activities to direct and control the accomplishment of agreed objectives" and control as "comparison of actual performance with planned performance, analysing variances and taking appropriate corrective and preventive action as needed." Accordingly, there has been a shift in thinking in recent years from tools and techniques and processes to practices and outcomes.

Table 11.1 establishes the purpose of project procurement management and sets out the boundaries for this knowledge area of project management. However, it must be stressed that both the PMBOK®Guide and ISO 21502 provide a general foundation and generic guidance for concepts and processes applicable to all types of projects which may be located within any industry. These documents do not provide industry-specific adaptations of these processes. This is recognized by the PMI who have published the Construction Extension (2016), which describes the generally accepted principles for construction projects that are not common to all general project types.

This chapter identifies the project procurement management body of knowledge for the construction industry and the recent shifts in thinking. It commences with the identification of the specificities of the construction industry and articulates the differentiators in practices between this industry and what is catered for in the generic body of knowledge for project procurement management. Thereafter, it identifies the need for and nature of a construction-specific body of knowledge for project procurement management and indicates the knowledge, skills, and attitudes required of practitioners in this field. The procurement challenges and needs faced in developing countries are identified as well as areas requiring further research.

Specificities of construction procurement

General

PMBOK®Guide and ISO 21502 provide a general foundation and generic guidance on concepts and processes applicable to all types of projects that may be located within any industry. These documents do not provide industry-specific adaptations of these processes. This is recognized by the PMI, who have published the Construction Extension (2016), which describes the generally accepted principles for construction projects that are not common to all general project types. This publication recognizes that construction projects:

- need to simultaneously address the geography, site conditions, communities, physical environments, existing infrastructure, as well as a wide range of stakeholder requirements;
- occur in an ever-changing, complex environment, often with a high degree of risk;
- often result in a one-of-a-kind product rather than mass-produced products;
- often require the integration of engineering disciplines; and
- may sometimes be performed in phases to provide an opportunity to review and refine the project design and implementation strategy, as well as validate the investment intention.

The PMI also recognizes that the construction industry is almost entirely based on a competitive market environment for project cost, schedule, and performance delivery.

The Construction Extension provides a contractor's and an owner's perspective on procurement in construction and contextualizes procurement processes and adds management of claims to project procurement management. It falls short of providing much needed standard processes, procedures, and methods that are foundational to the establishment of project management offices (PMO), i.e., what the PMBOK®Guide refers to as organizational structures that standardizes the project-related governance processes and facilitates the sharing of resources, methodologies, tools, and techniques. The Construction Extension is also silent on procurement in a developing country context.

Procurement characteristics

The procurement of general goods and services for consumption usually involves the direct acquisition of products that are standard, well-defined, and readily scoped and specified. The process normally involves the production of a specification, which then forms the requisition for goods and services. An immediate choice can be made in terms of the cost of goods and services satisfying the specified requirements, which can be paid for upon delivery. In contrast, it is usually not possible to directly acquire construction works in the way that general goods and services are acquired. The delivery of construction works involves the procurement, programming, and coordination of a network of suppliers of goods and services which are required to collectively deliver or alter construction works on a site in accordance with specific client requirements and objectives. This network can include different companies specializing in design, manufacture, supply, assembly, or construction.

There are many more risks to manage in construction procurement, due to unforeseen events during the delivery of the project. In addition, construction works requirements are often established from a perspective of desired performance, rather than a well-defined specification. A range of different combinations of goods and services with differing characteristics such as initial cost, reliability, life-cycle costs, and operating costs may satisfy the performance requirements. A construction product is usually delivered and paid for incrementally over a period (Watermeyer and Phillips, 2020).

Table 11.2 outlines the significant common differences between the procurement characteristics associated with the provision, alteration, refurbishment, and rehabilitation of construction projects and those for general goods and services (Watermeyer, 2018).

The procurement of general goods and services for consumption is transactional in nature and is commonly handled by a purchasing (buying) department. In the public sector, it is frequently treated as a general administrative function requiring a relatively low skill level rather than a professional strategic function and is commonly located within a finance department. Construction procurement, on the other hand, is the strategic process of sourcing a product or service in the delivery of construction works on a site, which focuses on the minimization of risks, value, and return on investment. Given that construction procurement is a strategic function, it should be linked to the department or directorate responsible for delivering construction projects and services. It should not be relegated to a back office function and treated the same as the procurement of general goods and services for consumption. It should be noted that the Association for Project Management (APM, 2017) warns against the handling of procurement by a specific purchasing resource or department rather than being a central competency within portfolio, program, and project management. They point out that to do so in complex projects frequently leads to "unforeseen issues developing, leading to time, cost and quality over runs."

Supply chains

ISO 26000:2010 defines a supply chain as "the sequence of activities or parties that provides products or services to the organisation." ISO 44001:2017 offers a more expansive definition, namely, the "relationship of organisations, people, activities, logistics, information, technology and resources engaged in activities and creating value from point of origin to point of consumption, including transforming materials/components to products and services for end users." Accordingly, a supply chain can be

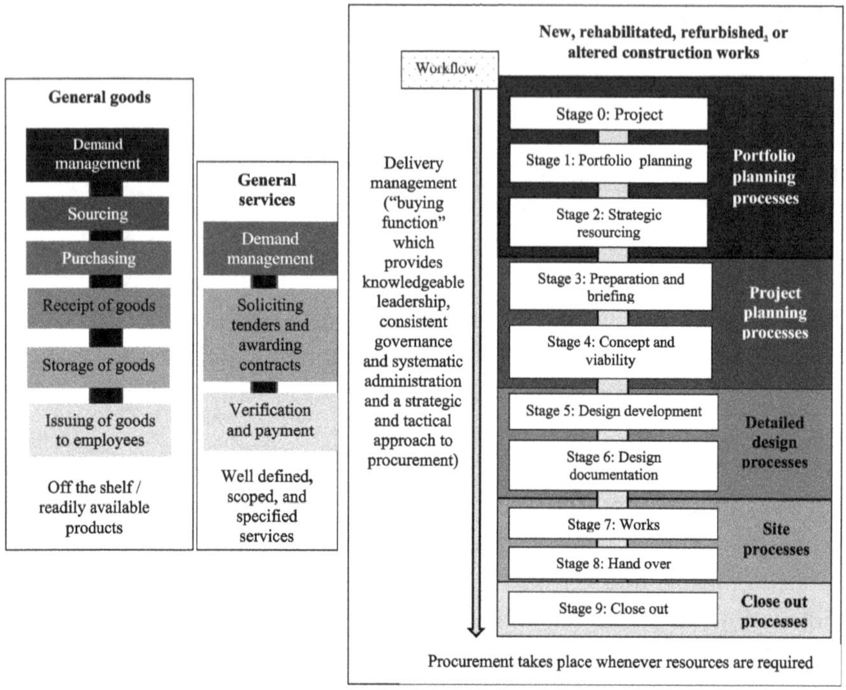

Figure 11.1: Commonly encountered supply chains.

regarded as the sequence of tasks (workflow) that provides products or services to the organization (see Figure 11.1).

Off-the-shelf or readily available products, once sourced and purchased, invariably need to be taken into some form of storage prior to being issued to employees. Demand for the supply of such goods is commonly linked to inventory levels to ensure continuity of supply (see Figure 11.1). The initial focus in services that are well-defined, scoped, and specified is on how frequent the service is required and over what period. Thereafter it shifts to the soliciting of tender offers and the awarding of contracts, followed by the verification that the services have been provided and the payment for such services as no decisions need to be made regarding the fitness for purpose of the service outputs (see Figure 11.1).

The supply chain for the provision of new, rehabilitated, refurbished, or altered construction works covers a wide and diverse range of goods and services, which are required to deliver a product or alter the condition of construction works on a site. This supply chain can be viewed as the flow of information from one set of tasks to the next, with decision points or gates at the boundaries between tasks, which provide the opportunity for ensuring that the proposed project remains within agreed mandates, aligns with the purpose for which it was conceived, and can progress successfully to the next task (see Figure 11.1). Procurement binds the participants in the supply chain (professionals, general contractors, specialists, and subcontractors) and defines the obligations, liabilities, and risks that link the parties together in a process that needs to deliver value for money (Watermeyer and Phillips, 2020). Delivery management is the critical leadership role played by a knowledgeable client to plan, specify, procure, and oversee the delivery of projects. Delivery management is required to translate the value proposition associated with a business case into project outcomes and is central to the performance of the supply chain in the delivery of construction work (DHET, 2021; Watermeyer and Phillips, 2020).

Accordingly, the process for the delivery of construction works projects involves the initial and subsequent recurring updating of planning processes at a portfolio level flowing out of an assessment of business needs. Thereafter it involves planning at a project level and the procurement and management of a network of suppliers, including subcontractors, to produce a product on a site.

The workflow associated with the planning, design, and execution of construction works projects (the project life cycle) indicated in Figure 11.1 is broken down into stages (collections of logically related activities in the delivery cycle) that culminate in the completion of a major deliverable. Each of these stages are linked to tasks associated with the supply chain required to deliver construction works projects. Decisions need to be taken on the acceptability of each end-of-stage deliverable (Watermeyer, 2018).

The typical stages indicated in Figure 11.1 are structured in such a manner that the viability of a project may be tested and monitored and controlled by the client delivery management team (those assigned to perform the "buying" function) as it progresses. It generates information which informs decisions at points in the process. Procurement takes place whenever resources external to the organization are required to progress an infrastructure project (Watermeyer, 2018).

Stage 0 (project initiation) admits projects into the pipeline of projects so that they can be further prepared prior to a decision being taken to progress or implement them. The management plan developed during stage 1 (portfolio planning) enables a client organization to prioritize projects admitted to the pipeline of projects, typically over a three- to five-year horizon, to ensure that projects are aligned with strategic objectives and to decide on how projects are to be financed prior to a decision being taken to further progress or implement them. Decisions on how projects identified and approved in the stage 1 management plan are to be planned, specified, procured, and overseen need to be captured in a procurement and delivery management strategy during stage 2 (strategic resourcing).

Stage 3 (preparation and briefing) establishes a strategic brief for the project to enable the professional team to advance the project. Stage 4 (concept and viability) results in a solution for the project which satisfies the strategic brief. The design or solution is commonly "frozen" at the end of stage 4. The decision taken at the end of stage 4 may authorize implementation, defer implementation, or terminate the project.

The development of designs during stage 5 (design development) includes the selection of materials and components. The design development report translates the concept report into a document, which paints a picture of what is to be delivered. Record information relates to what has been delivered. Accordingly, the record information provided during stage 8 (handover) is an updated version of the design development report.

Production information is developed during stage 6 (design documentation). This information enables manufacture, fabrication, and construction information to be produced by or on behalf of the contractor, in response to the production information that is provided.

There is a difference between achieving completion of the works in accordance with the provisions of the contract (stage 7) and the handing over of the works to the owner, end-user, or those responsible for the operation and maintenance of the works (stage 8). Upon completion or soon thereafter, risks associated with loss of, or wear or damage to, the works are no longer borne by the contractor. Record information, which is produced during stage 8, provides those tasked with the operation and maintenance of infrastructure with the information necessary to effectively do so. Stage 9 (close out) closes out not only the contractual provisions between the "buyer" and the "supplier" but also the project.

The client's business case, vision, values, and project priorities collectively make up the client's value proposition for a project. Activities associated with the planning, designing, manufacturing, fabrication, construction, installation, and commissioning need to translate the client's value proposition into project outcomes. Clients, to achieve project value, need to perform the following "buying" functions (Watermeyer and Phillips, 2020):

- plan — decide on what needs to be done, how it is to be resourced and achieved, and in what time frames, and set a budget;
- specify — define the client's functional and other requirements for the project clearly and precisely;
- procure — obtain project resources (internal and external) to execute project activities with care and effort; and
- oversee delivery — observe and define the execution of the project to realize the client's value proposition associated with a business case (promise of measurable benefits resulting from the project).

Client leadership is vital to the success of a project as it establishes the culture within which the project is delivered. Vision and values are two important tools in the exercising of client leadership. Vision provides direction and a sense of purpose while values provide trust and appropriate behaviors for successful outcomes. Client leadership creates an enabling environment for resources responsible for delivering projects to perform at their best (Watermeyer, 2018; DHET, 2021).

Accounting for and controlling expenditure

Procurement spending on general goods and services is frequently linked to an operational account in terms of which the contract price, the budget, and the purchase order (financial control which ensures that overpayment does not take place) are commonly the same value as risks are low. Accounting for expenditure in terms of this procurement regime is relatively straightforward. This is not the case for projects involving construction works.

Construction works are commonly delivered against an approved project budget. Expenditure needs to be accounted for on a project-by-project basis. Such projects may comprise several costs in addition to construction works contracts, for example, costs relating to land acquisition, statutory permissions, utility services and bulk contributions, free issue materials, information communication technology networks and furniture, fittings and equipment, and payments relating to the occurrence of client risk events. Costs can also emanate from several contracts linked to a particular project. Accordingly, accurate and up-to-date project record-keeping is required to keep track of project expenditure and to ensure that reliable data is available to make decisions on any course corrections sooner rather than later.

Projects in the public sector are commonly funded on an annual basis, often in terms of a program of projects. To avoid under-expenditure of budgets during a particular financial year, a degree of flexibility is permitted to change annual project cash-flow projections during the year, so that more money can be spent on faster moving projects in a particular financial year. This does not mean that overall project budgets or the purpose for which funds were approved are changed, but rather the rate of expenditure of approved project budgets can be allowed to vary (DHET, 2021). This can only be managed if reliable and up to date project costs and schedule data is maintained.

Approach to sustainable development

Sustainability is the state of the global system, including environmental, social, and economic aspects, in which the needs of the present are met without compromising the ability of future generations to meet their own needs. Sustainable development, on the other hand, is development that meets the environmental, social and economic needs of the present without compromising the ability of future generations to meet their own needs (ISO 6707-3:2017). It is rooted in the simple concept of providing a better quality of life for all, now and for generations to come. It is a way of looking at all resources that will lead to a higher quality of life for the current generation, without compromising that of future generations (Watermeyer, 2006).

ISO 20400:2017 defines sustainable procurement as "procurement that has the most positive environmental, social and economic impacts possible over the entire life cycle." This standard suggests that:

- the main principles are accountability, transparency, ethical behavior, full and fair opportunity, respect for stakeholders' interests, respect for human rights, the rule of law and international norms of behavior, innovative solutions, focus on needs, integration, analysis of all costs, and continual improvement;
- the core subjects are organizational governance, human rights, labor practices, the environment, fair operating practices, consumer issues, and community involvement and development; and
- the key considerations for sustainable procurement are managing risk (and opportunities), addressing adverse sustainability impacts through due diligence, setting priorities for sustainability issues, exercising influence, and avoiding complicity.

ISO 20400:2017 defines procurement narrowly and as such focuses on general goods and services. Construction works involve the combination of many goods and services in the development of a product on a site. Procurement in a construction context focuses not only on the acquisition process but also on the planning and contract management phases of the procurement process, i.e., the upstream and downstream activities of the procurement process. What is planned needs to be delivered in the face of many risks which may manifest and several competing objectives and impacts to achieve value for money (Watermeyer, 2018). What is promised during the acquisition phase needs to be delivered.

Value for money refers to a project that is well worth the money spent on it. It is the effective, efficient, and economic use of resources or the optimal use of resources to achieve intended outcomes (Watermeyer, 2013). Value for money is the attainment of a desirable or satisfactory outcome in relation to a carefully considered budget. The client's business case, vision, values, and project priorities collectively make up the client's value proposition for a project. A project that achieves the client value proposition is a project that achieves value for money. Activities associated with the delivery of construction works need to translate the client's value proposition through a number of activities and influencing and controlling actions into project outcomes that impact on the three aspects of sustainability (economic, environmental, and social) and result in a product (DHET, 2021 and Watermeyer, 2022).

There are accordingly significant differences in the approach to sustainable procurement as construction works commonly incorporates materials, products, components, and assemblies and involves a wide range of construction operations, often with competing impacts. Sustainable procurement in a construction works context is therefore concerned with achieving a balance between competing environmental, social, and economic impacts (changes that may be beneficial or adverse) within budgetary constraints and in the face of risks (the effect of uncertainty of objectives) that manifest during a protracted delivery process. Clients need to formulate and document their sustainability value propositions, brief those who are responsible for planning and designing construction works, and incorporate sustainability requirements in contracts entered.

A critical consideration is the service life of construction works, i.e., the period after installation during which construction works or its parts meets or exceeds the performance requirements. There is a need to forecast and control the cost of ownership as a high proportion of the life cycle costs may be set by the time that the construction works are complete. Life-cycle costs might also be required during the tender-evaluation process to compare the competitiveness of tenders received and to assess project affordability.

ISO 19208:2016 provides a framework for the specification of performance in buildings to satisfy user requirements (statement of need to be fulfilled) or societal expectations (what society deems acceptable). ISO 19208 considers performance as the "ability to fulfill required functions under intended use conditions, behaviour when in use or impact on economic conditions, the environment, society or quality of life." This standard recognizes four categories of performance, namely: reaction to agents, influence on human activities, impact on society, and changes in performance over time. The common drivers for objectives associated with contributions to sustainability for construction works as described in ISO 19208 are usage of resources such as energy and water, choice of building materials, construction methods and resources, waste disposal and resilience.

Standardizing procurement processes and procedures

General

All levels of government, public utilities, donor agencies, and international agencies invariably regulate procurement. Several public companies also regulate procurement. This is done in the interest of good governance and public or shareholder accountability. However, there is no uniformity in approach. The practice of developing separate procedures, guidelines, and drafting styles for procurement documentation for different categories of procurement (for example, supplies, services, works, disposals, and public–private and public partnerships) further complicates matters. It may also be argued that this fragmented approach to the regulation of procurement presents a significant barrier to trade and is not necessarily in the best interest of an organization. Those wishing to do business with an organization have to understand an organization's procurement culture to successfully gain access to business opportunities and to price risks associated with their procurement. This fragmented approach also works against the development of a procurement skills base within an organization and staff mobility between organizations (Watermeyer, 2005).

Public procurement, because of its nature and size, can have a significant impact on social and economic development (Arrowsmith, 1995). Governments in both developed and developing countries have responded to the use of procurement to attain policy objectives, in ways ranging from making it mandatory for officials to use procurement to attain socio-economic objectives to ruling out its use for such purposes (Arrowsmith *et al.*, 2000).

The starting point in the development of any procurement system is to determine the objectives for the system. Objectives associated with procurement systems typically relate to good governance (primary objectives) and, particularly in developing countries, to the use of procurement to promote social and national agendas (secondary or non-commercial objectives). These objectives also relate to sustainable development objectives to reduce negative impacts on the environment, including climate change and to contribute to the alleviation of poverty. The ISO 10845 series of international standards are framed around the following widely accepted system objectives:

- primary objectives: the procurement system shall be fair, equitable, transparent, competitive, and cost-effective.
- secondary objectives: the procurement system may, subject to applicable legislation, promote objectives additional to those associated with the immediate objective of the procurement itself.

These objectives or end outcomes may be applied to both the public and private sectors as well as to NGOs and donor organizations. Such objectives establish overarching performance requirements for a standardized procurement system. A system designed around these objectives promotes the economic, efficient, and effective use of resources in an accountable and developmental manner (Watermeyer and Phillips, 2020).

Components of a procurement system

General

A procurement system comprises (Watermeyer, 2011a):

- rules and guidelines governing the procedures and methods that can be applied;
- procurement documents, which include conditions associated with the tender process, evaluation criteria, conditions of contract and pricing mechanisms and which specify and describe the goods, services or works that are required and any other requirements and constraints relating thereto;
- governance arrangements which authorize, direct, empower, provide oversight, and limit the actions of management; and
- organizational policies which assign responsibilities for authorizing activities and confirming conformity with requirements, provide delegations for the awarding of a contract or the issuing of an order, establish ethical standards, limit choices in the usage and application

of particular selection methods, provide procedures for dealing with specific procurement issues, and establish secondary procurement goals and procedures.

ISO 10845 standards for construction procurement

The ISO 10845 series of construction procurement standards (Parts 1 to 4) creates a framework for the development and implementation of a procurement system that facilitates fair competition, reduces the possibilities of abuse, improves predictability of outcomes, and allows the demonstration of best value or cost-effective outcomes (Watermeyer, 2011b). It also standardizes components of the system that can be standardized at an international level and establishes the principles around which procurement systems can be managed and controlled as indicated in Figure 11.2 (Watermeyer, 2018).

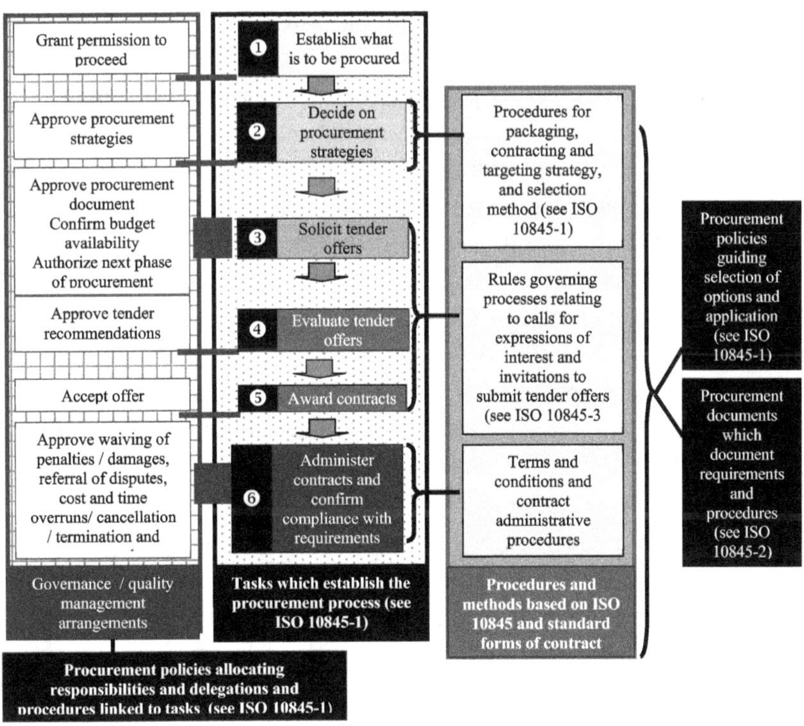

Figure 11.2: Tasks, processes, and controls associated with a procurement system.

ISO 10845-1 describes processes, methods, and procedures for the establishment within an organization of a procurement system that is fair, equitable, transparent, competitive, and cost-effective and establishes generic selection methods and procedures that are used in soliciting tender offers and awarding contracts. ISO 10845-2 establishes, in respect of supply, services, and construction contracts, a format for the compilation of calls for expressions of interest, tender and contract documents, and the general principles for compiling procurement documents. ISO 10845-3 establishes standard conditions of tender while ISO 10845-4 establishes standard conditions for the calling for expressions of interest. ISO 10845-2 enables ISO 10845-3, ISO 10845-4 and standard forms of contract to be readily referenced in procurement documents. Parts 1 to 4 of ISO 10845 can also be readily incorporated into procurement systems by reference in organizational policies or in legislation (Watermeyer, 2011a).

The approach to soliciting tenders from the market (selection methods) in ISO 10845-1 is different from that adopted by most multi-lateral organizations, international agencies, and legislatures which often deal with goods, services, and construction works separately. Typically, different sets of rules, guidelines, and regulations are established for these different categories of procurement. This compartmentalized approach is confusing and makes procurement unnecessarily complex. ISO 10845-1 introduces an alternative approach of first developing generic procurement methods that may be used in combination with each other, i.e., prequalification methods in the form of eligibility criteria and expressions of interest and methods, which provide opportunities for engaging with tenderers during the tender process. This enables either a transactional or strategic approach to be taken to approach the market for tender offers (see Figure 11.3). Combinations of the generic procedures and methods, with or without eligibility criteria, can be used to simulate the bespoke procurement methods adopted by multi-lateral organizations, international agencies, and legislatures for a particular category of procurement. At the same time, this approach provides procuring entities with a wide range of options in the pursuit of best-value procurement outcomes.

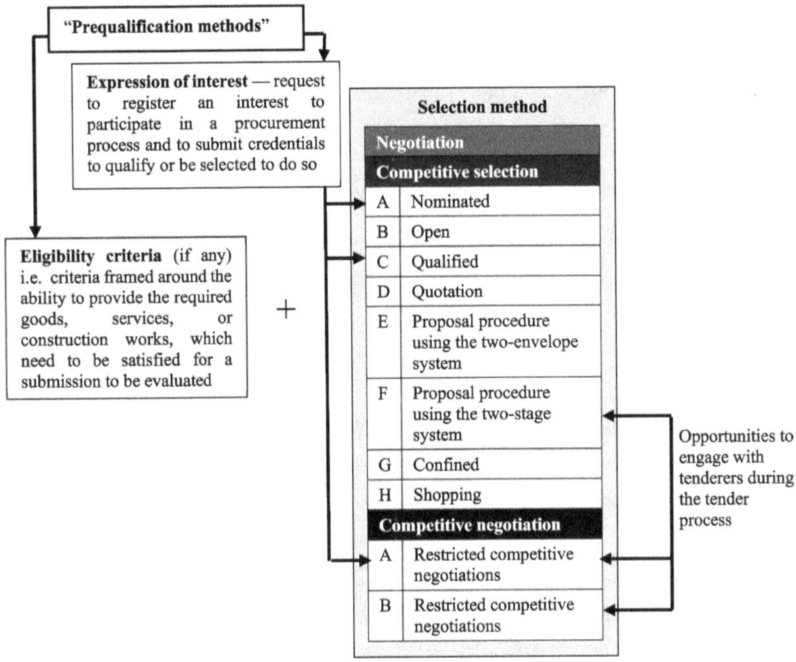

Figure 11.3: Approaches to soliciting tender offers from the market provided for in ISO 10845-1.

Standard forms of contract

Standard forms of contract can be drafted around significantly different objectives and principles such as master–servant relationship or collaboration between two experts, risk-sharing, or risk transfer. Standard forms of contract may also support open book approaches to the costing of changes due to the occurrence of risk events, foster collaborative working relationships, provide pricing structures that align payments to results and reflect a balanced sharing of performance risk, and deal with delays and disruptions efficiently and effectively. Standard forms of contract tend to be country-specific as they are developed by bodies within a particular country. There are, however, two international families of standard forms of contracts, namely, those published by the International Federation of

Consulting Engineers (FIDIC) and the Institution of Civil Engineers (The New Engineering Contract (NEC)). These standard forms of contract cover a range of contract types, contracting strategies, and approaches to managing risks (Watermeyer, 2018).

Procurement strategy and tactics

General

Project outcomes in projects involving construction works are sensitive not only to the decisions made during the planning, design, and execution of such projects but also to the manner in which resources are structured and procured to deliver such projects. There are a number of different approaches to the procurement of resources, each of which can result in different outcomes. Procurement strategy is all about the choices made in determining what is to be delivered through a particular contract, the contracting arrangements, how secondary procurement objectives are to be promoted, and which selection method will be employed to solicit tender offers. A procurement strategy commonly comprises (Watermeyer, 2018):

- a packaging strategy which organizes work packages into contracts or orders issued in terms of a framework agreement;
- a contracting strategy which governs the nature of the relationship the client wishes to foster with the contractor, which in turn determines the risks and responsibilities between the parties to the contract and the methodology by which the contractor is to be paid;
- a targeting strategy which leverages business, employment, and skills opportunities for target groups through the contracts that are entered into; and
- a selection method used to solicit tender offers from the market.

Procurement strategies are also formulated around procurement objectives that may relate to either the delivery of the product (primary objectives) or what can be promoted through the delivery of the product (secondary objectives), i.e., broader societal objectives. Procurement strategy is also informed by spend, organizational, market, and stakeholder analyses (Watermeyer, 2018).

Targeted procurement

ISO 10845-1 describes several targeted procurement procedures that create a demand for services or goods (or both) of, or to secure the participation of, targeted enterprises and targeted labor in contracts in response to the objectives of a secondary procurement policy. Such procedures can be used to promote a range of secondary procurement objectives linked to key performance indicators, including the granting of evaluation points in the evaluation process and financial incentives and the establishment of contractual obligations linked to key performance indicators and accelerated rotations on electronic databases (Watermeyer, 2000, 2006, 2010, 2018). ISO 10845-1 provides comprehensive guidance on the application of targeted procurement procedures. Parts 5 to 8 of ISO 10845 establish KPIs to measure the outcomes of a contract in relation to the engagement of target groups, and to establish a target level or performance for a contractor to achieve or exceed in the performance of a contract.

Small-scale enterprises can participate in procurement in one of two ways. They can either contract directly with a client, or act as a subcontractor, supplier, or service provider to a main contractor in the delivery chain. Clients can unbundle (break down) projects into smaller contracts to increase the participation of small and medium enterprises, which can result in inappropriate division of responsibilities, programming difficulties, duplication of establishment charges, and under-utilization of resources. This can have a negative impact on cost and time and place a considerable administrative burden on clients. Alternatively, ISO 10845-5, ISO 10845-6, or ISO 10845-7 can be incorporated in contracts to establish contractual obligations for the attainment of a specified contract-participation goal (KPI). The attainment of these goals necessitates that main contractors "unpack" their contracts into smaller contracts and procure the services of small businesses to perform such contracts and to administer them and, in so doing, remove this burden from clients. This approach to procurement facilitates local participation in contracts in a measurable, quantifiable, and verifiable manner.

Framework agreements

A framework agreement is an agreement between a client and one or more contractors, the purpose of which is to establish the terms governing orders to be awarded during a given period, in particular with regard to price and, where appropriate, the quantity envisaged. An order, on the other hand, is an instruction to provide work under a framework agreement. Framework agreements enable the client to procure on an as-instructed basis (call offs) over a set term without committing to any quantum of work. An order falling within the scope of the agreement may be issued during the term of the contract but not after the term. Such agreements do not bind the client to make use of such agreements to meet needs. The client may approach the market for work falling within the scope of work of the framework agreement, whenever it considers that better value in terms of time, cost, and quality may be obtained (ISO 10845-1:2020).

Framework agreements reduce a client's need to approach the market for goods and services and the number of relationships to be managed. They provide programming flexibility to manage expenditure relating to the delivery and multiple projects over time. They also enable lessons learned in one order to be taken to the next order and enable a team to work together on an integrated approach over a period of time. This also enables performance, including that of promoting secondary objectives, to be improved upon over time (Watermeyer, 2018)

Engaging the market

A client, where new or refurbished construction works is required, needs to answer the basic questions relating to (see Figure 11.4) (Watermeyer, 2018 and ISO 22058, 2022):

- the financing of the project on a "buy" or "make" basis, and
- if the decision is to "make," whether or not design responsibilities and / or responsibilities for the management of interfaces between direct contracts are to be retained or transferred.

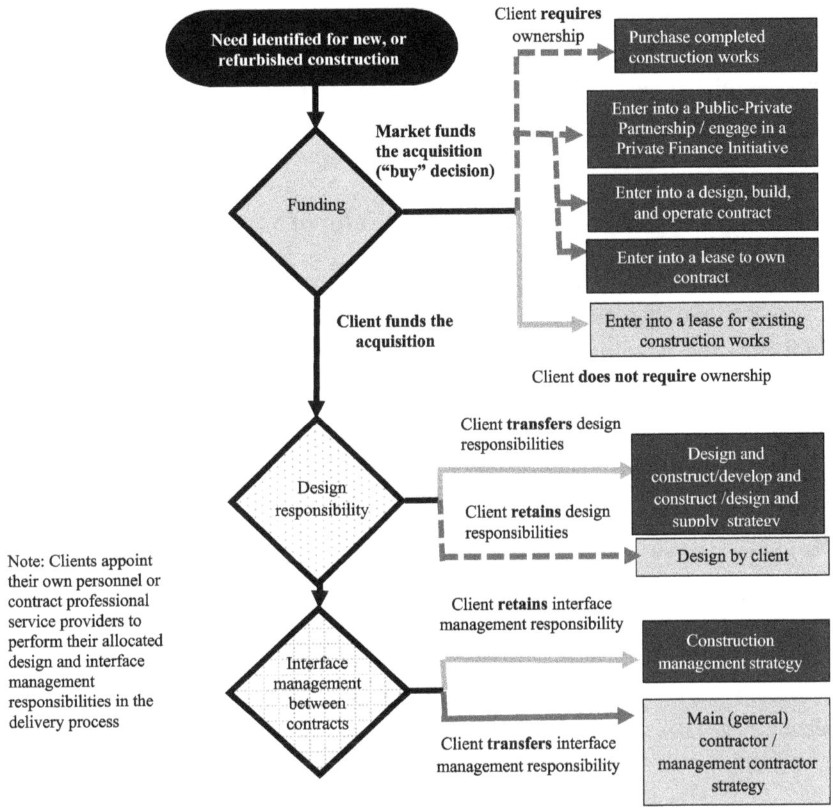

Figure 11.4: Common options to approach the market for new or refurbished construction works.

Procurement strategy determines the number of contracts that need to be procured and overseen as well as the capacity and capabilities of the client delivery management team that needs to be put in place to oversee the delivery of the required construction works (Watermeyer, 2018). Procurement tactics are required to successfully implement procurement strategies and, in so doing, improve project outcomes. They also impact upon the cost effectiveness of specific procurement transactions.

Procurement tactics commonly relate to the publicity to attract the right level of interest from the market, the sequencing and timing of the issuing of tenders and orders, and the setting up of procurement documents to ensure that contracts are awarded to the tendering entity that is most likely to deliver best value or a cost-effective solution and the setting up of the terms and conditions of contracts to achieve best results.

Developing and documenting procurement strategies

The procurement strategy that is decided upon for a particular procurement or category of procurement needs to be documented. Table 11.3 indicates the headings and content of an adopted strategy.

Table 11.3: Documenting a procurement strategy for construction works projects.

Aspect of strategy	Comments
Packaging strategy	Brief description of package framework/non-framework[a]
Design and interface management strategy	Design strategy: design by client/develop and construct/design and construct/design and supply[a] Interface management strategy: construction management/ management contractor/general contractor[a]
Contracting strategy	Contract type: construction/design, build and operate/professional service/service/supply[a] Standard form of contract: bespoke/ [name standard form of contract, for example FIDIC Red Book}[a] Pricing strategy: price-based (activity schedule/bill of quantities/ lump sum/percentage of cost of construction/price list/price schedule)/cost-based (cost plus/target cost/time based)/ performance-based[a]
Targeting strategy	Granting of tender evaluation points/accelerated rotations/ evaluation points in expressions of interest/financial incentives/ creation of contractual obligations[a,b]
Selection method	Negotiation procedure/competitive selection procedure (nominated/ open/qualified/quotation/proposal using a two-envelope system/ proposal using a two-stage system/confined market procedure)/ competitive negotiations (restricted/open)/order issued in terms of a framework contract[a]

Note: [a]delete options which do not apply; [b]describe so that readers understand the essence of the strategy and the KPI that is promoted.

Body of knowledge for construction procurement

The fundamentals of the body of knowledge associated with the planning, acquisition, and contract management phases of procurement in a construction project context are well established in the ISO 10845 series of international standards and the FIDIC and NEC families of standard contracts. Procurement strategy and tactics are well described in ISO 22058. These international publications address all aspects of the process which creates, manages, and fulfills contracts in the delivery of construction works projects.

What is still an emerging knowledge area is delivery management, which includes planning at a program and project level and the procurement and management of a network of suppliers including, as necessary, professional service providers, contractors, and subcontractors to design, scope, detail, and deliver infrastructure projects on a site (DHET, 2021). Two seminal guides on the role of the client: the Institution of Civil Engineers' Client Best Practice Guide (Kershaw and Hutchison, 2009) and the University of the Witwatersrand and Engineers Against Poverty's Client Guide for Improving Infrastructure Project Outcomes (Watermeyer, 2018) have been published, which are shaping this critical knowledge area.

Client teams, in performing the "buying" function, need to have not only the "hard" technical abilities but also the "soft" organizational and leadership skills of project delivery to successfully deliver projects. Leadership, organizational culture, mindsets, attitudes and behaviors of the client team have an impact on project performance. It is particularly important that those leading the client "buying" function have the requisite "soft" abilities to lead the client team. McKinsey and Company (2017) have undertaken some research into the "science" and "art" of delivering projects.

The need for organizations to work collaboratively to achieve satisfying project outcomes is increasingly being recognized. There is a need to shift the focus from traditional adversarial behaviors to behaviors, skills, and governance between and within organizations. Collaboration between individuals is relatively common but transitioning this to collaboration between organizations is more complex (Watermeyer, 2018). This is yet another emerging knowledge area in the delivery of construction-related projects which warrants further research.

Differences in approaches between developed and developing countries

A key question that needs to be asked is whether the body of knowledge needs to be adjusted for developing countries. One answer to this question lies in how sustainable development is approached. While the challenge of sustainable development is global, the strategies for addressing sustainability in construction works are local and differ in context and content from region to region. Such strategies need to reflect the context not only in the built environment but also in the social environment, which includes social equity, cultural issues, traditions, heritage issues, human health and comfort, social infrastructure, safety, and healthy environments. It may, in addition, particularly in developing countries, include poverty reduction, job creation, access to safe and affordable shelter and facilities, and mitigation of the loss of livelihoods.

Given the disparities in standards of living between developed and developing nations, the approach in general to the social component is very different. This results in different development priorities between the developed nations and developing nations, as indicated in Figure 11.5. The so-called "green" agenda addresses the issue of affluence and overconsumption and is generally more pertinent to affluent countries. On the other hand, the so-called "brown" agenda addresses the need to reduce the environmental threats to health that arise from inadequate shelter, poor

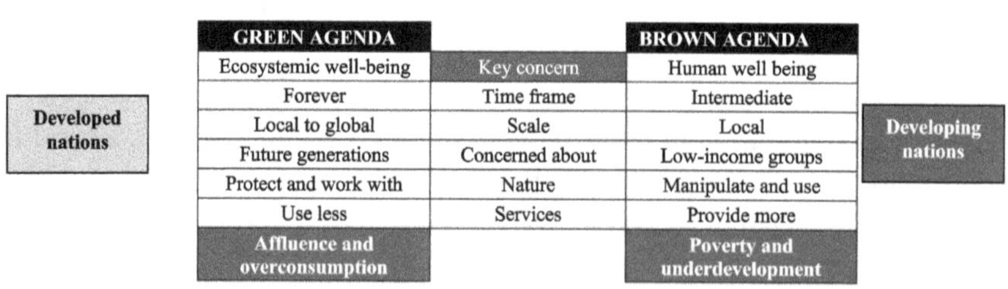

Figure 11.5: The "green" and "brown" agendas.

sanitary conditions, crowding, inadequate water provision, hazardous air and water pollution, and accumulations of solid waste. It is generally more pertinent in poor, under-serviced cities or regions. In nations with dual economies, the priorities differ regionally and within communities, depending upon where the poor and the affluent live (Watermeyer, 2006).

Accordingly, there are marked differences in the environment within which construction projects are undertaken and the strategies, tactics, and the solutions adopted to deliver projects. Relationships exist between employment opportunities, available skills, entrepreneurship, and the use of small-scale enterprises in the creation and maintenance of construction works. Projects can be structured and delivered in a manner that creates employment opportunities; promotes community involvement; imparts technical skills to the unskilled and semi-skilled members of the community; transfers administrative, commercial, and managerial skills to the community; retains, as far as is possible, the funds expended on the project within the community; and develops contractors from within the community in which they are to be constructed. The process of constructing assets can be just as important as the provision of the assets themselves (Watermeyer, 2006).

The "green" and "brown" agenda concept extends to construction industries within countries. The developed countries are well resourced in terms of skilled people, readily available materials and equipment, and project finance, whereas the developing countries commonly lack such resources. Different approaches need to be adopted to mitigate risks and to make contracts accessible to local contractors. For example, multiple framework agreements can be used to reduce the client's risk exposure and to lower the performance bond requirements as projects are delivered incrementally in a controlled environment (Watermeyer and Phillips, 2020).

It also needs to be recognized that client institutions have different levels of maturity in procuring and delivering construction works projects. A Client Maturity Model for Delivering Infrastructure Projects aimed at assisting clients to consistently produce successful delivery results for client organizations has recently been developed in South Africa (DHET, 2019). This model identifies four key processes, namely client governance and organizational practices, client leadership practices at a program level, client leadership practices at a project level, and infrastructure procurement practices. It enables organizations to determine the maturity of their organization on a self-assessment basis within one of five levels — ad-hoc (an improvised process capability), basic (a basic, disciplined process capability), structured (a fully established and institutionalized process capability), integrated (full integration with other organizational processes resulting in synergistic benefits), and optimized (processes focus on continuous improvement and adoption of lessons learned and best practices). Depending on the organization's annual infrastructure budget, the general scale, and nature of projects that are implemented and the environment within which projects are delivered, the investment necessary to achieve a high level of maturity may not be warranted. Accordingly, the level of maturity that an institution approaches its client "buying" functions with can vary between developed and developing countries.

Conclusion

The body of knowledge refers to the core teachings and skills required to work in a particular field or industry that is constantly evolving. The PMBOK®Guide and ISO 21502 establish a generic body of knowledge relating to project procurement management. However, these documents fail to address many of the critical issues required to mitigate the inherent risks and to address the complexities associated with the supply chain in delivering construction works projects. The project procurement management body of knowledge for construction works is well described in the ISO 10845 family of standards, ISO 22058 and the FIDIC and NEC suite of contracts with the exception of delivery management, i.e., the critical leadership role played by a knowledgeable client to plan, specify, procure, and oversee the delivery of projects. More research is required to establish the body of knowledge surrounding this client "buying" function, particularly in the field of "soft" organizational and leadership skills and collaborative working.

The underlying environment within which construction works projects are delivered and the resources available to deliver projects are the major differentiators between developed and developing countries. Whilst the fundamental knowledge areas remain the same, the strategic and tactical choices that are adopted in procuring and delivering construction works need to be environment appropriate. Accordingly, different options will be adopted and different procurement objectives and value propositions pursued to arrive at desired context specific outcomes. At the same time, the level of maturity in performing the client "buying" function can differ between developed and developing countries arising from resource constraints. Simply put, although the body of knowledge for project procurement management is the same, the manner, and extent of its application will differ.

More research is required to broaden the understanding of the linkage between client maturity and project outcomes, which may result in a range of differentiated approaches to the "client" buying function being developed. There is also a need for evidence-based research to inform decision-making in the development of procurement strategy and tactics in different contexts.

References

American Society of Civil Engineers (ASCE) (2008). *Civil Engineering Body of Knowledge for the 21st Century Preparing the Civil Engineer for the Future.* ASCE Second Edition.

Arrowsmith, S. (1995). Public procurement as an instrument of policy and the implementation of market liberalisation. *The Law Quarterly Review*, April, 235–284.

Arrowsmith, S., Meyer, G. and Trybus, M. (2000). *Non-commercial Factors in Public Procurement.* The Public Procurement Research Group, School of Law, Nottingham University.

Association for Project Management (2017). APM Guide to Contracts and Procurement. APM Knowledge, Princes Risborough, UK..

Department of Higher Education and Training (DHET) (2021). *University Macro-Infrastructure Framework: Infrastructure Management Guidelines for Universities.* Pretoria, South Africa.

Kershaw, S. and Hutchison, D. (Eds.) (2009). *Client Best Practice Guide. Institution of Civil Engineers.* Thomas Telford, Limited, London.

McKinsey and Company (2017). The art of project leadership: Delivering the world's largest projects. McKinsey Capital Projects and Infrastructure Practice, Sydney, Australia.

Project Management Institute (2016). *A Guide to the Project Management Body of Knowledge (PMBOK® Guide)*, 6th Edition. Project Management Institute Inc., Newtown Square, PA.

Project Management Institute (2016). Construction Extension to the PMBOK® Guide. Project Management Institute Inc., Newtown Square, PA.

Watermeyer, R and Phillips, P. (2020). Public infrastructure delivery and construction sector dynamism in the South African economy. NPC Economy Series — Background Paper. National Planning Commission, Pretoria.

Watermeyer, R. (2018). *Client Guide for Improving Infrastructure Project Outcomes*. School of Construction Economics and Management, University of the Witwatersrand and Engineers Against Poverty, Johannesburg and London.

Watermeyer, R.B. (2000). The use of targeted procurement as an instrument of poverty alleviation and job creation in infrastructure projects. *Public Procurement Law Review*, 5, 201–266.

Watermeyer, R.B. (2005). A generic and systemic approach to procurement: The case for an international standard. *Public Procurement Law Review*, 1, 39–61.

Watermeyer, R.B. (2006). Poverty reduction responses to the Millennium Development Goals. *The Structural Engineer*, 84(9), 27–34.

Watermeyer, R.B. (2010). Linking developmental deliverables to public sector contracts. Workshop on Designing Efficient Public Procurement Policies to Foster Technology Transfer and Development Capacity in Emerging Markets. PGlobal Global Advisory and Training Services Ltd., in cooperation with Istanbul Commerce, University, Istanbul, 1–2 October 2010.

Watermeyer, R.B. (2011a). Standardising construction procurement systems. Report. *The Structural Engineer*, 89(20), October.

Watermeyer, R.B. (2011b). Building trust — A platform for best practice construction procurement. Special Report. *ISO Focus +*, 24–26 September.

Watermeyer, R.B. (2022). Procurement and delivery management. In G. Ofori. (Ed.), *Research Companion to Construction Economics*. Elgar, Cheltenham, pp. 371–395.

https://doi.org/10.1142/9789811224720_0012

Chapter 12

Project Stakeholder Management in Developing Countries

Ezekiel Chinyio* and Eric-Kingkof Kofi Opoku-Ohemeng†

*University of Wolverhampton, UK
†Komplex Intelligent Solutions Plus (KIS Plus), British Virgin Islands

Abstract

The aim of this chapter is to discuss the concept and state of the art of stakeholder management. The objectives include the coverage of the key aspects of stakeholder management from the perspective of the literature, the synthesis of some problems of implementing stakeholder management in developing countries and formulation of solutions to these problems, and guidance on implementation of stakeholder management in developing countries. Twelve semi-structured virtual interviews with practitioners in some developing countries informed most of the contents of the chapter: the problems and solutions concerning stakeholder management in developing countries where the traditional type of procurement is still commonly used for project delivery. The content analysis of the interview data showed that, apart from the internal stakeholders of clients, design consultants, contractors and their teams of professionals, and other workers, another set of project stakeholders would include community organizations, trade unions, non-government organizations and sundry individuals, or groups. These many stakeholders present high chances of conflicting stakes. Power influences the prioritization of stakes in developing countries, i.e., the interests of more powerful stakeholders are accorded higher priority. Government and public establishments are often considered to be powerful; hence, there is often a general reluctance to challenge their stakes and those of the stakeholders associated with them. Moreover, some traditions and cultures are strong in communities, regions, or nations, and stakeholder engagements follow these norms. Some details of traditional protocols that are observed while negotiating conflicting stakes are often not documented, and the knowledge needed is sometimes deployed tacitly. Meanwhile, some socio-cultural protocols and government bureaucracy may slow down project procedures, but claiming for time extensions and other reliefs by project participants is virtually never done on these grounds. Another major influence in some developing countries is land ownership, which tends to be a leveraging factor on which some external stakeholders either bargain for compensation and concessions or attempt to disrupt a project. As "knowledge is power," there is scope for increasing the awareness and thus power of especially external stakeholders in developing countries.

Keywords: Culture, developing countries, expectations, negotiations, politics, project success, stakeholder management

Introduction to stakes and stakeholders

This chapter provides an overview of stakeholder management and aims to identify some good practices that could be adopted in its implementation. The objectives in the context of developing countries include: to highlight the key stakeholders in construction projects in these countries; to discuss the nuances of implementing stakeholder management; to explore the consequences of managing stakeholders in terms of project duration and cost; and to highlight some major challenges associated with stakeholder management on projects in these contexts.

A project stakeholder is an individual, group, or organization that may affect, be affected by, or perceived to be affected by, a project's decision, activity, or result (Project Management Institute, 2017). An organization in turn, relies on its stakeholders for certain benefits (Thompson, 2002; Johnson *et al.*, 2005). Thus, the influence of stakeholders is a two-way affair where two (groups of) persons or organizations affect each other. Engagements between stakeholders often involve developing and maintaining relationships amongst themselves (Lerbinger, 2006; Al Nahyan *et al.*, 2012).

Project stakeholders have a stake in (or expectation of) the performance of a project (Newcombe, 2003). These stakes or expectations of stakeholders are often dependent on what they want, such as project handover on a certain date. The expectations of stakeholders can change over time. Also, different stakeholders would have different expectations. For example, a subcontractor may be interested in getting regular jobs from a certain large contracting firm. Such a subcontractor may regularly offer discounts to the main contractor to try and influence the decision to grant it regular patronage.

A stake can also be a legal, moral, or presumed claim, and its influence can be directed at an organization's behavior, direction, process, or outcomes (Mitchell *et al.*, 1997). Savage *et al.* (1991) opined that a claim and its ability to influence must both be present before its source can be considered to be a stakeholder. This aligns with the view taken by Clarkson (1995, p. 106), who explains that stakeholders are those that "have, or claim ownership, rights, or interests in a corporation and its activities."

Stakeholders tend to be many, and in construction projects include: clients, users of built facilities, project managers, facilities managers, designers, legal authorities, employees, subcontractors, suppliers, providers of services, competitors, banks, insurance companies, the media, community representatives, neighbors, general public, government establishments, customers, regional development agencies, and visitors (Newcombe, 2003; Freeman and Currens, 2010; Pirozzi, 2019). These stakeholders will have various demands, rights, and expectations (Pedrosa-Ortega *et al.*, 2019; Pirozzi, 2019), which have the potential to influence an organization to change course or direction. Hence, an organization should proactively engage with, and manage, its stakeholders (Gibson, 2000; Sallinen *et al.*, 2011; Orndoff, 2005; Molwus *et al.*, 2017) to prevent any adverse consequences posed to the organisation's own projects, processes, and outcomes (Freeman, 1984). When organizations do not manage their stakeholders effectively, they could encounter difficulties that could affect them adversely and undesirably (Christopher *et al.*, 2002; Tete *et al.*, 2009; Yang *et al.*, 2011).

There could be many stakeholders to manage on a project, and the inter-relationships with them are often dynamic and sometimes complex. Stakes can last for short or long periods and form the basis on which a stakeholder would (try to) exert influence. The level of attention attached to stakes (saliency) also varies with time (Mitchell *et al.*, 1997; Pedrosa-Ortega *et al.*, 2019). Further, coalitions of stakeholders can emerge, either deliberately or accidentally, with the impact of increasing their joint saliency and influence (Newcombe, 2003; Bourne, 2010; Yang *et al.*, 2011). Hence, stakeholder management should be accorded high and constant attention. Organizations should meet the needs of their stakeholders optimally (Karim *et al.*, 2007; Remme and de Waal, 2020) and be wary of any "invisible stakeholders" (Yang *et al.*, 2009). The latter hints at the importance of stakeholder identification.

Conflicting expectations amongst stakeholders can take a while to resolve. Thus, this chapter provides guidance for managing stakeholders in construction project delivery in developing countries. The suggestions proffered in the chapter would help to minimize or forestall negative consequences that could arise from conflicting stakeholder demands and their associated resolution.

Stakeholder management on construction projects is subtle as it is often not stated as a requirement, or even as a process in the contract documents. However, it is prudent to adopt a systematic approach to the implementation of stakeholder management because ignoring it, or failing to practice it effectively can have grave impacts on projects. Thus, this chapter presents stakeholder management as a major contributor to project success.

The discussion in this chapter interchangeably refers to the stakeholders of an organization and/or project. These two sets are generally different but highly overlap, with organizational stakeholders subsuming the project stakeholders. However, the principles by which the two types of stakeholders should be managed are mostly the same hence the distinction between them is blurred in the chapter.

Structure of chapter

The types, attributes (features), and influence of stakeholders are discussed next. This is followed by consideration of the stakeholder management process, including the critical success factors, and the benefits and disadvantages. This theoretical discourse is followed by an overview of implementing stakeholder management in a developing country. This part of the chapter provides the theoretical underpinning in the form of a literature review, which introduces the concept of stakeholder management, its benefits, and consequences, and highlights the application of information and communications technology (ICT) in its implementation. The second half of the chapter is based on a field study of some practicalities that may be encountered in stakeholder management in developing countries. This study involved 12 virtual interviews with stakeholders in some developing countries in Africa, Asia, and the Caribbean. The information generated was evaluated by content analysis and, at the same time, screened by the authors for acceptability on the basis of "face validity." It should be noted that the information used in the discussion is limited; it is in no way representative of developing countries. Hence, the suggestions and conclusions in the chapter cannot be generalized. However, the study points to issues that might be beneficial for project managers in developing countries to note, and can be further explored in subsequent research.

Characteristics of stakeholders

Types of stakeholders

Organizations tend to have many and different types of stakeholders (Christopher *et al.*, 2002). Mitchell *et al.* (1997) identified seven types: Dormant, Discretionary, Demanding, Dominant, Dangerous, Dependent, and Definitive. These descriptors mostly relate to the behavior of each of the types of stakeholders. A dormant stakeholder may not exert influence either for a long time, or indefinitely. A demanding stakeholder will make constant requests while a dominant stakeholder will make strong claims and try to impose their interest on an organization and other stakeholders. Co and Barro (2009) warned that dangerous stakeholders possess power and time-sensitive stakes and have no regard for norms and rules, and hence they should be managed carefully.

Other categorizations of stakeholders include:

- internal or external to an organization (Savage *et al.*, 1991; Winch and Bonke, 2002; Achermann and Eden, 2011);
- direct or indirect (Smith and Love, 2004; Achermann and Eden, 2011): direct stakeholders are people who directly engage in the planning, executing, and administration processes of a project (Lester, 2007) while indirect stakeholders do not participate directly in the project (Lester, 2007; Cleland and Ireland, 2007);
- primary or secondary (Savage *et al.*, 1991; Hillman and Keim (2001): primary stakeholders have either a legal relationship with the project or a responsibility in the project management processes (Cleland and Ireland, 2007) while secondary stakeholders do not have such formal responsibility (Lester, 2007);
- critical or less critical (Calvert, 1995; Winch and Bonke, 2002);
- social or non-social: core, strategic, or environmental (Pedrosa-Ortega *et al.*, 2019; Achermann and Eden, 2011);
- market or non-market: market stakeholders are in an economic transaction relationship with the organization (Stevens *et al.*, 2005);
- political stakeholders (Karim *et al.*, 2007): both national and international (Holtbrugge *et al.*, 2007).

Influence of stakeholders

Stakeholders have certain features with which they can influence an organization or its projects. These include their interest, power, legitimacy, and proximity.

Interest

According to Cleland and Ireland (2007), stakeholders have vested interests in a project for a number of reasons, such as mission relevance, economic interest, legal rights, political support, health and safety, lifestyle, opportunism, and survival. Freeman *et al.* (2011) additionally stressed that moral interest is an important criterion for identifying who counts. The level of stakeholders' interests in a project is a key factor that can influence its success (PMI, 2004; Bourne and Walker, 2005; Eskerod and Vaagaasar, 2014). Remme and de Waal (2020) opine that common interests could inform the coalition of stakeholders, which in turn can strengthen their combined power or urgency.

Power

Contracts often assign certain powers to some stakeholders. Other pivotal roles such as providing specifications and funding empower the duty holders involved. The power of a stakeholder, if exercised solely from self-interest, can affect the progress on, or even survival of, a project (Yang *et al.*, 2009), although it can notably be based on illegitimate claims (Mitchell *et al.*, 1997).

Urgency

Urgency is the strength of feeling about an issue (Mitroff, 1983; Mitchell *et al.*, 1997). Urgency determines the extent to which stakeholders exert pressure (Bourne and Walker, 2006; Yang *et al.*, 2011). Stakeholders will likely agree to make concessions when their urgency is low.

Legitimacy

Legitimacy is the legal (and even moral) rights and interests of the stakeholders (Mitchell *et al.*, 1997). Its basis is the exchange relationship between the parties (Carroll and Buchholtz, 2011; Phillips, 2003; Suchman, 1995). Rights can be exercised or even enforced. A community that is opposed to a project can exercise their right to demonstrate against it, and this is a regulatory empowerment in most countries. For example, this right is granted by Article 11 of the Equality and Human Rights Commission which concerns "Freedom of Assembly and Association." Article 11 has been adopted by most countries, such as South Africa[1] and

[1] https://www.sahrc.org.za/home/21/files/SAHRC%20Community%20Protest%20 Pamphlet%20revised%2020%20March%202018.pdf [Accessed 05 September 2021].

Ghana.[2] Legitimacy is a core attribute in stakeholder–manager relationships (Clarkson, 1995; Donaldson and Preston, 1995; Freeman, 1984). The rights of stakeholders should be honored as much as, and to the greatest extent, possible.

Proximity

Proximity is the extent to which a stakeholder is involved in the project (Bourne, 2005). Bourne and Walker (2006) support the need to consider proximity while prioritizing project stakeholders. They developed a scale of 1 to 4 for rating stakeholders, where a stakeholder rated 1 is relatively remote from the project (i.e., does not have direct involvement in the processes), and 4 represents those that are directly working on the project (most of the time). The higher the proximity of a stakeholder the higher their chance of influencing the project.

Influence of multiple features

According to Harrison and Freeman (1999), each stakeholder group would have its own typology, and stakeholder relationships should be regarded as being multi-faceted and complex in nature, involving multiple objectives of the parties involved. Wolfe and Putler (2002) reinforce this pluralism and dynamism by asserting that the internal homogeneity or heterogeneity of each stakeholder group should be identified to facilitate their successful management. Some combined features of power, interest, and urgency have been used to map stakeholders in order to highlight their potential influence. Examples of stakeholder mappings that have considered these features are discussed in the following subsections.

Power and interest

A power–interest matrix helps project managers to determine which strategy to use to engage and communicate with project stakeholders (Olander, 2007). Indeed, the power–interest matrix illustrated in Figure 12.1 is fairly popular,

[2] https://www.rightofassembly.info/country/ghana [Accessed 5 September 2021].

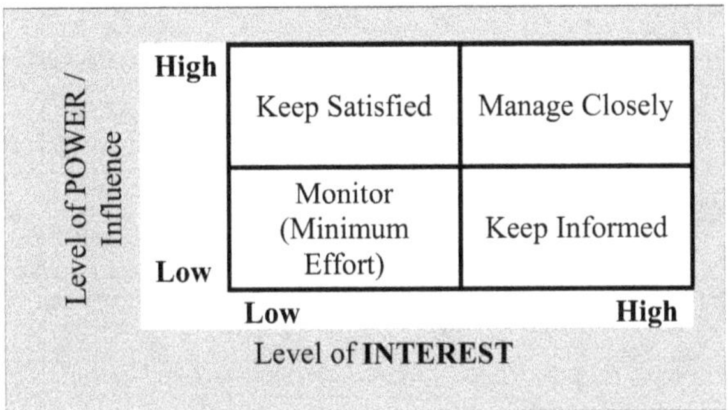

Figure 12.1: Power-Interest grid.

Source: Adapted from Newcombe (2003) and Winch (2004).

and it is often used to map stakeholders and prioritize and direct the attention that should be paid to them, as well as the type of response actions to deploy.

The Stakeholder Circle™ methodology

Bourne and Walker (2005) developed the Stakeholder Circle™ methodology for assessing and understanding the relative power and influence of stakeholders. This methodology considers the power, urgency (potential impact of their interests), and proximity of stakeholders to the project (manager). The project manager is represented by a solid small circle at the center of a bigger circle. Concentric inner circles then radiate from the inner core (project manager) to the extreme perimeter of the bigger circle. Areas within the concentric circles are used to denote the status of (groups of) stakeholders. The depth of an area (from the center) denotes the power of a stakeholder while the size of their area represents their level of influence. Color separation is used to differentiate between individuals and groups of stakeholders. A snapshot view of the circle provides the current position and potential impact of stakeholders, and this provides a basis for responding to their influences and engaging them effectively.

A typology by Mitchell *et al.* (1997)

Mitchell *et al.* (1997) presented a stakeholder typology, which maps stakeholders based on three key attributes: power, legitimacy, and urgency,

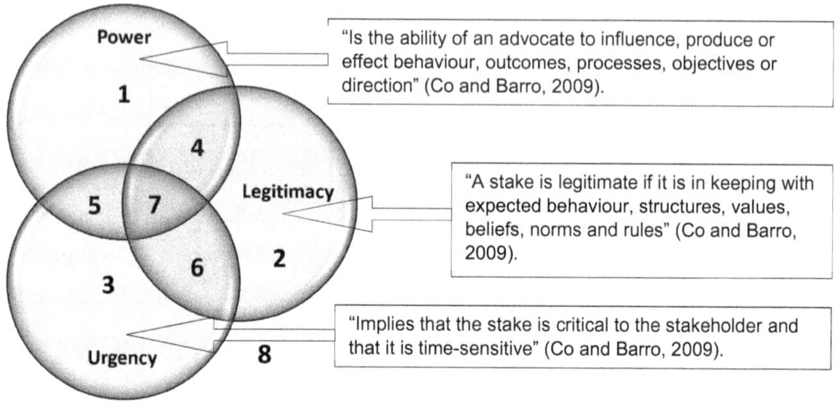

Figure 12.2: Classes of stakeholders.

Source: Adapted from Co and Barro (2009, p. 595) and Mitchell *et al.* (1997, p. 872).

Table 12.1: Stakeholder typology.

Class of stakeholder		Attribute(s)	Level of salience
Latent Stakeholders	Dormant	Power	Low
	Discretionary	Legitimacy	Low
	Demanding	Urgency	Low
Expectant Stakeholders	Dominant	Power & legitimacy	Moderate
	Dangerous	Power & urgency	Moderate
	Dependent	Legitimacy & urgency	Moderate
Definitive Stakeholders	Definitive	Power, legitimacy & urgency	High

Source: Adapted from Co and Barro (2009, p. 595).

as shown in Figure 12.2. An extension of this mapping can be used to identify three sub-groups of stakeholders: latent, expectant, and definitive (Table 12.1).

Social Network Analysis

Social Network Analysis (SNA) examines the patterns of structural relationships that develop among stakeholders over time. This analysis considers the interconnectivity between stakeholders and how they are positioned within a network; those that are highly connected or similar in attributes will be closer to each other in the network (Prell *et al.*, 2009). SNA can be used to identify invisible stakeholders who may influence a project largely while keeping a low profile (Bourne and Walker, 2006).

Complex nature of stakeholders' influences

Figure 12.2 and Table 12.1 show how stakeholder management can become very complex if the many features of the stakeholders are considered. If four or more stakeholders' attributes are considered, then mapping these on a two-dimensional representation becomes more complex. Larger organizations with many types of stakeholders that are exerting different influences will encounter this complexity. Further, stakeholders' attributes are dynamic (Co and Barro, 2009; Mitchell *et al.*, 1997). For example, a stakeholder lacking a specific attribute can become stronger and better able to project its interest by acquiring the attribute it does not have by cooperating with another stakeholder who has that specific attribute. The dynamic nature of stakes and stakeholders means that static stakeholder maps can only portray the situation at a particular point in time. Thus, ICT is increasingly being used to track and manage stakeholders and their stakes.

Harnessing software for stakeholder management

Digitization and data analytics provide information patterns and use software to record, track, share, and report stakeholder interaction activities. This ensures more effective connectivity and consistent communication that helps sustain and improve vital relationships. Borealis Software is one example that offers a real-time snapshot and history of all interactions and engagements with stakeholders via a customized dashboard (see Box 12.1). It is designed with an effective keyword search and filters to locate and efficiently find unique obligations, significantly reducing the time spent looking for information. The use of a software approach would prompt an organization when they need to act and suggest alternative responses in this regard.

Box 12.1: Boréalis software application for an oil and gas infrastructure project in North Vietnam.

Monkey Forest Consulting services was hired by an oil and gas infrastructure project in North Vietnam to assist its team with the implementation of a community relations strategy. Most households in the area relied on farming and fishing to subsist, and the project was going to transition them to a more urban environment and livelihood. There was a need to monitor the communities to ensure that they were adapting well.

Major concerns included the health impact of the project communities close to the project site; and some households that needed to be relocated. Relocating residents (i.e. stakeholders) is always a challenge worldwide. Communities will often resist relocation and if/when eventually they are convinced or forced to move, the amount of compensation becomes a big issue; and social lives are disrupted highly while people are relocating.

In this project in Vietnam, Monkey Forest Consulting services used the Boréalis Application successfully in its community engagement strategy while tracking the resettlement of several villages. It was able to build a strong relationship with the communities and maintain a social license to operate. The effect included:

- Successful resettlement and ongoing livelihood transition of almost 3,900 affected households.
- Development and deployment of strategic social investments aligned with communities' needs and good social risk management.
- Streamlining of the day-to-day management of the community relations activities.
- Raising the level of awareness of the communities about health and safety issues.
- Implementation of an efficient complaints and grievances management process.
- Implementation of a strong and effective engagement with over 1,000 stakeholders on a quarterly basis.

Source: Culled and adapted (with permission) from https://ressources.boreal-is.com/success-story/mfc?_ga=2.1971769.929161750.1601943606-1457813989.1596169443.

Stakeholder management process

Managing stakeholders requires a lot of decision-making, and finding the best ways to communicate with, and relate to, them. Implicit in stakeholder management is a set of principles and a process that involves their identification, assessment, and engagement (Chinyio and Olomolaiye, 2010).

Identification of project stakeholders

It is necessary to identify the stakeholders right from the strategic development stage of a project in order to obtain a good understanding of the possible positive and negative impacts each of them can have on the project. Some stakeholders have great power and can interfere with a project at various stages (Karlsen, 2002). Thus, it is important for the project team to know the stakeholders at every project stage, especially the key ones (Karim *et al.*, 2007; Salam and Noguchi, 2006). Reviews of, and reports on, past projects provide a good basis for identifying the stakeholders in the current and next project. Checklists of features of stakeholders and aspects of their identification as part of their management can be developed from past reviews and used as a basis to identify the stakeholders in the current project. This approach can be supplemented with brainstorming exercises and surveys involving an organization's employees.

Some stakeholders may be invisible or hidden (Yang *et al.*, 2009) and their identification could be missed. Also, some stakeholders may not show up at the beginning of a project, only to emerge subsequently when a matter relating to their interests arises. Hence, the identification of stakeholders should be sustained until the project is completed.

Assessing and responding to stakeholders' features and interests

The next task after identifying stakeholders is to assess their characteristics and (potential) influence on an organization. Stakeholders have the knowledge, tools, and interests to influence a project. Their attributes, such as their power, interest, urgency, proximity, and legitimacy, which have been discussed before, should be assessed. It is this assessment that enables accurate stakeholder mapping and development of appropriate actions and reactions towards them, i.e., engaging the stakeholders.

The assessment of stakeholders can be done by using the same techniques that are viable for their identification — the use of reviews of previous projects, checklists, brainstorming, and surveys among employees. Often, the two activities (identification of stakeholders and assessment of their features and interests) are distinct but interwoven.

Assessing stakeholders' positions provides a basis for prioritizing where attention should be placed in terms of addressing their needs; balancing these needs with the organization's objectives, and making any compromises which are necessary (McElroy and Mills, 2000; Freeman and Currens, 2010; Jepsen and Eskerod, 2009). Whenever it is not viable to meet the expectations of a stakeholder, it becomes vital to communicate with them and explain the reason why this cannot be done. On some occasions, it is necessary to make some trade-offs in order to placate some stakeholders. For example, in Box 12.1, Monkey Forest Consulting Services engaged with local communities who were being relocated against their will, and offered them better health and safety options.

The levels of importance of stakeholders' attributes can change in the course of a project. For example, a member of the design team would have high influence during the design phase and less power during the construction phase. Also, stakeholders could coalesce, which would raise their stakes and their potential to influence the project. Hence, stakeholders should be assessed continuously, at both the individual and group levels.

Tracking stakeholder management

The expectations of stakeholders should be addressed and not wished away. It is important to demonstrate to stakeholders that their expectations are not being ignored, or covered up. Regular or timely communication with stakeholders is quite important. This provides a basis to negotiate issues with the stakeholders and also offer them progressive feedback.

Stakeholder management is dynamic as the interests and other features of stakeholders change over the course of a project. Hence, more effective stakeholder management should involve a tracking approach that provides an up to date position of the situation on the project. Knowledge management is important when it comes to managing stakeholders, and ICT makes it viable to store the information in one place, retrieve it quickly, use it to inform and to remind an organization (when) to act, and provide suggestions on the appropriate courses of action.

Critical success factors in stakeholder management

Critical Success Factors (CSFs) highlight key aspects of practice that should not be allowed to slip if what is implemented is to be effective. The CSFs of stakeholder management are widely discussed in the literature, such as in Sallinen *et al.* (2011), Tarhini *et al.* (2015), Al Nahyan *et al.* (2012), and Molwus *et al.* (2017). Yang *et al.* (2010, p. 779) provide this indicative overview:

> (1) Undertaking social responsibilities; (2) Defining project mission; (3) Identifying stakeholders; (4) Understanding stakeholders' interests; (5) Exploring stakeholders' needs and constraints to projects; (6) Assessing stakeholders' behaviours; (7) Predicting the influence of stakeholders; (8) Assessing attributes of stakeholders; (9) Analysing conflicts and coalitions among stakeholders; (10) Resolving conflicts among stakeholders' demands; (11) Promoting good relationships with stakeholders; (12) Formulating appropriate strategies; (13) Predicting stakeholders' reactions; (14) Analysing the dynamism of stakeholders; and (15) Ensuring effective communication with stakeholders.

Benefits of stakeholder management

Stakeholder management is valuable and worthwhile (Karlsen, 2002; Olander, 2007; Walker *et al.*, 2008; Jepsen and Eskerod, 2008; Nauman and Piracha, 2016). On projects, stakeholder management helps the team to:

- Understand who the stakeholders are, and which stakeholder is more important or critical at each stage, and thus needs a high level of attention (McElroy and Mills, 2000; Freeman and Currens, 2010; Jepsen and Eskerod, 2009);

- Address the needs of the many stakeholders in the project;
- Not allow any of the stakeholders to undermine the objectives, values, goals, tasks, and priorities of the project (Jergeas *et al.*, 2000); and
- Avoid any setbacks that can be caused to the project by the stakeholders.

Difficulties in stakeholder management

Stakeholder management can face challenges such as:

- Silent stakeholders who do not indicate their interests can emerge and voice their demands at a later stage.
- The coalescing of stakeholders can lead to very powerful groups forming to influence a project. It is often difficult to know when these groups are coalescing.
- Clients or other powerful stakeholders may delay in providing relevant information, and this can cause disruption to the project's progress and affect its schedule.
- Some (dominant) stakeholders could be unyielding in negotiations where there are conflicting interests.

Stakeholder difficulties should be identified and addressed early in order to avoid the challenges they pose (Fraser and Zhu, 2008; Sallinen *et al.*, 2011).

Stakeholder management and issues in developing countries

The foregoing sections outlined the theoretical conception of stakeholder management. This section provides an overview of the implementation of stakeholder management in developing countries.

The developing countries are socially, economically, and politically heterogeneous. This section does not attempt to address stakeholder management in each developing country. Rather, it provides an indicative across-the-board approach to project delivery and stakeholder management.

In construction, the traditional contracting type of procurement is still commonly used in many developing countries where projects are mostly tendered publicly, and competitive tendering is used in selecting the contractor to do the job. The construction client would have a team of consultants while the contractor would have a supply chain. A third set of project stakeholders would include community organizations, trade unions, non-government (charitable) organizations, and sundry individuals or groups.

In developing countries, projects are procured by both the private-sector and public-sector organizations, which are ministries, departments, and parastatals. Projects by the private sector would include shopping malls, hotels, housing (estates), and premises for small-scale retail and other business activities. Public-sector projects could include roads, leisure facilities, offices, electrification schemes, dams, refineries, and sporting facilities. Some of these public-sector projects could be funded by the multi-lateral financial institutions (such as the World Bank, African Development Bank, and Asian Development Bank) and bilateral international development partners and philanthropic organizations.

Given the foregoing context, some challenges that could be faced in developing countries with respect to stakeholder management are discussed in the following subsections.

Conflicting stakes

Different stakeholders would expect different things from a project. For example, a contractor might feel that some components of a building project should be changed to minimize running costs whereas the designers may not want to implement the contractor's suggestion, as they would want the project to reflect their full signature. This hypothetical conflict of interest demonstrates how stakeholders' expectations could be divergent.

Conflicts of interest often come up in developing countries. For example:

- The politicians in power might want to build a golf course, while the environmentalists do not want such a sporting facility to take up greenfield land.

- The politicians might want to commence the construction of a road project now, before an election. However, the ministry responsible for procurement may not be ready for a quick start. While the politicians may be looking for a project to demonstrate their achievements and plans to the electorate as they campaign for the forthcoming elections, the ministry might be following procedures, which may be bureaucratic.
- A contractor might need to close a certain road during construction but parents and commercial drivers may want it to remain open for their school runs and business activities, respectively.
- The government in power may want to build a refinery but the party in the opposition may want to block this plan.
- The government may intend to build a road but the associated landowners may be unwilling to release their lands for the project.

Stakeholder conflicts can occur at any stage of a project. It is easier and usually cheaper to address disagreements at the early, design stages than in the construction phase. There can be some posturing at certain points on a project as some of the stakeholders may want to show that their opinions have greater influence than those of others. Due to varying factors, certain stakeholders' objectives may be deferred or rendered unachievable.

Stakeholders' wants often exceed their financial obligations. For example, the commissioning stakeholder might under-estimate or provide insufficient funding for projects but will always expect a high quality product. They also expect the project team to always treat their specific interests as the most important stakes. An extension of this consideration is when the interests of an individual dominates over the project's interest. For example, the project manager insists on buying materials from a particular supplier, but this vendor is always late with deliveries, thus holding back progress on the project. Sometimes, statutory or budget restraints can hinder the achievement of stakeholders' wishes. For example, a new regulation could block the importation of a certain material or component that had been specified in the project. It can be difficult to achieve all stakeholders' expectations. Even more problematic is when the interest of a particular stakeholder, an individual or group, is given precedence over that of the project.

Impacts of stakeholders' demands

Influential stakeholders can create scope creep, for example, when they lose interest in a project and withhold their support. Some stakeholders in positions of authority could also be very slow in making decisions or providing much needed information. In such circumstances, a project tends to incur delays and cost overruns. Some projects may even be abandoned; it is not unusual to see projects where construction was stopped for several months or even years in some developing countries. In some projects too, the original objectives could be changed or reduced significantly when the initial support of key stakeholders is no longer there. Ironically, contractors rarely claim for extra time and costs due to delays that arise by reason of a major stakeholder's indecision. They do so for two main reasons: (1) so that they will not be sidelined in future projects, and (2) so that any outstanding payments and entitlements on the current project will not be delayed further or rendered more complex.

Major factors in developing countries

Some prominent factors are at play in many developing countries, and these affect stakeholder engagements and project progress. Three big factors to be wary of are politics, culture, and religion.

Politics

Politicians have great power in developing countries. In many of the economies in developing countries, the ways of undertaking publicly funded projects could be highly political and sometimes regionally biased. Some ongoing projects have been stopped or deferred due to politicking with little or no resistance from relevant stakeholders and the public at large. Even public projects sponsored by international donors must get the proper sanction of the politicians in a developing country before these can proceed. Thus, before undertaking a project in any developing country, it is pertinent to know the power holders, influencers, and culture, especially as it relates to politics (see Box 12.2).

Box 12.2: Case example by Ronnie Lettsome.

I was involved in a hospital retrofitting project as a Principal Consultant with a prestigious organization that operates throughout the Caribbean. On one of the islands, I spearheaded the designs and project management of a small- to medium-size hospital that was located on the eastern side of the island. That side of the island was a part of the constituency of the Prime Minister in power. To familiarize myself with the country demographics, I had to conduct some community surveys to get familiar with the community (users of the facility) and gather feedback as to their wants and outcomes. This move allowed me to capture the much-needed baseline information and become aware of the issues present even though they were not presented to me by the main project stakeholders. The stakeholders' emphasis on the project was political but I had to stay impartial and combine all the information into the design to please both the stakeholders and the users of the facility.

Once the designs were partially completed, a town hall meeting was held where the layout and renderings of the proposed building were presented in an effort to finalize the drawings. The color rendering was yellow, which looked nice on the building. However, "yellow" represented the opposition party's colors. The Prime Minister gave his remarks after the presentation, indicating that "the building looks nice but not with that colour."

Rule 1. Know the party colors.

When the project was completed, I realized that the initial contact made with the community and users of the facility during the survey did help encourage community comradery and led members of the community to assist with donations of sanitary items. It also led the way for other donors who were members and citizens of the community but living abroad to participate by donating funds to the project for purchasing and repairing hospital beds and medical equipment and to enable the overall completion of the hospital. This was not expected from the community but it shows how important it is to maintain a strong line of communication with the stakeholders who are not just the government but the community/users of the facility. Once stakeholders are fully engaged in a project and you accomplish their wants and outcomes, where possible, it will increase the possibility of your project being a **SUCCESS**.

(Case study contributed by Ronnie Lettsome, Managing Director, Trojan Design and Development Ltd.)

Culture

Cultural norms and values are highly respected and observed in many developing countries. Culture could vary among towns and regions as a result of prevailing mixes of different ethnic groups. An example of cultural impact on a project is the case of a worker who might need a long holiday due to a family bereavement. The deceased could be a distant relative but the culture expects the wider family to mourn together for some days or weeks, participate in the burial and remain together for some days afterwards for other family responsibilities. Another scenario is where some workers demand concessionary holidays due to either a wedding in the family or some cultural events such as a festival. It is often difficult, if not impossible, to deny workers' requests in these regards. When permission is granted, the project manager might have to get a temporary replacement at higher cost and there could be time disruption on the project.

A project often involves people from different cultural backgrounds working together to achieve the goal of the project. However, cultural sensitivities can be high in developing countries. Foreign personnel may be employed and they come in with their different cultural perspectives. The project manager should take cognizance of the different cultures to avoid their interference with the effort to achieve the project's objectives. A good practice is to engage with the leaders and representatives of the community to seek advice on how to handle culturally sensitive issues. Community leaders are often skilled negotiators and communicators, capable of managing the expectations of the stakeholders they represent.

Organizational culture is another dimension to consider. The organizations involved in a project have different cultures. For example, with regard to communication, one organization may prefer virtual meetings or emails, while another might prefer face-to-face meetings. It may be worthwhile to engage in-house persons who are familiar with other organizations' cultures to lead with communications where necessary. Altogether, cultural differences are a big factor to consider in stakeholder engagements in developing countries.

Religion

In some countries or regions, religion can be a big factor in project management. In some instances, religion underpins the norms and cultures. Where that is the case, one has to respect the disposition of the locals as any sign of disrespect of their religion can generate high tension, and possibly, conflict.

A phlegmatic social climate

There tends to be a laid-back social behavior in some developing countries. A consequence of this could be lengthy turnaround times in response to requests for clarifications or information. Some stakeholders sometimes do not fully understand their roles, or do not possess the required competence to articulate their requirements. In other instances, stakeholder representatives do not assign adequate resources to their roles in the project until it is too late. Consequently, extra time and patience is often needed to sort out issues with some stakeholders in developing countries.

Engaging stakeholders

Engaging stakeholders is the key to managing them, and this should be sustained throughout a project's delivery. Negotiations may be held with all parties so that groups with conflicting demands understand their different points of view, restrictions, and the importance of delivering the expectations of each stakeholder. The project team should endeavor to maintain a balance among the stakeholders, given their competing interests. The project team should also differentiate between the main and secondary stakeholders and prioritize the main stakeholder's interests, if necessary.

The project team should broker compromise and identify the outcome that satisfies the majority of stakeholders. They should remain impartial, encourage open communication, and maintain an audit trail of decisions made and their rationale. A cost-benefit analysis can be carried out to identify or portray viable solutions from a neutral point of view for the consideration of all parties. Such an approach may lead to consensus and identification of ways forward quickly.

Information management

Communication is vital in stakeholder management. The project team expects stakeholders to provide all information as it relates to their wants, requirements, and outcomes, but this is often either not forthcoming, or delayed in developing countries. Some communities may take time to hold a meeting before articulating their views or providing the required information. Thus, the project team should anticipate delays and take them into account in their scheduling and costing.

The project team should make contact as soon as they need input from stakeholders. They should also get everyone pertinent involved so that all relevant parties will be in agreement with the end product. The team could hold regular meetings throughout the project to bring all queries and ideas together to deal with any issues.

Some suggestions

Managing personalities is important in stakeholder engagements and this requires the deployment of soft skills. So project teams should be diplomatic in their approach. They should exert their power with due care and circumspection although there may be occasions when they have to use it to break a deadlock. It is necessary to equip the project team with the softer skills needed to operate in a developing countries.

Companies operating in developing countries should ensure: commitment to fair negotiations and dealing on the interests of stakeholders; impartiality; and ability to respond quickly to situations. Such situations may impact on the estimated project cycle. Transparency, clear communication channels, and full understanding of projects are vital.

Organizations should be cautious when managing stakeholders in small communities because there is usually a limited pool for them to pick from. Keeping a good relationship with these stakeholders is paramount as they may need to transition with them from one project to another.

Be proactive

Any organization or practitioner operating in a construction project in a developing country should anticipate the different problems that may arise in the project's life cycle and find early solutions to these. Additional attention should be given to stakeholders who have, or appear to have, weaker expectations. It may be that they have trouble articulating their requirements and not that their expectations are less important. Sometimes, the project team might need to support some stakeholders to express their expectations by developing a skeletal list of requirements for them to populate or flesh out, and then use that as a basis to follow up. They can also provide stakeholders with choice options or alternatives that are more realistic and cost effective. This proactive approach can hasten decision making and avoid procrastination. A good practice is to produce periodic reports that have information that is of interest to the stakeholders; this will keep them updated on progress on the project.

Limitations

Some empirical data were collected from some key project stakeholders involved in project delivery in some developing countries. While the COVID-19 pandemic restricted this exercise to virtual discussions instead of full rigorous interviews, some valid and acceptable details were elicited in this process.

Future research

Future research on the subject may assess the specific impacts of external stakeholders on projects in developing countries, that is, the effects on project costs, duration, and other performance parameters. The appropriate use of IT for managing stakeholders in developing countries toward improved performance, such as increased productivity in projects, could also be explored.

Conclusion

On projects, stakeholder management is important, and it is needed. Each project will have stakeholders, and their many expectations will likely exceed what the project can deliver. Their needs may also be in conflict with the project's objectives. Compounding these issues are the transient nature of stakes and the potential of stakeholders coalescing to increase their influence on a project. Consequently, each project team should implement a principled approach that involves identifying, assessing, and managing stakeholders proactively. This should be done throughout the project.

In developing countries, there are certain subtle but fundamental factors that underpin some of the construction stakeholders' behaviors, demands, and interests. These include political, socio-cultural, and religious factors, and these are often highly valued. These factors may appear dormant but can be potent and should be recognized, taken into account, and specifically managed where relevant.

The use of IT is increasingly aiding the management of stakeholders. The Monkey Forest Consulting Services example (Box 12.1) demonstrates the applicability of IT in stakeholder management in a developing country. Contractors, clients, and other major stakeholders could employ this technology where feasible. The adoption of technology can be slower in developing countries. However, even after employing IT, soft and hard skills, and additional resources, the project team might not fully satisfy all stakeholders. The idea is to be objective and transparent and demonstrate to all stakeholders that they are important. They should endeavor to carry everybody along. This will earn them the support of the stakeholders, and they will either happily or reluctantly see how their expectations and interests either align or clash with both the project's objectives and other stakeholders' expectations. In developing countries, the project team should be proactive with stakeholder engagements and follow the principle of constantly identifying all stakeholders, assessing their concerns and (potential) influences, and responding to them.

References

Achermann, F. and Eden, C. (2011). Strategic management of stakeholders: Theory and practices. *Long Range Planning*, 44, 179–196.

Al Nahyan, M.T., Sohal A.S., Fildes, B.N. and Hawas, Y.E. (2012). Transportation infrastructure development in the UAE: Stakeholder perspectives on management practice. *Construction Innovation*, 12(4), 492–514.

Bourne, L. (2010). Stakeholder relationship management: Using the stakeholder circle methodology for more effective stakeholder engagement of senior management. In: Project Management Institute. *Proceedings of 7th Project*

Management National Benchmarking Forum — PMI Chapter, 24–26th November, Rio de Janeiro, Brazil.

Bourne, L. and Kasperczyk, S. (2009). Introducing a stakeholder management methodology into the EU. *Proceedings of Project Management Institute Global Congress*. 18–20 May, Amsterdam, Netherlands.

Bourne, L. and Walker, D.H.T. (2005) Visualizing and mapping stakeholder influence. *Management Decision*, 43(5), 649–660.

Bourne, L. and Walker, D.H.T. (2005). Stakeholder circle: The paradox of project control. *Team Performance Management*, 11(5/6), 649–660.

Bourne, L. and Walker, D.H.T. (2006) Visualizing stakeholder influence — Two Australian examples. *Project Management Journal*, 37(1), 5–22.

Calvert, S. (1995). *Managing Stakeholders: The Commercial Project Manager*. McGraw-Hill, New York.

Carroll, A.B. and Buchholtz, A.K. (2011). *Business and Society: Ethics, Sustainability and Stakeholder Management*, 8th Edition. South-Western College Publishing, Cincinnati, OH.

Chinyio, E. and Olomolaiye, P. (Eds.) (2010). *Construction Stakeholder Management*. Wiley-Blackwell, Oxford.

Christopher, M., Payne, A. and Ballantyne, D. (2002). *Relationship Marketing — Creating Stakeholder Value*. Butterworth-Heinemann, Oxford.

Clarkson, M.B.E. (1995). A stakeholder framework for analysing and evaluating corporate social performance. *The Academy of Management Review*, 20(1), 92–117.

Cleland, D.I. (2002). *Project Management — Strategic Design and Implementation*, 4th Edition. McGraw-Hill, London.

Cleland, D.I. and Ireland, L.R. (2007). *Project Management: Strategic Design and Implementation*, 5th Edition. McGraw-Hill, New York.

Co, H.C. and Barro, F. (2009). Stakeholder theory and dynamics in supply chain collaboration. *International Journal of Operations and Production Management,* 29(6), 591–611.

Donaldson, T. and Preston, L. (1995). The stakeholder theory of the corporation: Concepts, evidence, and implications. *Academy of Management Review*, 20(1), 65–91.

Eskerod, P. and Vaagaasar, A.L. (2014). Stakeholder management strategies and practices during a project course. *Project Management Journal*, 45(5), 71–85.

Fraser, C. and Zhu, C. (2008). Stakeholder perception of construction site managers' effectiveness. *Construction Management and Economics*, 26(6), 579–590.

Freeman, J.B., Penner A.M., Saperstein, A. Scheutz, M. and Ambady, N. (2011). Looking the part: Social status cues shape race perception. *PLoS ONE*, 6(9), 1–10.

Freeman, R.E. (1984). *Strategic Management — A stakeholder approach*. Pittman Publishing Company, Boston.

Freeman, R.E. and Currens, R. (2010). *Managing for Stakeholder: Survival, Reputation and Success*. Caravan Publishers, Lahore.

Gibson, K. (2000). The moral basis of stakeholder theory. *Journal of Business Ethics*, 26(3), 245–257.

Harrison, J.S. and Freeman, R.E. (1999). Stakeholders, social responsibility, and performance: Empirical evidence and theoretical perspective. *Academy of Management Journal*, 42(5), 479–485.

Hillman, A.J. and Keim, G.D. (2001). Shareholder value, stakeholder management, and social issues: What's the bottom line? *Strategic Management Journal*, 22(2), 125–139.

Holtbrugge, D., Berg, N. and Puck, J. (2007). To bribe or to convince? Political stakeholders and political activities in German multinational corporations. *International Business Review*, 16(1), 47–67.

Jepsen, A.L. and Eskerod, P. (2008). Stakeholder analysis in projects: Challenges in using current guidelines in the real world. *International Journal of Project Management*, 27(4), 335–343.

Jergeas, G.F., Williamson, E., Skulmoski, G.J. and Thomas, J.L. (2000). Stakeholder management on construction projects. *AACE International Transactions*, 12, 12.1–12.6. https://www-proquest-com.ezproxy.wlv.ac.uk/docview/208199241/DC128A6CB65C4366PQ/1?accountid=14685 [Accessed 6 November 2020].

Johnson, G., Scholes, K. and Whittington, R. (2005). *Exploring Corporate Strategy: Text and Cases*, 6th Edition. Financial Times Prentice Hall, Harlow.

Karim, S.B.A., Rahman, H.A., Berawi, M.A. and Jaapar, A. (2007). A review of the issues and strategies of stakeholder management in the construction industry. *Meeting and Conference on 'Management in Construction and Research Association'* (MICRA), 28–29 August, Shah Alam, Selangor, Malaysia, pp. 1–17. https://www.academia.edu/172847/Issues_and_Strategies_in_Stakeholder_Management [Accessed 25 August 2022].

Karlsen, J.T. (2002). Project stakeholder management. *Engineering Management Journal*, 14(4), 19–24.

Lerbinger, O. (2006). *Corporate Public Affairs: Interacting with Interest Groups, Media and Government*. Lawrence Erlbaum Associates, New Jersey.

Lester, A. (2007). *Project Management, Planning and Control: Managing Engineering, Construction and Manufacturing Projects to PMI, APM and BSI Standards*, 5th Edition. Elsevier Ltd., Amsterdam.

McElroy, B. and Mills, C. (2000). Managing Stakeholders. In R.J. Turner and S.J. Simister (Eds.), *Gower Handbook of Project Management*, 3rd Edition. Gower Publishing Ltd., Aldershot, pp. 757–775.

Mitchell, R.K., Agle, B.R. and Wood, D.J. (1997). Toward a theory of stakeholder identification and salience: Defining the principle of who and what really counts. *Academy of Management Review*, 22(4), 853–886.

Mitroff, I.I. (1983). *Stakeholders of the Organizational Mind.* Jossey-Bass, San Francisco, CA.

Molwus, J.J., Erdogan, B. and Ogunlana, S. (2017) Using structural equation modelling (SEM) to understand the relationships among critical success factors (CSFs) for stakeholder management in construction. *Engineering, Construction and Architectural Management*, 24(3), 426–450.

Nauman, S. and Piracha, M.S.S. (2016). Project stakeholder management — A developing country perspective. *Journal of Quality and Technology Management*, 12(2), 1–24.

Newcombe, R. (2003). From client to project stakeholders: A stakeholder mapping approach. *Construction Management and Economics*, 21(8), 841–848.

Olander, S. (2007). Stakeholder impact analysis in construction project management. *Construction Management and Economics*, 25(3), 277–287.

Orndoff, C.J.W. (2005). Promising new tool for stakeholder interaction. *Journal of Architectural Engineering*, 11(4), 139–146.

Pedrosa-Ortega, C., Hernandez-Ortiz, M.J., Garcia-Marti, E. and Vallejo-Martos, M.C. (2019). The stakeholder salience model revisited: Evidence from agri-food cooperatives in Spain. *Journal Sustainability*, 11(574), 1–14.

Phillips, R. (2003). *Stakeholder Theory and Organizational Ethics.* Berrett-Koehler, San Francisco, CA.

Pirozzi, M. (2019). Stakeholders, who are they? *PM World Journal*, 8(9), 1–10.

Prell, C., Reed, M.S. and Klaus, H. (2009). Stakeholder analysis and social network analysis in natural resources management. *Society and Natural Resources*, 22(6), 501–518.

Project Management Institute (2017). *A Guide to the Project Management Body of Knowledge (PMBOK Guide)*, 6th Edition. Project Management Institute, Newtown Square, PA.

Remme, J. and de Waal, A. (2020) High performance stakeholder management: What is needed? *Measuring Business Excellence*, 24(3), 367–376.

Salam, A. and Noguchi, T. (2006). Evaluating capacity development for participatory forest management in Bangladesh's Sal forests based on '4Rs' stakeholder analysis. *Forest Policy and Economics*, 8(8), 785–796.

Sallinen, L., Ahola, T. and Ruuska, I. (2011). Governmental stakeholder and project owner's views on the regulative framework in nuclear projects. *International Journal of Project Management,* 27(2), 131–141.

Savage, G.T., Nix, T.W., Whitehead, C.J. and Blair, J.D. (1991). Strategies for assessing and managing organizational stakeholders. *Academy of Management Executive*, 5(2), 61–75.

Smith, J. and Love, P.E.D. (2004). Stakeholder management during project inception: Strategic needs analysis. *Journal of Architectural Engineering*, 10(1), 22–33.

Suchman, M.C. (1995). Managing legitimacy: Strategic and institutional approaches. *Academy of Management Review*, 20(3), 571–610.

Tarhini, A., Ammar, H., Tarhini, T. and Masa'deh, R. (2015). Analysis of the critical success factors for enterprise resource planning implementation from stakeholders' perspective: A systematic review. *International Business Research*, 8(4), 25–40.

Tete, S., Mastrangelo, F., Bianchi, A., Zizzari, V. and Scarano, A. (2009). Collagen fiber orientation around machined titanium and zirconia dental implant neck: An animal study. *International Journal of Oral & Maxillofacial Implants*, 24(1), 52–58.

Thompson, J.L. (2002). *Strategic Management*, 4th Edition. Thomson, London.

Walker, D., Shelley, A. and Bourne, L. (2008). Influence, stakeholder mapping and visualisation. *Construction Management and Economics*, 26(6), 645–658.

Winch, G. and Bonke, S. (2002). Project stakeholder mapping: Analysing the interests of project stakeholders. In D.P. Slevin, J.K. Pinto and D.I. Cleland (Eds.), *The Frontiers of Project Management Research*. Project Management Institute (PMI), pp. 385–403.

Wolfe, R.A. and Putler, D.S. (2002). How tight are the ties that bind stakeholder groups? *Organization Science*, 13(1), 64–80.

Yang, J., Shen, G.Q., Bourne, L., Ho, C.M. and Xue, X. (2011). A typology of operational approaches for stakeholder analysis and engagement. *Construction Management and Economics*, 29(2), 145–162.

Yang, J., Shen, G.Q., Drew, D.S. and Ho, M. (2010). Critical success factors for stakeholder management: Construction practitioners' perspectives. *Journal of Construction Engineering and Management*, 136(7), 778–786.

Yang, J., Shen, G.Q., Ho, M., Drew, D.S. and Chan, A.P.C. (2009). Exploring critical success factors for stakeholder management in construction projects. *International Journal of Civil Engineering and Management*, 15(4), 337–348.

Yang, J., Shen, G.Q., Ho, M., Drew, D.S. and Xue, X. (2011). Stakeholder management in construction: An empirical study to address research gaps in previous studies. *International Journal of Project Management*, 29(7), 900–910.

Yang, R.J. (2014). An investigation in stakeholder analysis in urban development projects: Empirical or rationalistic perspectives. *International Journal of Project Management*, 32(5), 838–849.

Part 4

Additional Important Areas of Knowledge of Project Management in a Developing Country Context

https://doi.org/10.1142/9789811224720_0013

Chapter 13

Project Performance Indicators and Their Management in Developing Countries

Abimbola Windapo

The University of Cape Town, South Africa

Abstract

The concept of using indicators to assess performance originates from the practice of benchmarking used in many industries for improving business processes and products. What makes the concept of project success difficult and complicated in practice is that there is no consensus on how it should be measured, and the unlikelihood of reaching a consensus further complicates the management of projects. Scholars view the multiple ways of measuring success as being dependent on the interest and business goals of each project stakeholder. In developing countries, construction project environments are dynamic due to the involvement of multiple stakeholders, including communities with different interpretations of project performance indicators, who also prioritize them differently. Therefore, this chapter examines project performance indicators in the context of developing countries with the view to establish the important indicators common to project stakeholders and where there are usually conspicuous differences. The study uses a systematic literature review to gather the necessary information to answer the chapter's objectives. The outputs of the review include a conceptual model of project performance indicators common to developing countries. Furthermore, the chapter argues that project organizations play a crucial role in defining the terms of reference and accountabilities for all key roles in project delivery. Implications of this conceptual model for theory and practice are discussed. The establishment of these performance indicators will contribute to the improvement of project management in developing countries.

Keywords: Developing countries, procurement, project performance indicators, project performance management, project stakeholders, stakeholder analysis and theory

Introduction

In seeking to make economic and social progress, developing countries undertake various types of building and infrastructure projects, and lately, with the application of information and communication technologies (ICT) and e-government services. However, these projects face challenges such as cost deviation and poor stakeholder satisfaction with the final product (Liu *et al.*, 2011; Babatunde *et al.*, 2017; Banihashemi *et al.*, 2017; Windapo and Gcinulwazi, 2015). Nguyen (2007) identified the project management challenges in developing countries as bureaucratic red tape, inappropriate application of project management tools, governments' procrastination and indecisiveness, lack of consistent project organizational structures, and lack of transparency and accountability. The challenges highlighted by Adeyemi and Idoko (2008) were withdrawal by donors, shortage of foreign exchange, insufficient funds, low institutional and human capacity, poverty, and corruption.

Achieving project success is the objective of every project (Osei-Kyei and Chan, 2018). Hence, it is imperative to resolve these challenges. The metrics for measuring project success are referred to as project performance indicators (PPIs). PPIs have been described differently but with the same meaning. Mbugua *et al.* (1999) explained that PPIs predict project success and specify the measurable evidence necessary to prove that a planned effort has achieved the desired result. According to Ogunsanmi (2013), PPIs provide the measure of the overall effectiveness of projects.

Takim and Akintoye (2002) defined PPIs as the measures of the achievement of the project objectives.

These definitions of PPIs are fundamentally similar. Essentially, they point to the criticality of PPIs in the evaluation of project success. However, there are many ways of measuring success, and these are dependent on the interest and business goals of each of the project stakeholders (Freeman *et al.*, 2004), which means that the various stakeholders have different expectations and that the extent of project success depends on the PPIs that are selected for the project based on the needs of the stakeholders of the particular project. Project stakeholders are individuals or organizations that affect, or are affected by, the project objectives (Heravi *et al.*, 2015; Takim and Akintoye, 2002). They may be placed at risk by the project execution because their expectations are linked to the project outcomes (Tan *et al.*, 2005). For this reason, stakeholders seek to influence the course of the project to protect their interests, and the full participation of project stakeholders in project delivery has been linked to the level of project success (Orlu *et al.*, 2016).

The numerous PPIs available for evaluating project success is a major source of confusion for project managers. Also, the interests of project stakeholders are usually in conflict as a result of the differences in their expectations. The solution to the confusion and conflict concerning PPIs lies in their effective management. Freeman *et al.* (2004) observed that PPIs could be managed by standardization across project types or by overlapping the PPIs. This suggests that PPIs will best be managed when the expectations of different project stakeholders are standardized across project types, enabling the development of criteria for selecting essential PPIs for projects depending on the expectations of project stakeholders.

This chapter advances the notion that it is essential to develop criteria for selecting PPIs for projects toward managing expectations in order to manage project success. This is essential in developing countries because projects in the context of these countries have become highly bureaucratized and inefficient because of direct governmental involvement (Takim, 2009; Yanwen, 2012; Yapicioglu *et al.*, 2017). More importantly, projects in developing countries are experiencing the severity and complexity of implementation and shortage of strong leadership owing to the lack of project management capacity (Yanwen, 2012).

The failure of projects in developing countries is usually severe as it adversely affects the communities that lack access to economic and social infrastructure. In many countries, projects initiated, planned, or promised to improve the quality of life of the citizens are hindered in many ways. There are many examples of projects, including those intended to fulfill social needs such as housing and health facilities, which do not meet the needs and expectations of local communities. Examples are the Shagari Housing Project in Nigeria (Irouke *et al.*, 2017) and the Saglemi project in Ghana (Ansah, 2021), which have been left abandoned and unused after construction, owing to the differences in considerations of successive governments. Therefore, it is imperative to develop a system to identify essential PPIs from project stakeholders' expectations to manage construction projects in developing countries.

Several studies on project management in developing countries have given reasons for such a system. According to Yanwen (2012), it becomes essential to develop a sustainable project management system for the developing countries because the dependence upon developed countries and agencies for the delivery of successful projects in the developing countries is no longer economically, politically, and socially sustainable. Yanwen (2012) further explained that the adaptation of PPIs from developed countries has often proved impractical, owing to a lack of resources, shortage of efficient project management skills, and lack of well-established administrative procedures and systems in developing countries. Pillai *et al.* (2002) observed that project management competence and performance evaluation in the developing countries must be improved to reflect the needs and expectations of all the project stakeholders, and the unique project environment, economic realities, and cultural diversity.

According to Nguyen (2007), developing countries require a different project management system from that of developed countries. In contrast, Adeyemi and Idoko (2008) added that meeting the project stakeholders' expectations will be impossible due to the challenges to project management besetting developing countries. The understanding provided by these studies makes it clear that there is a lack of specific articulation on the management of PPIs in the project management literature. This chapter acknowledges the efforts of project management scholars in developing countries to enhance knowledge of project management in the developing

countries. Some of these studies have focused on identifying critical PPIs for projects in developing countries and not on their management in line with stakeholder expectations. For example, Khoury and Makkouk (2010) shed light on all the performance indicators that are necessary in order to successfully manage projects in developing countries. Faniran *et al.* (2000) presented an operating framework for achieving project success in developing countries by implementing front-end project management. Similarly, Majeed *et al.* (1998) explored the performance indicators of IT projects in public- and private-sector organizations in developing countries, focusing on Pakistan.

Various studies have also focused on project stakeholders' perceptions of PPIs. For example, Nurdiana *et al.* (2015) analyzed projects risks from the perspective of project stakeholders. Osei-Kyei and Chan (2017) explored the perceptual differences in the success criteria for public–private partnership (PPP) projects among PPP stakeholders. Hosseini *et al.* (2016) investigated stakeholders' perceptions concerning the critical success factors for the implementation of risk management systems for infrastructure projects in Iran. Ogunsanmi (2013) investigated key performance indicators that could improve the performance of PPP projects in Nigeria. Orlu *et al.* (2016) investigated stakeholders' perceptions of the success of waste management and infrastructure projects in developing countries. Tan-Mullins *et al.* (2017) evaluated the behavior of Chinese stakeholders engaged in large hydro-electric power projects in Asia and Africa. Wu *et al.* (2018) identified the key performance indicators of mega sustainable infrastructure projects from a stakeholder-network perspective. Yapicioglu *et al.* (2017) investigated stakeholders' perspectives on innovative strategies for infrastructure projects in Nigeria. Windapo and Gcinulwazi (2015) investigated whether there is a significant difference in the stakeholders' perception of PPIs for large engineering projects in South Africa.

However, these studies focused more on the perception of project stakeholders on PPIs and did not adequately consider the link between project stakeholders' interests and the management of the projects to attain the PPIs. This may be the reason for the project managers' lack of targeted management strategies to improve the level of success of projects in developing countries because stakeholders' perception is not the same as stakeholders' interests. Also, surveying project stakeholders' perceptions of PPIs is not the same as integrating project stakeholders' interests into PPIs and their management. Orlu *et al.* (2016) observed that the project stakeholders' interests are often not integrated into the PPIs for projects executed in developing countries.

The decisions on the essential PPIs for projects in the developing countries are usually based on the interests and considerations of the government, which, most of the time, are political interests (Orlu *et al.*, 2016; Babatunde *et al.*, 2017). To address this knowledge gap, this chapter examines PPIs in the context of developing countries with the view to establishing the important performance indicators common to project stakeholders and integrating their interests into the essential PPIs for projects in the developing countries. The understanding of these concepts which was gained was used as a platform to argue for a new PPI classification for project stakeholders. Moreover, on the basis of this understanding, the study develops a conceptual model of PPI management based on stakeholder interests. The practicality of the model was then demonstrated using the existing literature. The chapter concludes by considering the implications of the conceptual model for the theory and practice of project management in developing countries.

Research method

A systematic literature review was adopted as a methodological approach to gathering the necessary information needed to fulfill the objectives of the study. The systematic review was undertaken in four steps. The first step focused on identifying and collecting relevant literature through a database search and the use of keywords, titles, and abstracts. The keywords used included: "Project Performance Indicators," "Project Stakeholder Management," "Project Delivery in Developing Countries," "Project Procurement," "Project Stakeholders," "Stakeholder Analysis," and "Stakeholder Theory." The second step focused on screening the articles for the peer-review process, English Language as the language of publication, year of publication, and publication in prominent and high-quality journals. The third step focused on analyzing the objectives, findings, and conclusions of the selected articles. In the last step of the study, coherent and integrated arguments were produced from the synthesis of the selected articles.

Key PPIs common to project stakeholders in developing countries

Essential PPIs were identified using the perception of project stakeholders in developing countries, working in the context of PPPs/Infrastructural projects (Yuan *et al.*, 2009; Osei-Kyei and Chan, 2018; Ogunsanmi, 2013; Love and Holt, 2000), and Information Technology (Majeed *et al.*, 1998; Mitchell, 2006; Dombrowski *et al.*, 2013), International Development (Diallo and Thuillier, 2004), and Research and Development projects (Pillai *et al.*, 2002). These studies were undertaken using different research methods, including case studies and questionnaire-based surveys that sought to determine the perceptions of project stakeholders. The PPIs obtained from these studies which were found to be common to project stakeholders studied are presented in Table 13.1.

Table 13.1: PPIs common to project stakeholders working on Infrastructure and IT projects.

Project performance indicator	Reference
Quality	Almahmoud *et al.* (2012); Yuan *et al.* (2009, 2010, 2012); Love and Holt (2000); Dombrowski *et al.* (2013); Chan and Chan (2004); Diallo and Thuillier (2004)
Satisfaction — Client, end-users, Customer, project team, financiers, the need for public service	Meng (2012), Ogunsanmi (2013), Osei-Kyei and Chan (2018), Chan and Chan (2004), Cox *et al.* (2003), Pillai *et al.* (2002)
On-time project completion Short processing time	Majeed *et al.* (1998), Dombrowski *et al.* (2013), Mitchell (2006), Chan and Chan (2004), Diallo and Thuillier (2004)
High added-value	Dombrowski *et al.* (2013)
Cost	Diallo and Thuillier (2004), Cox *et al.* (2003), Griffith *et al.* (1999).
Health and Safety	Chan and Chan (2004), Emuze and Smallwood (2012)
Performance — Product, service; and financial, accuracy	Majeed *et al.* (1998); Love and Holt (2000)
Growth potential	Pillai *et al.* (2002)
Feedback	Pillai *et al.* (2002)
Cashflows	Pillai *et al.* (2002)

Table 13.1 shows that the more common project performance indicators identified by the studies reviewed are quality, satisfaction, and on-time delivery. In terms of quality, Chan and Chan (2004) present functionality, satisfaction, and technical specifications as indicators of quality-related project performance. Poor quality will increase the number of defects, which is another quality-related indicator (Almahmoud *et al.*, 2012), the word "quality" being associated with the idea of being free from defects (Nicholas and Steyn, 2008). Project team satisfaction, like client satisfaction, is subjective and measured by motivation, level of absenteeism, morale, trust (Meng, 2012); absence of legal claims (Pocock *et al.*, 1996) and teamwork (Chan and Chan, 2004; Cox *et al.*, 2003); and responsiveness and communication (Rad, 2003). Project team satisfaction is crucial to maintaining teamwork in the project, which is essential to the success of the project management effort, as Chan *et al.* (2002) observe.

While Cox *et al.* (2003) used time variation and early milestone delivery as time-related performance indicators, Chan and Chan (2004) used the speed of construction. Griffith *et al.* (1999) introduced "budget achievement," which refers to the level of success of the Project Manager in keeping within the authorized budget measured against the deviation from it as an indicator of cost-related project performance, while Cox *et al.* (2003) used unit cost, earned value, and earned man-hours. Most safety-related incidents occur during construction on site, and health- and safety-related PPIs are injuries (Chan and Chan, 2004) and fatalities (Emuze and Smallwood, 2012).

Other PPIs that have recently been suggested are employment generation, affordability, and life-cycle considerations. While the consideration of employment generation leads to emphasis on projects that create employment opportunities for priority groups and labor-intensive construction methodologies (GBCSA, 2014), affordability is measured using the proportion of households who pay more than 25 percent of their income on housing (Bourne, 1981). Ofori (1990) stipulates that a household that spends more than 30 percent of its income on housing is living in unaffordable housing. Life-cycle considerations cover the environmental aspects of the project activities. They embrace acquiring the materials used in construction, distance traveled, manufacturing methods, and the end-of-life fate of the building.

Although these studies focused on essential PPIs for different types of projects, a closer look at them showed that the essential PPIs reported by these studies are only superficially different. For example, Yuan *et al.* (2009) identified quality performance as one of the essential PPIs for infrastructural projects; Dombrowski *et al.* (2013) identified high quality as one of the essential PPIs for IT projects; while Diallo and Thuillier (2004) identified quality performance as an essential PPI for international development projects. This suggests a fundamental similarity among the essential PPIs for different types of projects. This similarity provides the opportunity to integrate essential PPIs across different types of projects to develop a framework to guide the effective management of the PPIs. Integrating the essential PPIs across different projects will provide effective means for managing PPIs (Freeman *et al.*, 2004). However, this will not be possible without integrating the interests of the project stakeholders (Orlu *et al.*, 2016).

Construction projects are dynamic due to the involvement of multiple stakeholders. According to Haponava and Al-Jibouri (2012), the project management team should align project deliverables with the stakeholder requirements and reach a compromise to achieve common objectives. The project stakeholders must be satisfied with the overall performance of the project. The following section presents an analysis of stakeholders in developing countries.

Analysis of stakeholders for projects in developing countries

According to Sharp *et al.* (1999), the following should be identified as project stakeholders: users, developers, legislators, and decision-makers, while Alexander and Robertson (2004) believed that project stakeholders should be identified as producers, sponsors, consumers, influencers, and consultants. Olander (2007) and Mulenburg (2007) argued that project stakeholders are to be classified as being internal or external stakeholders. Studies such as Diallo and Thuillier (2004), Ngacho and Das (2014), Toor and Ogunlana (2010), and Mladenovic *et al.* (2013) have identified different project stakeholders for projects in developing countries. Table 13.2 presents a summary of the contributions and expectations of the project stakeholders in developing countries. What is lacking in this analysis of

Table 13.2: Contributions and interests of different project stakeholders.

Project stakeholders	Contributions	Expectations
Government	Prime mover of projects, funding, acts on behalf of the end-users	Employment generation, conflict reduction
Local community	Support for projects, cooperation, community involvement, pressures and demands, project monitoring	Sense of ownership and control
Project management consultants	Technical advice and monitoring services	Profitability, learning and growth, absence of legal claims, safety
Contractors	Experience and expertise, manpower, innovation	Profitability, learning and growth, settlements of conflicts, meeting schedule, budget, and quality specifications
End-users	Agitation and demonstrations, involvement in needs definition and definition-making process, the contribution of ideas and requirements	Positive impacts on lives and properties, meet present and future requirements, usable life expectancy, level of service
International donor agencies and international organisations (for example, International Monetary Fund, World Bank, Overseas Economic Cooperation Fund)	Funding	Meet corporate priorities, conflict reduction, value for money
Civil right groups (activist and political groups)	Project monitoring, act as pressure groups	Positive impacts on lives and properties
Regulatory authorities	Standards and guidelines	Compliance with regulations
Financial institutions	Financial supports, provision of suitable bonds	Meet corporate priorities, conflict reduction, value for money

Source: Diallo and Thuillier (2004), Ngacho and Das (2014), Toor and Ogunlana (2010), and Mladenovic *et al.* (2013).

project stakeholders in developing countries is applying stakeholder theory and stakeholder analysis frameworks to integrate the contributions and interests of the project stakeholders.

Badewi (2016) provided empirical evidence to demonstrate that the power and interests of project stakeholders influence project success and should constitute the project benefits upon completion. McManus (2004) argued that project stakeholders care about projects because of their awareness that their interests and contributions are valued in the projects' benefits. Krane *et al.* (2012) empirically examined the dynamics of power play between the project stakeholders and its impact on project success. It was concluded in the study that project risks and uncertainties are best reduced by managing the project stakeholders according to their power. Johansen *et al.* (2014) theorized a unique relationship between project stakeholders and project benefits, which states that project stakeholders' power determines the opportunities, objectives, and uncertainties that arise from projects.

Di Maddaloni and Davis (2017) found a strong connection between the support from project stakeholders and the performance of infrastructure projects. The study singled out the power of the local community as a project stakeholder and suggested that seeking local community opinions in the initiation phase of the project and ensuring their support for project monitoring helps improve project performance. Wang and Huang (2006) evaluated the extent to which the roles of project stakeholders correlate with project success. They concluded that the roles of project stakeholders positively correlate with each other but that the key stakeholders play the most important roles in determining the project's success. Beringer *et al.* (2013) empirically established that project stakeholder behavior and project stakeholder management are key success factors for a project. Takim (2009) provided empirical insight into the process for managing the needs and expectations of project stakeholders in developing countries. The study identified a formalized process and priority criteria as the strategy for managing project stakeholders and performance.

Zhang *et al.* (2015) investigated the diverging and converging expectations of various stakeholders and concluded that, without integrating the stakeholders' expectations, the varying expectations of project stakeholders would negatively affect the project's success. Olander (2007) argued that projects attract interest from various stakeholders who express needs and expectations about the project. It is only by evaluating the stakeholders' expectations concerning the project that the needs and expectations of the project stakeholders can be managed. Kurniawan *et al.* (2014) concluded that each stakeholder must be made to understand the expectations of others before project commencement and at the end of the project. Chan and Oppong (2017) explained that the expectations of some stakeholders are more critical even though project stakeholders have diverse expectations. The study further explained that these expectations, if well analyzed, are always in the same direction. Newcombe (2003) argued that project stakeholders serve as multiple clients for infrastructure projects and that diverse expectations from different stakeholders must be analyzed and incorporated into the project expectations.

It is impossible to integrate the interests of the project stakeholders without identifying and managing their interests. Common methods by which stakeholders' interests are managed include stakeholder theory and stakeholder analysis. Olander (2007) and Mulenburg (2007) argued for a stakeholder analysis framework that will focus on the project stakeholders' direct involvement to prioritize their interests in the projects. Stakeholder theory provides the theoretical underpinning for analyzing the value that stakeholders seek, provides project managers with resources to find project success, and provides the means to balance the interests of different project stakeholders (Harrison and Wicks, 2013; Wu *et al.*, 2018). The postulations in stakeholder theory indicate that the value that stakeholders seek is their interests and that managing stakeholders' interests is a means to safeguarding project performance (Harrison *et al.*, 2010). The postulations of stakeholder theory also suggest that meeting project stakeholders' interests makes it possible to retain their support and participation in future projects. The postulations of stakeholder theory have been applied in project management studies to investigate community participation in tourism planning (Khazaei *et al.*, 2015), determine environmental disclosures in a developing country (Elijido-Ten, 2004), identify stakeholders for PPP infrastructure projects (McErlane *et al.*, 2016), and understand the diversity of stakeholders that influence agile software development (Power, 2010).

Stakeholder analysis is a derivative of stakeholder theory, which primarily entails identifying project stakeholders, the power and influence of project stakeholders, and the interests of project stakeholders. Stakeholder analysis accounts for the needs of the various stakeholders and provides a toolset for generating knowledge about stakeholders to understand their interests, intentions, and influence (Yang, 2014). In essence, stakeholder analysis suggests that prioritizing stakeholders' expectations will provide an effective means of managing their expectations according to the extent of their contributions.

Different frameworks have been proposed for analyzing project stakeholders. These frameworks have provided different methods of identifying and prioritizing project stakeholders' interests. The first set of frameworks, as proposed by Mitchell *et al.* (1997), Ballejos and Montagna (2008), and Agle *et al.* (1999), theorized that decision power and hierarchies must be employed when undertaking stakeholder analysis (i.e., stakeholder analysis based on legitimacy). Mitchell *et al.* (1997) identified seven levels of legitimacy for stakeholders. These are: dormant, discretionary, demanding, dominant, dangerous, dependent, and definitive stakeholders. Ballejos and Montagna (2008) grouped stakeholders into high-interest and high-power stakeholders, high-interest and low-power stakeholders, low-interest and high-power stakeholders, and low-interest and low-power stakeholders. Agle *et al.* (1999) argued that legitimate stakeholders should get a larger share of the project benefits. Sharp *et al.* (1999) and Alexander and Robertson (2004) were the proponents of a set of stakeholder analysis frameworks that argued that stakeholder analysis must be conducted based on function.

This study is aligned with the view held by Sharp *et al.* (1999) and Alexander and Robertson (2004) in the use of the function for conducting stakeholder analysis.

Conceptual model of the management of PPIs

This chapter develops a conceptual model of PPIs management in developing countries (see Figure 13.1) drawn from the review of the literature. The model builds on the criteria for project feasibility to establish the indicators for evaluating project performance. This follows the argument by Mechler (2005), which states that project feasibility provides social, economic, and environmental justification for projects. Project feasibility is a detailed and technical examination of the important aspects of project execution and implementation and provides information on the project's ability to succeed and on its technical, functional, and financial feasibility. Corrie and Atkins (1991) also opined that project feasibility covers the project definition, project output, and indicators for judging the project's performance. More so, project feasibility establishes whether a project is worthwhile in the light of its costs in terms of resource commitments and the project's expected benefits. This indicates that the criteria for assessing the feasibility of the project represent the project's expected benefits. Hence, the success of projects must be determined using the indicators to examine whether the project meets its expectations.

Second, the conceptual model builds on stakeholder theory and stakeholder analysis, considering the expectations and contributions of different stakeholders. This is in line with the decision power and hierarchy framework proposed for stakeholder analysis by Ballejos and Montagua (2005) since legitimacy, interest, power, expectations, contributions, function, and involvement of stakeholders depict the span of influence of the stakeholders on the project. To account for this assumption, the framework proposed by Ballejos and Montagua (2005) was modified to give two categories of project stakeholders: (i) high-power and high-interest stakeholders; and (ii) low-power and low-interest stakeholders. The modification becomes necessary because the power and interests of project stakeholders change over time throughout the project life cycle (Missonier and Loufrani-Fedida, 2014). Another reason is that project stakeholders can form coalitions to increase their power and interests, which they derive from legal sources, control of resources, possession of knowledge, or leadership authority (Saebo *et al.*, 2011). Therefore, merging project stakeholders into two categories provides a system of managing project stakeholders as collective units. Finally, the conceptual model disregards the type of projects and considers the powers and interests of project stakeholders as superior to the project type in determining essential project performance indicators.

The conceptual model proposes an integrated PPI approach to managing PPIs that are useful for benchmarking performance for all types of projects and ensuring the satisfaction of all project stakeholders in developing countries. In the conceptual model, the government, local community, international donor agencies, financial institutions, and regulatory authorities are characterized as having the highest level of power and interest. Although these categories of stakeholders can express their power differently, their powers always point toward the same interests. This makes their level of power or influence relate equally to their level of interests. Projects usually fail if this group of project stakeholders withdraws their support by exercising their powers (Chan and Oppong, 2017; Di Maddaloni and Davis, 2017).

The second group of project stakeholders (project management consultants, contractors, end-users, civil rights groups, unions, and trade associations) was characterized as having relatively low power and low interests. A lower level of interest characterizing these other groups of project stakeholders depends on their ability to provide funds and critical resources for projects. This group of stakeholders has enough power to claim their interests, but they do not have sufficient power to substantially derail projects owing to their lack of direct financial interests. Categorizing the project stakeholders into two groups reflects a trade-off between their power and provides a balance between their interests. Moreover, the two groups generate a strategy for managing PPIs and a principle by which the interests of the project stakeholders in the developing countries can be made consistent with the project expectations. This will improve the chances of project success in the developing countries since the success of projects depends on meeting the interests of the project stakeholders.

By combining the interests of the two groups of project stakeholders, the conceptual model identified three types of benefits (social, economic, and environmental benefits). These benefits lead to the identification of three different types of essential PPIs (social benefits indicators, environmental benefits indicators, and economic benefits indicators) for evaluating the success of projects. The expectations that these essential PPIs will meet, including employment generation, profitability and compliance with regulations, are summarized in Table 13.2.

The objective of the essential PPIs is to compare the actual and planned project performance (Yuan *et al.,* 2008). However, the criteria for project feasibility are those adopted to define the planned project performance; hence the essential PPIs were based on the criteria for project feasibility (i.e., social, economic, and environmental justification). The social justification aspect of project feasibility covers social benefits such as employment, housing, less crime, cheaper transportation, lower congestion for road users, better health, and lower health costs. The economic justification part of project feasibility is concerned with the cost savings of on the project. It also covers the ability of the project to generate a cash income for project stakeholders and enable a direct financial assessment to be made in terms of profitability and economic growth. The other element of economic justification that project feasibility provides is improvements in energy security, improving competitiveness, reducing the balance of payments deficit, and new business opportunities. The last part of project feasibility, which is environmental justification, covers environmental impacts or benefits of the project such as improved air and water quality, biodiversity and habitat protection, reduction in greenhouse gases, supporting industrial development, and reviving declining communities. The conceptual model demonstrates that project stakeholders are highly interested in the feasibility of projects and that project feasibility is a condition for project expectation or performance in developing countries.

Discussion

The conceptual model in Figure 13.1 integrates essential PPIs that support effective project management. The link in Figure 13.1 between the criteria for project feasibility and essential PPIs illustrates the identified

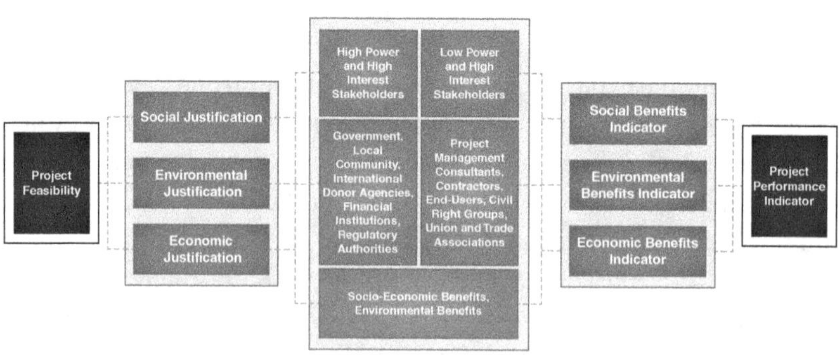

Figure 13.1: Conceptual model of PPIs management.

associations between projects' justifications and benefits indicators. Establishing the specific justifications and benefit indicators for projects depends on the project environment, types, and expectations. The model emphasizes the crucial role of the project stakeholder's influence (power and interest) as a prerequisite for determining the specific project benefits.

This concept resonates with earlier postulations made by Serra *et al.* (2015), Badewi (2016), McManus (2004), Krane *et al.* (2012), and Johansen *et al.* (2014). Serra *et al.* (2015) explained that the interest of project stakeholders creates strategic value for projects and serves as positive predictors of project success. The model also highlights a strong association between support from project stakeholders for a project and the actual performance of the project. This association is validated by studies such as Di Maddaloni and Davis (2017), Wang and Huang (2006), Kappelman *et al.* (2006), Beringer *et al.* (2013), and Takim (2009). However, the study indicated that the impact of project stakeholders on the level of project success highly depends on the intensity of engaging the key project stakeholders.

As postulated in the model, the main issue to be addressed to enhance project performance evaluation is to relate the performance indicators to the feasibility criteria. Such a link will enable the expectations of the project stakeholders and the project to be integrated and met easily. These postulations find support in previous studies such as Zhang *et al.* (2015), Olander (2007), Kurniawan *et al.* (2014), Chan and Oppong (2017), Newcombe (2003), and Takim (2009). This model could be explained as a novel method of managing PPIs in developing countries, and it is consistent with the argument that the power of the stakeholders determines their interests, and those interests are best managed through integration. In essence, in the absence of essential PPIs, project managers will evaluate project performance based on different interests from different project stakeholders. Also, the project performance evaluation process will be too complex and demanding. The conceptual model brought to light the methods of resolving the discrepancy between the perceptions of the project stakeholders on the PPIs. Several studies have reported different PPIs based on the perceptions of project stakeholders (Ogunlana, 2010; Ogunsanmi, 2013; Yuan *et al.*, 2012; Alwaer and Clements-Croome,

2010; Rodrigue *et al.*, 2013). This approach is problematic as it shifts the focus away from the interests and power of the project stakeholders and the impact they have on the PPIs. The proposed conceptual model addressed these concerns.

Conclusion

PPIs for projects executed in developing countries are usually based on political interests and reviewed using the project stakeholders' perceptions. This system disregards the project stakeholders' interests and fails to integrate the stakeholders' power and interests into the PPIs. Developing countries have limited resources, and this system of project performance evaluation further strains these resources. Also, this system of evaluation creates uncertainty and complexity in project performance evaluation which ultimately leads to incorrect evaluation and poor overall performance. Besides, previous studies have neither explored the impact of the power and interest of project stakeholders on PPIs in developing countries nor identified the leading causes of discrepancies between the perceptions of project stakeholders on PPIs for projects. This chapter examines PPIs in developing countries toward proposing a conceptual model for an integrated set of PPIs that encompasses the analysis of the power and interests of project stakeholders in developing countries.

The conceptual model contributes to a theoretical understanding of project stakeholders' interests in project performance and success. The contributions of the model are significant in that it provides a theoretical reference for a methodological and operational system for project delivery and performance evaluation in developing countries. The model identifies the key stakeholders for projects in developing countries and integrates their interests and power to derive an integrated set of PPIs that can be used to measure the overall project performance at any point in time during its life cycle. The set of PPIs identified in the model aligns with the criteria for project feasibility, supporting effective project management and combining the expectations of project stakeholders with project expectations. The project expectations are determined by the justifications provided for the project based on the outcome of the project feasibility.

More importantly, the conceptual model makes several significant contributions to the project management body of knowledge in developing countries. The model shows that support from key project stakeholders is a crucial precursor for project performance and success. It also provides a shift from a traditional project evaluation system to a systematic and analytical project evaluation approach. This expands the body of knowledge as it applies to project stakeholders and performance management in developing countries. The contributions of the model also highlight the underlying associations between project feasibility and project performance, providing a new perspective for addressing the problems associated with performance evaluation. This is novel to project management and provides areas for future research because it serves as a theoretical framework for researchers to identify, investigate, and integrate PPIs for different types of projects in developing countries.

In practical terms, the model contributes to raising the project managers' awareness of the project stakeholders' influence on the success of projects in developing countries. It provides a basis for increasing the level of support from project stakeholders in the context of project delivery challenges in developing countries. The model advances the point that the main factor that influences project performance and success is the support that project stakeholders provide for projects based on their satisfaction with the justifications for the projects and the interests or benefits they derive from the project's performance. Therefore, the chapter recommends the use of the three identified categories of performance indicators (social, economic, and environmental benefit indicators) to determine the PPIs for projects, meet project expectations, and meet the expectations of project stakeholders. Future research studies should examine how project organisations in developing countries use PPIs in managing projects and what PPIs various stakeholders consider as the most important.

Acknowledgments

This work is supported by the National Research Foundation, South Africa (Grant Number-120843). All opinions and conclusions are those of the author and are not necessarily attributable to the foundation.

References

Adeyemi, L.A. and Idoko, M. (2008). *Developing Local Capacity for Project Management — Key to Social and Business Transformation in Developing Countries*. Project Management Institute, Newtown Square, PA.

Agle, B.R., Mitchell, R.K. and Sonnenfeld, J.A. (1999). Who matters to CEOs? An investigation of stakeholder attributes and salience, corporate performance, and CEO values. *Academy of Management Journal*, 42(5), 507–525.

Alexander, I. and Robertson, S. (2004). Understanding project sociology by modeling stakeholders. *IEEE Software*, 21(1), 23–27.

Almahmoud, E.S., Doloi, H.K. and Panuwatwanich, K. (2012). Linking project health to project performance indicators: Multiple case studies of construction projects in Saudi Arabia. *International Journal of Project Management*, 30(3), 296–307.

Alwaer, H. and Clements-Croome, D.J. (2010). Key performance indicators (KPIs) and priority setting in using the multi-attribute approach for assessing sustainable intelligent buildings. *Building and Environment*, 45(4), 799–807.

Ansah, M. (2021). Decision to abandon Saglemi housing project 'senseless' — Hassan Ayariga. CNR Citi NewsRoom, April 27, 2021. https://bit.ly/3npOwYU [Accessed 10 September 2021].

Babatunde, S.O., Adeniyi, O. and Awodele, O.A. (2017). Investigation into the causes of delay in land acquisition for PPP projects in developing countries. Journal of Engineering, *Design and Technology*, 15(4), 552–570.

Badewi, A. (2016). The impact of project management (PM) and benefits management (BM) practices on project success: Towards developing a project benefits governance framework. *International Journal of Project Management*, 34(4), 761–778.

Ballejos, L.C. and Montagna, J.M. (2008). Method for stakeholder identification in inter-organisational environments. *Requirements Engineering*, 13(4), 281–297.

Banihashemi, S., Hosseini, M.R., Golizadeh, H. and Sankaran, S. (2017). Critical success factors (CSFs) for the integration of sustainability into construction project management practices in developing countries. *International Journal of Project Management*, 35(6), 1103–1119.

Beringer, C., Jonas, D. and Kock, A. (2013). The behavior of internal stakeholders in project portfolio management and its impact on success. *International Journal of Project Management*, 31(6), 830–846.

Bourne, L.S. (1986). The geography of housing. *Real Estate Economics*, 14(1), 173–174.

Chan, A.P. and Chan, A.P. (2004). Key performance indicators for measuring construction success. *Benchmarking: An International Journal*, 11(2) 203–221.

Chan, A.P. and Oppong, G.D. (2017). Managing the expectations of external stakeholders in construction projects. *Engineering, Construction and Architectural Management*, 24(5), 736–756.

Chan, A.P., Ho, D.C. and Tam, C.M. (2001). Design and build project success factors: Multivariate analysis. *Journal of Construction Engineering and Management*, 127(2), 93–100.

Corrie, R.K. and Atkins, W.S. (1991). *Project Evaluation*. Telford, London.

Cox, R.F., Issa, R.R. and Ahrens, D. (2003). Management's perception of key performance indicators for construction. *Journal of Construction Engineering and Management*, 129(2), 142–151.

Di Maddaloni, F. and Davis, K. (2017). The influence of local community stakeholders in megaprojects: Rethinking their inclusiveness to improve project performance. *International Journal of Project Management*, 35(8), 1537–1556.

Diallo, A. and Thuillier, D. (2004). The success dimensions of international development projects: The perceptions of African project coordinators. *International Journal of Project Management*, 22(1), 19–31.

Dombrowski, U., Schmidtchen, K. and Ebentreich, D. (2013). Balanced key performance indicators in product development. *International Journal of Materials, Mechanics and Manufacturing*, 1(1), 27–31.

Elattar, S.M.S. (2009). Towards developing an improved methodology for evaluating performance and achieving success in construction projects. *Scientific Research and Essays*, 4(6), 549–554.

Elijido-Ten, E. (2004). Determinants of environmental disclosures in a developing country: An application of the stakeholder theory. *Fourth Asia Pacific Interdisciplinary Research in Accounting Conference*, Singapore, 4–6 July.

Emuze, F.A. and Smallwood, J.J. (2013) Management concepts and project performance: Perceptions from the South African public sector environment. *Journal of the South African Institution of Civil Engineering*, 55(2). http://www.scielo.org.za/scielo.php?

Faniran, O.O., Love, P.E.D. and Smith, J. (2000). Effective front-end project management - A key to achieving project success in developing countries. In A.B. Ngowi and J. Ssegawa (Eds.), *Proceedings of the 2nd International Conference of the CIB Task Group 29 (TG29): Challenges Facing the Construction Industry in Developing Countries*, June, Gaborone, Botswana.

International Council for Research and Innovation in Building and Construction (CIB), Rotterdam.

Freeman, R.E., Wicks, A.C. and Parmar, B. (2004). Stakeholder theory and "the corporate objective revisited." *Organization Science*, 15(3), 364–369.

Green Building Council South Africa (GBCSA) (2014). *Technical Manual Green Star SA Office Design & Office As Built Version 1.1 2014*. 1.1 Edition, Green Building Council South Africa, Cape Town.

Griffith, A.F., Gibson, G.E., Hamilton, M.R., Tortora, A.L. and Wilson, C.T. (1999). Project success index for capital facility construction projects. *Journal of Performance of Constructed Facilities*, 13(1), 39–45.

Haponava, T. and Al-Jibouri, S. (2012). Proposed system for measuring project performance using process-based key performance indicators. *Journal of Management in Engineering*, 28(2), 140–149.

Harrison, J.S. and Wicks, A.C. (2013). Stakeholder theory, value, and firm performance. *Business Ethics Quarterly*, 23(1), 97–124.

Harrison, J.S. Bosse, D.A. and Phillips, R.A. (2010). Managing for stakeholders, stakeholder utility functions, and competitive advantage. *Strategic Management Journal*, 31(1), 58–74.

Heravi, A., Coffey, V. and Trigunarsyah, B. (2015). Evaluating the level of stakeholder involvement during the project planning processes of building projects. *International Journal of Project Management*, 33(5), 985–997.

Irouke, A., Vitalis, M. and Moses, A.A. (2017). An evaluation of Shagari Housing Programme: A case study of three towns: Abakaliki in Ebonyi State; Lokoja in Kogi State; Mbano in Imo State, Nigeria. *International Journal of Geography and Environmental Management*, 3(3), 58–67.

Johansen, A., Eik-Andresen, P. and Ekambaram, A. (2014). Stakeholder benefit assessment–Project success through the management of stakeholders. *Procedia-Social and Behavioral Sciences*, 119(2), 581–590.

Kappelman, L.A., McKeeman, R. and Zhang, L. (2006). Early warning signs of IT project failure: The dominant dozen. *Information Systems Management*, 23(4), 31–36.

Khazaei, A., Elliot, S. and Joppe, M. (2015). An application of stakeholder theory to advance community participation in tourism planning: The case for engaging immigrants as fringe stakeholders. *Journal of Sustainable Tourism*, 23(7), 1049–1062.

Khoury, W.E. and Makkouk, K. (2010). Integrated plant disease management in developing countries. *Journal of Plant Pathology*, 92, S35–S42.

Krane, H.P., Rolstadås, A. and Olsson, N.O. (2012). A case study of how stakeholder management influenced project uncertainty regarding project benefits. *International Journal of Information Technology Project Management (IJITPM)*, 3(2), 21–37.

Kurniawan, F., Ogunlana, S. and Motawa, I. (2014). Stakeholders' expectations in utilising financial models for public–private partnership projects. *Built Environment Project and Asset Management*, 4(1), 4–21.

Liu, J.Y.C., Chen, H.G., Chen, C.C. and Sheu, T.S. (2011). Relationships among interpersonal conflict, requirements uncertainty, and software project performance. *International Journal of Project Management*, 29(5), 547–556.

Love, P.E. and Holt, G.D. (2000). Construction business performance measurement: The SPM alternative. *Business Process Management Journal*, 6(5), 408–416.

Majeed, N., Shah, K.A., Qazi, K.A. and Maqsood, M. (1998). Performance evaluation of IT project management in developing countries. *The Bull Survey*, 14.

Mbugua, L.M., Harris, P., Holt, G.D. and Olomolaiye, P.O. (1999, September). A framework for determining critical success factors influencing construction business performance. *Proceedings of the Association of Researchers in Construction Management 15th Annual Conference*, Vol. 1, pp. 255–264.

McErlane, A., Heaney, G., Haran, M. and McClements, S. (2016). The application of stakeholder theory to UK PPP stakeholders. In: P.W. Chan and C.J. Neilson (Eds.), *Proceedings of the 32nd Annual ARCOM Conference*, 5-7 September 2016, Manchester, UK. Association of Researchers in Construction Management, Vol. 2, 863–872.

McManus, J. (2004, October). A stakeholder perspective within software engineering projects. *2004 IEEE International Engineering Management Conference* (IEEE Cat. No. 04CH37574), Vol. 2, pp. 880–884, IEEE.

Mechler, R. (2005). Cost-benefit analysis of natural disaster risk management in developing countries. Deutsche Gesellschaft fur Technische Zusammenarbeit, Eschborn.

Meng, X. (2012). The effect of relationship management on project performance in construction. *International Journal of Project Management*, 30(2), 188–198.

Missonier, S. and Loufrani-Fedida, S. (2014). Stakeholder analysis and engagement in projects: From stakeholder relational perspective to stakeholder relational ontology. *International Journal of Project Management*, 32(7), 1108–1122.

Mitchell, V.L. (2006). Knowledge integration and information technology project performance. *MIS Quarterly*, 919–939.

Mladenovic, G., Vajdic, N., Windsch, B. and Temeljotov-Salaj, A. (2013). Use of key performance indicators for PPP transport projects to meet stakeholders' performance objectives. *Built Environment Project and Asset Management*, 3(2), 228–249.

Mulenburg, G. (2007). Project Management: Effective Stakeholder Relationships. Raven's Brain v1.0.

Newcombe, R. (2003). From client to project stakeholders: A stakeholder mapping approach. *Construction Management and Economics*, 21(8), 841–848.

Ngacho, C. and Das, D. (2014) A performance evaluation framework of development projects: An empirical study of Constituency Development Fund (CDF) construction projects in Kenya. *International Journal of Project Management*, 32(3), 492–507.

Nguyen, N.M. (2007). The Challenges of transferring modern project management principles and methodologies to developing countries. *PMI Global Congress*, pp. 1–7.

Nurdiana, A., Wibowo, M.A. and Hatmoko, J.U.D. (2015). Sensitivity analysis of risk from stakeholders' perception Case study: Semarang-Solo highway project section I (Tembalang-Gedawang). *Procedia Engineering*, 125, 12–17.

Ofori, G. (1990). *The Construction Industry: Aspects of its Economics and Management*. Singapore University Press, Singapore.

Ogunlana, S.O. (2010). Beyond the 'iron triangle': Stakeholder perception of key performance indicators (KPIs) for large-scale public sector development projects. *International Journal of Project Management*, 28(3), 228–236.

Ogunsanmi, O.E. (2013). Stakeholders' perception of key performance indicators (KPIs) of public–private partnership (PPP) projects. *International Journal of Construction Supply Chain Management*, 3(2), 27–38.

Olander, S. (2007). Stakeholder impact analysis in construction project management. *Construction Management and Economics*, 25(3), 277–287.

Orlu, I.V., Longhurst, P. and Wagland, S. (2016). Beyond policies: managing solid waste in developing countries through stakeholders' perspective and infrastructural development. *Linnaeus Eco-Tech*, Kalmar, Sweden, November 21–23, 209.

Osei-Kyei, R. and Chan, A.P. (2018). Stakeholders' perspectives on the success criteria for public–private partnership projects. *International Journal of Strategic Property Management*, 22(2), 131–142.

Pillai, A.S., Joshi, A. and Rao, K.S. (2002). Performance measurement of R&D projects in a multi-project, concurrent engineering environment. *International Journal of Project Management*, 20(2), 165–177.

Pocock, J.B., Hyun, C.T., Liu, L.Y. and Kim, M.K. (1996). Relationship between project interaction and performance indicators. *Journal of Construction Engineering and Management*, 122(2), 165–176.

Power, K. (2010). Stakeholder theory and agile software development. *Proceedings of the 11th International Conference on Product-Focused Software*, pp. 97–98.

Rad, P.F. (2003). Project success attributes. *Cost Engineering-Morgantown*, 45(4), 23–29.

Reza Hosseini, M., Chileshe, N., Jepson, J. and Arashpour, M. (2016). Critical success factors for implementing risk management systems in developing countries. *Construction Economics and Building*, 16(1), 18–32.

Rodrigue, M., Magnan, M. and Boulianne, E. (2013). Stakeholders' influence on environmental strategy and performance indicators: A managerial perspective. *Management Accounting Research*, 24(4), 301–316.

Sæbø, Ø. (2012, September). E-government in Tanzania: Current status and future challenges. *International Conference on Electronic Government*, Springer, Berlin, Heidelberg, pp. 198–209.

Sæbø, Ø., Flak, L.S. and Sein, M.K. (2011). Understanding the dynamics in e-Participation initiatives: Looking through the genre and stakeholder lenses. *Government Information Quarterly*, 28(3), 416–425.

Serra, C.E.M. and Kunc, M. (2015). Benefits realisation management and its influence on project success and the execution of business strategies. *International Journal of Project Management*, 33(1), 53–66.

Sharp, H., Finkelstein, A. and Galal, G. (1999). Stakeholder identification in the requirements engineering process. *Proceedings, Tenth International Workshop on Database and Expert Systems Applications, DEXA 99*, Florence, Italy, pp. 387–391. doi: 10.1109/DEXA.1999.795198.

Takim, R. (2009). The management of stakeholders' needs and expectations in the development of construction projects in Malaysia. *Modern Applied Science*, 3(5), 167–175.

Takim, R. and Akintoye, A. (2002, September). Performance indicators for successful construction project performance. *18th Annual ARCOM Conference*, Vol. 2, pp. 545–555.

Tan, C.W., Pan, S.L. and Lim, E.T. (2005). Managing stakeholder interests in e-government implementation: Lessons learned from a Singapore e-government project. *Journal of Global Information Management (JGIM)*, 13(1), 31–53.

Tan-Mullins, M., Urban, F. and Mang, G. (2017). Evaluating the behaviour of Chinese stakeholders engaged in large hydropower projects in Asia and Africa. *The China Quarterly*, 230, 464–488.

Toor, S.-ur-R. and Ogunlana, S.O. (2010). Beyond the 'iron triangle': Stakeholder perception of key performance indicators (KPI) for large-scale public sector development projects. *International Journal of Project Management*, 28(4), 228–236.

Wang, X. and Huang, J. (2006). The relationships between key stakeholders' project performance and project success: Perceptions of Chinese construction supervising engineers. *International Journal of Project Management*, 24(3), 253–260.

Windapo, A. and Gicunulwazi, Q. (2015). Evaluation of the satisfaction metrics used by stakeholders on large engineering projects. *Journal of Engineering, Project, and Production Management*, 5(2), 82.

Wu, G., Qiang, G., Zuo, J., Zhao, X. and Chang, R. (2018). What are the key indicators of mega sustainable construction projects? — A stakeholder-network perspective. *Sustainability*, 10(8), 2939.

Yang, R.J. (2014). An investigation of stakeholder analysis in urban development projects: Empirical or rationalistic perspectives. *International Journal of Project Management*, 32(5), 838–849.

Yanwen, W. (2012). The study of complex project management in developing countries. *Physics Procedia*, 25, 1547–1552.

Yapicioglu, B., Mogbo, O.N. and Yitmen, I. (2017). Innovative strategies for transport policies in infrastructure development: Nigerian stakeholders' perspective. *International Journal of Civil Engineering*, 15(5), 747–761.

Yuan, J., Skibniewski, M.J., Li, Q. and Zheng, L. (2010). Performance objectives selection model in public–private partnership projects based on the perspective of stakeholders. *Journal of Management in Engineering*, 26(2), 89–104.

Yuan, J., Wang, C., Skibniewski, M.J. and Li, Q. (2012). Developing key performance indicators for public–private partnership projects: Questionnaire survey and analysis. *Journal of Management in Engineering*, 28(3), 252–264.

Yuan, J., Zeng, A.Y., Skibniewski, M.J. and Li, Q. (2009). Selection of performance objectives and key performance indicators in public–private partnership projects to achieve value for money. *Construction Management and Economics*, 27(3), 253–270.

Zhang, J., Dawes, S.S. and Sarkis, J. (2005). Exploring stakeholders' expectations of the benefits and barriers of e-government knowledge sharing. *Journal of Enterprise Information Management*, 18(5), 548–567.

https://doi.org/10.1142/9789811224720_0014

Chapter 14

Managing the Operating Environment of Projects in Developing Countries

Emmanuel Adinyira*,†, Kofi Agyekum† and George Ofori‡

*University of Johannesburg, South Africa
†Kwame Nkrumah University of Science and Technology, Ghana
‡London South Bank University, UK

Abstract

Any project's operating environment will have an impact on project management decisions and actions even in relatively stable environments. Whereas projects in developed countries are moderately sensitive to the operating environment, those in developing countries are highly sensitive to their environment. This issue is so mainly due to the varied, and in some cases, changing, nature of environmental factors of projects such as cultural, economic, political, social, physical, aesthetic, financial, legal, institutional, technological, and policy. It is a situation that presents a challenge for project management in developing countries. Failure to properly manage the unstable operating environment of projects is arguably the chief cause of the less-than-optimum project outcomes often recorded in developing countries. This chapter systematically examines the project operating environment in the context of developing countries. It highlights the significant differences and similarities in operating environments in developed and developing countries. The chapter advocates for workable approaches for the context of developing countries by discussing aspects of the project environment, suggesting ways in which it may be influenced to increase the probability of a successful outcome, and highlighting ways in which what is proposed for developing countries differs from what pertains in developed countries. Some recommendations for future research in this field of knowledge related to developing countries are presented.

Keywords: Projects, operating environment, environmental factors, developing countries, developed countries, new approaches

Introduction

Most projects clearly define their objectives, work scope, budget, and schedule, but all too often, the environment and context in which the project exists are neither fully understood nor clearly defined (Cusworth and Franks, 2013). This is a significant source of menace when it comes to project management. A clearly defined set of objectives, work scope, budget and schedule are essential to plan, implement, and control a project. If the project management team fails to fully understand their project environment and context, the project will likely be doomed to failure (Taherdoost and Keshavarzsaleh, 2016; Wideman, 1990). This is because the project environment and context drive performance as much as, if not more than, a clearly defined work scope, budget, or schedule. It is common to find in the project management literature the saying that "no two projects are ever the same, even if their objectives and work scope are" (see, for example, Aljohani *et al.*, 2017; Rao and Jigeesh, 2012; Cooke and Williams, 2004; Baum, 1978). This is because even projects with identical objectives and work scopes will inevitably be executed in different environments (Lock, 2000).

Though not listed as part of the knowledge areas in project management, a project's operating environment impacts how the project is managed. Thus, it should be studied for management decisions and actions to be determined on the project. It is therefore important for project managers to develop their capacities to understand the characteristics of the environment, to analyze it, and then to develop coherent management strategies for dealing with it in such a way as to enhance the chances of project success (Kuruoglu and Sorguc, 2000).

This chapter examines the project operating environment in the context of developing countries. It introduces the subject of the project environment and presents a description of the concept. The chapter highlights the significant differences and similarities between the project operating environment in developed and developing countries. It presents strategies to effectively influence the project environment in developing countries toward enhanced project success. At the end of the chapter, a future research agenda in relation to the project environment in developing countries is put forward.

Project operating environment explained

The operating environment of any project has an impact on the way the project is managed. It affects both a project's long-term effects arising out of the project's conceptual formulation, as well as its shorter-term impacts arising during execution (Wideman, 1990). Understanding the cultural, organizational, and social environments surrounding a project is important to any project manager's work. Therefore, it is an important subject that project managers must clearly understand. This section attempts to explain the project operating environment, its dimensions, its various factors, and how these can be influenced for the good of the project.

What is the project environment?

As put by Sidwell (1990), no project exists in a vacuum; it is subject to an array of influences, from regulatory control to political and industrial interventions. The project environment can be thought of in terms of the project time environment, the internal project culture, the original corporate culture, and the external social surroundings (Wideman, 1990). It encompasses various factors, many of which will directly impact the project outputs and the way it is implemented and how it is subsequently perceived (Lock, 1996). According to Collyer (2016), the term "project environment" includes such things as the industry, resources, processes, techniques, and so forth. These factors are dynamic and have a high probability of changing during a project's life cycle.

Although many project environmental factors are mentioned in existing studies (Luu *et al.*, 2006; Mafakheri *et al.*, 2007), the factors listed in the works of Walker and Hughes remain popular. Walker (1989) and Hughes (1989), in their respective studies, listed political, legal, institutional, cultural, sociological, technological resources, economic, financial, and physical (infrastructure) as the factors constituting the environment of projects. Both studies directed attention to these factors within the environment as posing more significant challenges to project success. These factors must therefore be focused on when managing a project's environment (Lock, 1996).

In a major review of project management theory, Bennett (1991) established that the environment interferes with projects' planned progress. The less predictable the environment and the greater its potential effects, the more it must be considered in managing projects' development. However, a review of project monitoring and evaluation results of World Bank projects indicates that many of the projects' critical problems are not under the project manager's direct control (Youker, 1992). This makes the issue of managing the environment of a project rather difficult. Understanding the project environment provides project managers with a structured approach to analyzing and handling possible internal and external constraints.

What are the dimensions of the project environment?

A project's environment is a "basket" of project time-related factors, internal project culture-related factors, corporate culture-related factors, and external related factors. These broad categorizations of the project environmental factors are often referred to in the literature as the Project Environment's dimensions.

- **Project Time Environment** — Every project typically goes through four distinct project phases: (1) Concept; (2) Planning; (3) Execution; and (4) Transfer. The first two phases are often referred to as the feasibility and engineering phases. At these phases, the project is built on paper, i.e., planned. The third phase is where actual physical implementation occurs, and the last phase is where commissioning is undertaken and completion approvals are acquired.

- **Internal Project Environment** — This environment describes what could be termed as the project culture. It reflects the leadership style and organizational structure for the project and can vary according to the project's size and nature. The project's internal environment is complex due to the varying internal stakeholder groups involved in the project. Various stakeholders have their own mini cultures brought together to make the project culture, thereby creating a complex culture that could result in project failure if not well managed.
- **Corporate Project Environment** — Corporate project culture or environment refers simply to the project workplace. It is manifested in the project workplace's organizational hierarchies, established policies, procedures, and authority lines, among others. Just as the internal culture, the corporate culture also directly impacts the success or otherwise of the project. The operationalization of key project decisions will be greatly influenced by the established policies and procedures governing the project workplace.
- **Project's External Environment** — Projects do not only have internal stakeholder groups but also, they have external stakeholder groups, such as the project's host community, government, and so on. If these external stakeholders are not well managed, that could lead to project failure irrespective of the success in managing the internal environment. Just as with the internal environment, the external environment could be equally complex, if not more complex, to deal with due to the varied attributes of the factors in this environment. Therefore, it is essential to develop a strategy to manage the external stakeholder environment, just as is the case for the internal environment.

Variability of environmental factors

Project environmental factors are subject to degrees of variability. As noted by Hughes (1989), their extent of changeability can be classified in terms of their degree of definition, stability, certainty, simplicity, and the ease with which they can be mitigated. Project environmental factors are defined from one project to another. The influence of these factors is often related to or expressed in terms of the factors' definitions. These definitions have everything to do with the perception of the stakeholders involved in the project. They can be looked at as the extent to which stakeholders perceive the effects of environmental factors on the project. These perceptions vary from stakeholder to stakeholder and, in many cases, are inconsistent over the project duration. Wideman (1990) stated that project environmental factors may be either constant or variable. Each factor could be in any state along a continuum of stability–instability (Hughes, 1989) with a degree of change in stability during the duration of the project.

Project environmental factors are also heavily affected by the degree of certainty surrounding each of them, i.e., the extent to which it can be predicted. The less certain the environmental factor is, the more difficult it will be to predict problematic areas, and the higher the variability to be expected. This degree of certainty or otherwise is also seen in terms of the complexity or simplicity associated with the factor. The variability of project environmental factors can also be considered in terms of the ease or otherwise with which each of them can be mitigated. This has to do with the extent to which it is in the power of the project management team to moderate the factor's adverse influences. According to Wideman (1990), some project environmental factors such as the politics of the nation concerned may be difficult to mitigate and would thus have a far greater adverse effect upon the project, while other factors such as the effect of technological complexity that could be addressed by employing suitably experienced consultants could be easier to mitigate.

A defined, stable, certain, simple, and mitigable project environment will be the best thing that happened to a project manager. However, that is rarely the case, especially in a less stable economic and political state as exemplified by most developing countries. For effective management of projects in such situations, the need to strategically influence the project environment becomes very important. The next sections introduce effective project operating environment management strategies.

Influencing the project's environment

The project environment, as earlier noted, is principally made up of the internal and external factors that have a significant influence on the management of a project (Wideman, 1990). Therefore, a project manager must be able to identify these factors and their impact and work in such a way as to influence the nature of the impact of such factors (Giri, 2019). Project management decisions or strategies should ensure that the negative impacts of project environmental factors are influenced to the extent that they are negated or mitigated while the positive impacts are influenced in how they are kept or enhanced (Tharp, 2012).

Projects fail or underperform due to the impact of many environmental factors (Taherdoost and Keshavarzsaleh, 2016). Even technical failure, when critically analyzed, will point to ultimate failure in managerial influences. Therefore, the role of management is vital to achieving project success (Taherdoost and Keshavarzsaleh, 2016). Active sponsorship and control management is essential. The project manager must be the authoritative agent in dealing with all parties and be the responsible and single formal contact with them (Wideman, 1990). According to Wideman (1990), no major technical, cost, schedule, or performance decisions must be made on a project without the project manager's participation. The project manager and other project team members must be competent enough to make the right decisions on the project to ensure success. The competence of the team around project management is therefore critical (Udo and Koppensteiner, 2004).

Influencing a project's external environment is also important, as it also characterizes uncertainty and risk to the successful accomplishment of a project (Liu *et al.*, 2019). Managing the external project environment involves developing a sound stakeholder environment. It involves understanding the behavior, motivation, and role of each of the various stakeholders and how this information may be used as an opportunity to improve both the perception and reception of the project (Liu *et al.*, 2019). According to Wideman (1990), one way to effectively deal with a project's external environment is to prioritize the required stakeholder linkages by conducting a stakeholder analysis. Such an analysis would be designed first to identify all the potential stakeholders who might have an impact on the project, then to determine their relative ability to influence it, and then to develop and maintain the necessary stakeholder linkages required to keep the project going.

Project operating environment in developing countries

The project environment in most developing countries poses unique challenges for project managers, leading them to presume cost and time overruns even before starting a project in such environments (Akanni *et al.*, 2015). Akanni *et al.* (2015, p. 91) postulate that "the less predictable the environment and greater its potential effects, the more it must be taken into account in managing the development of construction projects."

Variability of environmental factors in developed and developing countries

Turbulence and scarcity have been identified as two general characteristics that affect the project operating environment's development (Cushworth and Franks, 2013). These characteristics manifest themselves well within the project environment, with countries in the developed countries better equipped in dealing with these characteristics compared to those in the developing world. Table 14.1 presents a summary of the variabilities of some selected environmental factors that affect project operating environments in both developed and developing countries.

Youker (1992) noted that some project environmental factors pose more significant challenges than others. Therefore, such factors should be the focus of efforts to manage the project environment. Considering the impact of these environmental factors on the performance of projects in developing countries, Faniran *et al.* (2000) indicated a need to develop appropriate management tools and techniques to address these factors. Cusworth and Franks (2013) also indicated that, just as living organisms depend on their biological environment for survival, projects thrive on their environment to succeed. This suggests that there must be a continuous and constant interaction between the project and its environment.

Table 14.1: Comparison of environmental factors for developing and developed countries.

Developing countries	**Environmental factors**	**Developed countries**
Culture and religion play critical roles in every sphere of life	**Culture and religion**	Professional judgment holds sway over culture and religious beliefs
A distressing economy with unstable financial standing of firms	**Economic and financial**	Economic and financial features are centered on the level of general economic activities and the resources needed to undertake the work. Generally stable financial standing of firms
Unstable political grounds with ultimate decisions regarding public or social projects often in the power of politicians	**Political**	Politically stable environments, and in most instances with a two-party system where other parties can contribute. The influence of civil society is evident.
Stable tropical climates with minimal variation in most countries in most years	**Physical**	Very complex and unpredictable climate
Complex legal and regulatory environments. Laws and regulations may be scattered in several documents	**Legal and regulatory**	Well-defined laws and regulations easily available in written documents
Some professions are well represented by national professional institutions, but their regulatory roles are less mature	**Institutional**	National professional institutions represent various professions in the industry with mature regulatory functions
Technological progress is slow and influenced by more advanced countries such as China.	**Technological**	There is vast progress in all aspects of technology.
Unstable market conditions	**Market conditions**	Stable market conditions
Stakeholder influences felt in the operating environment but very difficult to manage because of the attributes of various stakeholders	**Stakeholder influence**	Stakeholder influences greatly felt in the project operating environment but well managed.

The environmental variables present in developing countries tend to differ from those in developed countries. There is a need to understand the complexities and unique features of these environmental variables in developing countries. This has become necessary because each project has its unique environment; hence, there is no definitive method for detailing the precise nature of a particular project's environment (Cushworth and Franks, 2013). However, understanding the characteristics of a particular environment, analyzing it, and developing coherent management strategies to deal with it provides project managers with basic ideas needed to control the environment of other projects. The project environments in developing countries have been found to pose special problems for construction projects managers (Cushworth and Franks, 2013). Some of the environmental and contextual shaping factors that need to be considered when developing a project management or execution plan are next discussed.

Cultural and religious environment

Construction project culture is defined as "the shared values, basic assumptions and beliefs that the participants involved in a project hold that determine the way they process the project and the relationship with each other in the project environment" (Zuo and Zillante, 2008, p. 357). Culture in this context can be defined as the degree of influence of indigenes' way of life on the project operating environment. There is a certain cultural and religious environment in which construction projects exist and it has the tendency to affect project performance. Such environmental factors that can dictate how the project management team may need to adjust the project execution plan may include, but are not limited to, personnel accommodation and work facilities, local holidays, acceptable working hours, restricted or protected areas, and security requirements and considerations. To William (2002), such factors may also include the customs, lifestyles, and values that characterize a society from its socio-cultural features. Engobo (2009) indicated that the demography of the population, educational levels, language, norms, values, among others, are all socio-cultural features that need to be considered in a project operating environment. Ignoring, or exhibiting cultural bias toward, any of these areas can result in adverse impacts on the project.

Culture can create differences among the people involved in construction projects, and if this situation is not properly managed, it can create misunderstanding among people within the project operating environment (Samaraweera and Senaratne, 2012). The project operating environment may be affected by different cultures (national, industry, organizational, and professional) at varying levels. For instance, Ofori and Toor (2009) opined that in a mega construction project with participants from different countries, one should not define the culture at the national level (considering the location) because although the foreigners may adopt the local culture, they maintain some ties with their roots. Hughes (1989) explained this by indicating that in some developed countries such as in the United Kingdom, the relatively recent influx of people with different racial backgrounds is creating continuing multi-racial traditions that are experienced in almost every sector of the economy, including construction. This makes culture a unique feature of the project operating environment.

Within developing country settings, especially in Africa, even if the people have the same ethnic roots, they might have various clans, and the people might belong to different religions. Culture in such countries may not be considered to be of great concern, especially where the project operating environment is deemed to be "national," or better still, "local." However, this can have consequences.

To Doh and Ramamurti (2003), approaches to the management of construction projects that are highly successful in the developed countries often fail in developing countries because of the disregard for their congruence with the internal operating culture of the construction industries of such nations. With the issue of religion, a study conducted by Kissi *et al.* (2020) in Ghana revealed that religion plays a critical role in every sphere of life, including construction performance measurement. In such developing countries, when managing project stakeholders, religion plays a critical role where effective communication is needed in community projects (Kissi *et al.*, 2020). This should be evident in how the project team involves the community in the project, such as how it approaches traditional leaders to inform them about the plans for their community's development. The outcome of such interactions can affect the project's operating environment.

Economic and financial environment

Economic and financial factors are imperative features of the project operating environment. During every project, resources are utilized to create assets. The assets having value and the resources having a cost indicate that the project's worth is directly affected by the economic and financial environment within which it is implemented (Yanwen, 2012). To Akanni *et al.* (2015), economic and financial features are centered on the level of general economic activities and the resources needed to undertake the work. Obalola (2006) indicated a difference between the economic and financial factors on a project. According to him, the economic aspect has to do with deploying resources, whereas the financial aspects are strictly limited to money.

The nature of the factors influencing the economic and financial environment causes high levels of uncertainty during project development because of the decisions required to be considered in the light of changes in the economy and related government policies, budgetary constraints, and foreign exchange shortages, among other things (Cannon, 1994). Every project manager is faced with the challenge of ensuring that a project is financially viable within a fluctuating economic environment. However, in developing countries which are diverse, and range from disaster-ravaged nations through failed states, to emerging economies (Lizarralde *et al.*, 2013), the economic and financial issues that have an impact on the project operating environments must be considered.

Political environment

The use of power and political behavior is one of the most powerful but frequently overlooked influencers of the successful management of projects (Pinto, 2000). According to Akanni *et al.* (2015), the political environment concerns government policies and decisions that influence projects. As an important feature of human organizations that permeates all levels of society, politics plays a significant role in determining progress on any construction project (Yanwen, 2012). Often, political influence comes in the form of having to deal with issues of bribery and corruption, managing differences between local and national policies, adapting to sudden changes in political power or influence, and resolving conflicts between different political factions. Yanwen (2012) further postulated that the political dimension might be viewed from two perspectives, i.e., national or international.

Nationally, projects face various forms of political interference in funding, seeking permission, and the like (Belassi and Tukel, 1996). This issue is paramount in developing countries, especially in Africa, where decisions regarding public or social projects lie with politicians. For instance, in Ghana, where the government is a major client of development projects (Damoah *et al.*, 2018), there is much politics within projects' operating environments. This hinders performance on projects, and therefore, economic growth (Damoah *et al.*, 2018).

According to Akanni *et al.* (2015), in developing countries, the government's significant role is in the form of a client, the administrator of the national economy, and a regulator. The implication of this is that through budgetary measures and monetary policies, the government can influence the level of demand for construction services (Akanni *et al.*, 2015). Furthermore, with the government's role in the project operating environment as the regulator of construction activities, development and building approval processes and enforcement of compliance with regulations can be politicized. Thomas and Martin (2004) stated that all construction projects are subject to various political and other influences. Thomas and Martin (2004) further indicated that project managers should be cognizant of the political issues that can create an uncertain project operating environment, such as unstable government, shifts in the economy, and changes in consumer demand.

Physical environment

Construction projects are affected by their natural setting, including its geological conditions, soils, climatic conditions, water resources, and any nearby ecological systems (Yanwen, 2012). The physical environment within which a project is situated may considerably impact its development (Akanni *et al.*, 2015). Apart from the natural conditions, such as those relating to the geographical location and site topography, access to roads, site drainage, and other infrastructure are all physical factors that affect construction projects (Bansal, 2020). Because construction projects are complex and unique (Bansal, 2020), it is always advisable to determine the physical environments before embarking on each project.

Specific physical settings surround a project sited in a particular location, and these settings may be the reason for the project's existence. Since the elements of such settings such as the local weather, are unpredictable, there is little the project manager can do to prevent their influence. Other features include geotechnical and topographical issues, site access constraints, utilities and local service availability, environmental sensitivities, and human and material resource availability. For instance, in the Gaza Strip, the influence of climate change on the operating environment of construction projects (i.e., project design and planning, construction workforce, equipment and materials, construction process, and so on) is well reported (El-Sawalhi and Mahdi, 2015). In the literature, emphasis is now being put on the need to incorporate the weather in construction scheduling and management because of its possible adverse impact on the project operating environment and the outcome of the project (Ballesteros-Peréz *et al.*, 2018). The impact of the other physical features on projects' operating environment in developed and developing nations is well reported in the literature. Project managers need to pay attention to the physical effects when planning for projects.

Legal and regulatory environment

The prevailing legal and regulatory environment affects projects. This environmental feature may impact project execution performance by placing conditions on specific parameters, such as prioritizing standards, adherence to site-specific and local environmental regulations, regulations that influence the availability of human and material resources, and local content requirements. The legal and regulatory environments facing organizations have become more complex and now affect businesses more directly and in many different ways (Akanni *et al.*, 2015).

Construction industries in all countries operate under planning and environmental regulations, codes of conduct or practice, safety regulations, and the like. Although these laws and regulations are well defined and easily available in standard documents in the developed countries, this is not the case in most developing countries. For example, in Ghana, Adjarko *et al.* (2016) identified numerous laws, regulations, and policies governing the construction industry's operations. However, this information was scattered in various documents, making it difficult for construction companies to gain access to it. This makes it difficult for companies to operate and for the construction industry to meet all legal and regulatory requirements. In some countries, these laws are alien, obsolete or incompatible with the countries' requirements, resources and necessary activities. Oladapo and Olotuah (2007) pointed out that in Nigeria, the construction laws and legislations were based on those of Britain; many of them were outmoded and out of synchronization with current trends and needs. Martin and Thomas (2004) suggested that since changes to such regulations are uncommon, stakeholders, especially project managers, should be prepared to face the problems that may arise due to such changes during the project lifecycle.

Institutional environment

Project managers need to be aware of the institutional frameworks they are operating in (Yanwen, 2012). Kerzner (1989) described the general institutional framework to encompass matters (such as the legal systems) within which the project-performing organization operates together with certain aspects of social organization (such as the land tenure and water rights systems). Ofori (2012) stressed the need for institutional frameworks to guide construction companies' activities in developed and developing countries.

Whereas some developed countries such as Australia, Hong Kong, Singapore, and the UK have realized the need for the continuous improvement and development of their construction industries through the establishment of administrative systems, most developing countries are yet to pay serious attention to such frameworks to guide the activities of their construction sectors. For instance, Ofori (2012) indicated that the reviews of the construction industries of the developed and newly industrializing countries have aimed at the radical restructuring of all aspects of the industries. Typical examples of such initiatives are the Construction 21 exercise in Singapore (Ofori, 2012), the then Construction Industry

Master Plan of Malaysia, and currently, initiatives for realizing Industry 4.0 in many of the developed nations.

These examples are relevant to the construction industries of most developing countries. It is observed that there is no shortage of appropriate initiatives in many developing countries such as Ghana, but the organizational and procedural frameworks needed to implement these existing national programs and suggested ideas are often lacking (Ofori, 2012). This notwithstanding, some African countries (such as Rwanda, Uganda, and South Africa) have gone beyond strategic reviews to prepare national construction industry policies (Ofori, 2012).

Technological environment

The availability of technological tools, skills, and experience can affect both the project's objectives and values through its impact on design complexity, human resource availability, speed and efficiency in project execution, adherence to scope and standards, reliability and operability of the end product, and safety in project execution and operation. Technology is an environmental aspect that should be considered when developing a strategic plan for a project (Akanni *et al.*, 2015).

According to Liu *et al.* (2019), the effect of technology accessibility on a project should be given due attention: "The lower the technology accessibility from the external environment for a project is, the fewer contractors there are who are capable of executing large scale and complicated projects" (Liu *et al.*, 2019, p. 283). According to Oladapo and Olotuah (2007), in measuring appropriate construction technology, the availability of locally made plant and equipment, skilled personnel, extent of local material resources, and the extent of utilizing such resources must be considered. However, in most developing countries, the construction industry is characterized by development projects that need and use technology and resources from developed countries. Many developing countries remain importers of technical workforce, equipment, spare parts, and other resources needed to undertake the construction projects they need in their current state. For example, in Nigeria, Akanni *et al.* (2015) reported that lack of technological know-how and shortage of managerial workforce are significant problems confronting construction operations. Liu *et al.* (2019) indicated that this is a serious issue because when technology accessibility is low, the duration, quality, cost, and risk-sharing on projects are affected.

Market conditions

The market conditions that affect the project operating environment include the level of competition in the project market and the number of eligible and qualified contractors in the market (Liu *et al.*, 2019). It is important to consider the market conditions in which projects are to be undertaken. Market conditions are dynamic and, depending on the overriding economic environment, can be either beneficial or detrimental to a project's performance. Varying market conditions may affect a project in several ways, like the financing of the project, human and material resource availability, and possibly, necessary changes to project scope and/or standards.

Construction companies have to compete among themselves for the same customers, implying that there must be continuous demand for companies' products and processes. Therefore, a particular company's operating environment has a major impact on its strategies and daily operations. According to Matyusz *et al.* (2012), market changes may require the ability to vary technologies and human resource requirements to react to the changes, among other things. Construction companies in developing countries are not so mature and this results in poor performance. One consequence of the lack of maturity is the influx of foreign construction companies into these countries to undertake significant infrastructure projects (Akunyumu *et al.*, 2021).

Stakeholder influence

Schepper *et al.* (2014) indicated that stakeholders' actions affect their targets and the overall project environment; a project is affected by the influences exerted on it by its controlling organization and other stakeholders. To have a conducive project environment and to be able to achieve its objectives, it is imperative to understand the interests of the stakeholders (Nguyen *et al.*, 2019), both the internal and external stakeholders. Winch (2004) indicated that although the internal stakeholders may support the project, the external ones may be in favor, against, or indifferent. The extent of their influence can generally be determined by stakeholder factors such as experience, culture, style, structure, maturity, risk attitude, interests, and priorities.

Among the numerous problems associated with external stakeholders regarding the project operating environment in developing countries are conflicts of all forms and socio-political risks, which hinder progress and might result in the premature termination of projects (Boutilier and Zdziarski, 2017). Stakeholder influences are experienced in all project environments irrespective of the location (i.e., whether in a developed or a developing country). However, with proper structures and systems in place, stakeholder influences are better managed in developed countries' project operating environments than in developing countries (Oppong, 2020; Eyiah-Botwe *et al.*, 2015). From a critical comparative review of related literature, Nguyen *et al.* (2018) were able to identify the three most critical strategies that external stakeholders use to influence projects: i.e., attempting to gain public attention and support for their cause, strengthening their position in the field, and using solution-seeking tactics. Project managers need mechanisms which enable them to respond to such actions.

Complexities of project operating environment in developing countries

Every project contains a certain degree of complexity, but there is no universally accepted definition of "complexity" (Bakhshi *et al.*, 2016). Several studies have defined complexity in various ways. Project complexity can be defined as "[consisting] of many varied interrelated parts" (Baccarini, 1996, p. 202) and characterized in terms of distinct differences (number of components in a project, such as tasks and specialists) and interdependency (the degree of interlinkages between the components) (Luo *et al.*, 2017). In the opinion of Vidal *et al.* (2011, p. 179), project complexity is "the property of a project which makes it difficult to understand, foresee and keep under control its overall behaviour even when given complete information about [the] project system." Sheard and Adviser-Mostashari (2012, p. 11) also defined project complexity as "the inability to predict a system's behaviour due to large numbers of constituent parts within the system and dense relationships among them." Following a critical review of related literature, Bakhshi *et al.* (2016) defined project complexity as "an intricate arrangement of the varied interrelated parts in which the elements can change and constantly evolve with an effect on the project objectives."

The literature has established that project complexities and environmental factors influence project success (Ishtiaq and Jahanzaib, 2017). Luo *et al.* (2017) assert that traditional project management methods are inadequate when applied in managing complex projects. The complexity of projects increases with changes in the environment, increased sophistication of the product, and increased time pressure (Williams, 1999). Dao (2017, p. 1) indicated that "most attributes of project complexity are constantly changing variables like project type, size, location, team experience, interface within a project, logistics/market conditions, geopolitical and social issues, and permitting and approvals."

According to Gidado (1996), the sources of project complexity factors can be grouped into two categories, namely:

- Category I: the components that are inherent to the operation of the individual task (for example, technical complexity, analyzability, and task difficulty) and uncertainty factors; and
- Category II: composed of elements necessary to form workflow and includes interdependencies among different kinds of technologies, the rigidity of sequence, and overlap of construction elements.

Bakhshi *et al.* (2016) also grouped project complexity factors into: project context, connectivity, diversity, emergence, size, autonomy, and belonging. Though other factors are significant, the analysis from Bakhshi *et al.* (2016) revealed that the project context, normally referred to as an environmental factor, is the most pronounced factor of complexity. The contextual factors they identified include local laws and regulations, networked environment, level of competition/market conditions, political issues, cultural configuration, and geological conditions (Bakhshi *et al.*, 2016).

In the opinion of Bosch-Rekveldt *et al.* (2011), although the contextual factors are softer aspects and influences from the environment, they contribute to project complexity, with a series of challenges encountered in trying to control them, in the case of developing countries. As seen in the preceding sections, these challenges appear in the form of the environment of varied culture and religion; the environment of changing economy and finance; environment of political instability; the environment of changing nature; the environment of misaligned legal and regulatory frameworks; the environment of the poor institutional framework; the environment of diversified technology; the environment of poor market conditions; and the environment of continuous stakeholder influence.

Approaches to the effective management of project operating environment in developing countries

Effective project management is the degree to which the project objectives have been attained on time and within budget and to the satisfaction of all stakeholders. These stakeholders may participate in the project directly or indirectly, closely or remotely, and collectively their attitudes, understandings, or vested interests contribute to the environment in which a project is created and undertaken. This environment needs to be managed just as surely as every other aspect of the project can be managed toward success (Wideman, 1990). Both external and internal causes can account for project failure. Given the differences in the project environment for developed and developing countries, there is the need for unique approaches that will work in the specific context of developing countries (Adams, 2017; Zuofa and Ochieng, 2012).

The project environment is one on which the project depends for its survival in the same way that a living organism depends on its biological environment (Cusworth and Franks, 2013). Therefore, there must be continuous interaction between the project and its environment. A hostile project environment increases project managers' difficulties and reduces the likelihood of success. It is vital that project managers in developing countries develop their abilities to understand the characteristics of their unique environment, be able to analyze it, and develop and adopt coherent management strategies for dealing with it in such a way as to enhance the chances of project success (Cusworth and Franks, 2013). Therefore, for a project manager to be effective in such hostile project environments, he/she will have to go beyond just understanding the environment to develop approaches for establishing supportive linkages, i.e., input-output linkages, actor factor linkages, and controls (Youker, 1987).

New workable approaches

The fundamental problem with managing the project environment in developing countries is the less stable and unpredictable nature of both the internal and external environments (Akanni *et al.*, 2015). Project management in such environments requires more flexible methods than is seen in the PMBOK. It requires project managers trained using focused project management training and human resource development programs to prepare them to cope with the dynamic internal environment. Sound stakeholder management training is also required to enable them to adequately handle the external environment's dynamic and complex nature (Smith, 2000). A study of culture, communication, and leadership for projects in dynamic environments by Collyer (2016) presented approaches for managing culture, communication, and leadership in environments particularly challenged by rapid change such as is evident in the project environment in developing countries. This chapter offers practical and theoretical insights that can be adapted to devise new workable approaches to how project managers can apply culture, communication, and leadership to better deal with the increasing challenge of an unstable project environment.

An effective project culture in a developing country project environment will be a goal-orientated culture that supports experimentation (Nguyen and Watanabe, 2017). This means there should be a small project team with a flat hierarchy and a culture supported by stakeholders. According to Drake (2016), one advantage of a flat structure in a dynamic environment is the team members' ability with situational awareness and specialist knowledge to make more timely and relevant decisions.

Processing a decision through multiple levels of a tall hierarchy can be a slow process, reducing the impact or relevance of the decision once made (Drake, 2016). Going with the smallest possible project team size possible to achieve the goal and selecting highly motivated multi-skilled staff members is highly recommended. For predictable or stable environments, process control (detailed procedures and plans) as preached by PMBOK is the best control mechanism, but in dynamic or unstable environments, where tasks are more often unique or uncertain, culture can have a much higher impact on performance (Ouchi, 1979). The project team should be ready to nurture the project culture through careful staff selection and training. It should be sufficiently flexible and pragmatic to allow for some level of experimentation.

Effective communication is vital in an unstable project environment. Timely and efficient communication is required in such environments. Abudi (2013) advocates increased emphasis on fast, timely, and succinct communication over slow, thorough communication. Collyer (2016) recommends formalizing direct communication channels that bypass organizational levels if required to aid more rapid communication.

Flexible leadership with rapid decision making is also vital in project environments in developing countries (Opfer and Abrams, 2004). The leader of the smallest possible project team should delegate tasks appropriately and make quick, reasonable decisions. Effective delegation is achieved by clearly communicating the project goal (Ahmed *et al.*, 2013). A challenge identified for decision making for leaders in dynamic environments is decision lag, i.e., decisions are not made in time to keep pace with the project. Collyer (2016) suggests three approaches that may mitigate decision lag: decision delegation, rapid feedback loops, and preplanned responses.

Table 14.2 presents highlights from Collyer's study (2016), outlining the major differences of project management approaches, i.e., project culture, communication, and leadership in the developed countries and the developing countries that appear to have relatively more dynamic project environments. Dynamism, in this context, is taken to be a dimension of a project representing the extent to which the project is influenced by rapid changes in the operating environment. As already seen, in a developed country, most project environments are largely predictable, with strategic

Table 14.2: Comparing approaches of project management in developing and developed country project environment.

Developing countries	Aspects of project management	Developed countries
Flexible Formal framework, informal core Collaborative, flat hierarchy Organic, experimental, adaptive Stakeholders expect and understand dynamic environments	**Culture** **Flexible, collaborative, organic, adaptive**	Rigid Formal Authoritarian, tall hierarchy Planned, strict, structured Stakeholders expect and understand static environments
A larger mix of informal with formal Includes rapid, informal, and practical Flat hierarchy Informal and formal inform each other	**Communication** **Rapid informal complementing less regular formal**	Focus on formal communication Slow, formal, thorough Tall hierarchy Formal informs informal
Explores through the jungle A clear view of the environment and goals Highly adaptable Knows the jungle Collaborates with a team Actions decided by the team Guides with goals Specialists deliver vision Team pursues goals	**Leadership** **Exploratory vision driven using collaboration and delegation**	Drives down a path A clear view of the path Highly structured Knows the path Leads a hierarchy Plans dictated centrally Manages with plan Workers follow plan Team is driven from above
Decisions focused on pragmatic expedience Speed capitalizes on a fleeting opportunity Intent and objectives set at the top Decisions made in the middle by people with situational/subject matter knowledge Action taken in time to capitalize on fleeting opportunities Decisions prepared in advance and executed when data are collected	**Decision making** **Rapid–adequate–in time**	Decisions focused on accuracy Accuracy achieves lasting perfection Intent and objectives set at top Decisions made at the top based on information passed up the hierarchy Action taken when confident of right decision Decisions are made after all data are collected

input mostly required at the start of the project. However, this is often not the case in developing countries (see Akanni *et al.*, 2015; Walker, 1989; Hughes, 1989). Here, the environment is difficult to predict, with targets moving all the time, thereby requiring strategic inputs throughout the project duration, calling for project management approaches suitable for dynamic projects.

Conclusion

Effective project management goes beyond monitoring and coordinating time, cost, and quality by planning, scheduling, and resource-levelling. It involves processes and activities to achieve specific project objectives according to the project acceptance criteria within agreed parameters. The PMBOK, in acknowledging this point, outlines knowledge areas, each of which contains all or some of the project management processes and activities. Outside the 10 project management knowledge areas, considered to cover all the areas in which work must be done to complete all projects, the management of the operating environment of any project has an impact on the way the project is managed and thus requires to be studied in its own right for appropriate management decisions and actions to be determined on the project. This chapter placed the spotlight on the project operating environment by projecting how the context of developing countries would have a different impact on, and implications for, it than in developed countries.

The project environment encompasses a variety of factors, many of which will directly impact the project outputs and the way it is implemented and how it is subsequently perceived (Lock, 1996). Walker (1989) and Hughes (1989) both listed in their respective studies, political, legal, institutional, cultural, sociological, technological resources, economic, financial, and physical (infrastructure) as the factors constituting the environment of a project.

Concerning the issue of culture and religion, it is evident that they play a crucial role in people's lives within developing countries such as those in Sub-Saharan Africa. This aspect is evidenced in the study undertaken by Kissi *et al.* (2020), where it was revealed that in Ghana, there is a significant positive relationship between religious elements of all the three major religions (i.e., Christianity, Muslim, and Traditional) and cost and schedule performance of construction projects. Several studies have revealed that national culture affects the activities of project organizations (see, for example, Owusu Ansah, and Louw, 2019; Nazariana *et al.*, 2017; Johns, 2006; Nelson and Gopalan, 2003; Hofstede, 2001). Furthermore, with regards to religion, though it is said to influence other aspects of life, its impact on the project operating environment has not received much coverage in the literature.

Also, regarding the economic and financial environment, the discussions revealed the unstable financial standing of project organizations in developing countries (Akanni *et al.*, 2015) compared to the relatively more stable economies of those in developed countries (Walker, 1989; Hughes, 1989). Most developing countries, especially in Africa, have unstable political situations (Akanni *et al.*, 2015). In contrast, in the developed countries, the political environment is stable (Walker, 1989; Hughes, 1989). There are also complex legal and regulatory environments within developing countries with laws and regulations concerning project operations scattered in several documents (Akanni *et al.*, 2015). However, in developed countries, laws and regulations concerning project operations are well defined and documented with appropriate implementation structures (Walker, 1989; Hughes, 1989). There is a greater technological advancement of project organizations in developed countries than in developing countries (Liu *et al.*, 2019). Finally, though stakeholder influence on the project is widely reported in the literature, evidence reveals that such influences are better managed in project organizations within the developed countries (Walker, 1989; Hughes, 1989) than developing countries (Akanni *et al.*, 2015).

The above situation means that the project manager will require unique approaches to managing projects' operating environment in developing countries which may influence the probability of successful project outcomes. A deep and broad understanding of both the internal and external environments of the project is vital. Project management training in this context should have a specific focus on human resource and stakeholder management. Training should particularly cover managing culture, communication, and leadership in such environments characterized by rapid changes. Training should provide project managers with the skills needed to mitigate the impact of project environment factors such as politics, culture, and religion; stakeholder influences; and market conditions.

An effective project culture in a developing country will be a goal-orientated culture that supports experimentation. It will require a project organization structure with a flat hierarchy and a culture supported by stakeholders. There should be an increased emphasis on fast, timely, and succinct communication. Also, a flexible leadership approach with rapid decision-making is important to the successful management of the project environment in developing countries.

Since it is evident that there are weaknesses associated with controlling project environment factors in developing countries, there is a need for these factors to be further investigated, especially in developing country settings. Developing countries' project environment complexity issues of importance for future research include lack of capabilities resulting in frequent contradictions in terms of project plans and actuals; lack of teamwork due to individual team members' monetary interest and ambitions; rigid vertical organization structure; and the general open market environment. These areas require good quality exploratory, explanatory, and predictive research to formulate guidance for better project management in developing countries.

References

Abudi, G. (2013). Managing communications effectively and efficiently. Paper presented at *PMI Global Congress 2013 North America*. Project Management Institute, New Orleans, LA; Newtown Square, PA.

Adams, A.B. (2017). Project management for developing countries: Back to the basics. *Dama International Journal of Researchers*, 2(4), 5–9.

Adjarko, H., Gemadzie, J. and Agyekum, K. (2016). Construction related environmental laws and policies in Ghana: A literature review. *Asian Journal of Science and Technology*, 7(5), 2984–2992.

Ahmed, R. Tahir, M.M. and Noor, A. (2013). Leadership is vital for project managers to achieve project efficacy. *Research Journal of Recent Sciences*, 2(6), 99–102.

Akanni, P.O., Oke, A.E. and Akpomiemie, O.A. (2015). Impact of environmental factors on building project performance in Delta State, Nigeria. *Housing and Building National Research Centre Journal*, 11, 91–97.

Akunyumu, S., Fugar, F.D.K. and Adinyira, E. (2021). An assessment of the readiness of construction firms for international construction joint ventures

(ICJVs) using the VERDICT model. *Journal of Engineering, Design and Technology*, [ahead-of-print]. https://doi.org/10.1108/JEDT-04-2021-0198.

Aljohani, A., Ahiaga-Dagbui, D. and Moore, D. (2017). Construction projects cost overrun: What does the literature tell us? *International Journal of Innovation, Management and Technology*, 8(2), 137.

Baccarini, D. (1996). The concept of project complexity — A review. *International Journal of Project Management*, 14(4), 2-1-204.

Bakhshi, J., Ireland, V. and Gorod, A. (2016). Clarifying the project complexity construct: Past, present and future. *International Journal of Project Management*, 34, 1199–1213.

Ballesteros-Peréz, Smith, S.T., Lloyd-Papworth, J.G. and Cooke, P. (2018). Incorporating the effect of weather in construction scheduling and management with sine wave curves: Application in the United Kingdom. *Construction Management and Economics*, 36(12), 666–682.

Bansal, V.K. (2020). Use of GIS to consider spatial aspects in construction planning process. *International Journal of Construction Management*, 20(3), 207–222.

Baum, W.C. (1978). The World Bank project cycle. *Finance Development* 15(4), 10–17.

Belassi, W. and Tukel, O.I. (1996). A new framework for determining critical success/failure factors in project. *International Journal of Project Management*, 14(3), 141–152.

Bennett, J. (1991). *International Construction Project Management: General Theory and Practice*, 2nd Edition. Butterworth-Heinemann, Oxford, UK.

Bosch-Rekveldt, M., Jongkind, Y., Mooi, H., Bakker, H. and Verbraeck, A. (2011). Grasping project complexity in large engineering projects: The TOE (Technical, Organisational and Environmental) framework. *International Journal of Project Management*, 29, 728–739.

Boutilier, R. and Zdziarski, M. (2017). Managing stakeholder networks for a social license to build. *Construction Management and Economics*, 35(8–9), 1–16.

Cannon, J. (1994). Why IT applications succeed or fail: The intersection of technical and organisational factors. *Industrial and Commercial Training*, 26(1), 10–15.

Collyer, S. (2016). Culture, communication, and leadership for projects in dynamic environments. *Project Management Journal*, 47(6), 111–125.

Cooke, L. and Williams, S. (2004). Two approaches to using client projects in the college classroom. *Business Communication Quarterly*, 67(2), 139–152.

Cusworth, J.W. and Franks, T.R. (2013). *Managing Projects in Developing Countries*. Routledge, London.

Damoah, I.S., Akwei, C.A., Amoako, I.O. and Botchie, D. (2018). Corruption as a source of government project failure in developing countries: Evidence from Ghana. *Project Management Journal*, 49(3), 17–33.

Dao, B., Kermanshachi, S., Shane, J., Stuart, A. and Hare, E. (2017). Exploring and assessing project complexity. *Journal of Construction Engineering and Management*, 143(5), 04016126.

Doh, J.P. and Ramamurti, R. (2003). Reassessing risk in developing country infrastructure. *Long Range Planning*, 36(4), 337–353.

Drake, G. (2016). Trust and growth in the workplace: An analysis of leadership in flat organisations. A Thesis submitted to Portland State University. https://pdxscholar.library.pdx.edu/cgi/viewcontent.cgi?article=1410&context=honorstheses [Accessed 12 September 2021].

El-Sawalhi, N. and Mahdi, M. (2015). Influence of climate change on the lifecycle of construction projects at Gaza Strip. *Korean Institute of Construction Engineering and Management Journal*, 5(2), 1–10.

Engobo, E. (2009). Social responsibility in practice in the oil producing Niger Delta: Assessing corporations and government actions. *Journal of Sustainable Development Africa*, 11(2), 113–115.

Eyiah-Botwe, E., Aigbavboa, C. and Thwala, W.D. (2015). Critical barriers affecting stakeholder management in the construction industry. https://core.ac.uk/download/pdf/54198685.pdf [Accessed 10 September 2021].

Faniran, O.O., Love, P.E.D. and Smith, J. (2000). Effective front-end project management- a key element in achieving project success in developing countries. https://citeseerx.ist.psu.edu/viewdoc/download [Accessed 8 August 2020].

Gidado, K. (1996). Project complexity: The focal point of construction production planning. *Construction Management and Economics*, 14(3), 213–225.

Giri, E.O.P. (2019). Study on the role of project manager in improving the project performance. *Technical Journal*, 1(1), 133–139.

Hofstede, G. (2001). *Culture's Consequences: Comparing Values, Behaviors, Institutions and Organizations Across Nations*. Sage Publications, Thousand Oaks, CA.

Hughes, W.P. (1989). Identifying the environments of construction projects. *Construction Management and Economics*, 7(1), 29–40.

Ishtiaq, F. and Jahanzaib, M. (2017). Impact of project complexity and environmental factors on project success: A case of oil and gas sector of Pakistan. *Journal of Basic and Applied Sciences*, 13, 351–358.

Johns, G. (2006). The essential impact of context on organizational behavior. *Academy of Management Review*, 31, 386–408. https://doi.org/10.5465/amr.2006.20208687.

Kerzner, H. (1989). Systems project management: A case study at the IRS. *Journal of Systems Management*, 40(1), 7–9.

Kissi, E., Agyekum, K., Adjei-Kumi, T., Debtah, C. and Ekow, D.M. (2020). Exploring the influence of religious elements on performance factors in developing countries: A case of the Ghanaian construction industry. *International Journal of Productivity and Performance Management*. https://doi.org/10.1108/ijppm-11-2019-0546.

Kuruoglu, M. and Sorguç, V.D. (2000). A suggestion of reorganisation of planning department for Turkish construction firms, *Proceedings of the 2nd Conference of Construction Management*, Turkey, June 15–17, pp. 31–42 [in Turkish].

Liu, B., Xue, B., Huo, T., Shen, G. and Fu, M. (2019). Project external environmental factors affecting project delivery systems selection. *Journal of Civil Engineering and Management*, 25(3), 276–286.

Lizarralde, G., Tomiyoshi, S., Bourgault, M., Malo, J. and Cardosi, G. (2013). Understanding differences in construction project governance between developed and developing countries. *Construction Management and Economics*, 31(7), 711–730.

Lock, D. (1996). *Project Management*, 6th Edition, Gower, Aldershot.

Lock, D. (2000). *Project Management*, 7th Edition. Gower Publishing Ltd, Burlington, VT.

Luo, L., He, Q., Jaselkis, E.J. and Xie, J. (2017). Construction project complexity: Research trends and implications. *Journal of Construction Engineering and Management*, 143(7), 04017019.

Luu, D.T., Ng, S.T., Chen, S.E. and Jefferies, M. (2006). A strategy for evaluating a fuzzy case-based construction procurement selection system. *Advances in Engineering Software*, 37(3), 159–171. https://doi.org/10.1016/j.advengsoft.2005.05.004.

Mafakheri, F., Dai, L., Slezak, D. and Nasiri, F. (2007). Project delivery system selection under uncertainty: Multicriteria multilevel decision aid model. *Journal of Management in Engineering*, 23(4), 200–206. https://doi.org/10.1061/(ASCE)0742-597X(2007)23:4(200).

Matyusz, Z., Demeter, K. and Szigetvari, C. (2012). The impact of external market factors on operational practices and performance of companies. *Society and Economy*, 34(1), 73–93.

Nazariana, A., Atkinsonb, P. and Foroudic, P. (2017). Influence of national culture and balanced organizational culture on the hotel industry's performance. *International Journal of Hospitality Management*, 63(2017), 22–32. https://doi.org/10.1016/j.ijhm.2017.01.003.

Nelson, R.E. and Gopalan, S. (2003). Do organizational cultures replicate national cultures? Isomorphism, rejection and reciprocal opposition in the corporate values of three countries. *Organization Studies*, 24, 1115–1151. https://doi.org/10.1177/0170840603247006.

Nguyen, L.H. and Watanabe, T. (2017) The impact of project organisational culture on the performance of construction projects. *Sustainability*, 9 (2017), 1–21.

Nguyen, T.H.D., Chileshe, N. and Rameezedeen, R. (2018). External stakeholder strategic actions in construction projects: A Vietnamese study. *Construction Management and Economics*, 36(8), 443–458.

Nguyen, T.H.D., Chileshe, N., Rameezedeen, R. and Wood, A. (2019). External stakeholder strategic actions in projects: A multi-case study. *International Journal of Construction Management*, 37(2019), 176–191.

Obalola, T.F. (2006). Evaluation of the effects of project environment on project performance on Lagos and Abuja, Nigeria. A dissertation submitted to Federal University of Technology, Akure, Nigeria.

Ofori, G. (2012). Developing the construction industry in Ghana: The case for a central agency. https://ghanatrade.com.gh/old/file/Developing%20the%20Construction%20Industry%20in%20Ghana%20BUILDING.pdf [Accessed 5 August 2020].

Ofori, G. and Toor, S. (2009). Research on cross-cultural leadership and management in construction: A review and directions for future studies. *Construction Management and Economics*, 27(2), 11–133.

Oladapo, R.A. and Olotuah, A.O. (2007). Appropriate real estate laws and policies for sustainable development in Nigeria. *Journal of Structural Survey*, 25 (3/4), 330–338.

Opfer, W.A. and Abrams, F. (2004). Leadership: An essential element of organisational project management maturity. Paper presented at *PMI Research Conference: Innovations*. Project Management Institute, London, England; Newtown Square, PA.

Oppong, G.D. (2020) External stakeholder management at the planning stage of construction projects in Ghana: Consults perspective. Ph.D Thesis submitted to the Department and Real Estate, Hong Kong Polytechnic University, Hong Kong.

Ouchi, W.G. (1979). A conceptual framework for the design of organisational control mechanisms. *Management Science*, 25, 63–82.

Owusu Ansah, M. and Louw, L. (2019) The influence of national culture on organizational culture of multinational companies. *Cogent Social Sciences*, 5(1), 1623648. https://doi.org/10.1080/23311886.2019.1623648.

Pinto, J.K. (2000). Understanding the role of politics in successful project management. *International Journal of Project Management*, 18(2000), 85–91.

Rao, N.S.N. and Jigeesh, N. (2012) A study of reasons behind delays in pharmaceutical projects. *IUP Journal of Operations Management*, 11(2), 19.

Samaraweera, A.U.A.A. and Senaratne, S. (2012). Understanding project culture in construction: A literature synthesis. *World Construction Conference*, 28–30 June, Colombo, Sri Lanka, pp. 314–321.

Schepper, S., Dooms, M. and Haezendonck, E. (2014). Stakeholder dynamics and responsibilities in public–private partnerships: A mixed experience. *International Journal of Project Management*, 32(2014), 1210–1222.

Sheard, S.A. and Adviser-Mostashari, A. (2012). Assessing the impact of complexity attributes on system development project outcomes. Stevens Institute of Technology, Hoboken, NJ.

Sidwell, A.C. (1990). Project management: Dynamics and performance, *Construction Management and Economics*, 8(2), 159–178. https://doi.org/10.1080/01446199000000014.

Smith, L.W. (2000) Stakeholder analysis: A pivotal practice of successful projects. Paper presented at *PMI Annual Seminars and Symposium*, Houston, TX. Project Management Institute, Newtown Square, PA.

Taherdoost, H. and Keshavarzsaleh, A. (2016) Critical factors that lead to projects' success/failure in global marketplace. *Procedia Technology*, 22(2016), 1066–1075.

Tharp, J. (2012). Project management and global sustainability. Paper presented at *PMI Global Congress 2012-EMEA*, Marseilles, France. Project Management Institute, Newtown Square, PA.

Thomas, E.U. and Martin, L. (2004). *Essentials of Construction Project Management*, 1st Edition. University of New South Wales Press Ltd., Sydney, Australia.

Udo, N. and Koppensteiner, S. (2004). What are the core competencies of a successful project manager? Paper presented at *PMI Global Congress 2004-EMEA*, Prague, Czech Republic. Project Management Institute, Newtown Square, PA.

Vidal., L.A., Marle, F. and Bocquet, J.C. (2011). Measuring project complexity using the analytic hierarchy process. *International Journal of Project Management*, 29(6), 718–727.

Walker, A. (1989). *Project Management in Construction*, 2nd Edition. BSP Professional Books, Oxford, UK.

Wideman, R.M. (1990). Managing the project environment, Chapter 5. In H. Reschke and H. Schelle (Eds.), *The Dimensions of Project Management*. Springer-Verlag, Berlin, pp. 1–356.

William, W. (2002). Citizenship questions and crisis in the Niger Delta: A critical reflection. *Nordic Journal of African Studies*, 11(3), 377–382.

Williams, T.M. (1999). The need for new paradigms for complex projects. *International Journal of Project Management*, 17(5), 269–273.

Winch, G.M. (2004). Managing project stakeholders. In P.W.G. Morris and J.K. Pinto (Eds.), *The Wiley Guide to Managing Projects*. Wiley, New Jersey, pp. 321–339.

Yanwen, W. (2012). The study on complex project management in developing countries. *Physics Procedia*, 25, 1547–1552.

Youker, R. (1987). *The Development Project Environment*. World Bank EDI, Mimeo.

Youker, R. (1992). Managing the international project environment. *International Journal of Project Management*, 10(4), 219–226.

Zuo, J. and Zillante, G. (2008). Construction project culture vs. national culture. *International Conference on Multi National Construction Projects*. http:www.irb.fraunhofer.de/CIBlibrary/search-quick-result-list.jsp?A&idSuche=CIB+DC12142 [Accessed 8 August 2020].

Zuofa, T. and Ochieng, E.G. (2012). Towards the advancement of project management practice in developing countries: The case of Nigeria. Paper presented at *PMI Research and Education Conference*, Limerick, Munster, Ireland. Project Management Institute, Newtown Square, PA.

https://doi.org/10.1142/9789811224720_0015

Chapter 15

Embedding Facilities Management Knowledge into Project Management in Developing Countries

Nayanthara De Silva and Ashan Senel Asmone

University of Moratuwa, Sri Lanka

Abstract

Project managers work toward achieving specific goals while avoiding the problems that arise when delivering projects effectively and efficiently within established project constraints. One important goal of Project Management (PM) is to achieve value for money (VfM) for the clients throughout the life cycle of the project. This is a goal commonly shared with their Facilities Management (FM) counterparts. Proper PM enables the FM to reach this goal through appropriate procurement strategies and value management practices, focusing on the life cycle, and bringing to the fore consideration of a facility's operational requirements that leads to achieving minimum operational cost. In developing countries, the need for PM to incorporate FM is even more critical as the operational budgets of facilities are usually insufficient to maintain an optimum facility performance level for most of the time. In this context, in developing countries, PM is of paramount importance for the success of FM. Similarly, FM has the potential to improve PM. This chapter explores the current situation in PM and attempts to build a body of knowledge for developing countries in terms of how PM relates to, and affects, FM, and vice versa. The chapter is based on a literature review and interviews with eight experts with experience in the fields of PM and FM. In this chapter, it is established that to operationalize the PM-FM integration in construction project delivery and to attain the untapped value available from Integrated Facilities Management (IFM), the way forward for developing countries includes embracing technological advancements, applying procurement methods favorable to FM, applying FM benchmarks, and involving value-laden, knowledge-based facility managers for business processes. This chapter contributes to the development of the PM body of knowledge by exploring the current practices of embedding FM knowledge into PM, and existing FM knowledge transfer models to PM.

Keywords: Facilities management, project management, developing countries, facilities management practices, integrated facilities management, facilities management knowledge gap

Introduction

It has long been held that construction industries play a crucial role in the economic growth of developing countries (Jnr, 1996; Ofori, 2012; Shehu *et al.*, 2014). However, the industries in these countries face obstacles in delivering projects, including a lack of skills and technology, poor communication and infrastructure, and a reliance on traditional delivery methods (Agyekum *et al.*, 2020; Durdyev *et al.*, 2019; Fathalizadeh *et al.*, 2021; Ghansah *et al.*, 2021; Ingle *et al.*, 2020; Pradhananga *et al.*, 2021; Shen *et al.*, 2020; Ullah *et al.*, 2020; Wijewickrama *et al.*, 2020). At the same time, the economic gap between the developing countries and the developed nations with significantly higher per capita incomes is widening (Punnett, 2013). Appropriate use of project management (PM) in developing countries is found to be useful in overcoming these obstacles (Lizarralde *et al.*, 2013).

PM professionals are involved in avoiding problems while delivering specific project goals effectively and efficiently within established project constraints (Meng, 2013). PM consists of 10 areas of the body of knowledge: scope, time, cost, quality, human resources, communications, integration, risk, procurement, and stakeholders, with each area playing an important role by itself and through the interconnection with the other areas (Reiss, 2013). Integration of knowledge of Facilities Management (FM) into PM by early engagement of a facility manager during the design and construction phases has been discussed by many researchers, who emphasize the life-cycle approach to projects (Kalantari *et al.*, 2017; De Silva, 2011).

FM is a continual process of planning, providing, and managing facilities through the changing needs of an organization. There are 11 core competency areas of FM: communication, quality, technology management, operations and maintenance, occupancy and human factors, finance and business, emergency planning and business continuity, leadership and strategy, real estate and property management, environmental stewardship and sustainability, and PM (IFMA, 2020; Kamaruzzaman *et al.*, 2018; Okereke, 2020). Thus, while PM is concerned with delivering construction projects on time and to budget, the FM team is responsible for the efficient operation of these built facilities.

The distinction between PM and FM can be laid out by considering the main characteristics of their subjects. Owing to the nature of projects, PM activities have a defined beginning and an end. On the other hand, FM is a continual process of managing the facilities through the changing needs of an organization (Alexander, 2013). PM and FM professionals, who have the common goal of ensuring the desired performance throughout the life cycle of facilities can, and should, co-create an ecosystem where they can effect a smooth exchange of information, materials, and services towards achieving that common goal (Kumaraswamy *et al.*, 2018). The common goal of both PM and FM professionals is achieving and maintaining a facility's operation throughout the entirety of a project's life cycle (Alsharif *et al.*, 2020). Therefore, PM enhances the value of FM through value management practices, focusing on the life cycle. PM then delivers a facility's operational requirements that lead to achieving a minimum operational cost (Bajpai and Misra, 2021).

In developing countries, operational budgets for facilities are insufficient to maintain an optimum facility performance level most of the time (Ebekozien *et al.*, 2021). In this context, in developing countries, PM is of paramount importance for the success of FM. Therefore, it is vital to explore the current situation in the PM industry and attempt to build a body of knowledge for developing countries in terms of how PM affects

FM and vice versa. This chapter aims to assess the FM practices in developing countries and identify the challenges they face in the context of transferring knowledge during PM phases. A review of the relevant literature and seven online interviews were conducted for this purpose. The interviewees were identified based on their exposure (to PM and FM), period of experience (minimum of 10 years), and their availability. Based on these criteria, eight leading experts with experience in more than two developing countries were interviewed online with the aid of an interview guide. These interviewees were:

- Expert 1 (E1): Over 30 years of experience in South Asia and Europe
- Expert 2 (E2): Over 10 years of experience in South Asia
- Expert 3 (E3): Over 10 years of experience in South Asia, Southeast Asia and the Middle East
- Expert 4 (E4): Over 30 years of experience in South Asia and Southeast Asia
- Expert 5 (E5): Over 20 years of experience in Southeast Asia
- Expert 6 (E6): Over 10 years of experience in South Asia and the Middle East
- Expert 7 (E7): Over 20 years of experience in South Asia and the Middle East
- Expert 8 (E8): Over 30 years of experience in South Asia.

The interview guide covered questions relating to the nature of PM-FM integration, its presence and application in developing countries, its shortfalls, and strategies applied to overcome these shortfalls. The interviews were recorded, transcribed, and analyzed using manual content analysis. The interview findings were used to supplement the findings from the literature review.

FM in the context of PM

For a client who is commissioning a building, the PM phase delivers the building project from the inception and planning stage. However, the ultimate value for the client or the facility user is achieved when the PM phase is effectively integrated with the FM phase with common goals

(Kumaraswamy *et al.*, 2010). Such integration should be "built-in" during the design itself, rather than be "bolted on" later; this must be initiated from the beginning of the PM phases (De Silva, 2011). This integration of PM and FM, leads to innovation to ensure "Value for Money" (VfM) for stakeholders, as illustrated in Figure 15.1. FM, which is supported by four pillars: people, place, process and technology, is often considered as the management of mainly operational services, but by introducing the concept of added value, the focus can be enriched toward the stakeholders' value (Jensen, 2012).

Historically, VfM has been recognized as a decision-making tool for the public sector in developed countries such as the UK, which pursues maximum public value (i.e., economic, social, environmental well-being) in utilizing public resources (Department for Transport, 2015). However,

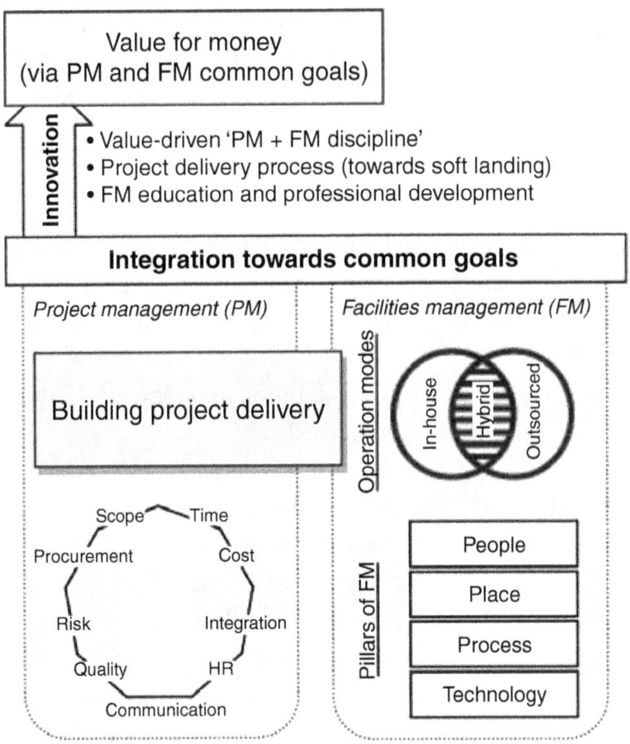

Figure 15.1: Conceptual framework.

it is often argued that the "value" is in the context of FM (Spencer and Winch, 2002). Thus, both FM and value management should be applied throughout a building's whole life cycle, starting with the early design stages. This must be a common goal shared by both PM and FM professionals. This was further elaborated upon by one Expert (E1) as:

> "(…) aligning and integrating the PM and FM professionals via common goals would ensure added holistic value far exceeding the conventional economic value of a building project, ultimately ushering in a more strategic focus on FM within client organizations as a 'VfM Service' (VfMS)(…)"

However, VfM frameworks are virtually non-existent in the context of developing countries (Almarri, 2021). This currently lost value would ideally benefit building end-users with more functional, comfortable, and safe buildings. This chapter identifies the opportunity for PM in developing countries to involve FM and work toward VfM. Figure 15.1 illustrates the conceptual framework that served as a guide for the study.

As shown in Figure 15.1, operationalizing FM has a number of forms including:

- in-house (such as in hotels and hospitality facilities where contract/temporary staff are employed through different labor contacts);
- outsourced (such as mainly in residential apartments and office spaces); and
- hybrid (such as in all types of facilities in which certain functions are either done in-house or outsourced).

The hybrid form of FM can vary and have a different meaning depending on the country, sector, and industry maturity levels. For example, it can be more of a 'soft' (managerially oriented) or 'hard' (technically oriented). For instance, FM in The Netherlands is mostly focused on the provision of services whereas in Austria, Germany, and the UK, FM is more concerned with technical aspects such as property and building management (Steenhuizen *et al.*, 2014). Further, modern facilities have become more imbued with cognitive capability and become anthropomorphized, requiring the modern facility managers to be more oriented towards soft services through technology solutions (Xu *et al.*, 2019).

FM practices in developing countries

FM first appeared as a profession in the US in 1975 and was propagated to Europe from there and to metropolises in Asia subsequently in the 1980s (Roper and Borello, 2013). Globally, FM has received much attention since the late 1980s and has made an ingress as a separate discipline within the property and construction industry (Alexander, 2013; Maas and Pleunis, 2001). Today, the FM industry in developed countries is aspiring toward establishing and improving increasingly more smart facilities and is focused on charting a new course for digitization, improved productivity, a sharing economy, greater safety, and sustainability (Bröchner *et al.*, 2019).

In developing countries, the FM profession appeared gradually in the 1980s (Quah, 1992). For example, it was first introduced into Nigeria in the early 1980s as a result of the relocation of two multi-national oil companies (Adewunmi *et al.*, 2012). It was introduced in Sri Lanka with the development of the World Trade Centre Colombo in 1993. South Africa has adopted FM as a means to enhance productivity while reducing operational costs in its industries and has seen steady growth in its application since the 1990s (Naidoo and Saheed Bayat, 2020). The authors further note that in China, while there is a rapidly growing FM market in the large cities and special economic zones, FM is virtually non-existent in other parts of the country due to entrenched cultural norms. In Brazil, on the other hand, where there is relatively higher outsourcing penetration, there is a higher FM industry growth, compared to other developing countries. FM was established as a specialized field in Malaysia in the 1990s (Kamaruzzaman *et al.*, 2018). Although there is no information on how and when FM emerged in Thailand, in the early stages of its appearance, it had been mainly focused on routine jobs such as cleaning and security services, pest control, landscaping, and the repair and maintenance works of building systems and further gained attention from academics and practitioners during the 2000s (Wisittigars and Siengthai, 2019).

Since then, the exponential growth of FM is reported in developing countries which have had a rising profile as emerging market economies (Ikediashi *et al.*, 2014; Sharma and Jain, 2016). Similarly, Kadzis (2015) noted a growth of FM in Latin America due to increased facility investments in rising regional economies. In India, changing attitudes due to growing understanding among building owners and occupiers about the life-cycle costs of a facility created new market opportunities for the FM industry (Sharma and Jain, 2016). Moreover, the growth of the FM profession in all these countries is influenced by multi-national companies and environmental sustainability compliance schemes. In line with these, the scope of the work of FM is widening, and that, in turn, has been fostering a potentially vibrant market for facility managers.

However, the FM practices in developing countries still face negative perceptions. There is a feeling that FM is an old-fashioned business which only concerns the cleaning, repair, and maintenance of buildings. There are differences between the perceptions between these developing countries and those in Europe and the US owing to a myriad of reasons, including those which are now outlined.

Differences in perceptions and culture: FM in developing countries is perceived as just a maintenance operation and an old-fashioned business which only concerns buildings, cleaning, repair, and maintenance, thereby restricting and limiting its adaptation (Kamaruzzaman *et al.*, 2018). According to E5, certain construction professionals have dubbed FM as "a nut-and-bolt job"; they do not consider FM as a professional function.

Infancy of the profession due to time lag between its emergence and its development to reach its maturity levels: Though in the early 1980s FM was introduced in some developing countries such as Nigeria and South Africa (Natukunda *et al.*, 2013), and India and Sri Lanka (expert E1), many other countries such as Malaysia (Kamaruzzaman *et al.*, 2018), Thailand (Wisittigars and Siengthai, 2019), and Uganda (Natukunda *et al.*, 2013) established it as a separate industry in the 1990s. Expert E1 stated that "lack of knowledge and skills caused mainly due to its late emergence are some of the reasons for the infancy and immaturity of the FM industry in developing countries."

Loosely defined sphere of FM activities: There is a wide and diverse scope of FM practice globally. The exact nature of FM and what FM encompasses are still up for debate, and there appears to be an unwillingness to meaningfully resolve the matter (Drion *et al.*, 2012). This has led to uncertainties and doubts in practice, especially in developing countries where the concept is still new. Expert E3 noted: "The scope of FM activities is described differently in different countries. For example, hard FM is the centrepiece of FM activities during the infancy stage of the FM industry everywhere."

Small industry with low volumes of the building stock: The market for FM in developing countries is comparatively smaller than those in the developed countries. For example, Sharma and Jain (2016) noted that market maturity, the level of understanding, and acceptance by clients in India are lower compared with Singapore, which is smaller in geographical size. They add that FM service providers in India are mostly unorganized small operators. Expert E1 has a similar view on Sri Lanka, and observed: "The FM industry in Sri Lanka is quite small, with the small volume of the building stock on which the FM services are outsourced."

Less recognition for the activity and the profession: FM activities are identified as administrative services, disregarding the strategic benefits of FM (Roper, 2017). Expert E2 observed that, in developing countries, even with standardized FM education and a breadth of competencies, organizations still hire facility professionals at the technical entry-level positions.

Fragmented and unsophisticated practice of FM: In Nigeria, Adewunmi and Ajayi (2016) observe a fragmented FM industry applying simple methods owing to the lack of investments in the use of technology for data analytics and communications among FM practitioners, and lack of client appreciation of the benefits of FM.

Position of FM in the organizational hierarchy: FM professionals are seldom involved in contributing to strategic functions of organizations. An apparent low-tier position is associated with FM in developing countries, that stems from either cultural or contextual barriers within the different layers of client organizations (Adewunmi *et al.*, 2015). For example, in Sri Lanka, the starting salary of facility managers is not as attractive as in the fields of engineering or quantity surveying and FM job positions are hardly at the strategic management level.

Archaic tenant–landlord relationships: Most clients in developing countries are individual developers with a business-as-usual attitude toward managing their facilities. Having to operate within these old paradigms has led to considerable barriers to the growth of the FM industry, as explained by Expert E3.

The above factors have affected the development of FM in developing countries and resulted in the slow progress in the growth of the industry into a mainstream business function. A soft approach with a managerial twist is not widely practiced in the FM industry in these countries. These issues in developing countries have prevented FM from attaining a strategic position in organizations as a knowledge-based profession.

Shortfalls in FM practices in developing countries

Even while cutting edge concepts such as "cognitive FM" (which is defined as active intelligent management of facilities (Xu *et al.*, 2019) are being discussed in the literature, in reality, the FM industry in developing countries such as in India, Malaysia, Nigeria, and Sri Lanka is characterized by a fragmented and unsophisticated market with various shortfalls, including inadequate knowledge and experience, less recognition, slow (or lack of) technology adoption, lack of awareness of FM, and lack of involvement of FM at the strategic level and in procurement practices. These are now discussed.

Knowledge and experience: Knowledge gaps of FM professionals hinder the growth of the FM industry. For instance, in Malaysia, the FM industry works only at operational and tactical levels in its services (Kamaruzzaman *et al.*, 2018). Whilst gaps in knowledge, skills, and capabilities necessary to adopt sustainable FM exist, local professional institutes are not building the knowledge and competencies needed. There is also a lack of knowledge on software tools such as building information modelling (BIM) (Kalantari *et al.*, 2017). In spite of the high volumes of investment and rapid development in China, a stable FM market has not emerged on the mainland, except in a few cities such as Shanghai and Beijing (Naidoo and Saheed Bayat, 2020). The Chinese FM market is relatively unsophisticated, restrictive, and limited (Gilleard, 2005). Similarly, in terms of maturity, even in India, where there are huge market revenues due to the geographical size of the country and the expanding economy, the FM market still has a long way to go (Sharma and Jain, 2016).

Recognition: FM is still contending to gain due recognition from building owners and users, despite its potential as a key driver of innovation, change, and organizational improvement (Bainbridge and Finch, 2009). This is even more apparent during the PM phase, where FM expertise is not integrated into the design, ultimately leading to a myriad of building issues during construction and in operation, which would have been avoidable if inputs had been provided by a competent FM consultant (De Silva, 2011). Moreover, as highlighted by Experts E2, E3, and E6, a perceived threat to the development of the FM industry results from a failure of potential clients to recognize its contribution to profitability, productivity, and regulatory compliance.

Technology: Limited use of technology such as information technology (IT) in the FM industry has set back its growth and improvements in its performance, due to the fragmented and unsophisticated nature of the subcontractor market for FM in developing countries where there are inadequate resources and a reluctance to bear the costs of investing in technology (Adewunmi and Ajayi, 2016). Moreover, a typically low level of expertise and non-existence of standards to measure the quality of performance in FM hinder the blending of technology into FM practice and industry.

Awareness: Facility owners and users at the back end of projects, as well as the clients and developers at the front end, are not aware of the competencies and potential strategic importance of a facility manager. Since FM has originated from the expansion of the role of a building manager or a maintenance manager, the industry expects the scope of work for FM to be the same as that of the building services engineer. FM is then perceived as a locus of technology that frequently falls short of shaping up as a forefront industry (Min *et al.*, 2016).

Strategic level involvement: The FM role can be proactive, and it can take the lead in implementing change in organizations to align the physical built environment and work processes with the organization's strategic intent (Pathirage *et al.*, 2008). Therefore, ideally, the facility manager should take a strategic position to influence and direct change for the benefit of both the owner and the core business organization (Støre-Valen and Buser, 2019). However, this development has faced many barriers in developing countries. Those highlighted in the literature include lack of steering mechanisms, financial skills, clients' understanding, process knowledge and an underpinning common knowledge and the lack of availability of methods, tools, and competencies related to the innovation process (see, for example, Häkkinen and Belloni, 2011). Therefore, a crucial challenge for facility managers is to gain attention at the strategic level in organizations and to talk the language of top management.

Outsourcing FM as a barrier to integration: In the past 20 years, there has been a clear trend toward the outsourcing of facilities services to external suppliers through formal contracts for the delivery of the core business (Ikediashi *et al.*, 2014; Atkin and Brooks, 2015). Proposing the incorporation of the role of FM into the outsourcing of goods and services, Kok *et al.* (2011) defined FM as a coordinating role between demand and supply of the facility. One perception is that the growth of FM organizations is a positive development, as it is generating specialized management and service delivery functions, new employment opportunities, and growth in the range of services offered, while encouraging the professionalization of FM and creating a separate and distinct industry sector (Drion *et al.*, 2012; Natukunda *et al.*, 2013). Contrary to the marketable benefits expected from the outsourcing of facility services, the expectation of "creating greater synergy between the client and the contractor from shared market advantage or shared costs and risk" has been hindered by a lack of performance-based service contracts (Ikediashi and Okwuashi, 2015; Lai *et al.*, 2006).

Moreover, the common practice of "reducing cost via FM outsourcing" in developing countries is challenged by the emergence of concepts such as VfMS (Natukunda *et al.*, 2013). This was underlined by these comments of E8: "(...) everybody is cost conscious. Everyone wants to get value for money (...) but when they outsource, they prioritize functionality and then the cost (and) not value for money or innovation."

The counter view would be that this growth has impeded innovation in FM and it has hindered the emergence of an intellectually coherent FM market and limited the opportunity for embedding FM knowledge into PM (Perera *et al.*, 2016). This is mainly because, when outsourced, the facility manager is an external party who acts mainly as a managing contractor and therefore, is less concerned with optimization opportunities. As Expert E2, who is an in-house facility manager, observed:

> "(...) design feedback is not sent to the client from parties engaged during PM, and by outsourced FM service providers. This causes repetitions in issues in facilities (...) Only the client-side FM is motivated by innovation and committed to providing feedback to seek VfMS (...) I have the freedom to do innovations (sic)."

Embedding FM knowledge into PM

FM is seen as a strategic management role, responsible for aligning people, work processes, and the physical environment according to an organization's strategic intent and ultimately to add value (Jensen *et al.*, 2012). Hence, embracing the facility manager's experience-based knowledge at the early design stages on the project would enable inputs toward operational efficiency to be made (Kalantari *et al.*, 2017; Meng, 2013; De Silva, 2011). However, facility managers are usually not sufficiently experienced or capable of being accepted as an equal dialog partner in the design process (Jensen, 2009). The operationalization of the concept of Facilities Management Knowledge Transfer (FMKT) would play a crucial role in embedding FM knowledge into PM. Jensen (2012) developed a topology for FMKT by introducing the concepts of front-end (such as requirements at the briefing stage) and back-end (i.e., performance at the commissioning stage) knowledge transfer. Multiple strategies can be used by facility managers to share potentially useful information during those stages, but there is little application of this in developing countries because early involvement of FM is still not a common practice in developing countries.

Many of the gaps and challenges in FM in developing countries which are identified in this study relate to information sharing and the project delivery process. Strategies proposed in the literature to overcome these gaps and challenges are now discussed.

Clients' involvement in FMKT

The success of FMKT is based on the existence of interaction and collaboration between the practitioners in the PM and FM phases (Jensen *et al.*, 2018), and as highlighted earlier, that is a challenging task due to high imbalance between those phases in developing countries. Ideally, the client should be the initiator in establishing those lines of communication. Best *et al.* (2003) emphasized that the client's role should become a strategic rather than operational function by considering FM as value-adding rather than cost-saving. Hence, the poor knowledge of the client or client's consultant about the benefits of FMKT has to be overcome in developing countries (Akdag and Maqsood, 2019).

Furthermore, governments and public agencies should formulate and enforce standards by which the clients of each large project are required to employ a qualified facility manager in the commissioning and handing over process. In this context, developing countries can learn lessons from Singapore and Hong Kong, which are known as trendsetters in Asia in the application of good FM practices with a high level of client understanding of the benefits of incorporating FM in the design and construction phases.

FMKT technologies

FMKT can be viewed as capturing building in-use experiences and embedding such FM knowledge into the PM phase to optimize the functionality of building projects. Communication is of paramount importance in the application of FMKT. Traditionally, these modes of communication include meetings with relevant stakeholders (inclusive of FM, discussing gaps and their causes, and possible solutions), monitoring and reporting, providing drivers (such as an operating platform) and incentives for stakeholders, and ensuring a lower turnover of stakeholders for a seamless transfer of knowledge. Moreover, with the rapid growth of the building sector, technology has enabled advancements of this protocol in terms of timeliness and effectiveness. For example, in the literature, BIM-enabled FM applications (BIM-FM) are found to facilitate FMKT (Matarneh *et al.*, 2018).

Liu and Issa (2014) assert that knowledge sharing between the FM and design professionals during the early stages of building projects has become possible with BIM, benefiting the safety, sustainability, and maintainability of buildings. BIM can store all kinds of information of systems and processes from the PM stages as big data, transcending the conventional CAD-based drawings. As noted by Golabchi *et al.* (2016), BIM technology can potentially contain a complete set of information of the life cycle of the building in the form of a digital model that allows automated decision making. It is widely projected to be a dominant technology in future; enabling digitization in FM. BIM-FM provides holistic operation and maintenance (O&M) that could include maintenance troubleshooting, scheduling, digital wayfinding, automated measurement and verification of equipment performance (such as those of air handling units and chillers), locating components, facilitating real-time data access, visualization and marketing, 3D visualization for facility operations and continuous commissioning (Becerik-Gerber *et al.*, 2012; Gao and Pishdad-Bozorgi, 2019).

Moreover, these technologies can facilitate smart O&M that includes optimization of energy, comfort, workspace, ICT asset management, and maintenance using predictive analytics. In this way, FM can strive to achieve lower O&M costs, provide more precise controls, and deliver cost-effective services for the occupants of buildings. For example, the application of advanced BIM technologies has been found to enable facility managers to realize time savings of up to 80 percent (Davtalab, 2017). At the same time, these technological advancements were found to deliver cost-effective services for the occupants (Marzouk and Zaher, 2020).

Furthermore, preventive/predictive maintenance programs can be run on digital platforms using BIM, Virtual Reality (VR), and other models that are developed during the design and construction phases (Wen and

Gheisari, 2020). However, practical approaches should be applied to link the design phase with the FM phase, through the PM phase, of a construction project; to effectively implement technologies such as BIM (Hosseini *et al.*, 2018; Wijekoon *et al.*, 2018). Even so, as Dixit *et al.* (2019) point out, application of BIM-FM tasks and decision-making seems limited because of the multiplicity of issues relating to technology execution and information management: technology, cost, and legal and contractual aspects. Authors further add that, with incompatibility between the building automation systems and other FM technologies with BIM, interchangeability of data in a shared platform would not be possible (Borhani *et al.*, 2017; Parsanezhad and Dimyadi, 2014). Moreover, the facility managers usually play a traditional role and thus have no incentive to adopt modern technologies. Thus, digitization in FM is not yet a reality in developing countries.

As Bui *et al.* (2016) indicated, only limited attention has been given to BIM implementation in the construction industry in developing countries due to high initial cost and lack of knowledge and experience, and thus, more work is needed to develop BIM-FM technologies. Hence, such credible models for sustained communication in developing countries have yet to be established. In this context, governments have a vital role to play in promoting the use of such technologies in large projects. As elaborated upon by Expert E1;

> "(...)currently nobody is using (BIM-FM). I don't think anybody is using that platform, maybe this happens in Singapore and UK, but I don't think BIM is used in many developing countries. Here, people are unaware (of BIM) other than a few companies or few specialists (...) We should promote the shift from CAD to BIM-FM with real-time data during O&M, possibly through mega-scale projects that are funded by foreign investors."

FM involvement in pre-construction, testing, and commissioning stages

Overemphasis on the technical aspects of building systems, while neglecting legal instruments such as warranties, bank guarantees, and insurance during the PM phase can adversely impact the overall project cost. This was highlighted by Expert E4: "FM expertise (knowledge) to leverage (or make provision for) the use of warranties, sureties, bankers guarantees, insurance during design and construction can save millions when it comes to downstream claims and payments." Conversely, if properly utilized with the experience-based FM knowledge during the PM phase, these instruments can yield benefits to the project when it comes to downstream claims and payments. In this regard, the facility managers need to have sound overall knowledge of what building projects must achieve so that they can contribute toward the aims of the client or business organization over the long term (Brown *et al.*, 2001).

In reality, in developing countries, there are no appointed facility managers by the time the facilities are commissioned and handed over. Their appointment during the early design stages is even rarer. For example, government hospital buildings in the Philippines that are equipped with critical building services are handed over to facilities personnel who have no proper knowledge of FM (Dela Cruz and Ortega-Dela Cruz, 2019). Many examples of similar issues in Sri Lanka due to the lack of involvement of FM during the commissioning stages were raised during the interviews with industry experts (E6 and E8). These included expensively built facilities being abandoned before the end of their service life due to the lack of expertise and experience of the technicians to whom these facilities are handed over and their consequent inability to address failures occurring during the operational stages. Most of these examples were on public-funded healthcare facilities. Other identified issues included: the clients getting into unsuitable service agreements with the suppliers, and early defects not being rectified during the defects liability period due to lack of proper testing or reporting after the handing over. These issues identified in Sri Lanka have also been found to be prevalent in other developing countries (Fatayer *et al.*, 2019; Olanrewaju *et al.*, 2010; Shafiq *et al.*, 2020). Therefore, there is a long way to go in developing countries, as a revolution is required: in the way project teams are appointed, in the way contracts are written, in the level of integration among members of the supply chain, and the roles and responsibilities of the experts in the whole industry in terms of establishing integrated facilities management (IFM).

Procurement practices

Procurement practices used in the PM phase are more established through standard conditions of contracts. However, there are many challenges in the FM phase with regard to contractual issues. These include: the absence of a standard form of contract; poor understanding of contract formation and the relevant provisions of contracts; inadequate definition of the scope of services; unclear roles, responsibilities, and targets; shortfalls in procedures for awarding contracts; and unfavorable contract terms (Ikediashi and Okwuashi, 2015; Ikediashi *et al.*, 2012; Lai *et al.*, 2004, 2006). De Silva *et al.* (2018) noted that developing a similar procurement protocol between PM and FM in the context of Sri Lanka is believed to be too novel and also the construction industry has no "room" for such innovative developments in the traditional system given the continuing chain of high-pressure projects.

IFM as a collaborative setting

The term "integration" in the context of linking the PM and FM phases is beset by paradoxes, among which is the variety of terms used — these include: Total Facilities Management (TFM), Total Asset Management (TAM), Facilities Project Management, and IFM. The discussion of emerging benefits from these concepts has stagnated; it has not moved on from the initial consideration of a few areas such as maintainability and sustainability (Asmone *et al.*, 2019). There has been less emphasis on other key issues such as operability and serviceability, concerning the whole life cycle of the building (Meng, 2013). Thus, creating a voice, such as through scholarly articles, has not led to significant progress. In practice, clients and developers are concerned about the increase in the initial cost which, in their perception, would result from the introduction of the role of the facility manager, and fail to see what facility managers have to offer in the design process, as well as the life-cycle benefits (Jensen *et al.*, 2014). This is even more the case when the client or developer is not among the end-users of the building. Moreover, when professionals operate in their silos, it leads to the emergence of many barriers for IFM. These include: client-side barriers (such as focus on capital cost, lack of awareness of the benefits), designer-side barriers (for example, low priority to life-cycle operability, less recognition of FM) and FM-side barriers (such as lack of knowledge and experience of the field) (Meng, 2013).

In India, a developing country with a large construction volume, IFM is practiced strictly in big projects carried out by private developers; it is not much used in public projects. Experts' view is that those who implement IFM have identified the financial benefits of such implementation. However, in neighboring Sri Lanka, the practice of IFM is carried out on only a handful of projects with international investors. As indicated by E2, this may be because construction projects are still profitable under current PM practices; thus, there is no incentive to change the *status quo*. This shows a disparity between the two different construction markets, where the life-cycle financial benefits are identified in one and ignored in another. Further militating against the implementation of IFM is the cost of obtaining experience-based FM knowledge during the PM phase, and the poor emphasis on whole life cost considerations to justify spending upfront to reduce the costs during the FM phase. This can be factored into the procurement practices and policies practiced in developing countries. However, adverse effects of short-term thinking in such practices are observable in a large number of building and infrastructure projects in developing countries.

"FM-favorable" procurement practices

The form of procurement of a building project has important implications for the extent to which FM knowledge transfer mechanisms are relevant or favorable (Jensen, 2012). To that end, a change in the existing procurement practices is necessary. The client should realize the strategic importance of the built-up space of their facility to their business and those of the end-users. In this context, the facility manager needs to be the client representative, from the early stages, to form the vision of the facility. As explained by E4, who is an expert in value-based FM, FM needs to be involved with the whole construction project, not only at the tail end; the facility manager has to be the clients' representative, involved from the beginning, even as early as when meeting the bankers to secure funds for the development.

Facility managers should be creating their unique value in this manner and should then be supported with the required investment, and remuneration for the value addition for which they are responsible. Thus, the FM process may involve whole life-cost analysis, projecting facility plans, and reviewing project proposals in the context of facility operation and core business requirements (El-Haram and Agapiou, 2002). Some enablers for FM-favorable procurement are now discussed.

Integrating FM operations through long-term contracts

Implementation of FM services such as hard FM through PPP (FM-PPP) is considered as a transition from a building contract to a service contract (Hashim *et al.*, 2016). Government-owned facilities such as hospitals, airports and harbors that provide round-the-clock critical services are potential facilities for FM-PPP contracts. In FM-PPP contracts, operational and maintenance costs of facilities can be estimated with increased certainty at the outset of projects, thus allowing the public sector to have knowledge of longer-term spending commitments and ensuring that the facility is properly maintained over the entire contract period. Thus, FM organizations have to play a strategic role in these contracts (Samuel, 2016).

PPP units have been set up in many developing countries to serve as the focal point for coordinating and managing the PPP programs. Different modes of PPP approaches are practiced in developing countries, based on the financial regulations of the local governments and the mode of operation of the project (Lu *et al.*, 2019). However, as mentioned by the World Bank Public–Private-Partnership Legal Resource Center (PPPLRC), PPPs can be susceptible to corruption unless they are carefully planned (PPPLRC, 2020). Moreover, the effective implementation of FM-PPP in developing countries is difficult without the realization of appropriate transitions and reforms (Almarri and Abuhijleh, 2017). For example, risk-sharing through shared gain/loss mechanisms is not well defined in long-term service contracts. There is a lack of understanding of FM-PPP and privatization among the public in developing countries. This, along with other constraints, such as interference from vested interests (such as the trades unions) and lack of policies, legal frameworks, and procedures were found to have imposed constraints on the effective implementation of FM-PPP contracts (Samuel, 2016). Moreover, FM-specific guidelines for PPP are not common at national program levels. As long as the clients do not understand the benefits of VfM in PPP, this procurement model would not be preferred by them. Hence, there must be a shared understanding of the strategic objectives of PPP between the owners and the facility managers (Brewer *et al.*, 2013).

Relational value networks

Relational contracting is a flexible procurement approach directed at optimizing project performance through the relational integration of all stakeholders of a project, by engaging them in "cross-linked value networks." Linking PM to FM, a relationally integrated value network (RIVANS) was recommended as a means of integrating the stakeholders of the PM and FM phases via crosslinks (Kumaraswamy *et al.*, 2010). Madhusanka *et al.* (2020) extended RIVANS developed by Kumaraswamy *et al.* (2010) to portfolio management to enable better team integration, thereby delivering greater value to meet long-term performance goals. However, this model was challenged by existing weak cross-links (i.e., lack of relationships among stakeholders) confronting the attempts to gain potential benefits through integration of PM and FM in developing countries (De Silva *et al.*, 2017).

FM benchmarking

In a competitive market, enterprises implement best practices for FM service providers to make breakthrough improvements and to operate cost-effectively (Adebanjo *et al.*, 2010). In particular, "whole life FM benchmarking" has been used by facility managers as an innovative tool aiming to optimize life-cycle cost, space requirements, and operational performance. However, it is more commonly used for comparing cost levels, while other aspects of FM such as "space," "quality," and "process" benchmarks are neglected (Wauters, 2005). For this good practice to be most effective, it should be positioned at the outset of the project. Thus, FM benchmarking could provide the facility managers with valuable information to improve the overall FM service delivery as VfMS, by being able to focus on either facility-related issues or business performance (Gilleard and Yat-lung, 2004).

Although FM benchmarking in Nigeria could help companies to have an external focus and find industry best practices by constantly comparing their performance against that of others, it has yet to gain wide acceptance and thus, there is a lack of professionalism and transparency in the industry (Adewunmi *et al.*, 2015; Adewunmi and Ajayi, 2016). They added that many organizations tend not to link strategic vision with the need to benchmark. According to an expert in the field of energy management in Sri Lanka, wastage of electrical power is significantly higher in the country due to high transmission and distribution losses. This observation is corroborated by reports from other developing countries (Hassan and Kamal, 2016; Jiménez *et al.*, 2014). Expert E7 highlighted that the country does "not need any more power plants to be built if energy losses from cables are minimised. But (there are) no benchmarks to define the limits for the wastage (...)." Since the application of benchmarking has yet to gain wide acceptance, setting up KPIs to guide effort towards maximizing operational efficiency, minimizing wastage, optimizing design/space, and so on, should be set as specific goals. Amos *et al.* (2020) proposed more specific KPIs for government hospitals in Ghana where FM practice is in its infancy, and generalized their observations to developing countries.

A soft establishment of FM benchmarks can be done through instruments such as national-level policies, indices, standards, certification, and awards. For example, with the emergence of the COVID-19 pandemic, the Sri Lanka Standard Institution (SLSI) published a standard on COVID-19 safety management system requirements for organizations (SLS 1672, 2020) for manufacturing and service organizations to maintain a pandemic-free environment, which facility managers can then use to benchmark their facilities.

Developing a shared communication protocol between PM and FM

One of the most commonly expressed frustrations with regard to communication between FM and PM (mainly during design and construction) is simply the use of abbreviations and acronyms (Kalantari *et al.*, 2017). RIVANS may build cross-links among stakeholders in PM and FM (Kumaraswamy *et al.*, 2018), while technologies such as BIM would enable information sharing in supply chains for continuous operation of a facility (Liu and Issa, 2014).

However, De Silva *et al.* (2018) noted that the construction industry in the developing countries has little time or "space" for such innovative developments in the traditional system unless otherwise learning from experiences from developed countries or encouraging effective information sharing system by a group of high-powered clients from mega-development projects.

Bridging the gap in body of knowledge

It is a requisite for the construction industry to achieve smooth operating smart, safe, comfortable, and energy-efficient facilities. Integrating experience-based FM knowledge has the potential to improve the functionality and overall efficiency of the building O&M and enhance tenant productivity and comfort, whilst providing an overall VfM facility. On the other hand, it has long been held that most, if not all, processes that most influence resource utilization and waste generation of a facility fall under the purview of FM (Shah, 2007). Hence, IFM as a collaborative concept is considered as an opportunity to share lessons learnt during the FM phase with the PM phase to design and build facilities with the desirable features, which ultimately contribute to the competitiveness of the enterprises using them, and the wellness of the occupiers.

The fragmentation between PM and FM in the traditional construction industry can be demonstrated in practical terms, yet the core competencies of both are required in order to strengthen and enhance the further development and more mainstream application of IFM. Thus, a radical change in the practice is required and some relevant recommendations for such changes are now considered.

Value-driven "PM+FM discipline"

VfM has been identified as a desirable goal that is common to both the construction and occupancy of buildings (Ive, 2006), and Expert E1 held that it should also be the centerpiece of IFM. When it comes to FM, VfM should be analyzed using whole life cost. In developing countries, FM practitioners often focus on managing costs rather than thinking in terms of "adding value" (Olanrewaju and Abdul-Aziz, 2015). There is a need for FM practitioners to check the appropriateness of the future facility operations during the building design (Isa *et al.*, 2017). An example drawn from the interviews in Sri Lanka was that the selection of the "best" suitable chiller in an air conditioning system needs to involve an analysis of the running cost to optimize it with the functionality. As held by E7, "(...) selecting a chiller with part-loading option or having variable speed drives would be the better energy saving option for the built environment when the demand for air conditioning is variable."

However, as noted by Expert (E3), "(...) without the contribution of their timely insights as FM practitioners during the PM phases, the designers of many building projects in Sri Lanka would install the least cost option although these have undesirable operational characteristics." This is highlighted as one of the perennial problems in the construction industry, which has a limited mindset when it comes to learning from experiences of the O&M phase of existing facilities (De Silva, 2011) as an aspiration to the status of a "value-driven PM+FM discipline" when new facilities are planned, designed, constructed, commissioned, and operated.

Project delivery process: Driving toward "soft landing"

The soft landing approach has been proposed by the UK government to minimize the knowledge gap in construction projects while paving a way for IFM (Philp *et al.*, 2019). It is suggested that the well-recognized RIBA

Plan of Work should encompass the soft landing approach, which enables a smooth handing over of constructed facilities (Way and Bordass, 2005). It is also considered as a client-driven management tool by which every team member has an opportunity to contribute positively (Gana *et al.*, 2018). Nor *et al.* (2019) suggested that soft landing should be used as a commissioning test tool for public universities in Malaysia. Developing countries have yet to investigate the adaptability of this approach to their construction industries (Samarakkody *et al.*, 2020). Moreover, Donohoe and Coggins (2015) noted that soft landing has not been greeted with universal acclaim; within the construction industry, there is sufficient interest to justify the use of soft landing as an alternative to the use of the retention sum to ensure delivery of buildings. Gana *et al.* (2018) revealed that strong relationships and teamwork needed to be established among stakeholders of a project for a soft landing approach to be successful. Thus, in developing countries, radical changes in the existing compartmentalized traditional thinking and practices are required to make soft landing a professional service in order to realize the "soft landing" of projects.

FM education and professional development

In FM education and professional development programs, creating opportunities for a facility manager to network with the PM team has not been fully addressed. Drion *et al.* (2012) pointed out a lack of "fit" between the FM profession and FM educators in institutions of higher education. FM education can develop potential professionals from the PM sphere to understand FM competencies, allowing for effective bridging between these professions. Therefore, FM education through Bachelor or Master programs can enhance the FM industry. Yet, these programs require certain changes in the core competencies they seek to build and should be supplemented by PM knowledge (Steenhuizen *et al.*, 2014). Proper education and professional development is essential to develop FM and PM to prosper with VfM practices, as asserted by E4 and E5. This sentiment is shared by Lizarralde *et al.* (2013), who found that in developing countries, PM is most often learned through professional practice rather than through formal education.

The International Facilities Management Association (IFMA), which is known as the world's largest and most widely recognized association for FM professionals, was established in 1980, and has chapters in developing countries such as India, Malaysia, and Nigeria. In line with IFMA's stress on networking, many developing countries, including India, South Africa, Malaysia, Thailand, and Sri Lanka have established local professional organizations. According to Wisittigars and Siengthai (2019), in 2008, the Thailand Facility Management Association was set up and became a key center for FM, and later, some universities started to offer FM programs. South Africa also has an organization, the South African Facilities Management Association, formed in 2011, that seeks to develop the area. In 2012, the Institute of Facilities Management Sri Lanka was established as an apex body for further developing the FM profession by actively functioning to improve competencies of FM practitioners.

Moreover, in Sri Lanka, as a result of rapid economic growth after it adopted an open economy in the early 1980s, a number of large-scale facilities of many types, such as housing, high-rise buildings and condominiums, hospitals, and industrial buildings have been constructed. With rapid urbanization, industrial development, and uplifting of the social standards of people, a market for FM has been created. With gradual increased demand for a problem-free built environment to work in, and to increase the effectiveness and efficiency of the business and its employees, a need for a separate profession arose. FM education was initiated in 2006 with the commencement of a Bachelor of Science degree program in Facilities Management. Its graduates are absorbed by different industries and sectors such as commercial, industrial, medical, housing, and construction for various positions including building operational management, maintenance management, social compliance and safety management.

Implications for developing countries

Developing countries have a gap to bridge when integrating PM with FM to achieve VfM in building project delivery. To bridge this gap, they can adopt lessons from the developed countries to overcome the various challenges, including lack of knowledge on, experience in, and awareness and recognition of, FM in developing countries. Figure 15.2 presents a

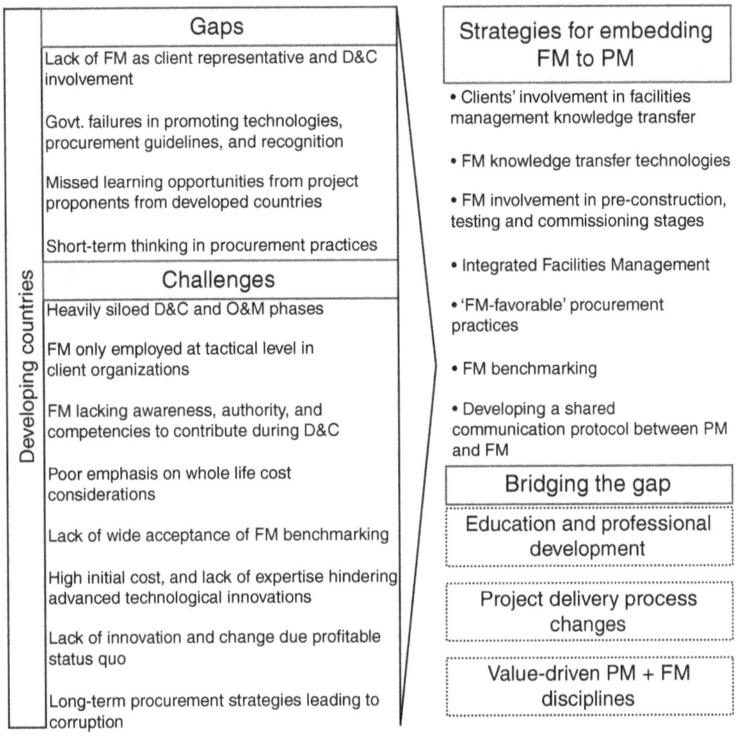

Figure 15.2: FM in the context of PM in developing countries.

framework of how this can be achieved by outlining different strategies for embedding FM knowledge into the PM phase, such that the identified gaps and challenges are overcome.

Some of the strategies discussed in this chapter have already been implemented either fully or in part in some developing countries. Hence, there exists knowledge on the success factors of such implementation. PM professionals can draw from such success factors to align their projects in such a way to draw most information from building in-use data by integrating the knowledge possessed by their FM counterparts. Ultimately, this approach can be used to execute an integration of operational processes across separate functional silos, integrating systems, people, and processes, with significant benefits for the fields of PM and FM in developing countries.

Conclusion

Professionals from the PM and FM fields should integrate their expertise to some degree by recognizing the value-adding role which can be provided throughout the entire life cycle of built items to improve the propensity for successful project delivery in forming built environments that are functional, comfortable, and safe to work and live in. The involvement of FM at the strategic level of organizations is important for this; it should be preceded by due recognition for the FM profession within the construction community such that FM professionals are welcomed by the PM team as bringing value addition, rather than being a cost burden and a necessary evil.

To operationalize the PM-FM integration in building project delivery and to realize the untapped value available from IFM, the way forward for developing countries includes embracing technological advancements and applying FM-favorable procurement methods, FM benchmarks, and shared communication protocols. A soft landing approach; value-laden, knowledge-based facility managers for business processes; and comprehensive FM education are foremost drivers in the development of the body of knowledge. This chapter contributes to the PM body of knowledge by exploring the current practices of embedding FM knowledge into PM (PM-FM), studying existing FM-to-PM knowledge transfer methods, and proposing innovative strategies for bridging the knowledge gap. This chapter is therefore useful for PM professionals; they can draw from success factors identified here to align their projects in such a way as to take advantage of building in-use information and integrate the knowledge possessed by their FM counterparts into their projects.

References

Adebanjo, D., Abbas, A. and Mann, R. (2010). An investigation of the adoption and implementation of benchmarking. *International Journal of Operations & Production Management*, 30(11), 1140–1169.

Adewunmi, Y., Omirin, M. and Koleoso, H. (2012). Developing a sustainable approach to corporate FM in Nigeria. *Facilities*, 30(9/10), 350–373.

Adewunmi, Y.A. and Ajayi, O.D. (2016). Attitudes of Nigerian facilities management professionals to the benefits of benchmarking. *Facilities*, 34(7/8), 468–492.

Adewunmi, Y.A., Omirin, M. and Koleoso, H. (2015). Benchmarking challenges in facilities management in Nigeria. *Journal of Facilities Management*, 13(2), 156–184.

Agyekum, K., Ghansah, F.A., Tetteh, P.A. and Amudjie, J. (2020). The role of project managers (PMs) in construction health and safety implementation in Ghana. *Journal of Engineering, Design and Technology*, 19(1), 245–262.

Akdag, S.G. and Maqsood, U. (2019). A roadmap for BIM adoption and implementation in developing countries: The Pakistan case. *Archnet-IJAR: International Journal of Architectural Research*, 14(1), 112–132.

Alexander, K. (2013). *Facilities Management: Theory and Practice*. Taylor & Francis, Abingdon, UK.

Almarri, K. (2021). Comparative analysis of the value for money factors of PPPs between the UAE and the UK. *International Journal of Construction Management*, 21(4), 416–426.

Almarri, K. and Abuhijleh, B. (2017). A qualitative study for developing a framework for implementing public–private partnerships in developing countries. *Journal of Facilities Management*, 15(2), 170–189.

Alsharif, M.A., Peters, M.D. and Dixon, T.J. (2020). Designing and implementing effective campus sustainability in Saudi Arabian universities: An assessment of drivers and barriers in a rational choice theoretical context. *Sustainability*, 12(12), 5096.

Amos, D., Musa, Z.N. and Au-Yong, C.P. (2020). Performance measurement of facilities management services in Ghana's public hospitals. *Building Research & Information*, 48(2), 218–238.

Asmone, A.S., Conejos, S. and Chew, M.Y.L. (2019). Green maintainability performance indicators for highly sustainable and maintainable buildings. *Building and Environment*, 163, 106315.

Atkin, B. and Brooks, A. (2015). *Total Facility Management*. Wiley Blackwell, Chichester.

Bainbridge, M. and Finch, E.F. (2009). Getting the attention the facilities manager deserves. *Facilities*, 27(7/8), 277.

Bajpai, A. and Misra, S.C. (2021). Analyzing key barriers for adoption of digitalization in Indian construction industry: A Case Study. In C.R. Panigrahi, B. Pati, B.K. Pattanayak, S. Amic and K.-C. Li (Eds.), *Progress in Advanced Computing and Intelligent Engineering*. Springer, Singapore, pp. 683–693.

Becerik-Gerber, B., Jazizadeh, F., Li, N. and Calis, G. (2012). Application areas and data requirements for BIM-enabled facilities management. *Journal of Construction Engineering and Management*, 138(3), 431–442.

Best, R., Langston, C.A. and De Valence, G. (2003). *Workplace Strategies and Facilities Management*. Routledge, Oxford.

Borhani, A., Lee, H.W., Dossick, C.S., Osburn, L. and Kinsman, M. (2017). BIM to facilities management: Presenting a proven workflow for information exchange. In *ASCE International Workshop on Computing in Civil Engineering 2017*, 51–58.

Brewer, G., Gajendran, T., Jefferies, M., McGeorge, D., Rowlinson, S. and Dainty, A. (2013). Value through innovation in long-term service delivery: Facility management in an Australian PPP. *Built Environment Project and Asset Management*, 3(1), 74–88.

Bröchner, J., Haugen, T. and Lindkvist, C. (2019). Shaping tomorrow's facilities management. *Facilities*, 37(7/8), 366–380.

Brown, A., Hinks, J. and Sneddon, J. (2001). The facilities management role in new building procurement. *Facilities*, 19(3/4), 119–130.

Bui, N., Merschbrock, C. and Munkvold, B.E. (2016). A review of building information modelling for construction in developing countries. *Procedia Engineering*, 164, 487–494.

Davtalab, O. (2017). Benefits of real-time data driven BIM for FM departments in operations control and maintenance. In *ASCE International Workshop on Computing in Civil Engineering (IWCCE 2017)*, Seattle, pp. 202–210.

Department for Transport. (2015). Value for money framework. London, UK. https://assets.publishing.service.gov.uk/government/uploads/system/uploads/attachment_data/file/918479/value-for-money-framework.pdf [Accessed 14 June 2021].

De Silva, N. (2011). Promoting the facilities management profession in the project development phase of high-rise buildings in Sri Lanka. *Built-Environment Sri Lanka*, 9(1–2), 37–44.

De Silva, N., Weerasinghe, N., Madhusanka, H.W.N. and Kumaraswamy, M. (2018). Enablers of relational integrated value networks (RIVANS) for total facilities management (TFM). *Journal of Financial Management of Property and Construction*, 23(2), 170–184.

De Silva, N., Weerasinghe, R., Madhusanka, H.W.N. and Kumaraswamy, M. (2017). Relationally integrated value networks (RIVANS) for total facilities management (TFM). *Built Environment Project and Asset Management*, 7(3), 313–329.

Dela Cruz, R.Z. and Ortega-Dela Cruz, R.A. (2019). Addressing facility management issues and challenges common among public health care institutions in a developing country. *International Journal of Healthcare Management*, 14(1), 107–113.

Department for Transport. (2015). *Value for Money Framework*, London, UK. https://assets.publishing.service.gov.uk/government/uploads/system/uploads/attachment_data/file/918479/value-for-money-framework.pdf [Accessed 14 June 2021].

Dixit, M.K., Venkatraj, V., Ostadalimakhmalbaf, M., Pariafsai, F. and Lavy, S. (2019). Integration of facility management and building information modeling (BIM). *Facilities*, 37(7/8), 455–483.

Donohoe, S. and Coggins, J.K. (2015). Soft landings or a bumpy touch down. *31st Annual Association of Researchers in Construction Management (ARCOM) Conference*, 31, 43–52.

Drion, B., Melissen, F. and Wood, R. (2012). Facilities management: Lost, or regained? *Facilities*, 30(5/6), 254–261.

Durdyev, S., Hosseini, M.R., Martek, I., Ismail, S. and Arashpour, M. (2019). Barriers to the use of integrated project delivery (IPD): A quantified model for Malaysia. *Engineering, Construction and Architectural Management*, 27(1), 186–204.

Ebekozien, A., Dominic Duru, O.S. and Dako, O.E. (2021). Maintenance of public hospital buildings in Nigeria — An assessment of current practices and policy options, *Journal of Facilities Management*, 20(1), 120–143.

El-Haram, M.A. and Agapiou, A. (2002). The role of the facility manager in new procurement routes. *Journal of Quality in Maintenance Engineering*, 8(2), 124–134.

Fatayer, F.A., Hassanain, M.A., Abdallah, A. and Al-Hammad, A.-M. (2019). Investigation of facilities management practices for providing feedback during the design development and review stages. *International Journal of Building Pathology and Adaptation*, 37(5), 597–614.

Fathalizadeh, A., Hosseini, M.R., Vaezzadeh, S.S., Edwards, D.J., Martek, I. and Shooshtarian, S. (2021). Barriers to sustainable construction project management: the case of Iran, *Smart and Sustainable Built Environment*, 11(3), 717–739. https://doi.org/10.1108/SASBE-09-2020-0132.

Fayasa, A.F., De Silva, N., Kumaraswamy, M. and Lai, J.H.K. (2020). Dimensions of space — Multi-disciplinary approaches. *13th Faculty of Architecture Research Unit (FARU) International Research Conference*, Sri Lanka.

Gana, V., Giridharan, R. and Watkins, R. (2018). Application of soft landings in the design management process of a non-residential building. *Architectural Engineering and Design Management*, 14(3), 178–193.

Gao, X. and Pishdad-Bozorgi, P. (2019). BIM-enabled facilities operation and maintenance: A review. *Advanced Engineering Informatics*, 39, 227–247.

Ghansah, F.A., Owusu-Manu, D.-G., Ayarkwa, J., Edwards, D.J. and Hosseini, M.R. (2021). Exploration of latent barriers inhibiting project management processes in adopting smart building technologies (SBTs) in the developing countries. *Construction Innovation*, 21(4), 685–707.

Gilleard, J.D. (2005). *Facility Management in China: An Emerging Market*. Hong Kong Chapter of IFMA, Hong Kong.

Gilleard, J.D. and Yat-lung, P.W. (2004). Benchmarking facility management: Applying analytic hierarchy process. *Facilities*, 22(1/2), 19–25.

Golabchi, A., Akula, M. and Kamat, V. (2016). Automated building information modeling for fault detection and diagnostics in commercial HVAC systems. *Facilities*, 34(3/4), 233–246.

Häkkinen, T. and Belloni, K. (2011). Barriers and drivers for sustainable building. *Building Research & Information*, 39(3), 239–255.

Hashim, H.A., Sapri, M. and Low, S.-T. (2016). Public private partnership (PPP) facilities management for healthcare services in Malaysia: The challenges of implementation, *Journal of Facilities Management*, 14(4), 350–362.

Hassan, S.Z. and Kamal, T. (2016). Evaluating the issues and challenges in context of the energy crisis of Pakistan. *Indian Journal of Science and Technology*, 9, 36.

Hosseini, M.R., Roelvink, R., Papadonikolaki, E., Edwards, D.J. and Pärn, E. (2018). Integrating BIM into facility management: Typology matrix of information handover requirements. *International Journal of Building Pathology and Adaptation*, 36(1), 2–14.

IFMA (2020). 11 core competencies of facility management. *International Facilities Management Association*. https://ifmacdn.azureedge.net/sfcdn/docs/default-source/marketing/pd-pages/11-core-competencies_oct2020.pdf?sfvrsn=2 [Accessed 20 December 2020].

Ikediashi, D. and Okwuashi, O. (2015). Significant factors influencing outsourcing decision for facilities management (FM) services: A study on Nigeria's public hospitals. *Property Management*, 33(1), 59–82.

Ikediashi, D.I., Mendie, A., Achuenu, E. and Oladokun, M.G. (2012). Key performance indicators of design and build projects in Nigeria. *Journal of Human Ecology*, 37(1), 37–46.

Ikediashi, D.I., Ogunlana, S.O. and Boateng, P. (2014). Determinants of outsourcing decision for facilities management (FM) services provision. *Facilities*, 32(9/10), 472–489.

Ingle, P.V., Mahesh, G. and Deepak, M.D. (2020). Identifying the performance areas affecting the project performance for Indian construction projects. *Journal of Engineering, Design and Technology*, 19(1), 1–20.

Ive, G. (2006). Re-examining the costs and value ratios of owning and occupying buildings. *Building Research & Information*, 34(3), 230–245.

Jensen, P.A. (2009). Design integration of facilities management: A challenge of knowledge transfer. *Architectural Engineering and Design Management*, 5(3), 124–135.

Jensen, P.A. (2012). Knowledge transfer from facilities management to building projects: A typology of transfer mechanisms. *Architectural Engineering and Design Management*, 8(3), 170–179.

Jensen, P.A., Maslesa, E., Berg, J.B. and Thuesen, C. (2018). 10 questions concerning sustainable building renovation. *Building and Environment*, 143, 130–137.

Jensen, P.A., van der Voordt, T., Coenen, C., von Felten, D., Lindholm, A., Nielsen, S.B., Riratanaphong, C., *et al.* (2012). In search for the added value of FM: What we know and what we need to learn. *Facilities*, 30(5/6), 199–217.

Jensen, P.A., van der Voordt, T.J.M., Coenen, C. and Sarasoja, A.-L. (2014). Reflecting on future research concerning the added value of FM. *Facilities*, 32(13/14), 856–870.

Jiménez, R., Serebrisky, T. and Mercado, J. (2014). *Sizing Electricity Losses in Transmission and Distribution Systems in Latin America and the Caribbean.* Inter-American Development Bank, Washington, DC.

Jnr, E.L.Q. (1996). Development projects through build-operate schemes: Their role and place in developing countries. *International Journal of Project Management*, 14(1), 47–52.

Kadzis, R. (2015). *Redefining the Executive View of Facility Management.* International Facility Management Association, Houston, TX.

Kalantari, S., Shepley, M.M., Rybkowski, Z.K. and Bryant, J. (2017). Designing for operational efficiency: Facility managers' perspectives on how their knowledge can be better incorporated during design. *Architectural Engineering and Design Management*, 13(6), 457–478.

Kamaruzzaman, S.N., Myeda, N.E., Zawawi, E.M.A. and Ramli, R.M. (2018). Developing facilities management (FM) competencies for Malaysia. *Journal of Facilities Management*, 16(2), 157–174.

Kok, H.B., Mobach, M.P. and Omta, O.S.W.F. (2011). The added value of facility management in the educational environment. *Journal of Facilities Management*, 9(4), 249–265.

Kumaraswamy, M., De Silva, N. and Madhusanka, N. (2018). Empowering collaborative total asset management and inspiring innovations through Rivans. *Infrastructure Asset Management*, 6(3), 140–154.

Kumaraswamy, M.M., Anvuur, A.M. and Smyth, H.J. (2010). Pursuing 'relational integration' and 'overall value' through 'RIVANS'. *Facilities*, 28(13/14), 673–686.

Lai, J.H.K., Yik, F.W.H. and Jones, P. (2004). Disputes arising from vaguely defined contractual responsibilities in building services maintenance contracts. *Facilities*, 22(1/2), 44–52.

Lai, J.H.K., Yik, F.W.H. and Jones, P. (2006). Critical contractual issues of outsourced operation and maintenance service for commercial buildings. *International Journal of Service Industry Management*, 17(4), 320–343.

Liu, R. and Issa, R. (2014). Design for maintenance accessibility using BIM tools. *Facilities*, 32(3/4), 153–159.

Lizarralde, G., Tomiyoshi, S., Bourgault, M., Malo, J. and Cardosi, G. (2013). Understanding differences in construction project governance between developed and developing countries, *Construction Management and Economics*, 31(7), 711–730.

Lu, J.Z., Chao, J.J. and Sheppard, J.R. (2019). *Guarantees for Mobilizing Private Investment in Infrastructure*. The World Bank, Washington, DC.

Maas, G.W.A. and Pleunis, J.W. (2001). *Facility Management*. Kluwer, Alphen aan de Rijn.

Madhusanka, N., Kumaraswamy, M.M., Pan, W. and Chan, S.Y.S. (2020). Relationally integrated value networks for total asset management in project portfolios. *Infrastructure Asset Management*, 1–12.

Marzouk, M. and Zaher, M. (2020). Artificial intelligence exploitation in facility management using deep learning, *Construction Innovation*, 20(4), 609–624.

Matarneh, S.T., Danso-Amoako, M., Al-Bizri, S., Gaterell, M. and Matarneh, R. (2018). Developing an interoperability framework for building information models and facilities management systems. In *Creative Construction Conference 2018*, Slovenia, pp. 1018–1027.

Meng, X. (2013). Involvement of facilities management specialists in building design: United Kingdom experience. *Journal of Performance of Constructed Facilities*, 27(5), 500–507.

Min, Z., Morgenstern, P. and Marjanovic-Halburd, L. (2016). Facilities management added value in closing the energy performance gap. *International Journal of Sustainable Built Environment*, 5(2), 197–209.

Naidoo, P.J. and Saheed Bayat, M. (2020). Evaluating the growth and evolution of facility management in innovating integrating and aligning business strategies to achieve a competitive advantage. *Management Studies and Economic Systems*, 5(12), 1–13.

Natukunda, C.M., Pitt, M. and Nabil, A. (2013). Understanding the outsourcing of facilities management services in Uganda. *Journal of Corporate Real Estate*, 15(2), 150–158.

Nor, J.M., Che-Ani, A.I., Chohan, A.H., Wahi, W. and Hussain, A.H. (2019). 'Building defects management program' under soft landings level 3 performances at Public Universities in Malaysia. *International Journal of Recent Technology and Engineering*, 8(2S2), 135–142.

Ofori, G. (2012). *New Perspectives on Construction in Developing Countries*. Routledge, Oxford.

Okereke, R.A. (2020). Evolving maintenance culture in Nigeria: The role of facilities management. *PM World Journal*, 9(7), 1–12.

Olanrewaju, A.L. and Abdul-Aziz, A.-R. (2015). Building maintenance processes, principles, procedures, practices and strategies. *Building Maintenance Processes and Practices*, 79–129.

Olanrewaju, A.L.A., Khamidi, M.F. and Idrus, A. (2010). Quantitative analysis of defects in Malaysian university buildings: Providers' perspective. *Journal of Retail & Leisure Property*, 9(2), 137–149.

Parsanezhad, P., and Dimyadi, J. (2014). Effective facility management and operations via a BIM-based integrated information system. In *CIB Facilities Management Conference*, CIB Working Commission W070 Facilities Management, Copenhagen.

Pathirage, C., Haigh, R., Amaratunga, D. and Baldry, D. (2008). Knowledge management practices in facilities organisations: A case study. *Journal of Facilities Management*, 6(1), 5–22.

Perera, B., Ahamed, M.H.S., Rameezdeen, R., Chileshe, N. and Hosseini, M.R. (2016). Provision of facilities management services in Sri Lankan commercial organisations. *Facilities*, 34(7/8), 394–412.

Philp, D., Churcher, D. and Davidson, S. (2019). *Government Soft Landings*. Centre for Digital Built Britain, Cambridge.

PPPLRC. (2020). Transparency, good governance and anti-corruption mechanisms public private partnership. https://ppp.worldbank.org/public-private-partnership/overview/practical-tools/good-governance-anticorruption [Accessed 8 September 2020].

Pradhananga, P., Elzomor, M. and Santi Kasabdji, G. (2021). Barriers and drivers to the adoption of sustainable construction practices in developing countries:

A case study of Venezuela. *Journal of Architectural Engineering*, 27(3), 5021005.

Punnett, B.J. (2013). *Management: A Developing Country Perspective*. Routledge, Oxford.

Quah, L.K. (1992). Facilities management, building maintenance and modernization link: Evolution of facilities management traced suggesting a need to re-divert attention back to underlying issues such as improvements in maintenance, modernization systems, and feedback process. *Building Research and Information*, 20(4), 229–232.

Reiss, G. (2013). *Project Management Demystified: Today's Tools and Techniques*. Routledge, Oxford.

Roper, K. and Borello, L. (2013). *International Facility Management*. Wiley Blackwell, Oxford.

Roper, K.O. (2017). Facility management maturity and research. *Journal of Facilities Management*, 15(3), 235–243.

Samarakkody, A.L., Perera, B. and Palliyaguru, R. (2020). Appropriateness of soft landings concept for avoiding malpractices in Sri Lankan building projects. *International Journal of Construction Management*, 1–13.

Samuel, A. (2016). *Policy Paper on Infrastructure Implementing Facilities Management Services through PPPs*. European Bank for Reconstruction and Development, London.

Shafiq, M.T., Al Seena, G., Al Saqqa, M. and Al Mansouri, S. (2020). Defects Management practice during DLP in the UAE Construction Industry, *International Conference on Industrial Engineering and Operations Management*, IEOM Society International, Dubai, UAE.

Shah, S. (2007). *Sustainable Practice for the Facilities Manager*. Wiley Blackwell, Oxford.

Sharma, H. and Jain, V. (2016). A study on evolution and growth of facility management services in India. *International Journal of Engineering Sciences & Research Technology*, 5(6), 537–551.

Shehu, Z., Endut, I.R., Akintoye, A. and Holt, G.D. (2014). Cost overrun in the Malaysian construction industry projects: A deeper insight. *International Journal of Project Management*, 32(8), 1471–1480.

Shen, W., Tang, W., Siripanan, A., Lei, Z., Duffield, C. F. and Hui, F. K. P. (2020). Understanding the green building industry in Thailand. In Z. Gou (Ed.), *Green Building in Developing Countries: Policy, Strategy and Technology*. Springer, Cham, pp. 161–180.

Spencer, N.C. and Winch, G. (2002). *How Buildings Add Value for Clients*, Thomas Telford, London.

Steenhuizen, D., Flores-Colen, I., Reitsma, A.G. and Ló, P.B. (2014). The road to facility management, *Facilities*, 32(1–2), 46–57.

Støre-Valen, M. and Buser, M. (2019). Implementing sustainable facility management: Challenges and barriers encountered by Scandinavian FM practitioners, *Facilities*, 37(9/10), 550–570.

Ullah, M., Khan, M.W.A., Kuang, L.C., Hussain, A., Rana, F., Khan, A. and Sajid, M.R. (2020). A structural model for the antecedents of sustainable project management in Pakistan. *Sustainability*, 12(19), 8013.

Wauters, B. (2005). The added value of facilities management: Benchmarking work processes, *Facilities*, 23(3/4), 142–151.

Way, M. and Bordass, B. (2005). Making feedback and post-occupancy evaluation routine 2: Soft landings–involving design and building teams in improving performance, *Building Research & Information*, 33(4), 353–360.

Wen, J. and Gheisari, M. (2020). Using virtual reality to facilitate communication in the AEC domain: A systematic review, *Construction Innovation*, 20(3), 509–542.

Wijekoon, C., Manewa, A. and Ross, A.D. (2018). Enhancing the value of facilities information management (FIM) through BIM integration, Engineering, *Construction and Architectural Management*, 27(4), 809–824.

Wijewickrama, M., Chileshe, N., Rameezdeen, R. and Ochoa, J.J. (2020). Quality assurance in reverse logistics supply chain of demolition waste: A systematic literature review, *Waste Management & Research*, 39(1), 3–24.

Wisittigars, B. and Siengthai, S. (2019). Crisis leadership competencies: the facility management sector in Thailand, *Facilities*, 37(13/14), 881–896.

Xu, J., Lu, W., Xue, F. and Chen, K. (2019). 'Cognitive facility management': Definition, system architecture, and example scenario, *Automation in Construction*, 107, 102922.

https://doi.org/10.1142/9789811224720_0016

Chapter 16

Distinct Project Management for Post-disaster Reconstruction Projects in Developing Countries

Roshani Palliyaguru*, Dilanthi Amaratunga†, Aravindi Samarakkodi† and Shavindree Nissanka†

**University of Vocational Technology, Sri Lanka*
†Global Disaster Resilience Centre, University of Huddersfield, UK

Abstract

Although post-disaster reconstruction has been the subject of a significant volume of research, particularly in developing countries, knowledge on differences in the application of Project Management (PM) theories, processes, activities, and practices between routine construction and specific post-disaster reconstruction projects is fragmented and thus needs to be established. This is the main purpose of this chapter. Thus, this chapter investigates the need for a special body of knowledge of project management for disaster reconstruction in developing countries, the nature of specific PM processes and activities that disaster reconstruction should adopt for generating successful project outcomes, and what the future holds for PM of disaster reconstruction in developing countries. In achieving the above aim and objectives, this chapter refers to, and analyzes, the challenges, conditions, and factors confronted by past (real-life) disaster reconstruction projects in developing countries such as Sri Lanka; discusses the extent to which traditional PM theories, processes, practices, and activities are appropriate and, in certain circumstances, inappropriate concerning the challenges confronted by disaster reconstruction projects in developing countries; and proposes changes required for the existing PM methodology for disaster reconstruction projects, with a special emphasis on developing countries.

Keywords: Post-disaster reconstruction, project management, project life cycle, developing countries

Introduction

The frequency and magnitude of natural-hazard-induced and human-induced disasters are increasing at an unprecedented scale all over the world, especially in developing countries (UNISDR, 2015; Liu *et al.*, 2017). Disasters triggered by natural hazards such as floods, droughts, or cyclones have the potential to cause large-scale damage on a regional, national, or even supranational scale worldwide (Hinzpeter and Sandholz, 2018). Disasters have a significant impact on the built environment of developing countries, which is usually higher compared to developed countries, by approximately more than 20 times (Barakat, 2003).

Post-disaster reconstruction is the phase that is viewed with a long-term eye on rebuilding or in other words "building back better" for the communities affected by a disaster (Lyons, 2009). There are several differences in the project cycle of routine construction and disaster-induced reconstruction, in terms of the time taken for project completion, the decision-making process and key decision-makers, procurement systems, funding arrangements, and especially the needs assessments. Accordingly, the key activities and personnel involved also differ (Capell and Ahmed, 2021). A typical construction project cycle seems to be more comprehensive in terms of its outcome compared to a reconstruction project and has a clear flow of activities starting from the identification of project needs. In reconstruction projects, the flow is not well established because they are not pre-planned; uncertainty is an inevitable feature of reconstruction projects. The situation could be further exaggerated in developing countries compared to developed countries due to the various tougher constraints prevailing in these countries such as tight financial situations, limited time, deficiencies in institutional arrangements, lack of capacity in the construction industry, various malpractices and corruption (Ahmed, 2011), lack of transparency, lack of stringent regulations, and lack of resources available for post-disaster reconstruction.

There are benefits from applying a Project Management (PM) approach to post-disaster reconstruction work (Kulatunga, 2011). The application of ineffective PM strategies during post-disaster reconstruction can further exaggerate the problems associated with reconstruction in developing countries. For instance, the application of conventional stakeholder management may not be appropriate for post-disaster reconstruction in developing countries because post-disaster construction requires the inputs of numerous irregular stakeholders such as community-based organizations, disaster management organizations, donors, and so on. Managing such irregular stakeholders requires more thoughtful approaches and processes. Hence, the question arises whether traditional PM theories, strategies, and practices can be equally applicable or adapted for post-disaster reconstruction in developing countries as well. This is the main question being addressed in this chapter.

In this setting, this chapter is an effort to establish the differences in the application of PM theories, processes, activities, and practices between routine construction and post-disaster reconstruction projects in developing countries. Within this frame of reference, the specific objectives of the chapter are:

- To present the need for a special body of knowledge of PM for post-disaster reconstruction in developing countries with reference to the complexities involved in, and the challenging nature of, post-disaster reconstruction;
- To present the nature of any specific PM processes and activities that post-disaster reconstruction in developing countries should adopt for generating successful project outcomes; and
- To present what the future holds for PM of post-disaster reconstruction in developing countries.

Limitations in the application of traditional PM to post-disaster reconstruction

PM is the "application of knowledge, skills, tools, and techniques to project activities to meet the project requirements" (PMI, 2017). The effectiveness and efficiency of projects rely on appropriate application and integration of the PM processes on the respective projects. PM processes are "a systematic series of activities directed toward causing an end result where one or more inputs will be acted upon to create one or more outputs" (PMI, 2017). According to the PMBOK Sixth edition, five PM processes are employed to deliver project objectives, namely, Initiating, Planning, Executing, Monitoring, and Controlling and Closing (Project Management Institute, 2017). Moreover, PM processes are also categorized by Knowledge Areas. A knowledge area is "an identified area of PM defined by its knowledge requirements and described in terms of its component processes, practices, inputs, outputs, tools, and techniques" (PMI, 2017). The 10 Knowledge Areas identified in PMBOK 2017, which are applied in practice in most projects are: Project Integration Management, Project Scope Management, Project Schedule Management, Project Cost Management, Project Quality Management, Project Resource Management, Project Communications Management, Project Risk Management, Project Procurement Management, and Project Stakeholder Management (PMI, 2017).

It is challenging when there are limited effective project (or program) management methodologies, training, and education that can be provided in planning and implementing (programs of) projects to ensure sustainable reconstruction following a disaster (Steinfort, 2017). Moreover, successful completion of post-disaster reconstruction projects with the incorporation of disaster resilience toward future hazards requires the application of specialized PM strategies. Reconstruction projects should be defined, pre-planned, and implemented in stages (Roosli and O'Keefe, 2012). According to Steinfort and Walker (2007), phases in reconstruction projects in general terms are well defined in short time frames yet can be recursive. However, there is limited continuity in projects with regard to longer-term gains from the reconstruction requirements (Jha, 2010).

When comparing PM life-cycle stages (process groups) with the post-disaster reconstruction processes, it can be observed that the project close-out needs to take place within the normal PM time frame, making it hard to manage the complexities inherent in reconstruction projects (Vahanvati and Mulligan, 2017). The authors also argued that the time-frame needs to be flexible, and sufficient time should be allocated to the planning phase in order to focus, even at this early stage, on the long-term, beyond the completion phase of the reconstruction project. While the "agile" or incremental strategy is the most often voted for solution (Kalkman and de Waard, 2017; Walker *et al.*, 2017), the following imperatives are found as measures to ensure longer-term benefits which contribute to building the resilience of communities (Vahanvati and Mulligan, 2017):

- allocating sufficient time for building and maintaining the community's trust;
- providing multiple choices for residents with regards to materials, skilled labor and technologies; and
- continued capacity building, extending beyond the completion of the project.

According to Walker *et al.* (2017), the literature on PM has said little about PM applications to disaster management and likewise, the literature on disaster management has said little about the management of the projects. Vahanvati and Mulligan (2017) argue that while traditional PM has clear benefits in ordinary contexts, it fails to address the complexity of post-disaster reconstruction projects. Hence, Vahanvati and Mulligan (2017) present a critique on the application of the traditional PM approach for post-disaster reconstruction. Moreover, there are several reasons pointed out by authors as to why the traditional PM approach has limitations in the context of post-disaster reconstruction:

(1) it focuses on a single project life cycle and usually, an inflexible time-frame for project completion (Vahanvati and Mulligan; 2017; Steinfort and Walker, 2007);

(2) it is not able to identify the complexities and unique challenges of large disaster settings (Vahanvati and Mulligan; 2017; Chang-Richards and Wilkinson, 2016); and
(3) it measures project success in terms of project outcomes rather than ongoing processes (Vahanvati and Mulligan; 2017; von Meding *et al.*, 2016).

"Project Management Methodology for Post-Disaster Reconstruction" of PMI and its limitations

"Project Management Methodology for Post-Disaster Reconstruction" (PDRM) is a PM method developed by the Project Management Institute (PMI) for reconstruction projects based on the "A Guide to the Project Management Body of Knowledge (PMBOK® Guide) — 3rd Edition" to enhance the quality, collaboration, consistency, and accountability on construction projects undertaken in disaster (crisis) rebuild environments (PMI, 2004). This was developed by nearly 80 PM volunteers and subject matter experts around the world, representing 20 countries as a prompt response to find better ways to manage the aftermath and recovery following the Indian Ocean Tsunami in 2004 and Hurricane Katrina in 2005. However, the scope is limited to individual/rudimentary projects. Although it is claimed that the application is suitable for development projects that aim at sustainability, this should be within the intended scope (individual/ rudimentary projects as aforementioned), which highlights the main gap in the application of this methodology. For the same reason, the real-time application in developing countries is also limited despite the authors' assertion that there are explicit benefits of this guide for the developing countries with minimal infrastructure (Chang-Richards and Wilkinson, 2016).

PDRM has not been updated since it was developed, and this has resulted in several issues. For instance, one of the important aspects affecting sustainable post-disaster reconstruction that is not covered in the third edition is the stakeholder engagement process (Steinfort, 2017). Thus, having been developed based on the PMBOK guide third edition, PDRM has placed emphasis on the traditional views about PM theories and not on the emerging views (Whitty and Schulz, 2007). Similarly, PDRM overlooks the cultural differences, which have a lot to do with stakeholder management. For instance, the risk management templates and the stakeholder engagement templates are silent about the potential issues that may arise as a result of cultural diversity, a major concern in developing countries in the domain of development. Several other concerns are raised with regards to these templates, the heart of PDRM methodology, as the PDRM limits its consideration to the iron triangle (time, cost, fitness for purpose) in defining a project's success, while the accountability for project success is required to be viewed from different stakeholders' perspectives (Steinfort, 2017) and can be considered in terms of the on-going processes rather than project outcomes (von Meding *et al.*, 2016). The weaknesses of PDRM have also been of much concern to authors such as Steinfort and Walker (2007). From the above discussion, it is evident that there is a need for a special body of knowledge of PM for post-disaster reconstruction in developing countries. This is the focus of the remaining sections of this chapter.

Need for a special body of knowledge of project management for post-disaster reconstruction in developing countries

United Nations Office for Disaster Risk Reduction (UNDRR, 2021) defines reconstruction as "the medium- and long-term rebuilding and sustainable restoration of resilient critical infrastructures, services, housing, facilities and livelihoods required for the full functioning of a community or a society affected by a disaster, aligning with the principles of sustainable development and "build back better," to avoid or reduce future disaster risk." Post-disaster reconstruction is not an easy task; it is challenging, chaotic, dynamic, and complex compared to routine construction work (Vahanvati and Mulligan, 2017; Bilau and Witt, 2016; Chang *et al.*, 2010). It typically entails the application of highly demanding processes (von Meding *et al.*, 2016; Amaratunga *et al.*, 2017), which are required to be performed under challenging and/or specific conditions, involving different stakeholders with limited capacity for handling multiple items of work, within a limited period of time, yet often requiring rapid reconstruction to restore the affected communities, with limited funds for managing such a wide spectrum of activities, compared to routine construction (Amaratunga *et al.*, 2017). These complex processes involve the interaction of economic, social, cultural, technological, political, and developmental factors. Developing countries are confronted with tough challenges, particularly in the implementation of post-disaster housing reconstruction projects (Ahmed, 2011). Hence, whereas most governments had ambitious plans for speedy and effective post-disaster recovery, a low success rate has been recorded in many parts of the world, especially in the developing countries. Substantiating this argument, Lyons (2009) asserts that "post-disaster reconstruction often fails in its stated objectives. These failures may be traced to the centralizing approaches generally taken to reconstruction, which are encouraged by the political economy of post-disaster situations." Chang *et al.* (2010) attribute the failures of most of the reconstruction projects to lack of resources for reconstruction, i.e., inadequate funding, lack of high quality physical and technical assistance, and so on.

A disaster typically results in an environment that makes the PM of reconstruction more difficult, and mere adherence to established PM processes, practices, inputs, outputs, tools, and techniques may be less effective and/or less appropriate in the effort to achieve desired outcomes. The application of PM for post-disaster reconstruction needs to particularly address the context-specific challenges to rebuild the affected built environment to an appropriate standard. As noted above, the context-specific challenges encountered on projects in developing countries include tight financial constraints, limited time, deficiencies in institutional arrangements, lack of capacity in the construction industry, financial malpractice, corruption (Ahmed, 2011), lack of transparency, lack of stringent regulations, and lack of resources available for post-disaster reconstruction projects. Thus, there are many ways in which the context of post-disaster reconstruction in developing countries differs from that of routine construction in industrialized countries, which needs to be taken into account in formulating a special methodology of PM for reconstruction.

Amaratunga *et al.* (2017) establish 13 key knowledge gaps in enhancing societal resilience to disasters, one of which is post-disaster PM. In the context of post-disaster PM, these 13 knowledge gaps reflect on time management, human resource management, leadership and people management, process and quality management, and materials and resource management. These knowledge areas closely relate to the 10 knowledge areas identified in the PMBOK (PMI, 2017). The fundamental similarities and changes required in the 10 traditional PM knowledge areas when they are applied to post-disaster reconstruction in developing countries are now discussed.

Project integration management

Due to the considerable level of uncertainty, urgency, complications, and challenges involved in post-disaster reconstruction, a high level of project coordination, together with rigorous management, is required to hold the project together (Zuo *et al.*, 2009; Moe and Pathranarakul, 2006). Accordingly, integrated reconstruction management is highlighted to be the key to the successful implementation of sustainable human resettlement projects (Ye and Okada, 2002).

Project integration management is composed of several steps, namely developing a project charter, developing the PM plan, directing and managing project work, managing project knowledge, monitoring and controlling project work, performing integrated change, and closing the project or phase. An approved project charter is required to formally initiate a project, and it basically establishes the relationship (partnership) between the two parties of the project, i.e., the requesting organization and the performing organization (PMI, 2017). Studies on construction project success conclude that a solid project charter that consists of clear and proper descriptions of authority contributes to the overall success of the project (Demirkesen and Ozorhon, 2017). The project charter, at a high level — for instance in the case of complex post-disaster reconstruction projects, enabling a common understanding of the key aspects such as the deliverables, roles and responsibilities, and milestones — establishes the foundation for stakeholder management. The PM plan defines how each task will be performed including the execution, monitoring and control, and closing (PMI, 2017). The subsidiary management plans cover all the PM knowledge areas and the baselines for each of them. Several authors have identified this planning component as a critical success factor for post-disaster reconstruction projects (Moe and Pathranarakul, 2006; Steinfort and Walker, 2007; Tatum and Terrell, 2012). With the development of the PM plan, the next step is directing and managing project work. This includes the execution of works as the plan specifies and accomplishing the goals and objectives (PMI, 2017). The next step includes managing tacit and explicit knowledge in the project, which is of paramount importance in post-disaster reconstruction PM.

Making informed decisions based on the available information is crucial in post-disaster reconstruction, which involves a large number of types of resources and variables, and a knowledge management system helps by providing timely information (Arain, 2011). The advantages of knowledge management in post-disaster reconstruction include: storing information for future use; facilitating learning from past experience for professionals; disseminating and growing a practice of performance-enhancing, better planning, time-saving, cost-cutting and providing better outputs to post-disaster reconstruction beneficiaries; and attracting new donors and other sources of funding and other resources (Amaratunga *et al.*, 2009). However, authors have concluded that despite the awareness the industry has, most of the organizations have failed to formally implement knowledge management in post-disaster housing reconstruction.

Monitoring and controlling is difficult in an environment where multiple organizations that do not usually work together are engaged (Kulatunga, 2011). A number of cases have been reported in developing countries that show overall failures in projects due to ineffective monitoring — for instance, ineffective monitoring of funds during post-disaster reconstruction in Sri Lanka (Nissanka *et al.*, 2008). Therefore, the establishment of proper monitoring and controlling systems is suggested as a tool to make post-disaster reconstruction projects a success (Fengler *et al.*, 2008).

Undertaking Integrated Change Control is a process that is carried out throughout the project and requires reviewing all change requests, and approving and managing those changes (PMI, 2017). Disaster reconstruction needs organizational and procedural measures that can regulate activities to survive in a dynamic environment (Ginige and Amaratunga, 2011), and it is advisable to have a change management and/or configuration management system to maintain the written records (Wedawatta *et al.*, 2018).

Project scope management

Scope management is a debatable area in post-disaster reconstruction projects in developing countries. The urgency of reconstruction, limited funds, political influences, poor coordination and communication among stakeholders, and limited policies and guidelines are the main causes of scope management difficulties. Causes that result in frequent scope changes in post-disaster reconstruction projects include: difficulty in reaching early consensus during the initiation phase due to the haste to meet essential needs, conflicting interests of different stakeholders and insufficient communication among them making it harder to identify the needs of the disaster-affected population, expansive work sites resulting in inaccurate information in the early project stages, the level of uncertainty due to the large number of influencing factors and, often, not conducting damage and risk assessments, time limitations in designing and planning, and requirements that are unique to the project (Alsaadi and Acar, 2021).

A post-disaster reconstruction project includes decisions and actions taken after a hazardous situation with a need for reinstating and refining the pre-disaster living conditions of the affected communities, while accommodating disaster resilience efforts to reduce future disaster risks (Moe and Pathranarakul, 2006). Owing to a lack of pre-preparation and proactive planning for reconstruction, decision-making in those projects takes an ad hoc nature. For example, especially in developing countries, decision-making related to project scoping and prioritizing in reconstruction is largely influenced by political agendas, power, funding agency regulations, and guidelines, with little involvement of local knowledge and neglecting local requirements. Lyons (2009) asserts that the past experiences show that post-disaster decision-making is influenced by economic, political, and humanitarian actors while the influence of real grassroot level beneficiaries/users remains minimal.

Scope management is usually linked to stakeholder management, time management, communication management, and risk management (Alsaadi and Acar, 2021). Project scope management comprises several steps: planning scope management, collecting requirements, defining scope, creating the Work Breakdown Structure (WBS), validating scope, and controlling scope. A main component in this process is the project scope management plan. This plan has received very little attention from the post-disaster reconstruction sector despite the necessity for it. However, considering the basic components that form the scope management plan, it can be argued that this lack of attention can be a result of the lack of awareness of the management of the scope owing to the urgency of the projects. The scope management plan includes the quality management plan, descriptions of project life cycle, and the development approach in which the contents are unique in post-disaster reconstruction projects. For example, the development approach for such projects is mostly from the agility perspective. The next step, collecting requirements, is the basis for defining the project scope as well as the product scope by managing stakeholder needs and requirements to meet the project objectives (PMI, 2017). Similar to routine PM, post-disaster reconstruction PM also involves producing unique products, and so previous projects will be dissimilar to what is required. Therefore, this makes a novel process necessary, and that includes requirement documentation and thorough identification of relationships among the requirements (Aliakbarlou *et al.*, 2017). Although the scope of a routine construction project is generally defined based on the availability of time and cost, the scope of work in disaster reconstruction is defined based on the amount of damage caused and the guidelines (and rules) available for restoration (Norling, 2013). In developing countries, the disaster victims are mostly the poorest communities who are often also already marginalized due to many reasons. Therefore, in developing the scope definition for post-disaster projects in developing countries, it is essential to be concerned about how reconstruction can address the sustainable livelihood of victims beyond the physical reconstruction and the departure of the implementing agencies.

The project manager constructs the WBS with the identification of all the activities that need to be carried out to perform the project tasks, and its importance does not lessen regardless of the type of project. While the WBS can be created through various approaches, in developing the WBS for disaster reconstruction projects, it is necessary to bear in mind and ensure that these projects tend to implement the small tasks incrementally as and when the situation demands (Walker *et al.*, 2017). A clear WBS is identified as a successful project (program) management tool that can deliver sustainable value for stakeholders in post-disaster reconstruction management (Steinfort, 2017). Next, the scope needs to be validated periodically throughout the project (PMI, 2017). These scope management components should also examine, in parallel, the effect on the community that is experiencing change with the implementation of the project (Sterling, 2008).

Project schedule management

One of the factors which contribute to the unique nature of disaster reconstruction is the limited time available for rebuilding and for resettling the affected communities (Masurier *et al.*, 2006). The main causes that result in time overruns in reconstruction project involve the absence of financial vision; poor anticipation of arrival times of resources as a result of complex logistical requirements and restrictions; scarcity of human and non-human resources in the development (disaster-affected) area; time limitations; and frequent changes in scope (Alsaadi and Acar, 2021). A study on the causes of delays in slum reconstruction projects in India revealed that the main causes of delays were the absence of clearly set out plans and targets for relocation of victims, not carrying out a risk assessment in the planning stage, issues in handling working capital, labor shortage on the site, and disagreement among parties about the quality snag list (Shah *et al.*, 2021) which are equally applicable to other developing countries. While these causes usually occur throughout the project life cycle, one can argue that schedule management is a task that requires all the other management aspects of PM to be successfully in place. Nevertheless, to manage the project time, PMI (2017) suggests steps, including: planning schedule management, defining activities, sequencing activities, estimating activity durations, developing schedule, and maintaining control in a systematic way to prevent time overruns in projects.

In planning schedule management, a documentation procedure related to the project schedule needs to be established. Particularly in post-disaster reconstruction projects, this needs to be advanced until the steps, such as preparing a disaster management plan, establishing a delivery framework that sets out a clear structure, and time allocation for each project objective, implementing time management processes, utilizing time management tools including software (such as Microsoft Project 2010, Primavera P6), developing capability and capacity, and implementing procurement strategies, are covered (Norling, 2013). Compared to usual construction projects, post-disaster reconstruction projects necessitate soft resources that need to be accounted for in defining activities. These include: the community's trust and its participation, the capacity of the implementer, institutional support, transparency, and accountability, and they demand a process-oriented approach instead of an outcome-oriented one (Vahanvati and Mulligan, 2017). However, as several experts suggest, in sequencing the activities, the agility perspective in post-disaster construction should take precedence (Kalkman and de Waard, 2017; Walker *et al.*, 2017). The next step involves estimating activity durations, which mostly depends on the timeframes imposed by the stakeholders, especially donors and the government in post-disaster reconstruction projects. The accountability and transparency of these parties involved in post-disaster reconstruction are increasingly critical, and that proves the need for effective schedule management, especially where there are problems with resources (Ismail *et al.*, 2014) as is frequently found to be the case in developing countries.

The schedule that is to be developed within the delivery framework should reflect realistic timeframes and the sequencing established in previous steps based on experts' knowledge on reconstruction projects, and the main consideration should be to avoid optimistically responding to the deadlines imposed by donors (Da Silva, 2010). With the development of the schedule, a systematic method should also be in place to control the schedule. This becomes a complex task owing to competing interests with regards to the time taken to deliver post-disaster reconstruction, and the usual long duration and the actual speed requirements.

Project cost management

Post-disaster reconstruction projects involve large amounts of financial and human resources. Post-disaster reconstruction differs from normal construction considering the funding arrangements (Bosher *et al.*, 2007; Freeman, 2004; Thayaparan *et al.*, 2010). Unlike routine construction work, disaster-induced reconstruction mostly arises instantly, and most developing countries have little or no preparation at all to face disasters at the time they occur. In developing countries, in addition to the responsibility governments bear for restoration and reconstruction of the public infrastructure, they are also responsible for reinstating/relocating the low-income households affected by such events. While a significant amount of funds is sourced through external aid from national and international donors, this phenomenon places a sudden and heavy ad hoc financial burden on government budgets. Such financial burden on central and local governments usually results in projects that are not sustainable or satisfactorily resilient due to the curtailing of the scope of the work and cost-cutting. Moreover, the difficulty in developing cost plans as a result of unrealistic estimates, largely depending on local sellers and imported building materials, make it difficult to get the best price, and political instability in the country, migrant/day labor and staffing, instability of exchange rates, inflation, lack of insurance systems, funding issues, failure of donors to act upon the promised commitments, and time overruns are identified as the causes that lead to cost overruns in post-disaster reconstruction projects (Alsaadi and Acar, 2021).

The PMBOK has established steps under effective cost management, which can be used to prevent the cost-related problems in reconstruction projects, such as planning cost management, estimating costs, determining the budget, and controlling costs. The first step, planning cost management, provides basic guidance and direction on how the project cost is managed. Post-disaster reconstruction projects should align with the notion "building back better," and that can increase the reconstruction costs (Pamidimukkala *et al.*, 2020). It is suggested that integrating Disaster Risk Reduction (DRR) into investment decisions is the most cost-effective way to reduce disaster risks; investing in resilience reaps its harvest mostly in the long run. This is discouraging the communities from investing in disaster resilience (CISL, 2016). Currently, there is little knowledge among the members of the communities on how to make their investments in assets meaningful, sustainable, and resilient as they deal also with the economic hardships and competing demands (Cutter *et al.*,

2013). To address this issue and prevent cost overruns, the best solution is to identify the factors that affect project cost and estimate ahead (Rouhanizadeh and Kermanshachi, 2019). Determining the budget and keeping the reconstruction cost within it is almost always a priority for practitioners, yet it is often difficult to realize it, due to the nature of reconstruction projects (Safapour *et al.*, 2020). This involves the issues arising as a result of the lack of information about the site/facility, insufficient space for construction, occupational health and safety-related problems, and engagement and involvement of building users earlier than expected (McKim *et al.*, 2000). Furthermore, the lack of reliable and continuous data records for quantifying the relationship between the natural disasters and the increases in cost indices is a major problem (De Silva, 2011).

To prevent these issues, authors have emphasized control mechanisms such as scope control, site control, safety control, and communication control. Therefore, one can argue that cost control on reconstruction projects is not only about the costs but also involves considering all the interdependencies by taking a holistic approach. Moreover, budgeting and financial planning, fund sourcing and financial management skills, financing to address disaster resilience, and financing flood adaptation strategies are among skills the built environment professionals should be equipped with (Perera *et al.*, 2016). Indeed, there are ongoing arguments regarding the feasibility of traditional manual cost estimation methods as the post-disaster situation makes it necessary to prioritize acting quickly in managing the project (Kermanshachi and Rouhanizadeh, 2018).

Project quality management

There are several causes of low quality in post-disaster reconstruction projects, including: inadequate funding, scarcity of materials and resources in the local market and consequent dependence on imported goods, issues with quality control, and unrealistic schedules (Alsaadi and Acar, 2021). The steps in project quality management outlined in PMI (2017) are planning quality management and managing and controlling quality. While the quality requirements and success factors depend on the type of the project (Ismail *et al.*, 2014), in reconstruction projects, they need to be evaluated and planned as lack of planning in the initial stages leads to overall low quality in post-disaster reconstruction projects (Alsaadi and Acar, 2021). Similarly, due to the inherent characteristics of disaster reconstruction projects, such as extensiveness and time limitation, monitoring and controlling quality is a challenge. Therefore, from the broader perspective, the success of post-disaster reconstruction projects demands a boundary-spanning approach through the understanding of sustainability-related impacts, beyond the technical scope (Vahanvati and Mulligan, 2017). Sanderson (2016) emphasized the need for project managers and leaders to move beyond their traditional roles to build up processes that involve people in places of uncertainty and rapid change.

The sustainability and resilience of post-disaster reconstruction projects face challenges of knowledge gaps in environmental impact assessment and management; sustainable design principles; waste production and pollution of land, water and air; sustainable retrofitting; and debris management (Amaratunga *et al.*, 2017). Moreover, in-depth understanding of the expertise, knowledge, and the know-how of how to mitigate the effects of hazards and threats is vital in designing and constructing a resilient built environment (Bosher *et al.*, 2007; Lorch, 2005), which in turn become vital in managing quality improvements of reconstruction projects. As part of quality assurance, ensuring that the reconstruction is disaster resilient is of paramount importance. In deciding how to embed disaster resilience to ensure that the project quality parameters are met, exploring the basic underlying characteristics of a given context for the products to be disaster resilient is vital. Disaster resilience has two properties: inherent resilience and adaptive resilience (Zhou *et al.*, 2010). The inherent capacity is defined for the normal circumstances, determined by the structure and functions of the system before, during, and after a disaster, until the structure and functions are destroyed. Adaptive resilience is the ability to resist and recover from the disaster after the hazardous event has taken place (Zhou *et al.*, 2010). Bruneau *et al.* (2003) define four properties of resilience: Robustness, Redundancy, Resourcefulness, and Rapidity, in relation to the resilience of both physical and social systems. These are also named as attributes of resilience in another study by Parker (2020). According to Ksenia *et al.* (2017), as shown in Figure 16.1, to make the highest positive impact on the outcomes, DRR should be

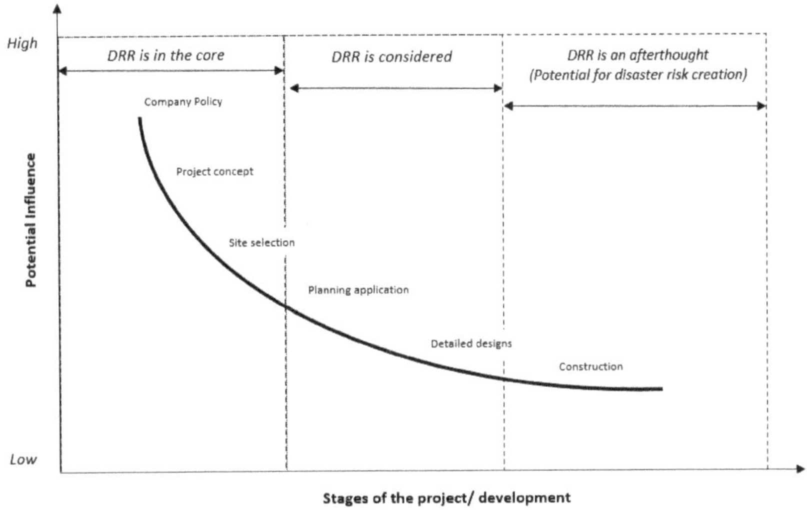

Figure 16.1: The 'Project influence curve.'
Source: Adapted from Bosher *et al.* (2016).

embedded in the project from its conceptualization and throughout the life cycle (Bosher and Chmutina, 2017). This requires the willingness to make additional investments in finance, human capital, equipment and organizational assets (Gallego-Lopez and Essex, 2016) as part of project quality management. In certain developing countries where corruption is common, there must be a stringent PM methodology in place to enable investments to be utilized effectively and efficiently to realize disaster resilience.

Thus, incorporating the resilience dimensions and properties into the quality management of post-disaster reconstruction projects in developing countries is essential, as otherwise, due to the loose regulations in place in these countries, there is a risk of failure to make reconstruction efforts sustainable and disaster resilient. Amaratunga *et al.* (2017) stress the necessity of proper governance, legal frameworks, and compliance toward attaining disaster resilient reconstruction. These could be addressed through holistic economic planning, urban planning and land-use practices, building codes and regulations, health and safety measures, and principles of accountability and transparency. Although legal measures are available for routine construction, aimed at attaining a safer and more sustainable environment, there are often few provisions in the legislation to facilitate reconstruction projects. This was evident in the aftermath of the tsunami disaster in Sri Lanka in 2004. The tsunami-induced reconstruction work had to be based on normal guidelines designed for new construction work. Their applicability to ensure the quality, sustainability, and resilience of reconstructed facilities in an exceptional situation, such as what prevailed in the aftermath of the tsunami, became questionable due to the context-specific differences between new construction and reconstruction projects.

Project resource management

Chang *et al.* (2009) assert that post-disaster housing reconstruction generally suffers from a lack of resources. Other challenges are lack of suitable resources (Russell, 2005), lack of access to available resources, and ineffective use of manpower. This significantly limits the prospects for successful recovery (Chang *et al.*, 2011). Such resource constraints were evident following the earthquake in Wenchuan, China, in May 2008 (Chang *et al.*, 2011); the Indian Ocean tsunami in Sri Lanka, India, and Bandar-Ache, Indonesia in 2004; and many other post-disaster reconstruction work in developing countries.

The effectiveness of resource management in post-disaster reconstruction depends on multi-stakeholder collaboration, market flexibility, donor management, and government intervention with donor engagement (Malalgoda *et al.*, 2014; Chang *et al.*, 2010). With the significant involvement of international donors in disaster rebuilding in developing countries, there is a tendency for professionals from overseas to be engaged in leading roles in offering professional services in the rebuilding process. Nevertheless, the importance of local professionals has risen over time as their understanding of how things work on the ground cannot be matched by the international experts who come to the scene in a post-disaster situation. Moreover, in a series of interviews, construction professionals involved in the post–2004 tsunami rebuilding in Sri Lanka believed that if the same professionals and teams engaged in the planning, designing, construction, and operation phases of a built facility were involved in the post-disaster rebuilding of that particular facility, they would rebuild the facility better. For that reason, the professionals believed that maintaining information databases of professionals who can supply various types of services is important. However, in many low-income developing countries, there is often a shortage of such skills, particularly in remote locations and in the poorest regions (Nofal and van de Lindt, 2020). Amaratunga *et al.* (2017) identify human resource management, leadership and people management, materials, and resource management as areas that need to be further investigated in relation to post-disaster PM.

It has been found that when funds start flowing in upon the occurrence of a disaster, the level of corruption also increases, and this has been common in the recent disaster-induced reconstruction work in developing countries. This is associated with the lack of oversight of post-disaster reconstruction (Jordan and Javernick-Will, 2014) and deficiencies in the PM of reconstruction. However, researchers such as Tierney and Oliver-Smith (2012) and Jordan and Javernick-Will (2014) report that opportunities for corruption arise when rebuilding is performed by the private sector. Public-sector reconstruction was also found to be prone to corruption in developing countries such as in Sri Lanka in the aftermath of the 2004 tsunami.

While project resource management processes involved in traditional PM — i.e., planning resource management, estimating activity resources, acquiring resources, developing the team, managing the team, and controlling resources — are equally important in post-disaster reconstruction in developing countries, the traditional inputs, tools, and techniques involved in the implementation of these processes become constrained or inappropriate in the post-disaster context. For example, inputs needed in the form of project documentation, PM plans, and work performance reports may not be available in post-disaster projects. Also, context-specific tools and techniques may be required. For example, striking a balance between centralized and decentralized decision-making is essential in post-disaster reconstruction. It is also necessary to consider the social, cultural, physical, and economic requirements of beneficiary communities. This is one of the reasons why community consultation and participation is encouraged in post-disaster decision-making although, as noted by Ahamed (2011), it is usually inadequately implemented. While the community-driven resourcing concept, where the affected communities rebuild their own houses, is a common approach in project implementation (Enshassi *et al.*, 2017; Bilau and Witt, 2016), community-related features like community participation and influence sometimes play a major role in donor-led resource procurement approach as well (Ahmed, 2011). These factors need to be taken into account in planning resources, estimating activity resources, and acquiring resources.

Furthermore, designers should support the use of local construction materials and their recycling and re-use of capabilities where possible (Da Silva, 2010; Barakat 2003), and the engagement of local skilled human resources. Also, special measures are needed in managing resources in developing countries, such as involving and empowering affected communities as well as developing teams, which, as defined by PMI (2017), is: "the process of improving competencies, team member interaction, and the overall team environment to enhance project performance."

Project communications management

Post-disaster reconstruction projects require well-developed communication links and relationships, based on trust and respect among the parties (Masurier *et al.*, 2006) including: (1) governmental/non-governmental organizations and disaster-affected communities; (2) internally within governmental/non-governmental organizations; and (3) between governmental/non-governmental organizations. The establishment of strong and reliable communication links and relationships between governmental/non-governmental organizations and disaster-affected communities enables communities to be aware of opportunities that become available for them to participate in the recovery and reconstruction phases (Sadiqi *et al.*, 2017); receive appropriate, timely, and relevant information about the reconstruction process; have knowledge of the assistance they receive from various organizations; and understand how to rebuild better. However, in developing countries, the involvement of multiple stakeholders from different disciplinary, social, and cultural backgrounds and the lack of technology available for communication among poor communities will require specifically designed user-friendly communication mechanisms. Both formal and informal communication with affected communities are essential. Both one-way and two-way communication are essential as the need for information dissemination and dialog are both equally important, and can facilitate recovery and limit the potential for setbacks and misunderstanding (Jha, 2010).

Amaratunga *et al.* (2017) identify the need for improvements in the soft skills of communication, community empowerment, leadership and people management, disaster awareness, working in alliances and partnerships, interdisciplinary working, and change management for successfully incorporating disaster resilience into the construction projects. It will be necessary to identify the roles and responsibilities of each stakeholder and develop proper communication links, which will facilitate sharing of good practice and resources (Malalgoda *et al.*, 2014).

Project risk management

According to PMI (2017), "Project risk management aims to exploit or enhance positive risks (opportunities) while avoiding or mitigating negative risks (threats)." Traditional project risk management includes risk management planning, identification of risks, analysis of risks, risk response planning, risk response implementation, and monitoring of risk (PMI, 2017). Risk management of post-disaster reconstruction also requires similar processes, but is subjected to a wide array of constraints such as limited budgets and time frameworks. Given the multitude of challenges involved in post-disaster reconstruction compared to routine construction, sources of risks affecting reconstruction projects are very wide.

The chaotic and disrupted nature of the environment following a disaster calls for enhanced risk management (Bilau and Witt, 2016). For example, apart from event-based risks and non–event-based risks, post-disaster reconstruction in developing countries should consider the associated risks in different types of housing or infrastructure approaches, such as a cash-based approach, owner-driven reconstruction, community-driven reconstruction, agency-driven reconstruction in situ, and agency-driven reconstruction in a relocated site (Enshassi *et al.*, 2017) and project types such as disaster-related housing projects, public projects, multiple-small reconstruction projects, international development projects, and projects by non-government organizations (Ismail *et al.*, 2014). Also, the risks associated with technological innovations, which are brought onto the scene in the aftermath of disasters, constitute another important consideration (Gharaati and Davidson (2008) cited in Bilau and Witt (2016)).

Traditional project risk management largely has a short-term focus rather than being concerned about the overall project life cycle or sustainability or resilience requirements of construction projects. It is predominantly concerned with the fact that unmanaged threats may result in issues such as project delays, cost overruns, performance shortfall, or loss of reputation (PMI, 2017). The European Union estimates that "climate change-related damage to infrastructure could grow tenfold under a business-as-usual case scenario" (UNDRR, 2020), and if the infrastructure is made more resilient, these impacts can be reduced (ADB, 2019). The vital necessity of mainstreaming disaster risk management into infrastructure planning has been highlighted by many authors (Prabhakar *et al.*, 2009; Trujillo *et al.*, 2015; Weekes and Bello, 2019). Accordingly, the need for integrating multi-hazard risk assessments into the post-disaster reconstruction needs to be given attention in order to bring a "sustainability" perspective into project risk management.

As Masurier *et al.* (2006) note, regulations should not be limited to being methods of disaster mitigation, but should facilitate reconstruction projects and not increase project risks. For example, the buffer zone regulation along the coastal line in Sri Lanka was enacted following the 2004 tsunami prohibiting all construction within close proximity to the sea, but it was later considered a controversial regulation that created many community problems. Among the main points that made the rule controversial was the massive relocation of the affected population further inland; giving poor considerations to possible alternative livelihoods for them and to their environmental, social and cultural problems (Ingram *et al.*, 2006); and the inequity and corruption in the application of the regulation to powerless persons as against powerful entities such as business developers. Thus, the rule which started with a 100-feet buffer from the sea, was later amended and the buffer reduced to 35 feet, and was finally ignored and abandoned with certain reconstruction activities, making it a poorly functioning rule. This failure resulted in the abandonment of some donor-driven projects, putting both projects and beneficiaries at risk, and also highlighted the deficiencies in the management of government–donor relations (Bilau *et al.*, 2015). Therefore, the root causes of risk need to be addressed, and inputs of valid traditional knowledge such as indigenous knowledge brought forward should be included in decision-making levels. Furthermore, the need for social and cultural awareness through developing cultural intelligence, and indigenous knowledge, becomes key in post-disaster reconstruction projects for handling communities and the transition processes, especially in developing countries (Amaratunga *et al.*, 2017).

Project procurement management

According to Sharif and Morledge (1996), "Procurement is a framework through which construction is brought about, acquired or obtained." It is suggested that client satisfaction is largely influenced by the selection of the most appropriate procurement strategy, and failure to do so is considered as a primary cause of project failure (Masterman, 1996). Procurement in the construction industry involves the acquisition of services, goods, material, plant, and equipment to plan, design, and build an item. Project procurement management includes the processes required for procurement decision-making, identifying potential contractors, obtaining tenders from contractors, selecting and awarding contracts, developing and administering contracts, managing procurement relationships, monitoring contract performance, making changes and corrections as appropriate, and closing out contracts (PMI, 2017).

The selection of an appropriate procurement strategy is generally based upon many factors: type, capability, and experience of the client; client's needs and wants in terms of time, cost, quality targets of the project; technical complexity of the project; location; extent of innovation required; project risks; and external factors such as the capability of local contractors, and availability of required skills from the construction industry (Sharif and Morledge, 1996; Masterman, 1996). While the same key concerns are relevant to procurement management of post-disaster reconstruction as well, there is a wide range of other complexities and challenges involved in reconstruction projects which need to be given significant attention. It is necessary in the adoption of procurement management approaches that those procurement methods and processes that involve time-consuming and costly procedures are avoided (Kulatunga, 2011). For instance, long and tedious procurement procedures, including contract drafting and other contractual procedures, can significantly affect the project duration (Kulatunga, 2011).

The need for unconventional procurement methods for reconstruction work is stressed by MacAskill and Guthrie (2017). Delivery routes such as the traditional procurement routes are discouraged for reconstruction projects, whereas integrated methods such as design-and-build routes are advocated (Kulatunga, 2011). Moreover, a procurement strategy adopted for a reconstruction project is generally expected to be part of the long-term sustainability efforts of the project and have the potential to positively contribute to local communities and economies in the disaster-affected regions by encouraging community participation in the overall procurement process (PMI, 2004, McGee *et al.*, 2008). The importance of incorporating community participation strategies into procurement management is stressed by Kulatunga (2011). Through this, the disaster-affected communities can be made more resilient and their lives sustainable. Accordingly, in reconstruction work, assessment of local community capacity for decision-making, and their involvement in physical construction work can be critical elements of the procurement strategy (Baraka, 2003, p. 34). Moreover, the modern construction world encourages construction procurement strategies that adopt traits such as trust between parties, greater transparency, accountability, risk sharing, and long-term sustainable partnerships for complex projects as they have a greater potential to provide win-win outcomes to parties. Kalkman and de Waard (2017) encourage a balance between trust and control of stakeholders, and also between contractual relationships and informal relationships, in reconstruction projects. Given the urgency and sensitive nature of reconstruction projects, leaving every matter for regulations and contracts to decide/control can lead to detrimental effects on reconstruction projects.

Nevertheless, the most appropriate procurement strategies for reconstruction may considerably vary depending upon the magnitude of the disaster and the economic status and coping capacity of the country (Kulatunga, 2011).

Project stakeholder management

As noted by various researchers, a wider range of stakeholders is involved in reconstruction projects compared to routine construction (Shafique and Warren, 2016). Generally, different stakeholders bring different interests to a construction project and accordingly they carry different responsibilities. Mojtahedi and Oo (2017) believe that stakeholders with power, legitimacy, and urgency attributes perform better in the disaster recovery processes. Nevertheless, the most important segment among all of the stakeholders comprises the individuals and/or communities who survived a disaster — i.e., those who were directly affected either by losing their loved ones, or physical properties, or both. The affected communities are the ones who have the right knowledge and understanding that is crucial for planning, designing, and executing the reconstruction projects. It is one of the reasons for considering effective community participation as a key factor in the success of post-disaster reconstruction projects (Wardak *et al.*, 2011). However, the affected communities become part of the post-disaster reconstruction process with a distressed state of mind and a great deal of grievances, causing several difficulties in the entire reconstruction process compared to routine construction, including in areas such as needs assessments, fund management, land acquisition, and relocation. For example, the road reconstruction work in Sri Lanka following the 2004 tsunami faced challenges in acquiring land for road widening work, establishing road boundaries, and upgrading/renewing drain systems as there were instances that some inhabitants had illegally acquired or encroached upon certain portions of land belonging to the state. However, the reacquisition of such plots of land was largely restricted in Sri Lanka due to the regulations being imposed by the agencies funding the reconstruction projects and consideration given to the grievances of disaster-affected people.

In reconstruction, initially, almost all stakeholders have a genuine interest, generosity, and a sympathetic mindset. This is common in developing countries such as Sri Lanka where large groups of people come forward to help the affected communities, demonstrating their selfless devotion. However, there is a risk of this initial approach changing when the projects drag on for long periods, and are subject to corruption and undue political influence. Thus, effective engagement of stakeholders is a challenging task in developing countries.

Integrating disaster resilience into post-disaster construction is a complex task that entails the input of many additional stakeholders such as community-based organizations, national disaster management organizations, non-governmental organizations, and research institutes (Venter, 2007). Therefore, in post-disaster reconstruction projects, it is necessary to have a multi-stakeholder approach which entails empowerment, team working, and collaboration among different parties (Amaratunga *et al.*, 2017). However, in reconstruction projects, the demarcation of responsibilities is often blurry and lines of authority are unclear (Bilau *et al.*, 2015; Moe and Pathranarakul, 2006). The lack of clarity in who needs to take up what functions leads to delays in the reconstruction projects (Pathirage *et al.*, 2012). Therefore, effectively identifying all relevant stakeholders and their interests, and assigning appropriate responsibilities is essential in ensuring the success of a project (Shafique and Warren, 2016). Considering the wide spectrum of construction activities involved in reconstruction and the wide range of stakeholders involved, it is necessary to institute mechanisms to optimize their inputs (Bosher *et al.*, 2016).

In the preceding sections, evidence is presented to show why and how PM of post-disaster reconstruction needs to adopt a context-specific approach to address the challenges posed by these projects, with special reference to developing countries. Considering the current status of the application of PM to post-disaster reconstruction, there is a need for certain fundamental changes to be introduced in the field going into the future, as discussed in the next section.

Future of project management of post-disaster reconstruction in developing countries

Effectively dealing with the long-term impact of a disaster in developing countries depends on several factors, including the extent to which the reconstruction process adopts an agile approach, draws on local materials and labor, removes corruption from the system, adopts community participation approaches, complies with an effective regulatory and policy framework for reconstruction, deals effectively with donors, manages the risks posed by a myriad of factors, and integrates disaster resilience and DRR strategies into the process of reconstruction and its outcomes. A PM method for post-disaster reconstruction in developing countries should incorporate the above factors which are not addressed in traditional PM. These future essentials are discussed below.

Disaster Risk Reduction and disaster resilience building

It is suggested that reconstruction projects should move beyond the traditional approach to PM to incorporate DRR and disaster resilience building as a priority into all the knowledge areas, enabling the respective PM processes and activities to take account of specific concepts, practices, and needs associated with DRR and disaster resilience building, leading to longer-term benefits beyond project completion. DRR mainly comes before the occurrence of the hazard during the pre-disaster stage and also after the occurrence of a hazard, during the post-disaster reconstruction stage, forming the basis of the "build to last" concept to prepare for the next probable hazardous condition (UNDRR, 2019). The global initiative, the Sendai Framework for DRR 2015–2030, was introduced in March 2015. One of the four main priorities of this framework is "Enhancing disaster preparedness for effective response, and to "Build Back Better" in recovery, rehabilitation, and reconstruction" (UNISDR, 2015). The DRR measures can be categorized in several ways and they are: policy and planning measures, physical preventative measures, physical coping, and/or adaptive measures and community capacity building measures (DFID, 2005, 2011).

A resilient system comprises several requirements: for example, it has to be preventive as well as recoverable after a hazard. Bosher (2008, p. 13) defines the feature of "disaster resilience" in the context of the built environment as being:

> "Designed, located, built, operated and maintained in a way that maximizes the ability of built assets, associated support systems (physical

> and institutional) and the people that reside or work within the built assets, to withstand, recover from, and mitigate for, the impacts of extreme natural hazards and human-induced threats."

Goal nine of the sustainable development agenda specifically addresses resilient infrastructure. It has this theme: "Build resilient infrastructure, promote sustainable industrialization and foster innovation." This reinforces the need to apply building back better principles for the infrastructure sector, especially as most of the costs of disasters are attributed to damage to the infrastructure and the built environment. Thus, it is essential that all traditional PM knowledge areas, especially project quality management, give due recognition to policy and planning, physical, technological, social, cultural, political, economic, and developmental concerns associated with concepts such as DRR and disaster resilience building within their processes and activities. This requires an attitudinal and radical change in the PM field.

Need for a new knowledge area

The specific needs of reconstruction projects suggest that it is necessary to introduce an additional Knowledge Area for PM, which covers "Health and Safety Management." Health and safety management is a priority area in routine construction work. Especially, in developing countries, this area receives little attention from lawmakers, policymakers, and construction practitioners. Considering the hazardous conditions and environments created in the aftermath of disasters, with debris, damaged buildings and infrastructure, some of which are unsafe, contaminated water, damaged power lines, and so on in the affected areas, reconstruction works are confronted with more severe health and safety challenges compared to routine construction work (Bilau and Witt, 2016). Therefore, a new PM knowledge area on health and safety management will be useful on reconstruction projects in developing countries.

Conclusion

It is stressed that the gross indirect costs of disasters are partly offset by the positive downstream effects of the rehabilitation and reconstruction efforts, such as increased activity in the construction industry. For example, the 2004 tsunami created a huge volume of construction demand in the housing and infrastructure reconstruction sectors in Sri Lanka. Similarly, the economic recovery of the developing countries most adversely affected by this tsunami was rapid, although it took longer in the coastal regions that were hit the hardest due to the context-specific challenges faced by the developing countries. The context of post-disaster reconstruction, especially in developing countries, differs from that of routine construction in many ways. This gives rise to the need for a special body of knowledge for PM of post-disaster reconstruction in developing countries. While the traditional PM theories, processes, practices, and activities have the potential to comprehensively address the needs of post-disaster reconstruction, there are circumstances in which they become inappropriate owing to the challenges confronted by disaster reconstruction projects in developing countries, as detailed throughout this chapter. Strong adherence to a disaster-induced reconstruction PM approach can provide solutions to many of the context-specific challenges. There is scope for in-depth research in future on each knowledge area of the PMBOK with the view to adapting each of them for post-disaster reconstruction in developing countries.

References

Ahmed, I. (2011). An overview of post-disaster permanent housing reconstruction in developing countries. *International Journal of Disaster Resilience in the Built Environment*, 2(2), 148–164. https://doi.org/10.1108/17595901111149141.

Alexander, D. (2004). Planning for post-disaster reconstruction. *I-Rec 2004 International Conference Improving Post-disaster Reconstruction in Developing Countries*, pp. 1–12.

Aliakbarlou, S., Wilkinson, S., Costello, S.B. and Jang, H. (2017). Client values within post-disaster reconstruction contracting services. *Disaster Prevention and Management: An International Journal*, 26(3), 348–360.

Alsaadi, O. and Acar, E. (2021). Challenges of post-disaster reconstruction projects: An empirical investigation according to project management knowledge areas. *American Journal of Management*, 21(4). https://doi.org/10.33423/ajm.v21i4.4557

Amaratunga, D., Haigh, R., Malalgoda, C. and Keraminiyage, K. (2017). Mainstreaming disaster resilience in the construction process: Professional education for a disaster resilient built environment: A report of the CADRE project: Collaborative Action towards Disaster Resilience Education. http://www.disaster-resilience.net/cadre/ [Accessed 3 March 2021]

Amaratunga, D., Haigh, R., Thanurjan, R. and Seneviratne, L.I.P. (2009). The role of knowledge management in post-disaster housing reconstruction. *Disaster Prevention and Management*, 18(1), 66–77. https://doi.org/10.1108/09653560910938556.

Arain, F.M. (2011). An information technology (IT) based approach for enhancing prompt and effective post-disaster reconstruction. *Business Review*, 6(2), 67–79.

Barakat, S. (2003). Housing reconstruction after conflict and disaster. Humanitarian Practice Network: Network Paper, 43 (December). http://www.odihpn.org/hpn-resources/networkpapers/housing-reconstruction-after-conflict-and-disaster [Accessed August 2012].

Bilau, A.A. and Witt, E. (2016). An analysis of issues for the management of post-disaster housing reconstruction. *International Journal of Strategic Property Management*, 20(3), 265–276. https://doi.org/10.3846/1648715X.2016.1189975.

Bilau, A.A., Witt, E. and Lill, I. (2015). A framework for managing post-disaster housing reconstruction. *8th Nordic Conference on Construction Economics and Organization, Procedia Economics and Finance*, 21, pp. 313–320.

Bosher, L. and Chmutina, K. (2017). *Disaster Risk Reduction for the Built Environment*. Wiley & Sons Ltd., Oxford, UK.

Bosher, L., Carrillo, P., Dainty, A., Glass, J. and Price, A. (2007). Realising a resilient and sustainable built environment: Towards a strategic agenda for the United Kingdom. *Disasters*, 31(3), 236–255. https://doi.org/10.1111/j.1467-7717.2007.01007.

Bosher, L., Chmutina, K. and Von Meding, J. (2016). Disaster risk reduction as a professional competency: A review of related training and education provision for built environment practitioners in the UK and Australia. *Proceedings of the International Conference on Building Resilience*, Auckland, New Zealand, 7–9 September 2016. https://hdl.handle.net/2134/22615

Bosher, L., Von Meding, J., Johnson, C., Arefian, F. F., Chmutina, K. and Chang-Richards, Y. (2016). Disasters and the built environment. Research roadmap. CIB W120 — Disasters and the Built Environment. CIB Publication 410. International Council for Research and Innovation in Building and Construction, Delft.

Bruneau, M., Chang, S., Eguchi, R., Lee, G., O'Rourke, T., Reinhorn, A., ... Winterfeldt, D. (2003). A framework to quantitatively assess and enhance the seismic resilience of communities. *Earthquake Spectra — EARTHQ SPECTRA, 19*. https://doi.org/10.1193/1.1623497.

Capell, T. and Ahmed, I. (2021). Improving post-disaster housing reconstruction outcomes in the Global South: A framework for achieving greater beneficiary satisfaction through effective community consultation. *Buildings*, 11, 145. https://doi.org/ 10.3390/buildings11040145.

Chang, Y., Wilkinson, S., Brunsdon, D., Seville, E., and Potangaroa, R. (2011). An integrated approach: managing resources for post-disaster reconstruction, *Disasters*, 35(4), 739–765.

Chang, Y., Wilkinson, S., Potangaroa, R. and Seville, E. (2010). Resourcing challenges for post-disaster housing reconstruction: A comparative analysis. *Building Research & Information*, 38(3), 247–264.

Chang, Y., Wilkinson, S., Seville, E. and Potangaroa, R. (2009). Capacity empowerment and building: integrated recovery management framework in China. *First International Conference on Disaster Management and Human Health: Reduction Risk, Improving Outcomes*, pp. 309–319.

Chang-Richards, Y. and Wilkinson, S. (2016). The insurance industry and integrated project management frameworks in post-disaster reconstruction: Recovery after the 2010 and 2011 Christchurch earthquakes. In P. Daly and M. Feener (Eds.), *Rebuilding Asia Following Natural Disasters: Approaches to Reconstruction in the Asia-Pacific Region*. Cambridge University Press, Cambridge, pp. 339–366. https://doi.org/10.1017/CBO9781139683548.014.

Chmutina, K., Jigyasu, R. and Bosher, L.S. (2017). Integrating disaster risk reduction including climate change adaptation into the delivery and management of the built environment. In I. Kelman, J. Mercer and J.C. Gaillard (Eds.), *The Routledge Handbook of Disaster Risk Reduction Including Climate Change Adaptation*. Routledge, Abingdon, p. 11.

Cutter, S.L., Ahearn, J.A., Amadei, B., Crawford, P., Eide, E.A., Galloway, G.E., ..., Zoback, M.L. (2013). Disaster resilience: A national imperative. *Environment: Science and Policy for Sustainable Development*, 55(2), 25–29. https://doi.org/10.1080/00139157.2013.768076.

Da Silva, J. (2010). *Key Considerations in Post-Disaster Reconstruction*. UK: Practical Action Publishing, Rugby, UK.

De Silva, L. (2011). Forecasting of cost escalations in post-disaster construction with special reference to Tsunami reconstruction in Sri Lanka. *Built-Environment Sri Lanka*, 9(1–2), 56–63.

Demirkesen, S. and Ozorhon, B. (2017). Measuring project management performance: Case of construction industry. *Engineering Management Journal*, 29(4), 258–277.

DFID (2005). *Natural Disasters and Disaster Risk Reduction Measures: A Desk Review of Costs and Benefits.* Environmental Resources Management's London Office, London. https://www.unisdr.org/files/1071_disasterriskreductionstudy.pdf [Accessed 22 March 2021].

DFID (2011). Defining Disaster Resilience. DFID Approach Paper, London, UK, pp. 1–20.

Enshassi, A., Chatat, T., von Meding, J. and Forino, G. (2017). Factors influencing post-disaster reconstruction project management for housing provision in the Gaza Strip, Occupied Palestinian Territories. *International Journal of Disaster Risk Science*, 8(4), 402–414.

Fengler, W., Ihsan, A. and Kaiser, K. (2008). *Managing Post-Disaster Reconstruction Finance — International Experience in Public Financial Management.* The World Bank, Washington, DC.

Freeman, P. K. (2004). Allocation of post-disaster reconstruction financing to housing. *Building Research & Information*, 32(5), 427–437.

Gallego-Lopez, C. and Essex, J. (2016). Designing for infrastructure resilience. *Evidence on demand,* Department for International Development, London.

Ginige, K. and Amaratunga, D. (2011). Capacity development for post-disaster reconstruction of the built environment. *Post-disaster Reconstruction of the Built Environment: Rebuilding for Resilience*, 1, 13–29.

Hinzpeter, K. and Sandholz, S. (2018). Squaring the circle? Integrating environment, infrastructure and risk reduction in Post-Disaster Needs Assessments. *International Journal of Disaster Risk Reduction*, 32, 113–124.

Ingram, J.C., Guillermo, F., Rumbaitis-del Rio, C. and Khazai, B. (2006). Post-disaster recovery dilemmas: challenges in balancing short-term and long-term needs for vulnerability reduction. *Environmental Science and Policy*, 9(7–8), 607–613.

Ismail, D., Majid, T.A., Roosli, R. and Ab Samah, N. (2014). Project management success for post-disaster reconstruction projects: international NGOs perspectives. *Procedia Economics and Finance*, 18, 120–127.

Jha, M.K. (2010). Natural and anthropogenic disasters: An overview. In M.K Jha (Ed.), *Natural and Anthropogenic Disasters.* Springer, Dordrecht. https://doi.org/10.1007/978-90-481-2498-5_1.

Jordan, E. and Javernick-Will, A. (2014). Successes and failures of the post-tsunami housing reconstruction program in Tamil Nadu, India. *Construction Research Congress 2014*, May 19–21, 2014, Atlanta, Georgia. https://doi.org/10.1061/9780784413517.123.

Kalkman, J.P. and de Waard, E.J. (2017). Inter-organizational disaster management projects: Finding the middle way between trust and control. *International Journal of Project Management*, 35(5), 889–899.

Keinänen, M. (Ed.) *CIB World Building Congress (WBC) 2016*, "Intelligent Built Environment for Life," Tampere Hall, Tampere, Finland.

Kennedy, J., Ashmore, J., Babister, E. and Kelman, I. (2008). The meaning of 'build back better': Evidence from post-tsunami Aceh and Sri Lanka. *Journal of Contingencies and Crisis Management*, 16(1), 24–36.

Kermanshachi, S. and Rouhanizadeh, B. (2018). Feasibility analysis of post-disaster reconstruction alternatives using automated BIM-based construction cost estimation tool. *Proceeding of CSCE 6th International Disaster Mitigation Specialty Conference, Montreal: Canadian Society of Civil Engineering*, pp. 13–16.

Krausmann, E., Girgin, S. and Necci, A. (2019). Global Assessment Report on Disaster Risk Reduction 2019: Natech. United Nations Office for Disaster Risk Reduction (UNDRR), New York, pp. 126–132.

Kulatunga, U. (2011). Project management of disaster reconstruction In D. Amaratunga and R. Haigh (Eds.), *Post-Disaster Reconstruction of the Built Environment: Rebuilding for Resilience*. Wiley, Chichester, pp. 133–150.

Le Masurier, J., Rotimi, J.O. and Wilkinson, S. (2006). Comparison between routine construction and post-disaster reconstruction with case studies from New Zealand. In *22nd Annual ARCOM Conference, 4–6 September 2006 Birmingham, UK. Association of Researchers in Construction Management*, Vol. 1, pp. 523–30.

Liu, B., Siu, Y.L. and Mitchell, G. (2017). A quantitative model for estimating risk from multiple interacting natural hazards: An application to northeast Zhejiang, China. Stochastic *Environmental Research and Risk Assessment*, 31(6), 1319–1340.

Lorch, R. (2005). What lessons must be learned from the tsunami? *Building Research & Information*, 33(3), 209–211. https://doi.org/10.1080/096132105 00070219.

Lyons, M. (2009). Building back better: the large-scale impact of small-scale approaches to reconstruction. *World Development*, 37(2), 385–398.

MacAskill, K. and Guthrie, P. (2017). Organisational complexity in infrastructure reconstruction — A case study of recovering land drainage functions in Christchurch. *International Journal of Project Management*, 35(5), 864–874.

Malalgoda, C., Amaratunga, D. and Haigh, R. (2014). Challenges in creating a disaster resilient built environment. *Procedia Economics and Finance*, 18, 736–744. https://doi.org/10.1016/S2212-5671(14)00997-6.

Masterman, L. (1996). Media education worldwide: Objectives, values and super-highways. *Africa Media Review*, 10, 61–75.

McGee, H.M., O'Hanlon, A., Barker, M., Hickey, A., Montgomery, A., Conroy, R. and O'Neill, D. (2008). Vulnerable older people in the community:

Relationship between the vulnerable elders survey and health service use. *Journal of the American Geriatrics Society*, 56(1), 8–15.

McKim, R., Hegazy, T. and Attalla, M. (2000). Project performance control in reconstruction projects. *Journal of Construction Engineering and Management*, 126(2), 137–141.

Moe, T.L. and Pathranarakul, P. (2006). An integrated approach to natural disaster management: Public project management and its critical success factors. *Disaster Prevention and Management: An International Journal*, 15(3), 396–413.

Mojtahedi, M. and Oo, B.L. (2017). Critical attributes for proactive engagement of stakeholders in disaster risk management. *International Journal of Disaster Risk Reduction*, 21, 35–43.

Nissanka, N.M.N.W.K., Kurusena, G. and Rameezdeen, R. (2008). Study of factors affecting post-disaster housing reconstruction. *BEAR 2008*, Sri Lanka.

Nofal, O.M. and van de Lindt, J.W. (2020). Understanding flood risk in the context of community resilience modeling for the built environment: Research needs and trends. *Sustainable and Resilient Infrastructure*, 7(3), 1–17.

Norling, B. (2013, May). Effective time management in post-disaster reconstruction. *Australian and New Zealand Disaster and Emergency Management Conference*, pp. 1–10.

Pamidimukkala, A., Kermanshachi, S. and Karthick, S. (2020, July). Impact of natural disasters on construction projects: Strategies to prevent cost and schedule overruns in reconstruction projects. In *Creative Construction e-Conference 2020*, Budapest University of Technology and Economics, pp. 49–57.

Parker, D.J. (2020) Disaster resilience — A challenged science. *Environmental Hazards*, 19(1), 1–9. https://doi.org/10.1080/17477891.2019.1694857.

Pathirage, C., Seneviratne, K., Amaratunga, D. and Haigh, R. (2012). Managing disaster knowledge: Identification of knowledge factors and challenges. *International Journal of Disaster Resilience in the Built Environment*, 3(3), 237–252.

Perera, S., Babatunde, S., Adeniyi, O. and Ginige, K. (2016). Community stakeholder perspective on construction industry-related needs and skills for enhancing disaster resilience, In K. Kähkönen and M. Keinänen (Eds.), *CIB World Building Congress (WBC) 2016, Intelligent Built Environment for Life*. May 30–June 3, Tampere Hall, Tampere, Finland, Vol. 1, pp. 396–407.

Prabhakar, S., Srinivasan, A. and Shaw, R. (2009). Climate change and local level disaster risk reduction planning: Need, opportunities and challenges. *Mitigation and Adaptation Strategies for Global Change*, 14(1), 7.

Project Management Institute (2004). *A Guide to the Project Management Body of Knowledge (PMBOK® Guide)*, 3rd Edition. Newtown Square, PA.

Project Management Institute (2017). *A Guide to the Project Management Body of Knowledge (PMBOK® Guide)*, 6th Edition. Newtown Square, PA.

Roosli, R. and O'Keefe, P. (2012). Learning and adaptation of disaster management and housing provision: The Malaysian experience. *Australian Journal of Emergency Management*, 27(3), 20–26.

Rouhanizadeh, B. and Kermanshachi, S. (2019, June). A systematic approach to analysis and prioritization of the socioeconomic policies and legal barriers to rapid post-disaster reconstruction. *7th CSCE International Construction Specialty Conference (ICSC)*, pp. 12–15.

Russell, T.E. (2005). *The Humanitarian Relief Supply Chain: Analysis of the 2004 South East Asia Earthquake and Tsunami*. MIT Thesis. Engineering Systems Division, Massachusetts Institute of Technology, Cambridge, MA.

Sadiqi, Z., Trigunarsyah, B. and Coffey, V. (2017). A framework for community participation in post-disaster housing reconstruction projects: A case of Afghanistan. *International Journal of Project Management*, 35(5), 900–912.

Safapour, E., Kermanshachi, S. and Jahan Nipa, T. (2020). A damage-based analysis of rework in reconstruction of infrastructure projects due to natural disasters. *Creative Construction e-Conference 2020*. Budapest University of Technology and Economics, pp. 55–62.

Sanderson, D. (2016). Building resilience. UNSW magazine — UNIKEN winter 2016. https://newsroom.unsw.edu.au/news/art-architecture-design/building-resilience [Accessed 1 April 2021].

Shafique, K. and Warren, C.M.J. (2016). Stakeholders and their significance in post natural disaster reconstruction projects: A systematic review of the literature. *Asian Social Science*, 12(10), 1–17.

Shah, M.N., Dixit, S., Kumar, R., Jain, R. and Anand, K. (2021). Causes of delays in slum reconstruction projects in India. *International Journal of Construction Management*, 21(5), 452–467. https://doi.org/10.1080/15623599.2018.1560546.

Sharif, A. and Morledge, R. (1996). Procurement strategies and national organisations: The dependency linkage. In *CIB W92 Symposium North Meets South: Developing Ideas*. Proceedings of CIB W92 — Procurement Systems: North Meets South: Developing Ideas, 14–17 January, Durban, South Africa.

Steinfort, P. (2017). Community and post-disaster program management methodology. *International Journal of Project Management*, 35(5), 788–801.

Steinfort, P. and Walker, D. (2007). A critique of the PMI Post-Disaster rebuild methodology. https://www.academia.edu/33047970/A_CRITIQUE_OF_THE_PMI_POST_DISASTER_REBUILD_METHODOLOGY [Accessed 20 March 2021].

Sterling, M. (2008). Project management methodology for post-disaster reconstruction. Paper presented at *PMI® Global Congress 2008* — Asia Pacific, Sydney, New South Wales, Australia. Newtown Square, PA: Project Management Institute.

Tatum, M.C. and Terrell, F. (2012). Hurricane reconstruction in the United States Gulf Coast. *International Journal of Disaster Resilience in the Built Environment*, 3(3), 199–219. https://doi.org/10.1108/17595901211263602.

Thayaparan, M., Siriwardena, M.L., Amaratunga, R.D.G., Kaklauskas, A. and Lill, I. (2010). Reforming HEI to improve skills and knowledge on disaster resilience among construction professionals. In *The RICS COBRA Conference 2010: Construction, Building and Real Estate Research Conference of the Royal Institution of Chartered Surveyors*. Paris, France, 2–3 September 2010.

Tierney, K. and Oliver-Smith, A. (2012). Social dimensions of disaster recovery. *International Journal of Mass Emergencies and Disasters*, 30(2), 123–146.

Trujillo, M., Baas, S., Ricoy, A., Battista, F., Herold, J. and Vantwout, T. (2015). Mainstreaming disaster risk reduction in agriculture: An assessment of progress made against the Hyogo Framework for action. Food and Agriculture Organization of the United Nations (FAO). Final report, USA, 96 pp.

UNDRR, U.O.f.D.R.R. (2020). Options for addressing infrastructure resilience. UNDRR Regional Office for Europe. *Working Paper*, Brussels. https://www.undrr.org/publication/working-paper-options-addressing-infrastructure-resilience [Accessed 28 March 2021].

UNISDR (2015). Making development sustainable: The future of disaster risk management. Global assessment report on disaster risk reduction. United Nations Office for Disaster Risk Reduction, GenevaUN-Water (2010). Climate change adaptation: The pivotal role of water.

UN Office for Disaster Risk Reduction (UNDRR) (2019). Parliamentary protocol for disaster risk reduction and climate change adaptation. Retrieved from Canada: http://parlamericas.org/uploads/documents/ENG_Protocolo_DRR_Online_Version.pdf

United Nations Development Programme (2004). *A Global Report-Reducing Disaster Risk: A Challenge for Development*. Bureau for Crisis Prevention and Recovery, New York.

United Nations Office for Disaster Risk Reduction (UNDRR). *Terminology*. https://www.undrr.org/terminology [Accessed 24 March 2021].

Vahanvati, M. and Mulligan, M. (2017). A new model for effective post-disaster housing reconstruction: Lessons from Gujarat and Bihar in India. *International Journal of Project Management*, 35(5), 802–817.

Venter, A. (2007). Integrated development planning as an approach to sustainable development. In G. Waldt (Ed.), *Municipal Management: Serving the People*. Juta and Company Ltd., Cape Town, South Africa, pp. 93–107.

von Meding, J., Wong, J., Kanjanabootra, S., Tafti, M. (2016). Competence based system development for post-disaster project management. *Disaster Prevention Management*, 25(3), 375–394.

Walker, B., de Vries, H.P. and Nilakant, V. (2017). Managing legitimacy: The Christchurch post-disaster reconstruction. *International Journal of Project Management*, 35(5), 853–863.

Wedawatta, G., Ingirige, B. and Sugathapala, K. (2018). Long-term sustainability and performance of post-disaster housing projects. *Chartered Institute of Building (CIOB) Bowen Jenkins Legacy Research Fund Research Report*. Aston University, Birmingham, UK.

Weekes, C. and Bello, O.D. (2019). Mainstreaming disaster risk management strategies in development instruments (II): Policy briefs for Barbados, Guyana, Saint Lucia, Suriname, and Trinidad and Tobago. Studies and Perspectives Series–ECLAC Subregional Headquarters for the Caribbean, No. 75 (LC/TS.2019/7; LC/CAR/TS.2018/3), Economic Commission for Latin America and the Caribbean (ECLAC), Santiago.

Whitty, S.J. and Schulz, M.F. (2007). The impact of Puritan ideology on aspects of project management. *International Journal of Project Management*, 25(1), 10–20.

Witt, E., Lill, I. and Nuuter, T. (2015). Comparative analysis of current guidance for the evaluation of building retrofit investments. *Procedia Economics and Finance*, 21, 321–328.

Ye, Y. and Okada, N. (2002). Integrated relief and reconstruction management following a natural disaster. Paper presented at the *Second Annual IIASA-DPRI Meeting*, Integrated Disaster Risk Management: Megacity Vulnerability and Resilience, IIASA, Laxenburg, Austria, 29-31 July, pp. 1–18.

Zhou, H., Zhou, H., Wang, J.a., Wang, J.a., Wan, J., Wan, J., ..., Jia, H. (2010). Resilience to natural hazards: A geographic perspective. *Natural Hazards*, 53(1), 21–41. https://doi.org/10.1007/s11069-009-9407-y.

Zuo, K., Potangaroa, R., Wilkinson, S. and Rotimi, J.O.B. (2009). A project management prospective in achieving a sustainable supply chain for timber procurement in Banda Aceh, Indonesia. *International Journal of Managing Projects in Business*, 2(3), 386–400. https://doi.org/10.1108/17538370910971045.

https://doi.org/10.1142/9789811224720_0017

Chapter 17

How Cost Estimators Develop Estimates: Experiences from the Indian Context

Shubham Bajaj* and Ashwin Mahalingam†

**Indian Police Service, India*
†Indian Institute of Technology, Madras, India

Abstract

Cost estimates in construction projects are often incorrect, leading to the well-known phenomenon of cost overruns. The literature suggests that estimation is a process that is mildly chaotic, infused with randomness, and not completely organized. While a number of behavioral, cognitive, and structural explanations are given for cost estimates not matching up to final project costs, the voice of estimators is rarely heard. Our goal is to understand the underlying micro-dynamics of construction cost estimating in the developing country context as well as to understand how we might restructure and eliminate biases that lead to incorrect estimates that then contribute to cost overruns. This chapter describes how project costs are estimated in the context of construction projects in India — one of the world's largest developing economies — through studying the experiences of the people involved in estimating projects. We find that several practices of estimation are pursued by different stakeholders who occupy different positions in the project value chain. While we did not find evidence of strategic misrepresentation, we did find some evidence of optimism bias in the estimates prepared. We conclude by recommending the creation of separate standards and practices for different types of firms and different levels of estimates.

Keywords: Cost estimating, India, construction, estimators, practices

Introduction

Cost estimation is a fundamental process underpinning the development of civil engineering projects. Virtually every undergraduate civil engineering curriculum the world over features a course or a module on quantity and cost estimation, covering aspects such as material take-offs, pricing, putting bids together, and the fundamentals of contracts. In some cases, students are encouraged to specialize in this area, as evinced by a number of graduate programs on Quantity Surveying with a focus on estimating, cost control, and contracts that continue to be popular in several Commonwealth countries in the developing world.

While the pivotal role played by cost estimators and the estimating process in the lifecycle of engineering projects is acknowledged by both academics and practitioners alike, the treatment given to this area in academic and practical bodies of knowledge is often idealized. In academia, estimation is often taught as a deterministic process, starting from the geometric calculation of quantities of materials, followed by an assessment of the cost of work of each building element by combining rates for material, equipment, and labor. Often these costs are combined into rates of work, further simplifying the process of cost estimation into determining quantities of work from drawings and multiplying these with their unit rates of work to obtain a cost for the project. A few strategic considerations involving the quantum of overheads and profits to be quoted are sometimes discussed, but otherwise the estimation process is considered to be objective and linear.

Professional organizations, such as the Project Management Institute (PMI), as part of its PMBOK framework, addresses this issue as well, albeit only recently. In 2011, PMI brought out a "Practice Standard for Project Estimating" that discusses best practices on how estimates can be created and managed (Kanabar and Warburton, 2011). This framework also discusses the "bottom up" approach of breaking a project up into different items of work and developing detailed estimates for each, as well as estimating based on analogous projects or through parametric techniques similar to the "rate analysis" methods described above.

Professional institutions of knowledge do acknowledge uncertainties and fuzziness in cost estimates and also advocate methods such as the use of Delphi techniques, where a number of experts are involved in the estimation process and consensus is sought between their estimates, and techniques such as PERT that deal with uncertainty in estimates (Kanabar and Warburton, 2011). While the practicality of these approaches in project settings and the frequency of their use in practice is debatable, these methods center on the notion that estimation is part art, part science, and subject to uncertainties, thereby allowing for subjectivities and inaccuracies ex-post.

The idealized notion of estimation as an exact science fails to pass muster when confronted by the vast evidence on cost overruns in the literature (Flyvjberg *et al.*, 2003). This evidence indicates that there often exists a difference between actual and estimated capital costs for projects (Flyvjberg *et al.*, 2018) clearly putting paid to the notion of cost estimating as an exact science. Developing countries are no exception. Take the case of India for instance. According to the Ministry of Statistics and Program Implementation (MoSPI), infrastructure projects developed by the central government sector costing INR 150 crore (US$22 million) and above are currently experiencing cumulative cost overruns of 20.1 percent of their planned cost[1]! Given that India plans to invest US$4.5 trillion in infrastructure projects in the next 20 years, the impact of this trend of cost overruns on the Indian economy, should it continue, can be debilitating. Of equal concern is the fact that several studies have shown that there has hardly been any reduction in the quantum and frequency cost overruns the world over in the last 70 years (Flyvbjerg *et al.*, 2002), indicating that this

---

[1] https://economictimes.indiatimes.com/news/economy/infrastructure/358-projects-worth-rs-3-53-lakh-crore-report-cost-overruns-mospi/articleshow/67060611.cms [Accessed October 9, 2020].

phenomenon is not new and that the underlying issues are systemic and institutionalized.

A considerable amount of research has been undertaken to understand why these cost overruns take place, and to be fair, the literature indicates that while in some cases this may be due to inaccuracies in the estimation process, in other cases they may be due to extraneous factors that are not within the control of the estimator. For instance, Meng (2012) points out that poor relationships across the supply chain lead to cost overruns. Subramani *et al.* (2014) identify the major causes of cost overruns to be slow decision-making, poor schedule management, increase in material, machine prices, poor contract management, poor design, delay in providing design, rework due to wrong work, problems in land acquisition, and delays between design completion and time of bidding, hardly any of which can be controlled by estimators.

In addition, there are several developing-country–specific studies that both reinforce these views and provide contextual factors that may have a greater influence on cost overruns in a particular context. In the Indian context, the most common causes of time and cost overruns in infrastructure projects have been identified as delays in land acquisition, delays in forest clearance, law and order problems, price escalation, high capital cost, poor performance of contractors, and delay in the supply of equipment (Narayanan *et al.*, 2018). In Ghana, Frimpong *et al.* (2003) conduct an extensive survey among owners, consultants, and contractors and conclude that periodic payment difficulties from agencies, poor contractor management, poor material procurement, poor technical performance, and escalation of material prices are key factors leading to cost overruns. Rosenfield (2014) suggests that premature tender documents, too many changes in owners' requirements or definitions, and tender-winning prices being unrealistically low are the root causes of cost overruns in Israel. In an interesting twist, Ahsan and Gunawan (2010) look at 100 international development projects sponsored by the Asian Development Bank in several Asian countries and find significant cost underruns. Complementary to the findings above, they identify factors such as competitive international bidding, changes in local tax and interest policies, and depreciation/devaluation of the local currency as contributing to improved cost performance on projects. It is important to note that at least the last two of these reasons are macro-economic in scope and therefore do not come under the sphere of influence of project managers.

On the other hand, some of the approaches suggested in the literature do point to behavioral and cognitive bias of the estimators to explain cost overruns. Chitkara (2011), for instance, identifies inadequate project formulation consisting of poor field investigations, inadequate project information, poor initial cost estimates, and lack of experience of the estimator as key drivers of cost overruns. Researchers such as Bent Flyvbjerg explain cost overruns on the basis of constructs such as "Optimism Bias" and "Strategic Misrepresentation" (Flyvbjerg *et al.*, 2002). Flyvjberg and his associates indicate persistent bias in infrastructure project appraisals, where costs are systematically underestimated and demand systematically overestimated either on purpose in order to ensure that projects are viewed as feasible and are embarked upon (Strategic Misrepresentation), or due to an inherent psychological tendency to feel confident of one's ability to control the future at the start of a project (Optimism Bias). They argue that cost variations are skewed toward the positive side (overruns) and one hardly finds any negative variations (underruns) to the estimated costs, implying that there is a pattern here and not merely chance happenstance (Flyvbjerg *et al.*, 2002, 2004, 2005, 2008, 2009). While such claims of strategic misrepresentation need to be investigated in closer detail using empirical data, this stream of literature suggests that the process of cost estimation is not deterministic, but is strategic, subjective, and consequently leads to inaccuracies.

Another group of experts led by Peter Love refute these claims while acknowledging the presence of agency in estimation. Love and associates argue that the major reason for cost overruns is the inability to predict numerous uncertainties in infrastructure projects and consequently the lack of complete information available to estimators (Love and Ahiaga-Dagbui, 2018). The degree of accuracy or completeness of information governs not only the accuracy of the estimate but also the range of assumptions that estimators will need to make as they try to arrive at a cost that is both competitive and defensible. Research on leadership and governance of construction projects by Gil and Lundrigan (2012), perhaps, offers a more holistic assessment of cost growth that aligns closely with the views of Love and Ahiaga-Dagbui (2018) above. That projects evolve is, essentially, at the core of their argument. For Love and Ahiaga-Dagbui (2018) and Gil *et al.* (2012), project cost overruns are not really a case of projects not going according to plan (budget), but the other way round — plans not going according to the project. Gil and Pinto (2018) take this argument a step forward and suggest that, as the project evolves, new stakeholders emerge who have an interest in the project, be they landholders, utilities, subcontractors, or vendors. As these stakeholders supply accurate information on their own spheres of influence to the project, the actual costs of the project become more apparent. This process of finalizing specific costs well after the initial estimates are undertaken then leads to cost overruns. Thus, Gil and Pinto (2018) attribute cost overruns to this polycentric governance system prevalent in construction, where no single party controls all the information flow on the project. This perspective appears less speculative than ones that emphasize strategic misrepresentation, and more rooted in the context of practice.

As debates rage between these schools of thought (see for instance, Flyvjberg *et al.*, 2018) Ahiaga-Dagbui and Smith (2014) attempt to bridge these ideas by suggesting that estimates of reliability and accuracy depend on two separate but often confused phenomena — underestimation and cost overruns. Arguments for underestimation include optimism bias that emanates from behavioral theories such as prospect theory, strategic misrepresentation, corruption, and the Dunning–Kruger effect (the tendency to overestimate competency or accuracy in judgment and the inability to see past one's own errors). On the other hand, arguments for cost overruns include scope changes, managerial or technical difficulties, risk and uncertainty, ground conditions, and price fluctuations.

Taken together, the studies discussed thus far provide one with a picture of project estimation as a process that is mildly chaotic, infused with randomness, and not completely organized. It is therefore imperative, that these dynamics be better understood and the current body of knowledge on estimation be augmented to take into consideration phenomena such as incomplete information and strategic considerations. While there is quite a bit of literature relevant to the process of cost estimation, most research studies ignore the key actor involved in the preparation of cost estimates — the cost estimator. After all, it is the estimator who derives the initial cost estimate on which a project's cost performance is evaluated, and it stands to reason that the estimator's behavior, their strategic objectives, and the processes they follow are to be unpacked if we are to contribute to the body of knowledge on cost estimating. How do estimators, particularly in the developing country context, undertake the practice of estimation? Do these practices of estimation indeed influence cost overruns on projects? Do they create expectations that projects are inherently unable to meet? It is to these questions that we now turn our attention.

The practice of cost estimation

Barley and Kunda's (2001) clarion call to "bring work back in" has motivated researchers across disciplines to go beyond the identification of factors and abstractions of behavior, to pay closer attention to the practice of how work is carried out in social and technical settings. This "practice turn" in studies of organizations has led researchers to look beyond "actors and their 'rational' actions and attempt to provide a rich and often descriptive understanding of the process of an organization and work in social settings" (Ramalingam and Mahalingam, 2018). This approach attempts to integrate the role of actions, material artifacts, discursive practices, and notions of power and interest to depict how work is produced and reproduced in the context of an organization and to analyze "social, technological, cultural and organizational phenomena" as they are dynamically "produced, reinforced and changed through ongoing and recurrent actions" (Bechky, 2006; Feldman and Orlikowski, 2011; Nicolini, 2011). The objective in this tradition is not to identify a theoretical framework with a generalizable set of "best" practices, or to characterize teams that have high performance, but rather to focus on building a grounded understanding of "work" and its situated and potentially contested (re) production.

Practices are often routinized, repetitive sequences of actions that actors undertake in order to do work. In the neo-institutionalist tradition, they comprise both action and structure that are mutually constituted as performative aspects and ostensive patterns (Feldman and Orlikowski, 2011). Performative aspects refer to the observable actions that constitute these practices or routines, while the ostensive patterns describe the structures, contexts, or norms that frame these actions. From a structurationalist perspective, practices constitute actions that are influenced by a pre-existing institutional structure. However, practices in turn reinforce these structures, and depending on their level of stability, might merely reconstitute existing practices or might leverage the action–structure duality to change both the actions performed and the structures within which they are performed. A practice perspective is therefore quite valuable in studying "how" work is performed, and in our case, provide us with some clues on how cost estimates are prepared and how this process of preparation might lead to the eventuality of cost-overruns.

To what extent then do we understand the practices that cost estimators adopt to estimate projects? The closest that we can get to this is a body of literature that suggests a variety of methods of cost estimation in construction projects. These methods can in turn be classified as traditional and non-traditional methods. The most popular traditional method used for cost estimation is the quantity rate analysis technique, while emerging non-traditional methods are either statistics or Artificial Intelligence based. The non-traditional methods are essentially data analysis techniques, which help in predicting future events that can have an impact on cost estimates. Some examples are regression analysis, reference class forecasting, case-based reasoning, neural networks, fuzzy inference, and Monte Carlo simulations (Shabniya and Dilruba, 2017). Some of these methods are briefly described below.

Quantity rate analysis

In this long-serving and highly popular method, the entire project is divided into small discrete work items, and a unit rate is established for each item. The unit rate is then multiplied by the required quantity to find the cost for the work item. All costs are added to obtain the estimated total construction cost (Shabniya and Dilruba, 2017). Most consultants and contractors still use traditional spreadsheets showing their rates for any type of work. Indirect costs are also calculated in the same way by using work breakdown structures.

Regression analysis

It is well known that estimators face many difficulties while estimating costs in construction projects. Reasons range from lack of information and limited cognitive ability to process information, to uncertainties in the future. Regression analysis is used to develop cost models that help in addressing such issues by analyzing or "fitting" data from previous projects. Construction costs are a function of many variables, such as the characteristics of the structure being built, socio-economic conditions, project characteristics, and the experience of the estimators. Regression analysis involves developing mathematical models that express the relationship between construction costs and their statistically significant independent variables (cost drivers) (Thomas and Thomas, 2016). These models are then populated by parameters specific to the project that is being estimated, in order to develop a cost estimate for the project.

Reference class forecasting

Reference class forecasting derives from the Prospect Theory, developed by Daniel Kahneman and Amos Tversky (Kahneman and Tversky, 2013) and was first applied in construction by Bent Flyvbjerg (Flyvbjerg, 2002) to analyze the cost performance on large British transportation projects. This, along with the Quantity Rate Analysis method, appears to be a very popular technique for developing estimates on projects. Similar to regression analysis, the data from past projects are used to predict the cost of similar future projects. However, in contrast to regression analysis, combinations of factors, socio-economic variables, and so on, are often left out. Similar past projects are identified, costs of different elements are taken from these previous projects, and escalation and a few other modification factors are used to find the cost of similar elements in a new project. While this method lends itself to developing quick estimates, a disadvantage is that the method is not very accurate and leads to a lot of errors in estimation.

Artificial intelligence based methods

Given the limitations to parametric cost modelling, as no two projects are the same and the number of variables to be modeled is often very high for methods such as regression analysis to yield effective results, researchers have started looking toward Artificial Intelligence/Machine Learning based techniques for cost estimation. Pearce *et al.* (1996) developed a technique using Artificial Neural Networks (ANN) for generating range estimates to evaluate the risk of cost escalation in building construction. They outlined a procedure for building a prototype model for cost estimation, and using an ANN model to generate estimates for construction projects. Hegaz and Amyr Ayed (1998) used a neural network approach to manage construction cost data and develop a parametric cost estimating model for highway projects. They introduced two alternative techniques to train the network's weights: simplex optimization (Excel's inherent solver function), and genetic algorithms (GAs). However, these approaches are not used extensively by practitioners at the moment, and lie squarely within the domain of researchers.

The efficacy of any cost estimation method can be analyzed on three parameters — accuracy, usability, and ease of understanding. It is clear that neither the traditional nor the non-traditional methods of estimation have achieved all three outcomes together. Additionally, irrespective of the merits and demerits of these approaches, the literature merely describes these methods and does not provide us with an understanding of the actual practices that estimators adopt. For instance, estimators often make subjective decisions while preparing cost estimates. What kinds of bias then are present in the minds of estimators as they prepare estimates? How are decisions actually taken by estimators? As Laryea and Hughes (2008) have noted, a number of risk models have been proposed in the literature, but there is no evidence that such formal models are used to price risks in the process of estimating. Rather "a set of complex, micro-economic factors" (Laryea and Hughes, 2008) are used to price risk and are often not incorporated in current analytical approaches.

Understanding estimator behavior through a behavioral economic lens could provide some answers. Behavioral economics is broadly the study of psychology as it relates to the economic decision-making processes of individuals and institutions. In contrast to traditional economic approaches that assume rationality and instrumentality on the part of individual decision-makers, behavioral economics acknowledges that cognitive bias is at the root of many human errors that arise from relying on heuristics and pre-determined notions or instances of bias for decision-making (Tversky and Kahneman, 1991). Developing cost estimates for construction projects is no exception. In addition to determining the costs of materials, machinery, and labor, estimation also involves identifying project complexities and quantifying these qualitative risks. In the process, several assumptions need to be made. These assumptions are influenced by the estimator's limited cognitive ability and inherent bias, especially when they are working under tremendous time constraints. When confronted with such situations, estimators often perform an informal reasoning process, sometimes referred to as preference construction (Shealy *et al.*, 2015) to quantify risks and hidden costs. These shortcuts are common in the estimation process and lead to cognitive bias. Shealy *et al.* (2015) suggest that approaches from behavioral science (loss aversion, role models, and combined interventions) can translate to, and improve, multi-stakeholder infrastructure planning decisions, of which cost estimation is one.

Recognizing this lack of emphasis in the extant literature on the practices, decision-making processes, and bias involved in how estimators estimate construction costs, this chapter attempts to fill this gap by understanding how estimators estimate, what bias they work under, how they make decisions, when they use techniques such as quantity rate analysis versus reference class forecasting, and so on. In particular, this chapter attempts to "declutter" the process of cost estimation prevalent, particularly in the developing country context, through adopting an ethnographic approach to understanding the perspective of seasoned estimators in India, as is elaborated upon in the next section. Specifically, while trying to understand how cost-estimators develop estimates, we seek to answer the following questions: *What sub-practices constitute cost estimating? Do estimators follow different approaches for cost estimation based on the type of organization, stage or project? What role do instances of bias and phenomena such as optimism bias/strategic misrepresentations have in the preparation of estimates?*

In doing so, we hope to not only better understand the underlying micro-dynamics of construction cost estimating in the developing country context but also to understand how we might restructure and eliminate biases that lead to incorrect estimates that then contribute to cost overruns. Thereby, we hope to add to the body of knowledge on this subject. We next discuss the methodology that we adopted for our study followed by a presentation of our observations and a discussion of our findings.

Methods

In order to study the practices of estimators in a developing country context, we chose to study estimators in India, given that both authors are based in India and had connections with a variety of firms in the country. Practices are best studied through ethnographic techniques — both direct observation and ethnographic interviewing methods (Spradley, 1979). Consequently, first-hand techniques such as personal interviews with estimators who estimate costs in construction projects were relied upon. The minimum experience of the informants selected for the study was greater than 10 years. This helped to ensure that data were being collected from experienced estimators who were using routinized practices for estimation. While most of the interviews were open-ended as recommended by the literature on ethnographic interviewing, a second round of interviews was often conducted (or a round was added at the end of the first interactions) where a semi-structured format of questioning was used to ensure that the informants spoke to the research questions that have been identified above. However, the informants were primarily encouraged to talk about their work and tell the researchers stories of what they did on a daily basis to help them understand practices that were prevalent in cost estimation. This allowed an understanding of practices followed by estimators in India to be induced.

A total of 14 professionals from 12 different organizations involved in construction were interviewed. All of the informants were involved in, and familiar with, the estimation process. In the first step, each of these stakeholders was interviewed personally; each was asked to explain their approach to estimating project costs in detail. The researchers' intuition was that there exists both a routinized process and some discretionary strategic considerations that go into preparing a budget estimate, and the objective of this initial set of interviews was to validate and arrive at an understanding of both these dynamics. Examples of the kinds of open-ended questions that were asked to start the discussions are:

- What is the sequence of actions taken while estimating costs for a construction project?
- How many people from the organization are involved in the estimation process and what roles do they play?

- What risks do estimators consider and how do they quantify risks that they foresee?
- How and where do estimators use their past experiences in the estimation process?

The interviews were recorded and transcribed. Detailed field notes were also taken at each interview. The details of the interviews and the informants are presented in Table 17.1 (the duration of the interview represents the total time spent with the informant. Due to their busy schedules, many of the interviews were broken into shorter chunks and multiple sessions were held with the informants).

In addition to these interviews, a few senior managers in these firms were also briefly interviewed to give insights into the strategic considerations used for preparing estimates. Construction is a very competitive industry, and hence strategic decisions that decide the profit margins and risk contingency are the real determinants of the final estimate. A second

Table 17.1: Details of interviews conducted for this study.

No.	Roles	Experience (years)	Organization type	Duration (hours)
1	Chief Estimator	20	Public Sector Client	2
2	Head of Estimation	25	Small Contractor	3
3	Head of Estimation	28	Medium Contractor	3
4	Senior Executive	30	Large Contractor	1.5
5	Senior Executive	30	Large Contractor	1.5
6	Senior Executive	15	Consultant	2
7	Head of Estimation	15	Consultant	2
8	Senior Executive	30	Public Client	2
9	Ex- CEO	35	Infrastructure Developer	3
10	Senior Manager	15	Large Contractor	1.5
11	Director	18	Consultant	3
12	Manager	10	Small Contractor	2
13	Estimator	10	Medium Contractor	1
14	Senior Executive	20	Private Client	2

round of interviews was also conducted with the informants indicated in Table 17.1 to clarify the remaining lacunas in understanding the process. In these second round of interviews, hypothetical scenarios were given to estimators in some cases to better understand their thought processes during the estimation process. Overall, 36 hours of personal interviews were conducted.

Data collected from the interviews was analyzed through standard coding techniques used in grounded theory generation (Corbin and Strauss, 2014). In particular the researchers carefully coded for sources of bias and heuristics used in the estimating process. An extensive matrix was developed comprising eight key stakeholders in the construction industry on the *X*-axis and 16 different parameters relating to estimation and outcomes on the *Y*-axis. These parameters resulted from the coding exercise that was undertaken. The stakeholders involved were divided into three main categories: Client, Consultant, and Contractor, as shown in Figure 17.1.

The key codes selected for comparison and analysis were divided into four categories: Routine processes, Strategic considerations, Risk estimation techniques, and Relation to overruns. These codes and their relevant subcodes are presented in Figure 17.2.

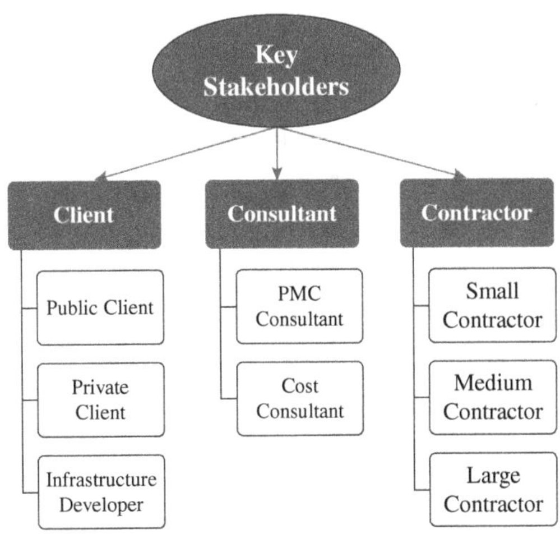

Figure 17.1: Characterization of stakeholders.

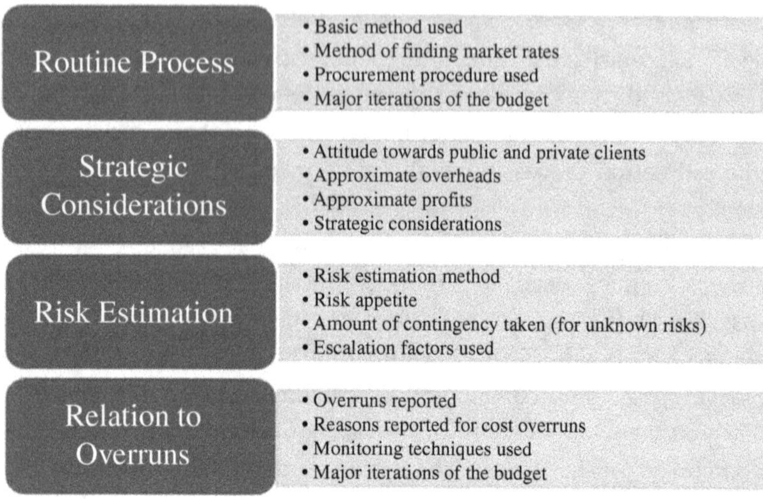

Figure 17.2: Parameters selected for comparing key stakeholders.

This analysis allowed the researchers to distinguish between the estimation methodologies of key stakeholders. It also gave an understanding of how the estimation process is related to underestimation of costs or cost overruns. The findings and observations are now unpacked in the next section.

How estimators develop cost estimates in India

As described in Figure 17.1, the informants were divided into eight stakeholder categories — Public Client, Private Client, Cost Consultant, PMC Consultant, Small Contractor, Medium Contractor, Large Contractor, and Infrastructure Developer. For the purpose of analysis, we clubbed public and private clients together as well as both types of consultants. Consequently, six key organization types were arrived at — Client, Consultant, Small Contractor, Medium Contractor, Large Contractor, and Infrastructure Developer.

We first individually describe each of these stakeholders and their approach to cost estimation. We then compare and contrast these approaches and present some insights and observations which will represent the key findings of this research.

How clients estimate

Data from two very different clients were analyzed from the public sector and the private sector. The public-sector client chosen was a university's engineering unit which develops academic buildings for the university campus. The researchers interacted with their Chief Estimator who had over 12 years of experience in cost estimation. This client did not follow a detailed method of cost estimation. Rather, they simply followed guideline values given by standards such as the Delhi Plinth Area Rates (DPAR) and Delhi Schedule of Rates, which were released by government departments on a regular basis. Thus, the client expended effort in taking off rough quantities from the drawings, and then merely used the rates given in these publications to come up with a cost estimate. A high-powered committee of university administrators then used this estimate to decide on the final budget and select consultants and contractors for the project. Subsequently, further work was taken on by the architects and consultants to prepare a Bill of Quantities (BoQ), which was then approved by the high-powered committee. Contractors were invited to submit their bids against this BoQ and the lowest bidder (L1) was selected. Risk estimation was not given much importance since most buildings were similar in nature and the client felt that uncertainties and risks were well known and controllable. Clearly, not much attention was paid to cost estimation by the client and most of the detailed work was done by the consultants and architects.

The private-sector client selected to be studied was a commercial developer. The researchers interacted with two executives within this firm — an estimator with over 10 years of experience and a senior executive closely involved in making major strategic decisions. In contrast to the public-sector client, this client reverse-engineered their estimates. Initially, market studies were done to determine revenues that could be generated from a commercial development. Using discounted cash flow models that fixed their internal rates of return, the cost of construction was then calculated. However, this cost was not shared with the firm's consultants. Simultaneously, an internal team would calculate the approximate value of the construction and use this to develop building specifications that would meet their target cost. These specifications would then be shared with their design consultants. Since these processes often took place in parallel, considerable information exchange was required between the client and the consultant, often resulting in a difference in objectives as defined by the client and as understood by the consultant.

How consultants estimate

Two consultants were interviewed — a Project Management Consultant (PMC) and a cost consultant. The researchers spoke to a senior estimator in the cost consultancy firm and a pair of senior executives at the PMC firm. Both types of consultants used very similar methods of cost estimation. However, the cost consultants had a larger data set to choose from. Both firms used the reference class forecasting technique — they referenced different items from old projects and modified their cost estimates for the current project as per the conditions and the needs of the new project. These consultants generally adopted the median value without going into too much detail and risk profiling since there was not much time given to them to prepare their estimates by their clients. Both consultants had a fairly large data set of old projects and a team to calculate various site-specific factors such as escalation and labor rates. However, the factors chosen were very subjective and were easily changed when clients asked them to reduce costs. As the executive of the PMC consultant explained:

> "Consultants use three things: Experience from past projects especially similar projects in the same location, quotations from contractors and for some items first principle methods. First principle method gives higher costs than the contractor actually bears and hence is avoided by the consultants."

In most projects, not all designs are shared with the consultants, and this led to iterative estimates that tend to be erroneous. The consultants we spoke to also did not pay much attention to risks in the projects and generally did not consider risk factors. Consequently, consultants tended to develop estimates that were likely to be lower than the actual costs — in keeping with the clients expectations of agreeing on an economical budget. The consultants we spoke to highlighted the trust deficit in the Indian construction industry and its impact on cost overruns.

How small contractors estimate

Small contractors are firms that construct projects that cost between US$10 million and US$30 million. The researchers spoke to the Head of Estimation and the CEO of a small contracting firm. This firm specializes in constructing industrial structures. These contractors appeared to follow first principle methods such as Quantity Rate Analysis. They had a robust data set of manpower and machinery required prepared for different items and used these to come up with very accurate estimates. In their words:

> "Estimation basically is a two-step process — estimating quantities and estimating rates. These two steps may have to run simultaneously as rates and quantities are interdependent. Firstly, quantity will be estimated by three to four people at the junior level. Then the rates will by estimated by the experienced people."

Any item in the BoQ is divided into three parts — material, machine, and labor. For each item or activity, the quantity of each of these three was precisely calculated to find the overall cost of the item. These contractors also cross-checked their estimate with previous project costs to validate their results. In the conversations, the contractors reported much lower cost overruns than the consultants. However, they did cite reasons such as inflation or sudden changes in labor costs as reasons for cost overruns in small projects.

The real challenge for these contractors was to balance risks, overheads, profits, and to win the bid. These strategic considerations are the major differentiating factor between the bids of different players. The informants noted that their estimates of profit margins and risk contingencies depended on many factors, such as the image of the client as a paymaster, competitors, past relations with the client, and whether the contractor was looking for experience in certain kinds of projects. Such contractors operated on very thin margins and therefore needed their estimates to be as precise as possible. With regards to assessing risks, small contractors appear to undertake projects that were mostly very similar in type and within a small geographic region. As a result, they had a good understanding of risks in and around the projects. However, their risk assessment systems broke down if the project was non-routine. The CEO whom the researchers interviewed explained that new kinds of projects generally resulted in cost overruns due to their inability to quantify risks accurately.

How medium-sized contractors estimate

Medium-sized contractors in India are contractors that construct projects that cost between US$30 and US$100 million. The firm from this segment that we chose to study operates in multiple cities and has a very diversified portfolio. The researchers spoke to the Head of Estimation in this firm, who had over 20 years of experience. The methods used by these contractors to develop estimates were very similar to that of small contractors. The key difference is in the level of sophistication of the estimate. Medium-sized contractors also followed the Quantity Rate Analysis approach and hence the routine part of their estimate was very robust. Unlike the small contractors, these contractors prepared two types of estimates — one for the bidding process by the tendering team and another by the project manager and team that are going to implement the project on the ground. Our informant clarified:

> "Two estimates are prepared; one is initial estimate during the time of bidding/tendering and the other one Accepted Cost Estimate (ACE) which is prepared after winning the bid. Initial bids objective is to win the project. It is prepared by a separate bidding team comprising experienced project managers heading it, while ACE is prepared by a separate team which also involves the project manager who is going to implement the project on the ground."

This firm had different departments within the organization, such as the quantity coordination team, tendering team, procurement team, and risk assessment team, to take care of different facets of estimation. Hence, the process of estimating was distributed and very organized, resulting in low overruns for the firm. The different departments gave their inputs to the tendering team, which then calculated direct costs of material, machine, and labor for the project. Finally, other indirect costs such as insurance and other overheads costs were added to arrive at the final estimate. Typical overheads for this firm were between 15 to 20 percent of direct costs. The strategic considerations that we discussed for small contractors also held for the medium-sized firm that we studied.

According to our informants, most medium-sized contractors have well-structured methods of risk assessment. They have a highly experienced central risk assessment team that divides the risks into project phases and assigns a contingency value to each risk. As the Head of Estimation explained, a contingency factor of 2 percent is generally kept for each risk but is often reduced during post-bid negotiations. Similar to small contractors, medium-sized contractors too bemoaned the lack of time available to prepare estimates and the consequent lack of detail in the estimates prepared.

How large contractors estimate

Large contractors are firms that develop projects that cost more than US$100 million. These firms have a complex structure and methodology to estimate costs. We interviewed six different professionals working in different segments of one of India's largest contracting firms.

Large contractors also use the Quantity Rate Analysis method but also couple this with reference class forecasting techniques. In the firm that we studied, a quantity team estimated the quantity of machinery, material, and labor for all the activities in the BoQ and sent the requirements to a procurement team. A centralized procurement team procured all major items such as cement, steel, electro-mechanical systems, and so on, leading to economies of scale. The use of such specialized teams resulted in reduced margins of error.

With regards to risks, the contractor who was interviewed in this segment decided their margins based on a number of strategic factors, including the state of the market, the government in power, and expectations of profit from the shareholders. A comprehensive risk matrix was prepared in which risks were categorized under several heads. Feedback was sought from external consultants to justify their risk assumptions. Most major risks, such as exchange rate risks and inflation risks, were managed by a central risk management team and risks were balanced from one project to another (using reference class techniques). The risk estimation process was therefore considerably more robust compared to what we observed in the small and medium-sized firms that we studied.

How infrastructure developers estimate

To analyze estimating processes in infrastructure development firms, the researchers spoke to an ex-CEO of a leading private infrastructure developer with over 20 years of experience in running projects as well as a senior executive in an on-going metro project. In infrastructure projects, clients often start by commissioning a Detailed Project Report (DPR). DPRs are prepared by consultants, who also provide an estimated cost based on their analysis of similar projects. The consultant's ability to conceive the project is limited by time and expertise. They estimate only on the basis of the given requirements and market conditions, which are subject to change during the long development phase of the project. Competitive bidding forces infrastructure developers to keep their bids as low as possible, as close to the consultants estimates as possible, and to be more optimistic and aggressive in their cost estimation. They underestimate the risk contingency needed and repose undue trust in their operational ability. As our informant observed:

> "Initially, most large-scale projects have funding constraints and this invariably brings aggression in all steps of the projects. Benefits are over estimated, costs are underestimated and risks are undermined and the result is a much better project on paper than on (the) ground."

Discussion: Varieties of estimation

The observations indicate that estimation practices vary widely depending on the kind of firm involved in preparing the estimates. Construction projects have three key stakeholders — the client, the design consultants, and the contractor. Generally, consultants prepare an initial estimate as per the requirements of the clients and manage the tendering process involved in selecting an appropriate contractor. Contractors then prepare separate estimates which they use to place their bids.

Consultants tend to use reference class forecasting based practices, where they analyze similar projects to estimate costs for new projects. These estimates are highly inaccurate. The consultants we interviewed revealed that their estimates were often wrong by as much as 20 percent (without any major changes in the scope of the project). On the other hand, contractors prepare their estimate using grounds-up Quantity-Rate-Analysis–based practices, where they meticulously calculate the quantity of material, manpower, and machinery involved in executing each task and what the costs of these parameters would be. The contractors interviewed reported a much smaller final deviation between their estimates and the actual costs of a project, reporting an average cost overrun of only 5 percent over their bid estimate (without any major change in the scope of the project). In general, as compared to the consultants, the techniques used by contractors to prepare cost estimates appear to be very robust. They tend to have better linkages with subcontractors and vendors and are well aware of the ongoing and upcoming market conditions, and are therefore able to price risks accurately. The former CEO of a leading infrastructure developer firm commented thus:

> "Initial Detailed Project Report is prepared by a consultant. Consultant's ability to conceive the project is limited by time and expertise. They can estimate only on the basis of given requirements and market conditions which are obviously subject to change during the long development phase of the project."

Consultants generally do not seem to undertake any risk analysis and this contributes to their estimates being inaccurate. Contractors, with their enormous on-site experience, market awareness, and incentive to bid correctly, estimate more accurately than the consultants. Therefore, for any benchmarking or calculating overruns, it is often better to use the estimates of the contractors rather than those of the consultants.

Differences between the estimation methodologies of various contractors

There were significant differences between the estimation methodologies used by small, medium-sized, and large contractors. Though all contractors broadly used the Quantity Rate Analysis method, specific practices, and in particular, the levels of detail considered, varied for each. Small contractors have a more simplistic and deterministic approach while medium-sized and large contractors use a mix of statistical and deterministic approaches. They used different scenarios to come up with their estimate. For large contractors, the decision on whether to bid or not to bid is also decided by market expectations. A senior executive of India's leading contractor firm who was interviewed commented:

> "In business, both top line (total volume of business) and bottom line (margins from each project) has to grow simultaneously. Everything is determined by the expectations of the market and shareholders. Shareholders expect the company to take on more and more projects. Therefore, many times such projects are selected which may not be very viable for the company."

We also found that small contractors have a single pre-bid and post-bid budget whereas both medium and large contractors have different pre-bid and post-bid budgets. The post-bid budget is prepared by the estimation team in confluence with the on-site team responsible for implementing the project. Thus, the responsibility to finish projects on time and under budget is shared between the execution and construction teams in these types of firms.

Another key difference was found in the practices used to estimate risks. Small contractors merely assumed a contingency factor based on past experience or intuition, whereas medium-sized contractors took a more systematic approach to risk analysis by breaking down risks into different phases, creating a checklist for each phase, and assigning risk-adjusted costs to each activity based on their experience and the risk appetite of the organization. Large contractors used a much more sophisticated and well-architected risk estimation framework. A seasoned estimator in a large contracting firm explained:

> "Large organisations have specialized people for managing risk called risk managers. Although the probability that they estimate is subjective, generally they prepare a risk chart and give different weightages to different risks."

It is also important to note that small and medium-sized contractors seemed highly risk averse and therefore not optimistically biased as Flyvbjerg (2002) may have us believe. However, we find some optimism bias when it comes to large contractors and infrastructure projects.

Are there instances of bias in estimation?

One of the research questions that the researchers set out to understand was the role of bias in estimate preparation. Construction is a competitive industry and hence contractors are by nature quite aggressive with their bid estimates. This is found across most levels — small, medium-sized, or large projects. Bidding psychology plays a key role in deciding the final cost estimate. It was found that small and medium-sized contractors cannot afford to be overly optimistic or aggressive with their bidding. Only in very few instances did these contractors bid optimistically, and only if they were very confident of the client's reputation as a generous paymaster. However, large contractors tended to be much more optimistic. A senior executive at one of the largest construction companies in India commented during one of the interviews:

> "You are always optimistic. Winning the project is more important. Optimistic but conscious call is taken to select break-in project, but have confidence in operational efficiency to turn it around later. The only difference will be how much optimistic I am, what is the profit margin I put over my bid. To win the bid I have to consciously under-assess the risks or my method of risk estimation should be different."

Therefore, while an optimism bias was present in these estimates as Flyvjberg would suggest, the researchers did not find any evidence of major strategic misrepresentation of estimates to clients to win bids on projects.

However, we noticed considerable variations between how contractors estimate costs for private projects and how they do so for government (public) projects. In private projects, impacts of risks are deemed to be much less compared to government projects as contractors and clients often negotiate ex-post and settle their disputes amicably. This scope for negotiations once a contract has been awarded is non-existent in government projects and therefore estimates for public works need to be done far more precisely. An estimator at one of India's leading contractors compared private and public projects thus:

> "Government officers can drag the project because no personal stake is involved. However, for private player time wasted is revenue lost. With government there is a very slim chance of negotiating later; hence we have to be more careful. In government projects, only L1 (lowest bidder) is taken into account, whereas in private projects one can award to other than L1. Also private player tends to keep higher contingencies as compared to government projects."

Hence, contractors admittedly load more risk in their bids in government projects. This can be as much as five percent of the project cost.

Conclusion

Our aim in this chapter was to explore the practice of estimation. Our analysis indicates that there are several practices of estimation pursued by different stakeholders who occupy different positions in the project value chain. Further, factors such as the size of the firm and the type of project also determine the practice of estimation used.

From a project lifecycle perspective, initial estimates prepared by clients and consultants are often simplistic and follow reference class forecasting based practices. This approach is necessitated by the fact that the duration for creating these estimates is highly compressed, and clients often do not have settled requirements at the start of the project. Vague notions crystallize much later on. These rather approximate estimates form the basis for the final evaluation of a project's performance, leading to erroneous judgments being drawn on cost overruns. For instance, a flash report of the MoSPI in 2018 concluded thus:

> "Total original cost of implementation of 1361 projects when sanctioned, was of the order of Rs. 678,634.82 crore but this was subsequently revised to Rs. 2,016,360.99 crore implying a cost overrun of 20.1%."

The baseline here was the approximate preliminary estimates provided, and therefore a large cost overrun was reported, where in reality, the difference between budgeted and actual costs may have been much closer when compared with the final detailed estimates.

As projects progress and contractors get involved, a different practice of cost estimation — the Quantity Rate Analysis technique — was observed. Here, detailed estimates are made by calculating the extent of labor, machinery, and material required, and sophisticated risk analysis calculations are performed to determine adequate but competitive buffers to be added to projects. The level of sophistication of these estimates varied in direct proportion to the size of the contractors involved. Public-sector clients also benefited from highly detailed estimates.

We also set out to investigate the role and presence of biases in the preparation of cost estimates. While we did not find evidence of strategic misrepresentation, we did find some evidence of optimism biases in the estimates prepared. However, these were often only within the purview of large contractors bidding on megaprojects, while smaller firms with lower margins often crafted more realistic estimates of what a project would cost.

Our study also has implications for the creation of a body of knowledge in the area of cost estimation for developing countries. It is clear that prescriptive practices and techniques need to be developed separately for different categories of firms who estimate with different levels of granularity and different levels of completeness of information. Furthermore, it is important to recognize that pre- and post-bid estimates may differ as may estimating procedures used for public versus private projects. Consequently, separate standards, practices and knowledge may need to be evolved for each of these cases.

We are aware that our study has several limitations — the overall number of informants is quite small and our findings are restricted to the developing country context of India. Our results are therefore more indicative than general. Notwithstanding this, we believe that our understanding of the field of cost estimation is quite nascent and that this study has shed some light on the micro-processes involved. Some of the propositions that we have raised vis-a-vis small versus large contractors, public versus private projects, and others are empirically testable and can spawn research directions that can greatly enrich our understanding of this field. It is also possible that this age-old tradition of cost estimation is not as stable as it seems. We did not find much evidence of the use of deep-technology such as Artificial Intelligence in the practical construction of estimates. However, given the theoretical advances that are being made in this field coupled with more relational contracting approaches, it is possible that we will see a sea change in the actors, actions, and structures involved in the practice of cost estimation. This may then further revolutionize the practice of cost estimation, requiring further updating of the extant body of knowledge in this area. Digitization has already influenced estimating. Building Information Models, for instance, are already able to calculate geometric quantities instantly and with minimal error. The stage is therefore set for a digital turn in this age-old practice of estimating costs on projects. We invite researchers to delve into these issues, particularly in the context of developing countries.

References

Ahiaga-Dagbui, D.D. and Smith, S.D. (2014). Rethinking construction cost overruns: Cognition, learning and estimation. *Journal of Financial Management and Property Construction*, 19(1), 38–54.

Ahsan, K. and Gunawan, I. (2010). Analysis of cost and schedule performance of international development projects. *International Journal of Project Management,* 28(1), 68–78.

Barley, S.R. and Kunda, G. (2001). Bringing work back in. *Organization Science*, 12(1), 76–95.

Bechky, B.A. (2006). Gaffers, gofers, and grips: Role-based coordination in temporary organizations. *Organization Science*, 17(1), 3–21.

Chitkara, K.K. (2011). *Construction Project Management — Planning, Scheduling and Controlling*, 2nd Edition. Tata McGraw Hill, New Delhi.

Corbin, J. and Strauss, A. (2014). *Basics of Qualitative Research: Techniques and Procedures for Developing Grounded Theory*. Sage Publications, Thousand Oaks, CA.

Feldman, M.S. and Orlikowski, W.J. (2011). Theorizing practice and practicing theory. *Organization Science*, 22(5), 1240–1253.

Flyvbjerg, B. (2008). Curbing optimism bias and strategic misrepresentation in planning: Reference class forecasting in practice. *European Planning Studies*, 16, 3–21.

Flyvbjerg, B. (2009). Survival of the unfittest: Why the worst infrastructure gets built — And what we can do about it. *Oxford Review of Economic Policy*, 25, 344–367.

Flyvbjerg, B., Ansar, A., Budzier, A, Buhl, S., Cantarelli, C., Garbuio, M., Glenting, C., Holm, M.S., Lovallo, D., Lunn, D., Molin, E., Rønnest, A., Stewart, A. and Van Wee, B. (2018). Five things you should know about cost overrun. *Transportation Research Part A: Policy and Practice*, 118(December), 174–190. https://doi.org/10.1016/j.tra.2018.07.013.

Flyvbjerg, B., Bruzelius, N. and Rothengatter, W. (2003). *Megaprojects and Risk: An Anatomy of Ambition*. Cambridge University Press, Cambridge, UK.

Flyvbjerg, B., Holm, M. and Buhl, S. (2002). Underestimating costs in public works projects. *Journal of the American Planning Association*, 68(3), 279–295. https://doi.org/10.1080/01944360208976273.

Flyvbjerg, B., Skamris Holm, M.K. and Buhl, S.L. (2004). What causes cost overrun in transport infrastructure projects? *Transport Reviews*, 24, 3–18.

Flyvbjerg, B., Skamris Holm, M.K. and Buhl, S.L. (2005). How (in)accurate are demand forecasts in public works projects? The case of transportation. *Journal of the American Planning Association*, 71, 131–146.

Frimpong, Y., Oluwoye, J. and Crawford, L. (2003). Causes of delay and cost overruns in construction of groundwater projects in developing countries; Ghana as a case study. *International Journal of Project Management*, 21(5), 321–326.

Gil, N. and Lundrigan, C. (2012). *The Leadership and Governance of Megaprojects*. Centre for Infrastructure Development (CID), Manchester Business School, The University of Manchester, UK.

Gil, N. and Pinto, J. (2018). Polycentric organizing and performance: A contingency model and evidence from megaproject planning in the UK. *Research Policy*, 47(4), 717–34.

Hegazy, T. and Amr Ayed (1998). Neural network model for parametric cost estimation of highway projects. *Journal of Construction Engineering and Management, ASCE*, 124(3), 210–218.

Kahneman, D. and Tversky, A. (2013). Prospect theory: An analysis of decision under risk. In L. Maclean and W. Ziemba (Eds.), *Handbook of the Fundamentals of Financial Decision Making*. World Scientific Publishing Ltd., Hackensack, pp. 99–127.

Kanabar, V. and Warburton, R.D.H. (2011). Leveraging the new practice standard for project estimating. Paper presented at *PMI® Global Congress 2011 —* North America, Dallas, TX. Newtown Square, PA

Laryea, S. and Hughes, W. (2008). How contractors price risks in bids: Theory and practice. *Construction Management and Economics,* 26(9), 911–924.

Love, P.E.D. and Ahiaga-Dagbui, D. (2018). Debunking fake news in a post-truth era: The plausible untruths of cost underestimation in transport infrastructure projects. *Transportation Research Part A: Policy and Practice*, 113, 357–368.

Meng, X. (2012). The effect of relationship management on project performance in construction. *International Journal of Project Management,* 30(2), 188–198.

Narayanan, S., Madhav Kure, A. and Palaniappan, S. (2018). Study on time and cost overruns in mega infrastructure projects in India. *Journal of The Institution of Engineers (India): Series A,* 100. https://doi.org/10.1007/s40030-018-0328-1.

Nicolini, D. (2011). Turning practically: broadening the horizon. *Journal of Organizational Change Management*, 24(2), 164–174.

Pearce, A.R., Gregory, R.A. and Williams, L. (1996). Range estimating for risk management using artificial neural networks. *Journal of Parametric Estimating*, 14(1), 88–93.

Ramalingam, S. and Mahalingam, A. (2018). Knowledge coordination in transnational engineering projects: A practice-based study. *Construction Management and Economics*, 36(4), 1–16. https://www.tandfonline.com/doi/full/10.1080/01446193.2018.1498591.

Rosenfield, Y. (2014). Root-cause analysis of construction-cost overruns. *ASCE Journal of Construction Management*, 140(1). https://doi.org/10.1061/(ASCE)CO.1943-7862.0000789.

Shabniya, V. and Dilruba, K.M. (2017). A review of construction cost forecasting techniques. *International Research Journal of Engineering and Technology (IRJET)*, e-ISSN: 2395-0056.

Shealy, T., Klotz, L., Weber, E.U., Johnson, E.J., Bell, R.J. and Harris, N. (2015). Alleviating biases in infrastructure decisions for sustainability: A summary of five experiments and a call to action for the engineering project management research community. *Proceedings of the Engineering Project Organization Conference,* Cle Elum, Washington.

Spradley, J. (1979). *The Ethnographic Interview.* Waveland Press Inc., Illinois.

Subramani, T., Sruthi, P.S. and Kavitha, M. (2014, June). Causes of cost overrun in construction. *IOSR Journal of Engineering*, 04(06).

Thomas, N. and Thomas, A. (2016). Regression modelling for prediction of construction cost and duration. *Applied Mechanics and Materials*, 857, 195–199.

Tversky, A. and Kanheman, D. (1991). Loss aversion in riskless choices: A reference dependent model. *The Quarterly Journal of Economics*, 106(4), 1039–1061. https://doi.org/10.2307/2937956.

https://doi.org/10.1142/9789811224720_0018

Chapter 18

Body of Knowledge in Developing and Implementing Construction Industry Improvement Programs

Gangadhar Mahesh*, Desalegn Girma Mengistu† and Mohan M. Kumaraswamy‡,§

*National Institute of Technology Karnataka, India
†Hawassa University — Institute of Technology, Ethiopia
‡The University of Hong Kong, Hong Kong SAR
§The University of Moratuwa, Sri Lanka

Abstract

Construction project performance is influenced by industry-wide issues, such as the business environment, sector-specific drivers and challenges, and country-specific issues. Imperatives for addressing such industry-level issues have led to industry improvement programs formulated and implemented by high-powered government-industry teams across the developed and developing countries. Despite these initiatives, the industry has yet to significantly improve its performance and image. The overarching goal of this chapter is to identify common core components and potentially critical elements of a Body of Knowledge (BoK) in developing and implementing Construction Industry Improvement Programs (CIIPs), with a particular focus on applying it to developing countries. In developing the BoK, CIIPs in Hong Kong, Singapore, the UK, and a few other countries are reviewed to identify important BoK themes. Lessons learnt and challenges unveiled from implementation and status reviews in the above jurisdictions are also discussed. The findings are compared with specific improvement programs and requirements of developing countries, with examples from India, Ethiopia, and Sri Lanka, so as to initiate development of the targeted BoK, that could hereafter help improve the planning and implementation of construction industry reform programs in developing countries in particular. The identified knowledge areas of CIIPs are: (i) Manpower Development, (ii) Enhancing Capacity, (iii) Institution Building, (iv) Improving Practices, and (v) Planning for Smoother Demand. The status of these knowledge areas and/or their components determines project performance. For example, the availability and competence of manpower in the industry affects productivity and hence the schedule performance of projects. Similarly, the capacity of construction firms affects most of the project performance parameters, such as the schedule, cost, and quality. While the specifics of these issues are addressed in other book chapters, it is clear that enabling optimal project performance and boosting project management maturity at the industry/national level calls for holistic industry improvements and overall, rather than piecemeal, developments.

Keywords: Construction industry improvement programmes, manpower development, capacity development, institution building, demand sustainability, key performance indicators

Introduction

Developing a Body of Knowledge (BoK) is a common practice for a specific profession, for example, a BoK for engineering disciplines by National Society of Professional Engineers (NSPE, 2013), and project management BoKs by different institutes and associations (Morris *et al.*, 2006). A BoK is expected to encapsulate the depth and breadth of knowledge, skills, and attitudes appropriate to enter a practice as a professional in charge of relevant activities that potentially impact the performance of the professional activities (NSPE, 2013). It indicates proven principles and the best practices for success of the profession and helps the practice to mature through time. The development of a BoK for a profession requires the consideration of the roles and ultimate objectives of the profession. Along similar lines, a generic BoK can be developed for common initiatives such as on Construction Industry Improvement Programs (CIIPs), that will enable the development of common principles and terminologies, and hence help in codifying and refining core knowledge and practices within a generally accepted framework. Considering the varying levels of achievements of CIIPs, and that a successful program of industry development in itself is a significant contribution to national development, a BoK for formulating and implementing CIIPs has been implicitly growing around the world for some decades. However, unlike discipline- or profession-specific BoKs, it remains unorganized and non-standardized, due to the reasons delineated below.

It is difficult to standardize a BoK of CIIPs, since unlike a profession-specific BoK, it is impractical to prescribe and regulate the CIIP methodologies that would necessarily vary with country-specific and time-specific industry issues, constraints, and priorities. Still, given the lessons learned to date, it is timely to develop a generally applicable common core BoK to avoid common pitfalls, while injecting usually successful strategies in formulating and implementing CIIPs in different countries. To attain this, it is necessary to identify common core components and potentially critical elements of the BoK, including key knowledge areas, for formulating and implementing CIIPs. It is also necessary to identify commonly critical activities under core CIIP processes of designing, implementing, and fostering continual improvement of the program.

The growing volume of knowledge in formulating and implementing CIIPs has been researched and key knowledge areas have been classified in seminal research and improvement programs, which are presented in Table 18.1. Differences in various jurisdictions and/or perceptions of researchers in terms of classification of the knowledge areas and/or components arise mainly from contextual terminology associated with the relevant knowledge areas. For example, the different nomenclatures used to describe such knowledge areas include: improvement measures (CIRC, 2001), contributing factors (Fox, 2003), drivers of change (Egan, 1998), and strategic thrusts (C21, 1999).

The target objectives in a particular context influence the definition and classification of the knowledge areas and their components. The difference could be in type and extent of improvement requirements and/or

Table 18.1: Summary of the knowledge areas and their components for CIIP as identified by different research and reform initiatives.

(Ofori, 1980) Strategies (Developing countries: Ghana)	(Ofori, 2015) Components of CID (Developing countries)	(Business Roundtable, 1983) What needs to be done (strategies) (USA)	(Aniekwu, 1995) Factors affecting construction industry (Nigeria)	(Egan, 1998) Drivers of change (UK)
1. Economic growth and stability 2. Government recognition 3. Planning demand 4. Revision of Procedures, codes and documents 5. Development of Materials 6. Manpower development 7. Adoption of appropriate Technology 8. Development of contractors	1. Technology development 2. Corporate development 3. Institution building 4. Materials development 5. Human resource development 6. Documentation, procedures and practices 7. Operating environment	1. Sharpening management's tools and techniques 2. Plugging the gaps in training and education 3. Harnessing research and technology 4. Maximizing worker productivity 5. Lifting government involvement	1. Contracting and contract administration practices 2. Business environment of the construction industry 3. Capacity and efficiency of the contractors 4. Capable institutions to cater for the progress of the industry 5. Research and development	1. Committed leadership 2. A focus on the customer 3. Integrated processes and teams 4. A quality driven agenda 5. Commitment to people

(*Continued*)

Table 18.1: *(Continued)*

(ISR, 1999) **Action Agendas** (Australia)	(C21, 1999) **Strategic thrust area** (Singapore)	(CIRC, 2001) **Improvement measures** (Hong Kong)	(CII, 2008) **Strategic directions** (Hong Kong)	(Fox, 2003) **Factors facilitating CID** (*International*)
1. Innovation and research 2. Promotion of IT application 3. Regulation and standards 4. Project delivery and business improvement 5. Environment issues 6. Training and skill development 7. Exports	1. Enhancing professionalism of the industry 2. Raising the skills level 3. Improving industry practice and techniques 4. An integrated approach to construction 5. Developing an external wing 6. A collective championing effort for the construction industry	1. Fostering a quality culture 2. Achieving value in construction procurement 3. Nurturing a professional workforce 4. Developing an efficient, innovative and productive industry 5. Improving safety and environmental performance 6. Devising a new institutional framework to drive the implementation of the change program for the industry	1. Formulating an industry-specific long-term vision and policy 2. Developing favorable factor conditions and resources 3. Fostering a best practice culture 4. Enhancing technical competency	1. Industry-led better practice and culture 2. Financial resources and investor confidence 3. Human skills and culture of transparency 4. Government policies and strategies supporting construction business 5. Research and development for construction 6. Self-reliant construction culture 7. Institutional support 8. Supportive attitudes from aid agencies

Table 18.1: (*Continued*)

(WEF, 2016) Transformation areas (*International*)	**(CIDB-Malaysia, 2015) Strategic Thrusts and Enablers (Malaysia)**	**(Ci3, 2016) Action Items (India)**	**(Wolstenholme, 2009) Big themes for future action (UK)**	**(CIDB-South Africa, 2017) Strategic Goals (South Africa)**
1. Technology, materials and tools 2. Processes and operations 3. Strategy and business model innovation 4. People, organization and culture 5. Industry collaboration 6. Joint industry marketing 7. Regulation and policies 8. Public procurement	1. Quality, Safety and Professionalism 2. Environmental Sustainability 3. Productivity 4. Internationalisation 5. Robust governance 6. Strong coordinating body 7. Effective industry collaborations	1. Identification and formulation of Key Performance Indicators 2. Construction project time and cost reduction strategies 3. Design processes and technology adoption 4. Design codes and standards 5. Human capital and productivity 6. Construction client's charter 7. Institutional platform	1. Understand the built environment 2. Focus much more on the environment 3. Find a cohesive voice for our industry 4. Adopt new business models that promote change 5. Develop a new generation of leaders 6. Integrate education and training 7. Procure for value 8. Suppliers to take the lead	1. Inclusive growing construction industry 2. Innovative and thriving construction environment 3. Reputable regulator 4. Working in alliance 5. Sound corporate governance

in terms of scope, based in turn on any currently pressing priorities, apart from any longer-term needs and vision. For example, as observed in Table 18.1, manpower development or its components are indicated in one way or another in all of the studies and initiatives. The differences are in descriptions. For example, in Ofori (1980) it is directly referred to as "manpower development"; in Business Roundtable (1983) as "plugging the gaps in training and education"; in ISR (1999) as "training and skill development"; in CIRC (2001) as "nurturing professional workforce"; in C21 (1999) as "rising skills level"; and in Ci3 (2016) as "human capital and productivity." Similarly, improving industry practices is covered under different descriptions and with different focal points, such as "improving industry practice and techniques" (C21, 1999); "promotion of IT application" (ISR, 1999); "efficient, innovative and productive industry" (CIRC, 2001); "technology development" (Ofori, 2015); and "adoption of new technologies, materials and tools" (WEF, 2016). Similarly, although the main objective is the same, the CIIPs have different themes, for example: "Constructing the Team" (Latham, 1994); "Rethinking Construction" (Egan, 1998); "Reinventing Construction" (MGI, 2017); and "Time for Change" (HKDB, 2018).

Analysis and synthesis of the knowledge areas and their components, as indicated in Table 18.1, to account for similarities, antecedents, precedents, and criticality led the authors to identify five knowledge areas: (i) Manpower Development, (ii) Enhancing Capacity, (iii) Institution Building, (iv) Improving Practices, and (v) Planning for Smoother Demand. However, the effectiveness and efficiency of formulating and implementing the CIIP is affected by the nature and challenges of the particular national industry scenario, with more needs in the developing countries. It is also important to understand the mutual interdependence of the knowledge areas, with the performance in one being often affected by the state of others. For example, improvement of one knowledge area should improve others; an example would be that enhancement of manpower development increases the capacity of the firms through alleviating challenges associated with a shortage of competent professionals in the industry, and enhancing the capacity of the firms in turn improves industry practices as more competitive firms will have the capability to adopt good practices.

Consequently, in the next subsection, the core process groups: (i) designing, (ii) implementing, and (iii) fostering continual improvement are discussed to identify and define the activities under the respective process groups. This is followed by another subsection in which the five knowledge areas are discussed to identify and define the dimensions/components of the knowledge areas, characteristics of each knowledge area, and/or the role of the stakeholders concerned in determining performance of the knowledge area. Subsequently, examples from India, Ethiopia, and Sri Lanka are presented with the view to indicating special requirements of developing countries. The final section includes concluding remarks on the CIIP process groups and the knowledge areas, with suggestions that attention should be paid to special requirements of developing countries in enhancing the effectiveness in formulating and implementing CIIP.

BoK in developing and implementing CIIPs

Processes in CIIPs

As defined by CIB TG29 (1998), construction industry development is "a deliberate and managed process to improve capacity and effectiveness of the construction industry to meet the national economic demand for building and civil engineering products and to support sustained national economic and social development objectives." CIB W107 (2015) acknowledges the changing paradigms of development and advocates evolving development strategies and processes that express local conditions, aspirations and control over resources, according women their rightful place in society, and considering religious and spiritual ethics and values when formulating the new paradigm. Essentially, it advocates local participation and institution building and encourages development and participation of professional institutions and trade associations. Achieving these objectives depends on the effectiveness of the different management processes in the formulation and implementation of CIIP and fostering of its continual improvement. The effectiveness of these processes is affected by the particular organization, its strength, and the established facilitating institutional systems. (This concept is discussed in detail below under "Institution Building.")

The status of CIIP knowledge areas in a specific jurisdiction depends on the nature and challenges of that construction industry. Understanding the operating environment, the enablers and barriers (structural and systemic), and the stakeholders' implementation capacity and their commitment are key to the success of CIIP. This can be called a situation analysis of the industry (Ssegawa-Kaggwa *et al.*, 2013), which is the first activity in designing a CIIP. Hence, the designing process of CIIP covers assessing the contextual scenario and setting realistic targets and Key Performance Indicators (KPIs) with the associated appropriate mechanisms of achievement that suit the context. The improvement trends of construction industries in different countries indicate that performance improvements require long periods of time (Wolstenholme, 2009; Kumaraswamy *et al.*, 2010; Ofori *et al.*, 2011). Hence, the KPIs, while being challenging, should not be over-ambitious; but they should be attainable in a reasonable timeframe. CIC (2015) indicated the expected attributes of KPIs: they should be relevant and important to the industry, quantifiable, have a recurrent supply of data, reflect future development, and be able to improve external accountability and verification. KPIs should help to monitor and track improvements of industry performance.

In addition, the CIIP has to be an integrated plan to account for the interdependent nature of the knowledge areas and their context within the objectives of national development. While KPIs as proposed by Egan (1998) and widely adapted in UK, which are primarily measured at the project and organization levels are useful, KPIs proposed by HKDB (2018), Kumaraswamy *et al.* (2017), and CITP (2016) better reflect the needs of KPIs for CIIPs as they acknowledge the interdependent nature of the knowledge areas and their context in the objectives of national development. The second process is effectively and efficiently implementing the designed improvement program. This needs the commitment and concerted effort of the stakeholders (Egan, 1998). The implementation mechanism may be in two modes: (1) enforcing the envisaged mandatory practices through regulatory tools; and (2) promoting benefits to stakeholders and supporting voluntary acceptance through creating conducive environments.

An example of the voluntary mode is in self-improvement initiatives, such as the Client Charter of Ci3 (Kumaraswamy *et al.*, 2017). The implementation can start on a voluntary basis and shift to being mandatory as the envisaged practice matures. For example, consider a firm's commitment to training and development to ensure continuing professional development (CPD) among its personnel to achieve the manpower development objective of the CIIP. Voluntary acceptance needs awareness development about short- and long-term benefits of the envisaged practice and importance of establishing KPIs for performance measurement. A CIIP's KPIs may not serve to measure internal performance of particular organizations. Hence, organizations need to develop their own performance indicators for their performance assessment (DETR, 2000; Kumaraswamy *et al.*, 2017), while considering how they may collectively contribute to the attainment of planned national industry KPIs.

The requirements of improvement initiatives in different knowledge areas would differ depending on the time under consideration (Ofori, 1980; Fox, 2003). Thus, there is a need for monitoring performance and amending respective strategies and targets (including the KPIs) of the knowledge areas over time, to reflect the changing nature of the industry. Hence, the purpose of the third process: fostering continual improvement. However, applying a truly reliable method for comparing construction costs is difficult due to the nature of the industry and its products. The problem above is exacerbated by the difficulties in the establishment of reliable construction purchasing power parities. (Best and Meikle, 2019). This process is also challenged by difficulties in collecting and processing industry performance data. Ideally, data collection can be integrated with the implementation mechanisms: it might comprise mandatory and voluntary aspects. However, problems associated with construction industry data, such as authenticity, reliability and accuracy (Windapo and Qongqo, 2011), suggest the importance of establishing a centralized data collection, processing, storage, and dissemination system to reduce such problems (Ofori, 1988). Extensive consultation with stakeholders will help to secure commitments to meet the targets of the CIIP and its data collection and analysis procedures (PSIB, 2005).

Knowledge areas of CIIPs

Manpower development

Most construction industry problems are directly or indirectly associated with the availability and competence of manpower in the industry.

According to Drucker (2006), "the only competitive advantage of developed countries is the availability of skilled labor resources." Availability of skilled manpower is dependent on policies for developing an adequate pool of competent manpower in the industry. The components of manpower development are: planning, production, and monitoring, with effective coordination of these elements (Oviawe *et al.*, 2017). The planning involves identification of relevant disciplines and occupational groups with the required competence and forecasting the demand. Manpower development is a long-term activity and therefore, there should be a sound mechanism for projecting requirements to facilitate the process (Wong *et al.*, 2012). For effective manpower planning, all stakeholders should collaborate in collating and compiling manpower requirements (CIRC, 2001); for example, as indicated by CII (2008), in Australia, relevant ministries form taskforces to propose strategic directions and closely monitor manpower development needs.

Similar to planning, production also needs the involvement of different stakeholders; with a coordinated effort of academic institutions, industry organizations, and government. After identifying the demand (quantity and quality), production needs continuous monitoring and periodic review of the objectives as circumstances change to ensure continual development (Ofori *et al.*, 2013). In producing competent professionals, academic institutions bear the major responsibility, their main focus being to equip the students with the required knowledge and skills (Naveed *et al.*, 2017). It is necessary to ensure the inclusion of required skills and knowledge in the curriculum, and that education is practice-based and relevant to the industry. Industry organizations are also partly responsible for developing entry-level professionals as they are required to liaise with, and be at least consulted by, the academic institutions in designing appropriate internship programs and providing internship opportunities.

Human resource management practices of the industry organizations play an important role in maintaining the competence of manpower, including ensuring CPD. Despite the strong link between manpower development and construction industry improvement, there are shortfalls, even negligence, in manpower development by construction firms in both developed and developing countries (Osabutey *et al.*, 2012). According to Loosemore *et al.* (2003), the consequences of ignoring human needs and focusing on organization and project requirements are: employee dissatisfaction, increased turnover, reduced commitment, industrial conflict, de-professionalization, more workplace accidents, and a continued poor public image. While affecting the respective organizations, this adversely affects industry-level manpower development as well.

In improving overall practices toward effective manpower development, especially in the context of developing countries, the government needs to play a central role in formulating policies that integrate the initiatives of all parties concerned (Osabutey *et al.*, 2012). It can influence manpower development through different mechanisms: regulations (such as registration systems) and facilitation of collaboration among industry organizations and between these organizations and universities. Specifically, coordination of manpower planning and monitoring in the construction industry needs governmental commitment, based on understanding the needs and challenges in existing manpower development practices in the particular context.

According to WEF (2016), manpower-related challenges facing the construction industry in future are prospective scarcity of skilled labor, increasing sophistication of technology which needs broader skills, and high volatility of workforce demand. Similarly, Deku (2014) identified these challenges to manpower development within the construction industry: lack of financial resources, lack of central development and regulatory agency, lack of appreciation of the role of human capital in organizational performance, cost of manpower development, slowness to change, high employee mobility, low level of education, and fragmentation of the industry. Also, according to Wong (2006), factors affecting manpower demand at industry level are: construction output, technological change, and wage level. The nature of work, economic changes, and demographic (social) factors were identified as important determinants affecting manpower planning in the Malaysian construction industry (Dom *et al.*, 2012).

Enhancing capacity

Enhancing the capacity of the firms, in turn, helps to improve industry practices as competitive firms will develop specific capabilities to adopt good practice and gain more opportunities to achieve project and business targets and boost professionalism. There is no generic definition and measurement for competitiveness, while factors affecting competitiveness change with time and context (Ericsson *et al.*, 2005). After an extensive review of the literature, Lu (2006, p. 25) defined contractor competitiveness as "the ability of a firm to bid successfully for construction projects, to provide construction services with superior quality, lower costs, and with shorter time than its domestic and international competitors, and in the long-run to consistently achieve superior firm performance."

Enhancing the competitiveness of firms needs identification of its dimensions and the determinant factors and devising effective improvement mechanisms. Ofori (1999) explained that a contractor development program must enable the firm to mature and develop commercial, managerial, and administrative skills; credibility in commercial circles; and experience in pricing contracts while accepting increasingly greater risk and contractual responsibility. Lu (2006), in developing a competitiveness assessment model, categorized the factors of competitiveness into these clusters: project management skills, organization resources, organization structure, relationships, competitiveness strategy, marketing ability, bidding techniques, technology, and research and development. These factors of competitiveness can be discussed under three dimensions: technical capacity, financial capacity, and management practices. Mengistu (2019) defines "technical capacity" as the equipment owned and related operational staff (adequacy and skills) to efficiently utilize the equipment, expertise in work methods, and the ability to foresee technological adoptions to maintain reputability; "financial capacity" as the ability to finance projects and arrange financial resources to run the business; and "management practice" as the application of a broad range of skills, and management knowledge and experience for efficient and effective delivery of the process.

These dimensions of competitiveness are interrelated (Bajracharya *et al.*, 2018) and are affected by different internal and external factors (Tang and Ogunlana, 2003). According to Wong and Ng (2010), common causes of failure of construction companies are: human capital issues, macroeconomic issues, adaptation to market conditions, and budgetary issues. The problems of local contractors in developing countries are: lack of qualified manpower, limited access to working capital, shortage of materials and machinery, and weak use of modern technology (Hillebrandt, 1999; IGC, 2012). At the industry level, major institutional challenges facing contractor development are: absence of a suitable legal framework governing contractors, limited training institutions, lack of management know-how, lack of drive to learn, non-timely payment of contractors by clients, procurement issues, absence of reliable credit facilities, absence of equipment pools, a corruption syndrome, limited research and information, and occupational health and safety concerns (Kiggundu, 1999).

Appropriate mechanisms for enhancing capacity depend on the particular local context. According to Ofori (1999), forms of assistance provided by different countries in small-scale contractor development programs are: finance, more project opportunities, training and advice, and resource supply (materials and equipment). Similarly, intervention areas for contractor development identified by ILO (1987) are: access to work, improvement of the business environment, and training and advisory services. The involvement of foreign contractors from developed construction markets is also considered as another means for enhancing capacity.

According to Ofori *et al.* (1999), the major factor determining local contractor development is the role of the government. They also emphasized that such help by government should not create dependency and it should be monitored and adjusted as the context changes. The characteristics of good contractor development programs are: identification of expertise required, who can provide the expertise, what is expected from the different categories of contractor, training programs, methods of evaluation, performance monitoring and assessment of progress, feedback mechanism, sanctions mechanism, and ensuring that deserving contractors are engaged (Ogbogbaidi, 1999).

Enhancing capacity should incorporate the development of all levels of construction organizations and material suppliers to enhance overall competitiveness at the industry level (Kumaraswamy, 2006). As shortage of supplies such as equipment, skilled labor, and construction materials is found to be a leading cause of economic risks for project performance (Kumaraswamy, 2006), enhancing the capacity of construction materials manufacturers to produce materials meeting relevant industry specifications and standards is important for improving construction industry performance.

Institution building

To foster the continual improvement of practices in the construction industry, it is necessary to develop an effective facilitating institutional system comprising the structures and mechanisms used to diffuse the practices to the industry and regulate the associated processes. These include: (i) the regulatory system; and (ii) the participation of professional and trade associations.

The performance of the construction industry depends on the efficiency of the regulatory system (Egan, 1998; ISR, 1999). The government acts as a regulator, a major client, and a promoter of the construction industry (CIRC, 2001), hence it can intervene through appropriate mechanisms to improve industry practices. Aniekwu *et al.* (2015) indicated that, being a major client, government can foster the initiation and diffusion of best practices in the industry, for example, through procurement systems, thereby aligning pre-qualification and other contractual requirements with industry development strategies. Compulsory registration of firms is another regulatory tool to use to raise standards and change industry behavior. Similarly, enforcing compliance with mandatory material standards helps to drive poor quality materials out of the market (CIDB-Malaysia, 2015). Fox (2003) also highlighted the strong influence of governments in creating conducive business environments by setting out policies that promote private firms and by combating corruption.

Attaining effective and sustainable change in the construction industry requires concerted efforts of the stakeholders. Professional institutions and trade associations have a significant importance in improving industry practices by highlighting major challenges needing policy intervention and strategy setting, diffusing practices to the industry, and self-regulating through good standard practices. They can drive the development of professional excellence, raising awareness, and setting and promoting high-quality standards (NAS, 2005). They also help the industry in maintaining and monitoring educational and professional qualifications for professionals and supporting continual professional development (Green, 2015). The institutional systems, efforts of the associations, and the regulatory system support and affect each other. Hence, it is important to strengthen the associations and create a conducive environment to maximize their contribution to industry development. If the associations are strengthened and provided with appropriate and adequate representation in the CIIP, the industry is likely to achieve self-regulation with time.

Sustaining the force of change throughout the industry value chain requires a common purpose and institutional reform that creates a conducive environment for stakeholders to act in concert to boost the various individual and collective interests of the industry (CIRC, 2001). This can be achieved through establishing a statutory organization that helps to reduce conflicting objectives and can monitor and develop the overall practice in the industry (Ofori, 1985). The Building and Construction Authority (BCA) in Singapore is playing such a role for the implementation of the recommendations of C21 (Ofori *et al.*, 2011). Similarly, different countries have institutions (CIIP organizations) with some differences in the circumstances of their genesis, and their mandates. Examples are: the Construction Industry Institute (CII) in the USA (CII, 2016), Ci3 in India (Ci3, 2017), Construction Industry Council (CIC) in the UK (CIC, 2017), Construction Industry Development Board (CIDB) in Malaysia (CIDB-Malaysia, 2017), and CIDB in South Africa (CIDB-South Africa, 2017). Some of them have statutory powers (those in Singapore, Malaysia, and South Africa), while others do not have any such authority (India, UK, and US). The role of such institutions should be properly defined and their functions clearly delineated together with the nature of the organization, its powers, duties, organization structure, and relationship with the industry.

Improving practices

Major areas where practices are addressed in construction industry performance improvement are: improving technology development (Ofori, 2015), IT application (ISR, 1999), and fostering the adoption of different management tools and systems (Egan, 1998; Kumaraswamy, 1998, 2006; CIRC, 2001; Behera *et al.*, 2015). It is important to assess shortfalls in management practice and adopt best practices to suit the context and/or contextualize the practices in order to improve performance under different knowledge areas of project management as discussed in other chapters of this book. Technology development and IT applications are discussed in subsequent paragraphs.

Researchers have suggested different conceptualizations of construction technology. Grosse (1996) referred to three types of technology that are defined in the business and management literature: product technology, process technology, and management technology. This classification is adopted by Osabutey *et al.* (2014) in the context of construction, considering the product technology as relating to hard elements (construction outputs, materials, plant, and equipment); management technology as concerning the soft elements (skills, knowledge, organization); and process technology as combining product technology with management technology to produce outputs. In this chapter, the concept proposed by Osabutey *et al.* (2014) is adopted. However, IT application (being more a part of soft elements), is discussed separately. Here, technology development includes improving construction methods, practices, and availability and accessibility of materials and equipment and practices to attain improved efficiency.

Technology development is costly, risky, and path-dependent, and hence it is more efficient for developing countries to simply acquire beneficial technologies developed in other countries through technology transfer (Fu *et al.*, 2010). Therefore, it is important to pay particular attention to the selection of an effective technology transfer mechanism or combination of mechanisms. According to Ofori (1994), vehicles for transferring technology include: joint ventures, supply of plant and equipment, subcontracting, strategic alliances, counterpart training, licensing, government-level technical aid, and attendance of conferences and seminars. The technology transfer process has been re-envisioned by some researchers as a two-way, mutually beneficial "technology exchange" (Kumaraswamy and Shrestha, 2002), based on each partner passing on technology components where it has greater strength, for example, the local knowledge-skills and organizational-information networks of the local partner in the developing country. Osabutey *et al.* (2014) emphasized that effective technology transfer is only attained through working together at the project level. However, stakeholders do not play equal roles in transferring technology to the local construction industry. Contractors often have little say in the selection of technology for particular projects as these are set out in the design and specifications (Loganathan *et al.*, 2017). Appropriate policies and incentives from government at a broad level and contractual incentives from clients can strengthen technology adoption.

Suitable IT applications can improve industry performance through an enabling role in construction (Yang *et al.*, 2012), including by facilitating information sharing at project and industry levels; helping to reduce conflict through better communication; and improving decision-making processes (Sommerville and Craig, 2006). However, their implementation is constrained by barriers at individual, organization, and project levels (Peansupap and Walker, 2006). Individual-level constraints include budget limits, commitment shortfalls in project participants, and issues of standardization and security. The organizational level constraints include: lack of experience, availability of time, low level of awareness of benefits of IT use, and lack of training. Constraints at the project level include: time available to share information, quality of personal contacts, and geographical distance. Miller *et al.* (2009) highlighted that perception of the value, benefit, and usability determines the effectiveness of implementation. These barriers constraining the wider application of technology need to be overcome in order to optimize the benefits for industry development and performance improvement.

Planning for smooth and sustainable demand

Sustainable investment in construction assures continuity of work for the organizations and workers, which is needed for sustainable capacity building and manpower development in the industry. Information about future demand and capacity of the industry is vital in planning the resources and skills to meet the demand and also for formulating policy, strategy, and business plans. Weddikkara and Devapriya (2001) identified factors that affect demand for construction as: government policies, economic conditions, construction prices and inflation, population growth and urbanization, foreign financial aid, and global and regional economic cooperation. Ideally, to realize the sustainable development of the construction industry, fluctuations in demand should be minimized (Ofori, 1980; Wong *et al.*, 2010). As the experience of the UK and South Korea indicates, this can be achieved through developing and applying forecasting models (CII, 2008).

For construction firms to optimize the benefit of smoother and sustainable demand, it is important for them to understand and prepare for the expected development of their national infrastructure stock. Over time, in the long term, the capital investment of a country can largely shift from new construction to repair, maintenance, and urban renewal works. As the market changes, the nature and challenges of the projects differ, requiring different skills and techniques. Therefore, appropriate adjustment and timely diversification of business models are crucial to survive in these transformative environments (CII, 2008).

Cases on improvement programs and special requirements of developing countries

As indicated earlier, CIIP processes are affected by different factors depending on the challenges, conditions, and priorities of construction industries in different jurisdictions. This section considers case examples of CIIP from three developing countries, focusing on the local requirements, institutional systems, and initiatives, with a view to eliciting some commonalities and differences that can contribute to the development of the CIIP BoK, with special reference to developing countries.

Construction industry improvement initiatives in India

The rapidly increasing demands which the fast-growing Indian economy makes from the country's construction industry has led to increased capacity. However, the high volume of more and higher quality housing and commercial and industrial infrastructure cannot be met by increased capacity alone. The industry faces systemic challenges, including: project time and cost overruns (Iyer and Jha, 2005, 2006), low productivity, lack of skilled labor (Loganathan and Kalidindi, 2015), quality shortfalls, health and safety issues, and low levels of technology adoption. These need to be addressed to improve performance levels. The institution responsible for policy on industry development is primarily the Ministry of Housing and Urban Development, but given the nature of construction, its ambit overlaps with other institutions such as the Ministry of Finance (procurement policy), Public Works Departments, and other departments responsible for project execution (implementation). Although there is a

Construction Industry Development Council in India (formed in 1996), it lacks statutory powers. This fragmentation of responsibility results in a lack of a unified long-term focus and a coordinated and reliable institutional structure.

The Construction Industry Improvement Initiative India (Ci3 India), a collaborative academia-industry venture, was launched in 2016 (Loganathan *et al.*, 2017), targeting significant and sustainable industry improvements through an industry development initiative championed by a group of large construction organizations with a long-term vision for value-driven project delivery. The major objectives of Ci3 India were: (i) to identify current and imminent critical issues in the construction industry in India; (ii) to prepare a roadmap for industry improvements in strategic high (and wide) impact domains; and (iii) to launch (a) system improvement initiatives, and (b) demonstration projects, in prioritized focus areas within the above strategic domains. The Ci3 India initiative identified 19 critical issues (Loganathan *et al.*, 2017), which led to the mobilization of the following "Action Teams" to address improvements under groupings of issues and tasks:

Action Team 1: Identification and Formulation of KPIs
Action Team 2: Construction Project Time and Cost Reduction Strategies
Action Team 3: (3A) Design Processes *and* (3B) Technology Adoption
Action Team 4: Design Codes and Standards (Note: mobilization was postponed, after noting the longer-term needs and complexities of this Action)
Action Team 5: Human Capital (including Labor, Technical, and Managerial, and Skills Development) and Productivity
Action Team 6: Construction Clients' Charter
Action Team 7: Institutional Platform for Construction Industry Improvement Initiative *India* (later named as Ci3).

Roundtables and workshops led to the formation of the above action teams and also to the consolidation of their outputs (Ci3, 2016). The enthusiasm generated at these fora to meet identified CIIP needs in India triggered a proposal to set up a Ci3 with similar objectives (Ci3, 2017a) to the CII USA. While this proposal is "on hold," Draft White papers were produced by the five main Action Teams (Ci3, 2017b) and were revisited in 2020 and consolidated at the Institute of Technology Madras into a Ci3 White Paper for presentation to relevant governmental and industry organizations and groups.

Some concepts, templates, and detailed examples may be drawn for development and comparisons in both India and elsewhere, from the Draft White papers (Ci3, 2017b). For example: (a) the "Clients Charter" in the Action Team 6 Draft White Paper that would help establish and diffuse a common client commitment to higher standards, and (b) suggested base KPIs aimed at short-, medium-, and long-term benchmarking to address the continuous improvement needs, in the Action Team 1 Draft White Paper (Ci3, 2017b; Kumaraswamy *et al.*, 2017).

Construction industry improvement initiatives in Ethiopia

There has been no dedicated CIIP in Ethiopia but there are aspects of general programs for national development that impinge on CIIP. These have manifested shortfalls in all important processes. Reviews of three national plans: *A Plan for Accelerated and Sustained Development to End Poverty (2005/6–2009/10)*; *Growth and Transformation Plan I [GTP I] (2009/10–2014/15)*; and *Growth and Transformation Plan II [GTP II] (2015/16–2019/20)* indicate that the recurring major themes to improve the construction industry are related to: manpower development, enhancing capacity, institution building, and improving practice. This suggests that the knowledge areas are already identified. However, while the first plan lacks clear KPIs, the KPIs adopted in GTP I and GTP II lack the required attributes, i.e., relevance and threshold reference value to be compared against, and some of them are ambiguous. Furthermore, there is no consistency among the targets and KPIs in the consecutive national plans. So far, there is no separate detailed plan, with clear targets and continual performance measurement and improvement practices, for what must necessarily be a long-term CIIP.

Different components of a CIIP have been tried so far. These relate to institution building, enhancing capacity, improving practice, and manpower development, and are now considered. The construction industry has passed through different periods, facing challenges associated with political ideologies and perception of the governments toward the industry that affects institution building (Desta, 2015). Recent trends indicate that the governance structure of the industry has been changing. In 2015, the Ministry of Construction was established as a central statutory body dedicated to construction industry development, being separated from the Ministry of Urban Development and Construction (MUDC) (FDRE, 2015). However, in 2018, it was reintegrated into MUDC. Such major changes in the governance structure, with various readjustments of the regulatory authorities and institutions, would create difficulties in achieving continuous improvement of the industry. The concern for improvement has been growing. A construction industry development policy framework was launched in 2013 (MUDC, 2013). The framework indicated challenges of the industry and set 10 targets to meet the vision for the construction industry. The challenges identified were: poor implementation capacity, regulatory framework problems (poor implementation and lack of revaluing practice), skill and knowledge gap in the industry, lack of manpower forecasting, registration and certification, poor capacity of stakeholders, poor involvement of business and professional associations, and poor information management in the industry.

The targets set were: (i) creating a conducive environment to deter corruption and unethical practices, (ii) manpower development, (iii) establishing a system that can ensure effectiveness and create competitiveness, (iv) establishing an institute to facilitate project management and technology development, (v) establishing a supply chain system for sustainable material supply, (vi) establishing modern systems to provide financial and equipment resources, (vii) setting a direction that facilitates collaboration of stakeholders for industry development, (viii) strengthening building design, construction supervision and usage permissions, (ix) establishing a system of planning for cross sectorial issues along with construction, and (x) preparing a detailed engineering and construction works program and a legal framework package for implementation. Generally, the provisions in the policy covered most of the knowledge areas and their components.

In the same year (2013), the Ethiopian Construction Project Management Institute was established, with the objective of facilitating the development of the industry through building the project management capacity of the key stakeholders (FDRE, 2013). The Construction Industry

Council (CIC) was established in 2017 with the objective of creating a stakeholders' forum which would engage in developing, and facilitating the implementation of, policies, programs, laws, and strategic issues that would lead to an efficient construction industry. However, so far, there is no evidence of progress since the establishment of the CIC.

Some of the powers and duties of MUDC need to be redefined and refined to avoid overlaps with those of other organs of government. It is difficult to clearly assign duties to any one party, owing to the nature of the construction industry, but the barriers can be reduced through efficient coordination mechanisms. It is important to recognize the importance of regulatory tools in shaping industry practice and devising integrated improvement mechanisms through regulatory tools (Milford, 2009). However, a review of the regulatory tools (the registration system; design approval and building permit system; and procurement practices) — except for a few hydropower and road projects — indicates that there are shortfalls in supporting components of the CIIP. The regulatory tools should be re-evaluated to meet CIIP targets. The codes, specifications and standards need to be flexible to enable the adoption of new technologies, and to be kept up-to-date, to diffuse best practices and improvements to the industry.

Some capacity enhancement initiatives have been undertaken in the building sector (MWUD, 2010) and road sector (ERA, 2016); both programs include contractors' and consultants' capacity development. The requirements for establishment of the companies are: academic qualifications and experience of the partners establishing the company. The support mechanisms include: providing projects with fixed reasonable price rates, supplying materials, providing construction equipment with credit, and providing training in management. However, these programs were fragmented, and their planning and implementation lack the characteristics of good capacity development programs discussed above. Other shortfalls are associated with the commitment of the companies engaged in the program. The contractors and consultants established through the programs were over-dependent on the support program; most of them failed to upgrade and sustain themselves in the market. Thus, the initiatives were not effective in attaining their goals.

Another initiative to improve practice seeks to reduce corruption. The Federal Public Procurement and Property Administration Agency requires procuring entities to disclose project information on its website (MoFED, 2010a). However, most reports of the Infrastructure Transparency Initiative (CoST) Ethiopia indicate that there is a problem in accessing project information from both the client and the consultant. Another initiative is the manpower development program of the Ethiopian Roads Authority (ERA) with the aim of developing a competent manpower pool in construction. ERA has been sponsoring postgraduate programs in specializations including: construction technology and management, geotechnical engineering, structural engineering, and road and transport engineering in more than six universities during the decade 2011–2012 to 2019–2020. The main shortcoming of the program is that the majority of the universities do not have adequate academic staff to deliver the program and have been teaching the courses mostly with guest lectures on a block basis. This affects the objective of the initiative in developing a competent manpower pool in the industry.

Construction industry improvement initiatives in Sri Lanka

Sri Lanka has seen a series of construction industry improvement initiatives since the mid-1980s. Benefits have been below expectations, and changes in government have led to lack of continuity and "champions" who have not been able to implement what they envisaged. The Institute for Construction, Training and Development (ICTAD) was set up in Sri Lanka in 1986 to develop the construction industry; it took over from a British-fund supported Construction Industry Training Project. ICTAD was initially funded by the World Bank but then moved on, as planned, to government funding and self-generated income from its training programs and other services. Its services included: training at all levels; development and advisory services, such as developing standard contract documents, guides, and construction statistics; and maintaining a system of registered contractors in different grades. ICTAD contributed by developing the industry incrementally through its development and training activities and earned the industry's respect, despite its lack of "teeth" to drive major changes.

Responding to recommendations to provide "regulatory teeth" to ICTAD, the 2014 Construction Industry Development Act No 33 led to the transformation of ICTAD into the Construction Industry Development Authority (CIDA). The Act provides for the following: (a) regulate, register, formalize and standardize the activities of the construction industry, (b) establish the National Advisory Council on Construction; (c) establish the Construction Industry Development Authority; (d) establish the Construction Industry Development Fund and the Fund of the Construction Industry Development Authority; (e) devise measures for the improvement and well-being of the industry-related professionals, manufacturers, suppliers, contractors, and craftsmen; (f) reach settlement of disputes related to construction activities; and (g) ensure public safety in the construction industry of Sri Lanka. Seven objectives and 33 functions of CIDA were also outlined when it was being set up (11 "areas of activity" are currently listed by CIDA (2020)).

Focusing on a good example, appropriate and proactive "project procurement" strategies and practices of large clients have been found to substantially influence construction industry growth trajectories, as well as the capacity development of construction organizations in many countries. In a study, Kumaraswamy (1998) confirmed major damages to a historically strong Sri Lankan construction industry and attributed them mainly to inappropriate procurement policies that, for example, discouraged prequalifying local companies for "large" projects. The first attempt to address this led to Sri Lanka Cabinet guidelines (ICTAD, 1988) on enforcing the then World Bank and similar Asian Development Bank (ADB) guidelines that provided a tender price advantage for suitably involving "domestic contractors" in large projects.

Specific reforms were recommended, based on a World Bank sponsored study on the "Domestic Construction Industry in the Roads Sub-Sector" in Sri Lanka (Kumaraswamy, 1998). This study highlighted some common shortfalls in foreign-funded projects in developing countries, such as the paradox of not prequalifying domestic contractors for megaprojects, because of inadequate experience, whereas, in the process, such contractors would be deprived of the opportunity to develop such a track record. The cost of large projects rose, since overseas organizations undertook projects that could have been done by competent local organizations, some of which were handling bigger projects overseas. Recommendations of the study included (ICTAD, 1992):

(a) rationalization of the system of registration, grading and prequalification of contractors;
(b) increasing opportunities for "Local Competitive Bidding" by reducing package sizes;
(c) extracting the funding component envisaged for equipment from a series of projects under a forthcoming ADB program and using it to finance and maintain a central specialized heavy equipment pool to serve domestic contractors;
(d) enforcing the then prevalent World Bank Procurement Guidelines (1992) and similar ADB guidelines for a 7.5 percent preference margin for domestic contractors in developing economies, along with safeguards provided by the Sri Lanka Cabinet guidelines (ICTAD, 1988) to safeguard against abuse by nominal joint ventures set up solely to gain a preferential advantage; and
(e) consideration of alternative Conditions of Contract, including the New Engineering Contract for projects.

Other recommendations included centralized information systems, import duty, and tax concessions for construction equipment and specific training programs in technical and managerial skills. Local roadworks contractors did benefit and develop their capacities based on implementation of most of the recommendations. However, the contract administration of many projects was still weak following a period where such experience had been denied to local professionals. This often resulted in cost and time over-runs on road projects, whether handled by both local or foreign contractors (Kumaraswamy and Raza, 2014).

Much remains to be done to "do the right things," while the knowledge on "how to do it right" is not lacking. What is lacking is the political will and commitment by a group of cross-industry champions to drive through the necessary improvements. CIDA is well-positioned as a potential vehicle to implement the reforms, to attain continuous improvement.

Focus areas for CIIPs in developing countries

A cross case analysis of the initiatives across the identified knowledge areas indicates that the common shortfalls in CIIPs in developing countries are: (1) lack of political will and commitment by a group of cross-industry champions to drive through the necessary improvements; (2) lack of a long-term plan and weak monitoring and controlling practices, for example, lack of consistency among the targets and KPIs in the consecutive plans, as observed in Ethiopia; (3) lack of strong institutions, points of responsibility, and dynamism in industry governance, for example, (i) overlap of MHUD's duties with other institutions in India, and (ii) overlap of MUDC's duties with other institutions and the frequent readjustments in Ethiopia; and (4) unorganized and short-term initiatives, for example, diverse components of fragmented initiatives observed in Ethiopia, such as those related to institution building, enhancing capacity, improving practice, and manpower development. The key to relatively successful programs has been the establishment of strong institutional frameworks with regulatory powers, and provision of facilitating environments, for example, the BCA in Singapore, and CIDB in Malaysia. While industry-led initiatives have their role in CIIP, the commitment of the most important stakeholder, i.e., the government, and other major clients, has been an essential ingredient for success in construction industry development.

Concluding remarks

Developing a generally applicable common core BoK on CIIPs can help to avoid common pitfalls, while injecting successful strategies in formulating and implementing CIIPs in different countries. There are common critical activities under the CIIP processes of designing, implementing, and fostering continual improvement of the program, for example: (1) designing an effective CIIP, including: (i) assessing the contextual scenario, (ii) setting realistic targets and KPIs, and (iii) devising appropriate mechanisms to achieve specific objectives that suit the context; (2) implementing the CIIP effectively and efficiently, including: (i) enforcing mandatory practices through regulatory tools, and (ii) promoting and supporting the acceptance of voluntary best practices, by creating a conducive operating environment; and (3) fostering continual improvement, including: (i) evaluating performance (data collection, processing, benchmarking and dissemination), and (ii) adjusting targets and KPIs to suit the context.

The common and critical knowledge areas in formulating and implementing CIIPs are: (1) Manpower Development, (2) Enhancing Capacity, (3) Institution Building, (4) Improving Practices, and (5) Planning for Smoother Demand. However, the effectiveness and efficiency of formulating and implementing a CIIP would depend on the nature and challenges of the particular national industry, with, invariably, more constraints in developing countries. The status of these knowledge areas and their components in a country at any time would largely determine project performance. Therefore, boosting the above knowledge areas and their components together would, in turn, boost project management maturity at industry/national level and holistically elevate project performance levels.

In summary, formulating and implementing construction industry improvement programs worldwide is seen to be growing, albeit in an ad hoc and unstructured manner. Moreover, it has not yet been consolidated into a coherent BoK that can be conveniently tapped into, for applications in a new country scenario. To address this pressing need, this chapter made a start in bringing together lessons learned from previous CIIPs and identified the common and critical knowledge areas for CIIPs in general, as above, so that these may be broadly targeted and/or prioritized by developing construction industries, with or without formal CIIPs. While providing a general roadmap and/or basic template to compare or "kick-off" with, country-specific CIIPs would need to be developed thereafter, depending on the specific strengths and weaknesses, as well as the particular contexts, constraints and priorities of that country.

References

Aniekwu, A.N. (1995). The business environment of the construction industry in Nigeria. *Construction Management and Economics*, 13(6), 445–55.

Aniekwu, A.N., Igboanugo, C.A. and Onifade, M.K. (2015). Critical issues in reforming the Nigerian construction industry. *British Journal of Applied Science & Technology*, 5(3), 321–32.

Bajracharya, A., Ogunlana, S.O., Goh, C.S. and Tan, H.C. (2018). Conceptualising the nexus of projects, finance and capacity in construction business. *Frontiers of Engineering Management*, 5(3), 289–297.

Behera, P., Mohanty, R.P. and Prakash, A. (2015). Understanding construction supply chain management. *Production Planning & Control*, 26(16), 1332–1350.

Best, R. and Meikle, J. (2019). The challenges of measuring and accounting for construction. In R. Best and J. Meikle (Eds.), *Accounting for Construction: Frameworks, Productivity, Cost and Performance*. Routledge, Abingdon, pp. 1–13

Business Roundtable (1983). *More Construction for the Money, Summary Report of the Construction Industry Cost Effectiveness Project*. New York. http://faculty.ce.berkeley.edu/tommelein/BRTMoreConstructionForTheMoney.pdf

C21 (1999). *Reinventing Construction*. Ministry of Manpower and Ministry of National Development, Construction 21 Steering Committee, Singapore.

Ci3 (2016). Completed Events page in Ci3 website, Construction Industry Institute India. http://www.ci3.in/completed_events.html.

Ci3 (2017a). Construction Industry Institute India, Home Page. http://ci3.in/

Ci3 (2017b). Action Team Draft White Papers, in Draft White Papers page, Ci3 website, Construction Industry Institute India. http://www.ci3.in/draft_whitepapers.html.

CIB TG29 (1998). Construction in developing countries. *Proceedings of the First Meeting of CIB Task Group 29 (TG29) on Construction in Developing Countries*, Arusha, Tanzania.

CIB W107 (2015). W107-construction in developing countries research roadmap — Report for consultation. International Council for Research and Innovation in Building (CIB), Rotterdam.

CIC (2015). Hong Kong Construction Industry Performance Report for 2013, Construction Industry Council. Hong Kong. http://www.hkcic.org/files/Document/KPI2013/KPI Report for 2013 (English).pdf.

CIC (2017). Construction Industry Council-UK, April 4. http://cic.org.uk/about-us/.

CIDA (2020). Construction Industry Development Authority. http://www.cida.gov.lk/sub_pgs/about_areas.html [Accessed 24 August 2020].

CIDB-Malaysia (2015). Construction Industry Transformation Programme (CITP) 2016–2020, Construction Industry Development Board Malaysia. Kuala Lumpur, Malaysia.

CIDB-Malaysia (2017). Construction Industry Development Board-Malaysia. http://www.cidb.gov.my/cidbv5/index.php/en/ [Accessed 4 April 2017].

CIDB-South Africa (2017). Construction Industry Development Board-South Africa, April 4. www.cidb.org.za [Accessed 4 April 2017].

CII (2008). Reinventing the Hong Kong Construction Industry for Its Sustainable Development. Construction Industry Institute, Hong Kong. http://158.132.160.118/bitstream/10397/2371/1/Full%20Report%20-%20Reinventing%20the%20Hong%20Kong%20Construction%20Industr.pdf

CII (2016). Construction Industry Institute-USA. https://www.construction-institute.org/scriptcontent/aboutcii.cfm?section=aboutcii [Accessed 19 December 2016].

CIRC (2001). Construct for Excellence, Construction Industry Review Committee. Hong Kong. http://www.devb.gov.hk/filemanager/en/content_735/reporte.pdf

Deku, G. (2014). *Impact of Human Capital Development on the Performance of Ghanaian Road Contractors*. MSc. Thesis, Kwame Nkrumah University of Science and Technology, Ghana.

Desta, S.S. (2015). *The Management of Construction Processes in Developing Countries: A Case Study of the Ethiopian Roads Authority*. Ph.D. Thesis, University of Cape Town, South Africa.

DETR (2000). KPI Report for The Minister for Construction. Department of the Environment, Transport and the Regions. London.

Dom, N., Kasim, N. and Shamsuddin, A. (2012). Framework of human resource planning (HRP) influencing factors for local workforce supply in Malaysian construction industry. *Journal of Technology Management in China,* 7(2), 177–197.

Drucker, P.F. (2006). *Small Business in the American Economy*. U.S. Government Printing Office, Washington, DC.

Egan, J. (1998). Rethinking Construction: The Report of the Construction Task Force, UK. London. http://constructingexcellence.org.uk/wp-content/uploads/2014/10/rethinking_construction_report.pdf

El-Sayegh, S.M. (2008). Risk assessment and allocation in the UAE construction industry. *International Journal of Project Management*, 26(4), 431–438.

ERA (2016). Road Sector Development Program-19 Years Performance Assessment Report, Ethiopian Roads Authority. Addis Ababa. http://www.era.gov.et/documents/10157/37f7faf1-4614-4abb-8be4-2146ffadfe27

Ericsson, S., Henricsson, P. and Jewell, C. (2005). Understanding Construction Industry Competitiveness: The Introduction of the Hexagon Framework. *Proceedings of the 11th Joint CIB International Symposium Combining Forces — Advancing Facilities Management and Construction through Innovation*, Helsinki, Finland, pp. 188–202.

FDRE (2013). Ethiopian Construction Project Management Institute Establishment. Federal Negarit Gazeta of the Federal Democratic Republic of Ethiopia, Council of Minsters Regulation No. 289/2013. Addis Ababa.

FDRE (2015). Definition of Powers and Duties of the Executive Organs of the Federal Democratic Republic of Ethiopia. Federal Negarit Gazeta of the Federal Democratic Republic of Ethiopia, Proclamation No. 916/2015. Addis Ababa.

Fox, P.W. (2003). Construction Industry Development: Analysis and Synthesis of Contributing Factors. Ph.D. Thesis, Queensland University of Technology, Queensland.

Fu, X., Pietrobelli, C. and Soete, L. (2010). The Role of Foreign Technology and Indigenous Innovation in Emerging Economies: Technological Change and Catching Up. Inter-American Development Bank Technical note No. IDB-TN-166 on Institutional Capacity and Financial Sector. https://publications.iadb.org/publications/english/document/The-Role-of-Foreign-Technology-and-Indigenous-Innovation-in-the-Emerging-Economies-Technological-Change-and-Catching-Up.pdf [Accessed 3 September 2021].

Green, B. (2015). Understanding the Value of Professionals and Professional Bodies. Chartered Institute of Building (CIOB), Bracknell, UK.

Grosse, R. (1996). International technology transfer in services. *Journal of International Business Studies*, 27(4), 781–800.

Hillebrandt, P.M. (1999). Problems of larger local contractors: Causes and possible remedies. *Proceedings of CIB-TG29, Contractor Development, UCCIDAH in Conjunction with Department of Civil Engineering and Department of Architecture, Makerere University*, Kampala, Uganda, pp. 25–33.

HKDB (2018). Construction 2.0, Time to change. Hong Kong.

ICTAD (1988). Development of Domestic Construction Contractors — Cabinet Paper 116 of 10/8/88. Publication ICTAD/ID/03, December 1988, Institute for Construction, Training and Development (ICTAD) renamed Construction Industry Development Authority (CIDA). Sri Lanka.

ICTAD (1992). Consultancy Reports on the 'Domestic Construction Industry in the Roads Sub-Sector', Inception Report in February 1992, the Interim Report in May 1992, the Draft Final Report in July and the Final Report in September 1992 — World Bank sponsored Study led by Team Leader (Technical): M.M. Kumaraswamy, Institute for Construction Training & Development (ICTAD). Renamed Construction Industry Development Authority (CIDA), Sri Lanka.

IGC (2012). The Challenges and the Way Forward for the Construction Industry in Mozambique. International Growth Center, Maputo, Mozambique.

ILO (1987). Guidelines for the Development of Small Scale Construction Enterprises. International Labour Office, Geneva.

ISR (1999). Building for Growth: An Analysis of the Australian Building and Construction Industries. Industry Science Resource, Canberra, Australia.

Iyer, K.C. and Jha, K.N. (2005). Factors affecting cost performance: Evidence from Indian construction projects. *International Journal of Project Management*, 23(4), 283–295.

Iyer, K.C. and Jha, K.N. (2006). Critical factors affecting schedule performance: Evidence from Indian construction projects. *Journal of Construction Engineering and Management*, (132)8, 871–881.

Kiggundu, B.M. (1999). Institutional Challenges to Contractor Development. *Proceedings of CIB-TG29, Contractor Development, UCCIDAH in Conjunction with Department of Civil Engineering and Department of Architecture,* Makerere University, Kampala, Uganda, pp. 161–67.

Kumaraswamy, M.M. (1998). Industry development through creative project packaging and integrated management. *Engineering, Construction and Architectural Management*, 5(3), 228–37.

Kumaraswamy, M.M. (2006). Accelerating construction industry development. *Journal of Construction in Developing Countries*, (11), 73–96.

Kumaraswamy, M.M. (2015). Source of time and cost over-runs in road works projects: pilot study. World Bank Group, Washington, DC. http://documents.worldbank.org/curated/en/2015/10/25127140/source-time-cost-over-runs-road-works-projects-pilot-study [Accessed 30 April 2020].

Kumaraswamy, M.M. and Raza, H. (2014, July). Pilot study on sources of Time and Cost over-runs in Roadworks projects. Report to the World Bank Colombo, Sri Lanka.

Kumaraswamy, M.M. and Shrestha, G.B. (2002). Targeting 'technology Exchange' for faster organisational and industry development. *Building Research & Information*, 30(3), 183–195.

Kumaraswamy, M.M., Mahesh, G., Mahalingam, A., Loganathan, S. and Kalidindi S.N. (2017). Developing a clients' charter and construction project KPIs to direct and drive industry improvements. *Built Environment Project and Asset Management Journal*, Special Issue on "Securing Clients' Objectives throughout Construction Project Life cycles," C. Ramanayaka and M. Sutrisna (Eds.), (7)3, 253–270.

Kumaraswamy, M.M., Ofori, G., Mahesh, G., Teo, E., Tjandra, I. and Wong, K. (2010). Construction industry improvement initiatives: are we really translating rhetoric into reality? In R. Rameezdeen, S. Senaratne and Y.G. Sandanayake (Eds.), *International Research Conference on Sustainability in*

Built Environment, Colombo, Sri Lanka, 18–19 June. ISBN: 978-955-9027-33-1, BEMRU, University of Moratuwa, Sri Lanka, pp. 116–125.

Latham, M. (1994). Constructing the team, Joint Review of Procurement and Contractual Arrangements in the United Kingdom Construction Industry. HMSO, London.

Loganathan, S. and Kalidindi, S. (2015). Masonry labor productivity variation: An Indian case study. *Proceedings of the first Indian Lean Construction Conference*, 175–185.

Loganathan, S., Srinath, P., Kumaraswamy, M., Kalidindi, S. and Varghese, K. (2017). Identifying and addressing critical issues in the Indian construction industry: Perspectives of large building construction clients. *Journal of Construction in Developing Countries*, 22(1), 121–144.

Loosemore, M., Dainty, A. and Lingard, H. (2003). *Human Resource Management in Construction Projects: Strategic and Operational Approaches*. Spon Press, London and New York.

Lu, W. (2006). A System for Assessing and Communicating Contractors' Competitiveness. Ph.D. Thesis, The Hong Kong Polytechnic University, Hong Kong, SAR.

Mengistu, D.G. (2019). Improving Determinant Factors to Facilitate Construction Industry Development in Ethiopia, Ph.D. Thesis, National Institute of Technology, Karnataka, India.

MGI. (2017). McKinsey Global Institute, Reinventing Construction: A Route To Higher Productivity. http://www.mckinsey.com/industries/capital-projects-and-infrastructure/our-insights/reinventing-construction-through-a-productivity-revolution.

Milford, R. (2009). Construction industry development in developing countries; Lessons and opportunities. *3rd International Conference on Concrete & Development*, Tehran, Iran, pp. 59–70.

Miller, A, Radcliffe, D. and Isokangas, E. (2009). A perception-influence model for the management of technology implementation in construction. *Construction Innovation*, 9(2), 168–183.

MoFED (2010a). The Federal Public Procurement Directive. FDRE, Ministry of Finance and Economic Development, Addis Ababa, Ethiopia.

Morris, P.W., Crawford, L., Hodgson, D., Shepherd, M.M. and Thomas, J. (2006). Exploring the role of formal bodies of knowledge in defining a profession — The case of project management. *International Journal of Project Management*, 24(8), 710–721.

MUDC (2013). Construction Industry Development Policy. FDRE, Ministry of Urban Development and Construction, Addis Ababa, Ethiopia.

MWUD (2010). Housing Development Program, 2006–2010 Implementation Report. Ministry of Works and Urban Development, Addis Ababa. http://www.mwud.gov.et/web/guest/reports.

NAS (2005). *Facilitating Interdisciplinary Research*. The National Academies Press, Washington, DC, USA. http://www.nap.edu/catalog/11153.

Naveed, M.H., Thaheem, M.J., Khurshid, M.B. and Farooqui, R.U.H. (2017). Performance assessment of Construction Engineering and Management (CEM) degree program in developing countries: Case of Pakistan. *International Journal of Construction Education and Research*, 13(1), 3–23.

NSPE (2013). *Professional Engineering Body of Knowledge*. Prepared by the Licensure and Qualifications for Practice Committee of the National Society of Professional Engineers, Alexandria, VA, USA, 60 pp. https://www.nspe.org/sites/default/files/resources/nspe-body-of-knowledge.pdf

Ofori, G. (1980). The Construction Industries of Developing Countries: The Applicability of Existing Theories and Strategies for Their Improvement and Lessons for the Future. The Case of Ghana. Ph.D. Thesis, University College London, UK.

Ofori, G. (1985). Managing construction industry development. *Construction Management and Economics*, 3(1), 33–42.

Ofori, G. (1988). A central data bank for construction. *Habitat International*, 12(1), 87–94.

Ofori, G. (1994). Construction technology development: Role of an appropriate policy. *Engineering, Construction and Architectural Management*, 1(2), 147–168.

Ofori, G. (1999). Construction contractor development: New directions. *Proceedings of CIB-TG29, Contractor Development, UCCIDAH in Conjunction with Department of Civil Engineering and Department of Architecture,* Makerere University, Kampala, Uganda, pp. 147–160.

Ofori, G. (2015). Nature of the construction industry, its needs and its development: A review of four decades of research. *Journal of Construction in Developing Countries*, 20(2), 115–135.

Ofori, G., Ai Lin, E.T. and Tjandra, I.K. (2011). A decade of change and improvement? An industry view of construction industry development in Singapore under Construction 21. *Proceedings of CIB, Management and Innovation for a Sustainable Built Environment*, Amsterdam, The Netherlands, pp. 1–13.

Ofori, G., Ai Lin, E.T. and Tjandra, I.K. (2013). Effectiveness of Construction 21: Enhancing professionalism in Singapore's construction industry. *Proceedings of the 19th International CIB World Building Congress: Construction and Society*, Brisbane, Australia, pp. 2457–2468.

Ofori, G., Pin, T., Leong, C. and Lean, S. (1999). Do foreign contractors help host-country construction industries to develop? Case of Singapore. *Proceedings of CIB-TG29, Contractor Development, UCCIDAH in Conjunction with Department of Civil Engineering and Department of Architecture,* Makerere University, Kampala, Uganda, pp. 90–99.

Ogbogbaidi, B. (1999). The role of the private sector in contractor development: The Shell Uganda experience. *Proceedings of CIB-TG29, Contractor Development, UCCIDAH in Conjunction with Department of Civil Engineering and Department of Architecture,* Makerere University, Kampala, Uganda, pp. 85–89.

Osabutey, E.L.C., Nyuur, R.B. and Debrah, Y.A. (2012). Human Resource Development in Construction. In G. Ofori (Ed.), *New Perspectives on Construction in Developing Countries*, Routledge, Abingdon, pp. 229–252.

Osabutey, E/L.C., Williams, K. and Debrah, Y.A. (2014). The potential for technology and knowledge transfers between foreign and local firms: A study of the construction industry in Ghana. *Journal of World Business*, 49(4), 560–571.

Oviawe, J.I., Uwameiye, R. and Uddin, P.S.O. (2017). Bridging skill gap to meet technical, vocational education and training school-workplace collaboration in the 21st century. *International Journal of Vocational Education and Training Research*, 3(1), 7–14.

Peansupap, V. and Walker, D.H.T. (2006). Information Communication Technology (ICT) implementation constraints: A construction industry perspective. *Engineering, Construction and Architectural Management*, 13(4), 364–379.

PSIB (2005). International Review of International Review of Benchmarking in Construction Contents. Process and System Innovation in Building and Construction, The Hague, The Netherlands.

Sommerville, J. and Craig, N. (2006). *Implementing IT in Construction.* Routledge, London and New York.

Ssegawa-Kaggwa, J., Ngowi, A.B. and Ntshwene, K. (2013). Using a situation analysis to identify the construction industry deficiencies in Botswana. *Journal of Construction in Developing Countries*, 18(1), 1–18.

Tang, Y. H. and Ogunlana, S.O. (2003). Selecting superior performance improvement policies. *Construction Management and Economics*, 21(3), 247–256.

Weddikkara, C. and Devapriya, K. (2001). Demand and supply trends and construction industry development: A case study in the Sri Lankan construction industry. *The Australian Journal of Construction Economics & Building*, 1(1), 91–105.

Windapo, A. and Qongqo, P. (2011). A comprehensive study of South African construction data sources. *International Conference on Management and Innovation for a Sustainable Built Environment*, Amsterdam, The Netherlands.

Wolstenholme, A. (2009). *Never Waste a Good Crisis: A Review of Progress since Rethinking Construction and Thoughts for Our Future*. Constructing Excellence, London.

Wong, J., Chan, A. and Chiang, Y.H. (2012). A critical review of forecasting models to predict manpower demand. *Australian Journal of Construction Economics and Building*, 4(2), 43–56.

Wong, J.M.W. (2006). Forecasting manpower demand in the construction industry of Hong Kong. Ph.D. Thesis, The Hong Kong Polytechnic University, Hong Kong, SAR.

Wong, J.M.W. and Ng, S.T. (2010). Business failure in the construction industry: A critical review and a future research agenda. *Proceedings of FIG Congress, Facing the Challenges — Building the Capacity*, Sydney, Australia, pp. 1–17.

Wong, J.M.W., Ng, S.T. and Chan, A.P.C. (2010). Strategic planning for the sustainable development of the construction industry in Hong Kong. *Habitat International*, 34(2), 256–263.

World Economic Forum (2016). *Shaping the Future of Construction: A Breakthrough in Mindset and Technology*. Cologny, Switzerland. https://www.bcgperspectives.com/Images/Shaping_the_Future_of_Construction_may_2016.pdf

Yang, L.R., Chen, J.H. and Wang, H.W. (2012). Assessing impacts of information technology on project success through knowledge management practice. *Automation in Construction*, 22(1), 182–191.

https://doi.org/10.1142/9789811224720_0019

Chapter 19

Project Leadership in Construction in Developing Countries

Shamas-ur-Rehman Toor* and George Ofori†

**Asian Infrastructure Investment Bank, China*
†London South Bank University, UK

Abstract

Leadership plays an important role in social settings; be it in the political arena, social environment, or business organization. The very nature of construction projects makes leadership even more essential. Construction projects are complex as they involve several stakeholders with diverse backgrounds and often competing needs. Large construction projects pose additional challenges due to added technical, managerial, and social complexity. Project managers tend to focus on managing the technical tasks, being conscious about the project budget and schedule, and meeting hard deadlines and other project parameters. Project managers often pay less attention to the importance of the human element, the team that delivers the tasks on the projects. This leads to poor team performance which, in turn, has an impact on project performance. The need for effective leadership in construction is acute owing to widely highlighted problems of the construction industry and poor performance on its projects: project delays, cost overruns, disputes, and a poor record of safety and environmental performance. Studies further indicate that the developing countries face even more severe problems in these regards, and that hinders their efforts to establish the physical foundation for their socio-economic development. The aim of this chapter is to highlight the importance of effective project leadership and its development in construction in the developing countries. The objectives are to explain leadership and its relevance to projects; to consider the special requirement of project leadership in construction; and to discuss the need for project leadership in construction in the developing countries. Finally, suggestions are made for project leadership development in the construction industries in the developing countries.

Keywords: Leadership, project leadership, leadership development, developing countries, research agenda

Introduction

Aim and objectives

The aim of this chapter is to highlight the importance of effective project leadership and its development in construction in the developing countries. The objectives are to:

- explain leadership and its relevance to projects, and in particular, construction projects;
- discuss project leadership and explore how to develop effective project leadership;
- discuss the need for project leadership in construction in the developing countries; and
- make proposals for the development of project leadership in the construction industries in the developing countries.

Features of construction and importance of leadership

It is well known that the success of a business venture largely depends on the quality of the leadership (Kotter, 2001). The nature of construction projects makes the role of leadership important (Ahmed *et al.*, 2021). As suggested by Ofori (2021), each construction project is unique in many regards (including its design and components, location, contractual provisions, and client and project team). The project is location-specific, being influenced by factors in the locality. The projects have a wide range of sizes and therefore costs, but the typical project is expensive and takes a long time to complete. The performance parameters are set out by the client. Thus, a construction project faces a great deal of risks. The World Economic Forum and Boston Consulting Group (2015) indicate how the risk-averse nature and price focus of clients, in turn, structure the nature of the construction industry as they lead to intense competition and low margins in the industry, which then hinders the ability of the firms to invest in technology, innovation, and in their people (or to attract talent). This tendency also results in a short-term focus on individual projects and tasks, rather than on strategic considerations and on people. It also impairs the ability of the organizations to enhance their capacity and capability to perform well on projects.

Construction projects comprise teams from a range of professional backgrounds, and often, countries, cultures, and socio-economic circumstances. A construction project manager today has to deal with a greater proportion of highly trained workers and the application of advanced technologies on site. Much of the work is also done off-site, as modern methods of construction are playing an increasingly large role in the industry (McKinsey, 2016; NHBC Foundation, 2018). Quality standards are also progressively more stringent. A construction project manager today also deals with an increasingly more demanding external environment which comprises statutes, regulations, and government policies that are becoming increasingly stringent. Moreover, a construction project has an extensive value chain, with a range of business partners, including suppliers and subcontractors, which have competitive pressures of their own. The stakeholders of the construction project are many and varied. Apart from the project team and the range of businesses in the value chain, they include the relevant government agencies, the end purchasers and direct beneficiaries, the community in the environs of the project, and pressure groups. Indeed, on large projects, this range of stakeholders includes the media. With this set of tasks and operating environment, which are in a state of flux, it is evident that the construction industry needs good leaders for its projects and companies, and at the level of the industry.

The advent of globalization has seen the extensive internationalization of construction activities, and, as a result, the players have faced several additional challenges (Low and Leong, 2000; Lewis, 2007; Jin *et al.*, 2013). In particular, in the developing countries, where construction activity in the large-project segment is dominated by foreign enterprises, cross-cultural interactions play a key role in negotiations, decision making, problem solving, and other aspects of business and technical operations. Cultural differences among project participants should lead to varieties in the way management and leadership approaches are designed and operationalized (Gerstner and Day, 1994; Loosemore and Lee, 2002; Wong *et al.*, 2007). Studies show that failure to appreciate differences in culture among the participants in a construction project can lead to undesirable consequences (Norwood and Mansfield, 1999). For example, Dahles and Wels (2002) observe that cultural issues are complex and can influence how a project leader deals with tensions and conflicts, uncertainties, and frustrations while negotiating and managing various national cultures, corporate identities, and business pressures and objectives on the construction project. APM (2021) states that, "Managing a team with culture and relationships in mind is key to good project management. Team ethos or team spirit plays an essential part in how everyone interacts with one another — a culture of trust and openness enables alignment to the project goals." Therefore, it is suggested that international firms should have managers who are culturally intelligent (Early, 2006). Selmer (2001) goes further to suggest that managers with these attributes can be used in a strategic way to develop business across borders. The virtual team with members in different countries has been a reality on large construction projects since the late 1990s (Chinowsky and Rojas, 2003; Vorakulpipat *et al.*, 2010; Hosseini and Chileshie, 2013).

It is suggested that that there is an increased need for leadership when working in a volatile environment and dealing with change (Kotter, 2001). Krahn and Hartment (2006) assert that leadership is important in a project environment (as projects generate change), and the characteristics can differ from one project to the next. The construction project is an endeavor to create a unique and usually complex item in a volatile and uncertain environment, which is intended to satisfy the aspirations of a large number of internal and external stakeholders. The need for leadership on such projects is evident; the role of project managers is changing, and their leadership capabilities should be enhanced. Krahn and Hartment (2006) observe that their research findings suggest that, when some project characteristics are present, such as a novel project which requires considerable innovation, more leadership-focused skills and competencies, such as people skills and vision, become more important. This also supports the assertion that the context within which the leadership occurs impacts the level of leadership needed.

Effective project management has become more challenging as the environment within which projects are delivered has become increasingly volatile and complex (Goodwin, 1993). Changes to the characteristics of the project and team, such as changing business relationships, new technologies, heterogeneous teams, and more diverse stakeholders are making project management more difficult (Manning, 2003; Thompsen, 2000). Project leadership is becoming more important to the field of project management in general (Heagney, 2018). The International Centre for Complex Project Management (2018) noted that leadership is necessary to deal with complex projects of all types, including emergence, change management, maintaining strategic outcomes focus, and working with multiple stakeholders.

Leadership is becoming increasingly more important. Lindgren and Packendorff (2009b) note that one of the consequences of the "projectification" of industries and societies is that project leadership has become an increasingly usual task for members of organizations. Thus, there is a growing demand for people with the ability to lead projects successfully. Krahn and Hartment (2006) observe that project leadership is an increasingly popular field of investigation, an area growing in relevance and importance as projects are being delivered in a more complex and uncertain environment.

Construction projects in developing countries

The challenges that face construction projects in developing countries are well cataloged. Mir *et al.* (2007) present some of the myriad problems encountered in construction industries in developing countries. These include: insufficient education and training; absence of government commitment; lack of long-term vision and planning for the industry; fluctuations in workload; ineffective budgeting; defective contract documents; corrupt procedures; payment-related delays; problems of bonding and insurance; lack of adequate financial resources; foreign exchange constraints; non-availability of equipment and spare parts; and poor information. Ofori (2021) provides a review of the characteristics of the construction industries in developing countries, which outlined similar issues.

Similarly, Rwelamila and Purushottam (2012) outline these "African project failure symptoms":

- clients and other stakeholders are dissatisfied with the final products or services;
- most of the project missions are archaic;
- there is the poor relationship in the project-oriented organization between project management and the project site means that adequate resources and authority are not provided;
- most projects do not have appropriate schedules and plans;
- there is little or no consultation of stakeholders;
- the personnel recruitment practices of the project-oriented organization lack planning, selection, and training;
- there is inadequate monitoring and feedback, hindering control during implementation;
- communication in the project-oriented organization is often ineffective;
- the troubleshooting strategies in the project-oriented organization are inadequate and teams are unable to deal with crises and deviations from plans;
- the persons appointed as project managers are technical experts and incompetent administratively, interpersonally, and in terms of project-specific expertise;
- there is excessive power and politics in the organizations, furthering self-interest;
- events in the operating environment have a negative impact on projects; and
- urgency is an elusive word in the countries.

The different context for projects found in developing countries is discussed in Chapters 2 and 4. Bredillet *et al.* (2012) noted an increase in the volume of projects in Africa and in their sizes and complexity. He observed that projects in Africa include many stakeholders with different and often divergent interests often influenced by historical and geopolitical factors. The context of projects in Africa is "very specific," being influenced by these historical and geopolitical relationships and the cultural and economic differences between Africa and its major trading partners.

Project leadership: An overview

Researchers and practitioners alike differentiate leadership from management (Zaleznik, 1977; Bennis and Nanus, 1985). It is suggested that, as the business environment experiences greater change, uncertainty, and volatility, more leadership is needed (Kotter, 2001; Dimov, 2004). Kotter (2001) considered management and leadership to be different but complementary. To him, management involves bringing order and consistency (including setting goals and budgets, establishing steps and schedules, allocating resources, solving problems, and monitoring the results). Kotter (2001) asserted that while management is important, the increases in the complexity and volatility to the business environment create a need for greater leadership. Leadership involves dealing with change and includes setting and communicating direction; developing vision; and aligning team members, stakeholders, and others. As Toor and Ofori (2008a, 2008b) argue, leadership is long-term, visionary, and purpose-oriented and seeks to attain innovation and change, while management is short-term and task-focused and aspires to achieve control and stability. Leaders and managers are different, as they apply different conceptualizations and approaches to work, exercise different problem-solving approaches, and exhibit different behaviors, owing to their different intrinsic and extrinsic motivations.

It is suggested that leadership is about influencing others: working primarily to establish a direction, aligning people, and inspiring and motivating them (Ekkert, 2019). For a project manager, the task is understanding the vision given to him or her by the organization and influencing others to follow that vision. Ekkert (2019) notes further that leadership is about embracing a vision (at both the strategic and tactical levels), communicating it, and then working to influence and inspire the team to execute that project. Bennis and Thomas (2002) suggested that leaders should have four competencies: adaptability (the ability to surpass adversity), engaging others (motivating others to a shared vision to achieve together and creating shared meaning), a compelling voice (effective communication of the shared vision), and integrity (the presence of authenticity and strong values).

Project leadership is a relatively new field of study, and thus it is relatively under-investigated. Sotiriou and Wittmer (2001) stated that whereas general leadership has been a focus of investigation for over a century, there has been relatively little empirical research on project leadership. Authors note challenges to the investigation of project leadership. Slevin and Pinto (1991) asserted that successful project management requires effective leadership. However, the study of project leadership is complicated by the fact that it is a topic that is simultaneously well known and little known. A second challenge is the wide range of meanings ascribed to the concept by different authors. Thite (1999) used the term "technical leadership" to refer to the leadership that is provided to technical and scientific personnel. Other authors considered project leadership to mean various different things, such as a skill for effective project management, while others thought it involved such elements as interpersonal relationships and facilitation (Gemmill and Wilemon, 1994; Kezsbom, 1994). Finally, some authors use the terms project leadership and project leader interchangeably with the terms project management and project manager respectively (Puccinelli, 1999; Sense, 2003).

There have also been some efforts to differentiate between project leadership and project management. Norrie and Walker (2004) note that, as the project managers' main task is to implement project plans to achieve pre-determined objectives within time and cost constraints, this limits their strategic thought process and impairs their vision for their people and organizations. Coleman and Bourne (2018) suggest that the skills required of a project leader are different from those proposed and developed for project management. Leadership is more about the future, dealing with people, and working outside the project with stakeholders, whereas many aspects of project management are inward- and backward-looking. The issue of working with outside stakeholders is most pertinent to developing countries, where community participation or even consultation is ignored, or not effective, even where it is enshrined in major policy documents such as national development plans, as in Uganda (see National Development Authority, 2015), although it is well known that stakeholder participation increases the likelihood of project success (Simushi and Wium, 2020).

Studies have found that the leader of a project is a highly critical success factor (Coleman and MacNicol, 2015). Jiang *et al.* (1998) and Krahn and Hartment (2006) asserted that the project manager is the most critical element for projects to be delivered successfully while Zimmerer and Yasin (1998) noted that the main cause of project failure is a lack of project manager leadership. Going further, Smith (1999) argues that projects do not fail due to lack of project management, but rather from a lack of project leadership. In other words, project management alone does not work. Thus, it is suggested that project management must go beyond managerial functionalism and a focus on short-term project goals, and progress toward project leadership (Bull, 2010; Madsen, 2015). Shenhar (2004, p. 571) suggests that strategic project leadership shifts the focus in project management "from efficiency only to effectiveness and efficiency; from operational issues to strategic, operational, and human; and from getting the job done, to getting the business results and winning in the market place."

The project managers are responsible for the operational performance and outcomes of their projects. They manage large budgets and control large volumes of other resources. They resolve disputes among parties involved in the project and they take critical decisions which can have a long-term impact on project health. They should be able to satisfy the distinct demands of each of the numerous stakeholders of the project they deal with. Such a short-term focus, while being necessary and important, is not sufficient. It is necessary to develop more sophisticated approaches to managing the performance on projects in a way which supports both specific project objectives and the wider business goals of the organization (Dainty *et al.*, 2006). As Gilbert (1983) suggests, project management must be complemented by project leadership that acts as a force of cohesion and a catalyst, makes possible the environment for creativity and motivation, and helps to achieve the strategic goals of projects. Similarly, Shenhar (2004) proposes that instead of the conventional focus on the project performance parameters of time, budget, quality, efficiency, and operational performance, companies should take a strategic look at their projects in order to create value for their clients and other stakeholders and enhance their corporate competitiveness. Going further, Norrie and Walker (2004) suggest a new perspective: projects should be completed on-time, on-budget, on-quality, and more importantly, on-strategy.

The wide commercial importance of each project for the organization is now being stressed. Shenhar and Dvir (2004) note that today, dynamic business environments and global competition require finding new ways to use projects as competitive weapons. Almost all projects are initiated with a business perspective and goal in mind. However, most projects are still managed with an operational mindset, focusing on delivering short-term results. Increasingly, project managers are required to grow and become real leaders. In a study on the future skills of project managers, Wiezel *et al.* (2013) found that leadership competencies for today's project managers rose to the top of the rankings for future competencies — above technical and management competencies. The project manager of the next decade will have to contend with deep underlying global forces and would need to respond quickly to unexpected breakthroughs and to innovations that come at an accelerated rate. The project manager role would require greater competence in communications, relationship building, complex decision making, business insight, risk management, diverse thinking, engagement with others, and coaching and mentoring. These new skills will be added to the fundamental attributes associated with project managers, such as integrity, accountability, initiative, and decisiveness.

Project Manager (2020) notes that project leaders inspire others to share their vision, motivate others to act on that vision, and encourage others and help them overcome obstacles in pursuit of that vision. Project leadership is about getting something done well through others. The Ethics Member Advisory Group of Project Management Institute (2014) notes that project management is, for the most part, an activity undertaken with others, and project managers depend on them for the success of their projects. Projects involve having these others do, or not do, just what is needed in an environment where the project manager has far less authority than responsibility. Thus, project leadership is team development and the creation of the right environment for the team. Ekkert (2019) notes that, to become a great project leader, humility is required. One should have an accurate view of one's own flaws when discussing areas for improvement. This combination of being "accurate" while being modest is among what gives a project manager the opportunity to earn the trust of his or her colleagues.

Project Manager (2020) notes that the core values of a strong leader are: communication; motivation of the project team, i.e., getting people to want to do what you need them to do; delegation; positivity, i.e., keeping a positive attitude regardless of the situation; trustworthiness, i.e., being able to instill a sense of trust; creativity, i.e., being aware that some problems cannot be solved in an usual manner and one must be open to taking chances to find unique solutions; feedback to the team and other stakeholders; responsibility, i.e., taking responsibility for the bigger picture and for one's behavior; commitment to the project; and flexibility, i.e., dealing with things as they change.

Owing to the large number of stakeholders involved, and the complex operating environments of many projects, the project manager should be a facilitator, a coordinator, a motivator, and a politician. Thus, the project manager should be a project leader (Briner *et al.*, 1996). Thite (2000) suggests that in the era of flatter organizational structures, outsourcing, and the engagement of knowledge workers (who need recognition, motivation, empowerment, and appreciation to perform well), boundaryless teams and virtual organizations, the task-oriented leadership style common on projects should be replaced by a participative, result-oriented style. Lewis (2003) presents the personal traits, principles, and examples of leaders and followers and considers how to move from project management onto project leadership.

The project management professional institutions have recently been stressing project leadership as well. For example, the Association for Project Management (APM) (2021) states: "A project team is a group of people working together in collaboration or cooperation towards a common goal. Some teams are co-located in the same geographic area; some span multiple organisations and virtual team-working is increasingly prevalent. In each case, the ability of the project professional to develop and lead teams is of vital importance";[1] and that: "Leaders need to adapt their style and approach to the needs of the team and the work that needs to be accomplished, this is called situational leadership. Leadership is the ability to establish vision and direction, to influence and align others towards a common purpose, and to empower and inspire people to achieve success." APM has commissioned several works on project leadership including Coleman and Bourne (2018); Kontantamer (2019); and MacKay (2021).

Nature of project leadership

What is project leadership? Cleland (1995, p. 86) defines project leadership as "a presence and a process carried out within an organizational role that assumes responsibility for the needs and rights of those people who choose to follow the leader in accomplishing the project results." To Kloppenborg *et al.* (2003, p. 15), project leadership is "the systemic application of leadership understanding and skills at each stage of a project life cycle." Norrie and Walker (2004, p. 48) define it as "the higher pursuit of the project team's creating purposeful, strategic action that will augment the organization's business strategy and achieve results within the norms and values of the organization."

Is there a difference between organizational and project leadership? Leadership and its conceptualization and research on it are usually viewed from the perspective of an organization. Ofori and Toor (2021) note that the nature of the project makes project leadership different from organizational leadership. Some of these features are that project leadership: focuses on a single, unique project with a defined life cycle and set objectives; is constrained by fixed, pre-determined performance parameters such as time, budget, and quality; mostly deals with short-term goals and objectives, but often has to find long-term, strategic solutions; coordinates a temporary, often loose, team formed from different organizations or across functional

[1] https://www.apm.org.uk/resources/what-is-project-management/what-is-project-team-management-and-leadership/

groups, the members of which are not accustomed to working with each other; deals with numerous stakeholders (individuals, groups, or organizations) with diverse backgrounds and often competing interests; deals with a changing composition and structure of the project as the work proceeds; faces an environment of uncertainty; does not enjoy direct control or formal authority over the teams and persons involved in the project; involves the performance of roles both within and outside the project; and must establish a fine balance between leadership and management. The complex and dynamic nature of projects poses distinct challenges to a leader, making his or her job multi-faceted and highly demanding.

Similarly, Coleman and Bourne (2018) suggest that project leadership is different from general leadership. Project leaders have to create, organize, develop, and disperse the project team, after disbanding the project organization. They also have to deal with change — they operate in an unstable and volatile environment and have to make fast judgment calls in ambiguous situations. Although many project leadership skills overlap with general leadership skills, simply developing general leadership skills is insufficient preparation for developing the leadership needed for major, complex projects. That leading a project involves necessary tasks outside the project is most notable from the perspective of developing countries, considering the relatively short duration of projects and the short learning curves they involve.

Project leadership in developing countries

The context of the developing countries can be illustrated with the eight project leadership survival skills developed by Coleman and Burke (2018):

(1) *anticipating* — being prepared for what could knock the project off course next; in the developing countries, the relatively difficult operating environment of the developing countries poses continual challenges in a routine manner
(2) *judgment and decision-making* — making timely decisions with incomplete information; in the developing countries, the information

is really incomplete, and timeliness is difficult to attain in the difficult operating environment

(3) *seeing it all* — feeling the totality of what is going on inside and outside the project; in developing countries, what would be going on outside the project is really wide-ranging, including politics, local culture, and traditions, and there are many inter-relationships and dependencies

(4) *building credibility and confidence* — belief in the leadership and the team; such credibility will develop if the leader behavior is contextually appropriate

(5) *being organizationally intelligent* — knowing when and how to engage with the organization; this leadership skill will also be important in developing countries

(6) *learning* — being open-minded and reflecting on and developing personal and team performance; in the developing countries, it is necessary for the project leader to be imaginative in dealing with the complex context and learn from experiences in order to improve performance subsequently

(7) *resolving conflicts and collaborating* — building a common purpose, despite the rules; in the developing countries, for conflict resolution to work, it should be firmly built on the local culture

(8) *creating the project culture and environment* — deliberately defining and creating the culture and environment to succeed; in the developing countries, this will be an important activity; again, it should be built on the local culture and recognize the role of the stakeholders.

Effective project leaders

What makes an effective project leader? There have been many studies on the behaviors and skills of project leaders, and Martin (2018) notes that project managers have a bewildering amount of leadership information to sift through to identify actions essential for them to progress to project leadership. Strang (2007) believes that effective project leaders are aware of their behavior, traits, and skills and they try to reconcile their traits and behaviors with the requirements of the situation and the context in which they operate. According to Toor and Ogunlana (2006), behaviors that are mentioned frequently in relation to project leadership include: visioning (Makilouko, 2004), inspiring (Dainty *et al.*, 2005), goal setting (Egbu, 1999), listening and empathizing (Odusami, 2002), considerate decision-making (Toor and Ogunlana, 2006), facilitating (Giritli and Topcu-Oraz, 2004), rewarding (Lee-Kelley and Leong, 2003), coaching/teaching (Giritli and Topcu-Oraz, 2004), people orientation (Fellows *et al.*, 2003), task orientation (Dulaimi and Langford, 1999), and management of conflict (Toor and Ogunlana, 2008).

Leadership abilities are highlighted as one of the most important qualities of the project manager (Chipulu *et al.*, 2013; Alvarenga *et al.*, 2019; Ahmed *et al.* (2021)). Competencies that are covered in the discussion of project leadership include team skills, interpersonal skills, project management skills, communication skills, organizational skills, and technical skills (Geoghegan and Dulewicz, 2008). MacKay (2021) establishes what good project leadership looks like and offers steps to achieving it. He shows that command and control behaviors are out-of-date; they are seldom effective in today's changed delivery environment and can actually be counter-productive to project success. Instead, he shows how the effective project leader evaluates the self, the team and the organizational culture to cultivate fit-for-purpose project leadership behaviors such as empowering team agility, synergy, and collaboration.

Similarly, Martin (2018) suggests that project leaders should remember seven principles: (1) the project leader should not fear losing control of the project if the team participates; (2) the leader should connect the project to the strategic goals of the organization, and let the team know why it is being done, what they are supposed to do, and how what they do affects others and fits into the whole picture; (3) every team member should understand the interdependencies in the project and see how their contributions are essential to getting the whole project completed successfully; and (4) the leader should show appreciation for the contributions of each individual on the team and for the team as a whole, ensure that they feel valued and solicit their feedback on how improvements can be made. Martin (2018) adds that the leader must: (1) build and maintain an environment of mutual trust and respect (honor diversity of thinking and other individual differences; keep to commitments; maintain confidences; value each person's inputs and ideas; eliminate blame; minimize interference; learn to understand members' unique experiences, emotions, biases, opinions, and agendas that lie in the background of group discussions; endeavor to learn about the aspirations and personal interests of their team members); and (2) empower the team (avoid micromanagement; maintain team ownership and accountability; set up a process which will give early warning signs if the project is off track; and ensure that people have the resources they need to get the job done). Project Manager (2020) notes that project leadership is difficult work; there is no single body of knowledge from which to learn it, and learning by doing is the only way forward. However, from the way successful leaders work, there are commonalities. Most leaders share attributes which can be pillars on which one can build project leadership: they are grounded and centered; they create solutions; they are analytical; they can evaluate risk; they can generate a sense of urgency; they are insightful; they build cohesion; they motivate people; and they achieve results. Leadership is fluid. It requires nuance.

Considering reviews like what has been outlined in this section so far, Krahn and Hartment (2006) note that much of what is written about what makes up the leadership of effective project managers takes the form of lists of important project manager skills and competencies, often sorted into groups such as technical, business, and social skills. Moreover, much of the literature is based not on empirical investigation but project manager opinion and is not necessarily well-reflected in bodies of knowledge. (Ahmed *et al.* (2021) make similar points on the literature.) Moreover, the lists are also static. Textbooks provide lists of project manager skills and competencies with descriptions (Gido and Clements, 2003), and professional associations — such as the Project Management Institute (PMI) — publish lists and groupings of project management skills and competencies, such as PMI's Project Manager Competency Development Framework (PMI, 2002). Papers in journals also lend insight into the key project manager skills and competencies to effectively lead projects and teams in diverse groups, including technical ability, detail-orientation, leadership, and human issues (Cowie, 2003; Dawes, 2002; Lampel, 2001). Krahn and Hartment (2006) suggest that the lists provide a starting point to understand what is important for a project manager, but it is difficult to deduce from the lists which skills and competencies are most important for a particular project manager in a particular context, particular elements of the work of the project manager, or if these should change with changes to the characteristics of the project.

Project leadership style

Much has been written about the style of the project leader. Slevin and Pinto (1991) emphasize that the leadership style of the project leader is determined by the situation on the project. Hence, the leader may have different styles during different stages of the project. Several researchers also agree that leadership style should vary according to the situation, and the leader must find a fit between his/her style, those who are being led, and situational factors (Gilbert, 1993; Kangis and Lee-Kelley, 2000). Ogunlana *et al.* (2002) also found that the relationship-oriented leadership style was more appropriate than the task-oriented style for project managers in Thailand. Odusami *et al.* (2003) found that the most appropriate leadership style for Nigerian project leaders is that of the "consultative autocrat." However, Makilouko (2004) studied multi-cultural projects and found that the majority of project leaders adopted a task-oriented leadership style. They also showed cultural blindness, ethnocentrism, parochialism, or in-group favoritism. A study by Owusu-Manu *et al.* (2021) found that democratic, transformational, and situational leadership styles were prevalent leadership styles in the Ghanaian construction industry; and that project managers favored the "growth mindset" as opposed to a "fixed mindset," which had a low positive relationship with autocratic and situational leadership styles but a low negative relationship with transformational leadership style.

In an often-referred-to study, Barber and Warn (2005) use the analogy of firefighting to describe a good project leader. They note that a proactive project leader pre-empts the problems and prevents them from occurring. Thus, an effective project leader is a "fire-lighter"; who is able to inspire a shared commitment, encourage reflection before action, and coach others to achieve demanding objectives.

The authentic leadership approach is highly recommended for project leaders. To George (2003), authentic leaders have a sense of purpose, practice solid values, lead with the heart, and establish connected relationships. Such leaders empower others. They are consistent and self-disciplined and do not compromise on their principles. Toor and Ofori (2008a) note that authentic project leaders have a good understanding of cultural sensitivities and are highly motivated and self-aware. They understand the demands of the project from the perspectives of the key stakeholders, and give their best to make the project a success for all of them. The Ethics Member Advisory Group of Project Management Institute (2014) stresses the merits of "authentic project leadership," noting that: "Generally, authentic leaders are positive people with truthful self-concepts who promote openness. By building trust, acting ethically, and generating enthusiastic support from their subordinates, authentic leaders are able to improve individual and project team performance."

The Ethics Member Advisory Group of Project Management Institute (2014) also advocates quiet leadership for project leaders; it shows that a direct linkage exists between project success, effective quiet leadership, building trust, and ethical behavior. It explains that quiet leadership is a way of thinking about people, organizations, and effective action and a way of understanding the flow of events and discerning the best ways to make a difference; it is about leading from the back, leading with actions over words, listening, and forming relationships. They draw attention to six quiet project leadership tips: own the project culture, act for the long term, build a high-performance team, use soft power, establish and maintain trust, and model ethical behavior.

Another style being highlighted recently is distributed leadership. Kontantamer (2019) notes that many authors argue that effective responses to complex situations are based on distributed team leadership approaches. For example, Cox *et al.* (2003) and Pearce (2004) suggest that: in situations of high interdependence, team members act as informal leaders in providing leadership to their peers; in situations where the task or problem requires significant creativity, the whole team acts as a source of leadership by collectively generating novel ideas; and in situations where the task or problem is complex, a specialized group collectively generates solutions. Muethel and Hoegl (2011) argue that virtual project teams can respond to the task and environment uncertainties by sharing team leadership functions. From this perspective, the ties project team members have to their local environments and the specialist expertise of different project team members are opportunities for effectively responding to uncertainty.

The concept of distributed leadership has been broadened. Müller *et al.* (2017) applied distributed team leadership approaches to define the "balanced leadership" approach. This approach suggests that project managers delegate their authority temporarily to project team members in situations that are appropriate for this delegation. Drouin *et al.* (2018) examined the balanced leadership approach in various countries and industries and showed that project managers often delegate decisions requiring technical expertise to their project team members. The importance of distributed team leadership is increasingly being recognized in academia, industry, and public-sector organizations. Drouin *et al.* (2021) observe that balanced leadership has emerged as a contemporary theory of the dynamics in the continuous transfer of leadership authority between project managers and project team members. Their four case studies on three continents identified the generic cognitive coordination mechanisms between project managers and team members. By extending the concept of the socio-cognitive space, their study shows that empowerment, self-management, and shared understanding of skills needs govern and legitimize the question of "who leads" at any point in time on the project.

Finally, servant leadership is advocated. Ekkert (2019) notes that Agile project frameworks such as Scrum focus on leadership from the angle of the scrum master's ability to lead from a servant leadership perspective by serving his or her team members first, looking out for their wellbeing, and focusing on removing impediments to their work. The focus is on accelerating the team's capabilities to accomplish the vision and serving the members in order to complete that vision. To do this, the project leader's influence must have been rooted in having earned respect, trust, and personal power and this should be related to how one motivates a team.

Project leadership in construction

What is the history of project leadership, and when was it adopted in construction? Ofori and Toor (2021) provide a brief account of its history. They note that the term "project leadership" emerged only in the last few decades when scholars recognized that project leadership needs to be distinguished from organizational leadership. Project leadership first appeared in the *International Journal of Project Management* in the early 1980s (Gilbert, 1983). Slevin and Pinto (1991) used the term for the first time in the *Project Management Journal*. In construction research, the term first appeared in *Construction Management and Economics* (in Liu *et al.*, 2003) and in *Engineering, Construction and Architectural Management* (in den Otter and Prins, 2003). Some books published in the 1990s had "project leadership" in their titles (see, for example, Briner *et al.*, 1990, 1996).

The recent history of project leadership is discussed in more detail by Toor and Ofori (2008a). They reviewed works on leadership in the construction management literature and observed that empirical works on the effectiveness and performance of construction leaders appeared in the 1980s (Bresnen, 1986; Bryman *et al.*, 1987). In the 1990s, the focus moved to the leadership style, attributes, and behaviors of project leaders (Dulaimi and Langford, 1999; Rowlinson *et al.*, 1993). Toor and Ofori (2008a) argue that leadership research in construction has relied on old frameworks and empiricism embedded in the positivist approach. There was increased interest in project leadership in the early 2000s. Studies have addressed behaviors, traits, and styles (Giritli and Topcu-Oraz, 2004), leadership models (Chan and Chan, 2005), cross-cultural issues (Wong *et al.*, 2007; Ofori and Toor, 2009); leadership development (Toor and Ofori, 2008a), emotional intelligence of leaders (Songer *et al.*, 2008), negative sides of leadership (Toor and Ogunlana, 2009), ethical issues (Toor and Ofori, 2009a), and authenticity and psychological well-being (Toor and Ofori, 2009b). The establishment of the CIB Task Group 64 on Leadership inspired a new era of research on construction project leadership (CIB, 2006). McCaffer urged researchers around the globe to form a global research institute concentrating on leadership development in construction. The Major Projects Leadership Academy was established in 2012 in the UK with the objective of transforming the implementation of government policy through world-class delivery of major projects. The academy seeks to: develop project leaders to become world-class at successfully delivering major projects; create a cadre of world-class project leaders, formed into an expert support network; and elevate the status of project leadership professionalism in central government. The United Kingdom Project Leadership Programme was established in 2015 with the aim of developing project leaders across government at the level below major projects and improving project delivery.

There is no agreement on the status of the field of project leadership. For example, Lindgren and Packendorff (2009b) note that project leadership is well on its way toward professionalization. Although the content and context of project leadership varies greatly, project leadership is now being constructed as a distinct and homogenous practice, by the associations in project management organizing certification in it, as they are promoting the project as a distinct work form and project managers as a distinct occupation. On the other hand, there is some dissatisfaction about the current body of knowledge. For example, Lindgren and Packendorff (2009a) criticize the existing works; they undertook a review of the literature on project leadership and found that the current research focuses exclusively on individuals and their leadership competencies rather than the leadership practices in project settings, and propose a new research agenda built on the current debate in leadership studies on distributed leadership perspectives. Coleman and Bourne (2018) note that the literature on project leadership is limited, although many organizations are using projects to deliver products, services, and change, making projects critical to the future of organizations. The interest in the subject has not been uniformly on an upward trajectory. Ofori and Toor (2021) note that the level of understanding of leadership is relatively poor and there is heavy dependence on managerial functionalism.

There is also criticism of the approach to, and quality of, research on project leadership in construction. Toor and Ofori (2008c) observe that most of the research adopts quantitative methods, while Toor and Ofori (2008b) suggest that there is little appreciation of leadership as a process, and too much focus is put on the motivational factors and the personal characteristics of project managers (Dulaimi and Langford, 1999). Toor and Ofori (2008b) note that leadership research in construction has been mostly a replication of what has already been done and found in mainstream management, and there is little innovation, and focus on practical implications. The ASCE journal, *Leadership and Management in Engineering*, started in January 2001, but folded in October 2013, although the editor argued that there was the need to move the subjects of leadership and management in engineering into equity with the technical subjects of engineering (Hayden, 2013). In Box 19.1, Lindgren and Packendorff (2009b) outline some problematic issues in the research on the field of project leadership.

Box 19.1: Project leadership research: Problems and promises for the future.

Lindgren, M. and Packendorff, J. (2009b) outline some problematic issues in the research in the field of project leadership.

Individual focus. There is a tradition of considering the project manager as an individual. However, current developments in leadership research emphasize teamwork and consider team leaders as facilitators, implying that important knowledge on leadership is in the relations among team members rather than in the leader as an individual (Pearce and Conger, 2003; Crevani *et al.*, 2007). Also, project managers often neither have the technical skills of their team members nor the power base of their superiors in the project-based structure.

Traits and "pseudo-traits" focus. There is an interest in the personalities of project managers, treating individuals as if they possessed certain traits, and some of the newer research use established psychometric tools to investigate traits in successful project managers. There are also several examples in the older literature of "pseudo-traits" — what good project managers should be able to do, or even what good project managers are supposed to do (*cf.* Barber and Warn, 2005) — presented in the form of requirements on the individuals considered for project leadership assignments. This might lead to people being seen as bearers of a set of unchangeable qualities rather than as active and developing actors. There is a risk that the empirical inquiry into project leaders' behavior results in a confusion of personality traits, competencies, actions, and familiarity with the project management toolbox (for example, see Strang, 2007). An alternative to the inquiry into the competencies and personalities would be an interest in leadership practices as they unfold during project processes (*cf.* Carroll *et al.*, 2008).

Project focus. One of the most important trends in the project management field is the moving of focus from single projects to multi-project management and project portfolio management (Engwall, 2003). However, project leadership research remains focused on the single project. Today, both project managers and project team members often work in several projects in parallel (Zika-Viktorsson *et al.*, 2006). Moreover, an increasing amount of leadership work is taking place in project management offices. The focus on single projects may have negative consequences, such as conserving old autonomous

Box 19.1: (*Continued*)

ideas about project leadership that are not suited to modern portfolio thinking, or indeed ways of working on projects, such as distributed or virtual teams.

Lack of theoretical reflexivity. Where different schools of thought in the general leadership research literature are drawn upon, they are usually treated as complementary evidence that can be used to inform the project management community on how to improve project leadership practices. These schools of thought rest upon different scientific assumptions and in several cases they are in direct conflict with each other. For example, a leadership theory explaining project success from leadership style is not complementary to one emphasizing personal traits in the individual leader or one viewing leadership as a process of group interaction. There is a need for discussions on the ontological, epistemological, and axiological foundations of research (*cf.* Lindgren and Packendorff, 2009a), instead of the usual assumption that project management is a field in its own right that can formulate its own leadership theories.

Lack of empirical research. One consequence of the shortage of thorough, theoretically informed research on project leadership is that the empirical foundations of all the normative advice may become weak. The field is in danger of tending to rely on exploratory research (often made decades ago) mapping empirical patterns rather than testing theoretical hypotheses or developing theory.

Lindgren and Packendorff (2009b) call for more empirical studies on project leadership, based on thorough and well-founded theoretical reasoning and on an interest in actual practices. A widened view and discussions on the foundations of project leadership research can contribute to a re-formulation of the project leadership ideals that fill the literature, and serve to re-masculinize work life than promoting new ways of working and living (Lindgren and Packendorff, 2006). Still, there are also promises for the future inherent in project leadership as a theoretical and practical field of inquiry. There seems to be increasing interest in using concepts and methodologies from general leadership research, and the level of sophistication in current research is also rising.

Source: Lindgren and Packendorff (2009b).

There is, recently, increased interest in leadership in construction. For example, studies have been undertaken on emotional intelligence and leadership style of construction project managers (Sunindijo *et al.*, 2007; Potter *et al.*, 2018); leadership competencies of project managers (Tabassi *et al.*, 2016; Muller and Turner, 2010); leadership communication in project management (Zulch, 2014); relationship between leadership style and project success (Liphadzi *et al.*, 2015); impact of leadership competence on project success; project leadership across team development process (2015); leadership style and innovation in construction (Zhang *et al.*, 2018; Ozorhon, 2014); and role of leadership in organizational culture and innovative behavior in construction projects (Zheng *et al.*, 2019).

There have been suggestions of a future research agenda for project leadership. For example, Shenhar and Dvir (2004) note that project management research must establish better connections between business strategy and project management. They have developed a framework for project management titled Strategic Project Leadership® built on a hierarchy of five components: strategy (to be formally defined for every project to fill the gap between a business strategy and a project plan); spirit (translating project strategy into an inspiring vision, building an environment where commitment is driving the project team); organization, processes, and tools; the lower components of processes and tools represent the traditional project management paradigm, and the higher levels represent the new approach.

A new journal

In 2019, Elsevier, publisher of the *International Journal of Project Management*, initiated production of a new open access journal, *Project Leadership and Society.* Huemann (2021), the first Editor in Chief, suggests that this journal "allows further growth and diversity and especially with the open access format provides a new attractive publication outlet for researchers and educators as well as pracademics to share their theory based but practice relevant findings to a wide audience." The scope of the journal is described as follows: "*Project Leadership and Society* opens up for novel and disruptive approaches to study projects and relate them to society, whereas society is considered in a broad sense, including policy, leadership and managerial practice. Articles study the interaction between *projects, project leadership, project management* on the one hand, and economic, social, political and organizational processes, on the other." Notably, it is specifically stated that: "All papers are expected to yield findings that have implications for *policy* or *practice*." In the context of this book, one of the first two special collections of papers of the journal was on: "Managing and Leading Projects in Africa" (Ika *et al.*, 2021), which "calls African researchers into action to give them a voice and share their valuable research on leading and managing projects in Africa and the impact of projects to developing the society."

Project leadership in the context of construction in developing countries

As discussed in Chapters 2 and 3, project performance in developing countries is particularly poor. Chapter 2 also presents shortfalls in the programs to attain the objectives and targets of the 2030 Development Agenda, with progress toward the attainment of many Sustainable Development Goals (SDGs) lagging behind the required trends. The quality of life of the populations in these countries has been further worsened by the impact of the COVID-19 pandemic.

A description of undertaking projects in the context of immature organizations mirrors the theme of this chapter, if one substitutes "developing countries" for "immature organizations" (Ethics Member Advisory Group of Project Management Institute, 2014):

> "We are frequently managing projects in organizations with limited maturity where processes for prioritizing projects and resources are far from rational and repeatable; indeed, the average maturity of organizations, when assessed on a five-point scale, falls at level two-and-a-half" (PwC, 2004, p. 9).
>
> "Organizations at this maturity level are characterized by informal processes that are not yet institutionalized, by a lack of adherence to standards, and by inattention to lessons learned; these are the types of organizations where the **culture of personality dominates**..." (Cain, 2013, p. 28).

> "This limitation of authority that characterizes the project manager's role propels the most successful project managers to demonstrate leadership (Juli, 2011, p. 11). Consequently, leadership is a key to unlocking the solution to motivating with limited authority in a low-maturity organization; it is the currency that is spent achieving project success. But not just any type of leadership will do. The leadership type must be authentic; it must be the type of leadership that is consistent with the personality orientation of the project leader" (George, 2004, p. 12).

Ika *et al.* (2021) present the Call for Papers for the special collection of *Project Leadership and Society* on "Managing and leading projects in Africa" in September 2021. They note that "there are untold stories about successes and failures in projects and the highs and lows of project leadership in Africa, especially when they are locally funded, not donor-driven." They also note that "projectification is gaining ground in Africa. So is the awareness of the role of projects in the growth and transformation of the continent." They outline some major programs, which add up to a massive total investment, to develop a varied range of infrastructure projects in Africa. They present an outline of project performance in Africa: underperformance in time, budget, and stakeholder expectations; and projects which are never completed. Further adding to the points made in Chapters 2 to 4 about the difficult operating environment for projects in developing countries, Ika *et al.* (2021) note the special situation in Africa:

> "Such project underperformance in Africa may be due to structural (political, economic, physical/geographic, sociocultural, historic, demographic, and environmental), institutional (for example, collusion/corruption, capacity building, lack of political support, too much political interference, governance, and principal-agent) and managerial (initiation, planning, implementation, and monitoring and evaluation) problems (Ika, 2012). For example, in addition to such silent killers as cronyism, collusion, and corruption, collective choice failure can undermine projects… (Damoah *et al.*, 2018).
>
> "Projects may also succumb to what Ika (2012) calls a one-size-fits-all-technical trap (for example, the misconception that a project is a project is a project), an accountability-for-results trap (for example, too much

> emphasis on keeping track of results and little on their delivery), a-lack-of-project-management-capacity trap (for example, shortage of project management skills), and a cultural trap (for example, underplaying local contexts and cultures). For instance, Rwelamila and Purushottam (2012) single out three project management capacity shortages: far too many accidental project managers; mostly inadequate project management training programs; and little strategic project management focus. Evidently, as the Covid-19 crisis has shown, context matters. Capacity and resilience levels vary from country to country. Indeed, "Africa is too big to follow one script" (The Economist, 2011). Thus, there is no one-size-fits-all approach to managing and leading projects in Africa (Ika, 2012)."

The special situation in the developing countries makes project leadership particularly important. Thus, it can be suggested that there should be an immediate transformation of the discourse on project management in developing countries to project leadership.

Suggestions for developing future project leaders in developing countries

The project leader should be culturally and socially rooted in the local systems and be able to engage effectively with all the stakeholders in the project. The leader should recognize and address the aspirations of each of the groups of stakeholders through appropriate actions on the project. The project leader should develop a comprehensive understanding of the project environment and engender awareness of it among the project team members, setting out appropriate paths for building capabilities to overcome resource, technology, and information constraints, as well as bureaucratic, political, and cultural barriers to efficiency on the project.

The project leader should establish a relationship between the leader and the led that can enhance team performance on the project. This involves: selecting talent with skills matched to the project's requirements, motivating, mentoring, coaching and guiding, building trust, developing the team, and building an appropriate project culture. In this way, the project leader develops more leaders in the followers. The project leader should build trust among their team members, empower them, and give them freedom to fulfill their job responsibilities. This involves effective team building and team development.

The effective project leader creates a vision, sells the vision to the team members, ensures their buy-in and ownership, and inspires and motivates them to carry out their tasks, providing the required resources and removing any possible obstacles. The project leader should also recognize the differences in the aspirations of team members and encourage each of them to align their self-interest with that of the project. Thus, the project leader should have human relations skills. The vision should include what the project can, and should, achieve in the future. This also requires the project leader to have a community orientation. The project leader should be capable of producing change. The leader should be future-oriented, while continuing to be contextually aware. The project leader should have a long-term perspective.

Conclusion

Project leadership in construction is important to developing countries owing to the complex nature of the operating environment that projects in those countries face. The need to deal with business and government organizations, communities, and people outside the project accentuates the need for leadership qualities. The influence of administrators and politicians has to be recognized and addressed or negotiated around.

That leadership is different from management has now been well established. Project management should progress to project leadership. In other words, leadership should not just be one of the competences of the project manager. In the developing countries, the development of project leaders should be given critical consideration.

References

Ahmed, R., Philbin, S.P. and Cheema, F. (2021). Systematic literature review of project manager's leadership competencies. *Engineering, Construction and Architectural Management*, 28(1), 1–30. https://doi.org/10.1108/ECAM-05-2019-0276.

Alvarenga, J.C., Branco, R.R., Guedes, A.L.A., Soares, C.A.P. and Silva, W. (2019). The project manager core competencies to project success. *International Journal of Managing Projects in Business*, 79(11). https://doi.org/10.1108/IJMPB-12-2018-0274.

Anderson, S.D. (1992). Project quality and project managers. *International Journal of Project Management*, 10(3), 138–143.

APM (2021). What is project team management and leadership? https://www.apm.org.uk/resources/what-is-project-management/what-is-project-team-management-and-leadership/ [Accessed 15 December 2021].

Barber, E. and Warn, J.R. (2005). Leadership in project management: From fire-fighter to fire lighter. *Management Decisions*, 43(7/8), 1032–1039.

Bennis, W.G. and Nanus, B. (1985). *Leaders: The Strategies for Taking Charge*. Harper and Row, New York.

Bennis, W.G. and Thomas, R.J. (2002). Crucibles of leadership. *Harvard Business Review*, 80(9), 39–45.

Bredillet, C.N., Thomas, J. and Musila, J. (2012). Africa's project context at the start of the 21st century. In C.N. Bredillet, J. Thomas and J. Musila (Eds.), *Managing Projects in Africa — Essentials from the Project Management Journal*. Wiley and PMI, Newtown Square, PA.

Bresnen, M.J. (1986). The leader orientation of construction site managers. *Construction Engineering and Management*, 112(3), 370–386.

Briner, W., Geddes, M. and Hastings, C. (1990). *Project Leadership*. Van Nostrand Reinhold, New York.

Briner, W., Hastings, C. and Geddes, M. (1996). *Project Leadership*, 2nd Edition. Gower, Farnham.

Bryman, A., Bresnen, M., Ford, J., Beardsworth, A. and Keil, T. (1987). Leader orientation and organizational transience: An investigation using Fiedler's LPC Scale. *Journal of Occupational Psychology*, 60, 13–19.

Bull, R.C. (2010). *Moving from Project Management to Project Leadership: A Practical Guide to Leading Groups*. CRC Press, Boca Raton, FL.

Cain, S. (2013). *Quiet: The Power of Introverts in a World That Can't Stop Talking*. Broadway Paperbacks, New York.

Carroll, B., Levy, L. and Richmond, D. (2008). Leadership as practice: Challenging the competency paradigm. *Leadership*, 4(4), 363–379.

Chan, A.P.C., Ho, D.C.K. and Tam, C.M. (2001). Design and Build project success factors; Multivariate analysis. *Journal of Construction Engineering Management*, 127(2), 93–100.

Chinowsky, P.S. and Rojas, E.M. (2003). Virtual teams: Guide to successful implementation. *Journal of Management in Engineering*, 19(3), 98–106.

Chipulu, M., Neoh, J. G., Ojiako, U. and Williams, T. (2013). A multidimensional analysis of project manager competences. *IEEE Transactions on Engineering Management*, 60(3), 506–517. https://doi.org/10.1109/TEM.2012.2215330.

CIB (2006). TG64: Leadership in construction: Introducing new CIB Task Group. CIB Newsletter, December. https://www.cibworld.nl/website/newsletter/0608/tg64.html

Cleland, D.I. (1995). Leadership and the project management body of knowledge. *International Journal of Project Management*, 13(2), 82–88.

Coleman, S. and Bourne, M. (2018). *Project Leadership: Skills, Behaviours, Knowledge and Values*. Association for Project Management, Princes Risborough.

Coleman, S. and MacNicol, D. (2015). *Project Leadership*. Gower, Farnham.

Cowie, G. (2003). The importance of people skills for project managers. *Industrial and Commercial Training*, 35(6), 256–258.

Cox, J., Pearce, C. and Perry, M. (2003). Toward a model of shared leadership and distributed influence in the innovation process: How shared leadership can enhance new product development team dynamics and effectiveness. In C.L. Pearce and J.A. Conger (Eds.), *Shared Leadership: Reframing the Hows and Whys of Leadership*. Sage Publications Ltd, Thousand Oaks, CA.

Crevani, L., Lindgren, M. and Packendorff, J. (2007). Shared leadership: A post-heroic perspective on leadership as a collective construction. *International Journal of Leadership Studies*, 3(1), 40–67.

Dahles, H. and Wels, H. (Eds.) (2002). *Culture, Organization and Management in East Asia: Doing Business in China*. Nova Science Publishers, Inc., New York.

Dainty, A.R.J., Cheng, M. and Moore, D. (2005). A comparison of the behavioural competencies of client-focused and production-focused project managers in the construction sector. *Project Management Journal*, 36(1), 39–48.

Dainty, A.R.J., Cheng, M., and Moore, D. (2006). What makes an effective project manager? Findings of a four-year program of research. In A. Songer, P. Chinowsky, and P. Carrillo (Eds.), *Proceedings of the ASCE/CIB 2nd Specialty Conference in Leadership and Management in Construction*, pp. 116–123. PM Publishing, Louisville, CO.

Damoah, I.S., Akwei, C.A., Amoako, I.O. and Botchie, D. (2018) Corruption as a source of government project failure in developing countries. *Project Management Journal*, 49(3), 17–33.

Dawes, T. (2002). Project management — An integrated approach. *The British Journal of Administrative Management*, 34, 24–26.

Den Otter, A.F.H.J. and Prins, M. (2003) Architectural design management within the digital design team. *Engineering, Construction and Architectural Management*, 9(3), 162–173.

Dimov, P.I. (2004). Leadership: When management is not enough. Paper presented at PMI® Global Congress 2004 — North America, Anaheim, CA. Project Management Institute, Newtown Square, PA.

Drouin, N., Muller, R., Sankaran, S. and Vaagaasar, A.-L. (2018). Balancing vertical and horizontal leadership in projects: Empirical studies from Australia, Canada, Norway and Sweden. *International Journal of Managing Projects in Business*, 11(4), 986–1006.

Drouin, N., Muller, R., Sankaran, S. and Vaagaasar, A.-L. (2021). Balancing leadership in projects: Role of the socio-cognitive space. *Project Leadership and Society*, 2(December). https://doi.org/10.1016/j.plas.2021.100031.

Dulaimi, M.F. and Langford, D.A. (1999). Job behaviour of construction project managers: Determinants and assessment. *Construction Engineering and Management*, 125(4), 256–264.

Early, P. (2006). Leading cultural research in the future: A matter of paradigms and taste. *Journal of International Business Studies*, 37, 922–931.

Egbu, C. (1999). Skills, knowledge and competencies for managing construction refurbishment works. *Construction Management and Economics*, 17(1), 29–43.

Ekkert, C. (2019). Project leadership: 3 insights into leading a team. *Encore*, 7 January. https://www.encorebusiness.com/blog/project-leadership-3-insights-leading-team/.

Engwall, M. (2003). No project is an island: Linking projects to history and context. *Research Policy*, 32(5), 798–808.

Ethics Member Advisory Group of Project Management Institute (2014). Quiet Leadership Tips for Project Success: How leading quietly saved the men of the shipwrecked endurance. Paper presented at PMI® Global Congress 2014 — North America, Phoenix, AZ. Project Management Institute, Newtown Square, PA. https://www.pmi.org/learning/library/leading-quietly-saved-shipwrecked-men-9309.

Fellows, R., Liu, A. and Fong, C.M. (2003). Leadership style and power relations in quantity surveying in Hong Kong. *Construction Management and Economics*, 21, 809–818.

Gemmill, G. and Wilemon, D. (1994). The hidden side of leadership in technical team management. *Research Technology Management*, 37(6), 25–32.

Geoghegan, L. and Dulewicz, V. (2008). Do project managers' leadership competencies contribute to project success? *Project Management Journal*, 39(4), 58–67. https://doi.org/10.1002/pmj.20084.

George, B. (2003). *Authentic Leadership: Rediscovering the Secrets to Creating Lasting Value*. Jossey-Bass, San Francisco, CA.

Gerstner, C.R. and Day, D.V. (1994). Cross-cultural comparison of leadership prototypes. *The Leaders Quarterly*, 5, 121–134.

Gido, J. and Clements, J.P. (2003). *Successful Project Management*, 2nd Edition. Thomson South-Western, Mason, OH.

Gilbert, P. (1983). Styles of project management. *Project Management Journal*, 1(4), 189–193.

Giritli, H. and Topcu Oraz, G. (2004). Leadership styles: Some evidence from the Turkish construction industry. *Construction Management and Economics*, 22, 253–262.

Goodwin, R.S.C. (1993). Skills required of effective project managers. *Journal of Management in Engineering*, 9(3), 217–226.

Hayden, W.M., Jr. (2013). How many oceans do we have? *Leadership and Management in Engineering*, 13(4). https://doi.org/10.1061/(ASCE)LM.1943-5630.0000251.

Heagney, J. (2018). *Fundamentals of Project Management*, 5th Edition. American Management Association, New York.

Huemann, M. (2021). Editorial — Our first year of full publication and our way forward. *Project Leadership and Society*, 2, December. https://doi.org/10.1016/j.plas.2021.100037.

Ika, L.A. (2012). Project management for development in Africa: Why projects are failing and what can be done about it. *Project Management Journal*, 43(4), 27–41.

Ika, L.A., Keeys, L.A., Tuuli, M.M., Sané, S. and Ssegawa, J.K. (2021). Call for papers special collection: Managing and leading projects in Africa. *Project Leadership and Society*, 2, December. https://doi.org/10.1016/j.plas.2021.100023.

International Centre for Complex Project Management (2018). Project leadership: The game changer in large-scale complex projects. Roundtable Series. https://www.iccpm.com

Jiang, J.J., Klein, G. and Margulis, S. (1998). Important behavioral skills for is project managers: The judgments of experienced is professionals. *Project Management Journal*, 29(1), 39–43. https://doi.org/10.1177/875697289802900108.

Jin, Z., Deng, F., Li, H. and Skitmore, M. (2013). Practical framework for measuring performance of international construction firms. *Journal of Construction Engineering and Management*, 139(9), 1154–1167.

Juli, T. (2011). *Leadership Principles for Project Success*. CRC Press, Boca Raton, FL.

Kangis, P. and Lee-Kelley, L. (2000). Project leadership in clinical research organizations. *International Journal of Project Management*, 18(6), 393–401

Kezsbom, D.S. (1994). Team-based organizations and the changing role of the project manager. *Transactions of American Association of Cost Engineers (AACE) International*, HF1.1.

Kloppenborg, T.J., Shriberg, A. and Venkatraman, J. (2003). *Project Leadership*. Management Concepts, Vienna, VA.

Kortantamer, D. (2019). *Leadership: Responding to Complexity — A Systemic Framework for Responding to Complexity in Government Transformation and Service Delivery Projects*. APM, Princes Risborough.

Kotter, J.P. (2001). What leaders really do. *Harvard Business Review*, 79, 85–98.

Krahn, J. and Hartment, F. (2006). Effective project leadership: A combination of project manager skills and competencies in context. Paper presented at *PMI® Research Conference: New Directions in Project Management*, Montréal, Canada. Project Management Institute, Newtown Square, PA. https://www.pmi.org/learning/library/leadership-project-manager-skills-competencies-8115.

Lampel, J. (2001). The core competencies of effective project execution: The challenge of diversity. *International Journal of Project Management*, 19(8), 471–483.

Lee-Kelley, L. and Leong, K. (2003). Turners five functions of project-based management and situational leadership in IT services projects. *International Journal of Project Management*, 21(8), 583–591.

Lewis, J. (2003) *Project Leadership*. McGraw-Hill, New York.

Lewis, T.M. (2007). Impact of globalization on the construction sector in developing countries. *Construction Management and Economics*, 25(1), 7–23.

Lindgren, M. and Packendorff, J. (2006). What's new in new forms of organizing? On the construction of gender in project-based work. *Journal of Management Studies*, 43(4), 841–866.

Lindgren, M. and Packendorff, J. (2009a). Project leadership revisited: Towards distributed leadership perspectives in project research. *International Journal of Project Organisation and Management*, 1(3), 285–308.

Lindgren, M. and Packendorff, J. (2009b). Project leadership as a research field: Antecedents, current research and a critique. Unpublished paper, KTH Royal Institute of Technology, Stockholm, Sweden. https://www.diva-portal.org/smash/get/diva2:1354244/FULLTEXT01.pdf

Liu, A., Fellows, R. and Fang, Z. (2003). The power paradigm of project leadership. *Construction Management and Economics*, 21(8), 819–829.

London, K. and Chen, J. (2007). Role of cultural capital towards the development of a sustainable business model for design firm internationalization. In T.C. Haupt and R. Milford (Eds.), CIB. *World Building Congress: Construction for Development*. CIB, Cape Town, South Africa, pp. 4–17.

Loosemore, M. and Lee, P. (2002). Communication problems with ethnic minorities in the construction industry. *International Journal of Project Management*, 20, 517–524.

Low, S.P. and Leong, C.H. (2000). Cross-cultural project management for international construction in China. *International Journal of Project Management*, 18(5), 307–316.

MacKay, G. (2021). *Evolving Project Leadership: From Command and Control to Engage and Empower*. APM, Princes Risborough.

Madsen, S. (2015). *The Power of Project Leadership*. Kogan Page, London.

Makilouko, M. (2004). Coping with multicultural projects: The leadership styles of Finnish project managers. *International Journal of Project Management*, 22, 387–396.

Manning, T.T. (2003). Leadership across cultures: Attachment style influences. *Journal of Leadership and Organizational Studies*, 9(3), 20–30.

Martin, P. (2018). 7 Principles of project leadership. *Matrix Management Magazine*, International Matrix Management Institute. https://www.matrix-managementinstitute.com/blog/7-principles-project-leadership/.

McCaffer, R. (1995). Editorial. *Engineering, Construction and Architectural Management*, 15(4), 2008.

McKinsey (2016). *Industry 4.0 after the Initial Hype: Where Manufacturers are Finding Best Value and How They Can Best Capture It*. McKinsey & Co.

Mir, A.H., Tanvir, M. and Durrani, A.Z. (2007). Development of Construction Industry — A Literature Review. *Pakistan Infrastructure Implementation Capacity Assessment*, Report No. 43185. World Bank, Washington, DC.

Muethel, M. and Hoegl, M. (2011). Shared leadership functions in geographically dispersed project teams. In G. Cattani, S. Ferriani, L. Frederiksen and F. Täube (Eds.), *Project-Based Organising and Strategic Management*, Emerald Group Publishing Limited, Bingley.

Müller, R., Sankaran, S. and Packendorff, J. (2017). Balanced leadership: A new perspective of leadership in organizational project management. In S. Sankaran, R. Müller and N. Drouin (Eds.), *Cambridge Handbook of Organizational Project Management*. Cambridge University Press, Cambridge, pp. 186–199.

Mustapha, F.H. and Naoum, S. (1998). Factors influencing the effectiveness of construction site managers. *International Journal of Project Management*, 16(1), 1–8.

National Development Authority (2015). *Second National Development Plan 2015/16–2019/20: Uganda Vision 2020*. Kampala.

NHBC Foundation (2018). *Modern Methods of Construction Who's Doing What?* Milton Keynes.

Norrie, J. and Walker, D.H.T. (2004). A balanced scorecard approach to project management leadership. *Journal of Project Management*, 35(4), 47–56.

Norwood, S.R. and Mansfield, N.R. (1999). Joint venture issues concerning European and Asian construction markets of the 1990s. *International Journal of Project Management*, 17(2), 89–93.

Odusami, K.T. (2002). Perceptions of construction professionals concerning important skills of effective project leaders. *Journal of Management in Engineering*, 18(2), 61–67.

Odusami, K.T., Iyagba, R.R. and Omirin, M.M. (2003). The relationship between project leadership, team composition and construction project performance in Nigeria. *International Journal of Project Management*, 21, 519–527.

Ofori, G. (2021). Professionalism in built environment research: Beyond integrity and good practice. *Engineering, Construction and Architectural Management*. https://doi.org/10.1108/ECAM-02-2020-0118.

Ofori, G. and Toor, S.R. (2021). *Leadership in the Construction Industry Developing Authentic Leaders in a Dynamic World*. Routledge, Abingdon.

Ogunlana, S.O., Siddiqui, Z., Yisa, S. and Olomolaiye, P. (2002). Factors and procedures used in matching project managers to construction projects in Bangkok. *International Journal of Project Management*, 20(5), 385–400. https://doi.org/10.1016/S0263-7863(01)00017-5.

Owusu-Manu, D.-G., Debrah, C., Amissah, L., Edwards, D.J. and Chileshie, N. (2021). Exploring the linkages between project managers' mindset behaviour and project leadership style in the Ghanaian construction industry, *Engineering, Construction and Architectural Management*, 28(9), 2690–2711. https://doi.org/10.1108/ECAM-03-2020-0149.

Pearce, C.L. (2004). The future of leadership: Combining vertical and shared leadership to transform knowledge work. *Academy of Management Executive*, 18, 47–57.

Pearce, C.L. and Conger, J.A. (Eds.) (2003). *Shared Leadership: Reframing the Hows and Whys of Leadership*. Sage, London.

PricewaterhouseCoopers (2004). *Boosting Business Performance through Programme and Project Management.* PricewaterhouseCoopers, London.

Project Manager (2020). The ultimate guide to… leadership in project management. https://www.projectmanager.com/leadership-in-project-management.

Puccinelli, B. (1999). Principles of a project leader. *Inform*, 13(1), 50.

Remington, K. (2011). *Leading Complex Projects.* Gower, Farnham.

Rowlinson, S., Ho, K.K. and PO-Hung, Y. (1993). Leadership style of construction managers in Hong Kong. *Construction Management and Economics*, 11, 455–465.

Rwelamila, P.D. and Purushottam, N. (2012). Project management trilogy challenges in Africa — Where to from here? *Project Management Journal*, 43(4), 5–13.

Rwelamila, P.D. and Purushottam, N. (2012). Project management trilogy challenges in Africa — Where to from here. In C.N. Bredillet, J. Thomas, J. Musila (Eds.), *Managing Projects in Africa — Essentials from the Project Management Journal.* Wiley and PMI, Newtown Square, PA.

Selmer, J. (2001). Expatriate selection: Back to basics? *International Journal of Human Resource Management*, 12(8), 1219.

Sense, A.J. (2003). A model of the politics of project leader learning. *International Journal of Project Management*, 21(2), 107.

Shenhar, A. and Dvir, D. (2004). Project management evolution: Past history and future research directions. Paper presented at *PMI® Research Conference: Innovations*, 11–14 July, London, UK. Project Management Institute, Newtown Square, PA.

Shenhar, A.J. (2004). Strategic project leadership: Toward a strategic approach to project management. *R&D Management*, 34, 569–578.

Simushi, S. and Wium, J. (2020). Time and cost overruns on large projects: Understanding the root cause. *Journal of Construction in Developing Countries*, 25(1), 129–146. https://doi.org/10.21315/jcdc2020.25.1.7.

Slevin, D.P. and Pinto, J.K. (1991). Project leadership: Understanding and consciously choosing your style. *Project Management Journal*, 22(1), 39–47.

Smith, G.R. (1999). Project leadership: Why project management alone doesn't work. *Hospital Material Management Quarterly*, 21(1), 88–92.

Songer, A., Chinowsky, P. and Butler, C. (2008) Leadership behaviour in construction executives: Challenges for the next generation. *Construction Information Quarterly*, 10(2), 59–66.

Sotiriou, D. and Wittmer, D. (2001). Influence methods of project managers: Perceptions of team members and project managers. *Project Management Journal*, 32(3), 12–20. https://doi.org/10.1177/875697280103200303.

Strang, K.D. (2007). Examining effective technology project leadership traits and behaviours. *Computers in Human Behavior*, 23, 424–462.

Sunindijo, R.Y., Hadikusumo, B.H. and Ogunlana, S. (2007). Emotional intelligence and leadership styles in construction project management. *Journal of Management in Engineering*, 23(4). https://doi.org/10.1061/(ASCE)0742-597X(2007)23:4(166).

Taylor, R. (2011). *Leadership: Stories, Lessons, and Uncommon Sense.* New Point Publications, Washington, DC.

The Economist (2011). The hopeful continent: Africa rising. December 3.

Thite, M. (1999). Identifying key characteristics of technical project leadership. *Leadership and Organization Development Journal*, 20(5), 253–261. https://doi.org/10.1108/01437739910287126.

Thite, M. (2000). Leadership styles in information technology projects. *International Journal of Project Management*, 18(2), 235–241.

Thompsen, J.A. (2000). Effective leadership of virtual project teams. Paper presented at the *2000 IEEE International Engineering Management Conference*, August, Albuquerque, NM.

Toor, S.R. and Ofori, G. (2008a). Leadership in the construction industry: Agenda for authentic leadership development. *International Journal of Project Management*. https://doi.org/10.1016/j.ijproman.2007.09.010.

Toor, S.R. and Ofori, G. (2008b). Taking leadership research into future: A review of empirical studies and new directions for research. *Engineering, Construction and Architectural Management*, 15(4), 352–371.

Toor, S.R. and Ofori, G. (2008c). Grounded theory as the most appropriate methodology for leadership research in the construction industry. In R. Haigh and D. Amaratunga (Eds.), *Proceedings of CIB International Conference on Building Education and Research: 'Building Resilience'*, pp. 1816–1831.

Toor, S.R. and Ofori, G. (2009a). Ethical leadership: Examining the relationships with full range leadership model, employee outcomes, and organizational culture. *Journal of Business Ethics*, 90, 533. https://doi.org/10.1007/s10551-009-0059-3.

Toor, S.R. and Ofori, G. (2009b). Authenticity and its influence on psychological well-being and contingent self-esteem of leaders in Singapore construction sector. *Construction Management and Economics*, 27(3), 299–313.

Toor, S.R. and Ogunlana, S.O. (2006). Successful project leadership: Understanding the personality traits and organizational factors. Paper presented at

CIB-W107, *International Symposium, Construction in Developing Economies: New Issues and Challenges*, January 18–20, 2006, Chile, Santiago.

Toor, S.R. and Ogunlana, S.O. (2008). Leadership skills and competencies for cross-cultural construction projects. *International Journal of Human Resources Development and Management*, 8(3), 192–215.

Toor, S.R. and Ogunlana, S.O. (2009). Ineffective leadership: Investigating negative attributes of project leaders and organizational neutralizers. *Engineering, Construction and Architectural Management*, 16(3), 254–272. https://doi.org/10.1108/09699980910951663.

Vorakulpipat, C., Rezgui, Y. and Hopfe, C.J. (2010). Value creating construction virtual teams: A case study in the construction sector. *Automation in Construction*, 19(2), 142–147. https://doi.org/10.1016/j.autcon.2009.11.016.

Wiezel, A., Badger, W. and King, C. (2013). *Project Management Skills of the Future, RT-281*. Construction Industry Institute, Austin.

Wong, J., Wong, P.N. and Li, H. (2007). An investigation of leadership styles and relationship cultures of Chinese and expatriate managers in multinational construction companies in Hong Kong. *Construction Management and Economics*, 25, 95–106.

World Economic Forum (WEF) and Boston Consulting Group (BCG) (2015). *Shaping the Future of Construction*. Geneva. https://www.weforum.org/global-challenges/projects/future-of-construction

Zaleznik, A. (1977). Managers and leaders: are they different? *Harvard Business Review*, 55(3), 67–78.

Zika-Viktorsson, A., Sundström, P. and Engwall, M. (2006). Project overload: An exploratory study of work and management in multi-project settings. *International Journal of Project Management*, 24, 385–394.

Zimmerer, T.M. and Yasin, M.M. (1998). A leadership profile of American project managers. *Project Management Journal*, 29(1), 31–38. https://doi.org/10.1177/875697289802900107.

Part 5

Project Management in a Number of Developing Countries

https://doi.org/10.1142/9789811224720_0020

Chapter 20

Infrastructure Projects and Project Management in Brazil: Challenges and Trends

Flavia de Souza, Fernanda Borges, Mariana Wyse, Tiely Mognhol and Silvio Melhado

Escola Politécnica
Universidade de São Paulo, Brazil

Abstract

The scene of Brazilian infrastructure has changed in recent years, highlighting the growing participation of the private sector and the falling public investments as a result of the constraints on the federal public expenditure as from 2016, the *Lava Jato* operation, and reduction in the number of available loans. Particularly, the *Lava Jato* operation led most Brazilian infrastructure corporations to fully rethink their processes and opened the way for new national and international companies. In the restructuring phase, project management has shown itself to be sensitive to the changes made. In this sense, fostering risk management in the corporations, combined with efficient cost management, tends to become a decisive factor to guarantee the results of projects. Integrated management solutions, obtaining licenses, regularization, and authorization also became essential to attain efficiency in the use of resources. Considering the scenario of infrastructure projects in Brazil, this chapter discusses the market and internationalization trends in infrastructure projects, and the current state of project management knowledge through diagnosis and cases. Aiming to contribute to a better comprehension of procurement, risk, cost, and stakeholder management, as well as by using Building Information Modelling (BIM) processes to support the efforts to address challenges in the sector, some recent research results are summarized. Further, ethics and governance as pillars for infrastructure project management are also discussed in the text. In the conclusion, we present some proposals about new management areas that can be truly relevant in infrastructure project management in a developing country.

Keywords: Construction, project management, infrastructure, developing countries, Brazil

Introduction

Increasing infrastructure investment is crucial for Brazil to succeed in accelerating its economic development, which demands improvement in infrastructure pertaining to factories, hotels, airports, roads, and so on. These investments result in job generation, drive the economy, and accelerate Gross Domestic Product (GDP) growth. The studies conducted by McKinsey & Company, Brazilian National Economic and Social Development Bank (BNDES), International Finance Corporation (IFC), and Inter-American Development Bank (IDB) (2019) point out that there is great potential for return on infrastructure investment. Considering the global average of infrastructure stock, which is about 70 percent of the GDP of countries, and assessing the average effects of investments in infrastructure in the long run, a 1 percent investment in the construction industry, after 10 years, is equivalent to an increase by about 1.6 percent a year in that country's GDP. However, for this to happen, the country has to show itself to be competitive and attractive for both domestic and foreign investors.

Being dependent on large works, the Brazilian infrastructure sector has been severely affected in recent years. In relation to the Brazilian GDP, these investments increased from 2003, growing from 1.5 percent in 2003 to a maximum value of 2.4 percent in 2013. Yet between 2014 and 2017, the increase in investments fell to 1.6 percent, due to issues related to the interruption of The Brazilian Federal Government Program for

Accelerating Growth (PAC); *Lava Jato* (or Car Wash)[1] operation; rise in inflation; reduction in the number of loans by BNDES, among others (Dutra, 2018). In 2018 and 2019, the investments in infrastructure increased slightly, and there was an expected recovery for the coming years, which has not been confirmed, owing to the COVID-19 pandemic.

Within this potential of increasing investments in infrastructure, it is worth highlighting the growing participation of the private sector, especially in the light of the constraints on the federal public expenditure as from 2016. Since public investments have been sharply reduced, even with the fall in private investments between 2012 and 2014, arising from the crisis of confidence due to the increase in public debt and the lack of good projects available for bidding, in 2018, the private sector accounted for 70 percent of the total investment in infrastructure, whereas this proportion of participation was 61 percent in 2010.

There is a bet on concessions and privatizations for the private sector to increase its investment in infrastructure in Brazil even more. One of the initiatives that can contribute to attracting investments in infrastructure is the new legal framework of basic sanitation (PL 4.162/2019), approved by the Federal Senate and under discussion in the House of Representatives, which provides for services to be rendered by private corporations, and the opening of bidding in the sector, including the ending of the preferences of the state-owned companies. Another element inducing the participation of private enterprises in investments in infrastructure is Decree nº 9377 of 17th of May 2018, which formalizes the strategies for disseminating *Building Information Modelling* (BIM) in public works. The Decree provides for three stages with progressive requirements, the first stage in January 2021 and the third and last step, in January 2028. The participation of private enterprises, especially design companies, will be crucial for implementing the technologies inherent in BIM in the public environment.

Another point is the trend regarding the participation of small companies in the investments in infrastructure, traditionally dominated by large

[1]The *Lava Jato* (Car Wash) Operation is a set of investigations started by the Brazilian Federal Police in 2014 aiming to investigate active and passive corruption crimes, fraudulent management, money laundry, criminal organisations, obstruction of justice, fraudulent exchange operations and receiving undue advantages connected to contracts signed with the state-owned oil company Petrobras.

firms. According to a survey conducted by the Brazilian Chamber of the Construction Industry (CBIC) (2019), in the infrastructure sector, the large contractors, with over 500 employees, form about 0.2 percent of the total. However, the annual gross revenue of those companies is substantial: 41 percent of the revenue is derived from infrastructure services. The public contracting process is important for managing the corporations, through the imposition of specific requirements. Borges (2019) analyzed the major regulations for contracting public works in Brazil (Table 20.1).

A study by Brazilian Association of Infrastructure and Base Industries (ABDIB) (2020) on private enterprises, public bodies, governments and

Table 20.1: Major regulations used to contract public projects in Brazil.

Contracting forms	Application	Explanation	Impact
Public Bidding Law — Law 8666/93	Institutes standards for bidding and contracts in public management; allows bidding of administrative contracts pertinent to construction works, services, purchases, concessions and renting.	Basic design approved by the competent authority; the executive design may be further developed during the execution of works and services.	Difficulty in integrating the work of designers and contractors; problems on the site, including rework; a large amount of detailing and complexity may cause corruption problems.
Concession Law — Law 8987/95	Provides for the regime of concessionaires and licensees of public services, the special character of their contracts and of their extension, as well as the expiry conditions, inspection and termination of the concession or license; users' rights; tariff policy; the obligation of keeping adequate service.	The concession allows greater efficiency in the provision of service by the private partner to the public agency, guaranteeing the following characteristics: regularity; continuity; efficiency; safety; "currentness" — "modernity" of techniques, equipment, installations, as well as improvement and expansion of the services; courtesy while rendering services; and fairness in prices.	Greater risk-sharing with the private partner; favoring the final beneficiary by adopting adequate inspection criteria; distancing of designers from contractors in cases where the work is executed by the concessionaire.

Table 20.1: (*Continued*)

Contracting forms	Application	Explanation	Impact
Differentiated Contracting Regime (RDC) — Law 12,462/2011	Established for major sports events, such as World Cup events and Olympic Games (the accelerated realization of Olympic Games in Brazil (Rio 2016) required a specific law of public contracts, called the Differentiated Contracting Regime (RDC)), and extended to meet the PAC, SUS and, among other actions, engineering works and services related to improvements in urban mobility or expansion of logistics infrastructure.	Increasing efficiency in public contracts; stimulating technological innovation in application, especially in infrastructure projects; integrated contracting — undertaking of all the stages by the same company (from design to full operation); bidding from a preliminary draft.	Agility in the bidding process; stimulus of innovation; design error costs are the responsibility of the contracted party; tends to transfer the risks and responsibilities to the contracted party.
Public–Private Partnership (PPP) — Law 11.079/2004	A form of public concession and of managing long-term public services, with risk and investment sharing between the public and private partners, and focused on creating infrastructure.	As a concession modality, PPP is only justified if the private partner can render services more efficiently than under public sector management, which includes undertaking basic and executive design projects; and started from the reform adopted by the Brazilian government in the quest to make PPP attractive to the private sector in areas in need of public investments.	Unclear risk transfer to the private partner; great diversity of interests; diversity of roles adopted by the government in the partnership; management of the schedules of the public and private partners; the contract has a longer term; and the non-institutional resolution of aspects, such as participation, transparency, responsibility and control

Source: Borges (2019).

sectoral players involved in investments in infrastructure, foresees an upward trend in the investments in the following areas: basic sanitation; social infrastructure (hospitals, schools); electric power; railways; roads; and urban mobility. The same study points out the challenges in implementing the infrastructure projects, for which project management is highly relevant: increasing operational efficiency, financial capacity, project structuring, public guarantees, uncertainties in the demand, and governmental fiscal constraints.

The aim of this chapter is to discuss some of the challenges and trends regarding infrastructure programs and projects in Brazil, pointing out the need for evolution regarding their management. Some of the aspects discussed are: procurement, stakeholders, internationalization, cost, and risk management, as well as ethics and governance. The first section after this introduction considers the management topics viewed as key challenges, in a review of recent research. The next section presents a case study, selected owing to its potential influence over the new trends in management practices adopted by the Brazilian public sector on sanitation works, recently established as a prioritized segment of infrastructure in the country. Finally, in the last section, a conclusion is drawn up from the empirical evidence, and potential further topics for research are outlined.

Current challenges and status of project management knowledge through diagnosis and cases

Procurement management: How concessions have contributed to infrastructure projects accomplishment

Filho (2003) reports that, in Brazil, the institution of public service concessions, widely practiced in the 19th century and early 20th century, lost momentum as direct intervention by the government increased. However, in the 1990s, concessions started to be revisited as alternatives to meeting collective needs, and considering the nation's fiscal crisis, private capital started to occupy a place in the implementation of public policies. In Brazil, the ordinary and administrative/private concession regimes are guided by Laws n° 8987/95, known as the Concession Law and by Law n° 11079/2004, known as the PPP Law.

Di Pietro (2005) explains that, in Brazil, the role of concessionaires is frequently played by public-sector organizations and government-controlled (private) companies and entities of a private legal nature, which are nonetheless integral parts of decentralized public management. Perez (2005) gives examples of these situations: basic sanitation state companies acting as concessionaires in different municipalities, such as Sabesp in the State of São Paulo; and companies under the controlling interest of the Federal Government or of the State Governments that have taken on the role of concessionaires of specific public services, such as Eletrobrás, Furnas, Cemig, and Cteep in the power sector.

In 1991, the Federal Government launched the National Privatization Plan (PND), aiming to reduce costs and to increase the efficiency of the services rendered by infrastructure companies. Hence, a significant movement was started to privatize the federal state-owned equity interest companies, in the steel, chemical, petrochemical, and power sectors, which encompassed the privatization of 68 companies. Out of these, in the power sector, up to the 2000s, there were 23 privatizations, 20 of which involved power distribution companies.

However, the disarticulation of government directives among the sector entities in the planned operationalization faced the risk of a crisis caused by the electric power brownout, as well as the variations in the exchange rate in the early 2000s. Besides that, the context in which privatizations were conducted, including a speculative bubble and short-term financing, reduced the investment capacity in the sector. The result was the hydro-power crisis in 2001, due to which rationing measures and power-saving were implemented, besides the need for tariff re-composition and emergency power acquisition.

More recently, the new proposal for privatizing the power sector, supported by the Brazilian Federal Government, based on the Investment Partnerships Program (PPIs), provides risk mitigation measures, by reducing the "physical guarantees" (minimum level of power generation that, if not met, causes compulsory acquisition of power in the market) so as to increase the attractiveness of privatization to investors. Besides the privatization of Eletrobrás, the major company in the sector in Latin America, the privatization of a series of hydropower plants of State companies, Cemig, Copel and CEEE also occurred.

The BNDES[2] Sectoral Study on the airport sector points out that, in the early 2000s, a growth in the GDP was observed, allowing the accessibility of new consumers to the civil aviation market. This generated pressure on the Brazilian airport infrastructure, where airports were mainly operated by the public sector (by the Brazilian Airport Infrastructure Company (Infraero)).

Since 2011, in its first stage, when a pilot model was tested in Natal (RN), six airports were auctioned in the municipalities of Guarulhos, Campinas, Brasília, Rio de Janeiro, and Belo Horizonte. In 2017, bidding was started under the PPI, totaling four bidding exercises in that year. In 2019, a new round of auctions promoted the private concession of another 12 airports. Currently, eight years after the first concession, 22 airport concessions have been granted, and they are processing over two-thirds of the passenger movement in the country and representing 19 percent of the number of airports offering commercial flights.

Perez (2006) states that, in its classical format, the concession was characterized by the concessionaire being remunerated by charging users tariffs. Yet the impossibility of reducing the concession to a uniform and single model led to the search for new revenue sources to the concessionaires, which currently also include the so-called "financial solidarity," characterized by the management offer of financial aid or subsidies to meet the concession objectives and, in specific circumstances, the management may also take on the responsibility for direct payment to the concessionaire. An example of the drawbacks in the realization of benefits of a large concession is that of Subway Line 6 (Orange) of the São Paulo Metro, which caused the termination of the contract by the State Government after the works were stopped in 2016, due to the lack of credit to the concessionaires affected by the *Lava Jato* Operation, and consequent paralysis of the works, after only 15 percent of the contract had been delivered. In February 2020, an agreement was concluded between a Spanish company and the former concessionaire to resume work on the project.

This complex scenario arises from concessions being subjected to economic regulation, since the public services, in this case, started to be

[2] Brazilian Development Bank.

undertaken in an economic competition regime, which means the creation of this new market segment would be regulated to prevent the occurrence of a monopoly, cartel, or trust (Perez, 2005). Thus, a legal framework to support a certain configuration for performing an economic activity or public service is expected to occur, aiming to have new competitors that, without a risk-sharing structure and possibly cost-sharing with the management, would not be interested in bidding for the concession contracts. The results from this scenario of the partnership materialization are the complex economic–financial balance equations of the concession contracts, which play an essential role in ensuring the realization of the objectives of the contract without burdening the parties involved.

The concessionaire financing partners, in turn, establish their own criteria for providing the funds. The funding bodies establish a set of requirements aiming to provide improvements in the management standards of the infrastructure projects, undertaking institutional strengthening, and establishing a governance structure and according greater relevance to the social-environmental aspects.

Brazil is a major recipient of resources for projects from the Inter-American Development Bank (IDB), totaling 84 out of 613 projects in its portfolio (~14 percent), with government guarantees, totaling US$12.3 billion in loans. The eligibility criteria demanded by IDB are associated with the institution's objectives, which demand, for example, developing sustainability plans and institutional strengthening projects, followed by standard monitoring reports determined by the bank.

The model for assessing companies to be funded involves a survey to assess the multi-sectoral dimensions, going through environmental issues (waste management, water, power and materials, biodiversity, land use, and climate change) and stakeholder management issues (relationships with workers, communities, clients, and suppliers). This trend, assessed by the Sustainable Investment Alliance, demonstrated that only 22 percent of the assets with professional management in the regions surveyed follow a responsible investment philosophy. The demand for considering environmental, social, and governance (ESG) issues, levered by the launching of the Principles for Responsible Investment (PRI), supported by the United Nations, was also adopted by the Brazilian financial institutions.

Stakeholder management: The challenges in infrastructure projects

Civil construction in Brazil is characterized by its slow technological evolution, which restricts the application of innovative concepts applied in other sectors (MDIC, 2010). Additionally, there are the difficulties posed by the regulations, which are introduced to ensure the transparency and good standing of the public contracts, which eventually imposed severe constraints on the evolution of the management process of public projects.

The complexity of infrastructure projects originates from factors regarding their size, as well as from technical and management difficulties. The latter includes the high number and diversity of stakeholders and characteristics of the environment in which these projects are undertaken, which include aspects of public management and the laws governing the procurement of these projects.

In general, during the implementation of a project, there is greater concern about the activities to be undertaken and little importance is given to the involvement of the different stakeholders (Verweij, 2015). The management of stakeholders is essential for a good performance and for meeting the objectives of the infrastructure projects, which involves "identifying the major stakeholders groups of the project, mapping their influence and managing their expectations over the entire project life cycle" (Carvalho and Rabechini, 2017). One of the sources of conflict is the large number of parts involved due to their fragmented actuation and their own interests, which occasionally diverge as regards the project objectives (Melhado, 2005). Thus, one of the major management challenges to these projects is understanding the interests and positions of stakeholders, coordinating their actions, and managing conflicts so that all the players focus on the final objectives of the project (Borges, 2020).

In Brazil, about 35 percent of the investments in infrastructure is from the public sector. Borges (2019) carried out two case studies involving large-sized infrastructure projects in the São Paulo Metropolitan Region: one was a sanitation project, and the other, a transportation project. According to the study conclusions, the major stakeholders to be taken into consideration in infrastructure project management are: client (generally the public); management team or manager; construction company; design companies; private partner; State Government; Municipal Governments; financing agencies; inspecting bodies; regulation agencies; other bodies connected to the State Government; civil society, users; and operation and maintenance teams.

Borges (2019) also analyzed the aspects concerning the public management environment and with the main laws used for bidding, which may influence the management of infrastructure projects. Table 20.2 presents a summary of the main actions to be put in practice for managing these projects and Table 20.3 presents the major consequences due to relationship issues among the parties involved, and the actions to be taken in project management to improve their effectiveness (Borges, 2019).

Table 20.2: Actions for managing infrastructure projects.

Aspect	Actions suggested for managing infrastructure projects
Institutions involved	Identifying public and private institutions; understanding their interests, institutional positions, cultures, and forms of activities on the project; undertaking continued assessment and monitoring.
Public and private corporations	Understanding the interests, positions and distinct forms of the public and private corporations; keeping the focus on the interests in the project when dealing with the different corporations; having a carefully written contract of the project; clarifying the transfer of risks to the private partner in the contract, if that exists.
Organization that conducts project management	Selecting, adapting, or creating specific project management methods and tools to apply on the project, including professionals who have expertise and experience in project management in the team.
Different government levels	Identifying the interests and positions of different levels of government regarding the project; anticipating the risks and the actions needed to improve the likelihood of project success.
Political and electoral aspects	Monitoring changes and risks from the electoral cycle.
Articulation with government bodies	Including a professional in the project management team dedicated to communicating with the different government organizations; enabling the understanding of the public interests and the public policies related to the project; understanding the requirements of the environmental licenses and of the inspecting organizations.

(*Continued*)

Table 20.2: (*Continued*)

Aspect	Actions suggested for managing infrastructure projects
Physical environment	Assessing and considering the physical environment in which the project will be implemented, from the feasibility study up to the operation and maintenance of the products and services; verifying incidences of interference with projects (design) and land regularization; identifying the stakeholders who will be affected in the place where the project will be implemented.
Financing forms	Analyzing the financing form and possible necessary actions for managing the project, including the financing agencies or organizations as stakeholders.
Mass media	Including the mass media as stakeholders; identifying the interests and position of the media; disseminating official information on the project in the appropriate channels (social networks, official sites); including a professional dedicated to the communication actions in the project team.
Design detailing	Assessing the risks inherent in the process of detailed design that each bidding process requires to start the planning and execution of the project; conducting planning with well-defined design projects with scope and requirements; executing the project with designs that have the necessary detailing; involving the contracted party responsible for executing the project as soon as possible in the life cycle and involving it in working with the designer to enable integrated solutions to be determined.
Specific stakeholders	Identifying the different stakeholders that emerge depending on each procurement type; identifying their interests and needs; assessing the roles and actions of each stakeholder according to the aspects specified by the procurement regime; analyzing how stakeholders should relate among themselves under the provisions of the procurement regime; structuring the decision-making process taking into consideration the specific stakeholders' behaviors and interests.
Lowest price bid procurement	Assessing impacts on management and foreseeing risks arising from competitions won based on the lowest price; conducting integrated control of changes to manage possible contractual additions; stimulating responsible, transparent and responsive behavior on the part of the professionals on the project.

Table 20.3: Consequences of the relationship issues among the parties involved.

Stakeholders	Possible consequences of relationship issues	Actions suggested for managing stakeholders
Client	Conflicts which are difficult to resolve; impact on the quality of the project, product and services	Having an efficient communication process; generating periodic status reports; holding periodic meetings to discuss the status of the project; having a clear definition of the project scope and limitations; surveying the client's needs and translating them into requirements; using an integrated information system.
Management team or manager	Communication problems and conflicts hinder decision-making and performance on the project	Having a team with expertise in project management; having a team with technical expertise on the project's subjects, or hiring consultants when necessary; applying project management tools and techniques; holding periodic meetings and upon request with the different stakeholders; conducting performance analyses to foster effective decision-making; using integrated information systems.
Constructor	Problems in the final quality of the products delivered; delays in deliveries; increase in the costs of the works; impact on the environment	Holding periodic meetings and upon demand with the client and the designer; generating performance analyses to monitor and control the work; having a clear attribution of roles and responsibilities to the parties involved; using integrated information systems; analyzing the contract in detail; continuously inspecting the execution of the work.
Designer	Insufficient design details; quality of products below that expected; reworks; increase in the project costs; delays in project deliveries; excessive design revisions	Involving the designer from the very beginning of the project life cycle; keeping communication channels open; keeping collaborative relationships; holding periodic meetings and upon request; using integrated information systems; conducting performance analyses for discussion and decision-making; periodically generating status reports.

(*Continued*)

Table 20.3: (*Continued*)

Stakeholders	Possible consequences of relationship issues	Actions suggested for managing stakeholders
Private partner (when relevant)	Increase in the project's costs; delays in deliveries; quality below what is expected	Having a clear attribution of roles and responsibilities; having a clear definition of the objectives and benefits of the project; maintaining continuous and transparent communication; holding periodic meetings on critical analyses to aid joint decision making.
State government	Conflict generation; interruption of the project	Having a clear definition of the scope and objectives of the project; conducting effective and continuous communication; having a clear decision-making process.
Municipal governments	Delays in the project deliveries	Including the municipal governments among the stakeholders of the project; maintaining continuous and transparent communication; generating and disseminating information on the project status; including scope and activities regarding the counterparts in the project planning.
Funding agencies	Funding suppression; Halting works; Delaying deliveries; Impairing the final delivery of the project	Restraining and regulating the requirements for funding indicated in the planning process; maintaining continuous communication; generating reports on the status of the project and information about meeting established commitments.
Inspecting bodies	Halting and delaying works	Including actions related to compliance and regulations applicable to project planning; generating and making available periodic reports with the status of the works and with the necessary information to these bodies.
Regulation agencies	Halting and delaying works	Including actions related to licensing and authorizations in the planning for the project.
Other bodies in the state government	To be determined on a case by case basis	Including the different bodies among the stakeholders of the project; including due actions in the planning for the project; defining other necessary actions on a case by case basis.

Table 20.3: (*Continued*)

Stakeholders	Possible consequences of relationship issues	Actions suggested for managing stakeholders
Civil society	Difficulties in executing the project; creating a negative image of the project to the society	Conducting public consultations to identify the possibly varied interests in, and necessary actions on, the project; communicating with transparency; fostering cooperation and the participation of the civil society in management of the project.
Future users	May turn into opponents of the project; source of possible conflicts and difficulties	Preparing and delivering reports with information on the status of the project.
Operation and maintenance teams	May turn into opponents of the project; source of conflicts and difficulties	Fostering the participation of the operation and maintenance teams over the entire life cycle of the project; including this group of stakeholders in the decision-making process whenever necessary; preparing and delivering reports with information on the status of the project.

Source: Borges (2019).

Internationalization in infrastructure projects: Multi-culturalism influences and difficulties in project management

Defining project success represents a challenge to be understood by project management (Ofori, 2003). For Carvalho and Rabechini (2015), the success of projects can be considered from different points of view, such as the stakeholders' perspective, the type of project, the temporal perspective (project duration), and the analysis unit (project or organization). In the case of multi-national companies, a primary factor for project success is obtaining a good assessment by the clients, since one of the objects of these companies is expanding their presence in the host country (Mognhol, 2019). While the performance of a company on the international market is considered a strategy, executing projects in another country poses a series of new managerial challenges, and the performance of a company in the international market can be different from its performance in its domestic market. The difference occurs mainly due to the culture, the macroeconomic environment, market regulations, financial institutions and entry barriers, such as competition policies, and the preference for domestic companies (Jin *et al.*, 2013).

It is more difficult for construction companies to meet their internationalization objectives than for firms in other sectors of the economy, due to the characteristics inherent in the infrastructure sector, such as the localization of the work and one-off nature of the project. As a result, the problems involved in the improvement of the sector internationalization process in construction has been the object of several research works in the last two decades, such as Ofori (2003), Gunhan and Arditi (2005), and Mutti (2018).

Foreign construction companies compete with local companies, and it is thus relevant to develop thorough project management strategies, besides analyzing the capacity of the competitors and the capacity to respond to the different context and fast changes in the market conditions (Mognhol, 2019).

Among the major challenges foreign contractors face on their entry into Brazil are: difficulty for a foreign engineer in obtaining a license from the Federal Engineering and Agronomics Council (Confea); language difficulties and those faced in understanding the local market particularities; high taxes on importation of items for projects and services; and the Law 8666 requirements for certifications proving previous experience and financial capacity to compete in bidding exercises. One of the strategies practiced by foreign companies to gain entry into the Brazilian construction market is participating in consortia. Another strategy is merging with or even acquiring smaller local companies.

The internationalization process of constructors also represents a new challenge to project management. These often originate in a wide cultural and behavioral diversity of all those involved in the project; this process is hindered even further by communication, knowledge-sharing, and decision-making barriers inherent in international contexts. Therefore, the wider the cultural differences among the countries involved in operations, the greater the problem and conflict trends among the teams. Analysis of these factors provides understanding of how far companies are culturally prepared to build up their professional capacities and to develop their project management practices, besides understanding how this environment supports such initiatives. Whether this is done through the implementation of processes or organizational changes, there is the need to manage teams with multi-cultural thinking, and to overcome cultural barriers, particularly as regards communication among stakeholders.

Problems concerning design, cost, and time overruns; lack of information in the form of records from previous projects; and communication noise are usual in construction and tend to be aggravated in a context of changes intrinsic in construction in other countries. These problems were evidenced from the results of a field study on four companies and six infrastructure construction projects executed in Brazil, two of the companies being national and the other two, foreign firms. The data were collected from project managers and team coordinators, by individual interviews based on a set of open questions (Mognhol, 2019).

The research showed lack of knowledge among those involved in implementing the management processes adopted by the companies; and they lacked managerial maturity to take on a stricter posture, in aiming at implementing or improving the processes. Consequently, in some cases, delays and economic losses occurred; in others, there was a shortfall in the expected results. Other difficulties concerned the management of the design processes, which did not really exist in some cases. The lack of a team dedicated to management at the design stage and to the client–designer–work interface caused errors and delays, which had a significant impact on the results of the projects studied.

The research showed that, in information and knowledge management, it is important to record the project data, especially for future reference. There was evidence that there had been a loss of time in seeking information that should have been stored, but which was lost upon the conclusion of the projects and the disbandment of the project team, which is quite usual on construction projects. The research also drew attention to the need to improve processes to record and to disseminate information and knowledge among the project teams.

Communication management was found to be effective for the external players and ineffective for internal players in the projects analyzed. The internal communication was informal, generating, among other problems, duplication of activities; and errors in the purchasing of materials and contract services. Table 20.4 presents key actions to be considered in order to

Table 20.4: Key actions in managing infrastructure projects in Brazil.

Process	Action	Benefits expected
Risk management	Identifying new risks and opportunities	Expanding the list of risks and opportunities identified in the local environment
	Analyzing the probability and impact of occurrence; and attributing a value to each risk and each opportunity	Taking into account contingency resources and preventing cost deviation
	Attributing responsibility for responding to, monitoring and controlling risks and opportunities	Ensuring the correct control of negative occurrences; potentializing positive occurrences Ensuring the correct planning of mitigation actions; enhancing the opportunities; and identifying new risks and opportunities
	Disseminating the matrix of risks and opportunities to all in the leadership team	Ensuring the active participation of stakeholders in the monitoring and control stage
Management of the project process	Assembling appropriately-sized and qualified design teams	Ensuring high quality design and design management
	Performing critical and compatibility analysis of the projects	Adopting good technical solutions for execution and prevent delays in the liberation of projects for construction
Management of information and knowledge	Recording information and lessons learned during the execution and at the end of the projects	Ensuring that high turnover of professionals turnover does not lead to lack of records and consequent loss of acquired knowledge
	Organizing the organization's database to enable necessary information and lessons learned to be referred to in future	Reducing uncertainties regarding the risks involved in the activities on the project; and assessing potential opportunities
Management of communication	Establishing formal and effective communication among the different (internal and external) teams	Optimizing the flow of information, flow quality, and fast information exchange

Source: Moghnol (2019).

increase the likelihood of project success in the challenging context that is the case in Brazil, with the potential growth in foreign investment.

According to a research study by the North American consultancy company, AT Kearney (2020), involving executives from the 500 major companies in the world, Brazil presented an improvement in the Direct Foreign Investment (DFI) rate, as shown in Figure 20.1. Ranking in 22nd place, Brazil is the only Latin American country in the 2020 ranking. Among the factors kindling the interest in investing in Brazil, the initiatives by the Federal Government aiming to expand privatization, especially in the infrastructure sector, should be emphasized.

Project management shows a specific aspect with respect to globalization, and that is, to operate in this environment, awareness of the local context is considered extremely necessary, and this includes legal and normative aspects. There is a need to adjust management practices to the existing culture, to reduce the impact of the cultural differences, and to ensure project success. In this sense, companies should be able to recognize their own capabilities to carry out projects in an international environment, as the uncertainties associated with the execution of projects in the domestic environment tend to be even greater in the foreign market.

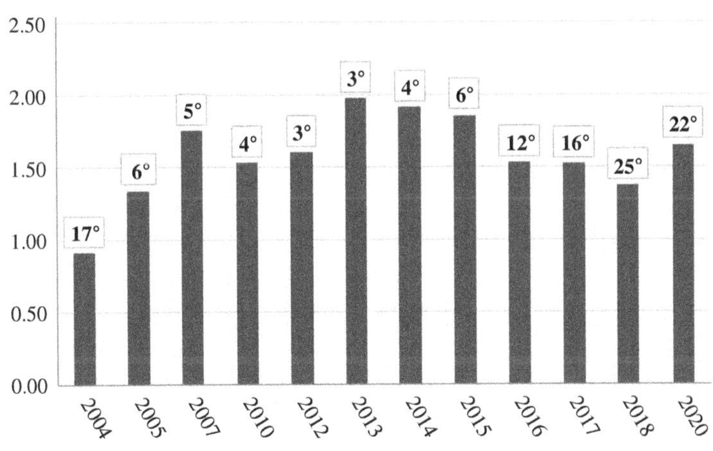

Figure 20.1: FDI confidence index by A.T. Kearney (0–3).

Note: There are no data for 2006, 2008, 2009, or 2011.

Cost management: Current challenges regarding contingency methods

Following the *Lava Jato* Operation, which dismantled corruption schemes in Brazil, the number of new and ongoing projects fell dramatically, forcing the players in the market for large and complex construction projects to rethink their budgeting and bidding processes, and their approach to the execution of work.

In the context of corruption, hidden payments were included and managed as part of the construction project budgets, and risk analysis and contingencies were ignored in the managing of costs on projects. After the *Lava Jato* operation, besides the reduction in opportunities for Brazilian companies in the heavy construction market, the competitiveness in both private and public bidding has become tougher.

The budgeting methods and cost control approaches adopted in Brazilian companies thus started to be questioned regarding the importance of managing risks at the projects budgeting stage. For many contractors and management companies, the use of risk management tools associated with cost management can be a good solution to eliminate or mitigate setbacks and to ensure real sustainability of their projects. In addition to applying risk management techniques to calculate the contingency estimates in the projects, using techniques already common in other areas has become relevant to decision making in budgeting, from the perspective of both investors and entrepreneurs in the industry. Corporate integrity programs became increasingly common and have guided the restructuring of several public and private companies. This also includes certification to ensure that the confidence of the market and investors is regained (Castelan, 2020).

Chong and Hopkins (2016) analyzed the variability in costs for different road works in various countries over the entire life cycle of the project, stressed the need to understand the nature of the variations, and proposed methods for effective predictions and precautions.

Baccarini (2005) noted that the definition of contingency as a "financial reserve" is probably more widely accepted among project managers and other stakeholders. In his study, he lists the most common methods in construction in the world. The more commonly adopted methods of contingency estimation include: Traditional Percentage, Method of Moments, and

Monte Carlo Simulation. In Brazil, the Traditional Percentage and Monte Carlo Simulation methods are most commonly used in infrastructure projects. Methods such as Regression Analysis and Artificial Neural Networks, which would be relevant alternatives, are not often applied in Brazil.

Considering the need to apply adequate cost management techniques, including budgeting, risk, and contingency management, Castelan (2020) researched how these processes have been applied by infrastructure contractors. The data were collected by an exploratory intersectional survey, answered by 41 professionals from Brazilian contractors' teams. Next, the results were submitted to an expert panel to discuss and validate the survey results.

Regarding the professionals' understanding of risk management and, consequently, of contingency calculation, it was possible to understand the most usual tools and how the risk management processes occurred during the execution of the works. According to the survey conducted by Castelan (2020), only 19.05 percent of the corporations retain professionals dedicated to Risk Management in the Brazilian market. The companies that have an area or professional dedicated to risk management are private infrastructure companies operating in the international market and which have concessions in their project portfolios. At least half of the respondents indicated that they know parameters associated with the organization's appetite for risks. Some 23.81 percent of the respondents also work for international concessionaires.

In the research, standing out among the responses regarding the method used for calculating contingency is the simple percentage method. The survey indicated delays and lack of collaboration among areas of expertise as a recurrent problem in the companies. However, the responses showed that small- and medium-sized companies, which tend to have less bureaucracy and better communication, manage to maintain a better relationship among areas of expertise and to more adequately use their references in the cost management process.

The infrastructure companies with over 10 years of experience were observed to perform better regarding cost control during the works execution stage. This was probably due to the fostering of cost control that a number of companies with large works have developed in recent years — for example, by involving mapping by drones and by implementing electronic notetaking with tablets and smart telephones.

Diagnosis of risk management in construction industry in Brazil

NBR ISO 31000 (ABNT, 2009) defines risk as the "effect of uncertainty in objectives." In agreement with this standard, corporations of all types and sizes face influences from internal and external factors that cause uncertainty about whether, and when, their objectives will be met. For Liu *et al.* (2013), risk management in civil construction is a poorly explored, yet fundamental process to ensure positive results for projects and corporations. Particularly, the transient nature of infrastructure projects, in addition to the significant number of players and other stakeholders, strong dependency on different resources and local and other factors, and a high potential of impacting the environment and society, gives this activity a significant degree of uncertainty and, therefore, exposure to risks. Recently, in Brazil, particularly after emblematic accidents, such as the collapse of a shaft during the excavation at the Pinheiros Station on Subway Line 4-Yellow of the City of São Paulo Metro, some infrastructure companies have introduced in their structures, areas or professionals specialized in risk management, including corporate-level ones, besides risks inherent in the production activities.

Nevertheless, observing the Brazilian scenario and how the subject is treated by the different groups and stakeholders, it is evident that risk management processes are not widely disseminated or consolidated in the Brazilian infrastructure companies. A survey conducted in 2018 and 2019 by De Padua and Souza (2019) showed that risk management in Brazil occurs quite informally, with gaps found in areas from identification, risk analysis, and management, up to the standardization of the corporations' internal processes and organizational culture. This research assessed the perceptions regarding risk frequency and impacts, the degree of informality in risk management, and the barriers to risk management application, drawing inspiration from the work by Tang *et al.* (2007) on risk management in China, which was adapted for application in Brazil.

The data collected in that survey were analyzed from the following perspectives: organization size and age; region in which the organizations operate; and specialization of the companies. From the number and characteristics of the respondents, the sample can be considered as being representative of the Brazilian civil construction industry. The typical profile for the majority of respondents includes a postgraduate degree and a managerial position held for less than five years in a contractor or management company, typically a big contractor with 30 years or more of existence.

In the questionnaire, respondents were asked about the most usual causes of risks in their construction projects (from the respondent's experience) and their assessment regarding the frequency and impact of the risks, on a 1 to 5 scale, where 1 represented "never" and 5 represented "always."

As a conclusion, from the answers, the most pressing causes of the most frequent and highest impact risks are: low quality of labor, inadequate or incorrect design, flaws in the quality control systems, problems at the worksite, inadequate management of the direct participants of the project, and flaws in the building systems and equipment. For the remaining items assessed, there was no significant difference in the assessment of the following causes: gaps in the participants' technical knowledge, flaws in safety, financial management problems, inadequate management of the indirect participants of the project, and flaws in equipment.

As shown in Figure 20.2, the analyses of the causes of the most frequent risks under the perspectives — corporations' size and age and corporations' region — indicate the same trends as the general analysis with regard to the identification of the major causes. However, when the data are analyzed under the specific groups' perspectives, it is evident that assessments on the part of designers are more severe than those of the other players — whereas the average general assessment for the labor item was 3.31, it was 4.0 for the designers. The situation was the same for the item associated with design — whereas the average assessment was 3.0, the designers' assessment was 3.5.

As in the analysis of frequencies, the information about impacts, under the perspectives of size of the corporations, age of the corporations, and players, indicated the same trends as those in the general analysis. Financial management problems are pointed out by companies with up to 20 years existence, by companies operating in the São Paulo region, and by design companies, as the aspect with the highest impact, and with considerable differences: 4.33, 3.86, and 4.17, respectively, as compared to the average of 3.34 in the general analysis. Moreover, the research

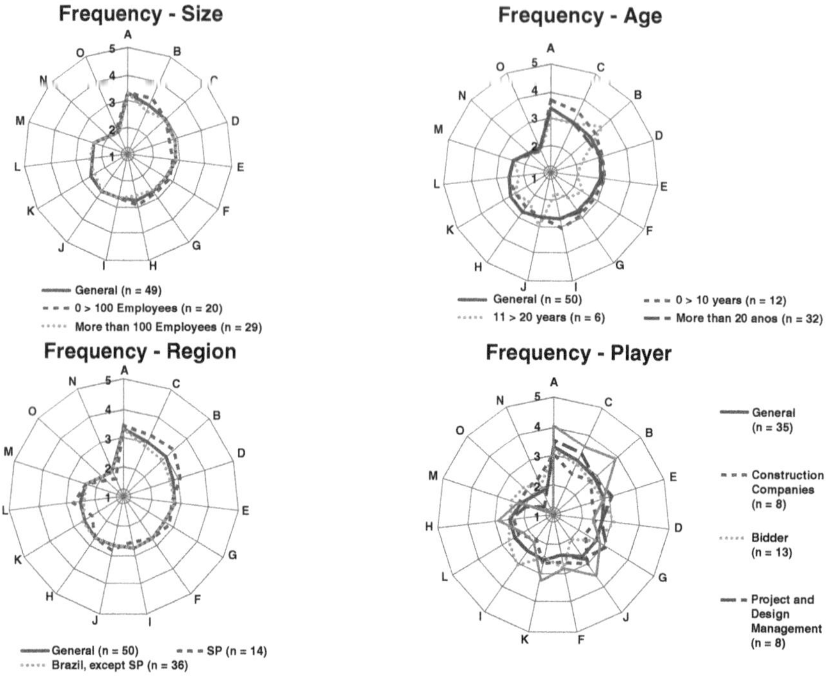

Figure 20.2: Analysis of the frequency of the causes under different perspectives.

Source: De Padua and Souza (2019).

assessed whether risk management practices are duly disseminated and also, whether the current risk management systems in the companies are formalized and adequate. The respondents were asked to rank from 1 to 5 the frequency in the application of the techniques listed, and processes for risk management; here, 1 meant "never" and 5, "always."

The non-existence of any assessment over 4 indicates that there are still gaps to be narrowed in risk management practices in Brazil. However, the responses show that the techniques and processes associated with risk management are known and applied. The following aspects stand out:

- the quantitative and semi-qualitative methods are those used with the lowest frequency
- the tools for identifying risks are more often accessed as compared to those for analyses, decision-making, and risk control

- the item of risk transference is the one with the lowest assessment (2.51) in the decision-making process as compared to the lowest assessment of the other items in the same category, such as accepting risks (3.11). Although the difference is not significant and the grade attributed indicates the existence of the transfer practice, the assessment indicates that practices associated with risk transfer (such as hiring adequate insurance coverage, and transfer of responsibility for losses by means of contractual agreements) are not fully disseminated in Brazil
- positively standing out in the items risk analysis and control is the involvement of key participants in the project.

The use of instruments for identifying the risks presents the same trends in the general analysis; however, from the players' perspective, the tools are considered to be more consolidated in the contractor and development companies than in the design and management companies. With regard to risk analysis, Figure 20.3 shows that the companies aged

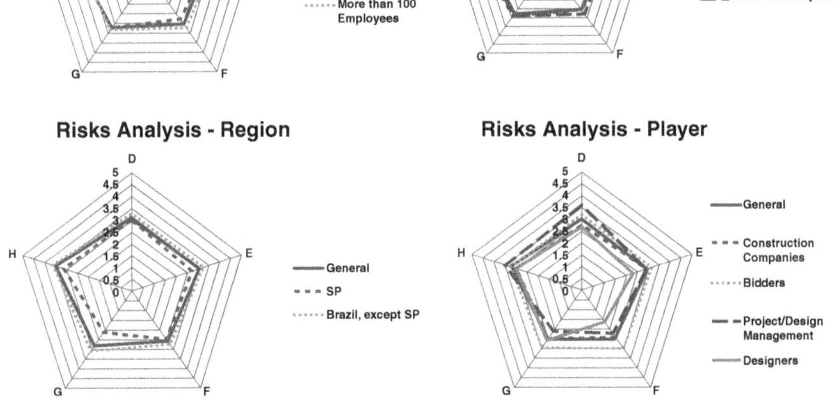

Figure 20.3: Application of instruments for analyzing risks, different perspectives.

Source: De Padua and Souza (2019).

0–10 years are those that mostly apply qualitative means and involve the key project participants in the analysis. In turn, among the players, the designers are those using qualitative techniques the least.

Concerning decision-making about risks, Figure 20.4 indicates that the management and contractor companies are on the way to consolidating the tools for risk mitigation, whereas the tools used in decision-making about risks are less often applied by designers. The risk control tools follow the same trends as those in the general analysis; when analyzed from the size, age, region, and player perspectives, the designers are the ones who less often apply risk control tools.

The assessment regarding the formality and whether the risk management systems are adequate, indicates that the companies are on the way to formalizing their risk management systems; yet, from the general assessments (=< 3.5), it can be stated that the systems are more informal than formal. Companies with over 100 employees and Contractors present a higher formalization level than the average (3 < Formalization < 3.5); Designers have the lowest formalization level (Formalization < 1).

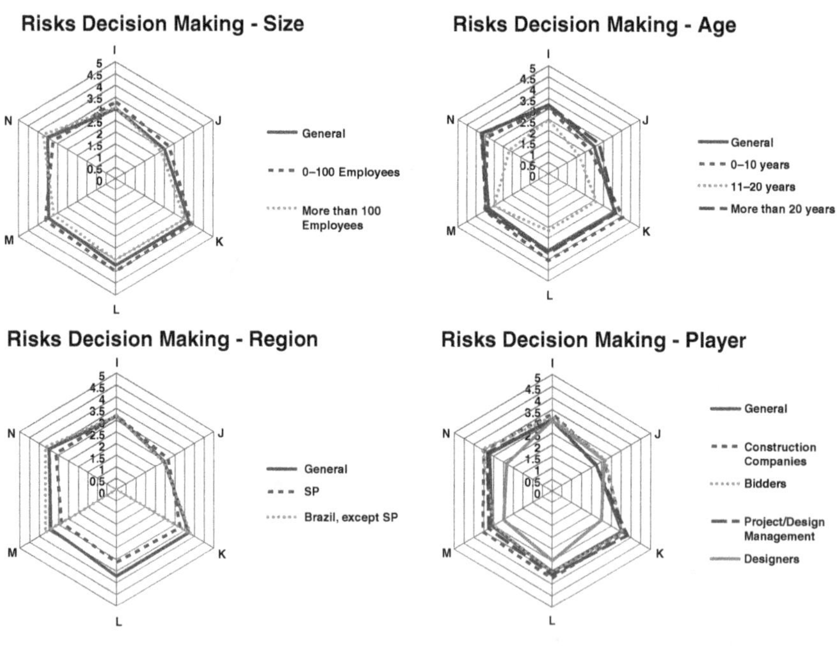

Figure 20.4: Decision-making about risks, different perspectives.

Source: De Padua and Souza (2019).

Furthermore, the grades related to how appropriate the systems are show that even the formalized systems are not adequate. As to the assessment of how adequate the risk management systems are, a rating of 3 is not exceeded, on a 1 to 5 scale. Standing out, designers and companies aged between 11 and 20 years were rated below 2. Contractors and companies aged between 0 and 10 years, had the highest ratings (3 < adequate < 4). "Inadequate or incorrect design" was the factor associated with the risks with the highest impact, which may be linked to the fact that the periods defined for planning, including designs, are not coherent with the projects' characteristics. Additionally, the high level of competition in the design market, with no price regulation, leads to the depreciation of the "design" product in Brazilian civil construction.

The last aspect assessed in the survey regarded the barriers to the application of risk management in Brazil. The question to be answered aimed at assessing the relevance of each of the barriers listed, from 1 to 5, where 1 assesses the barrier as "null," and 5 as "extreme." Table 20.5

Table 20.5: Barriers to risk management.

Barrier	Size	Age	Region	Player
Lack of knowledge and/or technique on risk management	3.45	3.14	3.14	3.31
Lack of data/historical information for analyzing risk behavior	3.35	3.1	3.1	3.23
Lack of incentive to implement risk management	3.3	3.16	3.16	3.17
Inefficacious application of risk management techniques	3.25	3.08	3.08	3.06
Lack of a formal risk management system in the organization	3.25	3.14	3.14	3.26
Lack of space in the organization for disseminating risk management culture/knowledge	3.2	3	3	3.09
Lack of mechanisms for joint risk analysis among the project participants	3.15	2.88	2.88	2.94
Divergent interpretations regarding the risk management techniques	3.15	3	3	3.11
Inadequate resource allocation for risk management	3	2.76	2.76	2.77
Non-efficacious monitoring	2.9	3.04	3.04	3.06
Insufficient design information to facilitate decision-making in risk management	2.8	2.86	2.86	2.86

Source: De Padua and Souza (2019).

shows that the barriers listed were associated with organizational and methodological issues and knowledge and issues associated with information quality, besides limitations associated with interpretation of the information for identifying and qualifying the risks. Although none of the barriers listed had been assessed as extreme, none of them obtained an assessment lower than 2.75 either, indicating that all the items are relevant barriers to risk management in Brazil.

For the São Paulo companies, all the barriers received at least 0.5 more in relevance than the companies from other regions in Brazil. Similarly, for the designer companies, all the barriers received at least 0.5 more in relevance than the companies from other regions in Brazil, except for the items, "inadequate resource allocation," "lack of mechanisms for joint risk analysis among the project participants," and "lack of space in the organisation for disseminating risk management culture/knowledge."

Ethics and governance as pillars for infrastructure project management compliance

Farias *et al.* (2019) presented a framework to analyze the process of compliance restructuring in a construction company involved in a corruption scandal. In the context of a globalized economy, and having to find capitalization alternatives, companies found in the stock market a way to avoid the elevated costs of a loan, therefore being required to adjust themselves to a series of corporate governance codes and regulations, especially those reflecting international standards of a consistent business ethical posture.

Brazilian Law No. 12846/2013 — the Anti-Corruption Law (Brasil, 2013) was passed to cover the responsibilities of companies as legal entities for the financial and ethical losses they had caused to the administration. It was executed by Federal Decree nº 8420 (Brasil, 2015), that states a series of parameters for the Integrity Program. Farias *et al.* (2019) state that the Integrity Program must be understood as an organic structure that will only function properly if there is harmony among the five pillars (selected from the Decree): (a) commitment and support from the directors of the company; (b) an independent party responsible for the Integrity Program (Compliance Area); (c) profile and risk analysis; (d) structure of rules and instruments; and (e) continuous improvement strategies.

They also state that the concept of compliance is, by definition, the abiding of the entire organization by applicable legislation. Therefore, it influences all of the organization's management systems, and should, ideally, be integrated into them. Also, besides the decree that implements the Anti-Corruption Law, there are two institutional initiatives that approach the implementation of compliance systems according to the standards NBR ISO 19600 (ABNT, 2014) and NBR ISO 37001 (ABNT, 2016). The first determines the obligations that an organization must be subjected to for compliance, and the second defines an anti-bribery system.

Farias *et al.* (2019) present a comparative approach of the three directives (see Table 20.6). Based on the framework developed by Farias *et al.*

Table 20.6: Comparison of compliance systems.

Differences	Federal Decree 8420/2015	ISO 19600/2014	ISO 37001/2016
Comprehensiveness	Covers the entire organization, sites, processes and products	The organization can define the scope it intends to implement	Restricted to anti-bribing practices
Entity that assesses/audits	Office of the Comptroller General	Any private consultancy or auditing company	Accredited Certification Body
Recognition	National	International	International
Requirements for the management/ integrity system	I. Commitment by the top management of the legal entity II. Conduct standards, code of ethics, policies and procedures for the integrity of staff members III. Conduct standards, code of ethics and integrity policies for third parties IV. Periodic training V. Periodic risk analysis VI. Accounting transparency VII. Internal controls to ensure reliability	1. Scope 2. Normative references 3. Terms and definitions 4. Organization Context 5. Leadership 6. Planning 7. Support 8. Operational 8.1 Planning and operational control 8.2 Establishing controls and procedures 8.3 Outsourced processes 9. Assessment and performance improvement	1. Scope 2. Normative references 3. Terms and definitions 4. Context of the organization 5. Leadership 6. Planning 7. Support 8. Operational 8.1 Planning and operational control 8.2 Due diligence 8.3 Financial controls 8.4 Non-financial controls 8.5 Implementation of anti-bribing controls 8.6 Anti-bribing commitments

(*Continued*)

Table 20.6: (Continued)

Differences	Federal Decree 8420/2015	ISO 19600/2014	ISO 37001/2016
	VIII. Specific procedures for preventing fraud and violations IX. Independence, structure and authority of the internal instance accounting for the integrity program X. Channels for reporting irregularities XI. Disciplinary measures; XII. Inhibition of detected irregularities or violations XIII. Appropriate procedures for contracting third parties XIV. Merging, acquisition, and corporate restructuring processes XV. Continued monitoring of the integrity program XVI. Transparency of donations to candidates and political parties		8.7 Presents, hospitality, donations and similar benefits 8.8 Managing anti-bribing inadequacy controls 8.9 Surveying concerns 8.10 Investigating and dealing with bribing 9. Assessment and performance improvement

Source: Adapted from Farias *et al.* (2019).

(2019), a case study was conducted with two additional companies, also involved in corruption scandals, in order to evaluate their compliance with the parameters in Brazilian Federal Decree nº 8420 regarding the Integrity Program, especially the five pillars stressed by Farias *et al.* (2019).

The central question presented in the case study was: "how did the compliance system implemented in the company influence its restructuring after the corruption scandals?" Agee (2009) establishes the need for the articulation of the many research questions reflecting the intentions and perspectives of those involved in social interactions. To ensure a thorough approach, the interviews were undertaken with a variety of people from different areas of the companies (such as compliance, engineering, human resources, legal, communications), in different roles, and with various positions in the hierarchy (such as board members, operational managers, and compliance analysts). Also, there were always two researchers present, ensuring the triangulation aspect of case studies that mitigates bias and adds depth to the collected information, as suggested by Denzin (2012).

The interview questions were based on the structure of the Brazilian Federal Decree 8420/2015, which implements the Anti-Corruption Law. They related to the five pillars to implementing the organic structure of an Integrity Program proposed by Farias *et al.* (2019): (a) commitment and support from company direction; (b) an independent party responsible for the Integrity Program (Compliance Area); (c) Profile and Risk analysis; (d) structure of rules and instruments; and (e) continuous improvement strategies. An outline of the data collected, as well as the information from the case study in Farias *et al.* (2019) is presented in Table 20.7.

Table 20.7: Interview data summary.

	Company A	Company B	Company C*
Anti-bribery management	The company has its own management board, with independent members. Most hired members have prior experience in governance and compliance.	The board hired a strategic consultancy to undertake the implementation of the compliance system and replaced the company president. The new one was identified by reference to ethical behavior.	Each of the company's businesses has a distinct management board with at least 20 percent of independent members.
Compliance management	The compliance area reports solely to the compliance committee, which reports directly to the management board. Ethics complaints and reports are evaluated by an external company. There is a	The compliance area reports solely to the compliance committee, which reports directly to the management board. On a monthly basis, reported issues are analyzed and responsive actions are taken. There are *compliance players* who	The compliance area reports solely to the compliance committee, which reports directly to the management board. The business branches have their own Chief Compliance Officers.

(*Continued*)

Table 20.7: (*Continued*)

	Company A	Company B	Company C*
	complementary structure of 54 *integrity players*, all volunteers.	help spread the compliance culture.	
Profile and risk analysis	An external company is responsible for checking third parties. Higher compliance risks require approval from two directors, one of whom must not be involved in the project. Risk management processes consider risks of noncompliance.	All third parties undergo a due diligence process before they are contracted. New projects, clients, suppliers, and partners have to be approved by a compliance analysis. There is a background check on new employees from a certain level upwards.	Due diligence processes are applied solely to third parties (business partners or suppliers), they are not applied in the company's personnel hiring processes. Risk assessments are periodically reviewed.
Structure of rules and instruments	The ethics code and company policy are guided by five values: respect, integrity, transparency, excellence and integration. These values are actively communicated to all employees. They use appropriate communication tools and language and also give open and easy access to information on compliance.	The company's organizational pillars are: compliance, operational excellence, and innovation, that are communicated to all employees. A monitoring device identifies operations with compliance risk, which are then investigated by the compliance area. On construction sites, there is a daily dialog and information on compliance is available.	Behavioral standards and an ethics code are explicitly expressed in the company policy, in accordance with transparency and ethics guidelines. There is a compliance policy also for third parties.
Continuous improvement strategies	The PDCA (Plan, Do, Check, Act) method is applied to each compliance initiative. Integrity players suggest what aspects of the compliance system should be strengthened. The company has recently begun to implement ESG controls. The company is currently preparing for ISO 37001 certification.	There is a yearly evaluation of the company's compliance culture among employees. The deficient items are reviewed by the compliance area. The company is affiliated with Brazilian Institute of Self-regulation, Ethics and Integrity in Infrastructure (IBRICS) and is contributing to the UN Anti-Corruption Collective Action.	The compliance system determines the capacity building plan and periodic training sessions. Adaptation requirements are evaluated through periodic risk assessments.

Source: Adapted from Farias *et al.* (2019).

A Brazilian case in the infrastructure sector: The PM body of knowledge developed by a sanitation company

Sabesp is a government-controlled (private) company, founded in 1973, involved in planning, executing, and operating basic sanitation services, including water collection, treatment, and distribution and sewage segregation and final disposal, in 375 municipalities of the State of São Paulo, a state which accounts for 32 percent of the GDP of Brazil.

It is among the major water and sanitation companies in the world (it is the fourth largest company serving the population), and the largest in Latin America, supplying water to over 28 million people and collecting sewage from over 24 million (67 percent of the population in the State of São Paulo).

In Brazil as a whole, Sabesp accounts for about 30 percent of the investments in sanitation, and its plans for the 2020–2024 cycle include investing about R$ 20.2 billion. Its stocks are traded in the Novo Mercado Brasil segment, Stock Exchange, Over-the-Counter (B3), and the New York Stock Exchange, in the form of American Depository Receipts (ADR Level III) since 2002. The State of São Paulo Government is the controlling shareholder, owning 50.3 percent of the shares.

Varoli *et al.* (2009) report that the large volume of investments of Sabesp and the relevance of its activities in the state as the main provider of basic infrastructure services led the company to reassess its organizational competence in project management in 2003. A series of actions which were set out to be taken over time (from 2004) are presented in Table 20.8. In its first cycle, structuring of the project management method was based on the perception of the external environment, the internal environment and of the model: "Structure, People, Processes and Tools," which is presented in Table 20.9.

The external environment indicated a new direction for the company toward a greater focus on environmental issues; it also meant a substantial increase in the inflow of financial resources from international and national development banks (such as IDB) and financing institutions (such as BNDES and Caixa Econômica Federal), besides the acceleration of growth in Brazil, which later became the PAC. Internally, it was

Table 20.8: Actions toward structuring the Sabesp project management.

2004	2005–2007	2008–2009	2010
Creation of TED — Department for developing project management Start of the project, "Revolutionising project management," based on the PMI project management practices	Definition of the methodological concepts and the project life cycle Design of the interrelated processes grid Creation of the project management methodology (PMM)	Assisting implementation of PMM in the units executing Sabesp projects	Publication of the company procedure for project management, consolidating PMM as a corporate practice

Table 20.9: Assisted implementation of MMP and revision of the methods of PMM and MMP.

2012	2013	2014	2015
Tietê Program (1st, 2nd and 3rd stages) Vale do Ribeira Program Clean Wave Program I Loss Reduction Program	Tietê Program (4th stage) Vale do Ribeira Program Clean Wave Program I and II Loss Reduction Program **Beginning of the MMP Revision**	Vale do Ribeira Program Clean Wave Program II Metropolitan Water Program (PMA) **PMM Integration in the MMP**	Clean Wave Program II Metropolitan Water Program (PMA) **MMP Integration in the SiiS**

necessary to consider a regional approach to corporate and project management, since up to the 1990s, all the contracts for projects and works were concentrated in a single company board, which was divided into semi-autonomous business units.

According to Varoli *et al.* (2009), in the first stage, the major critical factors identified by Sabesp were (i) planning and implementation of the Project Management Methodology, which demanded the setting up of an internal team, supported by external consultants; (ii) adapting the PMBOK® (Project Management Body of Knowledge) recommendations to reality in a participatory way (about 500 people were involved in the project); and (iii) managing the change process.

Among the main adaptations of the PMBOK® structure was the creation of specific processes for an area related to environmental management, which is a critical path item, and key point of the relationship with external stakeholders, including those responsible for issuing licenses and permissions for implementing the projects. The management of the change process occurred based on contracts assisted by the implementation of the Project Management Methodology (PMM).

One of the case studies on the project management methods on infrastructure projects Borges (2019) presented was the construction of an 83-km-long water supply system. He highlighted Environmental Management and Land Regularization as one of the specific knowledge areas necessary for successfully managing infrastructure projects. The management of Environmental and Land Regularization is emphasized by Sabesp at all stages of its project management approach.

The relevance of environmental management here is greater than in other kinds of construction, since infrastructure projects are large-sized and extensive, and therefore trigger greater environmental impact. Some issues to be considered from the early project definition stage include demands from environmental and inspecting bodies, besides communications and actions with the stakeholders. Some relevant aspects for such developments are temporary housing; reduction in noise and inconveniences for the neighboring community; and making available alternative transportation during the construction stage. Also, the impact caused by the materials to be used for the works, from their extraction, processing, transportation, utilization, up to being dismantled and recycled or disposed of should be considered. Such an environmental view is relevant at all stages of the project lifecycle, including the operation and maintenance stage.

The process of Land Regularization as a consequence of the physical scale of infrastructure projects should be managed from the preliminary design stage, foreseeing the places that will have to be expropriated or liberated for executing the works. The support of professionals from the legal section is needed since the management activities include negotiations, agreements, and often, lawsuits. To ensure the efficiency of the process, it is necessary to maintain communication with the stakeholders, fostering the participation of civil society, government bodies, and other stakeholders.

In the second phase of the initiative, called "Universalising Project Management in the Sabesp Ambit," the challenges identified were even greater, and the actions included: (i) introducing new processes, maintaining the competencies and experiences of its professionals; and (ii) connecting PMM computerization to corporate systems, to form a common data environment.

At the end of the two implementation cycles, the projects managed by PMM were observed to yield better values for the performance indicators (especially regarding schedule and cost) than those not based on PMM for their management.

From 2009, with PMM consolidated and undergoing improvement, a discussion was started on structuring a Management Methodology Program (MMP), and this developed from the perception of the need to extend the application of the management concept to the company. Its development occurred in the following years, up to 2011. Souza *et al.* (2011) describe the theoretical base of the structured MMP under three pillars: (i) conceptualization and establishment of Organizational Values and Principles; (ii) Institutional Policies, specifically the policy guiding Investment Management; and (iii) existing good management practices, especially those discussed by the Project Management Institute (PMI) in its *Project Management Body of Knowledge* (PMBOK) and by the Standard for Program Management. The Sabesp organizational values and principles are periodically revised in Strategic Planning cycles, conducted by the Integrated Planning Superintendence and count on the participation of all members of the company boards, having as a product the "Sabesp Strategic Directions." From this document, the Strategic Mapping is prepared, inspired by the Balanced Scorecard method.

The second MMP pillar deals with Institutional Policies, especially the institutional investment policy; based on it, the company's plans and investment programs are formulated. The requirements for conducting programs at Sabesp include: (a) being compatible with the Master Plans; (b) presenting Technical and Environmental Feasibility; and (c) presenting Economic-Financial and Social Feasibility. The third pillar means the connection to the Management Methodology Program, which gives a solid conceptual basis that is compatible with the other internal processes of the company.

The concept of the program defined in the Sabesp context was: "[The Program] is a set of interlinked projects managed in a coordinated manner to obtain benefits and control, not available in case they were managed individually" (Souza *et al.*, 2011). This concept was later updated to specify the company Structuring Programs: the Structuring Program is the set of interlinked projects, managed in a coordinated manner to potentialize results and benefits in a specific geographic region, not available if they were managed individually.

It has to be directly related to the strategic objectives and contain mostly projects encompassed by the Investments Planning; it may also contain initiatives (Martinelli *et al.*, 2017). The authors also state that three central requirements were determined for structuring the Management Methodology Program:

- Focus on the benefits managed along the Program's life cycle, unfolded into: Immediate Benefits (facilities delivered for operation — products of the projects and initiatives); Intermediate Benefits (facilities in operation); and Final Benefits (meeting the company's strategic objectives by implementing the Structuring Program);
- Integrated Solutions, either technical or financial, obtaining licenses, regularization, authorizations or establishing contacts, to attain efficiency in the use of resources by integrating the operational processes, including environmental management, conservation, recovery, and management of water resources; and
- Information system to communicate the current stage of the Program, thus providing the basis for decision-making by managers, the company board, and other stakeholders with power and influence over the Program, such as State Government officers.

From 2012, the MMP-assisted implementation was started in the company programs, followed by a methodological revision process and of the continuous improvement of the MMP, to meet the demand for simplifying and updating the tools (see Table 20.10). The revision led to integrating the PMM into MMP. Processes, forms, virtual environments, electronic sites, and databases were revised, focusing on improving usability and interactivity with users and in the interoperability among the

Table 20.10: Timeline for creating the Management Methodology Program.

2009	2010	2011
Initial discussions for formulating the Management Methodology Program	Definition of the program management processes Definition of the Sabesp program life cycle	Formulation of the Sabesp Management Methodology Program

company's internal systems. In 2015, the work of integrating MMP into the new corporate Enterprise Resource Planning system (ERP) was started; it was called the Sabesp Integrated Information System (SiiS).

In 2019, Sabesp commissioned a project to develop the potential of the Methodology in the planning process for projects and programs, systematizing the information to be supplied to the company board. The major drivers of the model proposed were:

- Ensuring better returns on investments from Governance, analysis of prioritization and projection of investments and benefits scenarios; Management Structuring Programs and, at superintendence and board level; and Guidance and Structuring of the Company portfolio and programs
- Helping to improve the units' expertise by assessing the performance of the activities at the project level and suggesting modifications that ensure meeting the deadlines, quality, and costs; analyzing the implementation planning of the works proposed by the companies contracted; verifying the adequacy of the planning of the program, and analyzing management and contractual indicators by the MMP tools
- Ensuring the expansion of the management environment by the governance of Programs and Projects; support to structuring, planning, and management of Structuring Programs, Projects, and Initiatives; Application of the Methodology for Managing Programs and Projects; and Data Collection in the Programs and Projects Management system.

Finally, it is worth highlighting the recent sanctioning of Law 14,026/20, the New Legal Sanitation Framework, which accelerates the universal application of the initiatives for rendering services in the sector, which enables investments to be better applied, and helps the companies to address to the demand for updated management mechanisms for their projects thus allowing investments to be better applied and also the application of updated management methods and tools for their projects.

Conclusion

The elements presented in this chapter illustrate how far infrastructure project management goes beyond the traditionally defined knowledge areas. The empirical evidence in the chapter identified some key factors of successful project management relevant to the infrastructure sector of a developing country. While all the management fields are involved in infrastructure projects, considering the Brazilian context, this chapter sought to reveal the importance of project management areas such as procurement, stakeholders, cost, and risk management, along with ethics and governance, environmental management, and regularization of land ownership.

Recent changes in the approach of infrastructure procurement, linked to the trends in concessions and PPP projects, have increased the importance of stakeholder management, in the context of more internationalized projects. Moreover, the *Lava Jato* operation led the vast majority of Brazilian infrastructure corporations to fully rethink their processes, and opened the way for new national and international companies. After *Lava Jato*, fostering risk management in the corporations, combined with efficient cost management, became a decisive factor to guarantee success on projects.

The weaknesses of public management caused problems relating to stakeholders' relationships, in the context of complex political, legal, economic, organizational, and ethical factors. The need for management actions here include examining the different responsibilities and interests of the public and private sectors; managing contracts and outsourcing; considering the different governments' levels of decentralization; taking into account the complexity of the stakeholders' roles; and bearing in mind the political issues which may influence decision making, as well as allowing undue behaviors. Added to that are the conditions of an increasingly and strongly internationalized market, and the requirements arising from the Brazilian policy on progressively adopting BIM on public projects. This stresses even more the movement for restructuring processes, methods, and tools for infrastructure project management. In Brazilian infrastructure projects, other management areas, such as environmental considerations and land registration, have tended to be expanded and requirements for the management of procurement, stakeholders, costs and risks, within an ethical environment, organizationally and technologically, increasingly made compulsory under the BIM implementation requirements.

The future development of the subject of this chapter should include the effect of the COVID-19 pandemic on the infrastructure sector and its project management practices. Beyond that, also the consequences of the application of digitization in construction, and the lessons learned from the application of digitization in the new procurement models. These subjects could be studied in further research in the context of infrastructure projects in Brazil.

References

A.T. Kearney. https://www.kearney.com/foreign-direct-investment-confidence-index/rankings.

Agee, J. (2009). Developing qualitative research questions: a reflective process, *International Journal of Qualitative Studies in Education*, 22(4), 431–447. https://doi.org/10.1080/09518390902736512.

Associação Brasileira Da Infraestrutura E Indústrias De Base (2020). *Barômetro da Infraestrutura Brasileira*, 3rd Edition. Junho.

Associação Brasileira De Normas Técnicas (ABNT) (2016). ISO 19600:2014 Sistema de gestão de compliance — Diretrizes, Rio de Janeiro.

Associação Brasileira De Normas Técnicas (ABNT) (2017). NBR ISO 37001:2016 Sistema de Gestão antissuborno — Requisitos, Rio de Janeiro.

Associação Brasileira De Normas Técnicas (ABNT). NBR ISO 31000:2009 Gestão de Riscos — Princípios e Diretrizes, Rio de Janeiro, 32 p.

Baccarini, D. (2005). Understanding project cost contingency: A survey. In: A.C. Sidwell (Ed.), *Proceedings of the Queensland University of Technology Research Week 2005*, Brisbane, 4-5 July. Queensland University of Technology, Brisbane, Australia. https://espace.curtin.edu.au/handle/20.500.11937/9641.

Banco Nacional De Desenvolvimento Econômico E Social (2019). *Relatório Seminário: Novo ciclo de investimentos em infraestrutura e a transparência na construção civil.* Abril.

Borges, F.V. (2019). Recomendações para a gestão de empreendimentos de infraestrutura. Dissertação de Mestrado, Escola Politécnica, Universidade de São Paulo, São Paulo. https://doi.org/10.11606/D.3.2019.tde-07052019-091445.

Brasil (2013). Lei nº 12.846, de 1º de agosto de 2013 — Dispõe sobre a responsabilização administrativa e civil de pessoas jurídicas pela prática de atos contra a administração pública, nacional ou estrangeira, e dá outras providências, Brasília, Brasil.

Brasil (2015). Decreto nº 8420, de 18 de março de 2015 regulamenta a Lei Nº 12.846, de 1º de agosto de 2013 e dá outras providências, Brasília, Brasil.

Câmara Brasileira Da Indústria Da Construção. Projetos. https://cbic.org.br/

Carvalho, M.M. and Rabechini, R. Jr. (2017). *Fundamentos em gestão de projetos: construindo competências para gerenciar projetos.* 4th ed. São Paulo: Atlas.

Castelan, E.L. (2020). *Análise de riscos e contingenciamento em obras de infraestrutura.* Monografia de Especialização em Gestão de Projetos na Construção. São Paulo: Poli Integra.

Chong, U. and Hopkins, O. (2016). An international experience on the evolution of road costs during the project life cycle. *Transport Policy*, 48, 60–66.

De Padua, R. and Souza, F. (2019). How risk management has been practiced in the Brazilian construction industry. *Proceedings of the CIB World Building Congress 2019*, Constructing Smart Cities, Hong Kong.

Denzin, N.K. (2012). Triangulation 2.0. *Journal of Mixed Methods Research*, 6, 80–88. https://doi.org/10.1177/1558689812437186.

Di Pietro, M.S.Z. (2005). *Parcerias na Administração Pública: concessão, permissão, franquia, terceirização e outras formas.* 4th ed. São Paulo: Atlas.

Dutra, H. (2018). Construção civil no Brasil: situação atual e projeções para 2018. https://www.sienge.com.br/blog/construcao-civil-no-brasil/.

Farias, A.B., Machado Jr., C., Silva, M.M., Messias, M. and Furlaneto, C.J. (2019). Reestruturação do Compliance em Construtora Envolvida em Escândalo de Corrupção. *Revista de Auditoria, Governança e Contabilidade*, 7(30), 31–46.

Gunhan, S. and Arditi, D. (2005). Factors affecting international construction. *Journal of Construction Engineering and Management*, 131, 273–282.

Hwang, B. and Lim, E.J. (2013). Critical success factors for key project players and objectives: Case study of Singapore. *Journal of Construction Engineering and Management,* 139(2), 204–215.

Jin, Z., Deng, F., Li, H. and Skitmore, M. (2013). Practical framework for measuring performance of international construction firms. *Journal of Construction Engineering and Management*, 1154–1167 ASCE, Setembro.

Justen Filho, M. (2003). As Diversas Configurações da Concessão de Serviço Público. Revista de Direito Público da Economia, Belo Horizonte, Editora Fórum, n.1, 95–136, Jan/Mar.

Liu, J.Y., Zou, P.X.W. and Gong, W. (2013). Managing project risk at the enterprise level: Exploratory case studies in China. *Journal of Construction Engineering and Management,* 139(9), 1268–1274.

Martinelli, M.A., Carolino, C.R., Silva, G.M., Ale, M.L. and Abaurre, M.W. (2017). Metodologia de Gestão de Programas e Empreendimentos (MGP): Desenvolvimento e Implantação. *Congresso ABES – FENASAN*. Anais... Sao Paulo, October 2 to 6, 2017.

MDIC (2010). Plano plurianual 2008–2011. Relatório de avaliação. Brasília: Ministério do Desenvolvimento, Indústria e Comércio Exterior, 2010.

Melhado, S.B. (2005). *Coordenação de projetos de edificações*. 1st ed. São Paulo: O Nome da Rosa.

Mognhol, T.Z. (2019). *Gestão de projetos em empreendimentos de infraestrutura: estudo comparativo de construtoras brasileiras e construtoras internacionais atuando no Brasil.* Dissertação de Mestrado, Escola Politécnica, Universidade de São Paulo, São Paulo.

Mutti, C.N., Bridi, P.E.H. and Miranda, A.M. (2018). *Tomada de decisão e estratégias para a internacionalização da construção*. Editora Secco, 1st edição.

Ofori, G. (2003). Frameworks for analysing international construction. *Construction Management Economics*, 21(4), 379–391.

Perez, M.A. (2006). O Risco no Contrato de Concessão de Serviço Público. Belo Horizonte, Editora Fórum.

Sabesp (2019). Companhia de Saneamento Básico do Estado de São Paulo. Edital da Concorrência SABESP CSS 00734/18 — Prestação de Serviços Técnicos Especializados de Apoio à Gestão e Governança de Programas e Empreendimentos da Sabesp.

Sabesp (n.d.). Companhia de Saneamento Básico do Estado de São Paulo. Perfil Institucional. http://site.sabesp.com.br/site/interna/Default.aspx?secaoId=505 [Accessed 16 August 2020].

Souza, F. Martinelli, M.A., Mendes, V., Brito, A.S., Varoli, J.J., Castro, M.V. and Leifert, S. (2011). Gerenciamento de programas com foco em benefícios — o desafio de novos horizontes. Artigo submetido ao Prêmio Mario Covas — Governo do Estado de São Paulo — Secretaria de Gestão Pública e da Fundação do Desenvolvimento Administrativo (Fundap).

Tang, W., Qiang, M., Duffield, C.F., Young, D.M. and Lu, Y. (2007). Risk management in the Chinese construction industry. *Journal of Construction Engineering and Management*, 133(12), 944–956.

Varoli, J.J., Mendes, V., Alves, L.O., Maia, S.R.D.A., Silva, A.A., Moguinho, F.A., Mingroni, R.T.P. and Tanikawa, Y. (2009). A Sabesp revoluciona a gestão de empreendimentos. Artigo vencedor do Prêmio Mario Covas — Governo do Estado de São Paulo — Secretaria de Gestão Pública e da Fundação do Desenvolvimento Administrativo (Fundap).

Verweij, S. (2015). Achieving satisfaction when implementing PPP transportation infrastructure projects: A qualitative comparative analysis of the A15 highway DBFM project. *International Journal of Project Management*, 33, 189–200.

https://doi.org/10.1142/9789811224720_0021

Chapter 21

Project Management in Developing Countries — A Case of Indian Construction Industry

Kumar Neeraj Jha*, Ajit Kumar Sinha[†],
Satish Kumar Viswanathan[‡], Santu Kar[§] and Sparsh Johari[§]

**Department of Civil Engineering,*
Indian Institute of Technology Delhi, Delhi 110016, India
[†]*Civil Construction Wing,*
All India Radio, New Delhi 110003, India
[‡]*Department of Atomic Energy, Anushakti Nagar,*
Mumbai, Maharashtra 400094, India
[§]*Department of Civil Engineering,*
Indian Institute of Technology Guwahati,
Guwahati, Assam 781039, India

Abstract

The projected size of the Indian construction industry by 2022 was around US$640 billion annually, mainly aided by government initiatives such as infrastructure projects and affordable housing schemes. In India, the construction industry is the second largest employment provider, with the participation of 16 percent of the country's working population. The construction industry in India is fragmented, with large-sized firms focusing across all the construction segments, medium-size firms being involved in niche activities, and mostly small firms operating as subcontractors. In comparison with the developed countries, the Indian construction industry is widely recognized as a labor-intensive industry, and the deployment of modern machineries and techniques is limited. Further, most of the Indian construction firms are reluctant to follow the relevant regulations fully. The above aspects play an influencing role in Indian construction firms' project management approach. The current chapter portrays an overview of the Indian construction industry. It covers the status of construction workers, status of Indian project performance, and the efforts made to improve them. In addition, the practices followed by the Indian construction industry in the key project knowledge areas such as project integration management, project scope management, project resource management, project communication management, project risk management, project procurement management, project stakeholder management, and leadership are also described.

Keywords: Project management, cost overrun, schedule overrun, worker's issues, disputes in construction, quality and safety in construction

Overview of Indian construction industry

The Indian construction industry is the second largest sector of the economy, next to agriculture, with a contribution of 8 percent to the country's GDP (GoI, 2020). This contribution is expected to be approximately 13 percent by 2025. India is expected to become the third-largest construction market in the world by 2025 (GoI, 2020). The construction industry is the key driver of socio-economic development in India. The gross value added (GVA) by the construction industry in India is estimated to be US$192 billion in 2019–2020 (GoI, 2020). The industry is expected to grow at an annual average of 6.6 percent between 2019 and 2028. Furthermore, an investment of US$4.5 trillion is required by 2040 to develop infrastructure in India.

The projected size of the Indian construction industry by 2022 was around $640 billion, mainly aided by government initiatives such as: "Smart City Mission," "Swachh Bharat Mission," "Atal Mission for Rejuvenation and Urban Transformation," "Pradhan Mantri Awas Yojana," and "Heritage City Development and Augmentation Yojana," and measures such as affordable housing schemes. The Government of India planned to construct 50 million houses by 2022 (GoI, 2020). Also, the size of the real estate market in India is estimated to be US$1 trillion by 2030 (India Services, 2020).

There has been a substantial increase in the Public–Private Partnership (PPP) projects penetration across the road, port, airport, power, and energy sectors in India. One of the major reasons for initiating the PPP mode of procurement in India was to bridge the gap between the investments required for infrastructure and the adequacy of what had been planned. An all-out effort is being made to ensure and attract private investments; this is more so because the "survival" of the investment is closely linked to the rate of return (RoR) on the investment made by the concessionaire.

The construction equipment industry is one of the emerging markets in India. Due to the increase in foreign investment, massive urban development, and huge government spending, it is expected that the size of the Indian construction equipment industry will cross US$4.7 billion by 2025 (Statista, 2021). The Indian construction equipment industry is classified into four segments — earthmoving, material handling, concrete mixing, and road construction equipment. The earthmoving equipment segment has the highest share in the Indian market. However, it is anticipated that the concrete mixing segment will have the fastest growth in the coming years. The growth of the equipment industry is expected to increase further owing to factors such as increasing size of the projects, requirement of completing the projects in a shorter time, and the increasing demand for customized equipment.

Employment opportunities and status of construction workers in India

Indian construction is labor intensive, and currently the share of employment in construction stands at about 16 percent of the country's working population. It is projected that the industry would employ over 67 million workers by 2022 (The Economy Survey, 2018) and is likely to be the largest employer. Construction workers are an important pillar of the Indian construction industry; however, their working conditions are a cause of concern. In general, they spend about 10–12 hours on work daily, in tough conditions. Even after a hard day of work, they are not looked after well in the places where they stay. Over 80 percent of the employment in construction constitutes a minimally skilled workforce, while the skilled workers account for around nine percent, and the remaining workers are distributed across work classes such as clerks, technicians, and professionals (Johari and Jha, 2020). Most of the workers are unskilled and have not undergone any training. Moreover, the workers migrate into the cities from the rural areas, and they participate in construction activities only during the non-harvesting seasons (Johari and Jha, 2020).

In general, the construction workers in India become associated with a construction site through a labor subcontractor. This is because most of the workers are illiterate and unaware of the job opportunities at the sites and therefore, a person who can bridge the gap between the job openings and the job seekers becomes a mediator, and is called a "labor subcontractor." The workers move with the subcontractor from one construction site to another and from one city to another as and when required by the construction companies. However, owing to such a system, the labor subcontractor becomes a master of the life of the workers. Decisions such as where the workers will stay, in what conditions, for how long they can work at one site, and when they can go back to their villages are generally taken by the labor subcontractor. Moreover, in most cases, the payment of the workers is also given by the client to the labor subcontractors, who then distributes the payments among the workers. In this process, the exact amount received by the workers is, more often than not, less than the minimum wage set by the government (FICCI and KPMG, 2014). Also, the wages are paid well after the scheduled date as provided for by the labor laws (Cotton *et al.*, 2005). Therefore, the living conditions of the Indian construction workers is so poor that they are deprived of even the basic elements of human dignity. The employment is casual and unregulated; the workers are employed on a fixed-term contract often provided by the subcontractors. Thus, the workers have neither social security protection nor the motivation to join the unions due to their short-term jobs and the fear of losing their jobs.

Generally, the rural to urban and inter-state migration of construction workers takes place for want of regular employment. According to Dhal (2020), migrants from rural areas have more earnings than they would have in rural areas, but their wages are lower than those of urban workers, and this gap is widening over time. Generally, these daily wage and migrant workers assemble early every morning at some select "pockets" (places) in cities, and make themselves available for work until noon before returning home if they do not get any work for the day. These pockets are known as "Labor Stands" or "Labor Chowks," and have an informal labor assembly varying from 50 to even 1,000 construction workers per day, without any regulation or coordination, and they provide a recruitment channel for hiring construction workers for the short term.

Governments and trade unions attempt to safeguard the welfare of workers; the government has formulated various laws to protect the interests and welfare of construction workers such as the Building and Other Construction Workers (Regulation of Employment and Conditions of Services) Act, 1996 (BOCWA) and Building and Other Construction Workers Welfare Cess Act, 1996. As per the Act, 1 percent of the cost of construction is collected towards the labor cess. The government launched various welfare schemes for construction workers, such as accident benefits, dependant benefits in the case of death, medical benefits including protection from critical illness, provision of meals, a stipend for training, maternity benefit, scholarships for children's education, and monetary support for the marriage of girl children of the construction workers. However, only registered workers are eligible for the benefits from the government, and most of the workers are not aware of such benefits. It is estimated that registered ration and beneficiary workers currently form about 12 percent of construction workers nationwide (Dhal, 2020).

The background information above has presented the role of the construction industry in the Indian economy, the opportunities available, and also the status of construction workers. The next sections describe the performance of the construction industry in terms of project cost, schedule, quality, safety, and disputes.

Performance of Indian construction industry

Cost performance

Cost is a primary measure of the success of a project. Unrealistic cost estimates and unexpected expenditure can change an otherwise successful capital investment into an investment failure. In construction projects, cost overrun is defined as the actual cost over budget and is also sometimes referred to as rising costs, increased costs, or budget overrun (Lee, 2008).

Data from the Ministry of Statistics and Programme Implementation (MoSPI) (2019) reveal that, as of December 2019, the total original cost of 1,701 central sector infrastructure projects (with a value of INR1,500 million and above) was INR20,657 billion, and their anticipated completion cost was likely to be about INR24,720 billion, which reflects an overall cost overrun of 19.66 percent of the original cost. Among all the sectors, water resource projects are facing the highest cost overrun (166.36 percent) followed by telecommunication projects (69.82 percent). The railways sector also shows a cost overrun of 69.82 percent, followed by shipping and ports (27.84 percent), highways (2.92 percent), and civil aviation (1.47 percent).

According to a report by the Project Management Institute (PMI) and KPMG (2019), the top 10 factors that have an impact on the cost performance of the central sector projects are: suboptimal detailed project report (DPR); scope creep; material price escalations beyond projections; poor selection of consultant; inadequate baseline/lack of planning; high cost of land acquisition; design changes and iterations; escalation in labor costs; ineffective utilization of labor; and inadequate availability of skilled workers.

The factors adversely affecting the cost performance of the Indian construction projects are: conflict among project participants, ignorance and lack of knowledge, presence of poor project-specific attributes and non-existence of cooperation, hostile socio-economic and climatic conditions, reluctance in making timely decisions, aggressive competition at tender stage, and short bid preparation time (Iyer and Jha, 2005). Likewise, a study by Tabish and Jha (2011) seeking to identify the success factors of Indian public-sector construction projects showed that the most significant factors influencing the cost overrun in Indian public projects are: political and social interference, lack of trust among project participants, lack of understanding of project scope, and poor pre-tender site investigation.

Many projects that reported cost overrun either directly or indirectly blame it on the lack of time for preparing their estimates. It is found that many Indian construction companies do not have a mechanism of forecasting realistic cost estimates (Vibhakar *et al.*, 2020). This is mainly due to the absence of standard cost norms and indices. Although some agencies such as the Office of Economic Advisor (OEA), Central Public Works Department (CPWD), and Construction Industry Development Corporation (CIDC) publish construction cost indices, these are mostly followed only on government projects. Most importantly, there is a common perception that these indices do not exactly reflect the market conditions.

The basis of estimating the cost of each item requires understanding of finance, market options, and the new technologies available. These aspects are absent in the Indian construction sector. The estimation of cost also requires careful evaluation by project managers and better coordination with various stakeholders (Meredith *et al.*, 2017).

Schedule performance

Project schedule management is a process of scheduling, monitoring, and controlling the activities of a project. Effective schedule management is essential for the timely completion of a construction project. The MoSPI (2019) report presented the status of 1,701 central sector infrastructure projects in India with a project cost of INR1,500 million and above. It showed that, of the 1,701 projects, 583 projects (34.27 percent) are delayed from their original schedules. Of these 583 delayed projects, 183 are delayed by one to 12 months, 129 projects are delayed by 13 to 24 months, 146 projects are delayed by 25 to 60 months, and 125 projects are delayed by 61 months and more. The average delay in these projects is 39.04 months. The details of sector-wise delayed projects are provided in Table 21.1.

Table 21.1 shows that all the atomic energy and heavy industry projects are facing huge schedule delays. The time overruns with respect to

Table 21.1: Schedule status of central sector infrastructure projects.

S. No.	Sector	Total projects	Delayed projects	Percentage of projects delayed (%)
1	Road transport and highways	867	217	25.03
2	Railways	312	151	48.39
3	Petroleum	151	54	35.76
4	Coal	107	39	36.45
5	Urban development	74	31	41.89
6	Power	70	52	74.28
7	Water resources	51	5	9.80
8	Health and family welfare	23	11	47.83
9	Civil aviation	13	5	38.46
10	Steel	9	8	88.89
11	Fertilizers	5	0	0
12	Mines	5	2	40
13	Atomic energy	4	4	100
14	Telecommunication	4	2	50
15	Heavy industry	1	1	100
16	Shipping and ports	1	0	0
17	Human resource department	4	1	25

Source: MoSPI (2019).

the original schedule of the projects in atomic energy are in the range of 36 to 133 months, whereas it is 6 months for the heavy industry projects. The sectors where there are schedule delays on more than 50 percent of the projects include the steel and power sectors; the steel sector has a time overrun of 16 to 62 months, and the power sector has a time overrun of one to 147 months. However, projects in the fertilizers and shipping and ports sectors are not facing any major schedule delay.

According to the joint report by PMI and KPMG (2019), in the pre-execution phase, delays in land acquisition and site handover and delays in regulatory approvals from several agencies are the primary reasons for the schedule delay in central sector projects. In the execution and closing phase, the primary reasons for the schedule delay are: inaccurate estimation of time of completion; project design and scope changes; lack of availability of resources such as project management professionals, skilled workers, good equipment suppliers, and contractors; inefficient contract management; ineffective project monitoring; coordination issues with project team or vendors; lack of awareness and application of modern scheduling tools and technologies; and payment delays.

In the case of private-sector projects, the commitment of the project participants and owner's competence are the success factors, and conflict among project participants are the failure factors for the schedule performance (Iyer and Jha 2006). Delegating authority to the project manager and down to other team members can enhance the team commitment, leading to improved schedule performance. Iyer and Jha (2006) suggested that taking timely decisions and regular monitoring of the project can improve the project's schedule performance.

Quality performance

Project quality management comprises quality control and quality assurance, which go hand in hand. To ensure success, the project leadership should ensure that all regulations, and provisions in relevant codes are unambiguously specified, and this has to be followed by strict enforcement and implementation which can only be ensured when a proper monitoring mechanism is in place.

In comparison to the other industries, the construction industry is always criticized for its poor performance, productivity, and quality. Construction is constantly under scrutiny for its quality. In India, the *cost of quality* (the amount of money spent in order to conform to the quality of construction work) is huge. Globally, it is estimated that about 6 to 15 percent of construction cost is wasted due to rework, and about 55 percent of the rework is due to inefficiency of workers and poor supervision, while 12 percent is due to material and system failures (Boukamp and Akinci, 2004). In India, these percentages could be even higher (Johari and Jha, 2020). Hence, it is imperative for the Indian construction industry to deploy an efficient and effective quality management system.

In many projects in India, project quality management plans (QMP) are prepared by the executing agencies. Thus, the quality of the end product is dependent on the executing agencies. Typically, a QMP includes material/vendor approval status, the status of approval of documents, details of testing activities in the project, and audit report. In some cases, clients/owners' organizations use outsourcing for ensuring quality by conducting the necessary tests for the materials used on the projects. In such cases, private parties are engaged to conduct the tests. However, clients/owners' organizations rarely have a standard template of the QMP; thus, there is a lack of uniformity and consistency in this document across the projects leading to poor quality of works in the projects in India (Hussain *et al.*, 2018).

Safety performance of construction projects in India

There are no readily available and reliable statistics on the number of people who are injured and killed in the construction industry. The present authors believe that the numbers presented in various reports are highly underreported. Even on large and prestigious projects, such as the construction of the Delhi Metro and Delhi International Airport, involving the extensive use of sophisticated equipment, advanced techniques of construction, and good subcontractors and workers, a large number of fatalities and major injuries have occurred. The problem of underreporting was also highlighted by Hamalainen *et al.* (2006) while carrying out a study on global estimates of occupational accidents for the International Labour Office (ILO). To estimate the fatalities in Indian construction, the study used information from Kazakhstan and Malaysia to formulate accident rates for India.

A study by Patel and Jha (2016) aimed to estimate the number of fatal accidents in the Indian construction sector. The study estimated the number of fatal accidents on construction projects in the National Capital Territory Delhi region, which was considered as a baseline (it covers 1483 square kilometers and has a population of about 16.78 million). The estimates were based on some reliable sources, which were later extrapolated to estimate the fatality at the national level based on a number of parameters: working population, accident rate, and cement consumption. In the extrapolation, it is assumed that the number of fatal accidents is proportional to the number of construction workers and cement consumption in a given state. The figures on the number of construction workers and the cement consumption, respectively, were obtained from records of the Census of India and Cement Manufacturers Association. Based on these figures, a minimum and maximum number of fatal accidents were worked out for all states and these were summed up as the estimate for the country.

According to the study, in the Indian construction industry, the number of people dying in construction could be anywhere from 11,614 to 22,080 annually. Even if the lower estimate is considered, this translates into a fatality rate (fatal accidents per 1,000 workers) of 0.22 in Indian construction, which is relatively higher when compared to the fatality rates of the developed countries. The estimate shows that there is a need for stakeholders to intervene to improve the situation and to make workplaces safe, and thus save lives.

Disputes

According to the World Bank's *Ease of Doing Business* report 2020, India was ranked 63rd among 190 countries, and it has registered an improvement of 23 places from the previous year (2019). However, when it comes to enforcing of contracts, India is ranked in 163rd position. As reported by the Ministry of Law and Justice, as in February 2020, there are about 36.5 million cases pending across various courts of India, of which 62,054 cases are pending in the Supreme Court, and 5.15 million cases in various High Courts. At the district and subordinate court levels, the number of pending cases stands at 34 million. In India, on an average, it takes around 1,420 days for a contract dispute to get resolved. This delay adds to the significant and incessant rise in the number of outstanding cases. The considerable delay in the dispute resolution mechanism leads to the frustration among the parties involved.

In India, the majority of the construction projects are carried out through contracts, and until recently, most of the public projects followed the standard contract conditions formulated by the CPWD and the Military Engineering Services (MES). The International Federation of Consulting Engineers (FIDIC) contract system is followed only when external funding sources such as the World Bank and Asian Development Bank are involved. As a developing nation, India is also going through a phase of infrastructure expansion due to globalization. With the increasing size and complexity of projects, the conditions of the contracts also tend to become more complicated, which in turn adds to the number of disputes and further delay in the settlement of disputes (Iyer *et al.*, 2008). Thus, it is vital to address the country's dispute management system in order to create a positive image among domestic and foreign players.

A study by Viswanathan *et al.* (2020) established that, in the Indian context, flawed or erroneous contract documents is the main factor causing disputes, followed by opportunistic behavior and unrealistic client expectations, and these factors merit attention to reduce construction claims and disputes, and delayed response to decisions. Based on the case studies in India, Iyer *et al.* (2008) identified the following critical clauses which lead to disputes in construction contracts in the order of criticality: final and binding power; time delay and extension; termination of contract; pricing of deviation and extra items by owner representatives; deviation limit/scope of work; and price escalation.

The preceding paragraphs have described the status of the Indian construction industry on the basis of various performance criteria such as cost, schedule, quality, safety, and disputes. It was observed that the performance on these criteria was not encouraging and a number of reasons account for this state of affairs. To address these issues and thus to improve the performance on projects, a number of improvements and initiatives have been implemented by various stakeholders. These are described in the following section.

Initiatives adopted to improve the performance in Indian construction industry

Cost and schedule

PMI and KPMG (2019) made some recommendations for improving project management in India, which include: (1) pre-planning and site readiness before mobilizing construction; (2) collaborative and agile planning; (3) reforming public procurement and contract management; (4) strengthening stakeholder management for land and regulatory issues; (5) improving governance, processes, and people capabilities; (6) implementing lean construction principles to realize productivity improvement; (7) embedding a culture of risk management; and (8) augmenting organizational skillsets. The report suggested that: a single window clearance mechanism be set up to simplify the regulatory approval process; an efficient transport and logistics system be set up to enable faster project implementation; and that PPP be promoted in infrastructure projects.

The milestones of various infrastructure projects in India are monitored using the Online Computerized Monitoring System (OCMS). The Government of India has launched the Pro-active Governance and Timely Implementation (PRAGATI) system, a unique information and communications technology (ICT) based multi-purpose, multi-modal interactive platform, to monitor and review important programs and projects of the central government as well those of the state governments (Zargar and Sheikh, 2018). The system facilitates real-time exchange of information among the key stakeholders and enables decision-making in projects to be expedited. Besides, eSuvidha-Project Management System (ePMS) has been developed by the government for fast-tracking the approvals for setting up and commissioning of public, private, and PPP projects. To digitize the land acquisition process, a web portal, Bhooomi Rashi, has been developed by the Ministry of Road Transport and Highway (MoRTH) with the help of the National Informatics Centre (PMI and KPMG, 2019). The measures which have been taken to improve the land acquisition process are discussed below.

Quality

In recent years, to improve the quality standards, India has enacted new policies and amended old and outdated regulations. For example, a new Act of Parliament established a Real Estate Regulatory Authority (RERA), which makes a contractor liable to pay for poor quality and workmanship of the construction project for the next five years following its commissioning. In addition, the National Building Code provides guidelines and the philosophy to accomplish the construction work from its inception to completion (planning, designing, construction, operation, and maintenance phases). As far as bid selection is concerned, all the public projects follow Quality and Cost Based Selection (QCBS).

Of late, the relatively newer nodal agencies responsible for construction and maintenance of greenfield and brownfield highway projects, such as the National Highway Authority of India (NHAI) and schemes dealing with the development of highway projects in the North-Eastern region of the country, and areas within the still under-developed regions, do have the latest wherewithal for quality standards and their enforcement. Related provisions in the concession agreement have been stipulated with provisions for penalty and/or incentives.

Thus, in India, the problem is not lack of regulatory standards, but the challenge is getting contractors and other businesses to understand, and comply with, the regulations. Therefore, India needs a system that can address the issues such as lack of technical expertise, slow pace of mechanization and technological upgrading, lack of training and skills, limited financial capabilities, and absence of quality certificates (Sinha and Jha, 2020).

Some of the leading organizations are implementing measures to address the quality-related issues in construction such as:

- Developing and maintaining a standard template of the quality management plan and ensuring its implementation
- Establishing a dedicated "Quality Cell" to improve the quality assurance system
- Testing of materials in approved test laboratories
- Ensuring an adequate number of tests following the codal provisions
- Analyzing test results and taking corrective measures if required.

Moreover, in recent years, the Government of India has undertaken various mega projects. Such large projects help in unlocking the vast resource of wealth, increase productivity, open up new markets for trade by attracting foreign investment, and improve the quality of life of millions. In a long run, mega projects will help in transforming India from underdeveloped to developed country category (Nyarirangwe and Babatunde, 2019). The mega projects deliver benefits far beyond the physical assets that are being built. Some of these advantages are optimum use of natural resources, increase of productivity, opening up of new markets for trade and commerce, improvement of the construction quality, creation of better infrastructure, and enhancement in the efficiency of the government.

Disputes

In order to improve the dispute resolution mechanism, the Indian Cabinet has recently approved an ordinance to amend the Commercial Courts, Commercial Division, and Commercial Appellate Division of High Courts Act. In a major step toward changing the dispute resolution mechanism in infrastructure projects in India, the government amended the Arbitration and Conciliation Act, 1996 by introducing the Arbitration and Conciliation (Amendment) Ordinance in 2015. This has brought in various amendments to expedite hearing as well as disposal of arbitration proceedings in a time-bound manner, along with others. The amendments of the Act of 1996 will facilitate achieving the goal of improving institutional arbitration by establishing an independent body to lay down standards, make the arbitration process more user-friendly and cost- and time-effective. Furthermore, KPMG (2019) recommends the following measures to improve the contract and claims management regime in India:

- Fast track the setting up of the proposed "Arbitration Council of India"
- Encourage mediation, conciliation, and arbitration to avoid litigation
- Incubate a pool of subject matter experts for arbitration
- Build up contract management capacity and continuously monitor contracts
- Build contingency and flexibility in contracts for various scenarios.

Safety

Based on the recommendation of the Second National Commission on Labor (2002), the central government has formulated the Occupational Safety, Health and Working Conditions (OSHWC) Act 2019. It is the amalgamation, simplification, and rationalization of the relevant provisions of a number of old labor laws related to industrial relations, wages, social security, safety and welfare, and working conditions. After its enactment, all these Acts being subsumed in it are repealed. The Act stipulates the safety measures to be taken at the construction site and responsibilities of various stakeholders; frames model rules for safety measures and emergency action plans; and outlines safety requirements of various construction elements. It is hoped that with the implementation of these laws, the safety and welfare of workers will be improved substantially.

The Directorate General, Factory Advice and Labour Institutes (DGFASLI) has been providing technical support over the years in drafting Central Rules/Model Rules; carrying out studies, surveys and safety audits; and conducting training programs, workshops, and seminars in this sectors for more than three decades (DGFASLI, 2020). Various new initiatives by the DGFASLI are:

- Expanding the Occupational Safety and Health (OSH) network in the Indian subcontinent
- International cooperation in capacity building
- Establishment and administration of the occupational disease awareness center
- Establishment of the Occupational Health Training Research and Development Centre
- Development of an OSH Profile in India.

The National Safety Council (NSC), set up by the Government of India under the Ministry of Labour, plays a major role in implementing safety, health, and environment (SHE) measures at the national level. Its activities include conducting specialized safety training programs, seminars, conferences, and workshops; providing services such as safety audits, risk assessment, material promotions; and preparing publications in the area of SHE (Saha, 2018). In India, March 4 of every year is celebrated as the National Safety Day; various campaigns are organized in the promotion of SHE across the country.

Training system for construction workers in India

Training is not a very old concept in India. During the Second World War, when there was a need to repair equipment and machinery, a big demand for a skilled workforce prevailed in the country, and this was met by the setting up of the independent body, the Directorate General of Resettlement and Employment (DGR&T). The DGR&T was established in 1945 under the Ministry of Labour and Employment (MoLE). The responsibilities of the Directorate General of Employment and Training (as the earlier DGR&T became) are: to create job opportunities, provide training facilities and services to the civilians, and to fill the gap between industrial demand and human resource development in the country.

In 2008, a new training system, the Skill Development Initiative Scheme (SDIS), was developed. Under SDIS, training is imparted in more than 90 trades in the construction sector (Johari and Jha, 2020). Another aspect of the scheme is that, for the first time, all the trade disciplines, from the helper category to the top management level in the construction industry, are taken into consideration for imparting training. Advantages such as the availability of career progression paths, higher stipend during training, and increased industry involvement are also associated with this scheme.

The SDIS was implemented through the National Skill Development Corporation (NSDC), which was formed in 2008 on the basis of the PPP model. This was done in order to raise the participation of private partners in the training system (Agrawal and Agrawal, 2017). Under the jurisdiction of NSDC, 38 sector skill councils (SSCs) have been created in India, of which the Construction Skill Development Council (CSDC) is one. In SDIS, training is imparted under the supervision of qualified trainers, at specific training centers accredited by the NSDC. The training is provided in a classroom without a practical component in actual working conditions. However, the curriculum, training material, and infrastructure for training are developed on the basis of the National Occupational Standards (NOS) which have been prepared by the CSDC.

Land acquisition and management

A major proportion of the Indian population is primarily dependent on agriculture for their sustenance. The general populace in India has a very low education level and thus, they are unable to participate in the benefits of industrial development (Chakraborty *et al.* 2018). It is here that relevant and modern techniques and methods are adopted for managing the land acquisition. The process usually does not involve taking the concerned landowners into proper confidence and thus, in general, an impression is created that the government is out to deprive them of their only asset. Indeed, many nations still resort to the principle of "eminent domain," which amounts to acquisition of private land almost forcibly (Gogoi, 2018).

However, with the passage of time, India has amended its rules to make the process of land acquisition more friendly, oriented toward the welfare of the population, and flexible. Thus, the rate of industrial development is likely to be more rapid in future. The central government has tried to bridge the trust deficit between the authorities responsible for land acquisition and the landowners. Normally, the cost of the land area contiguous to the land acquired for any project increases phenomenally once the project is initiated (Sinha and Jha, 2020). As a result, the landowners who have already sold or lost their land by way of acquisition for the project have a negative feeling of having been cheated. Therefore, it is felt that the upside of the appreciation in cost of the land, once the project gets underway, should also be shared with those who are displaced.

The promulgation of The Right to Fair Compensation and Transparency in Land Acquisition, Rehabilitation and Resettlement Act (RFCTLARR) 2013 (which took effect from April 1, 2014) is an enabler to smoothen the land acquisition process. Until it came into force, the land acquisition process was governed by the Land Acquisition Act 1894, and the issue of rehabilitation and resettlement was dealt with under a separate Government of India statute. However, under the RFCTLARR 2013, both the processes of land acquisition and the issues related to rehabilitation and resettlement have been integrated. Further, for the first time, the secondary beneficiaries such as the sharecroppers, the agricultural laborers who do not own land but are dependent on it for their survival, have also been covered under the new Act.

The new Act provides for the consent of 80 percent of the families before the land is acquired. There is also an opinion that the compensation should be completely at par with the market rates. In addition, there have been attempts to incorporate certain other relaxation provisions in the amendments to the law. However, Singh (2016) noted that there are some loopholes in the RFCTLARR 2013 Act, such as difference between the farmer's value of the land and the exchange value, and a lower proposed rate of compensation compared to the market value.

Project management practices in Indian construction industry

This section illustrates the key project management practices in the Indian construction industry. These include integration management, scope management, resource management, communication management, risk management, procurement management, stakeholder management, and leadership.

Project integration management

The success of a construction project depends on various facets of project management. Amongst those, project integration management plays a vital role by integrating processes and people in a construction project (Demirkesen and Ozorhon, 2017). Appropriate project coordination is key in integration management.

The construction project environment is not the same as those of other industries, particularly because work is fragmented among various participants and different sub-processes. The construction industry in India is fragmented, with large-sized firms working in all the construction segments, medium-sized firms in niche activities, and mostly small firms operating as subcontractors. The Indian construction industry comprises more than 200 firms in the corporate sector and there are about 120,000 "Class A" contractors registered with various government construction organizations. In addition, there are thousands of small contractors, which compete for small jobs, or work as subcontractors to prime contractors.

As noted earlier, a large number of central sector infrastructure projects are delayed with respect to their original schedules. One of the major reasons for this is the lack of project integration management, coordination, and monitoring, which often results in claims and disputes. In addition, the feedback mechanism and actions to remove bottlenecks are lacking in the Indian construction industry.

Studies show that "staff integration" is a foremost necessity in achieving project success in India (Thanki and Thakkar, 2018). In addition, "process integration," "supply chain integration," and "knowledge integration" are essential elements in project integration. Project integration can be achieved by coordination activities among project stakeholders (Demirkesen and Ozorhon, 2017). According to Iyer and Jha (2006), six activities are important in influencing the coordination rating of a construction project. These activities are: (1) preparation of a project quality plan in line with the contract specification; (2) arranging remedial work methods and programs for executing in case of defects or damage; (3) estimation of the optimum resource requirements; (4) development of a team spirit and receiving of constructive inputs from all participants in the project; (5) arrangement of required inputs such as drawings, specifications and technical details on time for execution; and (6) agreement on detailed methods of construction with all the parties.

Project scope management

Pre-project planning, including proper scope management in construction projects, plays an important role in achieving project success, and it can result in up to 20 percent cost savings and 39 percent schedule savings (Cho and Jr, 2001). Scope management is an integration of the sub-processes of scope definition, scope pricing, and scope control. Research has found that one of the notable reasons for poor management of scope is the presence of various uncertainties in construction projects (Subramanyan *et al.*, 2012). In construction projects, among the main causes of poor scope management are: lack of appreciation of roles among project participants, poorly defined responsibilities, and unequal bargaining among players.

According to KPMG (2019), for large capital construction projects in India, poorly defined project scope is the top cause of time overruns, and the second leading cause for cost overruns. In India, contracts are often one-sided and favor the owner. Thus, the risks and responsibilities mainly rest on the contractors and their bargaining power is much less. In addition, the involvement of representatives from the contractor and other vendors during the pre-project planning stage is limited, and opportunity is rarely provided to them to give their inputs during the planning phase. It is vital to understand the complete project scope to prepare feasibility reports and detailed project reports and subsequently, to meet the project success criteria.

Project resource management

To realize competitiveness and profitability, resource management is one of the most essential sets of activities in today's construction industry. Resources, such as human resource, finance, material, and equipment should be utilized in the most effective and efficient way. It is important to apply different management practices and principles to reduce the cost of resources under the constraint of optimum utilization of the available funds. Although resource management is one of the widely researched areas, its application in the construction industry has not been given adequate attention (Doloi *et al.*, 2012). In India, there is considerable scope for resource management. A massive workforce is employed in the Indian construction industry, and the demand for labor is increasing year by year.

In the case of materials, considering cement and steel production, India has an annual installed capacity of 510 million tons of cement and 138 million tons of steel. However, in 2019, India produced only 338 million tons of cement and 111.245 million tons of steel (IBEF, 2019; MOS, 2019). This is mainly because of insufficient funds, low quality of raw materials, and non-availability of skilled workers. Therefore, resource management becomes an important field of study to not only meet the current shortages of the resources in the industry but also to help in achieving the futuristic goals.

It was pointed out earlier that India would require an investment of US$640 billion in infrastructure by 2022 to enable sustainable utilization of its resources. In addition, the Indian construction industry is investing in the development of new technologies and techniques, such as Building Information Modelling (BIM), unmanned aerial vehicles, 3D printing, smart materials, advanced use of Geographical Positioning Systems (GPS), Artificial Intelligence (AI), and robotics. India possesses a rich demographic dividend, and thus, the requirements of the construction industry can be addressed comprehensively. Also, India has a rich pool of natural resources. Therefore, India can not only harness this advantage for its construction industry but can also take the lead in the supply of resources globally. However, in doing so, the Indian construction industry needs to develop, manage, and utilize its resources in such a way that the current requirements can be fulfilled along with the achievement of planned future business objectives.

Project communications management

The construction industry is complex and multi-dimensional, consisting of several stakeholders such as clients, contractors, engineers, architects, and site workers as well as suppliers. As they all work in a team, they require a collective, efficient, and effective communication. The Indian construction industry has adopted few of the advanced ICTs to improve the effectiveness of its communication. Technologies and software such as Electronic Document Management System, Enterprise Resource Planning, and E-commerce have been used in the Indian construction industry in the recent past. These new advanced technologies help the industry to improve record keeping, to make quick decisions, and to increase accountability, besides being less expensive and providing rapid and accurate communication. In India, BIM is still evolving. Concepts such as 5D BIM are being developed to integrate the schedule and cost with the 3D BIM of the project. Also, after the outbreak of the COVID-19 pandemic in India, it has been observed that the organizations relying on BIM have survived despite the impact of the pandemic (Ramya, 2020). This further gives a boost to the application of BIM in the Indian construction industry. However, the Indian construction industry is still far behind compared to other industries in the extensive utilization of ICT tools and techniques and ICT adoption has been slow in the industry (Ahuja *et al.*, 2009). The use of paper for engineering drawings, in-person meetings at site offices, and use of hard copy formats for issuing of materials and equipment are still the most common practices at Indian construction sites.

It is a paradoxical situation for India that while it has one of the most productive and advanced IT sectors in the world, this has had little influence in transforming the Indian construction industry (Dixit *et al.*, 2021). This is mainly because most of the work in India is executed by small and proprietary players. These small and medium enterprises (SMEs) do not have sufficient capital to invest in new and advanced, but relatively expensive information technologies (Kotturu and Mahanty, 2017). Moreover, lack of skilled staff, low awareness of information technologies, availability of cheap labor, and few quality checks further restrain these SMEs from using new and advanced information technologies in construction. Hence, it can be argued that the new technologies available in India, although less advanced in comparison to those in the developed world, are vested only with big contractors. Most of the SMEs, which constitute more than 95 percent of the total number of contractors in India, are still using the conventional tools for communication (Kotturu and Mahanty, 2017). Thus, there is a challenge to the Indian construction industry to make ICT tools more affordable and accessible for the Indian SMEs.

Another issue with the Indian construction industry is the lack of research and development (R&D) in the field of ICT. The use of advanced ICT technologies such as mixed reality, virtual reality, and augmented reality are still a distant dream for the Indian construction industry. One of the primary reasons is the lack of capital to invest. Less research implies not only less development of new technologies but also slow indigenization of already developed technologies. This is the primary reason why the Indian construction industry is not able to adopt the latest and advanced ICT techniques. Thus, there is a need to develop a robust and efficient R&D system in India.

Project risk management

Risk management is defined as a systematic controlling procedure for the predicted risk to be faced in an investment or a project (Xia *et al.*, 2018). The construction industry entails several risks. Throughout the project, construction companies may encounter a number of unforeseen events and risks. According to KPMG (2019), most of the Indian construction companies do not have a documented risk management process. Particularly, there is no formal system of risk planning, mitigation, and monitoring in place at the project or enterprise level. Thus, it is important to devise a risk management framework, considering internal/external risks at enterprise, project, and operations levels. Further, it is essential to identify the risks and transfer these risks to the suitable parties who can handle those risks.

The risk factors in Indian construction can be broadly categorized into: owner-specific, contractor-specific, consultant-specific, project-specific, project manager-specific, finance-specific, resource-specific risks, external environment-specific, and contract-clause-specific factors, as listed in Table 21.2.

The risks faced by Indian firms in the international construction market are broadly classified into four groups: (1) project-specific risk factors, (2) firm-specific risk factors, (3) market- and economy-specific risk factors, and (4) politically specific risk factors (Viswanathan, 2019). Among these factors, the project-specific risk factor has the most significant linear relationship with all the performance criteria, such as cost, schedule, firm, and overall project performance. As the international construction sector is project-based, the unmitigated project-specific risks are the primary causes of poor project performance. Thus, especially for firms from an emerging country like India, it is essential to deploy an efficient project management team in international construction projects.

Table 21.2: Risks in Indian construction industry.

Risk category	Risk description
Project-specific risk	Size of the project; Location uniqueness; Regulatory approvals; Type of project; Intense competition at tender stage; Tender selection methodology; Deviation of scope; Original contract duration is rigid; No clear definition of completion of work; Delay penalties; Legal disputes and lawsuits; Flow of finance; Insurance strategy; Exposure to accidents; Information management; Unanticipated impacts.
Owner-specific risk	Inadequate definition of project scope; Delay in handing over the site; Chances of facing financial crisis; Delay in revising and approving design documents by owner; Delay in payments by owner; Sudden termination of work by owner; Unreasonably high expectations of owner; Lack of vision/inability in identifying critical activities; Holding key decisions in abeyance; Changes made by owner during construction; Owner's lack of exposure to changing trends in industry.

(Continued)

Table 21.2: (*Continued*)

Risk category	Risk description
Contractor-specific risk	Delay in mobilization; Poor site management and supervision by contractor; Improper construction methods; Delays in subcontractors' work; Frequent change of subcontractors; Poor qualification/experience of the contractor; Holding key decisions in abeyance; Ignorance of impact of contract clauses; Chances of facing financial crisis.
Architect/consultant-specific risks	Insufficient data collection and survey before design; Inadequate experience of consultant with regard to type of project; Delay in performing inspection and testing by consultant; Inflexibility of consultant; Complex/non-executable design; Unclear and inadequate details in drawings; Chances of consultant leaving the project midway; Non-use of advanced engineering design software.
Project-manager-specific risk factors	Project manager's technical capability; Use of appropriate planning tools and techniques by project manager; Holding key decisions in abeyance; Lack of induction and training of human resources; Negative attitude of project manager; Lack of coordinating ability and rapport of project manager with other contractors at site; Reluctance of top management to maintain target schedule; Lack of leadership quality of project manager; Chances of project manager leaving the project; Tools and techniques.
Resource-specific risk	Selection of materials and equipment; Delay in materials delivery; Changes in material types and specifications during construction; Unrealistic variation in prices of materials; Improper selection of equipment; Equipment breakdowns; Shortage of equipment; Quality variations; Shortage of labor; Unqualified workforce; Poor inventory management.
External-environment specific risk	Unfavorable social environment; Unfavorable economic/market fluctuations; Unfavorable political environment; Changing government policies; Labor strikes; Natural calamities; Sudden unforeseen events.
Finance-specific risk	Financial policies; Liquidity; Cost of capital; Market risk; Credit risk; Operational risk; Profitability risk; Contingency risk.
Contract-clause-specific risk	Differing site conditions clause; Delay damages clause; Extension of time clause; Forfeiture of security deposit clause; Termination of contract clause; Responsibility for design clause; Defect liability period clause; Dispute resolution clause; Price escalation clause; Ambiguities in defining certain clauses.

Source: Viswanathan *et al.* (2020).

As a part of the study by Viswanathan (2019), where the researchers did the modelling to identify the causes of disputes in Indian construction projects, a number of case studies were undertaken on the leading Indian construction firms, such as Rail India Technical and Economic Service (RITES), Indian Railway Construction Company (IRCON), Larsen and Toubro (L&T), AFCONS, Shapoorji and Pallonji, Punj Lloyd, Engineers Projects (India) Limited (EPL), Engineers India Limited (EIL), and Tata Projects, that have a strong presence in many countries and segments of the international market. These case studies were undertaken to examine the strategies adopted by these companies to overcome the risks in the international market. Some of the strategies are: allocating contingencies; joint venturing; local participation; and entering into strategic alliances with international partners.

Project procurement management

Procurement management is an essential element of project management, which involves procurement of materials, equipment, and services in a construction project. Typically, materials and equipment account for 50–60 percent of the total project cost in a construction project (Caldas *et al.*, 2015). Therefore, effective procurement management is the key to the success of construction projects.

From the site visits and interviews conducted by Kar and Jha (2020) to examine the effect of material management issues on the schedule and cost performance of Indian construction projects, it was found that organizations in India adopt various functions in procurement management such as material planning; procurement; transportation and logistics; receiving, warehousing, and issuing; and material control.

In India, large companies carry out procurement management functions using a computer-based system, such as enterprise resource planning (ERP) and systems application products (SAP). However, often, the computer-based system does not integrate the construction schedule with procurement management. Furthermore, the system does not provide the inventory status of the materials and does not facilitate suppliers' performance evaluations. Sharing of information with suppliers and involvement of suppliers in the project front-end planning is rarely observed in the Indian construction industry. Moreover, contractors and owners in India usually do not enter into long-term agreements with suppliers. They attribute this to the temporary nature and uniqueness of each construction project. However, for the procurement of certain materials that are required for most construction projects, such as steel and cement, organizations enter into long-term agreements with trusted suppliers.

A study by Kar and Jha (2020) reveals the level of implementation of different best practices in procurement in the Indian construction industry; these are presented in Table 21.3. The table shows that many best practices

Table 21.3: Level of implementation of different best practices in procurement.

S N	Best practices in procurement	Level of implementation
1	Forming procurement team for the project	High
2	Involving material procurement team in the project front-end planning	Moderate
3	Identifying long lead materials	High
4	Preparing procurement plan for materials	High
5	Preparing delivery schedule for materials	High
6	Having suppliers' database system	High
7	Having multiple projects procurement database	Moderate
8	Developing long-term partnership with suppliers	High
9	Using reverse auctions for procurement of material	Moderate
10	Having a mature import/export compliance system	Moderate
11	Outsourcing to implement some material management functions	Low
12	Having systematic inspection process for procurement of material	High
13	Implementing agreements with transportation carriers	Moderate
14	Using on-site material tracking technologies (such as barcode, RFID, etc.)	Moderate
15	Levying liquidated damages on late deliveries of materials	Moderate
16	Giving incentives for early deliveries of materials	Low

Table 21.3: (*Continued*)

S N	Best practices in procurement	Level of implementation
17	Having a formal process to evaluate suppliers' quality control	High
18	Having central warehouses of materials	Moderate
19	Conducting post receipt preservation and maintenance of materials	Moderate
20	Having surplus-reducing program	Moderate
21	Using an integrated material management computer system	Moderate
22	Preparing project material status databases	High
23	Conducting materials management process audits	Moderate

adopted globally are either implemented at a "moderate" level or at a "low" level; and only a few practices have a "high" level of implementation in the Indian construction industry. However, none of the practices was found to have a very high level of implementation, which is a cause of concern in developing countries.

Project stakeholder management

Construction is a collaborative effort of different stakeholders. However, the inherent objectives of the stakeholders can vary greatly, and there is mistrust among stakeholders in the execution of most construction projects. The identification of the various stakeholders (ranging from stockholders to the community) is critical to ensuring unhindered development and completion of any project. It should be borne in mind that collaboration among all the stakeholders in the project team is most important, as only then are the right decisions taken at the appropriate time on any project.

In India, it has been observed that there is a lack of proper coordination and mechanism to take on board all project stakeholders. There have been many instances of different individuals, groups, and non-government organizations not connected to the projects jumping into the fray, which needs to be dealt with by the management through negotiation. Further, such groups normally work to not only counter any development but also incite other genuine stakeholders to put up resistance. Such cases frequently occur in countries beset with poverty (low level of income) and lack of adequate and proper education.

Lack of proper coordination is primarily due to the management team not paying genuine attention to the grievances. The management has, in general, a perception that overindulgence with them will hinder the progress of projects and as such tend to ignore them. This way, in many cases, the management gets the opportunity to get involved in unethical practices. Thus, taking along all the groups and entities, and instilling in them the importance of industrial development, is perhaps one major management style. However, this involves face-to-face interaction on the ground and spending sufficient time to convince groups of various hues. The authorities must sincerely work to secure the welfare of such stakeholders. Educating them and making them aware of their roles to be played positively shall ensure the stakeholders are managed as desired.

Project leadership

Over time, there is increasingly greater competition among the construction firms. This makes it necessary for the implementation of project management systems on their projects to be effective (Dulaimi, 2005). Therefore, the construction firms are seeking professionals who not only have technical skills but also have better management and leadership skills. However, the Indian educational system is still following the traditional task-oriented curriculum, which can only produce managers rather than leaders. Moreover, the construction industry is only working on the philosophy of management rather than leadership. This accounts for the reference to construction project managers rather than leaders. The focus of most of the construction managers is to achieve short-term goals that involve managing day-to-day construction activities and working according to the planned cost, schedule, and quality. In the focus on the achievement of the goals, there is also less consideration of the way the goals are achieved. Thus, construction managers are considered to be production-oriented, rather than being relationship-oriented people who have the skills to achieve long-term goals (Ofori, 2008).

The project managers should be very good in enhancing project certainty, the effective allocation of risk: price optimization, and achieving maximum value for money. Owing to the complexity of construction projects, flexibility in approach is necessary. Taking due consideration of the welfare of the team is another important objective. Effective project leadership requires a business plan comprising reliable information, output specifications, risk analysis, and procurement strategy with underlying transparency and fairness. The leader should have the most up-to-date information on the project; and should also have a group of transaction advisors in the team (Dainty, 2005). Therefore, in the Indian scenario, there is a huge leadership crisis in the construction industry, which needs to be addressed with measures such as further developing and improving the education and training system and developing appropriate performance standards.

Summary and conclusions

The Indian construction industry is the second largest employer and contributes more than 8 percent of India's GDP. The Indian government has pumped in huge amounts of money into the industry, and massive contracts are under execution in the construction industry. The government has also opened the doors of opportunities to the private sector in the Indian construction industry, and the PPP model is contributing to the growth of infrastructure. Moreover, the construction equipment sector is also expanding and new manufacturing facilities are being added in the country.

Despite the availability of such opportunities, the performance of the Indian construction industry is not yet up to the mark. According to MoSPI, more than 300 projects have significant cost and time overruns. In addition, the industry also faces issues such as poor quality, lack of skilled and trained workers, unfinished projects due to the lethargic dispute resolution mechanism, a poor construction safety record, and lack of finance. The Indian construction industry is taking steps to establish new benchmarks in terms of construction quality, schedule, cost, and safety. The industry is also investing its time, money, and efforts for enhancing its R&D facilities, indigenous capabilities, and expertise to realize technological upgrading and improvement of management capabilities for speedy economic development and upliftment of conditions of the citizens in the country. With these improvements, India is poised to play an important role in the global construction industry.

References

Agrawal, T. and Agrawal, A. (2017). Vocational education and training in India: A labour market perspective. *Journal of Vocational Education and Training*, 69(2), 246–265.

Ahuja, V., Yang, J. and Shankar, R. (2009). Study of ICT adoption for building project management in the Indian construction industry. *Automation in Construction*, 18(4), 415–423.

Boukamp, F. and Akinci, B. (2004). Towards automated defect detection: Object-oriented modeling of construction specifications. *Proceedings of 10th International Conference on Computing in Civil and Building Engineering*, Bauhaus-Universität Weimar, Weimar, Germany.

Caldas, C.H., Menches, C.L., Reyes, P.M., Navarro, L. and Vargas, D.M. (2015). Materials management practices in the construction industry. *Practice Periodical on Structural Design and Construction*, 20(3), 04014039.

Chakraborty, T., Das, S.K., Pathak, V. and Mukhopadhyay, S. (2018). Occupational stress, musculoskeletal disorders and other factors affecting the quality of life in Indian construction workers. *International Journal of Construction Management*, 18(2), 144–150.

Chmutina, K. and Rose, J. (2018). Building resilience: Knowledge, experience and perceptions among informal construction stakeholders. *International Journal of Disaster Risk Reduction*, 28, 158–164.

Cho, C.-S. and Gibson Jr., E. (2001). Building project scope definition using project definition rating index. *Journal of Architectural Engineering*, 7(4), 115–125.

Cotton, A.P., Sohail, M. and Scott, R.E. (2005). Towards improved labour standards for construction of minor works in low income countries. *Engineering, Construction and Architectural Management*, 12(6), 617–632.

Dainty, A., Cheng, M.I. and Moore, D. (2005). A comparison of the behavioural competencies of client-focused and production-focused project managers in the construction sector. *Project Management Journal*, 36(2), 39–48.

Demirkesen, S. and Beliz, O. (2017). Impact of integration management on construction project management performance. *International Journal of Project Management*, 35(8), 1639–1654.

DGFASLI (2020). The Directorate General, Factory Advice and Labour Institutes, Ministry of Labour and Employment, Government of India. https://dgfasli.gov.in/en/basic-page/institutes [Accessed 5 March 2021].

Dhal, M. (2020). Labor stand: Face of precarious migrant construction workers in India. *Journal of Construction Engineering and Management*, 146(6), 04020048.

Dixit, S., Stefańska, A., Musiuk, A. and Singh, P. (2021). Study of enabling factors affecting the adoption of ICT in the Indian built environment sector. *Ain Shams Engineering Journal*, 12(2), 2313–2319.

Doloi, H., Sawhney, A., Iyer, K.C. and Rentala, S. (2012). Analysing factors affecting delays in Indian construction projects. *International Journal of Project Management*, 30(4), 479–489.

Dulaimi, M.F. (2005). The influence of academic education and formal training on the project manager's behaviour. *Journal of Construction Research*, 6(01), 179–193.

FICCI and KPMG (2014). Skilling India: A look back at the progress, challenges and the way forward. http://ficci.in/spdocument/20405/FICCI -KPMG-Global-Skills-report.pdf [Accessed 20 January 2021].

Gogoi, M. (2018). The nexus between sovereignty and 'eminent domain' under the Land Acquisition Act, 1894, and the Land Act, 2013. *Social Change*, 48(2), 173–187.

GoI (2020). Make in India: Construction. http://www.makeinindia.com/sector/construction [Accessed 20 June 2020].

Hämäläinen, P., Takala, J. and Saarela, K. L. (2006). Global estimates of occupational accidents. *Safety Science*, 44(2), 137–156.

Hussain, S., Fangwei, Z., Siddiqi, A.F., Ali, Z. and Shabbir, M.S. (2018). Structural equation model for evaluating factors affecting quality of social infrastructure projects. *Sustainability*, 10(5), 1415.

IBEF (2019). Indian brand equity foundation. https://www.ibef.org/industry/cement-presentation [Accessed 25 August 2021].

India Services (2020). India Services Portal, Ministry of Commerce & Industry: Construction and related engineering services. https:www.indiaservices.in/construction [Accessed 20 June 2020].

Iyer, K.C. and Jha, K.N. (2005). Factors affecting cost performance: Evidence from Indian construction projects. *International Journal of Project Management*, 23, 283–295.

Iyer, K.C. and Jha, K.N. (2006). Critical factors affecting schedule performance: Evidence from Indian construction projects. *Journal of Construction Engineering and Management*, 132(8), 871–881.

Iyer, K.C., Chaphalkar, N.B. and Joshi, G.A. (2008). Understanding time delay disputes in construction contracts. *International Journal of Project Management*, 26(2), 174–184.

Jha, K.N. (2011). *Construction Project Management: Theory and Practice*. Pearson Education India, Delhi.

Johari, S. and Jha, K.N. (2020). Challenges to attract construction workers towards skill development training. *Engineering, Construction, and Architectural Management*, 27(2), 321–340.

Kar, S. and Jha, K.N. (2020). Examining the effect of material management issues on the schedule and cost performance of construction projects based on a structural equation model: Survey of Indian experiences. *Journal of Construction Engineering and Management*, 146(9), 05020011.

Kotturu, C.M.V. and Mahanty, B. (2017). Determinants of SME integration into global value chains: Evidence from Indian automotive component manufacturing industry. *Journal of Advances in Management Research*, 14(3), 313–331.

Lee, J.K. (2008). Cost overrun and cause in Korean social overhead capital projects: Roads, rails, airports, and ports. *Journal of Urban Planning and Development*, 134(2), 59–62.

Meredith, J.R., Shafer, S.M. and Mantel Jr., S.J. (2017). *Project Management: A Strategic Managerial Approach*. John Wiley & Sons, Hoboken, NJ.

MOS (2019). Ministry of Steel, Government of India. https://steel.gov.in/make-india [Accessed 18 July 2021].

MoSPI (Ministry of Statistics and Programme Implementation) (2019). 409th flash report on central sector projects. http://www.cspm.gov.in/english/publication.html# [Accessed 10 September 2020].

Nyarirangwe, M. and Babatunde, O.K. (2019). Megaproject complexity attributes and competences: Lessons from IT and construction projects. *International Journal of Information Systems and Project Management*, 7(4), 77–99.

Ofori, G. (2008). Leadership for future construction industry: Agenda for authentic leadership. *International Journal of Project Management*, 26(6), 620–630.

Patel, D.A. and Jha, K.N. (2016). An estimate of fatal accidents in Indian construction. In: P.W. Chan and C.J. Neilson (Eds.), *Proceedings of the 32nd Annual ARCOM Conference*, 5-7 September, Manchester, UK. Association of Researchers in Construction Management, Vol. 1, 539–548.

Project Management Institute (PMI) and KPMG (2019). Revamping project management. http://www.mospi.nic.in/sites/default/files/Kpmg1.pdf [Accessed 25 October 2020].

Ramya, G. (2020). Overcoming the impact of COVID-19 using integrated project delivery model. https://assets.researchsquare.com/files/rs-66806/v1/3a482c51-dc50-47c9-a63f-98aa23485e90.pdf?c=1598653382 [Accessed 5 July 2021].

Saha, R.K. (2018). Occupational health in India. *Annals of Global Health*, 84(3), 330.

Singh, S. (2016). Land acquisition in India: An examination of the 2013 Act and options. *Journal of Land and Rural Studies*, 4(1), 66–78.

Sinha, A.K. (2019). Development of framework for smooth and rapid execution of PPP road projects. A Doctoral Thesis, Indian Institute of Technology, New Delhi.

Sinha, A.K. and Jha, K.N. (2020). Critical analysis of contract clauses in road sector: Case study. *Journal of Legal Affairs and Dispute Resolution in Engineering and Construction*, 12(3), 05020005.

Statista (2021). Breakdown of the construction equipment market in India from 2015 to 2025, by segment. https://www.statista.com/statistics/1221244/india-construction-equipment-market-share-segment/ [Accessed 4 September 2021].

Subramanyan, H., Sawant, P.H. and Bhatt, V. (2012). Construction project risk assessment: Development of model based on investigation of opinion of construction project experts from India. *Journal of Construction Engineering and Management*, 138(3), 409–421.

Tabish, S.Z.S. and Jha, K.N. (2011). Identification and evaluation of success factors for public construction projects. *Construction Management and Economics*, 29(8), 809–823.

Thanki, S.J. and Thakkar, J. (2018). Interdependence analysis of lean-green implementation challenges: A case of Indian SMEs. *Journal of Manufacturing Technology Management*, 29(2), 295–328.

Vibhakar, N.N., Tripathi, K.K., Johari, S. and Jha, K.N. (2020). Identification of significant financial performance indicators for the Indian construction companies. *International Journal of Construction Management*, 1–11. https://doi.org/10.1080/15623599.2020.1844856.

Viswanathan, S.K. (2019). Identification and modelling of risk factors, mitigation measures, and entry strategies for Indian construction firms in international market. A Doctoral Thesis, Indian Institute of Technology, New Delhi.

Viswanathan S.K., Panwar, A., Kar, S., Lavingiya, R. and Jha, K.N. (2020). Causal modeling of disputes in construction projects. *Journal of Legal Affairs and Dispute Resolution in Engineering and Construction*, 12(4), 04520035.

Viswanathan, S.K., Tripathi, K.K. and Jha, K.N. (2020). Influence of risk mitigation measures on international construction project success criteria–a survey of Indian experiences. *Construction Management and Economics*, 38(3), 207–222.

Xia, N., Zou, P.X., Griffin, M.A., Wang, X. and Zhong, R. (2018). Towards integrating construction risk management and stakeholder management: A systematic literature review and future research agendas. *International Journal of Project Management*, 36(5), 701–715.

Zargar, T.A. and Sheikh, M.A. (2018). Good governance in India: Challenges and prospects. *IOSR Journal of Humanities and Social Sciences*, 23(2), 60–64.

https://doi.org/10.1142/9789811224720_0022

Chapter 22

Project Management in Brazil: A Reflection About the Brazilian Context and Its Impact on Social Housing Projects

Luciani Somensi Lorenzi*, Paulo Roberto Pereira Andery[†] and Patricia Elizabeth Ferreira Gomes Barbosa[†]

*Universidade Federal do Rio Grande do Sul (UFRGS), Brazil
[†]Universidade Federal de Minas Gerais (UFMG), Brazil

Abstract

Social housing projects have stood out in the Brazilian construction industry, whether due to the great social impact in a country with a large housing deficit, or due to government subsidies, especially in the last 10 years. These projects were less affected by the substantial economic downturn that characterized the industry. The management systems of these projects were conditioned by both financial and regulatory managerial systems based on ISO 9001 and other performance-based standards. The scope of this chapter is to describe these systems and discuss their influence on project management practices. Thus, this chapter first outlines the Brazilian construction industry and highlights the social housing projects. Next, it describes a set of circumstances that had a substantial impact on project management processes, including a set of public financing mechanisms for housing projects, which was conditioned on the implementation of a quality management system developed specifically for construction companies. This system, referenced in ISO 9001, specifies the normative requirements for the management of construction projects. It was harmonized with other projects that make up the Brazilian Habitat Quality and Productivity Program. Another significant initiative for project management, which has been disseminated, is the Brazilian Standard on Performance-Based Buildings (NBR 15.575), which, along with the implementation of various management systems, has been promoting substantial changes in project management processes including: better definition of design scope and design management processes, an improvement in the integration of the design and construction phases, and improvement of procurement processes; these are outlined in the chapter. A final section describes how some of these processes have been used in projects of another nature, mostly public and corporate projects.

Keywords: Social housing projects, performance-based project management, Brazilian construction industry

Introduction: A reflection on the context of civil construction in Brazil

The production chain of civil construction in Brazil is part of a context based on a scenario of uncertainties. The unstable scenario is because of the variations in the economy. On the one hand, the economic situation has varied significantly in the last 20 years. Since 2015, the country has undergone a recessionary process that resulted in a decline of about 30 percent, which is the deepest recession in the construction industry (CBIC, 2020). From the perspective of construction project management, this economic slowdown resulted in difficulty in obtaining funding, particularly for social housing projects, as well as uncertainty as to the speed with which the housing units produced would be sold, management of habitational units to be sold, and portfolio planning.

Although some larger companies have expanded their project portfolios, this uncertainty has led to a reduction in investments in technologies, from the perspective of both innovations in construction systems and the improvement of project management processes (Mendonça and Monetti, 2019). Even considering that in the last 10 years the financing mechanisms have been improved, through government policies, in most of the construction companies, especially the small ones, the possibility of obtaining financial support for the projects (for both contractors and end clients), if any, was not accompanied by improvements in the production and management systems (Shimbo, 2019).

As regards housing projects, the product definition often does not consider the contribution of engineering designers; the product design is usually dissociated from the design and planning of constructive solutions, and this imposes barriers on the project's constructability (Barbosa and Andery, 2015). Another point that makes management of construction projects difficult concerns professional qualifications. For example, Architecture courses in Brazil often do not address topics related to design and project management in their curricula. Topics such as "design for constructability" are little explored in class or in practical sessions. A similar situation is also seen in Civil Engineering courses, which offer an extensive curricular program, but with little emphasis on managing construction projects.

Many developers and construction companies have postponed investments to implement Building Information Modelling (BIM) methodologies. There are still few design and construction companies that use this collaboration platform, and even more, companies that involve all project designers in coordination and BIM collaboration processes are rare (Santos *et al.*, 2015; Vieira Calmon and Faroni, 2017). A change in this framework is expected to occur with the recent institution of a regulatory framework that requires public-sector projects to be developed using BIM.

Despite the scenario briefly outlined, the Brazilian government, in partnership with several market segments (design and construction professionals, the construction industry, regulatory agencies, funding agents, quality audit companies, and academics), has been developing for the past 20 years a program of housing policies that has been encouraging companies to implement formal quality management systems. Moreover, recent technical standards which have been released make it mandatory to implement processes to ensure the quality performance of the building.

The knowledge of the standards and their correct application in the process of design and on construction sites are still being developed, and end clients are still getting to know how they are used.

These aspects have significantly changed project management practices in Brazil. This chapter aims to outline these regulatory and quality management systems and highlight their impact on project management practices on housing projects, as well as other construction works. The chapter also points out the lessons learned that can be applied to other Brazilian construction projects. Regulatory and managerial systems which are mandatory requirements in applications for the provision of governmental finance for social housing projects are described. Their impacts on project management processes are then considered.

Project management in housing of social interest (HSI) in Brazil

Regulatory systems and their impact on project management of housing projects

A brief historical overview of managerial policies in Brazilian social housing can be useful in the discussion of their impacts on project management processes. A summary is now presented.

Owing to many different and complex causes, Brazil's housing deficit exceeds more than five million housing units (Gonçalves Junior *et al.*, 2014). Although several social housing financing programs have been introduced over the past 30 years, the most expressive and consistent program is called *Programa Minha Casa, Minha Vida* (MCMV), which means, "My House, My Life Program," which was developed to intensify the construction of large-scale homes and house building.

From its beginning in 1998 to 2018, the MCMV program delivered approximately 4.15 million housing units, with investments of around US$100 billion according to the Brazilian Regional Development Ministry (2018). It was carried out by financial institutions, mainly a public institution, Caixa Econômica Federal (CEF), that accounts for about 96 percent of housing finance in Brazil. In playing its decisive part in enhancing the viability of housing developments, CEF adopted the role of inducing improvements in the quality of buildings and introducing financing mechanisms, leading to innovations in materials and construction systems (Fernandes, Formoso and Fazenda, 2018). Taking a retrospective view, it is worth mentioning that CEF was the successor of the National Housing Bank (BNH) which, in the 1970s and 1980s, was the principal federal institution of urban development in Brazil; arguably, it has been the most significant organization in housing in Brazilian history. During this period, the first studies on quality in social interest housing were undertaken. Systemic problems of quality and performance of buildings were raised, and it was found that they were resulting from several causes, including the lack of processes for the correct identification and implementation of innovative construction systems.

In later periods, aiming to foster the quality of social housing, CEF promoted other studies on implementing innovative construction solutions, which generated several widely disseminated publications and technical bulletins. One example is the series of publications sponsored by the Habitare Program, dealing with performance specifications of materials and construction systems. The most significant milestone in the harmonization and consolidation of these documents was the publication of the "Technical Standards for Evaluation of Innovative Building Systems for Housing," which was configured as a first attempt to standardize and disseminate technological standards for housing of social interest, and fostered the implementation of performance concepts in such types of housing.

From there, the Brazilian Association of Technical Standards (ABNT) began the discussion of the subject to reach a consensus and transform it into a Technical Standard. In 2008, Brazil had the first version of the Building Performance Standard; it was restricted to housing construction of up to five floors in height. In 2013, the standard (NBR 15575) came into force in an expanded version. This standard did not include any restriction on the number of floors; it applied to all housing construction. Thus began a process of implementation of concepts of performance-based buildings in Brazil.

Because NBR 15575 is a non-prescriptive standard that does not identify and prescribe standardized solutions, several construction companies began to perform tests and computational simulations to evaluate their construction systems and validate the construction methods. With this being done, it is expected that the quality management processes of the companies incorporate the results obtained from the tests and computer simulations in order to set out design solutions and construction systems for implementation on similar new projects. In this way, the companies could have more security in the adoption of design solutions and the possible introduction of innovative technologies.

A significant step was subsequently realized by incorporating the performance standard in the Quality Management System demanded by financial institutions, as defined by the Brazilian Habitat Quality and Productivity Program (PBQP-H), which is discussed below. The text of the normative rules explicitly included the requirements to be in compliance with ABNT NBR 15575:2013, and its implementation became mandatory for obtaining housing financing.

As a funding organization that induces actions to ensure the performance of buildings, CEF establishes guidelines for standardized components and building systems, defines some specific design solutions to be adopted, and establishes minimum conditions of performance and functionality, creating a system of standards (building codes) specified in its Technical Manual. These actions were combined with the implementation, from 1998, of the Brazilian Habitat Quality and Productivity Program (PBQP-H), resulting from a multi-institutional articulation that aimed at the development of systemic actions to ensure the quality and productivity of the dwellings.

Thus, in Brazil, housing financing for developers, provided by CEF and other financial agents, is conditional on their compliance with the Brazilian Program of Quality and Productivity of Habitat PBQP-H. The program, which has the support of more than 2000 construction companies and hundreds of manufacturers of materials and construction systems, has three major projects: the Compliance Assessment System for Service and Construction Companies (SIAC), the National Technical Evaluation System (SINAT) of construction systems, and the Qualification System of Companies of Materials, Components and Construction Systems (SIMAC). SIAC induces the implementation of a quality management system in construction companies. This system uses as reference, ISO9001:2015, establishing the specific regulatory requirements for construction companies with the scope of building or infrastructure projects, making additional requirements, or specifying the requirements included in ISO9001:2015 more generically. SIAC requires that each project should have a specific Quality Assurance Plan, including the monitoring and control of construction processes and materials, the planning of logistics issues on construction sites, and the proper treatment of waste generated on site, among other aspects. Quality management processes recommended in project management practices began to be gradually introduced in construction companies.

Thus, a government program encouraged the attainment of quality and performance in the sense that, in order to obtain financing for the projects, the construction companies must ensure their adherence to performance and quality standards. A combination of technical guidelines for the granting of financing is associated with requirements regarding the implementation of quality assurance systems. This work structure has had a substantial impact on how construction companies organize their business management and project management systems, especially during the last five years. Recent Brazilian literature points to the fact that the implementation of quality management systems had a significant impact on the improvement of management processes of the companies. It has especially concerned the introduction of project quality plans, better control of construction materials, and procedures regarding construction tasks, based on quality and performance parameters (Barbosa and Andery, 2018).

The second project of the Program is the SIMAC, which develops actions to encourage manufacturers of materials and components to adopt systemic actions to improve the quality compliance of their products, with the normative references for each product or component. The program is divided into sector subprograms for each type of material (such as cement, mortars, blocks, steel and aluminium frames), conferring a quality certificate for the products. This project is directly related to the previous one (SIAC) to the extent that construction companies certified in the SIAC are committed to using materials and components certified in SIMAC.

The third element of the Program is the National Technical Evaluation System (SINAT) which aims to evaluate new products used in construction and stimulate technological innovation, increasing the number of technological alternatives available for housing production. SINAT is the organization that authorizes and supervises Technological Institutes of Evaluation (ITAs). It has, in its scope, the evaluation of the performance of buildings and their systems and consequently, this creates the demand for laboratories in the area of building construction to undertake tests, simulations and technical inspections. Specialists in building performance conduct all data and performance analysis of construction components and systems, and they are formally appointed by the PBQP-H. However, the lack of a laboratory structure in Brazil is one of the primary concerns of the construction industry. The demand for specialized performance services should imply an increase in construction laboratories, and qualified researchers and specialists in the area. Although there are approximately 30 laboratories accredited by the National Institute of Metrology (INMETRO), which defines and undertakes the accreditation of laboratories, most of them do not have capacity to evaluate the performance of buildings and systems. The lack of knowledge about the behavior of buildings and their systems in use throughout the service life may be associated with the lack of research in building construction in general. The adopted solution was the creation of a database of performance assessment.

In Brazil, designers and contractors often lack technical knowledge of construction systems, especially about their performance. There is no tradition in Brazil of considering performance data on construction systems, or establishing predefined performance criteria with inputs for the development of design solutions and definition of construction systems. The concern with the performance guarantee is recent and it was stimulated by the publication, in 2013, of the technical standard NBR 15575:2013, which defines requirements and criteria for the performance of dwellings. Owing to favorable climatic and other conditions, such as the absence of seismic shocks, small thermal variations and low incidence of strong winds, there were no significant innovations in the improvement of materials and construction techniques. An exception was the creation of some industrialized construction systems, focused on large-scale production, which was driven by cost reduction rather than improvement in performance.

Currently, the scenario is promising with respect to improvement in performance in the production chain of housebuilding in Brazil. There is an articulation between government, materials manufacturers and construction companies in order to create actions to ensure improved quality and performance in housebuilding through the PBQP-H.

Project management to ensure performance

As mentioned above, arguably the most effective impact of these regulatory and managerial standards was on Scope Management processes, as well as product development processes. In particular, the NBR 15575:2013 (Performance Standard) has led to important changes in product definition. Regarding project management to ensure performance, the market practices of housing projects are guided by the frameworks mentioned above. The conceptual structure of performance management throughout the enterprise's life cycle is presented schematically in Figure 22.1.

The conceptual framework for performance assurance is divided into three steps: pre-performance, performance, and post-performance. These three steps characterize the project life cycle with a focus on: designed and constructed performance; performance in use and operation; and post-performance, considering the case that the building can already be designed with a predefined purpose. Pre-performance is defined as pre-use and building operation. The objective of this stage is to enable, plan and design, build, and assure the potential performance of the building throughout its life cycle. The stage consists of four phases: expected performance, designed performance, building performance, and performance evaluation. These are now briefly outlined.

Phase I: **Expected performance**. Analysis of technical and economic feasibility associated with the initial development of preliminary solutions for the architectural and engineering design and the definition of components, elements, and construction systems.

Phase II: **Designed performance**. Integrated development of planning and design consisting of the Building Performance Profile (BPP) and architectural and engineering design, including the specifications of components, elements, and systems.

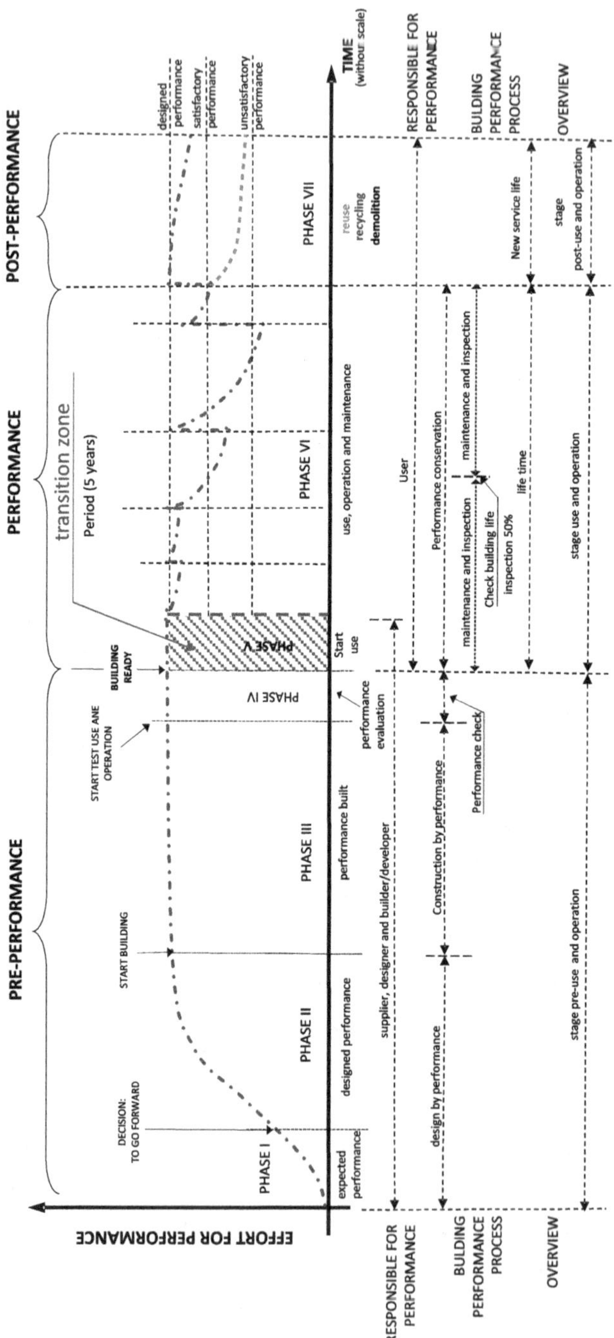

Figure 22.1: Performance management throughout the project life cycle.

Source: Adapted from Lorenzi (2022).

Phase III: **Building performance**. Execution on sites, with the use of Standard Execution Procedures considering the project specifications concerning performance.

Phase IV: **Performance evaluation**. Conducting inspections and performance tests to validate compliance with the requirements and performance criteria specified in the design.

In these four phases of pre-performance, three of the main parties responsible for performance: supplier, designer, and builder/developer, are involved. The supplier is responsible for having its products evaluated by performance, the designer for using performance-based concepts, and the builder/developer to build, based on the design and specifications by performance.

The **performance** stage is characterized by the building's use and operation. The objective of this step is to maintain the performance of the delivered building, and it is composed of two phases: the transition zone, and conservation, which are now discussed.

Phase V: The **Transition zone** is the five-year warranty period and relates to the integration of the builder/developer and user responsibilities for the conservation of the building, following the User Manual.

Phase VI: **Conservation** is composed of maintenance (the instructions are set out in the User Manual) and building inspection (established in ABNT NBR 16747:2020, a Brazilian Standard). The responsibility for the conservation of the building, after the transition zone, is exclusively that of the user. For the performance of a building to be satisfactory during its life, user participation is fundamental, as it is primarily responsible for building performance during use, operation and maintenance. During the first period of the building's use and operation, the construction company's action is very present, making the transition during the five years of the warranty period. Subsequently, it becomes the responsibility of the user exclusively to perform the maintenance and inspections. Phase VI is the longest in the pre-performance period, and is important in the effort to ensure that the building performs at acceptable levels. Failure to plan for, or perform, maintenance can lead to failure, or lack of satisfactory building performance, and might make necessary interventions significantly excessive and expensive.

The design life established in the pre-performance stage must be validated in the performance step (Phase VI). After 50 percent of the life of the building, an inspection is carried out to prove the design life. The Manuals of Use and Operation define the maintenance programs of buildings, associated with inspection procedures defined in the recent standard, NBR 16474:2020.

Post-performance (Phase VII) is the building's destination after performance: reuse, recycling, and demolition of the building. At this stage, the building fulfills its purpose, and the user alone determines its destination. In Brazil, reuse is the standard consideration for the residential buildings which are the subject of this chapter, since the Brazilian user's characteristic is to have only one dwelling during his/her entire life.

The management of the performance of buildings can also be characterized by the products generated during its process, such as design for performance, construction for performance, performance assessment, performance conservation, and post-performance destination. The relationship between these products is fundamental to meeting the performance of the building during its life cycle.

These concepts of performance management have led to progressive changes in design management practices and the management of construction execution processes in Brazil, with several developments, especially in two fields: (a) design procurement and management, including a more efficient system regarding the risk analysis of the project; and (b) control of construction processes, and performance evaluation through the use of Technological Control Plans.

Breaking with the historical discussion, real estate and construction companies integrate the business-modelling phase with the conceptual phase of building construction, leading to deep changes in Project Scope Management processes. Thus, design managers have began to participate in the initial stages of product definition and development of preliminary studies of architecture and engineering, introducing requirements and solutions associated with meeting safety, habitability, and maintainability requirements recommended in ABNT NBR 15575:2013 (Building Performance Standard). Other changes that affect Project Management practices can also be outlined.

Gradually, improvements are being introduced in the definition of design scope and design office contracts. This process was previously often neglected, and the definition of the scope was limited to the definition of commercial issues such as costs and design milestones. From the introduction of the performance-based design approach, designers began to incorporate the development of more detailed documentation into the design scope, highlighting compliance with the performance criteria. From the introduction of design management processes to ensure performance, this function began to differentiate between two sets of processes, referred to here as technical coordination and managerial coordination, with emphasis on the design issues in the project management system.

Technical coordination addresses the design interface and technical constraints of the architecture in order to design solutions to make compatible simultaneously the architectural programming, specifications, performance and quality assurance, aiming to realize improvements in constructability.

The introduction of performance assurance concepts is significantly changing the technical coordination process, which has improved procedures regarding the scope of contracting architecture and engineering design in its various phases, the more effective participation of stakeholders in the design development, and the incorporation of consultancy guidelines in order to meet specific requirements, for example, thermal, acoustic, and lighting performance. On the other hand, the performance evaluation results, which comprise tests of the construction systems, computational simulations, prototype inspections, and design analysis, are gradually forming a database of the companies and are being incorporated into their knowledge assets. At this point, this information begins to be systematized and validated.

In companies with a more developed project management system, the management coordination process works more effectively with the management practices, leading to better knowledge of the performance-based concepts, methods and procedures. Among other aspects related to this management of design coordination is a more in-depth analysis of risk management at both company and project levels, which has been translated into the standardization of constructive solutions for similar projects, and the management of contracts, which allows a contracting process with detailed defined scope, as mentioned above.

The concepts of quality assurance reinforce and give the design manager prominence to disseminate the strategies adopted and implement training of the construction team during the execution of critical activities to ensure performance. In addition, this professional induces the feedback of the solutions for a more efficient process from the technical and financial point of view and enables continuous improvement of the procedures adopted in the various phases of the design development process and the building's construction process.

Similarly, management coordination stands out for incorporating management models that enable the reduction of uncertainties and improvements in the product, being responsible for the interfaces between the development activities of the design specialties and the other processes throughout the production cycle of the project, contemplating dependencies associated with deadlines, cost and scope, in addition to the restrictions of the logistics of resources, as indicated in Figure 22.2.

The "Performance Standard" indicates that for specific performance requirements, minimum (always mandatory), intermediate, or higher performance levels can be achieved. This set of requirements forms the

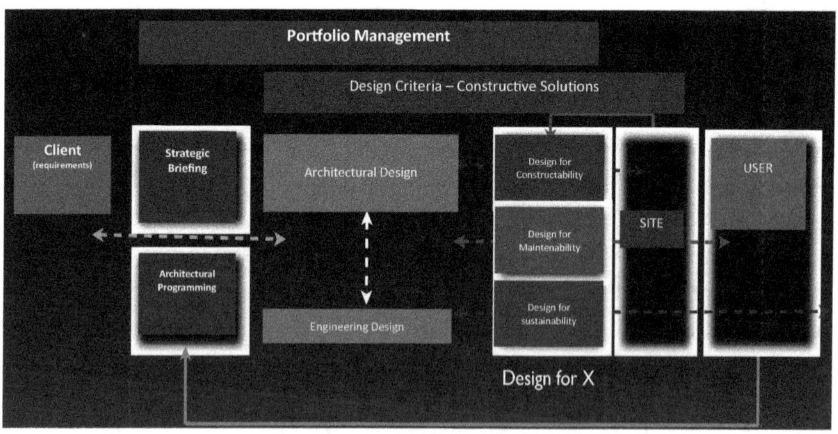

Figure 22.2: Stages of production of real estate developments.

Source: Adapted from Fabricio (2010).

Building Performance Profile, the definition of which has been required as design input under the Brazilian Quality and Productivity Program (*Programa Brasileiro de Qualidade e Produtividade* (PBQP-H)) Quality Management System. Thus, the coordinators start to define this profile.

At the interface between Phases II and III of Figure 22.1, and throughout the execution of the works, the conjunction between the requirements of the Quality Management System defined in the PBQP-H, as well as the introduction of regulatory mechanisms by the financing agencies gave rise to the improvement of Technological Control Plans in the building construction companies. Until then, this had been almost exclusively focused on the technological control of some critical materials for the works.

These Technological Control Plans define measures or procedures to be implemented in different design and site construction processes. In the definition of the product, in the preliminary design conceptual phase, the plan provides for the analysis of technical risks and the evaluation of environmental operating conditions. During the design development, this Technological Control Plan provides for calculations and/or simulations to verify whether the design solutions being developed meet the requirements of thermal, lighting and acoustic performance, and structural safety, as well as the building's use and conditions.

Throughout the process of the execution of the works, the Technological Control Plan provides for tests to verify that the construction systems are effectively meeting the performance requirements, as recommended in the conceptual structure of the Performance-Based Building criteria. From the introduction of these plans, it was observed that: (a) test results and performance simulations of construction systems become reference and design input for similar projects; and (b) these same elements serve as validators of constructive solutions foreseen in the design, as indicated above.

In the context of evaluating the performance of construction systems, pioneering work has been developed within the scope of the National System of Technical Evaluations (SINAT). The preparation and dissemination of "Performance Evaluation Sheets of Construction Systems (PES)" allows designers and construction companies to validate design solutions or building systems to the extent that they demonstrate the equivalence of these systems with those defined in the PES. Thus, tests or simulations which would have been required on projects can be replaced by officially validated technical references. Implementing performance assurance concepts has also induced significant changes in the relationship between material and construction systems suppliers and professionals involved in design development and execution of construction work.

During the execution stage, the Technological Control Plans continue to guide the simulations and validations carried out in the design phase. The procedures for performing the construction tasks on the site have been modified to meet the design criteria, and the specifications in the construction documents or consultants' guidelines aimed at specifying production parameters.

In some construction companies, the technological control plans developed jointly by the project and suppliers' teams have created a database that serves as a reference for standardization of constructive solutions that will serve as input into similar new constructions. Furthermore, they enable the performance standards and what can be considered to be the best practices to achieve higher levels of constructability.

As the guarantee of performance implies defining and complying with the conditions of use, operation, and, more recently, the conservation (maintenance and inspections) established in the User Manual, delivered to the user at the time of delivery of the house, it is not common for users to dedicate themselves to it. Although these manuals already existed since they were made mandatory in 1991 with the entry into force of the Consumption Defense Code (CDC), and are the object of a specific technical standard, almost all users do not read them.

The Brazilian real estate market has a long tradition of passivity concerning predictive or preventive maintenance of buildings. In practice, maintenance plans are rarely developed. The relationship between the construction team and the users can become litigious, either because the systems and components applied in the construction do not achieve the expected performance, or because there is a lack of user information on the correct use of the building. This lack of clarity in communication between the constructor and the user generates conflicts in defining each party's responsibilities, which are now decreasing due to the assumption of user responsibilities according to the performance-based criteria.

Summing up the discussion, the combination of requirements of quality management systems and the buildings' performance assurance induced significant changes in the design management processes and, in a broader sense, project management, encompassing the activities of product design, execution, and planning of the operation and maintenance.

Impact of quality and performance management processes on project management

The construction industry in Brazil introduced some changes that had a significant impact on the project and construction development process in order to meet the requirements of ABNT NBR 15575:2013 and the new market demand. These changes increased the effort employed in these processes resulting in better design management processes, with the valorization of design activities, better technical knowledge of the behavior in the use of the building and its systems, more qualified partners and better-elaborated contracts, with a clear definition of scope, responsibilities, and deliverables.

The design scope aligned with users' requirements, together with a differentiated posture of some suppliers, designers, and builders/developers, allowed the incorporation and integration of information at earlier stages of design phases, as well as during construction documents development processes. Among the aspects of most significant impact are the new structuring of the design process, including mechanisms regarding inputs, outputs, verification, critical analysis, and validation of performance requirements, as well as the execution of tests, computational simulations, and procedures for controlling material specifications, to demonstrate compliance with the normative requirements of performance, as established in the standard.

The incorporation of information allows the designer to design by performance and specify by performance the components, elements, and construction systems, allowing the understanding of the project's scope to establish the Design Life and Service Life of the building construction systems. The designer integrates the information from suppliers, constructors/developers, and users, as represented schematically in Figure 22.3.

The development of conceptualization and detailed design incorporating user requirements and information from the supplier and builder/

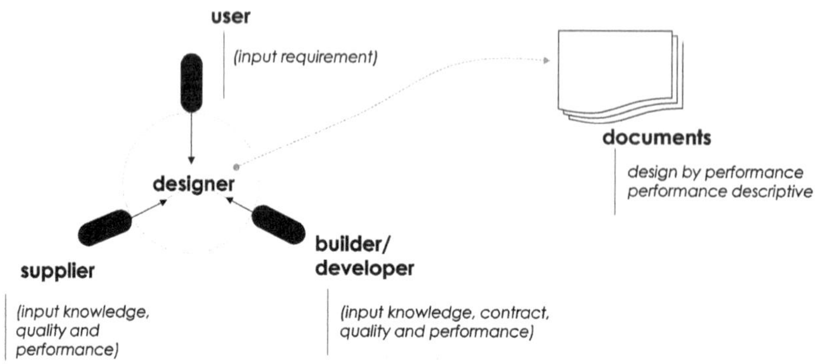

Figure 22.3: Information integration: Supplier, builder/developer, and user.

developer is a collaborative process that brings those involved together to validate the design's conformity. The summary of this collaboration is in the Building Performance Profile (BPE), as discussed above, which constitutes the integrated development of planning, project and specifications through the compilation of the knowledge of the supplier and the builder/developer as well as what is learnt from projects and the performance of the housing units.

One of the most significant changes that have been observed is the participation of design coordinators in the definition of the real estate product, although this is still in the preliminary stages of its development. Among the aspects that have been observed, the following stand out:

(i) more careful analysis of the technical risks involved in the development of projects, such as conditions of implementation on the ground, environmental impacts, and unusual operating conditions, such as constraints on the design of foundations or containments, the presence of contaminants in the soil, and the presence of more severe sources of noise; these aspects that were usually neglected; and
(ii) participation of technical and managerial coordinators in the definition of the performance levels required for the different construction systems, depending on the analysis of technical and commercial constraints.

The systemic vision of the coordinator is essential to ensure that the project meets the quality and performance requirements. According to

Barbosa and Andery (2018), there was an increase in the demand for the coordination of projects to incorporate in their work routines the hiring of specialized consultants for thermal performance analysis, as well as for lighting and acoustic performance, with the realization of simulations that guide project solutions.

Many Brazilian manufacturers of materials and construction systems are not aware of their responsibility for the evaluation of the performance of their products. The builder/developer seeks to know its product's performance, with large and medium-sized companies being the most up-to-date and prepared in this sense. A study conducted by the Brazilian Chamber of Construction (CBIC, 2020) and its associates found that 90 percent of construction companies and 59 percent of suppliers provide guidance on the use, operation, and maintenance of buildings in their products. On the other hand, those suppliers committed to their product's quality and performance became more active in providing information and guidance to designers, the supply sector, and construction teams. They played a more consultative role, facilitating the validation and dissemination of innovative solutions.

In construction companies which are more advanced in performance-based design practices, those responsible for supply management have taken a more proactive stance in identifying optimized constructive solutions in the trade-off between performance and cost. The introduction of performance assurance concepts has had a significant impact on the acquisition process. In some cases, the involvement of the suppliers of materials and construction systems was due to demands made directly by the construction industry.

Concerning the relationship between suppliers and builders, the introduction of performance requirements boosted the product supplier's responsibility to the construction industry, specifically for residential buildings, resulting in improved and performance-characterized products. Similarly, some of the builder/developer understood that there was an increase in their responsibilities and risks, and began to seek suppliers committed to the performance of their products. Another impact for the builder is in the quality control of the work with the incorporation of performance specifications in the Construction Tasks Execution Procedures, formalized procedures for executing constructive activities in the works.

Construction companies have also introduced new practices for managing projects during their use and operation concerning maintenance management. There was an advance in communication between builder/developer and user for awareness of reading, use, and application of the User Manual, which contains important information about maintenance requirements, guiding users on what to do, and with what periodicity.

Larger construction companies/developers have been developing Customer Relationship Management processes, including, in some cases, the development of software applications that allow users to monitor the maintenance conditions of buildings and also the systematizing of training for users and liquidators, which implies reducing the costs of technical assistance and corrective maintenance over the life of the building.

The user was positively impacted by the enhancement in the building's quality, with the knowledge of the projected performance expectation and the possibility of charging for the effectiveness of the performance of the builders. On the other hand, the user has to pay attention to the conservation of the building through inspections and maintenance throughout the life of the building.

Quality management had its role renewed with the implementation of performance management. The quality control process incorporated the building's pre-performance phases (see Figure 22.1), performing the control during the design and construction development processes until the delivery of the work. From the moment of delivery of the building to the user, the quality assurance in the building's performance stage comes into play, which addresses the conservation of performance divided into maintenance and building inspection (see Figure 22.1).

The combination of quality management with performance management helps in building confidence in the product, allowing construction companies/developers to innovate safely. This integration fills a gap in the uncertainties of the construction sector, aimed at incorporating new technologies and industrialization.

Construction companies with mature corporate managerial systems began to prioritize the production of prefabricated elements at scale, obtaining several benefits through rationalization of production, enhancing the effectiveness and efficiency of the process, and enabling the adoption of new technologies.

The buildings began to be analyzed systemically, and the detailed design had its importance recognized, as mentioned earlier (Ceotto,

2019). To ABDI (2015), companies in the construction industry must reassess and modernize their form of production through the industrialization of buildings and the adoption of new construction processes. This new context, has allowed companies to create new forms of management for the construction industry, introducing methods more directed to the sector's needs, such as requirements management, knowledge management, contract management, and, more recently, performance management.

Impact of changes in social interest housing in other construction projects

Part of the management impacts observed in *Social Housing Projects*, resulting from the implementation of quality management systems, and the introduction of performance-based building concepts associated with the Brazilian standard ABNT NBR 15575 were also observed in building projects for high-income clients, and some aspects were found to have been applied in commercial and corporate buildings. These typologies, when added to social housing projects, represent more than 70 percent of the Brazilian construction market (CBIC, 2020).

Among these impacts, some aspects can be highlighted:

(i) the coordination processes of the architecture and engineering design disciplines have been improved due to the fulfillment of thermal, acoustic, and lighting comfort requirements, more demanding in these constructive typologies, but also due to the increasing complexity of the projects as regards sustainability and facilities management requirements;

(ii) the concern with cost reduction is considered a requirement of design management, with the progressive introduction of target costing processes to make value improvement compatible with cost constraints; and

(iii) the Brazilian economic situation has favored the construction of rental projects and expanded the enterprises' building programmes to suit modality. For these projects, the requirements management processes have been improved as a function of the specific demands required by contracts and business models.

Thus, the changes induced by social housing management systems are gradually being applied to other projects, mainly as regards scope management, product definition and design development, and procurement practices.

A distinct reality is public projects, whether road projects, infrastructure works, or public buildings. These projects are technically conditioned by the Brazilian Bidding Law (Brazilian Government, 8,666, 1993). This law is focused on reducing corruption risks but makes the integration of design disciplines with the construction phase more difficult. A significant portion of public projects has cost and time overruns. The literature points out that the leading cause of these deviations is the changes in the project scope.

In this sense, it remains a challenge to transfer the recent advances in project management described above to public enterprises. Recent research has proposed models of integration between the stages of design and work, introducing concepts of value management and integration of design disciplines and phases, as determined in Concurrent Engineering practices (see, for example, Moreira and Andery, 2020).

Future prospects of HIS ventures project management

The understanding and application of project management is critical for the continuous improvement of the design process in Brazil. The constructive solution of Social Interest Housing (HIS) is industrialization, with a focus on sustainable production, less use of environmental resources, and modularization and standardization, enabling rationalization, which, in turn, leads to agility and productivity in construction. It can be suggested that, in five years, the scenario will be different due to the computerization of projects and the requirement to use BIM in public projects from 2021 onwards. These transformations are already happening at present, but only in a small group of companies in the civil construction sector.

These changes are associated with smart services to meet this new demand. The main directions for this change are in the future perspectives for the industry, which can be outlined as:

- the implementation of New Curricular Guidelines for Engineering, until 2023, with Project Management as one of the requirements;

- the intelligent use of the BIM process from the conception, design, and construction, to the conservation of the building to assist in meeting the project's useful life;
- interest among construction companies in the incorporation of Environmental, Social and Corporate Governance (ESG) considerations in projects; and
- the incorporation of new construction solutions for HIS, such as modular construction.

Because of this future perspective and the support for the improvement of the quality of HIS by government programs, it is possible to say that Project Management in Brazil has a great future, a path to follow, with a strong indication of improvements in the products and the construction process. In this way, it is expected that the Brazilian construction industry will have a productivity performance that puts the country in a better position on the international scene.

References

ABDI (2015). Agência Brasileira de Desenvolvimento Industrial (Brazilian Agency for Industry Development). Manual da Construção Industrializada (Industrialized Construction Manual) (in Portuguese). Brasilia. https://api.abdi.com.br//file-manager/upload/files/anual_construcao_industrializada_versao_digital.pdf [Accessed 15 August 2020].

Barbosa, P. and Andery, P. (2015). *Considerations on Constructability Improvement in the Design Processes of Construction Companies* (in Portuguese). Revista Construção, Belo Horizonte. http://www.fumec.br/revistas/construindo/article/view/3950 [Accessed 10 September 2020].

Barbosa, P. and Andery, P. (2018). Contribution to the analysis of the Brazilian Quality Assurance System SIAC in the implementation of NBR 15.575:2013 in construction companies (in Portuguese). In *Procedures of the Encontro Nacional de Tecnologia do Ambiente Construído ENTAC 2018 — Brazilian Meeting on Built Environment Technology*. ANTAC, Porto Alegre, pp. 2542–2548.

Brazilian Government (1993). Lei das Licitações. http://www.planalto.gov.br/ccivil_03/leis/l8666cons.htm [Accessed 10 September 2020].

Brazilian Regional Development Ministry (2018). Technical Report (April 2018).

CBIC (2020) Câmara Brasileira da Indústria da Contrução (Brazilian Construction Industry Chamber), Statistical Bulletin. http://www.cbicdados.com.br/home/ [Accessed 10 September 2020].

Ceotto, L. (2019). Da Encol até hoje — o que mudou na forma de construir? In *Encontro Nacional da Indústria da Construção — 91 ENIC*. Câmara Brasileira da Indústria da Construção, Rio de Janeiro.

Dos Santos, S., Vendrametto, O., González, M.L. and Correia, C.F. (2015). Profile of Building Information Modeling – BIM- tools maturity in Brazilian civil construction scenery. *Proceedings, IFIP International Conference on Advances in Production Management Systems (APMS)*, September, Tokyo, Japan, pp.291–298, 10.1007/978-3-319-22756-6_36.

Fabrício, M. (2002). Concurrent Design in Building Construction. Unpublished doctoral dissertation, Universidade de São Paulo, Brazil.

Fernandes, G., Formoso, C. and Tzortzopoulos-Fazenda, P. (2018). Method for automated requirement checking in social housing projects (in Portuguese). *Revista Ambiente Construído*, 18(4), 259–278.

Gonçalves Junior, C., *et al.* (2014). The impact of "My House, My Life" Housing Program in the Brazilian Economy: An analysis of input–output (in Portuguese). *Revista Ambiente Construído*, 14(1), 177–189.

Lorenzi, L. S. (2022). Building performance management: Vision integrating processes design, construction and conservation to minimize pathological manifestations (in Portuguese). *Boletines Técnico*, (1), 24–30.

Mendonça, M. and Montetti, E. (2019). Strategic management weaknesses and bottlenecks of residential Real Estate developers — An initial analysis with companies operating in the market (in Portuguese). In *Proceedings of the XIV Lares — International Latin America Real Estate Society Conference*. São Paulo: Latin American Real Estate Association.

Moreira, R. and Andery, P. (2020). Integração entre projeto e obra em empreendimento público rodoviário (in Portuguese). *Magazine Ambiente Construído*, 20(3), https://doi.org/10.1590/s1678-86212020000300417.

Shimbo, L. (2019). An unprecedented alignment: State, finance, construction and housing production in Brazil since the 2000s. *International Journal of Housing Policy*, 19(3), 337–353.

Vieira, D., Calmon, J. and Faroni, M. (2017). Building Information Modeling (BIM) in Brazil's Architecture, Engineering and Construction (AEC) Industry: A Review and a Bibliometric Study. *The Journal of Modern Project Management*, 5(1). https://www.journalmodernpm.com/index.php/jmpm/article/view/JMPM01304 [Accessed 15 September 2020].

https://doi.org/10.1142/9789811224720_0023

Chapter 23

Rules First or Practice First? The Paradox of Quality Management in Innovative Projects in Developing Countries: A China Case

Yan Ning* and Shang Gao†

**Nanjing University, PR China*
†The University of Melbourne, Australia

Abstract

Project quality management as one key area of the Project Management Body of Knowledge (PMBOK) of the Project Management Institute (PMI) is undertaken through the method of plan-do-check-act (PDCA). The PDCA cycle assumes that formal rules (such as regulations and codes) could work as the guidelines. However, these formal rules appear to be less systematic in developing countries, which might lead to a practical paradox. On the one hand, the absence of the formal rules may hinder the adoption of innovative quality management, especially for building and infrastructure projects as they involve operational safety, and that of the end-users and the public. In such a context, the development of rules should be prioritized. On the other hand, innovative projects are often taken as conduits to give rise to the emerging formal rules. This encourages innovative quality management practices to take place prior to setting the rules. How to deal with this paradox remains unknown, and addressing this question may have important implications for quality management in innovative projects in developing countries. This research aims to examine how stakeholders manage the paradox of quality management in innovative projects. China, a developing country, is taken as the empirical setting. One precast project was examined in-depth in order to delineate the trajectory of quality management and development of formal rules. Key findings are: (1) experimentation before full-scale application is necessary; (2) during the experimentation and on-going implementation, it is important to formalize quality management plans; and (3) it is important to engage a wider range of stakeholders (such as clients, contractors, supervisors, government agencies, and professional experts), who could jointly contribute their knowledge to the implementation of the new technology and increase the legitimacy of innovative quality management methods. These findings may inform the quality management of projects and enrich the application of the PMBOK in developing countries.

Keywords: Quality management, innovative projects, paradox, project management, developing countries, regulation deficiency

Introduction

Project management and delivery is context specific. As one of the main areas of the Project Management Body of Knowledge (PMBOK), project quality management is also sensitive to the context, especially for the building and infrastructure projects that involve the safety of the workers and end-users at the construction and operation phases respectively. There is a wide range of regulations, codes, and standards that need to be complied with for realizing the quality of the project design, construction, and materials. Project quality management is undertaken through the method of plan-do-check-act (PDCA), which assumes that formal rules (such as regulations and codes) could work as the guidelines.

When contracting parties intend to adopt innovative technologies in building projects, they have to consider whether there exists rules, codes, and standards that specify how technologies could be used, and what are the key parameters in relation to safety and quality requirements. An absence of these rules and regulations might possibly deter the players from the adoption of the technologies. However, for the developing countries, it is less feasible to develop all codes and standards first because the economic and societal development requires a large volume of buildings and infrastructure development in a timely manner. The delayed provision of buildings and infrastructure might further exacerbate the increasing societal demands. Thus, at the project level, it is critical to examine how contracting parties, in the light of an absence of rules and regulations, deal with the paradox of managing quality in innovative building projects. However, it is still less well theoretically developed in the context of developing countries such as China.

Therefore, this chapter aims to investigate how contracting parties deal with project quality management in innovative building projects in China. The findings could reinforce the importance of customizing project quality management in developing countries, a subject which is currently underexplored. The findings could also inform managers and enable them to cope with quality management in innovative building projects in developing countries. The remainder of the chapter is organized as follows: the next section presents the literature review of the importance of context and its impacts on project management. This is followed by the development of project management in China and the challenges for quality management in innovative building projects in China. Then, a case study of a precast building project is elaborated upon with the theme of quality management in innovative building projects.

The importance of context in project management

It is well accepted that project management practice is context-specific (Besner and Hobbs, 2013). Many studies provided different perspectives for understanding the context of the project. For example, Engwall (2003) suggested that the project management practices employed should be understood in relation to previous and simultaneous courses of the practices, to future plans, and to the norms of their current surroundings. Further, Engwall (2003) emphasized that project management needs to extend its temporal scope, analyzing how project practices evolve through history over prior, present, and future projects, as well as its organizational scope, analyzing how project practices relate to long-term institutions as well as simultaneous activities in their environment. Manning (2008) argued that projects get embedded in multiple systemic contexts through the constitution of the structural properties (i.e., tasks, times, and teams) that guide project activities. These structural properties are embedded into the organizations, networks, and fields. Organizations are collective actors whose members engage in and coordinate project activities; interorganizational networks are sets of longer-term relationships between legally independent organizations; and organizational fields are areas of institutional life constituted by organizations and their members. Morris and Geraldi (2011) presented a three-level framework, where Level 1 is technical — that is, operational and delivery-oriented; Level 2 is strategic — managing projects as organizational holistic entities, expanding the domain to include their front-end development and definition and with a concern for value and effectiveness; and Level 3 is institutional — managing the institutional context, and creating the context and support for projects to flourish and for their management to prosper. They argued that management here is done for, and on, the project rather than in, or to, it.

The PMBOK is criticized as having lost its context. Hällgren *et al.* (2012) explained that context relevance may be lost at two levels. The first loss occurs when the practice of project management is transferred, through generalization and standardization, into the "Best Practice" in PMBOK; and the second occurs when "Best Practice" is transferred back to education, research, certification, and practice.

Project management is described as adopting a phased "stage-gate" approach as the professional standard. Lenfle and Loch (2010) explained that the shift toward the stage-gate approach and loss of the context took root in the 1960s when the so-called McNamara Revolution at the US Department of Defense was cemented by the codes and practices of the department and the National Aeronautics and Space Administration (NASA), contemporary scientific writing, and the foundation of the Project Management Institute (PMI).

Project management development in China

Practice

In the 1960s, the mathematician Luogeng Hua introduced and promoted the program management techniques, which were combined with the Chinese philosophy of "overall planning method." This was similar to the development trajectory of the programming techniques in Western countries. Luogeng Hua also convened and facilitated the first training event of program management techniques in 1965, and then organized multiple groups to promote these methods at the provincial level across China, and in a wide range of sectors. At this stage, project management was particularly represented by program techniques.

Another milestone in the development of project management in China was the construction of the Lubuge hydropower project in 1982. This was known as the first infrastructure project using a World Bank loan in China. This project also assumed importance after the opening of the reforms in 1979. In accordance with the loan agreement, some packages of the project were opened to foreign bidders. In the end, a Japanese company, Taisei, won one contract and achieved great success. Taisei deployed 35 staff members and employed 420 local workers. Their high productivity and overall success was in significant contrast to the performance of the Chinese contractors in the project. The construction market also received a great shake up. The national newspaper, *The Peoples' Daily* called this a "Lubuge shock." Inspired by the Lubuge experience, several government departments jointly initiated reforms to the Chinese construction firms and emphasized heavily the project management model used by the Japanese firm. Also, the universities offering civil engineering courses started to offer courses on construction project management, as requested by the government departments.

As can be seen from these two events, the project management practice in China was heavily influenced by foreign practices. Once these practices had demonstrated advantages, they were quickly adopted by the government departments and further promoted through various governmental initiatives.

Research institutes and associations

In 1981, Luogen Hua and several other researchers established the Chinese Society of Optimization, Overall Planning and Economic Mathematics (OOPEM), which covers a wide range of themes (see Table 23.1). In 1991, the Project Management Research Committee (PMRC) was established under OOPEM. This was the first research institute on the subject in China.

Table 23.1: National level research societies and their project management committees.

National level research societies	Sub committee	Areas
Chinese Society of Optimization, Overall Planning and Economic Mathematics	Construction Management Research Committee	General project management
Chinese Management Society	Project Management Committee	General project management
The Architectural Society of China	Construction Management Research Committee	Construction projects

A decade later, PMRC became a member of the International Project Management Association (IPMA) and was authorized by IPMA to certify PM professionals. In PMRC, the committee members consisted of the academic and practice tracks; the latter were from a wide range of sectors. Also, C-PMBOK (China-PMBOK) was released by PMRC.

In 1999, the China International Talent Exchange Foundation started cooperation with PMI. They introduced PMBOK and Project Management Professional (PMP) certification. In 2000, they organized the first PMP certification examination, with 316 participants. Many other sectors also organized project management research organizations, for example, the Construction Project Management Committee under the China Construction Industry Association, the Project Management Working Committee under the China Association of International Engineering Consultants, and the Project Management Working Committee under the China National Association of Engineering Consultants.

In addition, there are many research organizations at the provincial level; they have their own research activities and working agendas. The establishment of the research bodies indicated that a large number of professionals are involved in the area of project management. They have a wide range of networking activities, competitions, conferences, and workshops.

Project management knowledge

PMRC issued the C-PMBOK in 2001. Some bodies of knowledge were organized for particular sectors. For example, the Standard for Construction

Project Management was published by the Construction Project Management Committee under the China Construction Industry Association. These bodies of knowledge played a significant role in promoting project management practices in different sectors and organizations. They also provided a clear framework on the managing of projects.

Training and education

Similar to many other countries, there are two major forms of PM certification in China, namely IPMP and PMP. By September 2019, participants in the PMP examination were almost 600,000; and 420,000 passed the examination. Valid PMP certification holders are close to 300,000. This represents close to one third of the total certified PM professionals worldwide. China became the second largest market for the PMP certification.

In terms of education, there are no PM programs at the undergraduate level in China yet. The most relevant major at the undergraduate level is Construction Management, which covers PM as a core module. Over 400 universities in China offer Construction Management related degrees. Additionally, degree courses in Software Engineering also have project management modules. At the post-graduate level, there is a part-time project management professional program, which has been incorporated into the Master of Engineering Management program since 2016. On all the relevant programs and majors, PM is mandated as a core module.

Quality management and good practices: Governance and compliance

There is a need for compliance with regulations, standards, and codes that govern construction, with registration and certification. These are also known as the "push" factors of quality management (CIOB, 2019). The code of quality management (CIOB, 2019) noted that, in the UK, quality management has no set of regulations, compared to Construction Design and Management Regulations (CDM); instead, there is a muddle with a reliance on compliance with standards, codes, and regulations, backed up by building control and contract terms and conditions. The plethora of rules, standards, and regulations is complex and not easily understood or accessible (CIOB, 2019, p.10). Similarly, in Australia, the Federal Government bears ultimate responsibility for the National Construction Code (NCC) and National Standards which are then enforced through State regulatory mechanisms. According to Shergold and Weir (2018), NCC sets minimum requirements for the design, construction, and performance of buildings throughout Australia. All the stakeholders have an obligation to ensure that work on the project complies with the legislation (CIOB, 2019).

In relation to registration and certification requirements, some countries, such as China and Singapore, choose to license contractors. The registration system can define the type of work, size of work, and so on, while according to CIOB (2019), the UK has chosen an open approach by allowing the industry to self-regulate without registration and licensing, except for specialist trades such as work involving the handling of asbestos.

Building inspection regime

In Australia, New Zealand, and most countries with effective regulations, it is a requirement that a building consent is granted by an approving authority (Building Consent Authority) before the commencement of construction work. Thus, a building authority reviews and inspects the work and processes to ensure that the proposed and completed built item complies with performance requirements as specified in the building codes. This offers protection to current and future owners (Rotimi *et al.*, 2015). The inspection regime relies on building inspectors, who are qualified building surveyors, or building inspectors acting on behalf of building surveyors.[1] Building surveyors and building inspectors are experts in both the building code of Australia and different interpretations and building regulations in their state or territory. Building surveyors and inspectors do not work directly for builders; instead, they are employed as consultants and are required to be independent to ensure that they can carry out their

[1] https://build.com.au/building-inspections-new-houses

work without any conflict of interest (Doing Business, 2014). In a similar fashion, Fang and Chen (2019) document the *Jianli* system in China's construction industry. Employed by the project owners, serving as specialists, one of the key responsibilities of *Jianli* is the undertaking of quality inspections.

ISO 9000 quality standards

ISO 9001 is the international standard for quality management. Quality Management Systems (QMSs) are policies and documented procedures in place to communicate and inform how a company delivers its products to customers. ISO 9001:2015 outlines a framework for improving quality and a vocabulary of understanding for any organization looking to provide products and services that consistently meet the requirements and expectations of customers and other relevant interested parties in the most efficient manner possible. According to Chini and Valdez (2003), ISO 9000 has brought advantages, mostly in the improvement of internal management systems and as a marketing tool for certified companies. The literature reports that ISO 90001 certifications are popular in developing countries, including Sri Lanka (Senaratne and Mayuran, 2015), Egypt (Magd and Curry, 2003), Indonesia (Willar *et al.*, 2015), and many others, but the number of ISO 9001 QMS certified organizations is still low. Construction firms in developed countries such as Singapore (Low and Fong, 2002) and the US (Chini and Valdez, 2003) acknowledged the importance of ISO 9000. The transition of ISO 9001 from Quality Assurance to Quality Management has also contributed to the improvement of building quality in Singapore (Low and Seet, 2011). However, caution should be exercised, and it is pertinent to note that implementing ISO 9000 alone did not add much to quality improvement (Zeng *et al.*, 2005).

The implication of lean on quality management

There is increasing discussion on the implications of the lean approach to production for quality management. "Lean" is the term used to describe a principle-based continuous quality improvement management system based on the Toyota Production System. Toyota popularized the term *andon*, which is a visual management tool used in a manufacturing system to highlight the status of the operations. Construction professionals are also attracted to such innovative quality management tools. In Brazil, where *andon* was adapted to a horizontal project (Biotto *et al.*, 2014; Kemmer *et al.*, 2006), the reported benefits were: the number of work stoppages was reduced significantly; communication was greatly enhanced; and transparency was enacted as production problems were readily reported, discussed, and analyzed.

Apart from the lean quality tool, at the system level, Andersson *et al.* (2006) acknowledged that Total Quality Management (TQM), Six Sigma, and lean have many similarities, especially concerning origin, methodologies, tools, and effects. They also noted that there is a lot to gain if organizations are able to combine these three concepts, as they are complementary. Further Bacoup *et al.* (2018) proposed a new method combining both ISO standards and Lean Management concepts to achieve certification with a Lean Quality Management System (LQMS).

Innovative practices

Singapore's Construction Quality Assessment System (CONQUAS) Standards could be a good reference point for many developing or developed countries seeking to produce a nation-wide, trade-oriented comprehensive and stringent quality assessment system. CONQUAS was first developed in Singapore and launched in 1989 (Building and Construction Authority, 2005). Its aim is to make quality assessment objective by measuring constructed works against workmanship standards and specifications using a sampling approach. CONQUAS covers most aspects of general building works. The assessment considers three components: structural, mechanical and electrical, and architectural finishes. The sum of the scores of the three components gives the CONQUAS score for the project. It is worth mentioning that, in developing CONQUAS, many studies and numerous trials were conducted to fine-tune its new test techniques and assessment standards. The CONQUAS 9th edition was launched in 2017 to promote the adaptation of design for manufacturing and assembly

(DfMA), which supports both high quality and productivity. Low *et al.* (1999) found that construction firms certified to the ISO9000 quality standards achieved higher CONQUAS scores than non-certified firms.

Research method: Case study

This study takes an explorative analysis approach based on a qualitative single case study design (Yin, 2017). A precast concrete (PC) project was selected as a typical innovative building project, and PC building projects were adopted as the empirical context. PC buildings have been heavily promoted in China since 2013, with the Chinese State Council stating that some pioneering regions in China should achieve 30 percent precast building in new building projects over the 10 years from 2013. The provincial governments then prioritized the development of PC buildings in their political agendas, to be aligned with the directions of the State Council. There have been many incentive schemes to promote the use of PC construction. In Nanjing (Jiangsu province), the construction industry has been expected to deliver at least a 30 percent PC ratio for new building projects since 2017. Since PC buildings are relatively new to the market, this suggests that PC building projects are innovative, and that QM would be largely exploration oriented. Thus, taking PC building as the empirical context was deemed suitable for examining QM in innovative building projects.

In the construction sector, rules and regulations are very important. Governmental departments have strong regulatory requirements on the project delivery and operation in order to ensure the safety of the construction workers and end users. The standards in China have four layers: national, industrial, local, and company level standards. Two categories exist at the national and industrial levels. These are mandatory and selective requirements. The building projects must comply with the mandatory standards and requirements in China. In cases where the work involves new technologies, emerging construction methods, and new materials which are not yet specified in the mandatory standards, the clients will call for consultation with experts and specialists to ensure that the deployment of the aforementioned innovation is a controlled risk. The results from the consultation are evaluated by the construction departments. Similarly, for overseas standards and the like, the clients are required to report to the construction departments.

Several governmental departments are involved in the monitoring process. For example, during the planning stage, the project's master plan has to be checked. This is followed by the checking of the construction drawings. The Construction Safety Department monitors the implementation of the safety standards and the quality department monitors the construction, supervision work, and acceptance work. It is a standard process that if innovative technologies, materials, design, and construction methods are used, contracting parties have to do their work in compliance with the rules and regulations. For example, it is required that the design uses new technologies and materials that might possibly impact the project quality and safety. There are not yet any national standards; thus, it is required to provide testing reports by the authorized organizations which have to carry out testing and assessment. Then the reports have to be evaluated by the construction technology expert committee organized by the government departments. After these procedures, the new technology and materials are approved for use on the specific project.

For the PC project, similar rules are also required to be complied with. When the design has a structural system that is not specified by the standards, it might possibly influence the project quality and safety. It is required to provide an expert assessment review organized by the local construction department. The design review department will perform their tasks based on the experts' reports.

Case project

This project provided an insightful perspective into the quality management practice in innovative building projects. The project was commenced in November 2017 and handed over in June 2018. First, the project was listed in four demonstration programs,[2] indicating its

[2](1) Demonstration Projects of the Ministry of Housing and Urban–Rural Development; (2) Demonstration Projects of Construction Industry Modernization in Jiangsu; (3) Demonstration Projects of Green Building in Jiangsu; and (4) Demonstration Projects of Renewable Energy in Jiangsu.

pioneering position. This project fell into the category of systemic innovation (Gann *et al.*, 2010), employing innovative architectural and structural design solutions. The innovation in design significantly influenced the QM in design, PC production, and construction. It was also the tallest building with PC sheer wall panels in Jiangsu Province. Second, this project achieved high performance, attracting attention from a wide range of outside visitors, including other companies, universities, and government agencies. It achieved three stars in green building. Table 23.2 shows the project profile. It has a plot area of approximately 23,000 m^2 and a construction area of about 95,000 m^2. The project consists of 918 standardized apartments in six buildings (see Figures 23.1 and 23.2).

The project was expected to showcase advanced PC technologies. The PC elements designed for this project included PC sheer wall panels (with thermal insulation); PC slab; PC column, balcony, beams, and staircases; PC and prefinished bath units; and PC interior wall panels. It was expected to achieve transferable and replicable technical solutions and to win the highest quality award at the national level. The project employed a design–bid–build (DBB) approach. The key stakeholders were the public developer, design consultant, contractor, the supervision company (*jianli* in Chinese), and PC suppliers. The public developer was the largest public housing provider in the local market. The client had high requirements regarding quality

Table 23.2: Profile of the building project.

Items	**Quantity**
Plot area (m^2)	22771.79
Construction area (m^2)	94121.02
Above ground area (m^2)	77333.86
Underground area (m^2)	16787.17
Floor area ratio	3.48
Building density	33.34%
Greening area ratio	20.84 %
Precast ratio	38%

Figure 23.1: Project design sketch.

Figure 23.2: Site work of superstructure.

performance; and it had won national quality awards for its previous projects. The contractor is stated-owned and headquartered in Shanghai. The PC elements were procured by the contractor. The design firm specializes in PC building design and is also a leading player in the local market.

Data collection

Data were collected through archival documents, in-depth interviews, and site visits. Multiple investigators and a mix of data collection methods were used to achieve theoretical triangulation and to enhance confidence in the source data and eventual findings (Eisenhardt, 1989).

Interviews

Two rounds of face-to-face interviews were carried out. The interviews were audio-recorded with the permission of the interviewees and notes were taken during each interview. The first round of interviews involved 11 participants from the five stakeholders (the public developer, the design consultant, the contractor, the supervision consultant, and the government departments). The investigation of multiple stakeholders helped to triangulate the empirical findings. The qualitative evidence was used to develop the framework. For each stakeholder, experienced managers were asked to describe the novelty of the project. The interview questions were guided by the central constructs of the resilience framework, which in turn aided the interpretation of the data. The second round of interviews had five participants to verify the proposed framework. The interviewees were asked to rate the appropriateness of the proposed framework. The evidence was used to refine the framework.

Site visits and archival data

Additional data were sourced from site visits and archival documents. Three site visits were made: on April 13, September 28, and October 13, 2017. During these visits, construction was at different stages and faced different quality problems. Multiple site visits helped in reaching a comprehensive understanding of the QM in its different stages. Archival documents were obtained from a set of research reports presented by each stakeholder. The challenges faced and the solutions used in the design, the PC production, the construction, and the quality inspection by the government agencies were summarized.

Data analysis

A multi-stage process for data analysis was adopted, following the systematic combining approach (Dubois and Gadde, 2002). The data analysis followed an iterative process in which data collection and data analysis had significant overlap and influenced each other. Key practices and categories were initially identified from the first round of interviews, relying on labels that could represent similar descriptions across multiple interviews. To collapse the list of practices, only the completely agreed-on practices were initially retained. Practices involving conflicts would be further verified through subsequent interviews. This juxtaposition of contradictory evidence could help to inspire the insights.

The data analysis of the second round of interviews was based on content analysis, and was used to verify and alter the proposed framework. All interviewees in the second round agreed with the appropriateness of the resilience framework combining planning, monitoring, responding, and learning. They also verified the comprehensiveness of practices under each category. In the end, the interviewees agreed that the resilience framework presents them with a clear picture of managing quality in the innovative building project.

Results

The uncertainties and ambiguities feature

The qualitative data shows that the level of novelty of the building project could be inferred from the regulatory uncertainties, the technical ambiguities, and uncertainties (see Table 23.3), which in turn posed challenges to QM.

As for regulatory uncertainty, several key specifications and codes of practice were still being developed. For example, no well-established inspection methods for grouting had yet been prepared for PC standards. This was a major concern for the construction quality inspection department. The architect gave one example, indicating that "from 2015 the floor slabs had to comply with requirements of both thermal and acoustic insulation. Only the thermal insulation needed to comply with the

Table 23.3: Ambiguity and uncertainties associated with quality management.

Categories	Examples
Regulatory uncertainty	• The specifications for the adopted precast technologies were not well established • The change of relevant specifications was unplanned • The regulations for precast buildings were changed in an unplanned manner
Technical ambiguity	• Difficult to decide how to deal with the quality problem when it arises • Difficult to fully anticipate the impacts of the quality problem • Difficult to identify the root causes of the quality problem • Difficult to fully inspect the quality problem • The inspection methods were not well established
Technical uncertainty	• Unanticipated quality problems • Novel precast technologies adopted • Multiple alterations to the quality management method • Multiple alterations to the construction plans

standard before 2015. The problem is that there were few materials available on the market to fulfill the double requirement... Another example was the prohibition on the use of thermal insulation mortar this year; it was permitted for use last year. We thus had to alter the plans." This indicates the presence of a high level of regulatory uncertainty.

The novelty of the building project could manifest itself as technical uncertainty or ambiguity. One strategic target of this project was to integrate advanced PC technologies with the highest precast ratio (38 percent) in buildings of comparable size and height in Jiangsu. A variety of innovative technologies was adopted with the aim of showcasing the latest PC technologies. Technical uncertainties gave rise to unexpected problems. For example, the project teams had no prior experience of using precast sheer wall panels. The site manager noted that: "We had no clear plan on how to manage quality, among many other issues, in the production of PC elements and the procedures." The technical manager mentioned that "this was new to us. If it were not new, we could have followed the standards." The quality manager added: "lots of issues are under exploration in PC buildings." The developer's project manager shared that: "We had no idea what quality problems might occur. We had to investigate the problems step by step." Giving an example, he explained that: "the quality focus actually shifted. Water leakage at the windows was not a problem in this PC building. But we had to focus on water leakage at joint gaps." The chief engineer added that: "in our previous experience, we had only focused on on-site construction. But in this PC project, because we procured the PC components, we had to be involved with the production shop, and to maintain close interaction with the PC designer and supplier. Additionally, we had to quality control the PC supplier's work."

The ambiguity and uncertainties caused significant challenges for the quality management in this innovative project. If the codes and regulations had to be established first, it would take a much longer time for PC buildings to be adopted. Then, the completion of the project would be delayed. Thus, project managers had to manage the project quality without well-established rules and regulations. In addition, the contracting parties faced great time pressure as they had to deliver the project as specified in the contract. Thus, they had to cope with a range of problems during the design, PC production and construction stages.

Quality management practice and development of the rules

Formalizing quality management plans

Due to a lack of standards, the first step was to formalize a quality management plan, which worked as a control tool for the quality management. However, the quality management could not be fully guided by the existing rules and regulations.

Scenario description and redundancy

Since the key quality issues were exploratory in nature, the project team began with full descriptions of specific quality scenarios. The goal was to portray the scenarios so that an accurate assessment would be possible. The design manager noted: "Having a clear understanding of the characteristics of the scenario, we prepared various contingency plans for quality control. For example, we designed multiple positions in which the insulation materials could be placed. Each design came with full documentation of the associated risks and their consequences." The quality manager stated that: "whatever we are concerned with regarding the plan will be fully documented and discussed by the team."

The project team were satisfied with the effectiveness of Building Information Modelling (BIM) as a tool for describing the scenarios for the design and construction methods. BIM was used by the team to detect clashes among the areas of the technical disciplines and to highlight the mistakes associated with openings, embedded conduits, and inserts.

Redundancy mindsets were instilled during the QM planning. According to the contractor, two PC suppliers were hired because the onsite schedule could be more reliable if there were two suppliers. The site manager asked: "What if the sole supplier failed to deliver some of the PC elements on time? We could do nothing but wait, leading to a waste of man-hours."

Another example concerns the use of two hoisters. The chief engineer noted: "It was mandatory to have one hoister when hoisting the components up. But we added another to assure safety. The additional one might seem redundant, but it provided higher safety guarantees." The final example is the Halfen connection system. The technical manager shared that: "The original connection system required 1.5 mm in-depth fastening, which was a pretty standard requirement. But we increased this to 2 mm. The quality inspection department was also concerned with the reliability of the system since it was the first time it was used in Nanjing. However, 2 mm connection bolts were not available on the local market and so we purchased them from Germany."

Scrutinizing plans

(1) QM Plan scrutinizing

QM plans are scrutinized in a collective manner, involving the client, contractor, designer, and supervisors. Given this collective routine scrutinizing, the construction plans improved continuously. The developer's project manager commented: "It was not often that we had to interrogate the drawings in cast in-situ projects. In this project, we participated in the whole process." The contractor also discussed the construction plans in detail with the foremen and construction workers. The quality manager noted: "Workers can sometimes provide valuable feedback. It was not one-way communication, but mutual consultation." Construction workers could propose alternative views based on their frontline experience. This allowed the construction plan to be easily accepted by workers, as it was open to adopting: "the construction workers' reasonable suggestions," as noted by the quality manager.

(2) Expert consultation

Expert consultation was adopted in scrutinizing the construction plan. The project manager pointed out: "we did not have well-established standards for some technologies used in precast sheer wall panels. We thus had to consult experts in the absence of standards and given the conflicts with the existing rules and regulations." The client organized more than 10 expert consultations, at which PC construction experts with direct experience in the field looked for weaknesses in the construction plan. Often, staff from government agencies (such as the Department of Quality and Safety Supervision, and Department of Construction) were also invited to attend. Consensus was ultimately reached on adopting specific processes. However, organizing the expert consultation was time-consuming and sometimes interrupted the construction process. Nevertheless, it was, acknowledged that the interruption was tolerable, given that the project team had strong social responsibilities to promote the technologies and to produce high-quality public housing. The client's project manager cautioned that: "it may be a significant burden for those in the private sector who are reluctant to invest resources."

Involvement of multiple stakeholders

The active involvement of the client was necessary; this was because the client was the driving force for adopting the new technologies, as it had to make the investment. The use of new technology also required additional investment, which depended on the client's support and engagement.

Conscientiousness

Since the project team had no prior experience of PC sheer wall construction, they were preoccupied with the possibility of failure and became very mindful of that task. The quality manager noted: "At the start of the project, we had high requirements for mindfulness. We emphasized focusing on the details. No concessions or compromises were allowed." There are two reasons for this: first, the innovation in structural design has a significant impact on structural stability and safety. Second, the project is highly exposed to the public, due to it being a demonstration project. The project team was therefore motivated to pay great attention to quality.

The chief engineer stated that: "Our engineers had to monitor the hoister and lifting inserts embedded in the PC component every morning. The safety supervisor had to do spot checks." The site manager emphasized: "We were concerned that crane operators and riggers did not have the confidence to handle it because the assembly demanded very high levels of accuracy … The largest PC element weighs 4.55 tons, so we had to be very careful." They also specified the responsibilities of the crane operators and rigger. The quality manager shared: "We highlighted the consequence of misbehaviors. Through these processes, we hope to increase the consciousness of the workers."

However, construction workers' "quality'" attitudes did not change significantly at the start. The contractor's general assessment of the construction workers was that they did not have a high level of consciousness or awareness. Many of the on-site workers had no experience of PC construction and were not ready for the stringent quality requirements. However, the workers did not recognize the severity of the problems. The site manager stated that: "We had to instil the right attitude and mindset constantly through effective monitoring and education. We aimed to instil the mindset that precast quality needs great awareness, unlike traditional construction methods."

Middle-level managers, on the other hand, had a very mindful attitude. The site manager commented: "For the on-site management staff, conscientiousness was an important factor of good quality. The more conscientious the mindset, the easier it was for us to implement management principles." For example, the quality inspection was traditionally undertaken by the quality division alone. However, on this project, according to the site manager: "all the staff would gather together, including the quality engineers from other divisions, to participate in the quality inspection." The site manager explained that: "since we had not touched on this before, managers in all divisions had to be very careful about quality performance."

Real-time on-site monitoring

The contractor used a multiple-checking approach to ensure the effectiveness of QM during different stages of the project. For example, prior to grouting, it prepared a checklist that required approval from the quality, technical, and site management divisions. During grouting, they recorded all sign-offs to ensure that all decisions and actions were traceable. They undertook a final inspection with participants from the quality, technical, and site management divisions. The quality manager shared that: "The collective efforts in site inspection have contributed to the high quality."

The quality manager provided another example related to panel lifting: "We had three rounds of checks. The first was during lifting: our engineers ensured that the location of the PC element was accurate. The second check was for the alignment between the aluminum formwork and PC elements. It was common that vibrations caused movement between the aluminum formwork and the PC elements. The third check was on the concrete after casting. By using multiple checks, the quality of the panel lifting was ensured. All the checks took place on the site." The quality manager also emphasized that: "The multiple-round checking method was developed during the construction."

At the beginning of the project, there were many technical problems that could be traced back to the production of the PC elements. The contractor decided to assign one engineer to be based in the factory, not only to provide detailed construction requirements but also to monitor the production and to give feedback to the contractor on the status of production and quality.

Sensitive to operations

The workers understood their job and were sensitive to each step in their work. The experience they gained in the early stages helped them to detect quality problems as they worked, as noted by the site manager: "Our engineers could learn a lot from the front-line construction workers." To motivate the construction workers to be sensitive to the operations, the contractor implemented a strict monitoring policy. The site manager described this: "When workers noticed that concrete came out of the grouting hole, they should fix it immediately. They knew that strict penalties would apply if they ignored the problem. But monetary penalties were not the only motivation; it was most important to change their mindsets, as they had to understand that precast building was totally different from the cast in-situ."

The managers and engineers were also sensitive to the QM operations. It was found that the contractor's technical and quality divisions stayed on site all day. Key activities, such as the grouting process, were video-recorded. The quality manager described how "after concrete cast-in, all the engineers and managers would come together to the site, checking all the key quality control areas."

Incentives for identifying problems

The project was open to industry visitors. The project team considered that any quality problem was a reputational risk, and so they focused on quality and problem solving. This required workers to identify problems as early as possible. According to the site manager, the contractors constantly encouraged the construction workers and foremen to report their observations and suggestions on quality issues. This was based on the premise that many of the experienced workers have excellent ideas, and that their contributions would help to realize continuous improvement to QM. In addition, the contractor responded rapidly to reported quality problems. The quality manager stated that: "If construction workers or foremen found any issue in the construction, they could report it to us, along with suggestions and countermeasures. We would then quickly follow up and assign an engineer to review the problem and verify the suggestions. We found that construction workers and foremen were happy to participate. Most importantly, this helped them to increase labour efficiency and reduce rework."

Open and timely communication

The project team initiated timely discussions to identify quality problems. As the site manager described, "Our communication is open. We can convey what we saw and what we thought directly to the person in charge." The project team used the instant message application, which has a group chat feature. When a quality problem was identified, it was quickly broadcast in the chat so that everyone in the group could see it. Anyone with the relevant expertise or experience could then provide a timely response and suggestions. This platform provided opportunities to clarify and resolve discrepancies between architectural, structural, and mechanical requirements. Since there were many voids and embedded conduits in the PC elements, any potential clashes were shared on the instant message application with photos and a brief description. The quality manager shared that: "it was quite efficient and convenient."

Joint problem-solving on site

The contractor preferred problems to be resolved at the actual place where the problem was located on site. As with the Toyota Way approach to problem solving (Liker, 2004), the project team encouraged different parties on site to thoroughly study the situation and the problem. The quality manager described how this was done: "once an on-site quality problem that the foremen could not solve was spotted, we would go to the place and help them out immediately. Meanwhile, we would be working with others in order to find a better solution." Joint problem solving on-site provided ready understanding of both situations and problems.

Also, tours of this demonstration project were arranged for a wide range of visitors. They provided some comments and suggestions on the quality management.

Experimentation and testing

Experimentation

The experimentation undertaken on the project took place in a full-scale pre-construction mock-up with a trialing-out purpose. The mock-up arrangement was a standardized unit of approximately 150 m^2, constructed using the construction techniques and materials that were expected to be used during construction on the project. The designer welcomed such experimentation explaining that: "numerous problems could not be detected on the 2D drawings and 3D models. We have had issues before, where the PC elements transported to the building site could not be installed because of inaccurate alignment. Experimentation was a great strategy to optimize the design solutions."

After the experimentation phase, the project team undertook a 360-degree review of the design, PC production, and construction. In the end, five groups of quality problems were identified and 29 sets of counter-measures were suggested. The experimentation exposed the problems before the project commenced. It provided an opportunity for fine-tuning the QM plans in a timely manner, and facilitated the learning of the construction workers, engineers and managers. The chief architect shared that: "setting up the experimentation had multiple purposes: (1) exposing quality problems before the real construction; (2) nurturing collaboration between different teams; (3) promoting craftsmanship; (4) aligning the design, PC production, and construction methods; and (5) preparing a reception area for visitors." All interviewees commented that they did not deal with any significant problems after the full-scale preconstruction mock-up. The full-scale construction mock up is an ideal method of engaging the construction parties (i.e., clients, designers, and construction teams) at all levels.

Learning by doing

Three practices discussed during the interviews demonstrate the application of learning by doing: these were interim reviews, sharing experience, and training.

(1) Interim reviews

The project team had three reviews at key milestones: mock-up completion (experimentation), ground floor completion, and tenth floor completion. The review at each stage had its own focus. The interim reviews enabled the team to summarize the key quality problems that occurred and to find effective solutions in a timely manner. This reduced the negative impact of quality problems on later stages of the project. The quality manager explained that: "The completion of the ground floor provided us with many meaningful quality data. We then had to determine what caused the defects. We listed all the possible causes, reviewed the statistics, and identified which ones most affected quality performance. All the factors were thoroughly examined."

(2) Training

Training was provided for the general construction workers and tradespersons. The contractor issued certificates to tradespersons who had been qualified to perform jobs, such as the grouting and crane operations. This certificate was valid only for this project. The training on the grouting was provided by the supplier. The site manager described an example of the training: "We required the crane operators to pass a test. We drew a rectangle on the ground and checked whether the driver could reach a small object within that boundary. Passing this type of test indicates that the drivers were competent to perform the lifting work."

(3) Sharing experience

Experience was effectively shared among the construction workers. They learned the techniques as soon as they were hired. The site manager shared that: "we often brought construction workers from other building sites to learn specific things, for instance, how to grout, how to clear grout holes, and many others. The construction workers thus had a chance to discuss with each other." The contractor also initiated intense cross-division experience sharing. The technical manager described this: "we had a routinized experience sharing session in which managers from other divisions shared their experience. Every division had to assign a staff member to share in a rotating manner."

Discussion

Project management needs to be considered in the context in which it is practiced. While there are formal steps for managing new technology adoption in innovative building projects, how contracting parties effectively manage project quality is still less examined. This study examined how contracting parties deal with quality management in innovative building projects where the codes and standards do not yet exist. A PC building project in China was selected as the case study which provided an example of how the context of the project might impact the evolution of the quality management practice.

The case study showed that there are significant barriers facing the adoption of new technologies. For example, contracting parties face a high level of regulatory uncertainties, technical ambiguities, and other uncertainties. Contracting parties might also encounter difficulties in deciding how to deal with the quality problem when it arises, or what the problem's root causes are. This was largely because there is a lack of formal standards. Apart from the contracting parties, the government departments are concerned with these issues too, as they did not have quality inspection and checking methods in place as they were not yet established. Thus, they worried about the appropriateness and robustness of accepting the project quality. The concerns from the government departments would then pass to the contracting parties, who had little confidence in their ability to persuade the government departments to accept the project quality. Also, additional upfront cost would have to be incurred in the adoption of the new technology, i.e., on the experimentation and identifying and solving the new problems. This might bring about a financial burden on the client. Since the project studied was a demonstration project, the parties received a substantial amount of subsidies from the PC-related funds; this helped to relieve the client's financial concerns.

Through the case study, it was found that it is important to engage a wider range of stakeholders who could jointly contribute their knowledge to the quality management plan. Also, engaging them during the process could ensure the transparency of the quality management methods. This would increase the acceptance of the innovative technology and quality management methods. Typical stakeholders include clients, contractors, supervisory firms, government department, and professional experts. Some of them have contractual relationships among them, for example, the client, contractor, and supervisory firms. Engaging these parties could be made possible through the contract which specifies each party's inputs and responsibilities for managing quality in innovative projects. In addition, some stakeholders rely on assistance from a larger community to which they belong. For example, contracting parties consult experts from their network and organize various kinds of expert consultation events. Also, visitors from other companies contribute their comments and suggestions on managing quality in the course of project implementation. Inputs from different parties increase the legitimacy of the innovative quality management methods, which subsequently enhance understanding of the technologies and their applications. This, in the end, enables the acceptance of quality management plans of new technologies.

While there is no set of standards available, it is important to formalize the inspection and quality check methods through the experimentation and on-going learning, which could help to standardize the quality management and increase the quality management level. It was realized that it is difficult to fully formalize the quality management plans at the start due to the lack of quality management standards. Thus, it is important to describe the various scenarios for the quality management plan. Also, it is critical to carry out experimentation through which contracting parties could have a better understanding of the scenario of the quality management and identify the key risks. However, the experimentation is only close to, but not, the real scenario. Thus, on-going learning would be critical at the implementation stage. In this project, the contractor undertook a timely review after completion of the first floor, third floor, and tenth floor. The review helped to stabilize the QM plans.

Overall, this study contributes to the existing knowledge on project quality management by presenting a context-contingency view. When managing a project in the context of an innovative structure and less specified formal rules, it is important to formalize the rules through experimentation and on-going learning by doing. It is an iterative process. It is important to engage a wide range of stakeholders during the rule formalization, and implement learning-by-doing.

Conclusion

Project management is context-sensitive, which indicates that quality management should be considered in the specific context. This study examined how quality is managed in two-layer contexts, namely, the innovative building and regulation contexts. In particular, this study examined how contracting parties cope with quality management in innovative projects in China. An in-depth case study was carried out; it involved an innovative PC building.

The key findings of the study are: (1) it is important to engage a wide range of stakeholders, who can increase the legitimacy of innovative quality management methods; (2) in innovative works, it is necessary to undertake experiments before full-scale application is necessary; and (3) during the experimentation and the project implementation, it is important to review and formalize the quality management plans, which could increase the quality management capabilities during the project process. It supports the proposition that practice shall be prioritized whilst formalizing the experience and learning into the development of rules.

There are also limitations in this research. First, the project studied was a demonstration project, which received governmental subsidies for the adoption of new PC technologies. These demonstration projects can play a pioneering role in inventing and diffusing new technologies; they might not be the common commercial cases where contracting parties prioritize their profit margins. As Chinese construction companies continue to increase spending to develop new, innovative products and technologies for application on their construction projects, the number of innovative projects is expected to increase. Therefore, it would be appropriate to undertake further research to extend the discussion of quality management in such a developing context. There is a case for including innovation management as part of the project management body of knowledge for developing countries.

References

Andersson, R., Eriksson, H. and Torstensson, H. (2006). Similarities and differences between TQM, six sigma and lean. *The TQM Magazine*, 18(3), 282–296.

Bacoup, P., Michel, C., Habchi, G. and Pralus, M. (2018). From a quality management system (QMS) to a lean quality management system (LQMS). *The TQM Journal*, 30(1), 20–42.

Besner, C. and Hobbs, B. (2013). Contextualized project management practice: A cluster analysis of practices and best practices. *Project Management Journal*, 44(1), 17–34. https://doi.org/10.1002/pmj.21291.

Biotto, C., Mota, B., Araújo, L., Barbosa, G. and Andrade, F. (2014). Adapted use of andon in a horizontal residential construction project. Paper presented at the *Proceedings of the 22nd Annual Conference of the International Group for Lean Construction: Understanding and Improving Project Based Production*. Oslo, Norway, June, pp. 1295–1305.

Building and Construction Authority (2005). *CONQUAS 21: The BCA Construction Quality Assessment System*. Singapore.

Chini, A. R. and Valdez, H. E. (2003). ISO 9000 and the US construction industry. *Journal of Management in Engineering*, 19(2), 69–77.

CIOB (2019). *Code of Quality Management — Guide to Best Practice Construction Quality Management*. Chartered Institute of Building, Bracknell.

Doing Business (2014). *What Role Should Risk-Based Inspections Play in Construction?* The World Bank, Washington, DC.

Dubois, A. and Gadde, L.-E. (2002). Systematic combining: An abductive approach to case research. *Journal of Business Research*, 55(7), 553–560.

Eisenhardt, K.M. (1989). Building theories from case study research. *Academy of Management Review*, 14(4), 532–550.

Engwall, M. (2003). No project is an island: Linking projects to history and context. *Research Policy*, 32(5), 789–808. https://doi.org/10.1016/s0048-7333(02)00088-4.

Fang, Q. and Chen, L. (2019). Understanding the role of Jianli in China: Practice perspective. *Journal of Professional Issues in Engineering Education and Practice*, 145(3), 05019004.

Hällgren, M., Nilsson, A., Blomquist, T. and Söderholm, A. (2012). Relevance lost! A critical review of project management standardisation. *International Journal of Managing Projects in Business*, 5(3), 457–485. https://doi.org/10.1108/17538371211235326.

Kemmer, S.L., Saraiva, M. A., Heineck, L. F., Pacheco, A., Novaes, M. d. V., Mourão, C. and Moreira, L. (2006). The use of andon in high rise building. Paper presented at the *Proceedings of the 14th Annual Conference of the International Group for Lean Construction*. Santiago, Chile, July, pp. 575–582.

Lenfle, S. and Loch, C. (2010). Lost roots: How project management came to emphasize control over flexibility and novelty. *California Management Review*.

Liker, J. K. (2004). *The Toyota Way: 14 Management Principles from the World's Greatest Manufacturer*. McGraw-Hill, New York.

Low, S. and Seet, K. (2011). Enhancing construction quality through TQM. *The Singapore Engineer Magazine*, 16–22.

Low, S.P. and Fong, E.T. (2002). Preparations for ISO 9001: 2000 — A study of ISO 9000: 1994 certified construction firms. *Construction Management & Economics*, 20(5), 403–413.

Low, S.P., Tan, K.B. and Ang, A.A.L. (1999). Effectiveness of ISO 9000 in raising construction quality standards: Some empirical evidence using CONQUAS scores. *Structural Survey*, 17(2), 89–108.

Magd, H. and Curry, A. (2003). An empirical analysis of management attitudes towards ISO 9001: 2000 in Egypt. *The TQM Magazine*, 15(6):381–390, DOI:10.1108/09544780310502714.

Manning, S. (2008). Embedding projects in multiple contexts — A structuration perspective. *International Journal of Project Management*, 26(1), 30–37. https://doi.org/10.1016/j.ijproman.2007.08.012.

Morris, P.W.G. and Geraldi, J. (2011). Managing the institutional context for projects. *Project Management Journal*, 42(6), 20–32. https://doi.org/10.1002/pmj.20271.

Rotimi, F.E., Tookey, J. and Rotimi, J.O. (2015). Evaluating defect reporting in new residential buildings in New Zealand. *Buildings*, 5(1), 39–55.

Senaratne, S. and Mayuran, J. (2015). Documentation management based on ISO for construction industries in developing countries. *Journal of Construction in Developing Countries*, 20(2), 81–95.

Shergold, P. and Weir, B. (2018). Building confidence: Improving the effectiveness of compliance and enforcement systems for the building and construction industry across Australia. Building Ministers Forum, Canberra. https://www.industry.gov.au/sites/default/files/July%202018/document/pdf/building_ministers_forum_expert_assessment_-_building_confidence.pdf.

Willar, D., Coffey, V. and Trigunarsyah, B. (2015). Examining the implementation of ISO 9001 in Indonesian construction companies. *The TQM Journal*.

Yin, R.K. (2017). *Case Study Research and Applications: Design and Methods*: Sage Publications, Thousand Oaks, CA.

Zeng, S., Tian, P., Tam, C. and Tam, V.W. (2005). Evaluation of implementing ISO 9001: 2000 standard in the construction industry of China. *Architectural Science Review*, 48(1), 11–16.

https://doi.org/10.1142/9789811224720_0024

Chapter 24

A Review of the Evolution of Project Management in South Africa

Clinton Aigbavboa, John Aliu and Wellington Didibhuku Thwala

University of Johannesburg, South Africa

Abstract

Project management (PM) skill is in high demand across the world. There is a shortage of skilled project managers in South Africa as the demand for PM skills in South Africa has increased significantly across a wide variety of industries. This shortage is exacerbated by the significant volumes of investment in infrastructure and services. The advent of the Fourth Industrial Revolution (4IR), has initiated a digital transformation across industries, including the PM profession. This revolution will drive the evolution of the PM profession in the years ahead and lead to the emergence of Project Management 4.0. Through a bibliometric approach, this chapter examines the evolution of the PM concept in South Africa by reviewing the various paradigm shifts in the profession from an "old" traditional model to the current "new" paradigm. This was achieved by mapping key knowledge areas and co-occurring keywords by identifying trends in research on the PM concept in the built environment domain within a 26-year period in works indexed in the Scopus database. The chapter also examines the implications of the 4IR for the PM profession and how project managers can leverage on this latest wave of digitalization. Finally, the chapter predicts both the hard and soft skills that project managers will be required to have in order to thrive in the fast-paced digital era and to make a meaningful contribution to the efforts to attain national aspirations in South Africa. The study concludes by presenting thought-provoking and practical ideas for the South Africa PM bodies, PM researchers, and higher education institutions as they revamp and restructure their curricula and research agenda to align with the coming mandate of Project Management 4.0.

Keywords: Construction education, construction management, engineering education, Fourth Industrial Revolution, project managers and project management education

Introduction

Project management (PM) is as old as humanity, and several large and complex construction projects were successfully completed during the early times despite the uncertainties and difficulties they faced at the time that could have rendered them a failure. Many of these projects were challenging in many ways; they required advanced planning, large scope and related changes, an enormous workforce, a considerable amount of time, and precise execution of new designs involving innovative technologies. In spite of the successful completion of these projects, there is little documentation of the organizational arrangements, methods, and techniques that were deployed in executing them. It is suggested that it was not until the 1950s that procuring and implementing agencies and executing companies began to adopt systematic tools and techniques to undertake complex projects (Seymour and Hussein, 2014). According to Chiu (2010), entities such as the United States Navy (founded in 1775) and the Manhattan Project (started in 1939) played a major role in the formulation and documentation of the principles of modern PM methods and techniques. The latter was undertaken during the Second World War and was critical to the development of the first set of nuclear weapons steered by the US and also involving the UK and Canada. Subsequent projects in the 1960s such as the space program (including the landing on the moon in 1969) further sparked the formulation and adoption of tools to manage large-scale projects. With technological advancements gaining momentum in the 1970s, PM software were developed by companies such as

Oracle. As personal computers (PCs) became more affordable in the 1980s and 1990s, PM tools such as PRojects IN Controlled Environments (PRINCE2) and Critical Chain Project Management (CCPM) were created by smaller companies (Marić, 2017) for the management of projects of all kinds regardless of the environment.

Also, since the turn of the twenty-first century, many industries and organizations have accepted, and have been applying, PM theories, tools, and techniques in their operations. PM courses are being taught in many universities, while PM is currently evolving at a fast pace and is becoming more of a science than an art (Seymour and Hussein, 2014). This has led to, and has also been aided by, the increased proliferation of software and applications, increased standardization of processes, and refinement of concepts. As an example, one of the significant advancements of PM is the development of Total Cost Management (TCM) thinking. According to the Association for the Advancement of Cost Engineering International (AACE), TCM refers to "a systematic approach to managing cost throughout the life cycle of any enterprise, program, facility, project, product or service" (Hollmann, 2006, p. 8).

The world is entering the era of the Fourth Industrial Revolution (4IR). Schwab (2017) suggested that this era of digitalization is characterized by a fusion of technologies, blurring the lines between the physical, digital, virtual, and biological spheres often referred to as cyber-physical systems. It is predicted that this will have major global impacts on economies, jobs, and education. While job losses have been predicted, a corresponding large number of new jobs will be created; thus, project managers must be willing to reskill, upskill and multi-skill themselves in response to the demand for new jobs and for the better management of projects.

This chapter has three major parts. First, it unearths how PM (both generally and in the South African context) has evolved, through a review of the various paradigm shifts in the profession from an "old" traditional model through the transition to a "new" form. Second, the implications of the 4IR on the PM profession and how project managers can leverage on the wave of digitalization are considered. Finally, the chapter predicts both the hard and soft skills that project managers will be required to possess to thrive in the fast-paced digital era and to make a meaningful contribution in South Africa as PM.

Evolution of project management

The Project Management Institute (PMI) describes a project as "a temporary group of tasks designed to produce a unique product, service or result" and PM as "the application of knowledge, skills, tools and techniques to project activities to meet the project requirements" (PMI, 2013). In the past, for projects to be considered a success, engineers, architects, and designers had to carefully consider all the processes from the initiation and planning phases, through the execution and monitoring, and to the completion stage of the project. Consequently, each successfully executed project should pave the way for the advancement of the techniques and processes applied on the next. However, the documentation of earlier projects is scarce mainly because there has been more interest in the outcomes rather than the methods adopted (Morris, 2013).

There is no agreed timeline on when and how PM came into existence and different researchers have provided several opinions on its emergence. According to Chiu (2010), in the book, *An Introduction to the History of PM: From the earliest times to A.D.1900*, Henri Fayol and Henry Gantt have been regarded as the forefathers of PM (Chiu, 2010). While this is debated, both are still regarded as the progenitors due to their significant contributions to the field. Fayol (1841–1925), a French mining engineer, played a pivotal role in equipping the French army before the First World War. It was during his role as the Managing Director of the leading steel company at the time that he outlined five functions of management and 14 principles of management that still guide managers on how to effectively execute them to this day. These five functions were: planning, organizing, commanding, coordinating, and controlling. However, Fayol's theory came under criticism from several scholars who believed that the philosophy did not fully reflect the managerial complexities faced by managers as they execute their daily activities. Despite those criticisms, Fells (2000), in a paper titled: "Fayol stands the test of time," argues that Fayol's elements of management have been reinforced by more recent works, and he also confirms that the five functions of management provide a general overview of present-day managerial functions (Fells, 2000).

As alluded to by Chiu (2010), the second father of modern PM is Henry Gantt (1861–1919). Gantt, an American mechanical engineer and management consultant, is best known for the development of the Gantt chart, which has been adopted in breaking up large projects into smaller manageable tasks. The Gantt chart, which is still widely used today and is considered as a vital tool in a project manager's toolkit (Seymour and Hussein, 2014), also takes into consideration the fact that some tasks and stages are dependent on each other. It is pertinent to note that one school of thought believes the chart was developed from earlier work by Karol Adamiecki, a Polish economist and engineer.

According to Snyder and Kline (1987), the modern PM era began in 1958 with the advent of tools such as the Program Evaluation and Review Technique (PERT) and the Critical Path Method (CPM). PERT was mainly developed to simplify the planning, scheduling, and processes of large-scale and complex projects such as the US Navy's Polaris nuclear submarine project in 1958 and the 1968 Winter Olympics in Grenoble, France. PERT visualizes the different scheduling scenarios of a complex and large-scale project and addresses the uncertainties that might hinder the start or completion of a project. CPM, the project modeling technique, was invented almost simultaneously with PERT. Its creation gained momentum when DuPont de Nemours Company decided to embark on the construction of a major chemical plant (Burke, 2013). Originally known as Project Planning and Scheduling (PPS), CPM was initiated when the company sought techniques to accurately estimate the cost and time of the project. The difference between the two techniques is that, simply put, PERT is event-oriented while CPM is activity-oriented (Burke, 2013).

Kwak (2005) highlighted four notable periods which mark the evolution of PM: before 1958; from 1958 to 1979; from 1980 to 1994; and from 1995 to the present day. Kwak (2005) explained that modern PM gained prominence between the 1900s and 1950s as the field was transformed from a craft system to human relations administrations. The first era (1900 to the 1950s) marked the advent of the Gantt Chart as well as an understanding of the concepts of job specifications and how they contribute to the successful completion of projects. Notable projects undertaken in this era, all in the US, included the Hoover Dam, Interstate Highway, and Manhattan Project, which many still consider as the project that ushered in the era of modern PM. According to Kwak (2005), the second era (from 1958 to 1979) was marked by significant technological advancement and the application of management science. This era marked the arrival of the first plain paper copier (Xerox 914) as well as the commencement of the application of PERT and CPM. The third era (from 1980 to 1994) witnessed the multi-tasking of PCs that had an impact on various aspects of business and work including PM. The improved efficiency of PCs paved the way for the development of PM software that were capable of processing complex data which were required to manage projects (Kwak, 2005).

The era of 4IR is based on the concept of cyber-physical systems, which allow for the representation of various business processes, production processes, and services to be represented in a virtual world through platforms that allow the interaction between humans, machines, goods, and services. This new era has triggered a digital transformation across several industries, including the construction industry. To gain competitive advantage, organizations must now utilize technology and data for strategy development and project planning, execution, and delivery. Technologies such as machine learning, automation, artificial intelligence (AI), and the Internet of Things have opened new possibilities for the workplace and especially for the smart management of projects. With project managers often at the sharp end of implementing change, the profession must be flexible and adaptive to this new wave of digitalization. For organizations, the impact of this revolution on production processes will not only influence the technological and infrastructural aspects, but also the organizational structures and management styles. In this era of digitalization, project managers will become the main drivers of projects that are of significant strategic importance for the future of organizations.

A key feature of the 4IR era is the emergence of hybrid project teams in which some team members will be virtual assistants (software and applications that possess learning and expressive skills that are similar to humans), while others will be tangible. This new wave of digitalization will also emphasize the innovativeness of projects and project teams are expected to become smaller and, as posited by Schwab (2017), more focused on specific objectives rather than the broader ones. It is suggested that automation will be the new norm as fringe business processes that do not require analytical and design skills will be gradually automated, which will see corporate structures replaced by more streamlined and seamless structures (Zhou *et al.*, 2015). Another feature of PM in the 4IR era is that companies will have new business operations models — for instance, a company can be involved in project conceptualization and implementation across various regions and with the aid of virtual team members from different countries and continents, creating a cultural challenge for project managers (Eberhard *et al.*, 2017). Furthermore, big data will become available and project managers will require an improved skill set to handle these data for project execution.

Evolution of project management in South Africa

South Africa, as a nation, is no stranger to the concept of PM. In the 1950s, the term placed emphasis on the process of budgeting, scheduling, and cost control. A few decades later, the concept of project information systems (that ran on mainframe computers) gained momentum. Since then, PM has been revamped in the country to involve a wide range of areas such as risk management, operations management, new product development, and systems thinking. A notable instance where PM was applied in the new political dispensation after the apartheid period was in the Reconstruction and Development Programme (RDP), which was initiated to enhance service delivery for the citizenry, and especially for the largely segregated and disadvantaged Africans. The RDP contained several initiatives, strategies and policy programs that were aimed to meet basic needs, develop human resources, build the economy, and democratize the state and society (ANC, 1994). Thus, PM was applied in nation building, through the RDP.

In recent times, several major projects have been undertaken in South Africa. These include the hosting of the 2010 FIFA World Cup; construction of the OR Tambo International Airport; the Gautrain rapid rail link project completed in 2010; construction of the Leonardo project between 2015 and 2019 (resulting in the tallest building in Africa); and refurbishments and upgrades of stadia, ports, and several landmark projects, such as the Mall of Africa and Discovery Building. Despite the magnitude and complexity of these projects, South Africa has fared well in their successful execution according to international standards and practices despite the limited expertise of its project managers compared with their counterparts in the developed countries (Ogunsanya *et al.*, 2016). While some attribute the limited expertise to weak political and economic conditions (Kissi and Ansah, 2016), others, such as Ahlemann *et al.* (2013) and Ika (2012) cite the inability to directly apply the Western concepts of PM in the African context as another major concern.

According to the South African Council for the Project and Construction Management Professions (SACPCMP), PM practices are controlled through six stages in the country. These are: "project initiation and briefing, concept and viability, design development, tender documentation and procurement, construction and contract administration and project close out" (SACPCMP, 2016). However, there are several schools of thought on the classes of knowledge that are essential for project managers to achieve success, and two stand out: generic, and industry-specific knowledge (Besner and Hobbs, 2008). The proponents of the generic knowledge school of thought opine that PM knowledge can be applicable across different sectors or industries. They further suggest that for a project manager to be successful, a project toolkit rather than the specific technical knowledge is important (Turk, 2007). This implies that a project manager in construction can rely solely on PM knowledge, rather than technical knowledge of the built environment.

The PMI Project Management Body of Knowledge (PMBOK) 4th edition listed nine generic knowledge areas that are requisite for project managers' success. They were: Communication Management, Cost Management, Human Resource Management, Integration Management, Procurement Management, Quality Management, Risk Management, Scope Management, and Time Management (PMBOK, 2008). A tenth area, stakeholder management, was added in the PMI PMBOK 5th edition of 2015. A further four areas have been incorporated in the PMI Construction Extension to the PMBOK and they are: claims management, environmental management, financial management, and safety management (PMI, 2008). These inclusions suggest that a generic school of thought does not fully suffice due to the dynamics and intricacies of the construction industry, and its projects and products. Hence, knowledge of the domain is essential for a project manager in construction. The proponents of the second paradigm assert that possessing knowledge of the industry is necessary to achieve success as a project manager. Unlike the previous paradigm, this school of thought believes that both industry-specific knowledge and PM knowledge should be mandatory for all project managers (Turk, 2007). The importance of industry knowledge was also highlighted by the SACPCMP, which states that for project managers to be successful in their projects in South Africa, they need to possess certain PM competencies and technical competencies (SACPCMP, 2015). In these regards, a project manager in construction should have: knowledge of construction science, knowledge of construction processes, knowledge of design processes, and knowledge of financial and cost factors.

Project management as a discipline in South Africa

Project Management as a discipline gained prominence in the US in the 1960s, in the UK in the 1980s, and in South Africa during the 2000s. There are several programs through which qualifications in PM can be obtained in South Africa. These include undergraduate and post-graduate degree programs, and diploma and certificate programs in PM. While some of the institutions offer a generic PM syllabus, others offer industry-specific programs on both an on-campus and distance-learning basis. Some of the shorter courses include the Higher Certificate in PM (course work) offered, for instance, by the Damelin Education Group, the Intensive PM Program (IPMP) (industry-specific) offered by the University of the Free State, and the Program in PM (PPM) (course work) offered by the University of Pretoria. MSc Degrees in PM are offered by both the University of Cape Town and the Nelson Mandela Metropolitan University. Generally, qualifications for PM courses are registered through the South African Qualifications Authority (SAQA) and are given appropriate National Qualifications Framework (NQF) levels.

Regulations and legislation on project management in South Africa

In the construction industry, the project manager should possess the relevant knowledge and skills to successfully execute the projects which tend to be technically complex and involve the bringing together of specialists in different areas. Robbins *et al.*, (2012) suggested that for project managers to effectively discharge their duties, they must exhibit interpersonal, technical, problem-solving, organizational skills and now, geopolitical knowledge. Project managers are also required to understand the politics and political environment of their organizations and be able to pay attention to details which is the embodiment of risk management; they must also possess management competencies. Ahsan *et al.* (2013) also noted that project managers should have adequate technical skills in Information and Communications Technology (ICT). The regulations and legislation on project management and the operations of project managers in South Africa are next considered.

Project and Construction Management Professions Act of 2000

In South Africa, PM is regulated through professional associations and statutory institutions. The South African Council for the Project and Construction Management Professions (SACPCMP) was created through the Act of Parliament of 2000. The essence of the Act is in its four main objectives. The first is ensuring that a juristic person be known as SACPCMP. Second, the Act seeks to provide for the registration of professionals, candidates, and specified categories in the project and construction management professions. Third, it provides for the regulation of the relationship between the SACPCMP and the overarching statutory organization, the Council for the Built Environment. Finally, the Act provides for matters connected therewith (South Africa Project and Construction Management Act, 2000). In Section 18 of the Act, there are several categories an individual may register for, and they include: professional, candidate, or specified categories recommended by the Council. The Professional portfolio is divided into professional construction manager or professional construction project manager, while the Candidate category is also divided into candidate construction manager or candidate construction project manager. An individual may only practice in any of these categories if they are registered with SACPCMP (South Africa Project and Construction Management Act, 2000).

South African Council for the Project and Construction Management Professions

Applications for registration by the SACPCMP are assessed on the basis of the applicant's theoretical knowledge and experience. The main requirement, a report, usually requires details of the applicant's work experience, successes, and milestones achieved while executing a project (this should reflect the 10 knowledge areas of PM), as well as challenges and shortcomings faced while undertaking these projects (SACPCMP, 2011). SACPCMP is a statutory organization that was established by Section Two of the Project and Construction Management Act, 2000 and is one of the six built environment councils (SACPCMP, 2011). According to SACPCMP, the council was formed to provide statutory professional certification, registration, and regulation of project and construction management professionals, to protect the public's interest, and to advance construction management and PM education and practice.

Project Management South Africa

PM South Africa (PMSA) is a SAQA-recognized professional association representing the interests of project, program, and portfolio management practitioners in South Africa. PMSA was established to create an enabling environment for professional development through a variety of activities and resources. Formerly known as the Project Management Institute of South Africa (PMISA), PMSA was formed in 1997 as a national association to represent PM professionals across all sectors in South Africa and to ensure quality in PM practices. The drive to create PMSA came from a realization that there was a need for a cross-sector forum for practitioners to meet and work together and for a national body to work with local organizations and the South African government in developing effective PM practices within South Africa.

Research method

A rationale of this study was to unearth the evolution of PM in South Africa by reviewing various paradigm shifts in the profession from an "old" traditional model to the current "new" paradigm. This was achieved via a bibliometric approach which identified and mapped key knowledge areas and co-occurring keywords by identifying research trends and patterns in PM from a South African perspective. The bibliometric analysis was used to map PM areas under several research themes obtained by keywords clusters. The collection of data for this study focused on literature in the Scopus database (Thelwall, 2018). According to Aghimien *et al.*, (2019), Web of Science (ISI) had earlier been considered as the major database for scientific research. However, since Elsevier Science introduced Scopus in 2004, it has gained popularity among researchers from various fields and has been adopted in various review works (Oliveira *et al.*, 2018; Tseng *et al.*, 2019). Scopus has been more widely adopted than other databases owing to its wide coverage of various peer-reviewed literature and quality web sources (Conforti *et al.*, 2018; Zhong *et al.*, 2019).

Published journal and conference papers in the built environment were targeted as reliable sources on the PM subject. Journal articles were considered owing to the reliable, high quality, in-depth, and peer-reviewed scholarly information they provide (Zheng *et al.*, 2016; Aghimien *et al.*, 2019). Conference proceedings, according to Ben-Daya *et al.* (2019) have been recognized as reliable sources of literature to be reviewed for academic work. Therefore, conference proceedings that addressed PM-related issues were included in this study. Special attention was paid to the search schema as shallow searches may exclude some important documents. Using the Scopus database, the following retrieval schema were entered into the catalog: (TITLE-ABS-KEY) ("project management") AND ("South Africa") AND ("project success") AND ("project management skills"). The "TITLE-ABS-KEY" indicates either a journal or conference article title, abstract, and keywords. For this study, the time frame considered was between 1994 and 2020. This period was considered because 1994 marked the commencement of the post-apartheid era in South Africa. The literature search was conducted in July 2020, and an initial search produced 443 articles with the above-named keywords. The extracted 443 articles were refined based on three parameters: (a) field (must be within the built environment); (b) publication language (English); and (c) publication type (journal articles and papers in conference proceedings). A total of 214 articles were finally extracted and used for the analysis as shown in Figure 24.1.

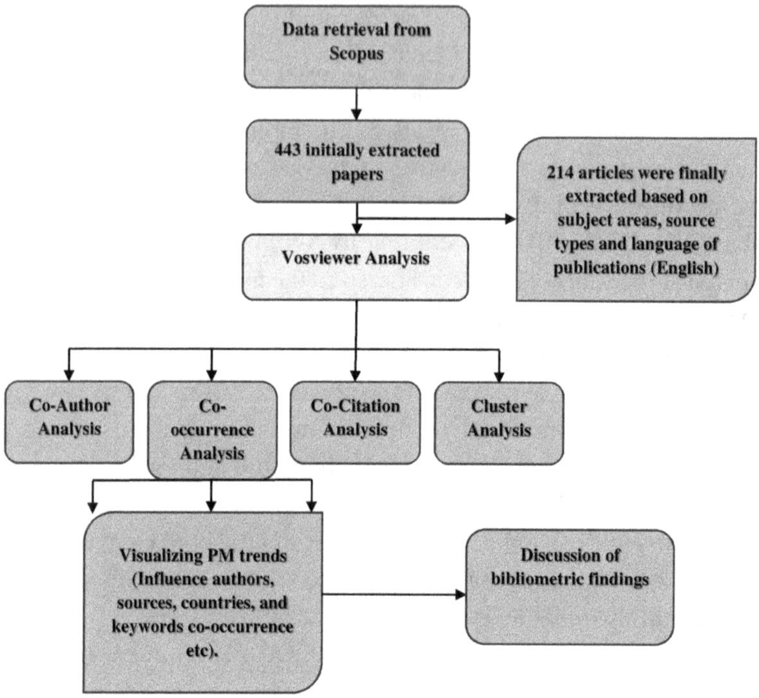

Figure 24.1: Outline of research method.

To explore the trends in PM studies, this study adopted the VOSviewer text-mining tool (Li *et al.*, 2020) to analyze the bibliometric connections based on certain results such as analysis of publications per year, publications per author and co-authorship network, co-authorship per country, and analysis of co-occurrence of keywords. VOSviewer is a software tool for creating maps based on network data and is particularly useful for visualizing large bibliometric networks and exploring the maps in seamless ways (Van Eck and Waltman, 2014; Li *et al.*, 2020).

Bibliometric results, analysis, and discussions

Publication per year

From the 214 extracted articles on PM-related themes, 84 were journal articles while 130 were from conference proceedings. As shown in

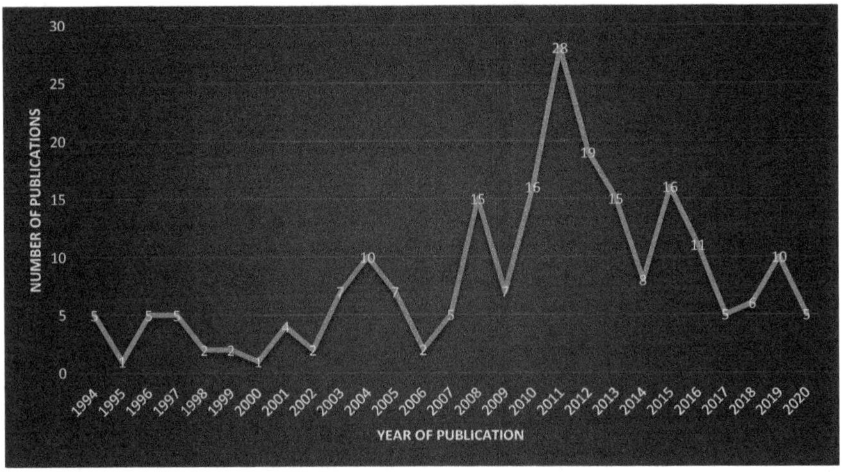

Figure 24.2: Number of publications per year (1994–2020).

Figure 24.2, 21 articles on the subject of PM were published during the early years of the post-apartheid era, between 1994 and 2000. However, a significant number of articles were published between 2008 and 2015, the highest number recorded within a seven-year span (with a total of 124 articles). During this period, South Africa embarked upon several landmark construction projects, and hosted the 2010 FIFA World Cup, which involved the construction of football venues and related infrastructure and facilities across the country. Some of these large-scale projects were responsible for the spike in PM studies, which is evident in Figure 24.2. It is also worth noting that the concept of 4IR gained attention in 2011 (Schwab, 2017) and has contributed to the increased number of articles from 2011 onward, as is evident in the subjects of the papers.

Publications per affiliation of author

The extracted papers were analyzed by the affiliation of the author. The top five affiliations were: University of Cape Town (UCT), 23 documents; University of Johannesburg (UJ), 21 documents; Nelson Mandela University, formerly known as Nelson Mandela Metropolitan University (NMMU), 20 documents; University of Pretoria (UP), 12 documents; and Council for Scientific and Industrial Research (CSIR), 11 documents, as

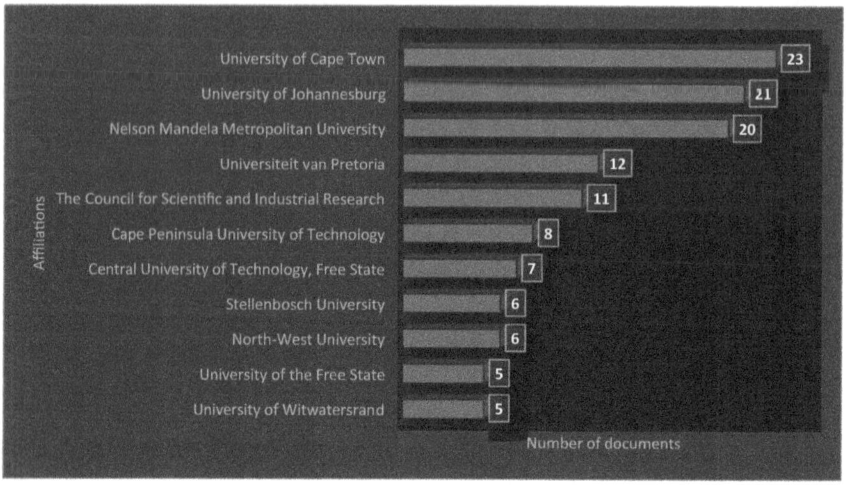

Figure 24.3: List of documents by affiliation.

shown in Figure 24.3. Cape Peninsula University of Technology, Central University of Technology Free State, and Stellenbosch University also had records with eight, seven, and six documents, respectively.

The publications per document source

Further analysis was carried out to determine the titles of the sources of the extracted papers. The 214 extracted articles were published in 114 different journals and conference proceedings, out of which 66 have only one publication under the stipulated time frame. Table 24.1 provides a breakdown of only those sources with at least five published papers on the subject of PM within the time frame. The yardstick of five papers was set on the basis that PM has been widely discussed in the body of knowledge in South Africa. Hence, it was useful to explore which of the sources have contributed significantly to the discussion within the specified time frame. The impact factors of the journals were also considered.

As shown in Table 24.1, *Journal of Engineering, Design and Technology (JEDT)* leads the way with 22 papers and 88 citations. JEDT focuses on a wide range of topics pertaining to PM such as project risk management, cost and life cycle issues, design strategies, human factors, process control, and several others. Table 24.1 also revealed the impact

Table 24.1: Number of publications per source.

Journal title	Documents (1994–2020)	Citations	Journal impact factor
Journal of Engineering, Design and Technology	22	88	0.760
Environmental Impact Assessment Review	19	95	4.135
Energy Policy	16	78	5.042
Renewable Energy	14	33	6.274
Habitat International	10	51	4.310
Transportation Research Record	7	20	0.960
South African Journal of Industrial Engineering	6	15	0.530
Sustainability	6	77	2.576
Journal of The South African Institution of Civil Engineering	5	32	0.404
Public Administration and Development	5	33	1.555
Journal of African Business	5	34	1.418

factor of each journal. Over 65 percent of the articles were published in high impact journals; this highlights the quality of the extracted publications.

Analysis of publications per author and co-authorship network

The authorship network shows that 385 authors (lead authors and collaborators) contributed to the extracted 214 articles. With the minimum number of documents per author set at three, only 13 authors met the threshold as shown in Table 24.2.

From Table 24.2, the author who has published the highest number of articles on the PM subject within the period under review is Smallwood (20 publications, with 39 citations). The authors with the highest number of citations are Aigbavboa (42 citations from 17 publications) and Thwala (35 citations from 14 publications). Although Haupt has just three publications on PM, those works have been cited 22 times, which highlights the impact of the publications in the PM discourse. Figure 24.4 shows the

Table 24.2: Number of publications per author.

Authors	Affiliation	Number of documents	Total citations
Smallwood, J.	Nelson Mandela University, South Africa	20	39
Aigbavboa, C.	University of Johannesburg, South Africa	17	42
Thwala, W.	University of Johannesburg, South Africa	14	35
Emuze, F.	Central University of Technology, South Africa	10	5
Bowen, P.	University of Cape Town, South Africa	4	3
Cattell, K.	University of Cape Town, South Africa	4	3
Haupt, T.	University of Johannesburg, South Africa	3	22
Agumba, J.	University of Johannesburg, South Africa	3	5
Govender, K.	Nelson Mandela University, South Africa	3	1
Martin, L.	Cape Peninsula University of Technology, South Africa	3	1
Verster, P.	University of the Free State, South Africa	3	1
Root, D.	University of Cape Town, South Africa	3	0

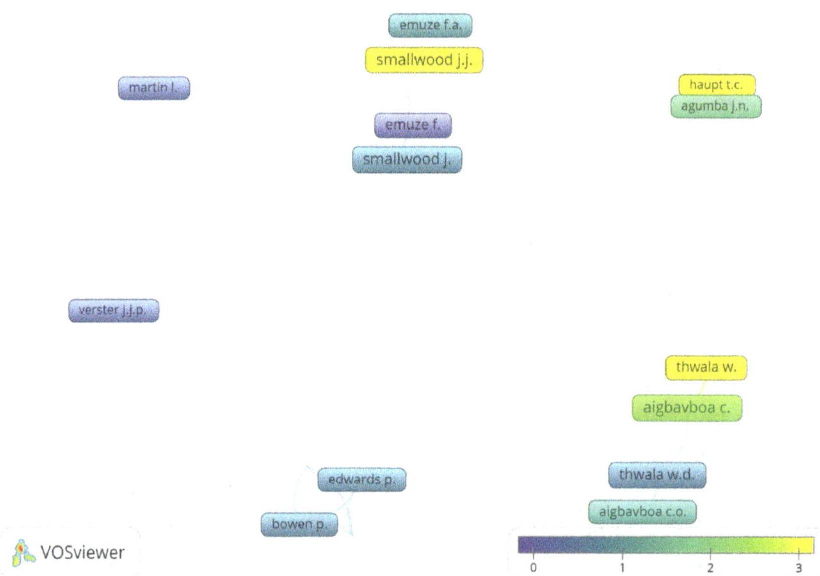

Figure 24.4: Overlay visualization co-authorship network.

overlay visualization of the co-authorship network, with six clusters of co-authorship observed.

At the beginning of 2010, Verster, Martin, Root, and Smallwood were actively involved in the production of PM articles, as seen in the deep blue color. However, the most active authors between 2012 and 2016 are Aigbavboa and Thwala, as shown in the pale green cluster on the right side of the map. The visualization also revealed that South Africa authors seldom collaborate in producing works on the subject of PM.

Analysis of co-occurrence of keywords

Based on the bibliographic data gathered, a co-occurrence map was created to examine the co-occurrence of keywords, which has shaped the PM discussion in South Africa. For this study, the number of keywords extracted was set at five, which agrees with the minimum number recommended by Aghimien *et al.* (2019). Therefore, for a keyword to be extracted, it must have at least five co-occurrences in the author and source indexed keywords. The analysis revealed a total number of 1,724 keywords for all 214 extracted articles. Out of these keywords, 73 met the threshold of five co-occurrences. According to Van Eck and Waltman (2014), the closer the keywords are to each other, the higher their occurrence. The 73 co-occurring keywords and their five different clusters are shown in the network visualization map in Figure 24.5.

As shown in Figure 24.5, the main keywords, "project management" is annotated and can be found in the center among the keywords.

- *Cluster 1* is the central subject "project management" represented in the red region on the map with 22 co-occurring keywords. Some of these keywords are: "environment impact," "public policy," "urban planning," "civil engineering," "social aspects," "regional planning," "industrial management," and "cost effectiveness." This cluster contains keywords that are firmly related to the general discussions on, or relating to, *Project Management*. These keywords mostly relate to the definition of PM as presented by the PMI, which describes PM as "the application of knowledge, skills, tools and techniques to project activities to meet the project requirements" (PMI, 2013). Therefore,

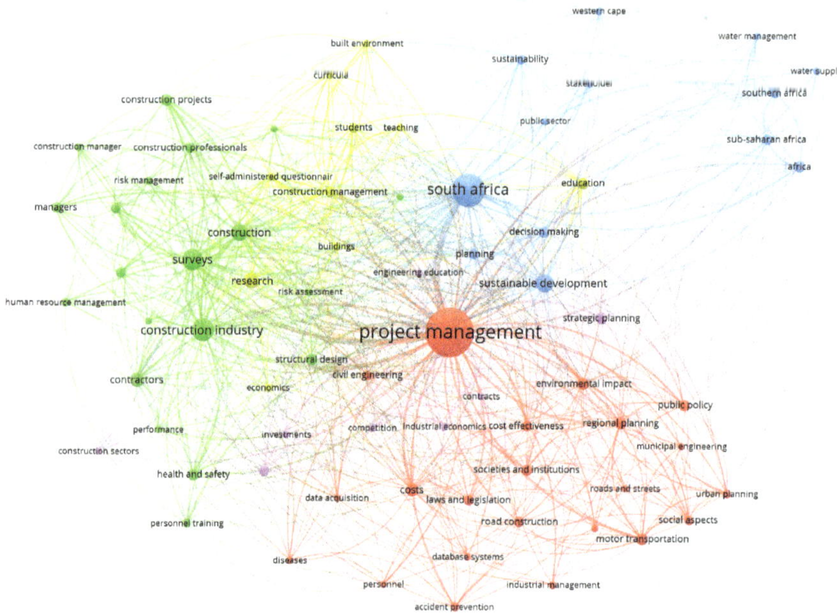

Figure 24.5: A network visualization of keyword occurrence.

for a project to be considered a success, the processes from the initiation and planning phases through execution and monitoring to the completion stage of the project must be sufficiently managed. This aligns with the PM studies of Shenhar (2008) and Morris (2013). These clusters also relate to the traditional roles of project management, which is to achieve project objectives within the expected cost, quality, scope and time and within other defined parameters (Ika, 2012).

- *Cluster 2*, the green cluster, has 20 keywords including: "budget control," "construction projects," "risk assessment," "performance," "structural design," "human resource management," "health and safety," and "risk management." Therefore, this cluster is seen to be considering issues relating to the risk aspects of PM. According to PMI (2004), a major element of the essence of risk management is to attain project objectives by employing a logical method of defining, evaluating, and acknowledging risks. As noted by Olsson (2007) and Borkovskaya (2018), risk management remains one of the most important features of PM and when risks are not minimized, construction projects are impacted negatively, which can affect the satisfaction of the deadlines for the completion of the projects. Abazid and Harb (2018) state that risks can occur at various stages of a construction project.

- *Cluster 3*, represented in blue, has 13 keywords which include: "decision making," "planning," "sustainability," "sustainable development," and "public sector." This cluster also relates to the social impacts of projects, assessment of project performance, and several other PM dimensions (SACPCMP, 2016) which are elements of PM in the South African context. It is pertinent to note that studies around sustainability and project management have begun to emerge, although this is occurring at a slow rate. For example, Silvius *et al.* (2012) and Gareis *et al.* (2013) stated that construction projects are now described as temporary organizations which have begun to include strands of sustainability discussions into their operations and thinking. These have led to discussions on the three dimensions of sustainability: social, economic, and environmental (Bebbington and Dillard, 2008). These dimensions of sustainability are further discussed by Kaplan and Norton (2001); Gore (2006); Higgins (2010); Dempsey (2011), and Martens and De Carvalho (2014). Furthermore, several sustainability principles for project management were proposed by Silvius *et al.* (2012).
- *Cluster 4*, represented in yellow, has 10 keywords including: "built environment," "construction management," "curricula," "education," "research," and "teaching." This cluster relates to the training of project managers. Most of the keywords align with PM as a discipline. PM qualifications are obtained in various ways. While some of the institutions offer a generic PM syllabus, others offer industry-specific programs, on both online and on-campus bases (Burger, 2013). Through these academic programs, several skills such as interpersonal, technical, problem-solving, ICT and organizational skills are developed (Robbins *et al.*, 2012; Ahsan *et al.*, 2013).
- *Cluster 5*, represented in purple, has eight keywords which include "construction sector," "contracts," "investments," and "strategic planning." This cluster relates to the domain and activities underpinning PM. As mentioned above, many industries and organizations have adopted PM theories, tools, and techniques in their operations. This

Figure 24.6: PM keywords word cloud.

proliferation of applications is being accompanied by increasing standardization of processes and investments, and refinement of concepts (Seymour and Hussein, 2014).

The PM keywords were further analyzed to examine their occurrences (total mentions) using a word cloud via the Wordle software (Feinberg, 2013). The word cloud is shown in Figure 24.6. An inspection of the word cloud reveals themes and the progression of the PM concept and subject matter between 1994 and 2020.

Toward a new paradigm of project management in South Africa

In the early days of PM in South Africa, the focus was primarily on the planning and execution of construction projects. Also, the integration of time, cost, and quality into the planning of construction projects was key as it was evident that change in one parameter could affect the others. Through the years, the concepts of scope management and the organization breakdown structure (OBS) became critical considerations, which indicated that the scope management of projects was performed through an organizational structure (Burke, 2013). In the early 1990s, more flexible organizational structures, which were considered to be more efficient, became more prominent. At the time, it was widely thought that, by adopting a management-by-projects approach, public institutions could assign their work to many small project teams, which would be able to quickly respond to innovation, new ideas, and market completion. The 1990s also saw an increase in the application of information technology and communicating through the Internet. There are now several dimensions, linking multiple construction projects with corporate strategies to enhance corporate competitiveness. Today, establishments handling several projects are required to make complex decisions in the structuring and restructuring of their portfolios to ensure the appropriate allocation of resources to individual projects based on their strategic relevance. The use of technology in making these decisions has gained prominence. IT systems, software, and adequately skilled project professionals are being utilized to manage many projects simultaneously. Aspects of digitalization triggered by the advent of 4IR have begun to gain momentum, marking the beginning of a new trend in research on the PM concept in South Africa.

Under the leadership of the current state President, Cyril Ramaphosa, the "4IR" theme has become the leading mantra of new policy initiatives designed to move the nation forward and out of the COVID-19–induced economic crisis. One such example is the inaugural Digital Economy Summit in Johannesburg in 2019, under the theme "Advancing the African Agenda on the Fourth Industrial Revolution through Digital Transformation." President Ramaphosa tasked the educational institutions to revisit and revamp their curricula in what he referred to as a "skills revolution." The President further stated that "...we are introducing subjects such as coding and data science and analytics at the primary school level to prepare our young people for the jobs of the future"... (Ramaphosa, 2019). Subsequently, the President established a 30-member "Presidential Commission on the Fourth Industrial Revolution" to advise the government on leveraging opportunities presented by 4IR.

These initiatives by the South African government highlight its readiness to become a major player in the 4IR era. However, in achieving the objectives of this 2030 mandate, the role of education cannot be overstated as this was the second of the seven listed priorities to be addressed by the 4IR. Accordingly, new subjects are to be introduced to prepare students for

4IR careers, including data science and analytics, AI, blockchain, additive manufacturing, robotics, and quantum computing. Therefore, this chapter recommends that to train project managers who are 4IR proficient, higher education institutions should modify the science and technology curriculum to enable students to develop and acquire competencies in the areas of advanced simulation, AI, cloud computing, data science, data communication, information technologies, real-time inventory operations, robotics, and system automation. This implies that the PM curriculum should be infused with 4IR thinking within the conventional primary sciences of the profession, with greater emphasis on digital literacy.

The adoption of 4IR technologies in PM is not without its challenges. Organizations may struggle to leapfrog to 4IR technologies due to the high investment and implementation cost of exploring the new technologies. The cost of training and educating employees and the necessary consultancy fees are all barriers to technology adoption Akanmu and Anumba (2005). Despite these challenges facing the adoption of 4IR technologies, the merits make the embracing by the PM profession of this new wave of digitalization worthwhile.

Conclusion and recommendations

One of the objectives of this chapter was to examine the evolution of the PM concept in South Africa through a review of the various paradigm shifts in the profession from an "old" traditional model to the current "new" paradigm. This was achieved via a bibliometric approach, which identified and mapped key knowledge areas and co-occurring keywords by identifying trends and patterns in research on the PM concept within the built environment domain within a 26-year period and indexed in the Scopus database. A total of 443 articles published between 1994 and 2020 were extracted from the Scopus database and used for the analysis. Based on the articles, several analyses were conducted using VOSviewer to examine the patterns and trends of PM research in South Africa. These include publications per year, publications per author, and co-authorship network. In addition, the co-occurrence of keywords was critically reviewed to determine the research themes and clusters. Based on the extracted clusters, PM research within the built environment domain in South Africa has placed significant focus on the traditional process of planning, execution, delivery, and maintenance of construction projects. Keywords such as "innovation," "digitalization," "Fourth Industrial Revolution," "4IR," and "digital tools" were among several less-frequently occurring keywords found during the analysis, a knowledge gap observed by this study, and a focus on the present and the future. These keywords gained increased mentions from 2015 onward, sparking a paradigm shift and research trend in the PM concept in South Africa. This innovative era will be the "new normal," and project managers who are often at the sharp end of implementing changes must be flexible and able to adapt to this new wave.

Due to the rapidly changing world of work caused by technological advances such as automation, project managers in South Africa will be required to possess a highly specialized skill set to be relevant and competent in their spheres of influence. As noted in the chapter, the 4IR era is innovation-driven and fast-paced, thus leading to increased skills complexity in the workforce of the future. Therefore, the PM profession will shift from the conventional approaches of doing things as planning and monitoring tools become sophisticated, smarter, and intelligent. The findings from the study highlight the need for project managers in South Africa to possess both technical/hard and non-technical/soft skills in the 4IR era. This study also revealed that technical skills would equally be important for project managers of the future. These technical/hard skills include digital skills, programming skills, data analytics, cybersecurity skills, data coding, drone knowledge, machine learning, data mining, and cloud computing knowledge.

One of the ways higher education institutions in South Africa offering PM programs can educate and train graduates in the 4IR era is by incorporating interdisciplinary and multi-disciplinary approaches. As discussed in this chapter, multi-disciplinary knowledge is required in the workforce of the future. More so, lifelong learning abilities will become essential for the workforce of the future as project managers must be willing to re-skill, up-skill, and multi-skill themselves in response to the demand for new expertise. Lifelong learning can take many forms, including attending conferences, seminars and team workshops, participating in innovation challenges and taking skills courses and certifications. As discussed in this chapter, the world is evolving, and PM will be required to follow suit. From the preceding discussions, 4IR skills requirements call for a reassessment of the importance of qualifications obtained from Technical and Vocational

Education and Training (TVET) in South Africa and beyond. TVET institutions are increasingly vital in the digital transformation ecosystem, as they often develop a technically skilled workforce. Technical institutions must be strengthened, supported, and revamped since technical and practical skills are key for project managers. In response to the innovations accompanying the 4IR, the PM profession is shifting to a new paradigm of knowledge orientation, which is supported by the three cardinal pillars of skills and competencies — education, research, and development. Also, this era of digitalization and automation could trigger a paradigm shift in how academic institutions train students. They could be compelled to reduce the need to train students for the highest possible qualification and increase the need to obtain expertise in 4IR related technologies in PM practice.

References

Abazid, M. and Harb, H. (2018). An overview of risk management in the construction projects. *Academic Research International*, 9(2), 73–79.

African National Congress (1994). The reconstruction and development programme: A policy framework. African National Congress, Marshalltown, South Africa.

Aghimien, D.O., Aigbavboa, C.O., Oke, A.E. and Thwala, W.D. (2020). Mapping out research focus for robotics and automation research in construction-related studies: A bibliometric approach. *Journal of Engineering, Design and Technology*, 18(5), 1063–1079. https://doi.org/10.1108/JEDT-09-2019-0237.

Ahlemann, F., El Arbi, F., Kaiser, M.G. and Heck, A. (2013). A process framework for theoretically grounded prescriptive research in the project management field. *International Journal of Project Management*, 31(1), 43–56.

Ahsan, K., Ho, M. and Khan, S. (2013). Recruiting project managers: A comparative analysis of competencies and recruitment signals from job advertisements. *Project Management Journal*, 44(5), 36–54.

Akanmu, A. and Anumba, C.J. (2015). Cyber-physical systems integration of building information models and the physical construction. *Engineering, Construction and Architectural Management*, 22(5), 516–535. https://doi.org/10.1108/ECAM-07-2014-0097.

Bebbington, J. and Dillard, J. (2008). Social sustainability: An organizational-level analysis. In J. Dillard, V. Dujon and King (Eds.), *Understanding the Social Dimension of Sustainability*. Routledge, Abingdon, pp. 173–189.

Ben-Daya, M., Hassini, E. and Bahroun, Z. (2019). Internet of things and supply chain management: A literature review. *International Journal of Production Research*, 57(15–16), 4719–4742.

Besner, C. and Hobbs, B. (2008). Project management practice, generic or contextual: A reality check. *Project Management Journal*, 39(1), 16–33.

Borkovskaya, V. (2018). Project management risks in the sphere of housing and communal services. *MATEC Web of Conferences*, Vol. 251, p. 06025, EDP Sciences.

Burger, M. (2013). Project management in the built environment: The need for industry specific knowledge. Doctoral Dissertation, University of the Free State, South Africa.

Burke, R. (2013). *Project Management*, 5th Edition. ABC Press, Cape Town.

Chiu, Y.C. (2010). *An Introduction to the History of Project Management: From the Earliest Times to AD 1900*. Eburon Academic Publishers, Delft.

Conforti, A., Mascia, M., Cioffi, G., De Angelis, C., Coppola, G., De Rosa, P., Pivonello, R., Alviggi, C. and De Placido, G. (2018). Air pollution and female fertility: A systematic review of literature. *Reproductive Biology and Endocrinology*, 16(1), 117.

Dempsey, N., Bramley, G., Power, S. and Brown, C. (2011). The social dimension of sustainable development: Defining urban social sustainability. *Sustainable Development*, 19(5), 289–300.

Eberhard, B., Podio, M., Alonso, A.P., Radovica, E., Avotina, L., Peiseniece, L., Sendon, M.C., Lozano, A.G. and Solé-Pla, J. (2017). Smart work: The transformation of the labour market due to the fourth industrial revolution (I4.0). *International Journal of Business and Economic Sciences Applied Research*, 10(3), 47–66.

Fells, M.J. (2000). Fayol stands the test of time. *Journal of Management History*, 6(8), 345–360. https://doi.org/10.1108/13552520010359379.

Gareis, R., Huemann, M., Martinuzzi, A., Weninger, C. and Sedlacko, M. (2013). Project management and sustainable development principles. Project Management Institute, Newtown Square, PA.

Gore, A. (2006). *An Inconvenient Truth: The Planetary Emergency of Global Warming and What We Can Do About It*. Rodale.

Higgins, P. (2010). *Eradicating Ecocide: Laws and Governance to Stop the Destruction of the Planet*. Shepheard-Walwyn, London.

Hollmann, J.K. (2006). Total cost management framework to be released at AACE international's 2006 annual meeting. *Cost Engineering*, 48(5), 8.

Ika, L.A. (2012). Project management for development in Africa: Why projects are failing and what can be done about it. *Project Management Journal*, 43(4), 27–41.

Kaplan, R.S., Robert, N.P.D.K.S., Kaplan, R.S. and Norton, D.P. (2001). *The Strategy-Focused Organization: How Balanced Scorecard Companies Thrive in the New Business Environment*. Harvard Business Press, Boston, MA.

Kissi, E. and Ansah, S.K. (2014). Professional Project Management practices and its constraints in developing African countries: A literature review. *Covenant Journal of Research in the Built Environment*, 1(2). https://journals.covenantuniversity.edu.ng/index.php/cjrbe/article/view/144.

Kwak, Y.H., 2005. A brief history of project management. In E.G. Caryannis, Y.H. Kwak and F.T. Anbari (Eds.), *The Story of Managing Projects: An Inter Disciplinary Approach*. Praeger, Westport, CT, pp.1–9.

Li, C.Z., Zhao, Y., Xiao, B., Yu, B., Tam, V.W.Y., Chen, Z. and Ya, Y. (2020). Research trend of the application of information technologies in construction and demolition waste management. *Journal of Cleaner Production*, 263, 1 August, Article number 121458. https://doi.org/10.1016/j.jclepro.2020.121458.

Marić, A. (2017). Comparison of project management frameworks and tools and their impact on project success. *2nd International Scientific Conference LEAN Spring Summit 2017*, January.

Martens, M.L. and De Carvalho, M. (2014). A conceptual framework of sustainability in project management. *Proceedings of the Project Management Institute Research and Education Conference 2014*, Portland, OR.

Morris, P. (2013). Reconstructing project management reprised: A knowledge perspective. *Project Management Journal*, 44(5), 6–23.

Ogunsanya, O.A., Aigbavboa, C.O. and Thwala, D.W., 2016. Challenges of construction procurement: A developing nation's perspective. In *Proceedings, IV International Conference of Socio-economic Researchers* (ICSR 2016 Serbia). Zlatibor, Serbia, 27–29 May, pp. 205–217.

Oliveira, A.S., de Barros, M.D., de Carvalho Pereira, F., Gomes, C.F.S. and da Costa, H.G. (2018). Prospective scenarios: A literature review on the Scopus database. *Futures*, 100, 20–33.

Olsson, R. (2007). In search of opportunity management: Is the risk management process enough? *International Journal of Project Management*, 25(8), 745–752.

PMI (Project Management Institute) (2004). *A Guide to the Project Management Body of Knowledge (PMBOK® Guide)*. Project Management Institute, Newtown Square, PA.

Project Management Institute (2013). GAC Accreditation High Standard of Quality for Project Management Degree Programs. http://www.pmi.org/~/media/PDF/Professional-Development/GAC/GAC_brochure.ashx

Ramaphosa, C. (2019). Address by President Cyril Ramaphosa to the 1st South African Digital Economy Summit. Gallagher Convention Centre,

Johannesburg, 5 July. https://www.gov.za/speeches/president cyril-ramaphosa -south-african-digital economy-summit-5-jul-2019-0000.

Robbins, S.P., De Cenzo, D.A. and Coulter, M.A. (2012). *Fundamentals of Management: Essentials Concepts and Applications*. Pearson Higher Ed., New York.

Schwab, K. (2017). *The Fourth Industrial Revolution*. Crown Publishing Group, New York.

Seymour, T. and Hussein, S. (2014). The history of project management. *International Journal of Management & Information Systems (IJMIS)*, 18(4), 233–240.

Shenhar, A.J. (2008). Unleashing the power of project management. *Industrial Management-Chicago Then Atlanta*, 50(1), 14.

Silvius, A., Schipper, R., Planko, J., van den Brink, J. and Köhler, A. (2012). *Sustainability in Project Management*. Routledge, London.

Snyder, J.R. and Kline, S. (1987). Modern project management: How did we get here — Where do we go? *Project Management Journal*, 18(1), 28–29.

Thelwall, M. (2018). Dimensions: A competitor to Scopus and the Web of Science? *Journal of Informetrics*, 12(2), 430–435.

The South African Council for the Project and Construction Management Professions (SACPCMP). (2016). GNR.136 of 13 September 2016: Guideline Scope of Services and Recommended Guideline Tariff of Fees, 2014, Government Gazette No. 42697. Pretoria.

Tseng, M.L., Islam, M.S., Karia, N., Fauzi, F.A. and Afrin, S. (2019). A literature review on green supply chain management: Trends and future challenges. *Resources, Conservation and Recycling*, 141, 145–162.

Turk, W. (2007). 21st century Project Management competencies. *Defense AT & L.*, 22–25, January-February.

Van Eck, N.J. and Waltman, L. (2014). Visualizing bibliometric networks. In Y. Ding, R. Rousseau and D. Wolfram (Eds.), *Measuring Scholarly Impact: Methods and Practice*, Springer, Heidelberg, pp. 285–320.

Zheng, X., Le, Y., Chan, A.P.C., Hu, Y. and Li, Y. (2016). Review of the application of social network analysis (SNA) in construction project management research. *International Journal of Project Management*, 34(7), 1214–1225.

Zhong, B., Wu, H., Li, H., Sepasgozar, S., Luo, H. and He, L. (2019). A scientometric analysis and critical review of construction related ontology research. *Automation in Construction*, 101, 17–31.

Zhou, K., Liu, T. and Zhou, L. (2015). Industry 4.0: Towards future industrial opportunities and challenges. *2015 12th International Conference on Fuzzy Systems and Knowledge Discovery* (FSKD), IEEE, pp. 2147–2152.

Part 6

The Future: Project Management Body of Knowledge for Developing Countries

https://doi.org/10.1142/9789811224720_0025

Chapter 25

Developing the Field of Knowledge of Project Management: The Perspective of the Developing Countries

George Ofori

London South Bank University, United Kingdom

Abstract

The field of project studies has a growing body of knowledge which receives contributions from many disciplines. This is important as the project has become ubiquitous in business organizations and in life in general. At what stage is this body of knowledge in its development? How relevant is it to the developing countries? How can the needs, concerns, and attributes of the developing countries be appropriately reflected in it? This chapter considers the development of the body of knowledge of project studies from the perspective of developing countries. It begins with a consideration of the current myths and misconceptions in the practice of project management and research in project studies, such as the tendency to consider all projects to be the same, and the low level of attention paid to the context of projects. It proceeds to discuss the theoretical development of project management, including its interdisciplinarity. The level of development of the field is next discussed, and it is noted that there are disagreements on the level of maturity of the field and the extent to which the lack of progress in the field is responsible for the poor performance on projects. The future of project management is next considered, starting with the challenges facing project management, and setting out some suggestions by authors for further research. The discussion then adopts a developing country perspective and takes up the subject of decolonizing project studies. It goes on to make proposals on what a Project Management Body of Knowledge for the developing countries should look like.

Keywords: Project management, myths, level of maturity, developing countries, further development, decolonization

Introduction

The aim of the study is to consider how to develop the field of knowledge of project management from the perspective of the developing countries. The objectives are to discuss: some of the misconceptions and disagreements in project management, consider the state of development and level of maturity of the area of knowledge, discuss its appropriateness to the context of developing countries and how it can be developed into the future, and introduce consideration of the decolonization of the project management field of knowledge.

Some myths and misconceptions in project management

Issues with "uniqueness" of projects

The definition of a project requires modification; not all projects have some of the commonly agreed features of a project as set out in Chapter 2 of this book, such as a fixed time constraint or defined scope. Hodgson and Cicmil (2007) note that the project has been singled out as an object to be managed, thereby establishing projects and the management of projects as homogenous, universal, and distinct phenomena, despite the actual internal variety. However, Lenfle *et al.* (2019) note that the growing role of innovation in the strategy of firms has led them to engage in uncertain ventures, frequently organized in the form of projects. This questions the standard model of project management. First, for exploratory projects, neither the goal nor the means to reach it can be clearly defined at the outset. They are mostly first-of-a-kind projects, exploring new technology, uses, business models, or strategic opportunities. Lenfle *et al.* (2019) observe that, regarding the contextuality of project organizing, research has shown that it is difficult, if not impossible, to assume that standard project methods can be efficiently transferred to exploratory projects.

Similarly, Loch *et al.* (2006) show the irrelevance of standard risk management methods for projects with unforeseeable uncertainties or what they refer to as "unknown unknowns." They propose managerial strategies to cope with these unknown-unknown situations, namely "selectionism" (exploration of different solutions simultaneously) and learning (exploration of different solutions one after the other) and discuss their managerial implications. Kreiner (2020) uses the recent controversy between Hirschman and Flyvbjerg in their perspectives on a project to trace the academic imposition of a narrow notion of a project and to consider how to open the field to new types of issues, approaches, and lessons.

Thus, the definition of a project cannot be rigid. For that reason, that suggested by Gareis (2006, pp. 2–3) relating to a project in a non-project oriented organization is pertinent: "a temporary organisation of a project-oriented company for the performance of a relatively unique short- to medium-term strategically important business process of medium or large scope."

The "one size fits all" conceptualization

Another myth is the assumption of uniformity among projects. Shenhar and Dvir (2004) note that a common misconception in project management is that all projects are the same; that project managers can use similar tools for all projects; and that managers would succeed if they would use a universal set of tools and techniques. They consider the tendency to use a fixed approach to project management as leading to project failures and delays. They cite the example of NASA's Space Shuttle Program in the 1970s and 1980s, which suffered from extensive problems, delays, and engineering challenges because the projects were managed with the wrong project management style that did not fit their level of complexity, uncertainty, and risk. Shenhar and Dvir (2004) note that the project management literature and research has not yet fully responded to the "One Size Does Not Fit All" challenge; most studies do not distinguish between different project types and environments. Thus, it is evident that the standard project management approach often requires modification in order to succeed. This calls into question the universal applicability of frameworks such as the Project Management Body of Knowledge (PMBOK) of the Project Management Institute (PMI) and other project management bodies of knowledge and frameworks. These points are highly relevant to project management in developing countries.

Krahn and Hartment (2006) note that it is assumed in many areas of the project management literature — for example, as reflected by the static nature of lists of project manager skills and competencies — that all projects involve the same work and can be managed most effectively with the same project manager skills and competencies. For example, Shenhar (2001) used technological uncertainty to differentiate among project types. Others have also considered different characteristics as a way by which to better understand the needs of the project. Krahn and Hartment (2006) observed that, based on their investigation, it is clear that different project characteristics require a different mix of key project manager skills and competencies. Müller and Turner (2007) and Malach-Pines *et al.* (2009) are examples of authors who propose frameworks for selecting project managers considering the nature of the project.

Importance of context

Yet another misconception in project studies and project management is the tendency to ignore the context of projects. Lenfle *et al.* (2019) note that, in project studies, context specificity is a possible problem because there is a risk that trivial context effects are underappreciated. This further indicates that the idea that "one size fits all" within project studies is illusory (Shenhar and Dvir, 2004, 2007). Hence, different forms need to be identified according to project characteristics, such as the project's purpose and the institutional context in which it is embedded. For example, Lenfle *et al.* (2019) remark that the project motivations and coordination issues are not the same in different contexts. Krahn and Hartment (2006) note that the environment within which the project manager works is impacted by the type of project being managed or the characteristics of the project as well as the business environment, team characteristics, and other factors. However, the impact of these on elements of projects, such as team composition and project manager selection, is seldom taken into consideration.

Similarly, Eskerod and Larson (2018) note that project management theory draws on reductionism (simplifying the description of a complex phenomenon in order to better grasp it). For example, because project stakeholder management theory has been influenced by this approach, the simplicity of the stakeholder conceptualization makes it difficult for project representatives to predict stakeholder behavior. Eskerod and Larson (2018) offer a new perspective on stakeholder analysis based on a richer and more holistic "shadows of the context" approach in contrast to the reductionist approach, which only considers, on the part of stakeholders, "What's in it for me?" Finally, and even more conceptually, Martinsuo and Geraldi (2020) investigate the relationship between project portfolios and their contexts based on four theoretical alternatives: institutional theory, stakeholder theory, resource dependence theory, and sensemaking theory. The results explain the mechanisms connecting project portfolios with their context, and call for a reformulation of portfolio success.

The one-person conceptualization

The notion of an individual being "the project manager" is also questioned. Lindgren and Packendorff (2009) suggest that the tradition of considering the project manager as an individual runs against current developments in leadership research, which emphasize teamwork and consider team leaders as facilitators. Such a narrative as in the concept of shared leadership implies that the relationships among team members are rather more important than the one leader (see, for example, Pearce and Conger, 2003). Also, project managers often neither have the technical skills of their team members nor the power base of their superiors in the project-based structure (see, for example, Bakker *et al.*, 2016).

Theoretical development of project management: research on project management

Interdisciplinarity of project studies

Project studies is an interdisciplinary and transdisciplinary field. Geraldi *et al.* (2020) note that the field of project studies has gained increasing attention from scholars around the world and across disciplines, including organizational theorists and business scholars (Clegg *et al.*, 2002; Sydow *et al.*, 2004); sociologists (Scott *et al.*, 2011); psychologists (Chiocchio *et al.*, 2015); historians (Scranton, 2014); and economists (Hirschman, 2015 [1967]), who explore project-based organizing and its implications for individuals, organizations, and society. For example, geography scholars study the linkages between temporary organizations and networks (Grabher, 2002; Thiel and Grabher, 2015). Some have studied the psychological aspects of project work, including work-life issues and problems associated with identity and project overload (Zika-Viktorsson *et al.*, 2006).

This diversity of interest has fostered cross-fertilization of the field of project studies with other fields of inquiry (Söderlund, 2011). It is suggested that the field is gaining academic legitimacy and theoretical sophistication. It has extended beyond its traditional engineering orientation (Morris, 2012), as researchers show the importance of considering projects as political, social, and cultural entities that span multiple contexts, enabling people to understand the multi-faceted and processual nature of contemporary projects (Söderlund, 2011). Moreover, it is suggested that project scholars are now rejuvenating the engineering heritage of the field to understand the socio-material nature of projects and solve society-related problems on projects (Orlikowski, 2007).

It is pertinent to note that not all authors fully welcome the merits of the interdisciplinarity of project management. Davies *et al.* (2018) point out that to make the interdisciplinary development of project studies beneficial, project scholars should draw from different fields and engage in different sets of theories. They highlight the need for metatheories (such as learning theory and institutional theory) to advance the field and facilitate interaction and mutual learning among different fields. Similarly, Orlikowski (2007) suggests that there should be close interdisciplinary collaboration among scholars from, among others, engineering, project studies, organization studies, and social studies. However, Kreiner (2020) challenges project scholars not to accept ideas from other fields, but instead to draw inspiration from these ideas and "do the rethinking ourselves."

Level of development of the field

The body of knowledge on the field of project management has been continually developed. For example, Bredillet (2006, 2010) outlines nine schools of project management thinking that have emerged over the years:

- Optimization School (1950) — *Earned Value Management*: Optimize project duration by mathematical processes
- Modelling School (1960) — *Integrating hard-soft systems*: Use of hard and soft-systems theory to model the project
- Governance School (1970) — *Project management offices (PMOs), portfolio management, project selection, regulatory compliance*: Govern the project and relationships among participants
- Behavior School (1975) — *Virtual teams, human resource management in project-oriented companies*: Manage relationships among people on the project
- Success School (1985) — *Refinement of success criteria, stakeholder satisfaction, causes of failure*: Define success and failure and identify causes
- Decision School (1990) — *Anchoring estimates, organization strategy and impact on portfolio, portfolio management decisions*: Information processing through the project life cycle
- Process School (1980) — *Project categorization, refinement of processes, project audits and reviews, maturity models*: Find an appropriate path to the desired outcome

- Contingency School (1995) — *Clarify differences in approaches, methods of adaptation, link to success criteria*: Categorize the project type to select appropriate systems
- Marketing School (2000) — *Strategy/tactics for business success, linking projects and strategy, align senior level thinking to projects, customer relationship management and public relations on projects*: Communicate with all stakeholders to obtain their support.

There is no consensus on the level of development and maturity of the field of knowledge of project management. Some authors suggest that it is relatively theoretically underdeveloped despite the widespread and critical nature of projects; they consider the field to lack theories, concepts, and frameworks. For example, Shenhar and Dvir (2004) note that project management research has not yet established its place among the traditional academic disciplines of management. They also suggest that the poor performance on projects, which is often highlighted, stems from a gap between what needs to be known about projects and what is known. According to Nicholas and Steyn (2008), project management still lags far behind its potential. For example, while procurement management is deemed to be a critical determinant of project success (see, for example, Watermeyer, 2018), the OECD (2021, p. 8) notes that: "Despite decades of theoretical study and experimentation in practice, "how to" actually procure infrastructure still lacks a complete and evidence-based guide, relying heavily on subjective perception and judgment. Sufficient evidence is now available to conclude that mistakes in the procurement strategy of a project can lead to infrastructure that is too costly and/or does not bring the expected quality/value. Moreover, delivery on-time and on-budget, while important, is not necessarily a sign that a procurement is going well."

On the other hand, the broader view is that authors consider the field of project studies to be well established, as discussed in the previous section. For example, Geraldi *et al.* (2021) note that in recent years, project-related papers in top journals have contributed to improved academic recognition of project studies and the knowledge of theoretical concepts from other fields.

Another problem is that very few of the works on organization studies are published in leading management journals, as found by Kloppenborg and Opfer (2002) in a dedicated study. On the other hand, some note that disproportional focus on publishing might negatively influence engagement of researchers with practice (Söderlund and Maylor, 2012) and lead to the situation where researchers lose touch with the realities of managers. According to Nicholas and Steyn (2008), project management still lags far behind its potential.

Relationship between theory and practice in development of project management

Most of the body of knowledge on project management is based on experience and lessons learned from good practice. Geraldi *et al.* (2021) note that researchers on project studies have always had their ears close to the ground, trying to understand new management problems and challenges; and research in project studies has benefited from an understanding of the empirical field and a mutually beneficial relationship with project practitioners. Not all authors are happy with the linkage between theory and practice in these regards. Kreiner (2020, p. 400) suggests that "the field of project management has erected an impressive edifice of knowledge that apparently hinders us in learning anything from experience except what we already know." The field of project management needs theory development to stimulate more research to foster its further development.

Considering the path of development of the field, Geraldi and Söderlund (2018) suggest that project organizing is a growing field of scholarly inquiry and management practice; the study and practice of projects have extended their level of analysis beyond mainly focusing on individual projects to considering micro- and macro-level concerns around projects. They observe the emergence of what they refer to as *type 3 research*, which reconciles the need for theoretical development and engagement with practice and suggests pragmatic avenues to research projects and project organizing.

Some of the gaps in project studies are important to the field of construction. For example, Sydow and Braun (2018) suggest that existing conceptualizations of projects as temporary organizations do not capture their interorganizational facets fully despite the increasing importance of what is called "interorganizational projects." In a study particularly relevant to the construction project, they consider how the interorganizational dimension may be theorized and introduce three facets of analyzing interorganizational projects that help to advance the theory of the temporary organization: the multi-level perspective, the processual understanding of relationships, and modes of interorganizational governance. Similarly, Wright and Boswell (2002) examined published works in the *International Journal of Project Management* spanning a 20-year period, and found the project to be at an under-researched level of analysis in Human Resource Management, and they drew attention to topics which are not normally considered, including careers on projects, and participation on projects, subjects which are of interest to construction.

Researchers on project management, especially in construction, have been debating the appropriateness of the methods of research adopted to study project management. For example, Simushi and Wium (2020), in a review, noted that conventional research on project performance has tended to use research methods that are ill-suited for an in-depth understanding of the actuality of managing projects, as was also suggested by AlSehaimi *et al.* (2013). The studies depend on the opinions of practitioners and are not project-specific and do not consider the contextual reality of projects, thus making them "superficial, replicative and stagnated" as noted by Ahiaga-Dagbui *et al.* (2015). This has affected the approach to the project management strategies and solutions which are proposed. Ahmed *et al.* (2021) reviewed the literature on the project manager's leadership competencies and found that almost all of the studies adopted quantitative methods, the majority had relatively small sample sizes, and most of them did not categorize, or indicate the ranking of, leadership competencies.

A more detailed discussion of decolonization is now undertaken (this further develops the consideration in Chapter 4 of this book).

Decolonizing project studies to develop the PMBOK for developing countries: Detailed consideration

The general situation

There has been a debate on decolonizing educational curricula and research in many countries over the past two decades which is relevant to project studies. Mkasi *et al.* (2018) notes that the earliest account of the use of the word "decolonization" was in 1836 by a French writer advocating withdrawal from Algeria. The term decolonization re-surfaced in the 1950s and 1960s, when it was used by historians and political scientists to describe the process through which many regions in Africa, Asia, and the Middle East broke free from European hegemony (see, for example, O'Brien, 2006; Thomas and Thompson, 2014; Crawford *et al.* 2021). Frantz Fanon, the French-Congolese psychiatrist, considered decolonization a power struggle between two groups: the colonizer and the colonized (Fanon, 1967; see also Sitole, 2016).

Many authors note that colonial education classified indigenous African thought as pre-logical, pre-critical, and inferior (Department of Education, 2008; Kapoor, 2009; Adebisi, 2016). Similarly, Munroe *et al.* (2013) note that, in Canada, policies of colonization, assimilation, integration, and systemic discrimination, which imposed European knowledge and ways of learning, eroded the nature, scope, and effective functioning of cultural systems of Aboriginal peoples (Comeau and Santin, 1995; Regan, 2010). Indigenous ways of learning and knowledges were negated and diminished. Wingfield (2017) notes that the decolonization of education means that a nation must become independent with regards to the acquisition of knowledge, skills, values, beliefs, and habits.

After political independence, many developing countries made efforts to decolonize higher education (Heleta, 2016), as universities attempted "...to decolonise the disciplines, to strip them of their Eurocentric cognitive and civilisational conceits" (Zeleza, 2009, p. 112). They sought to rediscover and re-evaluate their past and envision their future (Mudimbe, 1985, p. 206). It is suggested that these attempts have not decolonized higher education and research in most former colonies (Adebisi, 2016). Radcliffe (2017, p. 329) notes that now, the forms of knowledge "through which the world is apprehended and explained and modelled for the future are deeply rooted in post-Enlightenment Euro-American claims to be able to pronounce universal truths and to theorise the world." To Adebisi (2016), this deprives the world of a wider range of ways of knowing, pedagogy, and epistemologies. Connel (2007) refers to output-driven, Anglophone-oriented scholarship being imposed on southern and extra-university scholars. In the 2016 "Rhodes Must Fall" educational decolonization movement in South Africa, students and some academics sought to decolonize the university curriculum "by ending the domination of Western epistemological traditions, histories and figures" (Molefe, 2016, p. 32) and world views and put African and global perspectives at the center of education and research (Shay, 2016; Heleta, 2016). This was part of a new wave of decolonization of education and research.

Decolonizing various fields of knowledge

It is suggested that much of the work on decolonization has focused on the Humanities. Mkasi *et al.* (2018) note that they could not find many prior work on decolonization of engineering, as there is uncertainty regarding the meaning of decolonization in the sciences particularly because science is generally viewed as universal, making decolonization, in the manner described by the humanities, a more difficult task to conceptualize. Lokugamage *et al.* (2020) note that with increased interest in social justice, consideration is being given to decolonizing medical education and producing doctors who can meet the needs of diverse populations. They explore "recentering" indigenous healing systems and discuss the concepts of *medical pluralism* and *cultural humility* which challenge the biomedical view of health. They conclude that encouraging healthcare educators and professionals to adopt a "decolonizing attitude" can address power imbalances in health and improve person-centered care.

Decolonizing management, development, and project studies

Effort has been made to decolonize management studies. Girei (2017) notes that in the past decade, the West-centric character of management knowledge has been critically addressed, highlighting its role in the reproduction of global and historical inequalities and power asymmetries between the West and the rest of the world. Girei (2017) searches for methodologies and research practices committed to supporting efforts to decolonize management knowledge, based on empirical work in Uganda, and provides an example of how to take into account sensitivities from post-colonialism and critical management. Jammulamadaka *et al.* (2021) edited a special issue of *Organization* contributing to efforts to decolonize management and organizational knowledge. They suggest that a robust pluriversal discussion on the *how* and *why of decolonization* is vital. The authors suggest a radical ontological plurality that replaces the classical division between theory and praxis. It advocates praxistical theorizing that embraces decolonizing knowledge by moving into the realm of affect and embodied, other-oriented reflexive, communicative praxis. Ruggunan (2016) encourages South African scholars in management studies to reflect more deeply on their own positionality as knowledge producers.

Similarly, ODI (2021) notes that, over several years, the international development sector has faced repeated calls for its decolonization in theory and practice but hegemonic understandings of development and who it should serve continue to dominate. There are issues with sources of funding, power dynamics in methodology, and bias in profiling of research. There is an urgent need to reflect on decolonizing development and how research can be undertaken through a decolonization lens to make an impact within the communities in which development workers operate and elevate the voices needed to build for the future.

In project studies, it is acknowledged that there should be conscious effort to increase diversity among authors of papers published in the leading journals. Geraldi *et al.* (2021) suggests that, to enable this, institutional rules (on research and publication) should respond to the local conditions. Cultural sensitivity is essential for both reviewers and authors to prevent ethnocentrism. Special care should be given to stimulate empirical studies in, for example, Latin America, the Middle East, Africa, and Eastern Europe, as these can represent a rich and complex field of project studies.

Decolonizing engineering

Considering the decolonization of engineering, Muller (2018) distinguishes between retrospective approaches, which deconstruct colonial norms and values to understand their impact on the present, and prospective approaches, which consider what to do next. Should the priority be to break down the old or simply to recognize the flawed foundation and build a durable new future? In another study in South Africa, Fomunyam (2017) drew these conclusions: decolonizing the engineering curriculum is long overdue; the language of instruction, pedagogy, teaching, and learning and practice requires further interrogation to enhance the training of engineers; decolonization is a complex process requiring resources and commitment; the implications of decolonizing the engineering curriculum are far reaching, and the program would be strengthened and improved as decolonization unfolds; and decolonization is a mechanism to ensure that engineers focus on local problems and local development. As Mkasi *et al.* (2018) note, the concept of decolonizing engineering education is an emotive subject, which means different things to different people, and there is a lack of neutrality on the part of participants. The study found that the concept of decolonization is considered applicable to engineering education by students. The findings indicate that curriculum reform is a crucial part of decolonizing engineering education. Primary focus should be given to developing a curriculum inclusive of knowledge from different backgrounds, devoid of dominant Western influence culturally and historically, and free of bias such as toward a certain race or gender, by developing a locally centric education, in this case, Afrocentric education, of which the use of an African language is a crucial element.

On the decolonization of the built environment, much work is being done in South Africa. Newport (2017) suggested that built environment educators have a responsibility to challenge accepted norms under colonial systems and determine how to facilitate the creation of built environments that reflect the needs and aspirations of their society. Osman and Musonda (2017) explore why societies build and what governs building processes and find that the reasons for building go beyond the need for shelter and includes status, power, social convention, values, and ideas on aesthetics. They investigated the idea of community, multiple voices, and multiple decision-makers in the practice of architecture and suggested that it is a way to decolonize architectural education, as it is at odds with institutions teaching future architects, and institutes that regulate its practice which remain colonized.

Decolonizing research

In a study in Australia, Hart and Whatman (1998) note that the colonizers controlled the definition of what was essentially a subjugated culture, reserved the power to distinguish authentic aspects of the living traditions of the colonized, and compiled the "knowledge" about them, and adjudicated what is genuine in any claims they made. They suggest that the university curriculum, teaching methodologies, and research endeavors have a history of development that contributed to this dispossession. Considering more enterprising and collaborative approaches to learning, studying, and researching, where a recognition of Indigenous systems of knowledge is given voice and meaning, will lead to a rediscovery of the country that has endless potential.

In built environment research, Denny-Smith *et al.* (2019) note that in Australia, Indigenous procurement policies encourage the construction sector to provide new training, employment, and business opportunities for Indigenous people suffering from economic and social disadvantage. However, the success of these policies is often distorted by the failure of policy evaluations to account for Indigenous perceptions of social values which differ from non-Indigenous values. This can distort the allocation of funds to Indigenous communities and exacerbate the marginalization of the communities these policies are meant to help. The authors reconceptualize approaches to measuring Indigenous social value in an Indigenous social procurement policy context using a novel approach to Indigenous social impact research that recognizes the legitimacy of Indigenous perspectives. They argue that culturally appropriate focus groups ("yarning" discussion groups) are appropriate in research.

Similarly, Keikelame and Swartz (2019) note that it is becoming increasingly important for researchers to critically reflect on approaches that can have a positive impact on the health outcomes of indigenous people. They used an African lens to reflect upon some issues raised from interviews and focus group discussions. The major issues they raise are about important structures such as power, trust, cultural competence, respectful and legitimate research practice, and recognition of individuals' and communities' health assets in a decolonizing research process. They argue for alternative approaches that are culturally appropriate for health research and for improved health outcomes of marginalized groups, such as participatory and transformative research methods.

The very nature of research has been studied, with the view to decolonizing it. Ndlovu-Gatsheni (2017) notes that research is a terrain where the interests of the "researcher" are pitted against those of the "researched." The core concern is that research is still steeped in the Euro-North America–centric worldview. Researching continues to give the "researcher" the power to define. The "researched" appear as "specimens." He defines research methodology as a process of seeking to know the "Other," who becomes the object rather than the subject of research. That is why methodology needs to be decolonized. The process of its decolonization is an ethical, ontological, and political exercise rather than simply one of approach and ways to produce knowledge. Mkasi *et al.* (2018) asserted that decolonizers are concerned about whose problems are solved by the application of science. Of interest would be a question such as, "in engineering education, what African societal challenges need a transformation within the engineering curriculum in order to be addressed?" They state that: "Knowledge, including scientific knowledge, can be African centered, but it is believed it does so only when it is entangled in African realities, lexicons and matrices and shaped by these contexts" (Naude, 2017).

How is decolonization achieved?

Some authors urge caution in the discourse on decolonization. To Wingfield (2017), the term "decolonization of education" is being misinterpreted among South African students in their call for total rejection. She suggests that curricula be developed that incorporate locally developed knowledge and also build on the best knowledge skills, values, beliefs, and habits from around the world, and international best practices. Guattari (2001) argues that one cannot create new ways of living by reversing technological advancement and going back to old ways and methods that suited different contexts. Mkasi *et al.* (2018) also urge caution and a balance, stating that, while the removal of Western discovered science from engineering will result in an education that is no longer able to solve engineering problems, efforts must be invested in including African knowledge and wisdom within the engineering curriculum as well as in developing new knowledges.

As noted above, decolonization is not easy to achieve. To Smith (1999), it has these elements: deconstruction and reconstruction; self-determination and social justice (seeking legitimacy for knowledge embedded in their histories and how they view reality); ethics related to the protection of indigenous knowledge systems; language; internationalization of indigenous experiences; and history and critique (enabling the historically marginalized to communicate from their frames of reference). Garuba (2015) suggested two approaches of decolonization of the curriculum. The first is to add to the curriculum content from previously colonized places and peoples. The second approach is to "rethink how the object of study itself is constituted" and reconstruct it. Higher Education South Africa (2014, p. 7) suggests that change at universities must entail "engaging with ontological and epistemological issues in all their complexity, including their implications for research, methodology, scholarship, learning and teaching, curriculum and pedagogy." Le Grange (2016) noted that deconstruction and reconstruction concerns discarding wrong formulations; investigating distortions of colonized people's experiences, negative labeling, and deficient models about the colonized; and retelling their stories and envisioning the future. Moreover, Dei (2000, p. 13) notes that systems of knowledge are dynamic and influence each other; thus, holding on to a dichotomy "between good [Indigenous] and bad [conventional/ Western] knowledges" is not useful. Thus, decolonization of the curriculum involves change that does not necessarily involve destroying Western knowledge, but in decentering it.

What does a decolonized field look like? Chilisa (2019) proposes the Indigenous Research Paradigm, whose guidelines promote critical thinking and upholding of ethical behavior, instilling values focusing on indigenous knowledge systems. It acknowledges ontological, socially constructed, multiple-realities shaped by the connections of people to their environment and cosmology. Its research and data collection methods are participatory, transformative, and draw from indigenous knowledge systems.

Inviting "the others" in

In many fields, researchers are being encouraged to take interest in developing countries. George *et al.* (2016) reviewed papers on management studies in Africa and identified these challenges addressed and solutions proposed: *navigating institutional voids*, by designing around weak institutional infrastructure and overcoming human and financial resource constraints to seek value-creating opportunities; *building capabilities*, by promoting managerial capacity, positive employee behavior, and ethical values; and *enabling opportunities*, by implementing new market-entry strategies, governance modes, and organizational designs. Efforts to encourage research on developing countries include funding schemes requiring partnership with such countries' institutions or supporting exploration of issues in developing countries, such as the Global Challenges Research Fund (GCRF) of the UK government.

There have been attempts to study the development of project management in developing countries. Ika and Saint-Macary (2014) edited a special issue of the *Journal of African Business*, which had papers on projects ranging from major continental initiatives through the agricultural sector and then the construction industry. More recently, Ika *et al.* (2021) made a rousing call for papers on managing and leading projects in Africa. An extract from that call is presented in Box 25.1.

Box 25.1: A call to research and action.

"Project management research has focused little on African contexts, as in the broader business and management literature (Kiggundu and Lamont, 2015; Zoogah *et al.*, 2015; Kolk and Rivera-Santos, 2018). Exceptions include Bredillet *et al.* (2012) and Ika and Saint-Macary (2014), two special issues dedicated to project management in Africa. The call for papers for this special collection on African Project Management Research aims to fill this gap. The special collection, which consists in a three-year pilot project, focuses on managing and leading projects in Africa and purports to give a voice to African or Africa-friendly scholars with interest in investigating managing and leading projects. We encourage African researchers to bring a uniquely African perspective that is embedded in the project management experience in the African contexts. We are particularly motivated by the idea that, just as Africa contributed to the emergence and development of the Sustainable Development Goals (Fukuda-Parr and Muchhala, 2020), Africa can also shape project management theory and practice (Ika, 2012) and contribute to the global knowledge ecology of project management.

"Project management scholars have a unique opportunity to fill the dearth of research by "bringing in Africa" (George *et al.*, 2016) into the conversation in, on, and around projects (Geraldi and Söderlund, 2018). Africa offers different, unique, if not "extreme" topics, contexts, empirical settings, and ways

Box 25.1: (*Continued*)

of seeing the world as compared to other settings, like North America, Europe, and, to some extent, East Asia (Barnard, 2020; Ika *et al.*, 2020). The idiosyncratic nature of these particular contexts, we argue, can help test whether project management theories and practices are designed to be context-free or one-size-fits-all, context-bound or different across contexts, or context-specific or only applicable in a given context (Kolk and Rivera-Santos, 2018).

"Against this backdrop, this special collection is critical for a number of reasons. We live in a project society (Lundin *et al.*, 2015). Project management should help tackle societal if not global challenges such as pandemics, poverty reduction, sustainability, and climate change (Morris, 2013; Ika *et al.*, 2020). In the face of complexity and uncertainty, countries need resilience to tackle these challenges (Naderpajouh *et al.*, 2020) and deal with the unintended consequences of their transformational projects (Hirschman, 1967; Ika, 2018). …

"Project management capacity and social capital are key project success conditions (see Ika and Donnelly, 2017 and Amoako-Gyampah *et al.*, 2021 for Ghana; Chileshe *et al.*, 2021 for Tanzania). A sound appreciation of cultural and contextual differences can help deliver more successful projects (Muriithi and Crawford, 2003; Ika and Donnelly, 2017). Results-Based Management (RBM) and other approaches to project management can help achieve project benefits (Ika *et al.*, 2010; Ssegawa and Muzinda, 2016)."

Source: Ika *et al.* (2021).

Developing countries as a source of project studies ideas

Indeed, research based on the developing countries can help in advancing the definition of a "project." Kreiner (2020) sheds new light on the debate in project studies between Hirschman and Flyvbjerg (2014) on the hiding hand principle — a theory that examines how ignorance in the formative stage of projects may be benevolent as it underestimates not only the costs but also people's ability to respond creatively to obstacles. Kreiner suggests that while Flyvbjerg values getting things right at the outset, Hirschman opens the opportunity for getting things right at the end. Reflecting on how Hirschman's ideas have been accepted in project studies, Kreiner discusses how values and assumptions might encourage project scholars and practitioners to learn the same lessons over and over again.

How suitable are the PMI's PMBOK and other generic frameworks for developing countries?

The 10 *knowledge areas* outlined in the PMBOK (Sixth Edition) are outlined in Table 25.1, together with an outline of factors which make a different approach in developing countries necessary.

Table 25.1: Knowledge areas of project management in PMI BoK (Sixth Edition).

Knowledge area	Processes and activities	Developing country factors requiring a different management approach
Project integration management	Identifying, defining, combining, unifying and coordinating the various processes and project management activities.	Fragmented industry, many small players and agencies making various contributions. Need for more co-ordination and monitoring.
Project scope management	Ensuring that the project includes all the work required to complete the project and that no additional work is undertaken.	Lack of appreciation of roles among participants; responsibilities not always clear; unequal bargaining power among players means management involves political skills.
Project schedule management	Managing the completion of the project within the stipulated time.	Inaccurate estimating of time; lack of application of IT scheduling tools; absence of productivity norms for planning; worker attitudes and absenteeism; lack of monitoring of progress and enforcement of time performance targets; bureaucracy in administration of aspects of public projects; involvement of administrative procedures of lenders; delays in payment.
Project cost management	Planning, estimating, budgeting, financing, monitoring, administering and controlling costs to enable the project to be completed within the approved budget.	Many contributors to cost increases; delays in payments; absence of national cost norms and indices makes estimating difficult. Finance is important in there
Project quality management	Ensuring that the project will satisfy the needs for which it was undertaken.	Quality management systems non-existent or not enforced; inadequate definition of quality and monitoring arrangements; low level of establishment of materials quality standards; low level of enforcement of quality standards, codes and regulations.

Table 25.1: (*Continued*)

Knowledge area	Processes and activities	Developing country factors requiring a different management approach
Project resource management	Processes for organizing, managing, and leading the project team.	Shortages of qualified personnel and materials; resources go beyond human resource to include material, financial, technological, and information. Each of these requires systematic management. Legislation and weak enforcement; many items imported; local content regulations; quality of local inputs; health and safety
Project communications management	Ensuring appropriate planning, collection, creation, distribution, storage, retrieval, management, control, monitoring, and the eventual disposal of project information.	Information, communication, and their management a key project management issue, need for effective regime.
Project risk management	Conducting planning, identification, analysis, response planning, and controlling risk on a project.	Risks in these contexts are more numerous, wider and more potentially harmful; risks and their management are not well understood.
Project procurement management	Purchasing products, services, or results needed to undertake the project.	Enforcing procurement regulations is a challenge owing to entrenched interests; local content regulations; supply chain management is challenging; client's procurement and contract administration procedures have a major impact on the project. The procurement process should have a development orientation — companies and persons as well as the industry — of projects should be awarded to companies which are in a position to contribute most to the development of the industry.
Project stakeholder management	Identifying all people or organizations within and outside the project who are impacted by the project, or who can influence it, analyze their expectations and impact on the project, and develop strategies for effectively engaging these persons and organizations in project decisions and execution.	Research has found that effective community participation stimulates project success. Ofori (2021) notes that, whereas it is required by law in some developing countries, it seldom happens. Stakeholder identification is important; wider range of stakeholders including non-government organizations, community organizations, and traditional structures. The stakeholders require education and awareness building to play their roles; stakeholder development is a project activity; stakeholder welfare should be a key objective.

In the conventional, standard conceptualization of project management, these 10 topics are considered to cover all the areas in which work has to be done in order to complete all projects. However, as shown in the table, it is possible to outline, under each of the 10 areas, ways in which the context of a developing country would have a different impact on, and implications for, the area which is different from what pertains in an industrialized country.

The developing countries need a sound, appropriate framework for project management. The National Institution for Transforming India and Quality Council of India (2020, preface) notes in *The Indian Infrastructure Body of Knowledge* (INBoK) that:

> "There are multiple challenges to infrastructure development in India, including regulatory clearances, land acquisition, resettlement and rehabilitation... The government has set up various bodies to tide over such obstacles and is continuing to improve them."
>
> "However, one aspect which needs attention is the successful adoption of globally accepted program/project management practices. The country is in the transformation phase and with such large-scale initiatives planned, there is a growing demand for structured program/project management practices, to manage these programs and implement them successfully. Program/project management practices, when implemented successfully, can bring in synergies, integration, and a common language to all these complex program initiatives."

Indeed, these 10 areas do not cover all the tasks which require to be undertaken in order to enable the project to be completed in a developing country. For example, as noted in Chapter 4, the INBoK includes areas not covered in the generic bodies of knowledge such as PMBOK, including: Interface and Integration Management; Change Management; Concessionaire/Contractor Compensation Management; Supply Chain Management; and Value Creation and Benefits Improvement. The National Institute of Chartered Program and Project Professionals (2020) notes that: "...the INBoK is a technical guidebook that imbibes the best practices in program and project management from leading experts, basic principles of international standards for program/project management like ISO, AACE, etc., and contextualises it for the Indian infrastructure landscape."

Finally, the completion of the built item does not mark the end of the construction project. In many ways, it is the beginning, as the efficient management of the operation of the building is a major indicator of project success (Ofori, 2016). Commissioning of the completed built item is highlighted as an important activity (California Commissioning Collaborative, 2006). The maintenance needs of the built item should also be given due attention in project management. Thus, Commissioning, Operating, and Facilities Management should be a specific area of knowledge in project management in developing countries.

Some of the additional areas relevant to developing countries are now outlined.

Industry development

Developing countries need to develop capabilities at all levels of their construction industries and their related aspects and component parts, as they invest in the projects they need for their development (Rwelamila and Ogunlana, 2015; Rwelamila and Abdul-Rashid, 2021; Ofori, 2021). Various countries have formulated policies and strategies for this purpose; examples include Ethiopia (Ministry of Urban Development and Construction, 2012) and Sri Lanka (National Advisory Council on Construction, 2014). Thus, contributing to the building of the industry at large is one of the necessary tasks of the project team. The indicators could include: extent of meeting regulatory prescripts; technology and knowledge transfer; provision of employment; mentoring of smaller companies; and management of the project value chain. Project performance should be measured as "on-schedule, on-quality, on-strategy and on-development contribution." Performance on this set of criteria can be included in the procurement determination for future projects. In this way, the country will develop its industry one project at a time.

Operating environment of the industry

The operating environment has an impact on the way projects are managed, and it requires to be studied in its own right in order for management decisions and actions to be determined on the project. Styhre (2020) claims that projects should be understood in their "broader financial, regulatory, and political context wherein projects are developed, operate, and evolve." Narayanan and Hueman (2021) studied the activities of project managers in a construction company in India and concluded that labor and supplier markets in the country are underdeveloped, and the projects had to bear the cost of this development. It is necessary to highlight that projects create their own ecosystems and spheres of influence; for large projects, the latter can be quite extensive, and involve many aspects beyond the physical considerations, including economic, social and political. Biesenthal *et al.* (2018) suggest that increasingly, it is evident that the problem areas attached to large projects stretch beyond technical issues: they must be considered as socio-technical endeavors embedded in complex institutional frames, and study how to deal with institutional differences in the environment of megaprojects.

Some project studies scholars indicate factors external to the project as main causes of time and cost overruns and other instances of poor performance. Ameh *et al.* (2010) found environmental factors such as the economy, inadequate raw materials, and competition. Muianga *et al.* (2014) identified government, environment, and the economy; shortage of materials and equipment; and fluctuations of materials and equipment. Morris and Geraldi (2011, p. 20) suggested that project management should look beyond the preoccupation with "delivering undertakings on time, on budget, and on scope." Its conceptualization should consider these three levels:

- Level 1 — Technical level which is concerned with operating and effective delivery of the project on time, budget and scope
- Level 2 — Strategic level concerned with managing the project as an organizational entity and including the front-end
- Level 3 — Institutional level, which is focused on creating conditions to support and foster the project, both in its parent organization and its external environment; "Management here is done *for* and *on* the project rather than *in* or *to* it" Morris and Geraldi (2011, p. 20). They suggest that management at this level offers greatest potential for improvement in performance.

Taking inspiration from Morris and Geraldi (2011), Simushi and Wium (2020) suggest that a project be viewed as being performed in three environments: the project environment in which the participants operate; the organization environment, which combines the strategic and technical levels of Morris and Geraldi (2011), where the project is defined, designed, and managed; and the external environment where activities and processes outside the project and organization environment take place, which affects the operations of the project. They suggest that the last environment type could include the legal system, culture, community groups, the media, and the political system. In the study in South Africa, Simushi and Wium (2020) found that projects incurred time and cost overruns owing to a combination of factors originating from the external environment. The root cause of time and cost overruns were found to be lack of project-specific experience, decisions in the past in the external and organization environments, community resistance and pressure, delayed project start, insufficient client budgets, and procurement requirements of the client. Simushi and Wium (2020) note that community resistance and pressure affected both the organization and project environment, leading to delayed project start, insufficient budgets, and procurement short cuts, resulting in redesigns, reworks, request for additional project funding, and project time and cost overruns.

Writing in the US, Horsey and de la Garza (2014) present a process to improve the deployment of best practices in project management in unfamiliar locations by reducing the gap in the deployment of best practices domestically against the added challenges of deployment abroad. Some 61 issues which are commonly encountered in such deployments were identified and grouped into nine categories: business customs; social and cultural; regulations; market and political conditions; geography and logistics; legal and contracts; human resources and workforce; safety and security; and communications. The research developed the International Readiness Passport, which can increase a company's confidence when planning work abroad by establishing readiness to estimate and bid for work in unfamiliar countries; and provide a gap analysis to help identify risks and provide potential solutions to mitigate those risks.

Writing from their experience, Stuckenbruck and Zomorrodian (1987, p. 167) note that the project management approach "has potential for revitalizing the sluggish and ineffective management practices often encountered in developing countries. However, its unqualified adoption is strongly rejected." They concluded (p. 167):

> The application of project management is recommended only when certain technical, political, and environmental conditions are met. Even then, it will only work when it is incorporated into an indigenous framework based on local values, beliefs, and behavioural patterns. It is argued that, even when all cultural and political aspects are properly considered, careful consideration of other factors, such as the nature of the task, the type and size of the project, and the technology, must be considered in order to ensure the success of the endeavour.

In a McKinsey and Devex Development Agency Effectiveness Survey of 1,210 respondents undertaken by Lovegrove *et al.* (2011), only 36 percent of those surveyed said that most aid projects achieve their intended impact. Seven factors, which are mostly outside the control of project management teams, were found as having a significant or fundamental impact on the tasks of development agencies: increased pressure to show impact; greater scrutiny over donor budgets; the landscape changing rapidly, as new topics emerge on the development agenda; aid recipients have more diverse needs; pressure for partner country ownership is increasing; new players and funding sources are proliferating; and there are increasing calls for more coordination across agencies. More than 50 percent of the participants believed that overhead costs, high fees, and inefficient (sometimes even questionable) contracting and procurement processes contribute to at least 10 percent leakage in the aid system. For a majority of respondents, four areas stand out as needing improvement: planning for financial sustainability, ensuring stakeholder skills to sustain the program, forward-planning allocations, and evidence-based resource allocation. The delivery of those projects needs to change because taxpayers are demanding greater accountability from their governments, and thus donors funded by governments are demanding greater accountability and returns on investment.

In their South African study, Simushi and Wium (2020) note that time and cost overruns are a persistent problem on large projects despite the apparent progress of the project management profession. The root cause was found to be a lack of project-specific experience by the project team, external and organizational decisions in the past, community resistance and pressure on the project team, and scope change drive from stakeholders. Simushi and Wium (2020) considered that their study confirmed the theory that the limited approach to the management of the project environment by excluding the external and organization environments is a major handicap in a large project management strategy. They proposed that an effective strategy to reduce time and cost overruns should involve not only the management of the project environment but also the organization and external environments.

Supply chain management

Each construction project relies on an extensive supply chain and this should be particularly managed, as its performance has an impact on that of the project. The nature of the construction supply chain in the developing countries is highlighted by many authors as a major constraint on projects (Ofori, 2021). Narayanan and Hueman (2021) develop a model of the practices which are undertaken by project managers to address the challenges of organizational fields in the context of an emerging economy, based on a study of project managers' activities in a construction firm in India. The study illustrates how the micro-activities of project managers and the actions of senior management address the emerging economy challenges. They suggest that the activities of project managers in major construction projects may act as a mechanism of transition in emerging economies. The project managers undertook many field building activities that were crucial for the success of their projects; these activities were simultaneously addressing major gaps in the economic infrastructure of India. Thus, the study shows that project managers in the construction industry are not just engaged in project execution, but are active participants in the economic transition of a country.

Assessing project performance

The criteria for assessing performance on projects have been widely studied (Rwelamila, 2012; Ofori, 2016). APM notes that a project is usually considered to be a success if it achieves the objectives according to their acceptance criteria, within an agreed timescale and budget, adding that "time, cost and quality are the building blocks of every project."[1] Other project performance criteria that are discussed include: health and safety; environmental performance (sustainability), client satisfaction; and the satisfaction of other stakeholders, in particular, the community. Davis (2018) investigates the possibility that project failure is a result of the interpretations of the criteria and factors used for success by multiple stakeholder groups and presents a model encompassing the important attributes needed to measure project success across different stakeholder groups. The subject of determining the appropriate project performance criteria is still under development (Ofori, 2021).

There appears to be a bias in the focus of knowledge on project management; projects are marked by time pressure. For example, Delisle (2019) suggests that the modern experience of time in project management is one of increasing time pressure, acceleration and scarcity, as time management and deadlines are put at the forefront of the discipline. Delisle (2019) sought to uncover the way time is conceived in two project management bodies of knowledge. Her study showed that both standards draw on a quantitative and objective conception of time and evoke acceleration and time scarcity, and reveals that project management standards reflect and contribute to those temporal phenomena of acceleration and time scarcity.

Concluding remarks

Construction is undertaken differently in different countries (Davis *et al.*, 2000). There are, frequently, comparisons of practices in different countries to derive good practice and other ideas for emulation (Bennett *et al.*, 1987; Xiao and Proverbs, 2002). There is no such thing as a "construction process." While the structure of the construction industry, the roles of the practitioners, and documentation used in the developing countries are based on those of the former colonial powers, the business procedures and practices in the industry tend to be contextually based. There is ample evidence that the approach to the management of a

[1] https://www.apm.org.uk/resources/what-is-project-management/

project in the developing countries should be different from what has been developed for, and been applied in, the industrialized countries. There is a critical need to develop a separate body of knowledge for project management for the developing countries.

To enable the emergence of such a volume and foster its effectiveness in application, it is necessary to decolonize project studies. The research agenda proposed in this book (see, especially, Chapter 26) will be useful in contributing to the design of the tasks.

References

Adebisi, F. (2016). Decolonising education in Africa: Implementing the right to education by re-appropriating culture and indigeneity. *Northern Ireland Legal Quarterly*, 67(4), 433–451.

Ahiaga-Dagbui, D.D., Smith, S.D., Love, P.E.D. and Ackermann, F. (2015). Spotlight on construction cost overrun research: Superficial, replicative and stagnated. In A.B. Raiden and E. Aboagye-Nimo (Eds.), *Proceedings of 31st Annual ARCOM Conference*. Association of Researchers in Construction Management, Lincoln.

Ahmed, R., Philbin, S.P. and Cheema, F. (2021). Systematic literature review of project manager's leadership competencies. *Engineering, Construction and Architectural Management*, 28(1), 1–30. https://doi.org/10.1108/ECAM-05-2019-0276.

AlSehaimi, A., Koskela, L. and Tzortzopoulos, P. (2013). The need for alternative research approaches in construction management: The case of delay studies. *Journal of Management in Engineering*, 29, 407–413. https://doi.org/10.1061/(ASCE)ME.1943-5479.0000148.

Ameh, O.J., A.D. Soyingbe and K.T. Odusami (2010). Significant factors causing cost overruns in telecommunication projects in Nigeria. *Journal of Construction in Developing Countries*, 15(2), 49–67.

Bakker, R.M., DeFillippi, R.J., Schwab, A. and Sydow, J. (2016). Temporary organizing: Promises, processes, problems. *Organization Studies*, 37(12), 1703–1719. https://doi.org/10.1177/0170840616655982.

Bennett, J., Flanagan, R. and Norman, G. (1987). *Capital and Counties Report: Japanese Construction Industry*. Centre for Strategic Studies in Construction, University of Reading, Reading.

Biesenthal, C., Clegg, S., Mahalingam, A. and Sankaran, S. (2018). Applying institutional theories to managing megaprojects. *International Journal of Project Management*, 36(1), 43–54.

Bredillet, C.N. (2006). The future of project management: Mapping the dynamics of project management field in action. In D.I. Cleland and R. Gareis (Eds.), *Global Project Management Handbook: Planning, Organizing and Controlling International Projects*, 2nd Edition. McGraw Hill, New York, pp. 3-3–3-24.

Bredillet, C.N. (2010). Blowing hot and cold on project management. *Project Management Journal*, 41(3), 4–20. https://doi.org/10.1002/pmj.20179.

California Commissioning Collaborative (2006). *California Commissioning Guide: New buildings*. Sacramento, CA.

Chilisa, B. (2019). *Indigenous Research Methodologies*, 2nd Edition. Sage Publications, Los Angeles.

Chiocchio, F., Kelloway, E.K. and Hobbs, B. (2015). *The Psychology and Management of Project Teams*. Oxford University Press.

Clegg, S.R., Pitsis, T.S., Rura-Polley, T. and Marosszeky, M. (2002). Governmentality matters: Designing an alliance culture of interorganizational collaboration for managing projects. *Organization Studies*, 23(3), 317–337. https://doi.org/10.1177/0170840602233001.

Comeau, P. and Santin, A. (1995). *The First Canadians: A profile of Canada's Native People Today*. James Lorimer & Co, Toronto, ON.

Connel, R. (2007). *Southern Theory*. Polity, Cambridge.

Cotula, L., Toulmin, C. and Hesse, C. (2004). *Land Tenure and Administration in Africa: Lessons of Experience and Emerging Issues*. International Institute for Environment and Development, London.

Crawford, G., Mai-Bornu, Z. and Landström, K. (2021). Decolonising knowledge production on Africa: Why it's still necessary and what can be done. *Journal of the British Academy*, 9(s1), 21–46. https://doi.org/10.5871/jba/009s1.021.

Davies, A., Manning, S. and Söderlund, J. (2018). When neighboring disciplines fail to learn from each other: The case of innovation and project management research. *Research Policy*, 47(5), 965–979. https://doi.org/10.1016/j.respol.2018.03.002.

Davis, K. (2018). Reconciling the views of project success: A multiple stakeholder model. *Project Management Journal*, 49(5), 38–47. https://doi.org/10.1177/8756972818786663.

Davis, L. and Everest (2000). *Spon's European Construction Costs Handbook*, 3rd Edition. Spon Press, London.

Delisle, J. (2019). Uncovering temporal underpinnings of project management standards. *International Journal of Project Management*, 37(8), 968–978. https://doi.org/10.1016/j.ijproman.2019.09.005.

Dei, G. (2000). Rethinking the role of indigenous knowledges in the academy. *International Journal of Inclusive Education*, 4(2), 111–132.

Denny-Smith, G., Loosemore, M., Barwick, D. Sunindijo, R. and Piggott, L. (2019). Decolonising indigenous social impact research using community-based methods. Association of Researchers in Construction Management, ARCOM 2019 — *Proceedings of the 35th Annual Conference, 2019*, pp. 64–73. http://hdl.handle.net/10453/139908.

Department of Education (2008). *Report of the Ministerial Committee on Transformation and Social Cohesion and the Elimination of Discrimination in Public Higher Education Institutions*, Final Report. Department of Education, Pretoria.

Eskerod, P. and Larson, T. (2018). Advancing project stakeholder analysis by the concept 'shadows of the context'. *International Journal of Project Management*, 36(1), 161–169. https://doi.org/10.1016/j.ijproman.2017.05.003.

Fanon, F. (1967). *The Wretched of the Earth*. Penguin, Harmondsworth.

Fomunyam, K.G. (2017). Decolonising the engineering curriculum in a South African University of Technology. *International Journal of Applied Engineering Research*, 12(17), 6797–6805.

Flyvbjerg, B. (2014). What you should know about megaprojects and why: An overview. *Project Management Journal*, 45(2), 6–19. https://doi.org/10.1002/pmj.21409.

Gareis, R. (2006). Project management: A business process of the project-oriented company. In D.I. Cleland and R. Gareis (Eds.), *Global Project Management Handbook: Planning, Organizing and Controlling International Projects*, 2nd Edition. McGraw Hill, New York, pp. 2-1–2-28.

Garuba, H. (2015). What is an African curriculum? *Mail & Guardian*, 17 April. http://mg.co.za/article/2015-04-17-what-is-an-african-curriculum.

George, G., Corbishley, C., Khayesi, J.N., Haas, M.R. and Tihanyi, L. (2016). Bringing Africa in: Promising directions for management research. *Academy of Management Journal*, 59(2), 377–393.

Geraldi, J. and Soderlund, J. (2018). Project studies: What it is, where it is going. *International Journal of Project Management*, 36(1), 55–70. https://doi.org/10.1016/j.ijproman.2017.06.004.

Geraldi J., Söderlund J. and van Marrewijk, A. (2021). Bright and dark spots in project studies: Continuing efforts to advance theory development and debate. *Project Management Journal*, 52(3), 227–236. https://doi.org/10.1177/87569728211004064.

Girei E. (2017). Decolonising management knowledge: A reflexive journey as practitioner and researcher in Uganda. *Management Learning*, 48(4), 453–470. https://doi.org/10.1177/1350507617697867.

Grabher, G . (2002). Cool projects, boring institutions: Temporary collaboration in social context. *Regional Studies,* 36(3), 205–214. https://doi.org/10.1080/00343400220122025.

Guattari, F. (2001). *The Three Ecologies* (Trans. I. Pindar and P. Sutton). Athlone Press, London.

Hart, V.G. and Whatman, S.L. (1998). Decolonising the concept of knowledge. *HERDSA: Annual International Conference,* 7–10 July, Auckland, NZ. https://eprints.qut.edu.au/27531/.

Heleta, S. (2016). Decolonisation of higher education: Dismantling epistemic violence and Eurocentrism in South Africa. *Transformation in Higher Education,* 1(1), a9. http://dx.doi.org/10.4102/the.v1i1.9.

Hirschman, A.O. (2015 [1967]). *Development Projects Observed.* The Brookings Institute Press, Washington, DC.

Higher Education South Africa (2014). South African Higher Education in the 20th Year of Democracy: Context, achievements and key challenges. Presentation to the Portfolio Committee on Higher Education and Training, Cape Town, 5 March.

Hodgson, D. and Cicmil, S. (2007). The politics of standards in modern management: Making 'the project' a reality. *Journal of Management Studies*, 44, 431–450.

Horsey, T. and de la Garza (2014). *Deploying Best Practices in Unfamiliar Countries*, Research Report RR294-11. Construction Industry Institute, Austin, TX. https://www.construction-institute.org/resources/knowledgebase/knowledge-areas/business-and-project-processes/topics/rt-294/pubs/rr294-11.

Ika, L. and Saint-Macary, J. (2014). Special issue: Why do projects fail in Africa? *Journal of African Business*, 15(3), 151–155. https://doi.org/10.1080/15228916.2014.956635.

Ika, L.A., Keeys, L.A., Tuuli, M.M., Sané, S. and Ssegawa, J.K. (2021). Call for papers special collection: Managing and leading projects in Africa. *Project Leadership and Society*, 2. https://doi.org/10.1016/j.plas.2021.100023.

Jammulamadaka, N., Faria, A.J.G. and Ruggunan S. (2021). Decolonising management and organisational knowledge (MOK): Praxistical theorising for potential worlds. *Organization*, 28(5), 717–740. https://doi.org/10.1177/135050842110 20463.

Kapoor, D. (2009). Education, decolonization and development: Perspectives from Asia, Africa and the Americas. In D. Kapoor (Ed.), *Education, Decolonization and Development: Perspectives from Asia, Africa and the Americas*. Sense Publishers, Boston, pp. 1–6.

Kaya, H.O. and Seleti, Y.N. (2013). African indigenous knowledge systems and relevance of higher education in South Africa. *The International Education Journal: Comparative Perspectives,* 12(1), 30–44.

Keikelame, M.J. and Swartz, L. (2019). Decolonising research methodologies: Lessons from a qualitative research project, Cape Town, South Africa, *Global Health Action*, 12(1). https://doi.org/10.1080/16549716.2018.1561175.

Kloppenborg, T. J., and Opfer, W. A. (2002). The current state of project management research: Trends, interpretations, and predictions. *Project Management Journal*, 33(2), 5–18. https://doi.org/10.1177/8756972802033 00203.

Krahn, J. and Hartment, F. (2006). Effective project leadership: A combination of project manager skills and competencies in context. Paper presented at *PMI® Research Conference: New Directions in Project Management*, Montréal, Canada. Project Management Institute, Newtown Square, PA. https://www.pmi.org/learning/library/leadership-project-manager-skills-competencies-8115.

Kreiner, K. (2020). Conflicting notions of a project: The battle between Albert O. Hirschman and Bent Flyvbjerg. *Project Management Journal*, 51(4), 400–410. https://doi.org/10.1177/8756972820930535.

Le Grange, L. (2016). Decolonising the university curriculum. *South African Journal of Higher Education*, 30(2), 1–12. http://dx.doi.org/10.20853/ 30-2-709.

Lenfle, S., Midler, C. and Hällgren, M. (2019). Exploratory projects: From strangeness to theory. *Project Management Journal*, 50(5), 519–523. https:// doi.org/10.1177/8756972819871781.

Lindgren, M. and Packendorff, J. (2009b) Project leadership as a research field: Antecedents, current research and a critique. Unpublished paper, KTH Royal Institute of Technology, Stockholm, Sweden. https://www.diva-portal.org/ smash/get/diva2:1354244/FULLTEXT01.pdf

Lokugamage, A.U., Ahillan, T. and Pathberiya, S. (2020). Decolonising ideas of healing in medical education. *Journal of Medical Ethics,* Online First, 06 February. https://doi.org/10.1136/medethics-2019-105866.

Lovegrove, N., Gebre, B., Lee, T. and Raj Kumar, R. (2011). McKinsey-Devex survey results: Practitioners see need for new approaches to system-wide reform, 19 December. https://www.devex.com/news/mckinsey-devex-survey-results-practitioners-see-need-for-new-approaches-to-system-wide-reform-77026.

Malach-Pines, A., Dvir, D. and Sadeh, A. (2009). Project manager-project (PM-P) fit and project success. *International Journal of Operations and Production Management*, 29(3), 268–291. https://doi.org/10.1108/01443570910938998.

Martinsuo, M. and Geraldi, J. (2020). Management of project portfolios: Relationships of project portfolios with their contexts. *International Journal of Project Management*, 38(7), 441–453. https://doi.org/10.1016/j.ijproman.2020.02.002.

Ministry of Urban Development and Construction (2012). *Construction Industry Policy*. Addis Ababa.

Mkasi, M., Emwanu, B. and Kuchwa-Dube, C. (2018). The concept of decolonisation within engineering education. *Proceedings of the International Conference on Industrial Engineering and Operations Management*, Pretoria and Johannesburg, South Africa, October 29–November 1, IEOM Society International. http://ieomsociety.org/southafrica2018/papers/299.pdf.

Molefe, T.O. (2016). Oppression must fall: South Africa's revolution in theory. *World Policy Journal,* 33(1), 30–37. http://dx.doi.org/10.1215/07402775-3545858.

Morris, P.W.G. (2012). A brief history of project management. In P.W.G. Morris, J.K. Pinto and J. Söderlund (Eds.), *The Oxford Handbook of Project Management*. Oxford University Press, pp. 15–36.

Morris, P.W.G. and Geraldi, J.G. (2011). Managing the institutional context for projects. *Project Management Journal*, 42(6), 20–32. http://dx.doi.org/10.1002/pmj.20271.

Mudimbe, V.Y. (1985). African gnosis philosophy and the order of knowledge: An introduction. *African Studies Review*, 28(2/3), 149–233. http://dx.doi.org/10.2307/524605.

Muller, M. (2018). Decolonising engineering in South Africa — Experience to date and some emerging challenges. *South African Journal of Science*, 114(5/6), Art. #a0270, 6 pages. http://dx.doi.org/10.17159/sajs.2018/a0270.

Müller, R. and Turner, R. (2007). The influence of project managers on project success criteria and project success by type of project. *European Management Journal*, 25(4), 298–309. https://doi.org/10.1016/j.emj.2007.06.003.

Munroe, E.A., Borden, L.L. and Orr, A.M., Toney, D. and Meader, J. (2013). Decolonizing aboriginal education in the 21st Century. *McGill Journal of Education*, 48(2), 317–338.

Narayanan, V.K. and Hueman, M. (2021). Engaging the organizational field: The case of project practices in a construction firm to contribute to an emerging economy. *International Journal of Project Management*, 39(5), 449–462.

National Advisory Council on Construction (2014). *National Policy on Construction*. Ministry of Housing and Construction, Colombo.

National Institute of Chartered Program and Project Professionals (2020). Indian Infrastructure Body of Knowledge. https://nicpp.in/indian-infrastructure-body-of-knowledge.

National Institution for Transforming India and Quality Council of India (2020). The Indian Infrastructure Body of Knowledge (INBoK): A technical baseline to the practice of program and project management in India. Delhi.

Naude, P. (2017). *Decolonising Knowledge: In What Sense Is an 'African' Ethic Possible? — Ex Africa Semper Aliquid Novi*. University of Stellenbosch, Stellenbosch, South Africa.

Ndlovu-Gatsheni, S. (2017). Decolonising research methodology must include undoing its dirty history. *Journal of Public Administration*, 52(1). https://hdl.handle.net/10520/EJC-b1cd74dfa.

Newport, I. (2017). Decolonizing thought practices with discussion approaches for built environment educators. In S. Giloi and H. Botes (Eds.), *Proceedings of the 14th National Design Education Conference 2017*, 27–29 September, Tshwane, South Africa, pp. 213–223.

Nicholas, J.M. and Steyn, H. (2008). *Project Management for Business, Engineering, and Technology: Principles and Practice*, 3rd Edition. Butterworth-Heinemann, Oxford.

O'Brien, P. (2006). Historical traditions and modern imperatives for the restoration of global history. *Journal of Global History*, 1(1), 3–39.

ODI (2021). ODI Bites: Decolonising international development. https://odi.org/en/events/odi-bites-decolonising-international-development/.

OECD (2021). Procurement strategy in major infrastructure projects: Piloting a new approach in Norway. Paris. https://dx.doi.org/10.1787/38996343-en.

Ofori, G. (2012). Reflections on the great divide: Strategic review of the book. In G. Ofori (Ed.), *Contemporary Issues in Construction in Developing Countries*. Spon Press, Abingdon, pp. 1–19. https://doi.org/10.4324/9780203847350.

Ofori, G. (2016). Construction in developing countries: Current imperatives and potential. In K. Kahkonen and M. Keinanen (Eds.), *CIB World Building Congress 2016 on Intelligent Built Environment for Lives*. Tampere, 30 May–3 June, Tampere University of Technology.

Ofori, G. (2021). Construction in developing countries: Need for new concepts and theorising of contextual specificities to the global corpus of knowledge. *Proceedings, West Africa Built Environment Research (WABER) Conference*, 9–10 August, Accra, Ghana.

Orlikowski, W.J. (2007). Sociomaterial practices: Exploring technology at work. *Organization Studies*, 28(9), 1435–1448. https://doi.org/10.1177/0170840607081138.

Osman, A. and Musonda, I. (2017). 'Community' as the basic architectural unit: rethinking research and practice towards a decolonised education. In S. Giloi and H. Botes (Eds.), *Proceedings of the 14th National Design Education Conference 2017*, 27–29 September, Tshwane, South Africa, pp. 224–233.

Pearce, C.L. and Conger, J.A. (Eds.) (2003). *Shared Leadership: Reframing the Hows and Whys of Leadership*. Sage Publications Ltd, Thousand Oaks, CA.

Radcliffe, S.A. (2017). Decolonising geographical knowledges. *Transactions of the Institute of British Geographers*, 42, 329–333. https://doi.org/10.1111/trans.12195.

Regan, P. (2010). *Unsettling the Settler Within: Indian Residential Schools, Truth Telling, and Reconciliation in Canada*. UBC Press, Vancouver, BC.

Ruggunan, S.D. (2016). Decolonising management studies: A love story. *Acta Commercii*, 16(2). https://hdl.handle.net/10520/EJC-552348364.

Rwelamila, P.D. (2012). Construction project performance in developing countries. In G. Ofori (Ed.), *Contemporary Issues in Construction in Developing Countries*, Spon Press, New York, pp. 318–346.

Rwelamila, P.D. and Ogunlana, S. (2015). *W107 — Construction in Developing Countries Research Roadmap — Report for Consultation*. International Council on Research and Innovation in Building and Construction (CIB), Rotterdam.

Rwelamila, P.D. and Abdul-Aziz, A.-R. (2020). *Improving the Performance of Construction Industries for Developing Countries: Programmes, Initiatives, Achievements and Challenges*. Routledge, Abingdon.

Shay, S. (2016). Decolonising the curriculum: It's time for a strategy. *The Conversation*, 13 June. https://theconversation.com/decolonising-the-curriculum-its-time-for-a-strategy-60598.

Scott, W. R., Levitt, R.E. and Orr, R.J. (Eds.) (2011). *Global Projects: Institutional and Political Challenges*. Cambridge University Press, Cambridge.

Scranton, P. (2014). Projects as a focus for historical analysis: Surveying the landscape. *History and Technology*, 30(4), 354–373. https://doi.org/10.1080/07341512.2014.1003164.

Shenhar, A.J. (1992). Project management style and the space shuttle program: A retrospective look. *Project Management Journal*, 23(1), 32–37.

Shenhar, A.J. (2001). One size does not fit all projects: Exploring classical contingency domains. *Management Science*, 47(3), 394–414.

Shenhar, A. and Dvir, D. (2004). Project management evolution: Past history and future research directions. Paper presented at *PMI® Research Conference: Innovations*. London, England, 11–14 July. Project Management Institute, Newtown Square, PA.

Shenhar, A. and Dvir, D. (2007). *Reinventing Project Management: The Diamond Approach to Successful Growth and Innovation*. Harvard Business School Press, Cambridge.

Sithole, T. (2016). Frantz Fanon: Africana existentialist philosopher. *African Identities*, 14(2), 177–190. https://doi.org/10.1080/14725843.2015.1117385.

Simushi, S. and Wium, J. (2020). Time and cost overruns on large projects: Understanding the root cause. *Journal of Construction in Developing Countries*, 25(1), 129–146. https://doi.org/10.21315/jcdc2020.25.1.7.

Smith, L. (1999). *Decolonising Methodologies: Research and Indigenous Peoples*. Zed Books, London.

Söderlund, J. (2011). Pluralism in project management: Navigating the crossroads of specialization and fragmentation. *International Journal of Management Reviews*, 13(2), 153–176. https://doi.org/10.1111/j.1468-2370.2010.00290.x.

Söderlund, J. and Maylor, H. (2012). Project management scholarship: Relevance, impact and five integrative challenges for business and management schools. *International Journal of Project Management*, 30(6), 686–696. https://doi.org/10.1016/j.ijproman.2012.03.007.

Stuckenbruck, L.C. and Zomorrodian, A. (1987). Project management: The promise for developing countries. *International Journal of Project Management*, 5(3), 167–175.

Styhre, A. (2020). Thinly and thickly capitalized projects: Theorizing the role of the finance markets and capital supply in project management studies. *Project Management Journal*, 51(4), 378–388. https://doi.org/10.1177/8756972820931278.

Sydow, J. and Braun, T. (2018). Projects as temporary organizations: An agenda for further theorizing the interorganizational dimension. *International Journal of Project Management*, 36(1), 4–11. https://doi.org/10.1016/j.ijproman.2017.04.012.

Sydow, J., Lindkvist, L.and DeFillippi, R. (2004). Project-based organizations: Embeddedness and repositories of knowledge: Editorial. *Organization Studies*, 25(9), 1475–1489. https://doi.org/10.1177/0170840604048162.

Thiel, J. and Grabher, G. (2015). Crossing boundaries: Exploring the London Olympics 2012 as a field-configuring event. *Industry and Innovation*, 22(3), 229–249. https://doi.org/10.1080/13662716.2015.1033841.

Thomas, M. and Andrew Thompson, A. (2014). Empire and globalisation: From 'High Imperialism' to Decolonisation. *The International History Review*, 36(1), 142–170. https://doi.org/10.1080/07075332.2013.828643.

Watermeyer, R. (2018). *Client Guide for Improving Infrastructure Project Outcomes*. Engineers Against Poverty and University of the Witwatersrand, Johannesburg.

Wright, P.M. and Boswell, W.R. (2002). Desegregating HRM: A review and synthesis of micro and macro human resource management research. *Journal of Management*, 28(3), 247–276.

Wingfield, B. (2017). What "decolonised education" should and shouldn't mean. *The Conversation*, February 14. https://theconversation.com/what-decolonised-education-should-and-shouldnt-mean-72597.

Xiao, H. and Proverbs, D. (2002). Construction time performance: An evaluation of contractors from Japan, the UK and the US. *Engineering, Construction and Architectural Management*, 9(2), 81–89. https://doi.org/10.1108/eb021208.

Zeleza, P.T. (2009). African studies and universities since independence: The challenges of epistemic and institutional decolonization. *Transition*, (101), 110–135. http://dx.doi.org/10.2979/trs.2009.-.101.110.

Zika-Viktorsson, A., Sundström, P. and Engwall, M. (2006). Project overload: An exploratory study of work and management in multi-project settings. *International Journal of Project Management*, 24(5), 385–394. https://doi.org/10.1016/j.ijproman.2006.02.010.

https://doi.org/10.1142/9789811224720_0026

Chapter 26

Future of Project Management in Developing Countries

George Ofori

London South Bank University, UK

Abstract

This chapter completes the book. It begins with a discussion of the nature of the construction industry and the construction process, in order to highlight the peculiar nature of construction activity and the need for special actions in managing it, which cannot be adequately covered by generic frameworks. This is followed by a consideration of the importance of projects in developing countries, including the problems of the construction industry in those countries. The next section presents a brief summary of the discussion in the book. The possible implications of a developing country body of knowledge (BoK) are then discussed. Consideration of the future of project management, including the need for its improvement, challenges facing it, and an agenda for research in the future, is followed by a focus on two possible research areas: Benefits Management and Project Value. A case for the decolonization of project management is followed by suggestions of areas of research on project management in developing countries. The final section completes this last chapter and the book by proposing a definition for project management in developing countries before discussing actions to bring about the body of knowledge of project management for developing countries, including research and particular activities.

Keywords: Project management, body of knowledge, developing countries, research, decolonization, the future

Introduction

Nature of construction

Table 2.2 in this book presents some information on the nature of a construction project. In this chapter, it is pertinent to discuss the nature of the construction project into more detail. Its peculiar features are well highlighted. These include: location specificity; involvement of many organizations; high expense and long duration of each project (Hillebrandt, 2000); involvement of many participants; and influence of the client's desires and demands. Other peculiar features can be outlined for the project-dependent construction industry, the construction process and the constructed product. All these, taken together, signify the risks and uncertainties associated with construction.

The concept of Volatile, Uncertain, Complex and Ambiguous (VUCA) was first used in 1987 and based on the leadership theories of Warren Bennis and Burt Nanus. It was the response of the US Army War College to the sudden collapse of Soviet Union when the certainty of there being only one enemy was removed; this resulted in new ways of seeing and reacting.[1] As suggested by Ofori (2021), VUCA describes the construction industry in many ways, as typified by the nature of the construction industry, the project and the process. It also describes the construction product, the construction company and the construction practitioner. VUCA reflects the Volatility of the environment; Uncertainty of various factors influencing the project and its success; Complexity of the task on construction projects; and Ambiguity of the requirements and contributions of the participants. Indeed, VUCA describes the construction industry in the developing countries even more appropriately, in terms of their context. Thus, "Project Management in a VUCA Environment" typifies the

[1] https://www.vuca-world.org/

management of construction projects in the developing countries. In such a situation, there is the need for novel approaches to the management of projects. However, the existing bodies of knowledge of project management were not formulated with VUCA situations in mind. The framework guiding project managers requires considerable adaptation to make it suitable for application in such contexts. At the same time, there is also a shortage of project management skills in these countries. This situation makes this book necessary.

Much has been written about project management in a VUCA world (see, for example, Bosch-Rekveldt, 2011; Bierwolf *et al.*, 2017; Mikkelsen *et al.*, 2020). Pells (2019) identifies six fresh perspectives for project management in a VUCA world: Break large projects into smaller, more manageable projects and focus on strategy, stakeholders and benefits; Reverse Environmental Impact Analysis — analyze the impact of changing conditions and environmental factors on the projects; Stakeholder Intelligence — understand the stakeholders' changing attitudes and issues over the course of the project; Benefits Engineering — rather than value engineer scope to meet cost and schedule goals, adjust benefits to maximize value and customer satisfaction; "DARPA" versus "The Hunger Games" — harness diversity, new knowledge, and team-based innovation to create new solutions; and Strategic Agility — consider when and how to adapt agility and agile project management. These ideas are relevant to project management in developing countries, especially on construction projects.

Summary of the book

This book was compiled with the view to making a case for a Body of Knowledge for Project Management in Developing Countries (DCPMBOK). The 26 chapters in the book are categorized under the following headings:

- Introduction — chapters which introduce the book, and its main subject
- Project management in developing countries
- Project management knowledge areas with developing country perspectives and considerations

- (Adding to knowledge): necessary areas of project management, especially in a developing country context
- Project management in various developing countries
- The future: project management body of knowledge for developing countries.

Synopses of the chapters in the book are presented in Chapter 1. From the discussion in this book, these points can be made:

- Projects are common in all sectors of the economy and all aspects of life; there is said to be a "projectification" of society, and project management is a skill that can be applied in all forms of activity, in all sectors of the economy, in public administration and in social settings. Thus, performance on projects has an impact on competitiveness in business, in productivity at the national level and thus, in national socio-economic development
- Project management is most needed in developing countries. Whereas most of the projects in these countries are basic, the dynamics of the environments in which they are undertaken are complex. Their management is more demanding and, indeed, requires greater sophistication in approach than in the industrialized countries
- The current conceptualization of project management and the framework guiding its practice were drawn from, and formulated for application in, the circumstances prevailing in industrialized countries. It has been suggested, since the 1960s, that they do not fit the situation in developing countries
- Projects around the world, in most sectors, and especially large infrastructure projects, exhibit underperformance as judged according to most of the set performance parameters. Project performance in developing countries is even worse
- There is a need to develop the body of knowledge of project management further to bring it on par with other areas of management studies; there are also myths and misconceptions in the current body of knowledge which need to be addressed
- There is a need to decolonize project studies and project management
- A body of knowledge of project management in developing countries is necessary, and there is some urgency in formulating it because of

the importance of projects for all forms of activities, and the need for the developing countries to realize efficiency and effectiveness in the projects they undertake.

In the discussion in the next section, the argument for the DCPMBOK is reinforced by further exploring the importance of projects for developing countries, and therefore, the need for an appropriate framework for managing projects in their context.

Importance of projects in developing countries

What makes project management critical in developing countries? It is necessary to deliver projects effectively in those countries in order to enable the countries to meet the large volume of outstanding current and future needs of construction works, which is essential for their long-term economic and social development. Effective project management will enable the national budgets to go farther and support the completion of a larger physical volume of work. It will enhance the affordability of the built items, and shorten the time clients and/or end users have to wait for key items. It will also enable external stakeholders to participate effectively in projects, thus enhancing the contextual suitability of the built items. Moreover, completion of the items to good levels of quality will enhance durability and reduce maintenance costs.

Some points are made in Chapter 4 on the peculiar features of construction projects in developing countries. Long *et al.* (2004) note that although many studies have been undertaken into the factors affecting delays, cost overruns, quality, safety, and productivity, and other problems in specific types of projects, these studies seldom discuss common and general problems of construction projects. They observe that comprehensive studies on these problems are essential, and that since the problems are contextual, the studies need to focus on a specific geographical area, country, or region. From their study, they identify these main factors of the problems of large construction projects in Vietnam: incompetent designers/contractors; poor estimating and change management; social and technological issues; site related issues; and improper techniques and tools.

Much is expected of the construction industry in the developing countries by way of project performance. An area where this is most needed is in addressing the impact of disasters, which are increasing in frequency and level of destruction (Sheffield, 2020). Direct economic losses from disasters were estimated to be US$3 trillion between 1998 and 2017; climate-related disasters formed 77 percent of the total (Aon, 2020). Over that period, climate-related and geophysical disasters claimed some 1.3 million lives. More than 90 percent of all disasters were caused by floods, storms, droughts, heatwaves, or other extreme weather events. It has been found that poverty is a major underlying driver of disaster risk; and over 90 percent of internationally reported deaths due to disaster occur in low- and middle-income countries (UN, 2018). Disasters kill 130 people for every one million people in low-income countries, compared to 18 per one million in high-income countries (IFRC, 2020). The discussion on the project management of post-disaster reconstruction from the perspective of developing countries in Chapter 16 is highly pertinent. Considering the increasing frequency of climate-induced disasters, a project management framework which facilitates the undertaking of such highly demanding projects in the already challenging circumstances of developing countries is critically needed.

Construction projects have an influence on their district economies and the social wellbeing of the communities. The larger projects have wider influence. Moreover, projects in the developing countries are expected to have even wider socio-economic impact in the locality and in the region. Thus, Watermeyer (2018) outlines possible targets of a construction project (beyond the narrow ones of budget, schedule and quality). In rural areas, projects can be used to enhance income through work opportunities (Watermeyer, 2018). Other objectives of projects in developing countries include (Watermeyer, 2018): strengthening of indigenous building materials and methods, transfer or development of skills, and job opportunities for small and medium enterprises. These objectives and potential attainments cannot be realized unless there are due adjustments to the current project management framework, principles, and norms. For example, attaining the employment generation potential requires a new definition of, and modelling for, construction productivity in developing countries which involves consideration of job creation and decent jobs and a balance of time, cost, quality, and health and safety. It is argued in Chapter 13 that it is necessary to consider a wide range of project performance indicators in developing countries.

The discussion here shows that an even broader range of benefits from construction projects can be realized.

From the discussion in this section, owing to the peculiar features of construction, it is appropriate that the PMI has a special supplement to the PMBOK on construction. However, this supplement is still inadequate for dealing with the issues of the construction industries and projects in developing countries where the peculiarities of the construction industry are further accentuated by the circumstances of the developing countries.

Why is project management needed in developing countries?

In the developing countries, the project is of even greater strategic significance to the nation, the beneficiaries, and the organizations involved in delivering it than in the industrialized nations. This implies that appropriate decisions need to be taken on every aspect of every project. For example, in planning (location), the project has the potential to stimulate the local economy and improve the wellbeing of the community. In design, thought should be given to addressing the contextual fit with the local needs with community involvement or consultation; and selection of materials and technologies. In procurement, the appropriate selection of the preferred bidder can influence the development of local companies. Similarly, during the construction stage, contractors can enhance their performance and also help to develop smaller companies and their own personnel with appropriate policies and practices. In the operation stage, maintenance and possible refurbishment can ensure appropriate levels of performance over the life of the built item.

Whereas these considerations are not different on projects in the industrialized countries, in the circumstances of the developing countries, there is greater importance of social value and benefits management than the existing generic project management frameworks provide for. Finally, leadership is key, among many factors. The discussion here shows that there is a need for either: (1) deepening the existing areas of knowledge in the project management framework; or (2) adding new areas of knowledge, such as Project Operating Environment Management, and Project Benefits Management, to the generic framework.

Problems of construction in developing countries

The problems of construction in developing countries are well cataloged and have been presented in many of the chapters in this book. A summary of these problems at the industry, company, and project levels is now presented.

At the industry level, the government is a major client, regulator, and administrator of the industry. The government can use regulations to set standards and requirements and enforce compliance. The government's role as a client gives it the opportunity to use its bargaining power to drive and shape change in the industry. There is the potential to use each project to develop the industry as a whole; this can be realized through strategic procurement. Construction brings together many different areas of professional and technical specialization. The different professions do not usually collaborate. Ullal and Tombesi (2021) note that industry constraints regularly identified in studies include: limited managerial expertise; inadequate access to credit for construction firms; inappropriate or poorly implemented regulations; and widespread prevalence of corruption. There is continued prevalence of standard arrangements of procurement and contracting in these countries despite widespread recognition in the literature of adverse conditions and negative implications for industry development. They outline six critical dimensions of development in construction: availability of trade, management and professional expertise; availability of materials, components, and equipment; availability of credit for construction firms; quality of regulation; reliability of legal frames; and prevalence of corruption.

At the company level, construction industries have the typical fragmented structure, with a myriad of transient micro- and small firms, most of which have little prospect of development (see, for example, Eyiah, 2001; Soemardi *et al.*, 2021). The differing priorities of clients and construction firms, for example, with regard to price determination and risk allocation means that the industry is not set up for effective performance as it is almost compelled to adopt a short-term perspective, minimizing investments and even medium-term commitments. On almost all projects, the construction company does not have any say in the design, materials and some methods of construction. The level of risks in construction are among the highest of any sector. The industry has a high rate of mortality among its firms.

At the project level, the challenges include (Ofori, 2016, 2018; Ullal and Tombesi, 2021) land acquisition and settlement with owners and occupiers. The usual failure to address this issue often leads to community opposition, which causes delays and in some cases, abandonment of the project. Another problem is bureaucracy in development control (processing and granting planning permission) and building control. There are special challenges in the administration of the works. On public-sector projects, delays in payments are a common problem. Project governance is a challenge. There is political interference, which sometimes involves corruption, as well as extra-contractual demands which often cause scope creep. There are resource constraints including materials shortages (mainly owing to the reliance on imports), skills shortages, and low technology level, including internet connectivity. Commissioning and Closing also receives inadequate attention. Ullal and Tombesi (2021) present studies on causes of project delays in some African countries. The top five in Uganda were (Alinaitwe *et al.*, 2013): change of work scope and/or changes in material specifications; delayed payment to contractors, subcontractors, and/or suppliers; poor monitoring and control, such as due to incompetent and/or unreliable supervisors; high inflation, insurance and interest rates; and political insecurity and instability. In Zambia, the main causes were (Kaliba *et al.*, 2009): delayed payments; the financial process; financial difficulties; contract modification; and economic problems.

What is the impact on the related project parameters and knowledge and action areas, of these features of the developing countries with respect to the construction industry? Some of the manifestations of the peculiar environment are: (a) the institutions (a great deal of bureaucracy, political interference, weak administrative institutions); (b) regulatory framework (weak and/or obsolete laws and regulations or a strong body of laws and regulations with weak or non-existent enforcement); (c) corruption and/or patronage; (d) the market (clients with no knowledge of construction and projects); and (e) the business infrastructure (weak supply and value chains).

How will a dedicated PMBOK for developing countries help in addressing these problems? The PMBOK for developing countries should consider the peculiar features of construction as well as the context of the developing countries. In addition to advocating for the improvement of aspects of the construction industry, the framework should offer guidance on how to operate well despite the existence of the constraints.

Developing country BoK and its implications

A running theme in most of the chapters of this book is that a PMBOK for developing countries (DCPMBOK) should be formulated. Why should developing countries have a unique PMBOK? As discussed in Chapter 2, each project is unique. The uniqueness of projects is highlighted in sharp relief in the developing countries as the local context exerts its influence. An example here is the nature of the local community, and its reaction to projects in general, and to the particular project. The operating environment and context are very important in influencing performance and outcomes; these are different from what pertains in industrialized countries.

Will the new framework be less demanding and inferior compared to the mainstream bodies of knowledge? A PMBOK for developing countries should be more elaborate than the existing frameworks. Rather than simplifying or excluding any of the areas of knowledge, these will have to be even more developed, and relevant additional ones incorporated, considering the difficult operating context. For example, the Indian Infrastructure Body of Knowledge (InBoK), developed for infrastructure projects in India, is not simple. Indeed, project management knowledge in developing countries can inform and improve the development of the whole body of knowledge on project studies.

Will a unique PMBOK for developing countries mean a downward spiral of ineffectiveness and inefficiency on projects? If appropriately developed and effectively applied, such a guide will enhance performance in the developing countries, and enable the countries to meet their range of needs. It can be argued that such a PMBOK will have lessons for the industrialized countries, and for project management in general — for example, in the areas of stakeholder management and the related aspects of benefits management.

This chapter continues by considering the future path of the development of project management.

Future of project management

Need for improvement

The current body of knowledge and practice of project management point the way for further development as they suggest topics which will be of interest. Authors such as Kloppenberg and Opfer (2002) and Tanaka (2004) have provided useful ideas. These topics include: more emphasis on professionalism; stress on governance, i.e., transparency and empowerment; greater attention to the environment; more focus on risk management, including contingency planning and risk mitigation; greater disaster awareness; larger role for non-government organizations (NGOs) and activists; attention to business and project continuity issues; leadership to the fore; stress on strategic project management, linking project to corporation; greater focus on communications planning; assessing value delivered by project teams; ICT as a facilitator and a challenge; effective management of outsourcing; and standardization of project management techniques and tools. These points on the future of project management lay the ground for research in the subject, as considered below.

Challenges facing project management

How important will project management be in future? What skills will a project manager require in future? Some researchers argue that, in future, the project manager's job will become a skill that is part of many required job responsibilities (Stanleigh, 2010). Others argue that a special type of skill set is required for effective project management. In a US Construction Industry Institute research project, Wiezel *et al.* (2013) investigated the skill set that will be required by the project manager of the future to enable companies to use the competency forecast for recruiting and professional development. They found that the duties and responsibilities of construction project managers were undergoing a significant shift. Four drivers would require project managers to have different competencies from what they now need to address stakeholder and project team member needs: the evolution of technology; greater access to information; rapidly evolving workforce demographics; and changing organizational structures. These factors will change how the industry approaches projects, how it forms project teams, and how it manages the flow of information.

There is a consensus that the future project manager should be more strategic and connected, developing skills beyond traditional project management practices. Haughey (2021) outlines future challenges, including: globalization and the need for increased speed-to-market with products and services; projects becoming larger, more complex, and increasingly challenging to manage; teams becoming more diverse and spread across the world; and work moving offshore. He remarks that the world is changing, and project management will need to change with it. The KPMG, AIPM, and IPMA (2019) global study suggests that in an environment of constant change and upheaval, organizations must be able to adapt and implement quickly and build an agile delivery mindset that works for their particular circumstances. They should invest in new technologies, such as collaboration tools and artificial intelligence, to enable quicker and more effective use of project management data to support decision-making and be committed to project governance.

Project managers of the future should be able to adapt to constant and rapid change, uncertainty, and disruptions. Seymour and Hussein (2014) note the following challenges for the future project manager as the dynamics and environment of organizations evolve, driven by factors including globalization, progressively limited resources, increasing competition, and growing numbers and influence of stakeholders: larger and more complex projects and involvement of a greater variety of multidisciplinary teams; need to adapt to new technologies; importance of learning specialized techniques and tools that will work best on each project; filtering the abundant data to capture the right information; understanding the big picture; effectively communicating with others; and working with people in different countries and/or from different cultures and in the changing demographics of the workforce.

Wiezel *et al.* (2013) observe that the future challenges will require a different way of thinking, learning and managing by project managers: (a) Think Differently — there will be a shift in focus from technical and management skills to cognitive and leadership skills; (b) Learn Differently — project management education will require an interactive team setting with a skilled facilitator and will emphasize leadership; and

(c) Manage Differently — the new way of educating project managers can be used to gain insight into the real problems of the organization.

Box 26.1 presents a summary of challenges to civil engineers in the report of a study commissioned by the Institution of Civil Engineers (ICE) in the UK.

Box 26.1: Engineering rebellion: The future.

A study commissioned by the Institution of Civil Engineers (ICE) into the future of civil engineering identified that the infrastructure sector must both adapt and change its approach if it is to meet the needs of society. The study identifies the strategic trends and disruptors shaping the sector and the skills profile of the practitioners. It recommends that instead of merely focusing on the individual member, a professional institution must offer something of value to every member of the infrastructure team.

The study notes that the climate crisis, urbanization, the pandemic, and a demand for inclusivity are all accelerating and putting different pressures on the natural and built environment. In response, taxpayers, infrastructure owners, and investors are seeking a wider range of outcomes for their money. This has led to the traditional role of the professional in the construction industry to be questioned. Would their role need to change, and could this be more about investigating and identifying what infrastructure owners and users actually want and need?

The study identified six interconnected strategic trends that are interacting and shaping the infrastructure industry. These are the climate crisis and the UN Sustainable Development Goals (SDGs); accelerating digital transformation; flatlining productivity; growing complexity; competition for the future workforce and demand for increased diversity; and value replacing volume as the basis for financial reward.

In light of these strategic trends, the study identifies seven disruptors to the traditional role of the professional in construction:

- Net zero and sustainability benefits will become central to project outcomes.
- Business models will demand greater collaboration to deliver more value through the asset lifecycle.
- Diversity — people will need to come into the industry from a much wider set of routes and backgrounds.

Box 26.1: (*Continued*)

- Digitization will create a demand for people with the adaptability needed to understand and work with a wide and rapidly changing set of digital technologies.
- Productivity will need to improve rapidly. Engineers will need to master the skills and behavior that will allow innovative practices, techniques and materials to be deployed.
- Systems thinking will be needed at the project, network and system-of-systems levels.
- Upskilling will be constant — civil engineers will need to adopt a proactive attitude to lifelong learning.

The study's main advice to ICE was to "think differently" and support civil engineers to work more effectively in multi-disciplinary teams as this will help to deliver more effective outcomes.

Achieving net zero carbon and the wider SDGs is the moral and technical challenge of this generation. ICE needs to think about what that means for the license to operate it provides to professionals and how it can better support them to take their key sustainable development competencies to higher levels.

The leader of the study team planted this thought that has to be considered: "What if we've been asking the wrong questions all along? What if coming up with a single definition of the future engineer in the face of such change is a recipe for inflexibility when what we need is agility? What if society and client needs from infrastructure no longer map to the old professional disciplines? Or if the future is collaboration between people from a more diverse range of backgrounds?"

Source: Engineering Rebellion Steering Group (2021).

Agenda for research in the future

There is a growing body of work on future directions for project management research. Söderlund (2004) suggests that project management theory should be built by addressing these questions:

(i) Why do project organizations exist?
(ii) Why do project organizations differ?

(iii) How do project organizations behave?
(iv) What is the function of, or value added by, the project management unit?
(v) What determines the success or failure of project organizations?

It is evident that the answers to these questions in developing countries would differ from what is experienced in the industrialized countries and has been covered in the literature. Of relevance to construction, Denicol *et al.* (2020) suggest five avenues for future research that should consider examining megaprojects as large-scale, interorganizational production systems: designing the system architecture; bridging the gap with manufacturing; building and leading collaborations; engaging institutions and communities; and decomposing and integrating the supply chain.

Much has been written on future research agendas for the field of project management, as well as on aspects of it. For example, Gauthier and Ika (2012) offer a new ontological framework to stimulate project management research. They suggest that the ontological question should be viewed as a six-facet diamond that represents a set of root assumptions about projects, indicating that whenever a researcher emphasizes a specific facet, the researcher leaves out the other five facets in the work. They call for attention on the ground ontological assumptions of project management research in order to transcend the abstract epistemological and methodological debates and concentrate on what really divides the different theoretical positions.

The editors of *Project Management Journal*, Muller and Klein (2020) consider implications for research on projects, programs, and portfolios, which might have been brought about or accelerated by the COVID-19 pandemic to help potential authors to find contemporary topics and phenomena to study. To answer this question, they asked the editorial board members of the journal for their input on:

(a) The changing nature of the studies we expect in projects, programs, portfolios, and their management. What new or different perspectives do we anticipate?
(b) What new or different research questions will be addressed? and

(c) What new or different methodologies, techniques, theories, or philosophical perspectives can be foreseen for future studies?

Finally, in editing a special issue of the *Project Management Journal* on project studies, Geraldi *et al.* (2021) found *bright spots* in four areas: project organizing (organizing and collaborating in and between projects), project value (organizing value in and through projects), project citizenship (living in and through projects), and project scholarship (reflecting on project theorizing and scholarship). They highlighted three dark spots: a lack of diversity in the project scholars' ethnicities, geographies, and genders; absence of disciplines that extend beyond management and organization studies; and a dark spot in modes of reflexivity. The first "dark spot" of "a lack of diversity in the project scholars' ethnicities, geographies and genders" points to a need for decolonizing project studies.

Some possible research areas

It is pertinent to discuss some topics on project studies that are particularly relevant to developing countries, on which research is necessary.

Benefits management

Benefits management is an emerging subject of research and practice. It is particularly necessary in developing countries to include in the management of projects, deliberate efforts to ensure that the intended benefits are realized. It is suggested that setting effective target benefits supports project investment decisions, clear project management direction, and post-project success (Zwikael *et al.*, 2018). Effective target benefits should be specific, challenging but attainable, and comprehensive. Aubry *et al.* (2021) note that benefits management has recently gained in popularity but remains difficult to implement and undertake in organizations. In their study, they find that defining benefits is a complex task, because the concept of "benefit" is understood in various ways. They show that benefits management is not a linear activity. They uncover some of the social and political aspects of benefits management, which are often neglected because of the challenges involved in managing benefits. In another study, Svejvig and Schlichter (2020) report on a four-year action research study which considered benefits management at a detailed, practical level and evaluated the benefits management practices applied. They provide a structured evaluation of the process as it is currently practiced to uncover the weaknesses, and suggest an integrative management model with three layers: instrumental, practical, and reflective.

Svejvig *et al.* (2019) study project acceleration and benefit management and note that accelerating time to impact is a key challenge for organizations today. They consider a Danish initiative targeted at increasing the speed at which project benefits are attained, and analyze why some projects were able to achieve benefits faster than others. They identified reasons for the differences and grouped them in a conceptual model: the "house of time to impact" with three areas: valuing speed, owning speed, and entraining speed in the organization. Zwikael *et al.* (2018) note that target benefits such as "reduced operational costs" are strategic project goals that enhance organizational performance if successfully realized. Based on goal setting theory, they present three studies to develop and validate a scale to measure effective target benefits. The proposed scale comprises three dimensions: specificity (such as specific target values); attainability (such as the capacity to realize the target benefits); and comprehensiveness (for example, reflecting the views of key stakeholders). This scale can be used to assess the target benefits of proposed projects, contributing to more informed project investment decision making and the subsequent benefit management process.

Project value

A second research area in project studies, which is of practical relevance to developing countries, is that of value. Styhre (2020) studied finance not only as a value but also as an essential aspect of project management. He argues that finance capital increasingly defines projects, as the supply of finance determines the conditions under which projects are initiated, planned, and managed. In contrast, Martinsuo (2020) argues that such *hard value* in financial analysis and instruments obfuscates the *true value* of a project. She advocates for an alternative perspective of project value based upon the concept of values as beliefs, that is, subjective, idiosyncratic, and dynamic. Zerjav (2021) offers another, different, angle to value based on a fundamental question: "Why do organizations participate in projects?" He discusses different rationales that project owners, project-based firms, and the actual project use to justify their participation in projects and explores patterns of value creation and destruction in each type of organization. He suggests that a situated view on value is preferable to a universal view.

In construction, Value Management is an established, structured approach that has been recommended in many studies for application on projects in the UK, including the Egan Reports (Connaughton and Green, 2006; Kelly *et al.*, 2004); and is often adopted on construction projects in some countries, such as Hong Kong (Fong and Shen, 2000; Yu *et al.*, 2018). Tutesigensi *et al.* (2021) note that value management is not applied widely and systematically in construction projects in developing countries, and that this limits the achievement of value for money. They studied the state of value management practice in Uganda and found that its application was rudimentary, inconsistent, and misguided. They suggest that the practice of the approach in Uganda can be improved by raising awareness and the standard of application, and offer 10 strategies for such improvement.

Decolonizing project studies and project management

The subject of decolonizing project studies and the project management body of knowledge is discussed in Chapters 4 and 25 of this book. It is pertinent to outline some of the main elements of decolonization in the literature including those identified by various authors, such as Smith (1999) and Le Grange (2016). They are:

- deconstruction and reconstruction (discarding what has been wrongly written, and "interrogating distortions of people's life experiences, negative labelling, deficit theorizing, genetically deficient or culturally deficient models that pathologized the colonised ... and retelling the stories of the past and envisioning the future" (Chilisa, 2012, p. 17))

- self-determination and social justice (seeking legitimacy for knowledge that is embedded in their own histories, experiences and ways of viewing reality)
- finding new ways of living and new approaches in responding to current events as potential carriers of new possibilities (Pindar and Sutton, 2001)
- ethics (formulation, legislation, and dissemination of ethical issues related to the protection of indigenous knowledge systems)
- language (adopting appropriate language which makes the knowledge accessible to those who need to apply it; this includes terminology and jargon)
- internationalization of indigenous experiences (international scholars sharing common experiences, issues and struggles of colonized peoples in global and local spaces)
- history and critique (concerns a critical appraisal of the imperial model of the academy that continues to deny the colonized and historically marginalized other space to communicate from their own frames of reference).

It is suggested that decolonization is not an event but a process and it is not necessarily easy to achieve. It should also be noted that decolonization does not mean rejecting the existing body of knowledge as a whole. For example, Guattari (2001) argues that one should avoid the temptation to create these new ways of living by reversing technological advancement and going back to old formulas when the world was a different place and social relations were much stronger. It is important to recognize that, as Dei (2000) notes, bodies and systems of knowledge are dynamic, and continually influence each other. Thus, it is not useful to hold on to a dichotomy "between good [Indigenous] and bad [conventional/Western] knowledges" (Dei, 2000, p. 113). To Dei (2000, p. 113), decolonization of the curriculum involves a process of change that does not necessarily involve destroying Western knowledge but in decentering it or perhaps de-territorializing it.

These principles should guide the decolonization of project studies and the project management body of knowledge:

- introducing new areas of knowledge that are particularly needed in developing countries, as discussed below
- building on the generic project management frameworks to extend the level of analysis and make them more suitable to the context of the developing countries, such as…
  - considering the traditional governance structures of the host community as (an external) part of the project organization
  - incorporating active client development into the management of the project
- considering every project from a strategic standpoint, beyond the client and the project team, and making project management an active part of construction industry development and nation building — "making a difference one project at a time"
- stressing forward extension of, and links from, projects to enhance knowledge and performance.

Some areas of improvement in generic project management which are relevant to developing countries

Project management requires major changes to make it appropriate for developing countries. Some points on the generic frameworks are now outlined.

(1) The 10 knowledge areas of project management in the PMI PMBOK need to be extended to include such topics as...
   (i) Managing the Operating Environment
   (ii) Managing Project Benefits
   (iii) Managing the Facility.
(2) The nature of projects in developing countries makes it necessary for the project manager to have leadership skills. Thus, Project Leadership should be one of the key components of the DCPMBOK.
(3) Some of the existing knowledge areas of the generic frameworks should be broadened to cover other issues...

   (i) Project Cost Management should include value; it is also the appropriate area under which to cover the subject of sustainability and climate emergency on the project
   (ii) Project Resource Management should include team development and acculturation

(4) Project Sustainability and Climate Management should be given attention in the DCPMBOK.

(5) Project management of disaster reconstruction also requires due consideration, in particular, owing to the increasing frequency of climate-induced disasters.

Apart from the areas of knowledge considered above, several other subjects require further study and exploration of mainstream project management. Some of these are now considered.

Instead of the silo approach to the setting and monitoring of project performance parameters, a consolidated approach should be taken, as a trade-off, balancing and interrelating effort is necessary in order to optimize project performance rather than making major achievements in one as against the other(s). Project Integration Management should consider this issue, and it should also include the "project health card." This should be used consistently on projects to deal with issues as they arise on the particular project rather than perform historical post-mortems. A reason is that knowledge management is not effective in construction owing to the uniqueness of projects.

Projectification and its implications are ripe for further exploration. For example, construction and other project-based sectors can teach other sectors much from their peculiar nature. There can be mutual learning by the project-based organizations and routinized ones doing occasional projects as the project approach is found to be necessary.

It would be appropriate to take up the fundamental task of proposing a definition for project management in developing countries. There is a need to study how to reconcile and mix the attainment orientation of the major generic frameworks with the social awareness and impact focus of the approach taken by development-oriented organizations such as PM4NGOs.

Finally, Ofori (2016) suggests that it is important to consider options for leapfrogging in terms of technology development when considering how to develop the body of knowledge and practice for developing countries. The DCPMBOK should encourage and facilitate leapfrogging.

Action

Research

It is crucial to get to the bottom of why projects continue to exhibit significant underperformance despite the application of comprehensive project management frameworks and advanced information technology tools. The possible reasons are:

- the targets are wrong and not properly set
- the framework of management or aspects of it was or were not suitable to the project
- the framework or aspects of it was or were wrongly applied
- the framework is not appropriate to the management of any project
- projects are not amenable to management.

Some relevant questions are: Who sets the project parameters? How accurate are they? Are cost and time targets set through competition, based on the lowest bidder (or the one who makes the biggest error) appropriate as determinants of performance and success?

Researchers on project studies and as that field relates to the developing countries should focus on developing the elements of a contingency approach to project management and project leadership, which can help to address the needs and circumstances of the developing countries.

The research and concept development process should be directly based on practice in the developing countries so that the ideas are authentic and the most appropriate DCPMBOK guide will be developed. This calls for a new paradigm on project studies and in the practice of project management. Researchers on projects in developing countries need to adopt a new lens through which to view project principles, processes, outcomes, and results. Considering the project-based nature of construction, this call should be taken up, in particular, by researchers on Construction Project Management.

The external stakeholders can have a specific and special role. Their interface with the project team can be a key part of the management of the project. There is a need for innovation and openness to participation by stakeholders. The project organization structure should cover their involvement and participation in a systematic manner. It would be relevant to consider the possible involvement of the traditional social system in the management of projects.

Activities

Developing the DCPMBOK in practice should be a collaboration among the leading international project management institutions. The chapters of these institutions in developing countries should work together with the professional institutions in construction and their umbrella regional organizations to formulate the DCPMBOK. A Task and Finish Group could be set up by these units, with the mandate to develop such a PMBOK in each of the major regions of the developing world. This approach should lead to a generic framework for each region that countries can modify in accordance with their local needs and circumstances.

The stages of the development of the DCPMBOK could be:

(1) Appoint a formulation team comprising project managers and other project practitioners
(2) Analyze the key project management frameworks, such as those of the PMI, APM, IPMA, PM4NGOs, and ISO21500:2012, and identify their strengths and weaknesses
(3) Identify areas of incompatibility of the key generic framework with the developing country context. Make reference to existing works on the subject such as the chapters in this book
(4) Review frameworks formulated specifically for developing countries such as the InBoK
(5) Analyze the regional situation with respect to project management. For example, determine the factors which influence performance on

projects in the region. Identify good practice and get to the root of their origins and success

(6) Develop the regional project management framework

(7) Establish a mechanism for reviewing performance on the regional framework, and indicate what will be examined in such a review

(8) Appoint a standing committee for the task of monitoring and reviewing the performance of the framework.

At the local, country level, repeat step 5 above and from there, continue with:

(1) Analyze the local situation with respect to project management. For example, determine the factors which influence performance on projects in the country. Identify elements of good practice and get to the root of their origin and success

(2) Develop a local framework

(3) Collect data on project performance and maintain a database of project information, appropriately categorized

(4) Review the local framework with a similar frequency as the regional one, but out of phase with the regional schedule.

Concluding remarks

Project management is most needed in developing countries because while projects in these countries may be basic, the dynamics are complex. This shows that generic project management frameworks will not work in the context of developing countries. It is pertinent to note that the developing countries are dissimilar, and they have different needs and issues concerning projects. So, a regional approach would be advisable. Countries can then make local amendments as necessary to deal with details of their particular situations.

A definition for project management in developing countries is required. There is a need for the body of knowledge to capture the reality on the ground in these countries if they are to be effective in application in the project contexts in those countries. The definition should recognize the constraints on the ground, and consider a wider range of parameters and main targets (beyond cost, time and quality) such as benefits management. Thus, the definition of project management in developing countries should end in: "taking into account and applying the specific operating environment."

What do we mean by "project" and "project management"? This book is about project management in developing countries. The discussion covers projects in general, before focusing on construction projects. It also covers the subject in a general form relating to all countries before concentrating on the developing countries.

Whose main responsibility will it be to develop, maintain, and manage the framework? It is in the interest of the major professional institutions to contribute to the efforts to develop a developing country PMBOK because: (a) the analysis of the difficulties in the contexts can add to knowledge in project studies and inform the development of subsequent editions of the mainstream generic frameworks; and (b) the document that is produced will aid practice for all firms and practitioners operating in the developing countries. Indeed, the DCPMBOK will effectively reduce the information asymmetry between foreign and local firms in the developing countries and shorten the learning curve of the latter. Thus, it should be of interest to the construction industries and practitioners around the world. It will be a key component of the preparation of practitioners for projects abroad.

Then comes the question, "Is the project culture bound?" The notion that the project is a Western concept is a misconception, as all civilizations have undertaken projects in their history. Such a notion undervalues the lived experience of the people of the developing countries. The now-heralded process of projectification is not the preserve of any group of countries or any part of the world. Therefore, the conceptualization of projects and their management should be more culturally and contextually sensitive.

Now, how do we end the book? How do we draw the common threads together? First, projects require to be systematically, effectively, and efficiently managed. This is true in the developing countries as much as in the industrialized countries, and even more so. Second, the project outcomes indicate that there should be further development of project management. A third main thread is that the context of projects in developing countries is different from those in the industrialized nations, where the concept of project management emerged and the body of knowledge was put together. Fourth, it is evident that there is a need to decolonize the field of project studies and the practice of project management. Finally, it is necessary to formulate the DCPMBOK and progressively upgrade and update it accordingly.

References

Alinaitwe, H., Apolot, R. and Tindiwensi, D. (2013). Investigation into the causes of delay and cost overrun in Uganda's public sector construction projects. *Journal of Construction in Developing Countries*, 18(2), 33–47.

Aon plc (2020). Weather, Climate and Catastrophe Insight, 2019 Annual Report. Chicago, IL.

Aubry, M., Boukri, S.E. and Sergi, V. (2021). Opening the black box of benefits management in the context of projects. *Project Management Journal*, 52(5), 434–452. https://doi.org/10.1177/87569728211020606.

Bennis, W.G. and Nanus, B. (1985). *Leaders: The Strategies for Taking Charge*. Harper and Row, New York.

Bierwolf, R., Romero, D., Pelk, H. and Stettina, C.J. (2017). On the future of project management innovation: A call for discussion towards project management 2030. *2017 International Conference on Engineering, Technology and Innovation (ICE/ITMC)*, 689–698. https://doi.org/10.1109/ICE.2017.8279952.

Bosch-Rekveldt, M., Jongkind, Y., Mooi, H., Bakker, H. and Verbraeck, A. (2011). Grasping project complexity in large engineering projects: The TOE (Technical, Organizational and Environmental) framework. *International Journal of Project Management*, 29(6), 728–739.

Chilisa, B. (2012). *Indigenous Research Methodologies*. Sage Publications, Los Angeles.

Connaughton, J.N. and Green, S.D. (2006). *Value Management in Construction — A Client's Guide*. CIRIA SP129. CIRIA, London.

Dei, G. (2000). Rethinking the role of indigenous knowledges in the academy. *International Journal of Inclusive Education*, 4(2), 111–132.

Denicol J., Davies A. and Krystallis, I. (2020). What are the causes and cures of poor megaproject performance? A systematic literature review and research agenda. *Project Management Journal*, 51(3), 328–345. https://doi.org/10.1177/8756972819896113.

Engineering Rebellion Steering Group (2021). *Engineering Rebellion: A Study Into the Future of Civil Engineering*. Institution of Engineers, London.

Eyiah, A.K. (2001). An integrated approach to financing small contractors in developing countries: A conceptual model. *Construction Management and Economics*, 19(5), 511–518. https://doi.org/10.1080/01446193.2001.9709627.

Fong, P.S.-W. and Shen, Q. (2000). Is the Hong Kong construction industry ready for value management? *International Journal of Project Management*, 18(5), 317–326. https://doi.org/10.1016/S0263-7863(99)00028-9.

Gauthier, J.B. and Ika, L.A. (2012). Foundations of project management research: An explicit and six-facet ontological framework. *Project Management Journal*, 43(5), 5–23. https://doi.org/10.1002/pmj.21288.

Geraldi J., Söderlund J. and Marrewijk, A. van (2021). Bright and dark spots in project studies: Continuing efforts to advance theory development and debate. *Project Management Journal*, 52(3), 227–236. https://doi.org/10.1177/87569728211004064.

Guattari, F. (2001). *The Three Ecologies*. Trans. Ian Pindar and Paul Sutton. The Athlone Press, London.

Haughey, D. (2021). A brief history of project management. https://www.projectsmart.co.uk/history-of-project-management/brief-history-of-project-management.php [Accessed 12 January 2022].

Hillebrandt, P.M. (2000). *Economic Theory and the Construction Industry*, 3rd Edition. Macmillan, Basingstoke.

International Federation of Red Cross and Red Crescent Societies (IFRC) (2020). *World Disasters Report 2020: Come Heat or High Water.* IFRC, Geneva.

Kaliba, C., Muya, M. and Mumba, K. (2009). Cost escalation and schedule delays in road construction projects in Zambia. *International Journal of Project Management*, 27(5), 522–531. https://doi.org/10.1016/j.ijproman.2008.07.003.

Kelly, J., Male, S. and Graham, D. (2014). *Value Management of Construction Projects*, 2nd Edition. Wiley Blackwell, Chichester.

Kloppenberg, T. and Opfer, W. (2002). The current state of project management research: Trends, interpretations and predications. *Project Management Journal*, 33(2), 5–18.

KPMG, Australian Institute of Project Management and International Project Management Association (2019). *The Future of Project Management: Global outlook 2019 — Summary report*. https://home.kpmg/content/dam/kpmg/au/pdf/2019/future-of-project-management-global-outlook-2019-summary-report.pdf [Accessed 15 January 2022].

Le Grange, L. (2016). Decolonising the university curriculum. *South African Journal of Higher Education*, 30(2), 1–12. http://dx.doi.org/10.20853/30-2-709.

Long, N.D., Ogunlana, S., Quang, T. and Lam, K.C. (2004). Large construction projects in developing countries: A case study from Vietnam. *International Journal of Project Management*, 22(7), 553–561. https://doi.org/10.1016/j.ijproman.2004.03.004.

Martinsuo, M. (2020). The management of values in project business: Adjusting beliefs to transform project practices and outcomes. *Project Management Journal*, 51(4), 389–399. https://doi.org/10.1177/8756972820927890.

Mikkelsen, M., Marnewick, C. and Klein, L. (2020). On stupidity in project management — A critical reflection of PM in a VUCA world. *The Journal of Modern Project Management*, North America, 8, September. https://journalmodernpm.com/index.php/jmpm/article/view/JMPM02412 [Accessed 20 January 2022].

Muller, M. (2018). Decolonising engineering in South Africa — Experience to date and some emerging challenges. *South African Journal of Science*, 114(5/6), Art. #a0270, 6. http://dx.doi.org/10.17159/sajs.2018/a0270.

Muller, R. and Klein, G. (2020) The COVID-19 pandemic and project management research. *Project Management Journal*, 51(6), 1–3, https://doi.org/10.1177/8756972820963316.

Ofori, G. (2018). Construction in developing countries: Need for new concepts. *Journal of Construction in Developing Countries*, 23(2), 1–6. https://doi.org/10.21315/jcdc2018.23.2.1.

Ofori, G. (2021). Construction industry development in developing countries: New challenges and proposed agenda in VUCA world. Presented at the *1st International Conference & Symposium on Construction Industry Development (I-CENTROID2021)*, Padang, Indonesia, 24–25 August.

Pells, D.L. (2019). Six fresh eggs: A half dozen new ideas for managing projects in a rapidly changing VUCA world. Presented at the *13th Annual UT Dallas Project Management Symposium*, Richardson, TX, May; *PM World Journal*, VIII(VIII), September. https://pmworldlibrary.net/wp-content/uploads/2019/09/pmwj85-Sep2019-Pells-six-fresh-eggs.pdf [Accessed 20 January 2022].

Pindar, I. and Sutton, P. (2001). Translators' introduction. In F. Guattari (Ed.), *The Three Ecologies*, I. Pindar and P. Sutton (Trans.). The Athlone Press, London.

Seymour, T. and Hussein, S. (2014). The history of project management. *International Journal of Management and Information Systems*, 233–240. https://doi.org/10.19030/ijmis.v18i4.8820.

Sheffield, P. (2020). The future is already here — Civil engineering at the cutting edge. *Civil Engineering*, 173(1), 3–9.

Smith, L. (1999). *Decolonising Methodologies: Research and Indigenous Peoples*. Zed Books, London.

Söderlund, J. (2004). Building theories of project management: Past research, questions for the future. *International Journal of Project Management*, 22(3), 183–189. https://doi.org/10.1016/S0263-7863(03)00070-X.

Soemardi, B.W., Kusuma, B., Pribadi, K.S. and Yuliar, S. (2021). Technological capabilities of medium-sized contractors in Indonesia. *Journal of Construction in Developing Countries*, 26(2), 1–15. https://doi.org/10.21315/jcdc2021.26.2.1.

Stanleigh, M. (2010). *The Future of Quality and Project Management*. Business Improvement Architects, Toronto. https://bia.ca/the-future-of-quality-and-project-management/ [Accessed 5 January 2022].

Styhre, A. (2020). Thinly and thickly capitalized projects: Theorizing the role of the finance markets and capital supply in project management studies. *Project Management Journal*, 51(4), 378–388. https://doi.org/10.1177/8756972820931278.

Svejvig, P., Geraldi, J. and Grex, S. (2019). Accelerating time to impact: Deconstructing practices to achieve project value. *International Journal of Project Management*, 37(5), July, 784–801. https://doi.org/10.1016/j.ijproman.2018.12.003.

Svejvig, P. and Schlichter, B.R. (2020). The long road to benefits management: Toward an integrative management model. *Project Management Journal*, 51(3), 312–327. https://doi.org/10.1177/8756972819896485.

Tanaka, H. (2004). The changing landscape of project management. *Fourth International Project Management Workshop*, ESC Lille, 16–20 August.

Tutesigensi, A., Kibwami, N. and Matege, S.B. (2021). The status of value management practice on construction projects in Uganda and strategies for improvement. *Journal of Construction in Developing Countries*, 26(2), 251–267. https://doi.org/10.21315/jcdc2021.26.2.12.

Ullal, A. and Tombesi, P. (2021). Dimensions and correlates of development in construction. *Journal of Construction in Developing Countries*, 26(2), 37–64. https://doi.org/10.21315/jcdc2021.26.2.3.

United Nations (2018). *Sustainable Development Goals Report 2018*. New York.

Watermeyer, R. (2018). *Client Guide for Improving Infrastructure Project Outcomes*. Engineers Against Poverty and University of the Witwatersrand, Johannesburg.

Wiezel, A., Badger, W. and King, C. (2013). *Project Management Skills of the Future*, RT-281. Construction Industry Institute, Austin.

Yu, A.T.W., Javed, A.A., Lam, T.I., Shen, G.Q. and Sun, M. (2018). Integrating value management into sustainable construction projects in Hong Kong. *Engineering, Construction and Architectural Management*, 25(11), 1473–1500. https://doi.org/10.1108/ECAM-03-2017-0049.

Zerjav, V. (2021). in *Why do Business Organizations Participate in Projects? Toward a Typology of Project Value Domains. Project Management Journal*, 52(3), 287–297. https://doi.org/10.1177%2F87569728211001663.

Zwikael, O., Chih, Y.-Y. and Meredith, J.R. (2018). Project benefit management: Setting effective target benefits, *International Journal of Project Management*, 36(4), May, 650–658. https://doi.org/10.1016/j.ijproman.2018.01.002.

www.ingramcontent.com/pod-product-compliance
Lightning Source LLC
LaVergne TN
LVHW010538300926
849162LV00002B/165
* 9 7 8 9 8 1 1 2 2 4 7 1 3 *